# THE AMERICAN PEOPLE

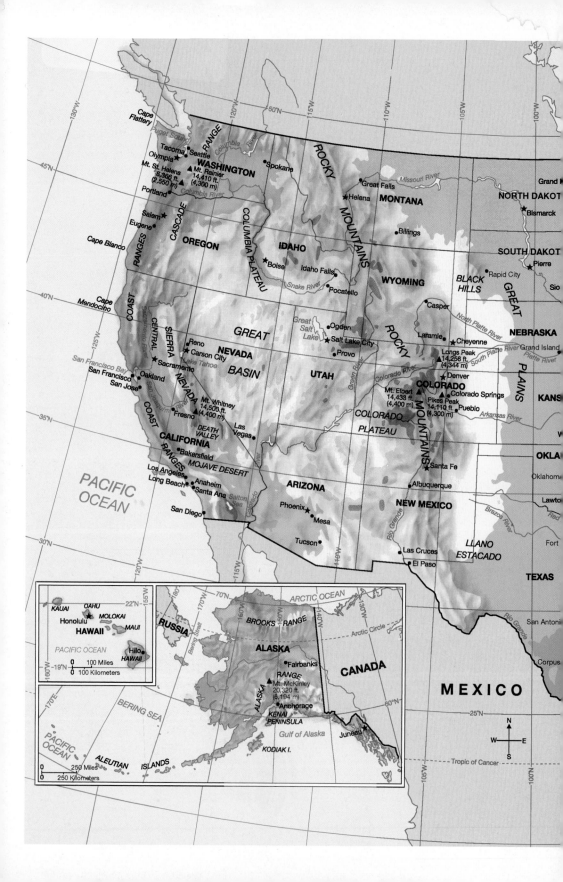

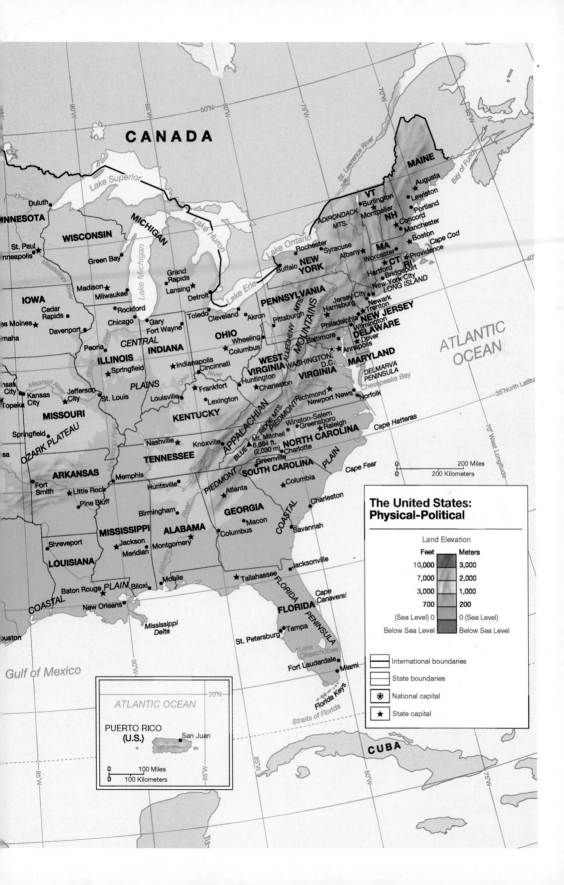

# THE AMERICAN PEOPLE

## Creating a Nation and a Society

Brief Fourth Edition

## Volume II: From 1865

**Gary B. Nash**
*University of California, Los Angeles*
**General Editor**

**Julie Roy Jeffrey**
*Goucher College*
**General Editor**

John R. Howe
*University of Minnesota*

Peter J. Frederick
*Wabash College*

Allen F. Davis
*Temple University*

Allan M. Winkler
*Miami University*

New York   San Francisco   Boston
London   Toronto   Sydney   Tokyo   Singapore   Madrid
Mexico City   Munich   Paris   Cape Town   Hong Kong   Montreal

Publisher: Priscilla McGeehon
Acquisitions Editor: Ashley Dodge
Development Manager: Lisa Pinto
Senior Development Editor: Dawn Groundwater
Executive Marketing Manager: Sue Westmoreland
Media Supplements Editor: Patrick McCarthy
Supplements Editor: Kelly Villella
Production Manager: Mark Naccarelli
Project Coordination, Text Design, and Electronic Page Makeup: Elm Street Publishing
    Services, Inc.
Cover Designer/Manager: Nancy Danahy
Cover Illustration: James Henry Daugherty, American 1887–1974, "Untitled" (detail)
    19th–20th Century, 26.3 x 34.4 cm, Fine Arts Museums of San Francisco, Achenbach
    Foundation for Graphic Arts, 1963. 30.25783
Photo Researcher: Photosearch, Inc.
Manufacturing Buyer: Roy Pickering
Printer and Binder: R. R. Donnelley & Sons Company/Crawfordsville
Cover Printer: The Lehigh Press, Inc.

For permission to use copyrighted material, grateful acknowledgment is made to the
following copyright holders. Page 819, George H. Gallop, *The Gallop Poll: Public Opinion,
1935–1971*, vol. 2 (New York: Random House, 1972). © American Institute of Public
Opinion. Page 897, "The Times They are A-Changin'" by Bob Dylan. Copyright © 1963,
1964 by Warner Brothers Music, Inc. Copyright renewed 1991 by Special Rider Music. All
rights reserved. International copyright secured. Reprinted by permission. Page 957,
*Newsweek*, 11/20/00 "Divided We Stand," p. 19. © Newsweek, Inc. All rights reserved.
Reprinted with permission.

**Library of Congress Cataloging-in-Publication Data**
The American people : creating a nation and a society / Gary B. Nash, general editor . . .
[et al.].—Brief 4th ed.
    p.   cm.
    Includes bibliographical references and index.
    ISBN 0-321-09434-4 (set).—ISBN 0-321-09432-8 (v. 1).—ISBN 0-321-09430-1 (v. 2).
    1. United States—History.   I. Nash, Gary B.

    E178.1 .A4927  2003
    973—dc21                                                              2002016010

Please visit our website at http://www.ablongman.com

ISBN 0-321-09434-4 (Single Volume Edition)
ISBN 0-321-09432-8 (Volume I)
ISBN 0-321-09430-1 (Volume II)

3 4 5 6 7 8 9 10—DOC—05 04 03

# Brief Contents

# DETAILED CONTENTS

# RECOVERING THE PAST

# TECHNOLOGY CHANGES THE AMERICAN PEOPLE

# MAPS

# PREFACE

The Yoruba people of West Africa have an old saying: "However far the stream flows, it never forgets its source." Why, we wonder, do such ancient societies as the Yoruba find history so important, while modern American students question its relevance? This book aims to end such skepticism about the usefulness of history.

As we begin the twenty-first century in an ethnically and culturally diverse society caught up in an interdependent global system, history is of central importance in preparing us to exercise our rights and responsibilities as a free people. Studying history cannot make good citizens, but without a knowledge of history, we cannot understand the choices before us and think wisely about them. Lacking a collective memory of the past, we lapse into a kind of amnesia, unaware of the human condition and the long struggles of men and women everywhere to deal with the problems of their day and to create a better society. Unfurnished with historical knowledge, we deprive ourselves of knowing about the huge range of approaches people have taken to political, economic, and social life; to solving problems; and to surmounting the obstacles in their way.

History has a deeper, even more fundamental importance: the cultivation of the private person whose self-knowledge and self-respect provide the foundation for a life of dignity and fulfillment. Historical memory is the key to self-identity: to seeing one's place in the long stream of time, in the story of humankind.

When we study our own history, we see a rich and extraordinarily complex human story. This country, whose written history began with a convergence of Native Americans, Europeans, and Africans, has always been a nation of diverse peoples—a magnificent mosaic of cultures, religions, and skin shades. This book explores how American society assumed its present shape and developed its present forms of government; how as a nation we have conducted our foreign affairs and managed our economy; how science and technology have changed our lives; how as individuals and in groups we have lived, worked, loved, married, raised families, voted, argued, protested, and struggled to fulfill our dreams and the noble ideals of the American experiment.

Several ways of making the past understandable distinguish this book from traditional textbooks. The coverage of public events like presidential elections, diplomatic treaties, and economic legislation is integrated with the private human stories that pervade them. Within a chronological framework, we have woven together our history as a nation, as a people, and as a society. When, for example, national political events are discussed, we analyze their impact on social and economic life at the state and local levels. Wars are described not only as they unfolded on the battlefield and in the salons of diplomats but also on the home front, where they have been history's greatest motor of social change. The interaction of ordinary and extraordinary Americans runs as a theme throughout this book.

Above all, we have tried to show the "humanness" of our history as it is revealed in people's everyday lives. Throughout these pages, we have often used the words of unnoticed Americans to capture the authentic human voices of those who participated in and responded to epic events such as war, slavery, industrialization, and reform movements.

## GOALS AND THEMES OF THE BOOK

Our primary goal is to provide students with a rich, balanced, and thought-provoking treatment of the American past. By this we mean a history that treats the lives and experiences of Americans of all national origins and cultural backgrounds, at all levels of society, and in all regions of the country. It also means a history that seeks connections between the many factors—political, economic, technological, social, religious, intellectual, and biological—that have molded and remolded American society over four centuries. And, finally, it means a history that encourages students to think about how we have all inherited a complex past filled with both notable achievements and thorny problems. The only history befitting a democratic nation is one that inspires students to initiate a frank and searching dialogue with their past.

To speak of a dialogue about the past presumes that history is interpretive rather than an agreed-upon account of what happened in the past and why history unfolded as it did. Students should understand that historians are continually reinterpreting the past. New interpretations may result from the discovery of new evidence, but more often they emerge because historians reevaluate old evidence in the light of new ideas that spring from the times in which they write and from their personal views of the world.

Through this book, we also hope to promote class discussions, which can be organized around seven questions that we believe are basic to the American historical experience:

1. How has this nation been peopled, from the first inhabitants to the many groups that arrived in slavery or servitude during the colonial period to the voluntary immigrants of today? How have these waves of newcomers contributed to and reshaped the American cultural mosaic? To what extent have different immigrant groups preserved elements of their ethnic, racial, and religious heritages?

2. How and to what extent have Americans developed a stable, democratic political system flexible enough to address the wholesale changes occurring in the last two centuries? To what degree has this political system been consistent with the principles of our nation's founding?

3. How have economic, scientific, and technological changes affected daily life, work, family organization, leisure, sexual behavior, the division of wealth, and community relations in the United States?

4. How did the European settlement of the Americas alter the landscape, and how have environmental factors shaped American society? How have Americans changed in attitudes and policies concerning the natural and human-built environment?

5. In what ways has religion united and divided the American people? Has religion served more to promote or retard social reform in our history? Whatever

their varied sources, how have the recurring reform movements in our history dealt with economic, political, and social problems in attempting to square the ideals and realities of American life? How has religious belief shaped our country's relations with the rest of the world?

6. What has been the role of our nation in the world? To what extent has the United States served as a model for other peoples, as an interventionist savior of other nations around the globe, and as an interfering expansionist in the affairs of other nations?

7. How have American beliefs and values changed over time? How have they varied between different groups: women and men; Americans of many colors and cultures; people of different regions, religions, sexual orientations, ages, and classes?

In writing a history that revolves around these themes, we have tried to convey two dynamics that operate in all societies. First, we observe people continuously adjusting to new developments, such as industrialization and urbanization, over which they seemingly have little control; we realize that people are not paralyzed by history but are the fundamental creators of it. They retain the ability, individually and collectively, to shape the world in which they live and thus in considerable degree to control their own lives. Second, we emphasize the connections that always exist among social, political, economic, and cultural events.

## STRUCTURE OF THE BOOK

The chapters of this book are grouped into six parts that relate to major periods in American history. The titles for each part suggest a major theme that helps to characterize the period.

Each chapter has a clear structure, beginning with a chapter outline and then a personal story, called *American Stories*, recalling the experience of an ordinary or lesser-known American. Chapter 22, for example, is introduced with the story of Edmund P. Arpin, Jr., who, along with hundreds of other men, enlisted in the Army after the United States declared war on Germany during the Great War. This brief anecdote serves several purposes. First, it shows the overarching theme that while looking for adventure and glory, Arpin, like many men, would never again feel the same sense of common purpose at war's end. Second, the personal story reminds us that ordinary as well as extraordinary people shaped our history. At the end of *American Stories*, a *brief overview* links the biographical sketch to the text by elaborating the major themes of the chapter.

We aim to facilitate an exciting engagement with history for students in other ways as well. Every chapter ends with pedagogical features to reinforce and expand the presentation. A *timeline* reviews the major events and developments covered in the chapter. The *conclusion* briefly summarizes the chapter's main concepts and developments, revisits the individual described in *American Stories*, and serves as a bridge to the following chapter. A list of *recommended readings* provides supplementary sources for further study and research; an annotated selection of historical novels and films, called *Fiction and Film*, is new to this edition. An annotated section of suggested Web sites, *Discovering U.S. History Online*, offers students electronic resources relating to chapter content and themes. In addition, each map, figure, and table has been chosen to relate clearly to the narrative. *Captions* are specially written to help students understand and interpret these visual materials.

## THE BRIEF FOURTH EDITION

This Brief Fourth Edition is condensed from the very successful full Fifth Edition of *The American People,* with its balance of political, social, and economic history. While we have eliminated detail and extra examples, and have compressed the text, we have retained the interpretive connections and the "humanness" of history—the presentation of history as revealed through the lives of ordinary as well as extraordinary Americans and the interplay of social and political factors.

### Format and Features

The Brief Fourth Edition continues the new format and more compact size of the previous brief edition. The four-color design enhances the value of the maps and graphs and gives the book a vibrant appearance. This makes the book accessible, easy to read, and convenient for students to carry to and from class.

This new edition is enhanced by additions to one of the most popular features of *The American People:* the two-page sections entitled *Recovering the Past.* Ten RTPs, as the authors affectionately call them, introduce students to the fascinating variety of evidence—ranging from novels, political cartoons, and public opinion polls to documentary photographs, autobiographies, and popular music—that historians have learned to employ in reconstructing the past. Each RTP gives basic information about the source and its use by historians and then raises questions—called *Reflecting on the Past*—for students to consider as they study the example reproduced for their inspection. Also, this edition has a new feature: *Technology Changes the American People.* Six of these features, including topics on wireless communication and air conditioning, trace the extraordinary impact that technology and science have had on the American people while putting the nation in the forefront of global technological changes. This feature also concludes with *Reflecting on the Past* questions for students to consider.

### Chapter Changes

Throughout the Brief Fourth Edition there are new materials on the role of religion, the environment, science and technology, and the American West. The structure and organization of the text—parts, chapters, sections, and subsections—reflect the full Fifth Edition. We have also significantly reorganized topics from the past 20 years. Chapter 30 concentrates on the revival of conservatism and the end of the Cold War. Chapter 31 examines the post-Cold War period of the Clinton administration, economic and social change, the election of 2000, and new foreign policy challenges.

Other chapter-by-chapter changes include the following:

- *Chapter 22* features a new discussion of the great flu epidemic
- *Chapter 23* includes new material on the technology of flood control
- *Chapter 24* points out the limitations of the New Deal for African Americans
- *Chapter 26* has increased coverage of computers in connection with the edition's goal of highlighting technology; features new material on the experiences of Native American, Latino, and African American communities in the postwar United States
- *Chapter 27* refocuses the analysis of the Cold War as a result of new materials now available to scholars; provides additional material on Eisenhower and on anti-Communism at home, including the ways in which an anti-homosexual effort played a part in the anti-Communist crusade
- *Chapter 29* has stronger coverage of the Civil Rights Movement and additional material on Native American rights; as part of the effort to highlight the importance of science and technology, there is an expanded discussion of birth control and the development of the pill and more material on nuclear regulation

In the Brief Fourth Edition, we have tried to present American history in its rich complexity but in a form that students will find comprehensible and interesting. Additionally, we have tried to provide the support materials necessary to make teaching and learning enjoyable and rewarding. The reader will be the judge of our success. The authors and Longman welcome your comments.

## ACKNOWLEDGMENTS

The authors wish to thank the following reviewers who gave generously of their time and expertise and whose thoughtful and constructive work has contributed greatly to this edition:

Patrick Ashwood, Hawkeye Community College
Arthur H. Auten, University of Hartford
Jolane Culhane, Western New Mexico University
Keith Edgerton, Montana State University at Billings
Trace Etienne-Gray, Southwest Texas State University
Kathryn H. Fuller, Virginia Commonwealth University
Barbara Green, Wright State University
Gretchen Grufman, Dominican University
Thomas D. Hamm, Earlham College
Carol Sue Humphrey, Oklahoma Baptist University
Xaio-bing Li, University of Central Oklahoma
Suzanne Marshall, Jacksonville State University
George W. McDaniel, St. Ambrose University
Ting Ni, St. Mary's University
Robert G. Rockwell, Mt. San Jacinto College
David E. Ruth, Pennsylvania State University

Randi Storch, State University of New York at Cortland
Seth Wigderson, University of Maine at Augusta
Nelson E. Woodard, California State University, Fullerton

Over the years, as previous editions of this text were being developed, many of our colleagues read and criticized the various drafts of the manuscript. For their thoughtful evaluations and constructive suggestions, the authors wish to express their gratitude to the following reviewers:

Richard H. Abbott, Eastern Michigan University; John Alexander, University of Cincinnati; Kenneth G. Alfers, Mountain View College; Terry Alford, Northern Virginia Community College; Gregg Andrews, Southwest Texas State University; Robert Asher, University of Connecticut at Storrs; Harry Baker, University of Arkansas at Little Rock; Michael Batinski, Southern Illinois University; Gary Bell, Sam Houston State University; Virginia Bellows, Tulsa Junior College; Spencer Bennett, Siena Heights College; Jackie R. Booker, Western Connecticut State University; Linda J. Borish, Western Michigan University; James Bradford, Texas A&M University; Thomas A. Britten, Briar Cliff College; Neal Brooks, Essex Community College; Jeffrey P. Brown, New Mexico State University; Dickson D. Bruce, Jr., University of California, Irvine; David Brundage, University of California, Santa Cruz; Steven J. Bucklin, University of South Dakota; Colin Calloway, Dartmouth University; D'Ann Campbell, Indiana University; Jane Censer, George Mason University; Vincent A. Clark, Johnson County Community College; Neil Clough, North Seattle Community College; Stacy A. Cordery, Monmouth College; Matthew Ware Coulter, Collin County Community College; David Culbert, Louisiana State University; Mark T. Dalhouse, Northeast Missouri State University; Bruce Dierenfield, Canisius College; John Dittmer, DePauw University; Gordon Dodds, Portland State University; Richard Donley, Eastern Washington University; Dennis B. Downey, Millersville University; Robert Downtain, Tarrant County Community College; Robert Farrar, Spokane Falls Community College; Bernard Friedman, Indiana University–Purdue University at Indianapolis; Bruce Glasrud, California State University, Hayward; Brian Gordon, St. Louis Community College; Richard Griswold del Castillo, San Diego State University; Carol Gruber, William Paterson College; Stephen A. Harmon, Pittsburgh State University; Colonel William L. Harris, The Citadel Military College; Robert Haws, University of Mississippi; Jerrold Hirsch, Northeast Missouri State University; Frederick Hoxie, University of Illinois; John S. Hughes, University of Texas; Link Hullar, Kingwood College; Donald M. Jacobs, Northeastern University; Delores Janiewski, University of Idaho; David Johnson, Portland State University; Richard Kern, University of Findlay; Robert J. Kolesar, John Carroll University; Monte Lewis, Cisco Junior College; William Link, University of North Carolina at Greensboro; Patricia M. Lisella, Iona College; Jeff Livingston, California State University, Chico; Ronald Lora, University of Toledo; Paul K. Longmore, San Francisco State University; Rita Loos, Framingham State College; George M. Lubick, Northern Arizona University; Suzanne Marshall, Jacksonville State University; John C. Massman, St. Cloud State University; Vernon Mattson, University of Nevada at Las Vegas; Arthur McCoole, Cuyamaca College; John McCormick, Delaware County Community College; Sylvia

McGrath, Stephen F. Austin University; James E. McMillan, Denison University; Otis L. Miller, Belleville Area College; Walter Miszczenko, Boise State University; Norma Mitchell, Troy State University; Gerald F. Moran, University of Michigan at Dearborn; William G. Morris, Midland College; Marian Morton, John Carroll University; Roger Nichols, University of Arizona; Elizabeth Neumeyer, Kellogg Community College; Paul Palmer, Texas A&I University; Albert Parker, Riverside City College; Judith Parsons, Sul Ross State University; Carla Pestana, Ohio State University; Neva Peters, Tarrant County Community College; James Prickett, Santa Monica Community College; Noel Pugash, University of New Mexico; Juan Gomez-Quiñones, University of California, Los Angeles; George Rable, Anderson College; Joseph P. Reidy, Howard University; Leonard Riforgiato, Pennsylvania State University; Randy Roberts, Purdue University; Mary Robertson, Armstrong State University; David Robson, John Carroll University; Judd Sage, Northern Virginia Community College; A.J. Scopino, Jr., Cental Connecticut State University; Sylvia Sebesta, San Antonio College; Phil Schaeffer, Olympic College; Herbert Shapiro, University of Cincinnati; David R. Shibley, Santa Monica Community College; Ellen Shockro, Pasadena City College; Nancy Shoemaker, University of Connecticut; Bradley Skelcher, Delaware State University; Kathryn Kish Sklar, State University of New York at Binghamton; James Smith, Virginia State University; John Snetsinger, California Polytechnic State University at San Luis Obispo; Jo Snider, Southwest Texas State University; Stephen Strausberg, University of Arkansas; Katherine Scott Sturdevant, Pikes Peak Community College; Nan M. Sumner-Mack, Hawaii Community College; Cynthia Taylor, Santa Rosa Junior College; Thomas Tefft, Citrus College; John A. Trickel, Richland College; Donna Van Raaphorst, Cuyahoga Community College; Morris Vogel, Temple University; Michael Wade, Appalachian State University; Jackie Walker, James Madison University; Paul B. Weinstein, University of Akron-Wayne College; Joan Welker, Prince George's Community College; Michael Welsh, University of Northern Colorado; Kenneth H. Williams, Alcorn State University; Mitch Yamasaki, Chaminade University; and Charles Zappia, San Diego Mesa College.

Gary B. Nash

Julie Roy Jeffrey

# SUPPLEMENTS

## For Qualified College Adopters

*Teaching the American People.* Written by Julie Roy Jeffrey and Peter J. Frederick with Frances Jones-Sneed of Massachusetts College of Liberal Arts, this guide is based on ideas generated in "active learning" workshops and is tied closely to the text. In addition to suggestions on how to generate lively class discussion and involve students in active learning, this supplement also offers a file of exam questions and lists of resources, including films, slides, photo collections, records, and audiocassettes. Available in print and online at www.ablongman.com/nashbrief4e/instructor

*Test Bank.* This test bank contains more than 3500 objective, conceptual, and essay questions. All questions are keyed to specific pages in the text.

*Test Gen 4.0 Computerized Testing System.* This flexible, easy-to-master computerized test bank includes all the test items in the printed test bank. The software allows you to edit existing questions and add your own items. Tests can be printed in several different formats and can include figures such as graphs and tables. It comes with *QuizMaster,* a program that enables you to design Test Gen-generated tests your students can take on a computer rather than in printed form. Available on a cross-platform CD-ROM for both Windows and Macintosh.

*Longman American History.com* (longmanamericanhistory.com). Available at a discount to adopters of the text, this new website combines quality educational publishing with the immediacy and interactivity of the Internet. At LongmanAmericanHistory.com, you will find a rich collection of primary sources, comparative case studies, and interactive maps as well as audio and video clips, images, and internet links, all organized according to the chapters of the text.

The American People, *Brief Fourth Edition Companion Website* (www.ablongman.com/nashbrief4e). This website, designed specifically for this book, is an invaluable tool for both students and instructors. It contains student resources such as self-testing and chapter outlines, and instructor resources such as the instructor's manual, testing ideas, and maps and charts from the full version of the book.

*Video Lecture Launchers.* Prepared by Mark Newman, University of Illinois at Chicago, these video lecture launchers (each two to five minutes in duration) cover key issues in American history from 1877 to the present. The launchers are accompanied by an instructor's manual.

*"This Is America" Immigration Video.* Produced by the American Museum of Immigration, this video tells the story of American immigrants, relating their personal stories and accomplishments. By showing how the richness of our culture is due to the contributions of millions of immigrant Americans, the videos make the

point that America's strength lies in the ethnically and culturally diverse backgrounds of its citizens.

*Discovering American History Through Maps and Views.* Created by Gerald Danzer of the University of Illinois at Chicago, the recipient of the AHA's 1990 James Harvey Robinson Prize for his work in the development of map transparencies, this set of 140 four-color acetates is a unique instructional tool. It contains an introduction on teaching history through maps and a detailed commentary on each transparency. The collection includes cartographic and pictorial maps, views and photos, urban plans, building diagrams, and works of art.

*Comprehensive American History Transparency Set.* This vast collection of American history map transparencies includes more than 200 map transparencies ranging from the first Native Americans to the end of the Cold War, covering wars, social trends, elections, immigration, and demographics. Also included are a reproducible set of student map exercises, teaching tips, and correlation charts.

*Text-Specific Map Transparencies.* A set of 30 transparencies drawn from *The American People,* Fifth Edition, is available.

*Longman American History Atlas Overhead Transparencies.* These 69 acetates from our four-color historical atlas were especially designed for this volume.

*A Guide to Teaching American History Through Film.* Written by Randy Roberts of Purdue University, this guide provides instructors with a creative and practical tool for stimulating classroom discussion. The sections include "American Films: A Historian's Perspective," a list of films, practical suggestions, and bibliography. The film listing is presented in narrative form, developing connections between each film and the topics being discussed.

## For Students

*Longman American History.com* (longmanamericanhistory.com). Available at a discount to adopters of the text, this new website combines quality educational publishing with the immediacy and interactivity of the Internet. At LongmanAmericanHistory.com, you will find a rich collection of primary sources, comparative case studies, and interactive maps as well as audio and video clips, images, and internet links, all organized according to the chapters of the text.

The American People, *Brief Fourth Edition Companion Website* (www.ablongman.com/nashbrief4e). This website, designed specifically for this book, is an invaluable tool for both students and instructors. It contains student resources such as self-testing, chapter outlines, Web activities, and links to outside sources; instructor resources such as the instructor's manual and testing ideas; and our unique syllabus manager that gives instructors and students access to the up-to-date syllabus at any time from any computer.

*Study Guides and Practice Tests.* This two-volume study guide, created by Julie Roy Jeffrey and Peter J. Frederick, and revised by Ken Weatherbie of Del Mar College, includes chapter outlines, significant themes and highlights, a glossary, learning enrichment ideas, sample test questions, exercises for identification and interpretation, and geography exercises based on maps in the text.

*Timeline to accompany* The American People, *Brief Fourth Edition.* Created especially for this edition of the text, this ten-page, fold-out, full-color, illustrated timeline is designed to be hung on a wall and referred to throughout the semester. Arranged in an easy-to-read format around important political and diplomatic, social and economic, and cultural and technological events in United States history, it gives students a chronological context in which to place their knowledge.

*Longman American History Atlas.* This full-color historical atlas includes 69 maps, all designed especially for this course. This valuable reference tool is available shrinkwrapped with *The American People* at low cost.

*Mapping America: A Guide to Historical Geography.* Each volume of this workbook by Ken Weatherbie of Del Mar College contains 18 exercises corresponding to the map program in the text, each concluding with interpretive questions about the role of geography in American history. This free item is designed to be packaged with *The American People.*

*Mapping American History: Student Activities.* Written by Gerald Danzer of the University of Illinois at Chicago, this free map workbook for students features exercises designed to teach students to interpret and analyze cartographic materials as historical documents. This free item is designed to be packaged with *The American People.*

*Retracing the Past, Fifth Edition.* This two-volume reader is edited by Ronald Schultz of the University of Wyoming and Gary B. Nash of the University of California, Los Angeles. These primary and secondary source readings cover economic, political, and social history with special emphasis on women, racial and ethnic groups, and working-class people.

*America Through the Eyes of Its People: Primary Sources in American History, Second Edition.* This one-volume collection of primary documents portrays the rich and varied tapestry of American life. It contains documents by women, Native Americans, African Americans, Hispanics, and others who helped to shape the course of U.S. history along with student study questions and contextual headnotes. Available free when bundled with the text.

*Sources of the African-American Past.* Edited by Roy Finkenbine of University of Detroit at Mercy, this collection of primary sources covers key themes in the African-American experience from the West African background to the present. Balanced between political and social history, it offers a vivid snapshot of the lives of African Americans in different historical periods and includes documents representing women and different regions of the United States. Available at a minimum cost when bundled with the text.

*Women and the National Experience, Second Edition.* Edited by Ellen Skinner of Pace University, this primary source reader contains both classic and unusual documents describing the history of women in the United States. The documents provide dramatic evidence that outspoken women attained a public voice and participated in the development of national events and policies long before they could vote. Chronologically organized and balanced between social and political history, this reader offers a striking picture of the lives of women across American history. Available at a minimum cost when bundled with the text.

*Reading the American West.* Edited by Mitchell Roth of Sam Houston State University, this primary source reader uses letters, diary excerpts, speeches, interviews, and newspaper articles to let students experience what historians really do and how history is written. Every document is accompanied by a contextual headnote and study questions. The book is divided into chapters with extensive introductions. Available at a minimum cost when bundled with the text.

*A Short Guide to Writing About History, Fourth Edition.* Written by Richard Marius of Harvard University and Melvin Page of East Tennessee State University, this short guide introduces students to the pleasures of historical research and discovery while teaching them how to write cogent history papers. Focusing on more than just the conventions of good writing, this supplement shows students first how to think about history and then how to organize their thoughts into coherent essays.

*New! Longman-Penguin Putnam Inc. Value Bundles.* A variety of classic texts are available at a significant discount when packaged with *The American People,* Brief Fourth Edition. Ask your local sales representative for details.

*Library of American Biography Series.* Edited by Oscar Handlin of Harvard University, each of these interpretive biographies focuses on a figure whose actions and ideas significantly influenced the course of American history and national life. At the same time, each biography relates the life of its subject to the broader theme and developments of the times. Brief and inexpensive, they are ideal for any U.S. history course.

# ABOUT THE AUTHORS

**Gary B. Nash** received his Ph.D. from Princeton University. He is currently Director of the National Center for History in the Schools at the University of California, Los Angeles. Among the books Nash has authored are *Quakers and Politics: Pennsylvania, 1681–1726* (1968); *Red, White, and Black: The Peoples of Early America* (1974, 1982, 1992, 1999); *The Urban Crucible: Social Change, Political Consciousness, and the Origins of the American Revolution* (1979); and *Forging Freedom: The Formation of Philadelphia's Black Community, 1720–1840* (1988) and *First City: Philadelphia and the Forging of Historical Memory* (2002). A former president of the Organization of American Historians, his scholarship is especially concerned with the role of common people in the making of history. He wrote Part I and served as a general editor of this book.

**Julie Roy Jeffrey** earned her Ph.D. in history from Rice University. Since then she has taught at Goucher College. Honored as an outstanding teacher, Jeffrey has been involved in faculty development activities and curriculum evaluation. Jeffrey's major publications include *Education for Children of the Poor* (1978); *Frontier Women: The Trans-Mississippi West, 1840–1880* (1979, 1997); *Converting the West: A Biography of Narcissa Whitman* (1991); and *The Great Silent Army of Abolitionism: Ordinary Women in the Antislavery Movement* (1998). She is the author of many articles on the lives and perceptions of nineteenth-century women. She wrote Parts III and IV in collaboration with Peter Frederick and acted as a general editor of this book.

**John R. Howe** received his Ph.D. from Yale University and taught at Princeton before moving to the University of Minnesota. He has been active on College Board committees seeking to improve the academic preparation of high school students for college work. A former Vice President and Program Chair of the American Studies Association, his teaching interests include the American Revolution and early American politics, with special emphasis on ties between the lives of ordinary Americans and major historical events. His major publications include *The Changing Political Thought of John Adams* (1966), *From the Revolution Through the Age of Jackson* (1973), and a book examining the uses of language in American political writing scheduled for publication in 2002. His current research focuses on the social politics of oral discourse in early America.

**Peter J. Frederick** received his Ph.D. in history from the University of California, Berkeley. Innovative student-centered teaching in American history has been the focus of his career at California State University, Hayward, and since 1970 at Wabash College (1992–1994 at Carleton College). Recognized nationally as a distinguished teacher (awarded the Eugene Asher Award for Excellence in Teaching by the AHA in 2000) and for his many articles and workshops for faculty on teaching and learning, Frederick has also written several articles on life-writing and a book, *Knights of the Golden Rule: The Intellectual as Christian Social Reformer in the 1890s*. He coordinated and edited all the "Recovering the Past" sections and coauthored Parts III and IV.

**Allen F. Davis** earned his Ph.D. from the University of Wisconsin. A former president of the American Studies Association, he is a professor of history at Temple University and Director of the Center for Public History. He is the author of *Spearheads for Reform: The Social Settlements and the Progressive Movement* (1967) and *American Heroine: The Life and Legend of Jane Addams* (1973). He is coauthor of *Still Philadelphia* (1983), *Philadelphia Stories* (1987), and *One Hundred Years at Hull House* (1990). He is currently working on a book on masculine culture in America. Davis wrote Part V of this book.

**Allan M. Winkler** received his Ph.D. from Yale. He is presently teaching at Miami University. An award-winning historian, his books include *The Politics of Propaganda: The Office of War Information, 1942–1945* (1978); *Modern America: The United States from the Second World War to the Present* (1985); *Home Front U.S.A.: America During World War II* (1986); and *Life Under a Cloud: American Anxiety About the Atom* (1993). His research centers on the connections between public policy and popular mood in modern American history. Winkler wrote Part VI of this book.

# The American People

# CHAPTER 16
# The Union Reconstructed

## CHAPTER OUTLINE

- The Bittersweet Aftermath of War
- National Reconstruction Politics

- The Lives of Freedpeople
- Reconstruction in the States
- Conclusion: A Mixed Legacy

## AMERICAN STORIES
### Blacks and Whites Redefine Their Dreams and Relationships

In April 1864, a year before Lincoln's assassination, Robert Allston died, leaving his wife Adele and his daughter Elizabeth to manage their many rice plantations. With Union troops moving through coastal South Carolina in the winter of 1864–1865, Elizabeth's sorrow turned to "terror" as Union soldiers arrived and searched for liquor, firearms, and valuables. The women fled. Later, Yankee troops encouraged the Allston slaves to take furniture, food, and other goods from the Big House. Before they left, the Union soldiers gave the keys to the crop barns to the semifree blacks.

After the war, Adele Allston swore allegiance to the United States and secured a written order for the newly freed African Americans to relinquish those keys. She and Elizabeth returned in the summer of 1865 to reclaim the plantations and reassert white authority. She was assured that although the blacks had guns, "no outrage has been committed against the Whites except in the matter of property." But property was the issue. Possession of the keys to the barns, Elizabeth wrote, would be the "test case" of whether former masters or former slaves would control land, labor and its fruits, as well as the subtle aspects of interpersonal relations.

Nervously, Adele and Elizabeth Allston confronted their ex-slaves at their old home. To their surprise, a pleasant reunion took place as the Allston women greeted the blacks by name and caught up on their lives. A trusted black foreman handed over the keys to the barns. This harmonious scene was repeated elsewhere.

But at one plantation, the Allston women met defiant and armed African Americans, who ominously lined both sides of the road as the carriage arrived. An old black driver, Uncle Jacob, was unsure whether to yield the keys to the barns full of rice and corn, put there by slave labor. Mrs. Allston insisted. As Uncle Jacob hesitated, an angry young man shouted: "If you give up the key, blood'll flow." Uncle Jacob slowly slipped the keys back into his pocket.

The African Americans sang freedom songs and brandished hoes, pitchforks, and guns to discourage anyone from going to town for help. Two blacks, however, slipped away to find some Union officers. The Allstons spent the night safely, if restlessly, in their house. Early the next morning, they were awakened by a knock at the unlocked front door. There stood Uncle Jacob. Silently, he gave back the keys.

◆◆ ◆◆ ◆◆ ◆◆

The story of the keys reveals most of the essential human ingredients of the Reconstruction era. Defeated southern whites were determined to resume control of both land and labor. The law and federal enforcement generally supported property owners. The Allston women were friendly to the blacks in a maternal way and insisted on restoring prewar deference in black-white relations. Adele and Elizabeth, in short, both feared and cared about their former slaves.

The African-American freedpeople likewise revealed mixed feelings toward their former owners: anger, loyalty, love, resentment, and pride. They paid respect to the Allstons but not to their property and crops. They wanted not revenge, but economic independence and freedom.

Northerners played a most revealing role. Union soldiers, literally and symbolically, gave the keys of freedom to the freedpeople, but did not stay around long enough to guarantee that freedom. Although encouraging blacks to plunder the master's house and seize the crops, in the crucial encounter, northern officials had disappeared. Understanding the limits of northern help, Uncle Jacob handed the keys to land and liberty back to his former owner. African-American freedpeople realized that if they wanted to ensure their freedom, they had to do it themselves.

This chapter describes what happened to the conflicting goals and dreams of three groups as they sought to redefine new social, economic, and political relationships during the postwar Reconstruction era. Amid vast devastation and bitter race and class divisions, Civil War survivors sought to put their lives back together. Victorious but variously motivated northern officials, defeated but defiant southern planters, and impoverished but hopeful African-American freedpeople could not all fulfill their conflicting goals, yet each had to try. Reconstruction would be divisive, leaving a mixed legacy of human gains and losses.

## THE BITTERSWEET AFTERMATH OF WAR

"There are sad changes in store for both races," the daughter of a Georgia planter wrote in the summer of 1865. To understand the bittersweet nature of Reconstruction, we must look at the state of the nation after the assassination of President Lincoln.

### The United States in April 1865

Constitutionally, the "Union" faced a crisis in April 1865. What was the status of the 11 former Confederate states? The North had denied the South's constitutional right to secede but needed four years of war and more than 600,000 deaths to win the point. Lincoln's official position had been that the southern states had never left the Union and were only "out of their proper relation" with the United States. The president, therefore, as commander in chief, had the authority to decide how to set relations right again. Lincoln's congressional opponents retorted that the ex-Confederate states were now "conquered provinces" and that Congress should resolve the constitutional issues and direct Reconstruction.

Politically, differences between Congress and the White House over Reconstruction mirrored a wider struggle between the two branches of the national government. During war, as has usually been the case, the executive branch assumed broad powers. Many believed, however, that Lincoln had far exceeded his constitutional authority, and his successor, Andrew Johnson, was worse. Would Congress reassert its authority?

In April 1865, the Republican party ruled virtually unchecked. Republicans had made immense achievements in the eyes of the northern public: winning the war, preserving the Union, and freeing the slaves. They had enacted sweeping economic programs on behalf of free labor and free enterprise. But the party remained an uneasy grouping of former Whigs, Know-Nothings, Unionist Democrats, and antislavery idealists.

The Democrats were in shambles. Republicans depicted southern Democrats as rebels, murderers, and traitors, and they blasted northern Democrats as weak-willed, disloyal, and opposed to economic growth and progress. Nevertheless, in the election of 1864, needing to show that the war was a bipartisan effort, the Republicans nominated a Unionist Tennessee Democrat, Andrew Johnson, as Lincoln's vice president. Now the tactless Johnson headed the government.

Economically, the United States in the spring of 1865 presented stark contrasts. Northern cities and railroads hummed with productive activity; southern cities and railroads lay in ruins. Southern financial institutions were bankrupt; northern banks flourished. Mechanizing northern farms were more productive than ever; southern farms and plantations, especially those along Sherman's march, resembled a "howling waste."

The widespread devastation in the South affected southern attitudes. As a later southern writer, Wilbur Cash, explained, "If this war had smashed the Southern world, it had left the essential Southern mind and will . . . entirely unshaken." Many white southerners braced to resist Reconstruction and restore their former life and institutions; others, the minority who had remained quietly loyal to the Union, sought reconciliation.

Socially, nearly four million newly freedpeople faced the challenges of freedom. After initial joy and celebration in jubilee songs, freedmen and freedwomen quickly realized their continuing dependence on former owners. A Mississippi woman said:

> I used to think if I could be free I should be the happiest of anybody in the world. But when my master come to me, and says, Lizzie, you is free! it seems like I was in a kind of daze. And when I would wake up in the morning I would think to myself. Is I free? Hasn't I got to get up before day light and go into the field of work?

For Lizzie, and four million other blacks, everything—and nothing—had changed.

## The United States in 1865: Crises at the End of the Civil War

### Military Casualties

360,000 Union soldiers dead
260,000 Confederate soldiers dead
620,000 Total dead
375,000 Seriously wounded and maimed
995,000 Casualties nationwide in a total
           male population of 15 million
           (nearly 1 in 15)

### Physical and Economic Crises

The South devastated; its railroads, industry, and some major cities in ruins; its fields and livestock wasted

### Constitutional Crisis

Eleven former Confederate states not a part of the Union, their status unclear and future states uncertain

### Political Crisis

Republican party (entirely of the North) dominant in Congress; a former Democratic slaveholder from Tennessee, Andrew Johnson, in the presidency

### Social Crisis

Nearly 4 million black freedpeople throughout the South facing challenges of survival and freedom, along with thousands of hungry demobilized white southern soldiers and displaced white families

### Psychological Crisis

Incalculable stores of resentment, bitterness, anger, and despair throughout North and South

# Hopes Among the Freedpeople

Throughout the South in the summer of 1865, optimism surged through the old slave quarters. The slavery chain, however, broke slowly, link by link. After Union troops swept through an area, "we'd begin celebratin'," one man said, but Confederate soldiers would follow, or master and overseer would return and "tell us to go back to work." The freedmen and women learned, therefore, not to rejoice too quickly or openly.

Gradually, though, African Americans began to test the reality of freedom. Typically, their first step was to leave the plantation, if only for a few hours or days. "If I stay here I'll never know I am free," said a South Carolina woman who went to work as a cook in a nearby town. Some freedpeople cut their ties entirely—returning to an earlier master, or, more often, going into towns and cities to find jobs, schools, churches, and association with other blacks, safe from whippings and retaliation.

Many blacks left the plantation in search of a spouse, parent, or child sold away years before. Advertisements detailing these sorrowful searches filled African-American newspapers. For those who found a spouse or who had been living together in slave marriages, freedom meant getting married legally, sometimes in mass ceremonies common in the first months of emancipation. Legal marriage was important morally, but it also established the legitimacy of children and meant access to land titles and other economic opportunities. Marriage brought special burdens for black women who assumed the double role of housekeeper and breadwinner. Their determination to create a traditional family life and care for their children resulted in the withdrawal of women from plantation field labor.

Both white southerners and their former slaves suffered in the immediate aftermath of the Civil War, as illustrated by this engraving from *Frank Leslie's Illustrated Newspaper*, February 23, 1867. (The Granger Collection, New York)

Freedpeople also demonstrated their new status by choosing surnames. Names connoting independence, such as Washington, were common. Revealing their mixed feelings toward their former masters, some would adopt their master's name while others would pick "any big name 'ceptin' their master's." Emancipation changed black manners around whites as well. Masks fell, and expressions of deference disappeared. For African Americans, these changes were necessary expressions of selfhood, proving that race relations had changed, while whites saw such behaviors as "insolence."

Other than a persisting desire for education, the primary goal for most freedpeople was getting land. "All I want is to git to own fo' or five acres ob land, dat I can build me a little house on and call my home," a Mississippi black said. Only through economic independence, the traditional American goal of controlling one's own labor and land, could freedpeople like Lizzie be certain that emancipation was real.

During the war, some Union generals had put liberated slaves in charge of confiscated and abandoned lands. In the Sea Islands of South Carolina and Georgia, blacks had been working 40-acre plots of land and harvesting their own crops for several years. Farther inland, freedmen who received land were the former slaves of Cherokees and Creeks. Some blacks held title to these lands. Northern philanthropists had organized others to grow cotton for the Treasury Department to prove the superiority of free labor. In Mississippi, thousands of ex-slaves worked 40-acre tracts on leased lands ironically formerly owned by Jefferson Davis. In this highly successful experiment, they made profits sufficient to repay the government for initial costs, then lost the land to Davis's brother.

Many freedmen expected a new economic order as fair payment for their years of involuntary work. "Give us our own land," said one, "and we take care ourselves; but widout land, de ole massas can hire us or starve us, as dey please." Freedmen had every expectation that "forty acres and a mule" had been promised. Once they obtained land, family unity, and education, some looked forward to civil rights and the vote.

## The White South's Fearful Response

White southerners had equally strong dreams and expectations. Middle class (yeoman) farmers and poor whites stood beside rich planters in bread lines, all hoping to regain land and livelihood. White southerners responded with feelings of outrage, loss, and injustice. Said one man, "my pa paid his own money for our niggers; and that's not all they've robbed us of. They have taken our horses and cattle and sheep and everything."

A dominant emotion was fear. The entire structure of southern society was shaken, and the semblance of racial peace and order that slavery had provided was shattered. Having lost control of all that was familiar and revered, whites feared everything—from losing their cheap labor to having blacks sit next to them on trains. Ironically, given the rape of black women during slavery, southern whites' worst fears were of rape and revenge. African-American "impudence," some thought, would lead to legal intermarriage, and "Africanization," the destruction of the purity of the white race. African-American Union soldiers seemed especially ominous. These fears were groundless, as demobilization of black soldiers came quickly, and rape and violence by blacks against whites was extremely rare.

Believing their world turned upside down, the former planter aristocracy tried to set it right again. To reestablish white dominance, southern legislatures passed "Black codes" in the first year after the war. Many of the codes granted freedmen the right to marry, sue and be sued, testify in court, and hold property. But these rights were qualified. Complicated passages explained under exactly what circumstances blacks could testify against whites, own property (mostly they could not), or exercise other rights of free people. Forbidden rights were racial intermarriage, bearing arms, possessing alcoholic beverages, sitting on trains (except in baggage compartments), being on city streets at night, or congregating in large groups. Many of the qualified rights guaranteed by the Black codes were only passed to induce the federal government to withdraw its remaining troops from the South. This was a crucial issue, for in many places marauding whites were terrorizing virtually defenseless African Americans.

Key provisions of the Black codes regulated freedpeople's economic status. "Vagrancy" laws provided that any blacks not "lawfully employed" (by a white employer) could be arrested, jailed, fined, or hired out to a man who would assume responsibility for their debts and behavior. The codes regulated black laborers' work contracts with white landowners, including severe penalties for leaving before the yearly contract was fulfilled. A Kentucky newspaper was blunt: "The tune . . . will not be 'forty acres and a mule,' but . . . 'work nigger or starve.'"

# NATIONAL RECONSTRUCTION POLITICS

The Black codes directly challenged the national government in 1865. Would it use its power in the South to uphold the codes, white property rights and racial intimidation or to defend the liberties of freedpeople? Although the primary drama of Reconstruction pitted white landowners against African-American freedmen over land and labor in the South, in the background of these local struggles lurked the debate over Reconstruction policy among politicians in Washington. This dual drama would extend well into the twentieth century.

## Presidential Reconstruction by Proclamation

After initially demanding that the defeated Confederates be punished for "treason," President Johnson adopted a more lenient policy. On May 29, 1865, he issued two proclamations setting forth his Reconstruction program. Like Lincoln's, it rested on the claim that the southern states had never left the Union.

Johnson's first proclamation continued Lincoln's policies by offering "amnesty and pardon, with restoration of all rights of property" to most former Confederates who would swear allegiance to the Constitution and the Union. Johnson revealed his Jacksonian hostility to "aristocratic" planters by exempting ex-Confederate government leaders and rebels with taxable property valued over $20,000. They could, however, apply for individual pardons, which Johnson granted to nearly all applicants.

In his second proclamation, Johnson accepted the reconstructed government of North Carolina and prescribed the steps by which other southern states could reestablish state governments. First, the president would appoint a provisional governor, who would call a state convention representing those "who are loyal to the United States," including persons who took the oath of allegiance or were otherwise pardoned. The convention must ratify the Thirteenth Amendment, which abolished slavery; void secession; repudiate Confederate debts; and elect new state officials and members of Congress.

Under Johnson's plan, all southern states completed Reconstruction and sent representatives to Congress, which convened in December 1865. Defiant southern voters elected dozens of former officers and legislators of the Confederacy, including a few not yet pardoned. Some state conventions hedged on ratifying the Thirteenth Amendment, and some asserted former owners' right to compensation for lost slave property. No state convention provided for black suffrage, and most did nothing to guarantee civil rights, schooling, or economic protection for the freedmen. Eight months after Appomattox, the southern states were back in the Union, freedpeople were working for former masters, and the new president was firmly in charge. Reconstruction seemed to be over.

## Congressional Reconstruction by Amendment

Late in 1865, northern leaders painfully saw that almost none of their moral or political postwar goals were being fulfilled and that the Republicans were likely to lose their political power. Would Democrats and the South gain by postwar elections what they had lost by civil war?

Congressional Republicans, led by Congressman Thaddeus Stevens of Pennsylvania and Senator Charles Sumner of Massachusetts, decided to set their own policies for Reconstruction. Although labeled "radicals," the vast majority of Republicans were moderates on the economic and political rights of freedmen.

Rejecting Johnson's position that the South had already been reconstructed, Congress exercised its constitutional authority to decide on its own membership. It refused to seat the new senators and representatives from the old Confederate states. It also established the Joint Committee on Reconstruction to investigate conditions in the South. Its report documented white resistance, disorder, and the appalling treatment and conditions of freedpeople.

Congress passed a civil rights bill in 1866 to protect the fragile rights of African Americans and extended for two more years the Freedmen's Bureau, an agency providing emergency assistance at the end of the war. Johnson vetoed both bills and called his congressional opponents "traitors." His actions drove moderates into the radical camp, and Congress passed both bills over his veto— both, however, watered down by weakening the power of enforcement. Southern courts regularly disallowed black testimony against whites and acquitted whites of violence, and sentenced blacks to compulsory labor.

In such a climate, southern racial violence erupted. In a typical outbreak, in May 1866, white mobs in Memphis, encouraged by local police, rampaged for over 40 hours of terror, killing, beating, robbing, and raping virtually helpless African-American residents and burning houses, schools, and churches. Forty-eight people, all but two of them black, died. The local Union army commander took his time restoring order, arguing that his troops had "hated Negroes too." A congressional inquiry concluded that Memphis blacks had "no protection from the law whatever."

A month later, Congress sent to the states for ratification the Fourteenth Amendment, the single most significant act of the Reconstruction era. The first section of the amendment promised permanent constitutional protection of the civil rights of blacks by defining them as citizens. States were prohibited from depriving "any person of life, liberty, or property, without due process of law," and all people were guaranteed the "equal protection of the laws." Section 2 granted black male suffrage in the South, inserting the word "male" into the Constitution for the first time. Other sections of the amendment barred leaders of the Confederacy from national or state offices (except by act of Congress), repudiated the Confederate debt, and denied claims of compensation to former slave owners. Johnson urged the southern states to reject the Fourteenth Amendment, and 10 immediately did so.

The Fourteenth Amendment was the central issue of the 1866 midterm election. Johnson barnstormed the country asking voters to throw out the radical Republicans and trading insults with hecklers. Democrats north and south appealed openly to racial prejudice in attacking the Fourteenth Amendment. Republicans responded by attacking Johnson personally and freely "waved the bloody shirt," reminding voters of Democrats' treason and draft-dodging. Self-interest and local issues moved voters more than such speeches, but the result was an overwhelming Republican victory. The mandate was clear: presidential Reconstruction had not worked, and Congress could present its own.

### Reconstruction Amendments

#### Constitutional Seeds of Dreams Deferred for 100 Years (or More)

| Substance | Outcome of Ratification Process | Final Implementation and Enforcement |
|---|---|---|
| **Thirteenth Amendment—Passed by Congress January 1865** | | |
| Prohibited slavery in the United States | Ratified by 27 states, including 8 southern states, by December 1865 | Immediate, although economic freedom came by degrees |
| **Fourteenth Amendment—Passed by Congress June 1866** | | |
| (1) Defined equal national citizenship; (2) reduced state representation in Congress proportional to number of disenfranchised voters; (3) denied former Confederates the right to hold office | Rejected by 12 southern and border states by February 1867; radicals made readmission depend on ratification; ratified in July 1868 | Civil Rights Act of 1964 |
| **Fifteenth Amendment—Passed by Congress February 1869** | | |
| Prohibited denial of vote because of race, color, or previous servitude | Ratification by Virginia, Texas, Mississippi, and Georgia required for readmission; ratified in March 1870 | Voting Rights Act of 1965 |

Early in 1867, Congress passed three Reconstruction acts. The southern states were divided into five military districts, whose commanders had broad powers to maintain order and protect civil and property rights. Congress also defined a new process for readmitting a state. Qualified voters—including backs but excluding unreconstructed rebels—would elect delegates to state constitutional conventions that would write new constitutions guaranteeing black suffrage. After the new voters of the states had ratified these constitutions, elections would be held to choose governors and state legislatures. When a state ratified the Fourteenth Amendment, its representatives to Congress would be accepted, completing its readmission to the Union.

## The President Impeached

Congress also restricted presidential powers and established legislative dominance over the executive branch. The Tenure of Office Act, designed to prevent Johnson from firing the outspoken Secretary of War Edwin Stanton, limited the president's appointment powers. Other measures trimmed his power as commander in chief.

Johnson responded exactly as congressional Republicans had anticipated. He vetoed the Reconstruction acts, hindered the work of Freedmen's Bureau agents and limited the activities of military commanders in the South, and removed cabinet officers and other officials sympathetic to Congress. The House Judiciary Committee charged the president with "usurpations of power" and of acting in the "interests of the great criminals" who had led the rebellion. But moderate House Republicans defeated the impeachment resolutions.

In August 1867, Johnson dismissed Stanton and asked for Senate consent. When the Senate refused, the president ordered Stanton to surrender his office, which he refused, barricading himself inside. Now the House quickly approved impeachment resolutions, charging the president with "high crimes and misdemeanors." The three-month trial in the Senate early in 1868 featured impassioned oratory, similar to the trial of President Bill Clinton 130 years later. And as with Clinton, evidence was skimpy that Johnson had committed any constitutional crime justifying his removal. With seven moderate Republicans joining Democrats against conviction, the effort to find the president guilty fell one vote short of the required two-thirds majority. Not until the late twentieth century (Nixon and Clinton) would an American president face removal from office through impeachment.

Moderate Republicans may have feared the consequences of removing Johnson, for the man in line for the presidency, Senator Benjamin Wade of Ohio, was a leading radical Republican. Wade had endorsed woman suffrage, rights for labor unions, and civil rights for African Americans in both southern and northern states. As moderate Republicans gained strength in 1868 through their support of the presidential election winner, Ulysses S. Grant, radicalism lost much of its power within Republican ranks.

## Congressional Moderation

Congress's political battle against President Johnson was not matched by an idealistic resolve on behalf of the freedpeople. State and local elections of 1867 showed that voters preferred moderate Reconstruction policies. It is important to look not only at what Congress did during Reconstruction, but also at what it did not do.

With the exception of Jefferson Davis, Congress did not imprison Confederate leaders, and only one person, the commander of the infamous Andersonville prison camp, was executed. Congress did not insist on a long probation before southern states could be readmitted. It did not reorganize southern local governments. It did not mandate a national program of education for the freedpeople. It did not confiscate and redistribute land to the freedmen, nor did it prevent Johnson from taking land away from those who had gained titles during the war. It did not, except indirectly and with great reluctance, provide economic help to black citizens.

Congress did, however, halfheartedly grant citizenship and suffrage to freedmen, but not to freedwomen. Northerners were no more prepared than southerners to make African Americans equal citizens. Proposals to give black men the vote gained support in the North only after the presidential election of 1868, when General Grant, the supposedly invincible military hero, barely won the popular vote in several states. To ensure grateful black votes, Congressional Republicans, who had twice rejected a suffrage amendment, took another look at the idea. After a bitter fight, the Fifteenth Amendment, forbidding all states to deny the vote to anyone "on account of race, color, or previous condition of servitude," became part of the Constitution in 1870.

# Recovering the Past

## Novels

We usually read novels, short stories, and other forms of imaginary literature for pleasure, for the enjoyment of plot, style, symbolism, and character development. "Classic" novels such as *Moby Dick, Huckleberry Finn, The Great Gatsby, The Invisible Man,* and *Beloved,* for example, are not only written well, but also explore timeless questions of good and evil, of innocence and knowledge, of noble dreams fulfilled and shattered. We enjoy novels because we often find ourselves identifying with one of the major characters. Through that person's problems, joys, relationships, and search for identity, we gain insights about our own.

Even though they may be historically untrue, we can also read novels as historical sources, for they reveal much about the attitudes, dreams, fears, and ordinary everyday experiences of human beings in a particular period. In addition, they show how people responded to the major events of that era. The novelist, like the historian, is a product of time and place and has an interpretive point of view. Consider the two novels about Reconstruction quoted here. Neither is reputed for great literary merit, yet both reveal much about the various interpretations and impassioned attitudes of the post–Civil War era. *A Fool's Errand* was written by Albion Tourgée, a northerner; *The Clansman,* by Thomas Dixon, Jr., a southerner.

Tourgée was a young northern teacher and lawyer who fought with the Union army and moved to North Carolina after the war to begin a legal career. He became a judge and was an active Republican, supporting black suffrage and helping to shape the new state constitution. Because he boldly criticized the Ku Klux Klan, his life was threatened many times. When he left North Carolina in 1879, he published an autobiographical novel about his experiences as a judge challenging the Klan's campaign of violence and intimidation against the freedpeople.

The "fool's errand" in the novel is that of the northern veteran, Comfort Servosse, who, like Tourgée, seeks to fulfill humane goals on behalf of both blacks and whites in post–Civil War North Carolina. His efforts are thwarted, however, by threats, intimidation, a campaign of violent "outrages" against Republican leaders in the county, and a lack of support from Congress. Historians have verified the accuracy of many of the events in Tourgée's novel. While exposing the brutality of the Klan, Tourgée features loyal southern Unionists, respectable planters ashamed of Klan violence, and even guilt-ridden poor white Klansmen who try to protect or warn intended victims.

In the year of Tourgée's death, 1905, another North Carolinian published a novel with a very different analysis of Reconstruction and its fate. Thomas Dixon, Jr., was a lawyer, state legislator, Baptist minister, pro-Klan lecturer, and novelist. *The Clansman,* subtitled *A Historical Romance of the Ku Klux Klan,* reflects turn-of-the-century attitudes most white southerners still had about Republican rule during Reconstruction. According to Dixon, a power-crazed, vindictive radical Congress, led by scheming Austin Stoneman (Thaddeus Stevens), sought to impose corrupt carpetbagger and brutal black rule on a helpless South. Only through the inspired leadership of the Ku Klux Klan was the South saved from the horrors of rape and revenge.

Dixon dedicated *The Clansman* to his uncle, a Grand Titan of the Klan in North Carolina during the time when two crucial counties were being transformed from Republican to Democratic through intimidation and terror. No such violence shows up in Dixon's novel. When the novel was made the basis of D. W. Griffith's film classic, *Birth of a Nation,* in 1915, the novel's attitudes were firmly implanted on the twentieth-century American mind.

**Reflecting on the Past** Both novels convey Reconstruction attitudes toward the freedmen. Both create clearly defined heroes and villains. Both include exciting chase scenes, narrow escapes, daring rescues, and tragic deaths. Both include romantic subplots. Yet the two novels are strikingly different. Even in these brief excerpts, what differences of style and attitude do you see in the depictions of Uncle Jerry and Old Aleck? What emotional responses do you have to these passages? How do you think late nineteenth and early twentieth century Americans might have responded?

## A Fool's Errand                                                   Albion Tourgée (1879)

When the second Christmas came, Metta wrote again to her sister:

"The feeling is terribly bitter against Comfort on account of his course towards the colored people. There is quite a village of them on the lower end of the plantation. They have a church, a sabbath school, and are to have next year a school. You can not imagine how kind they have been to us, and how much they are attached to Comfort . . . . I got Comfort to go with me to one of their prayer-meetings a few nights ago. I had heard a great deal about them, but had never attended one before. It was strangely weird. There were, perhaps, fifty present, mostly middle-aged men and women. They were singing in soft, low monotone, interspersed with prolonged exclamatory notes, a sort of rude hymn, which I was surprised to know was one of their old songs in slave times. How the chorus came to be endured in those days I can not imagine. It was—

'Free! free! free, my Lord, free!

An' we walks de hebben-ly way!

"A few looked around as we came in and seated ourselves; and Uncle Jerry, the saint of the settlement, came forward on his staves, and said, in his soft voice,

"'Ev'nin', Kunnel! Sarvant, Missuss! Will you walk up, an' hev seats in front?'

"We told him we had just looked in, and might go in a short time; so we would stay in the back part of the audience.

"Uncle Jerry can not read nor write; but he is a man of strange intelligence and power. Unable to do work of any account, he is the faithful friend, monitor, and director of others. He has a house and piece of land, all paid for, a good horse and cow, and, with the aid of his wife and two boys, made a fine crop this season. He is one of the most promising colored men in the settlement: so Comfort says, at least. Everybody seems to have great respect for his character. I don't know how many people I have heard speak of his religion. Mr. Savage used to say he had rather hear him pray than any other man on earth. He was much prized by his master, even after he was disabled, on account of his faithfulness and character."

## The Clansman                                                   Thomas Dixon, Jr. (1905)

At noon Ben and Phil strolled to the polling-place to watch the progress of the first election under Negro rule. The Square was jammed with shouting, jostling, perspiring negroes, men, women, and children. The day was warm, and the African odour was supreme even in the open air . . . .

The negroes, under the drill of the League and the Freedman's Bureau, protected by the bayonet, were voting to enfranchise themselves, disfranchise their former masters, ratify a new constitution, and elect a legislature to do their will. Old Aleck was a candidate for the House, chief poll-holder, and seemed to be in charge of the movements of the voters outside the booth as well as inside. He appeared to be omnipresent, and his self-importance was a sight Phil had never dreamed. He could not keep his eyes off him . . . .

[Aleck] was a born African orator, undoubtedly descended from a long line of savage spell-binders, whose eloquence in the palaver houses of the jungle had made them native leaders. His thin spindle-shanks supported an oblong, protruding stomach, resembling an elderly monkey's, which seemed so heavy it swayed his back to carry it.

The animal vivacity of his small eyes and the flexibility of his eyebrows, which he worked up and down rapidly with every change of countenance, expressed his eager desires.

He was already mellow with liquor, and was dressed in an old army uniform and cap, with two horse-pistols buckled around his waist. On a strap hanging from his shoulder were strung a half-dozen tin canteens filled with whiskey.

One casualty of the Fourteenth and Fifteenth amendments was the goodwill of women who had worked for suffrage for two decades. They had hoped that male legislators would recognize their wartime service in support of the Union and were shocked that black males got the vote but not loyal white (or black) women. Elizabeth Cady Stanton and Susan B. Anthony, veteran suffragists and opponents of slavery, campaigned against the Fourteenth Amendment, breaking with abolitionist allies like Frederick Douglass, who had long supported woman suffrage yet declared that this was "the Negro's hour."

When the Fifteenth Amendment was proposed, suffragists wondered why the word *sex* could not have been added to the "conditions" no longer a basis for denial of the vote. Disappointment over the suffrage issue helped split the women's movement in 1869. Anthony and Stanton continued their fight for a national amendment for woman suffrage and a long list of other rights, while other women concentrated on securing the vote state-by-state. Abandoned by radical and moderate men alike, women had few champions in Congress and their efforts were put off for half a century.

Congress compromised the rights of African Americans as well as women. It gave blacks the vote but not land, the opposite of what they wanted. Almost alone, Thaddeus Stevens argued that "forty acres . . . and a hut would be more valuable . . . than the . . . right to vote." But Congress never seriously considered his plan to confiscate the land of the "chief rebels" and give a small portion of it, divided into 40-acre plots, to freedpeople, which would have violated deeply held beliefs of the Republican party and the American people on the sacredness of private property. Moreover, northern business interests looking to develop southern industry and invest in southern land liked the prospect of a large pool of propertyless African-American workers.

Congress did pass the Southern Homestead Act of 1866, making public lands available to blacks and loyal whites in five southern states. But the land was poor and inaccessible, and most black laborers were bound by contracts that prevented them from making claims before the deadline. Only about 4,000 African-American families even applied for the Homestead Act lands, and fewer than 20 percent of them saw their claims completed. White claimants did little better.

## THE LIVES OF FREEDPEOPLE

Union army Major George Reynolds boasted late in 1865 that in the area of Mississippi under his command he had "kept the negroes at work, and in a good state of discipline." Clinton Fisk, a well-meaning white who helped found a black college in Tennessee, told freedmen in 1866 that they could be "as free and as happy" working again for their "old master . . . as any where else in the world." Such pronouncements reminded blacks of white preachers' exhortations during slavery to work hard and obey masters. Ironically, Fisk and Reynolds were agents of the Freedmen's Bureau, the agency intended to aid the black transition from slaves to freedpeople.

### The Freedmen's Bureau

Never in American history has one small agency—underfinanced, understaffed, and undersupported—been given a harder task than was the Bureau of Freedmen, Refugees and Abandoned Lands. Its name is telling; its fate epitomizes Reconstruction.

The Freedmen's Bureau performed many essential services. It issued emergency food rations, clothed and sheltered homeless victims of the war, and established medical and hospital facilities. It provided funds to relocate thousands of freedpeople. It helped blacks search for relatives and get legally married. It represented African Americans in local civil courts to ensure that they got fair trials and learned to respect the law. Working with northern missionary aid societies and southern black churches, the Bureau became responsible for an extensive program of education.

The Bureau's largest task was to promote African Americans' economic well-being. This included settling them on abandoned lands and getting them started with tools, seed, and draft animals, as well as arranging work contracts with white landowners. But in this area the Freedmen's Bureau, determined not to instill a new dependency, more often than not supported the needs of whites to find cheap labor than blacks to become independent farmers.

Although a few agents were idealistic New Englanders eager to help freedpeople adjust to freedom, most were Union army officers more concerned with social order than social transformation. Working in a postwar climate of resentment and violence, Freedmen's Bureau agents were overworked, underpaid, spread too thin (at its peak only 900 agents were scattered across the South), and constantly harassed by local whites. Even the best-intentioned agents would have agreed with Bureau commissioner General O. O. Howard's belief in the nineteenth-century American values of self-help, minimal government interference in the marketplace, the sanctity of private property, contractual obligations, and white superiority.

On a typical day, overburdened agents would visit local courts and schools, file reports, supervise the signing of work contracts, and handle numerous complaints, most involving contract violations between whites and blacks or property and domestic disputes among blacks. A Georgia agent wrote that he was *"tired out* and *broke down* . . . . Every day for 6 months, day after day, I have had from 5 to 20 complaints, *generally trivial* and of no moment, yet requiring consideration & attention coming from both Black & White." In finding work for freedmen and, to avoid dependency, imploring freedwomen to hold their husbands accountable as providers, agents often sided with white landowners by telling blacks to obey orders, trust employers, and accept disadvantageous contracts. One agent sent a man who had complained of a severe beating back to work: "Don't be sassy [and] don't be lazy when you've got work to do."

Despite numerous constraints, the agents accomplished much. In little more than two years, the Freedmen's Bureau issued 20 million rations (nearly one-third to poor whites), reunited families and resettled some 30,000 displaced war refugees, treated some 450,000 people for illness and injury, built 40 hospitals and hundreds of schools, provided books, tools, and furnishings—and even some land—to the freedmen, and occasionally protected their economic and civil rights. The great African-American historian and leading black intellectual of the twentieth century, W. E. B. Du Bois, wrote that "In a time of perfect calm, amid willing neighbors and streaming wealth," it "would have been a herculean task" for the bureau to fulfill its many purposes. But in the midst of hunger, sorrow, spite, suspicion, hate, and cruelty, "the work of any instrument of social regeneration was . . . foredoomed to failure." But Du Bois, reflecting the varied views of freed-people themselves, recognized that in laying the foundation for black labor, future land ownership, a public school system, and recognition before courts of law, the Freedmen's Bureau was "on the whole successful beyond the dreams of thought-ful men."

## Economic Freedom by Degrees

Despite the best efforts of the Freedmen's Bureau, the failure of Congress to pro-vide the promised 40 acres and a mule forced freedmen and women into a new dependency on former masters. Blacks made some progress, however, in degrees of economic autonomy and were partly responsible, along with international eco-nomic developments, in forcing the white planter class into making major changes in southern agriculture.

First, a land-intensive system replaced the labor intensity of slavery. Land ownership was concentrated into fewer and even larger holdings than before the war. From South Carolina to Louisiana, the wealthiest tenth of the population owned about 60 percent of the real estate in the 1870s. Second, these large planters increasingly specialized in one crop, usually cotton, and were tied into the inter-national market. This resulted in a steady drop in postwar food production (both grain and livestock). Third, one-crop farming created a new credit system whereby most farmers, black and white, rented seed, farm implements and ani-

Sharecroppers and tenant farmers, though more autonomous than contract laborers, remained dependent on the landlord for their survival. (Brown Brothers)

mals, provisions, housing, and land from local merchants. These changes affected race relations and class tensions among whites.

This new system took a few years to develop after emancipation. At first, most African Americans signed contracts with white landowners and worked very much as during slavery. All members of the family had to work to receive their rations. The freedpeople resented this new semiservitude, refused to sign the contracts, and sought a measure of independence working the land themselves. Freedwomen especially wanted to send their children to school rather than to apprenticeships, and insisted on "no more outdoor work," preferring small plots of land to grow vegetables near cities rather than to return to rural plantations.

Many blacks therefore broke contracts, ran away, engaged in work slowdowns or strikes, burned barns, and sought other means of negotiation. In the Sea Islands and rice-growing regions of coastal South Carolina and Georgia, where slaves had long held a degree of autonomy, resistance was especially strong. On the Heyward plantations, near those of the Allstons, the freedmen "refuse work at any price," a Freedman's Bureau agent reported, and the women "wish to stay in the house or the garden all the time."

Blacks' insistence on autonomy and land of their own was the major impetus for the change from the contract system to tenancy and sharecropping. Families would hitch mules to their old slave cabin and drag it to their plot, as far from the Big House as possible. Sharecroppers received seed, fertilizer, implements, food, and clothing. In return, the landlord (or a local merchant) told them what and how much to grow, and he took a share—usually half—of the harvest. The cropper's half usually went to pay for goods bought on credit (at high interest rates) from the landlord. Thus sharecroppers remained tied to the landlord.

Tenant farmers had only slightly more independence. Before a harvest, they promised to sell their crop to a local merchant in return for renting land, tools, and other necessities. From the merchant's store they also had to buy goods on credit (at higher prices than whites paid) against the harvest. At "settling up" time, income from sale of the crop was compared to accumulated debts. It was possible, especially after an unusually bountiful season, to come out ahead and eventually to own one's own land. But tenants rarely did; in debt at the end of each year, they had to pledge the next year's crop. World cotton prices remained low, and whereas big landowners still generated profits through their large scale of operation, sharecroppers rarely made much money. When they were able to pay their debts, landowners frequently altered loan agreements. Thus peonage replaced slavery, ensuring a continuing cheap labor supply to grow cotton and other staples in the South.

Despite this bleak picture, painstaking, industrious work by African Americans helped many gradually accumulate a measure of income, personal property and autonomy, especially in the household economy of producing eggs, butter, meat, food crops and other staples. Debt did not necessarily mean a lack of subsistence. In Virginia the declining tobacco crop forced white planters to sell off small parcels of land to blacks. Throughout the South a few African Americans became independent landowners—about 2 to 5 percent by 1880, and near 20 percent in some states by 1900.

Changes in southern agriculture affected middle class and poor white farmers as well, and planters worried about a coalition between poor black and pro-Unionist white farmers. As a Georgia farmer said in 1865, "We should tuk the

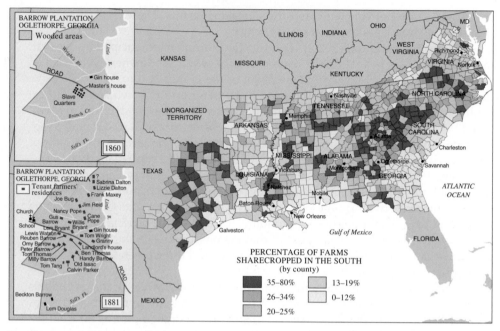

**THE RISE OF TENANCY IN THE SOUTH, 1880**   Although no longer slaves and after resisting labor
contracts and the gang system of field labor, the freedmen (as well as many poor whites) became tenant
farmers, working on shares, in the New South. The former slaves on the Barrow Plantation in Georgia, for
example, moved their households to individual 25–30 acre tenant farms, which they rented from the
Barrow family in annual contracts requiring payment in cotton and other cash crops. Note that the highest
percentage of tenants were in the "black belt."

land, as we did the niggers, and split it, and giv part to the niggers and part to me
and t'other Union fellers." But confiscation and redistribution of land was no
more likely for white farmers than for the freedmen. Whites, too, had to concentrate on growing staples, pledging their crops against high-interest credit, and facing perpetual indebtedness. In the upcountry piedmont area of Georgia, for example, the number of whites working their own land dropped from nine in ten
before the Civil War to seven in ten by 1880, while cotton production doubled.

Reliance on cotton meant fewer food crops and greater dependence on merchants for provisions. In 1884, Jephta Dickson of Jackson County, Georgia, purchased over $50 worth of flour, meal, meat, syrup, peas, and corn from a local
store; 25 years earlier, he had been almost completely self-sufficient. Fencing laws
seriously curtailed the livelihood of poor whites raising pigs and hogs, and restrictions on hunting and fishing reduced the ability of poor whites and blacks
alike to supplement incomes and diets.

In the worn-out flatlands and barren mountainous regions of the South, poor
whites' antebellum poverty, ill health, and isolation worsened after the war. Many
poor farmers were even less productive than black sharecroppers. Some became
farmhands at $6 a month (with board). Others fled to low-paying jobs in cotton
mills, where they would not have to compete against blacks.

The cultural life of poor southern whites reflected their lowly position and
their pride. Their emotional religion centered on camp meeting revivals. Their

ballads and folktales told of debt, chain gangs, and drinking prowess. Their quilt making and house construction reflected a marginal culture in which everything was saved and reused.

In part because their lives were so hard, poor whites clung to their belief in white superiority. Many joined the Ku Klux Klan and other southern white terror groups that emerged between 1866 and 1868. But however hard life was for poor whites, things were even worse for blacks. The freedpeople's hopes slowly soured. Recalled an African-American Texan, "We soon found out that freedom could make folks proud but it didn't make 'em rich."

## Black Self-Help Institutions

Many African-American leaders realized that because white institutions could not fulfill the promises of emancipation, freedpeople would have to do it themselves. Traditions of black community self-help survived in the churches and schools of the antebellum free Negro communities and in the "invisible" cultural institutions of the slave quarters. Emancipation brought a rapid increase in the growth of membership in African-American churches. The Negro Baptist Church grew from 150,000 members in 1850 to 500,000 in 1870, while the membership of the African Methodist Episcopal Church increased fourfold in the postwar decade, from 100,000 to over 400,000 members.

African-American ministers continued to exert community leadership. Many led efforts to oppose discrimination, some by entering politics; over one-fifth of the black officeholders in South Carolina were ministers. Most preachers, however, focused on sin, salvation, and revivalist enthusiasm. An English visitor to the South in 1867 and 1868 noted the intensity of black "devoutness." As one woman explained: "We make noise 'bout ebery ting else ... I want to go to Heaben in de good ole way."

The freedmen's desire for education was as strong as for religion. A school official in Virginia said that the freedmen were "down right crazy to learn." In addition to black teachers from the churches, "Yankee schoolmarms taught black children and adults." Sent by aid societies such as the American Missionary Association, these high-minded young women sought to convert blacks to Congregationalism and their version of moral behavior. In October 1865, Esther Douglass found "120 dirty, half naked perfectly wild black children" in her schoolroom near Savannah, Georgia. Eight months later, she reported that they could read, sing hymns, and repeat Bible verses and had learned "about right conduct which they tried to practice."

Such glowing reports waned as white teachers grew frustrated with crowded facilities, limited resources, local opposition, and absenteeism caused by fieldwork. In Georgia, for example, only 5 percent of black children went to school for part of any one year between 1865 and 1870, as opposed to 20 percent of white children. Blacks increasingly preferred their own teachers who could better understand them. To train African-American preachers and teachers, northern philanthropists founded Howard, Atlanta, Fisk, Morehouse, and other black universities in the South after 1865.

African-American schools, like churches, became community centers. They published newspapers, provided training in trades and farming, and promoted

Along with equal civil rights and land of their own, what the freedmen wanted most was education. Despite white opposition, one of the most positive outcomes of the Reconstruction era was education in freedmen's schools. (Valentine Museum, Richmond, Virginia)

political participation and land ownership. These efforts made black schools objects of local white hostility. As a Virginia freedman told a congressional committee, in his county, anyone starting a school would be killed and that blacks were "afraid to be caught with a book." In 1869, in Tennessee alone, 37 black schools were burned to the ground.

White opposition to black education and land ownership stimulated African-American nationalism and separatism. In the late 1860s, Benjamin "Pap" Singleton, a former Tennessee slave, urged freedpeople to abandon politics and migrate westward. He organized a land company in 1869, purchased public property in Kansas, and in the early 1870s took several groups from Tennessee and Kentucky to establish separate black towns in the prairie state. In following years, thousands of "exodusters" from the Lower South bought some 10,000 infertile acres in Kansas. But natural and human obstacles to self-sufficiency often proved insurmountable. By the 1880s, despairing of ever finding economic independence in the United States, Singleton and other nationalists advocated emigration to Canada and Liberia. Other African-American leaders, notably Frederick Douglass, continued to press for full citizenship rights within the United States.

# RECONSTRUCTION IN THE STATES

Douglass's confidence in the power of the ballot seemed warranted in the enthusiastic early months under the Reconstruction Acts of 1867. With President Johnson neutralized, Republican congressional leaders finally could prevail. Local Republicans, taking advantage of the inability or refusal of many southern whites to vote, overwhelmingly elected their delegates to state constitutional conventions in the fall of 1867. Guardedly optimistic and sensing the "sacred importance" of their work, black and white Republicans began creating new state governments.

## Republican Rule

Contrary to early pro-southern historians, southern state governments under Republican rule were not dominated by illiterate black majorities intent on "Africanizing" the South. Nor were these governments unusually corrupt or extravagant, nor did they use massive numbers of federal troops to enforce their will. By 1869, only 1,100 federal soldiers remained in Virginia, and most federal troops in Texas were guarding the frontier against Mexico and hostile Indians. Lacking strong military backing, the new state governments faced economic distress and increasingly violent harassment.

Diverse coalitions made up the new governments elected under congressional Reconstruction. These "black and tan" governments (as opponents called them) were actually predominantly white, except for the lower house of the South Carolina legislature. Some new leaders came from the old Whiggish elite of bankers, industrialists, and others interested more in economic growth and sectional reconciliation than in radical social reforms. A second group consisted of northern Republican capitalists who headed south to invest in land, railroads, and new industries. Others included Union veterans, and missionaries and teachers inspired to work in Freedmen's Bureau schools. Such people were unfairly labeled "carpetbaggers."

Moderate African Americans made up a third group in the Republican state governments. A large percentage of black officeholders were mulattos, many of them well-educated preachers, teachers, and soldiers from the North. Others were self-educated tradesmen or representatives of the small landed class of southern blacks. In South Carolina, for example, of some 255 African-American state and federal officials elected between 1868 and 1876, two-thirds were literate and one-third owned real estate; only 15 percent owned no property at all. This class composition meant that black leaders often supported policies that largely ignored the economic needs of the African-American masses. Their goals fit squarely into the American republican tradition. Black leaders reminded whites that they were also southerners, seeking only, as an 1865 petition put it, "that the same laws which govern white men shall govern black men [and that] we be dealt with as others are—in equity and justice."

The primary accomplishment of Republican rule in the South was to eliminate undemocratic features from prewar state constitutions. All states provided universal male suffrage and loosened requirements for holding office. Underrepresented counties got more legislative seats. Automatic imprisonment for debt was ended, and laws were enacted to relieve poverty and care for the handi-capped. Many southern states passed their first divorce laws and provisions granting property rights to married women. Lists of crimes punishable by death were shortened.

Republican governments financially and physically reconstructed the South by overhauling tax systems and approving generous railroad and other capital in-vestment bonds. Harbors, roads, and bridges were rebuilt; hospitals and asylums were established. Most important, the Republican governments created the South's first public school systems. As in the North, these schools were largely segregated, but for the first time rich and poor, black and white alike had access to education. By the 1880s, African-American school attendance increased from 5 to over 40 percent, and white from 20 to over 60 percent. All this cost money, and so the Republicans also greatly increased tax rates and state debts.

These considerable accomplishments came in the face of opposition like that expressed at a convention of Louisiana planters, which labeled the Republican leaders the "lowest and most corrupt body of men ever assembled in the South." There was some corruption, mostly in land sales, railway bonds, and construction contracts. Such graft had become a way of life in postwar American politics, South and North. Given their lack of experience with politics, the black role was remarkable. As Du Bois put it, "There was one thing that the White South feared more than negro dishonesty, ignorance, and incompetence, and that was negro honesty, knowledge, and efficiency."

The Republican coalition did not survive. The map on page 489 shows that Republican rule lasted for different periods in different states. It lasted the longest in the black belt states of the Deep South, where the black population was equal to or greater than the white. In Virginia, Republicans ruled hardly at all. Conserva-tive Virginia Democrats professed agreement with Congress's Reconstruction guidelines while doing as they pleased and encouraging northern investors to re-build shattered cities and develop industry. In South Carolina, African-American leaders' unwillingness to use their power to help black laborers contributed to their loss of political control to the Democrats. Class tensions and divisions among blacks in Louisiana helped weaken the Republican regime there.

## Violence and "Redemption"

Democrats used violence to regain power. As one southern editor put it, "We must render this either a white man's government, or convert the land into a Negro man's cemetery." The Ku Klux Klan was only one of several secret organizations that forcibly drove black and white Republicans from office. Although violence was terrible throughout the South, North Carolina and Mississippi typify the pattern.

After losing a close election in North Carolina in 1868, conservatives waged a concentrated terror campaign in several piedmont counties, areas of strong Unionist support. If the Democrats could win these counties in 1870, they would most likely win statewide. In the year before the election, several prominent Re-publicans were killed, including a white state senator and a leading black Union League organizer, who was hanged in the courthouse square with a sign pinned to him: "Bewar, ye guilty, both white and black." Scores of citizens were flogged, fired from their jobs, or driven in the middle of the night from burning homes and barns. The courts consistently refused to prosecute anyone for these crimes, which local papers blamed on "disgusting negroes and white Radicals." The conservative campaign worked. In the election of 1870, some 12,000 fewer Republicans voted in the two crucial counties than had voted two years earlier, and the Democrats swept back into power.

In Mississippi's state election in 1875, Democrats used similar tactics in what became known as the "Mississippi Plan." Local Democratic clubs formed armed militias, marching defiantly through black areas, breaking up Republican meetings, and provoking riots to justify killing hundreds. Armed men posted during voter registration intimidated Republicans. At the election itself, voters were either "helped" by gun-toting whites to cast a Democratic ballot or chased away. Counties that had given Republicans majorities in the thousands managed a total of less than a dozen votes in 1875!

Democrats called their victory "redemption." As conservative Democrats resumed control of each state government, Reconstruction ended. Redemption succeeded with a combination of persistent white southern resistance, including violence and coercion, and a failure of northern will and persistence.

Congress and President Grant did not totally ignore southern violence. Three Force acts, passed in 1870 and 1871, gave the president strong powers to use federal supervisors to ensure that citizens were not prevented from voting by force or fraud. The third act, also known as the Ku Klux Klan Act, declared illegal secret organizations that used disguise and coercion to deprive others of equal protection of the laws. Congress created a joint committee to investigate Klan violence, and in 1872 its report filled 13 huge volumes with horrifying testimony. Grant, who had supported these measures, sent messages to Congress proclaiming the importance of the right to vote, issued proclamations condemning lawlessness, and dispatched additional troops to South Carolina, where the violence against blacks was the worst. However, reform Republicans lost interest in defending

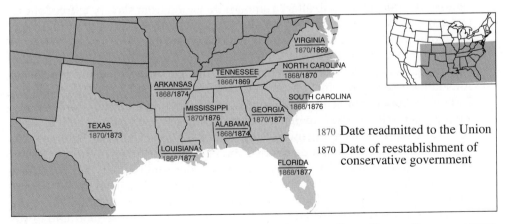

**THE RETURN OF CONSERVATIVE DEMOCRATIC CONTROL IN SOUTHERN STATES DURING RECONSTRUCTION**
Note that the length of time Republican governments were in power to implement even moderate Reconstruction programs varied from state to state. In North Carolina and Georgia, for example, Republican rule was very brief while in Virginia it never took place at all. "Redemption," the return of conservative control, took longest in the three Deep South states where electoral votes were hotly contested in the election of 1876.

African Americans, and regular Republicans decided that they could do without black votes. Both groups were much more concerned with northern issues. In 1875, Grant's advisers told him that Republicans might lose important Ohio elections if he continued protecting African Americans, so he rejected appeals by Mississippi blacks for troops to guarantee free elections. He and the nation "had tired of these annual autumnal outbreaks," the president said.

The success of the Democrats' Mississippi Plan in 1875, repeated a year later in South Carolina and Louisiana, indicated that congressional reports, presidential proclamations, and the Force acts did little to stop the reign of terror against black and white Republicans throughout the South. Despite hundreds of arrests, all-white juries refused to find whites guilty of crimes against blacks. The U.S. Supreme Court backed them, in two 1874 decisions throwing out cases against whites convicted of preventing blacks from voting and declaring key parts of the Force acts unconstitutional. Officially the Klan's power ended, but the attitudes (and tactics) of Klansmen would continue long into the next century.

## Reconstruction, Northern Style

The American people, like their leaders, were tired of battles over the freedpeople. The easiest course was to give citizenship and the vote to African Americans, and leave them to fend for themselves. Americans of increasing ethnic diversity were primarily interested in starting families, finding work, and making money. Slovakian immigrants fired furnaces in Pittsburgh; Chinese men pounded in railroad ties for the Central Pacific over the Sierra Nevada mountains and across the Nevada desert; Yankee women taught in one-room school houses in Vermont for $23 a month; Mexican vaqueros drove Texan cattle herds to Kansas; and Scandinavian families battled heat, locusts, and high railroad rates on farmsteads in the Dakotas.

At both the individual and national levels, Reconstruction, northern style, meant the continuation of the enormous economic revolution of the nineteenth century. Although failing to effect a smooth transition from slavery to freedom for freedpeople, Republican northerners did accelerate and solidify their program of economic growth and industrial and territorial expansion.

As North Carolina Klansmen convened in dark forests in 1869, the Central Pacific and Union Pacific railroads met in Utah, linking the Atlantic and the Pacific. As southern cotton production revived, northern iron and steel manufacturing and western settlement of the mining, cattle, and agricultural frontiers also surged. As black farmers haggled over work contracts with landowners in Georgia, white workers were organizing the National Labor Union in Baltimore. As Elizabeth and Adele Allston demanded the keys to their barns in the summer of 1865, the Boston Labor Reform Association was demanding that "our . . . education, morals, dwellings, and the whole Social System" needed to be "reconstructed." If the South would not be reconstructed, labor relations might be.

The years between 1865 and 1875 featured not only the rise (and fall) of Republican governments in the South, but also a spectacular surge of working-class organization. Stimulated by the Civil War to improve working conditions in northern factories, trade unions, labor reform associations, and labor parties flourished, culminating in the founding of the National Labor Union in 1866. Before the depression of 1873, an estimated 300,000 to 500,000 American workers enrolled in some 1,500 trade unions, the largest such increase in the nineteenth century. This growth inevitably stirred class tensions. In 1876, hundreds of freedmen in the rice region along the Combahee River in South Carolina went on strike to protest a 40-cent-per-day wage cut, clashing with local sheriffs and white Democratic rifle clubs. A year later, also fighting wage cuts, thousands of northern railroad workers went out in a nationwide wave of strikes, clashing with police and the National Guard.

As economic relations changed, so did the Republican party. Heralded by the moderate tone of the state elections of 1867 and Grant's election in 1868, the Republicans changed from a party of moral reform to one of material interest. In the continuing struggle in American politics between "virtue and commerce," self-interest was again winning. Abandoning the Freedmen's Bureau as an inappropriate federal intervention, Republican politicians had no difficulty handing out huge grants of money and land to the railroads. As freedpeople were told to help themselves, the Union Pacific was getting subsidies of between $16,000 and $48,000 for each mile of track it laid. As Susan B. Anthony and others tramped through the snows of Upstate New York with petitions for rights of suffrage and citizenship, Boss Tweed and other machine politicians defrauded New York taxpayers of millions of dollars. As Native Americans in the Great Plains struggled to preserve their sacred Black Hills from gold prospectors protected by U.S. soldiers, corrupt government officials in the East "mined" public treasuries.

By 1869, the year financier Jay Gould almost cornered the gold market, the nation was increasingly defined by its sordid, materialistic "go-getters." Henry Adams, descendant of two presidents, was living in Washington, D.C., during this era. As he explained in his 1907 autobiography, *The Education of Henry Adams,* he had had high expectations in 1869 that Grant, like George Washington, would restore moral order and peace. But when Grant announced his cabinet, a group of army cronies and rich friends to whom he owed favors, Adams felt betrayed, charging that Grant's administration "outraged every rule of decency."

Honest himself, Grant showed poor judgment of others. The scandals of his administration touched his relatives, his cabinet, and two vice-presidents. Outright graft, loose prosecution, and generally negligent administration flourished in a half dozen departments. The Whiskey Ring affair, for example, cost the public millions of dollars in tax revenues siphoned off to government officials. Gould's gold scam received the unwitting aid of Grant's Treasury Department and the knowing help of the president's brother-in-law.

Nor was Congress pure. Crédit Mobilier, a dummy corporation supposedly building the transcontinental railroads, received generous bonds and contracts in exchange for giving congressmen money, stock, and railroad lands. An Ohio congressmen described the House of Representatives in 1873 as an "auction room where more valuable considerations were disposed of under the speaker's hammer than any place on earth."

The election of 1872 showed the public uninterested in moral issues. "Liberal" Republicans, disgusted with Grant, formed a third party calling for lower tariffs and fewer grants to railroads, civil service reform, and the removal of federal troops from the South. Their candidate, Horace Greeley, editor of the New York *Tribune,* was also nominated by the Democrats, whom he had spent much of his career condemning. But despite his wretched record, Grant easily won a second term.

## The End of Reconstruction

Soon after Grant's second inauguration, a financial panic, caused by railroad mismanagement and the collapse of some eastern banks, started a terrible depression that lasted throughout the mid-1870s. In these hard times, economic issues dominated politics, further diverting attention from freedpeople. As Democrats took control of the House of Representatives in 1874 and looked toward winning the White House in 1876, politicians talked about new Grant scandals, unemployment and public works, the currency, and tariffs. No one said much about freedpeople. In 1875, a guilt-ridden Congress did pass Senator Charles Sumner's civil rights bill to put teeth into the Fourteenth Amendment. But the act was not enforced, and eight years later the Supreme Court declared it unconstitutional. Congressional Reconstruction, long dormant, was over. The election of 1876, closest in American history until 2000, sealed the end.

As their presidential candidate in 1876, the Republicans chose a former governor of Ohio, Rutherford B. Hayes, partly because of his reputation for honesty, partly because he had been a Union officer (a necessity for post-Civil War candidates), and partly because, as Henry Adams put it, he was "obnoxious to no one." The Democrats nominated Governor Samuel J. Tilden of New York, a well-known civil service reformer who had broken the corrupt Tweed ring.

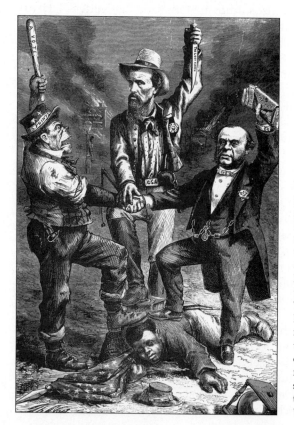

Under a caption quoting a Democratic party newspaper, "This is a white man's government," this Thomas Nast cartoon from 1868 shows three white groups, stereotyped as apelike northern Irish workers, unrepentant ex-Confederates, and rich northern capitalists, joining hands to bring Republican Reconstruction to an end almost before it began. The immigrant's vote, the Kluxer's knife, and the capitalist's dollars would restore a "white man's government" on the back of the freedman, a Union soldier still clutching the Union flag and reaching in vain for the ballot box. No single image better captures the story of the end of Reconstruction. (*Harper's Weekly*, September 5, 1868)

# Timeline

| | | | |
|---|---|---|---|
| **1865** | Civil War ends | **1869** | Georgia and Virginia reestablish Democratic party control |
| | Lincoln assassinated; Andrew Johnson becomes president | **1870** | Fifteenth Amendment ratified |
| | Johnson proposes general amnesty and Reconstruction plan | **1870s–1880s** | Black "exodusters" migrate to Kansas |
| | Racial confusion, widespread hunger, and demobilization | **1870–1871** | Force acts |
| | | | North Carolina and Georgia reestablish Democratic control |
| | Thirteenth Amendment ratified | **1872** | General Amnesty Act |
| | Freedmen's Bureau established | | Grant reelected president |
| **1865–1866** | Black codes | **1873** | Crédit Mobilier scandal |
| | Repossession of land by whites and freedmen's contracts | | Panic causes depression |
| **1866** | Freedmen's Bureau renewed and Civil Rights Act passed over Johnson's veto | **1874** | Alabama and Arkansas reestablish Democratic control |
| | Southern Homestead Act | **1875** | Civil Rights Act |
| | Ku Klux Klan formed | | Mississippi reestablishes Democratic control |
| | Tennessee readmitted to Union | **1876** | Hayes-Tilden election |
| **1867** | Reconstruction acts passed over Johnson's veto | **1876–1877** | South Carolina, Louisiana, and Florida reestablish Democratic control |
| | Impeachment controversy | **1877** | Compromise of 1877 |
| | Freedmen's Bureau ends | | Rutherford B. Hayes assumes presidency and ends Reconstruction |
| **1868** | Fourteenth Amendment ratified | | |
| | Impeachment proceedings against Johnson fail | **1880s** | Tenancy and sharecropping prevail in the South |
| | Ulysses Grant elected president | | |
| **1868–1870** | Ten states readmitted under congressional plan | | Disfranchisement and segregation of southern blacks begins |

Tilden won a popular-vote majority and appeared to have enough electoral votes for victory—except for 20 disputed electoral votes, all but one in Louisiana, South Carolina, and Florida, where some federal troops remained and where Republicans still controlled the voting apparatus despite Democratic intimidation. To settle the dispute, Congress created a commission of eight Republicans and seven Democrats who voted along party lines to give Hayes all 20 votes and a narrow electoral-college victory, 185 to 184.

As in the election of 2000, outraged Democrats protested the outcome and threatened to stop the Senate from officially counting the electoral votes, preventing Hayes's inauguration. There was talk of a new civil war. But unlike the 1850s, a North-South compromise emerged. Northern investors wanted the government to subsidize a New Orleans-to-California railroad. Southerners wanted northern

dollars but not northern political influence—no social agencies, no federal enforcement of the Fourteenth and Fifteenth amendments, and no military occupation, not even the symbolic presence left in 1876.

As the March 4 inauguration date approached, the forces of mutual self-
interest concluded the "compromise of 1877." On March 2, Hayes was declared
president-elect. After his inauguration, he ordered the last federal troops out of
the South, sending them west to fight Indians, appointed a former Confederate
general to his cabinet, supported federal aid for economic and railroad development in the South, and promised to let southerners handle race relations themselves. On a goodwill trip to the South, he told blacks that "your rights and interests would be safer if this great mass of intelligent white men were let alone by
the general government." The message was clear: Hayes would not enforce the
Fourteenth and Fifteenth amendments, initiating a pattern of executive inaction
that lasted to the 1960s. But the immediate crisis was averted, officially ending
Reconstruction.

❧❧ ❧❧ ❧❧ ❧❧

# CONCLUSION

## *A Mixed Legacy*

In the 12 years between Appomattox and Hayes's inauguration, victorious northern Republicans, defeated white southerners, and hopeful black freedpeople each
wanted more than the others would give. But each got something. The compromise of 1877 cemented the reunion of North and South, providing new opportunities for economic development in both regions. The Republican party achieved its
economic goals and generally held the White House, though not always Congress, until 1932. The ex-Confederate states came back into the Union, and southerners retained their grip on southern lands and black labor, though not without
struggle and some changes. The Allstons' freedpeople refused to sign work contracts, even when offered livestock and other favors, and in 1869, Adele Allston
had to sell much of her lands, albeit to whites.

In 1880, Frederick Douglass wrote: "Our Reconstruction measures were radically defective . . . . To the freedmen was given the machinery of liberty, but there
was denied to them the steam to put it in motion . . . . The old master class . . . retained the power to starve them to death, and wherever this power is held there is
the power of slavery." The wonder, Douglass said, was "not that freedmen have
made so little progress, but, rather, that they have made so much; not that they
have been standing still, but that they have been able to stand at all."

Freedpeople had made strong gains in education and in economic and family
survival. Despite sharecropping and tenancy, black laborers organized themselves
to achieve a measure of autonomy and opportunity in their lives. The three great
Reconstruction amendments, despite flagrant violation over the next 100 years,
held out the promise that equal citizenship and political participation would yet
be realized.

## Discovering U.S. History Online

*African-American Perspectives: Pamphlets from the Daniel A. P. Murray Collection, 1818–1907*
http://memory.loc.gov/ammem/aap/aaphome.html
A Library of Congress collection filled with links to Reconstruction topics and political speeches and manuscripts from the Federal Writers' Project interviews with ex-slaves in the 1930s.

*The Church in the Black Community*    http://docsouth.unc.edu/church/index.html
From the Documenting the American South collection of primary materials at the University of North Carolina.

*Civil War and Reconstruction, 1861–1877: Reconstruction and Rights*
http://lcweb2.loc.gov/ammem/ndlpedu/timeline/reconstruction.html
Overview of era with oral histories of whites and primary accounts of violence against blacks.

*Finding Precedent: The Impeachment of Andrew Johnson*    http://www.andrewjohnson.com/
Follow the unprecedented case from the pages of *Harper's Weekly.*

*Freedom: A Documentary History of Emancipation, 1861–1867*
http://www.inform.umd.edu/ARHU/Depts/History/Freedman/home.html
A rich collection of primary sources from the Freedom and Southern Society Project of the University of Maryland, containing superb links to four completed of nine projected volumes of collected documents.

*From Slavery to Freedom: The African-American Pamphlet Collection, 1824–1909*
http://memory.loc.gov/ammem/aapchtml/aapchome.html
Personal accounts, public orations, organizational reports and speeches from many African-American leaders of the era.

*In Black Culture: Images of African-Americans from the 19th Century*
http://digital.nypl.org/schomburg/images_aa19/
From the New York Public Library-Schomburg Center for Research in Black Culture, a huge collection of visual images by artists, engravers and photographers capturing elements of African-American life in the nineteenth century.

*Toward Racial Equality: Harper's Weekly Reports on Black America, 1857–1874*
http://blackhistory.harpweek.com
Fascinating text and imagery found in the pages of *Harper's Weekly* magazine.

## Fiction and Film

W. E. B. Du Bois's *The Quest of the Silver Fleece* (1911) is a little-known novel by the sociologist-historian about the lives of sharecroppers during Reconstruction. Howard Fast's *Freedom Road* (1944) is a novel about the heroic but ultimately failed efforts of poor whites and blacks to unite for mutual benefit during the era. Ernest Gaines's *The Autobiography of Miss Jane Pittman* (1971), framed as an autobiography, is a gripping fictional account of a proud centenarian black woman who lived from the time of the Civil War to the era of civil rights. Albion Tourgee in *A Fool's Errand* (1879), as described in the "Recovering the Past" section, takes the viewpoint of a sympathetic white judge toward helping the freedmen in North Carolina during Reconstruction.

Toni Morrison's *Beloved* (1988), an extraordinary novel set near Cincinnati in 1873, with flashbacks, is about the lasting traumas of slavery as black women especially seek to put their lives together and pursue their dreams of freedom. The film by the same name (1998), though slow moving, follows the time disconnections of the novel well with many moving scenes. *Birth of a Nation*, the classic 1913 film by D. W. Griffith portraying heroically the rise of the Ku Klux Klan as the defender of white supremacy and womanhood, is based on Thomas Dixon's *The Clansman* (1905), described in the "Recovering the Past" section of the chapter. A quite different film portrayal is seen in Oscar Micheaux's *Within Our Gates* (1919), the first feature film by an African American, available from the Library of Congress early American film collection.

# Recommended Reading

### The Bittersweet Aftermath of War

W. E. B. Du Bois, *Black Reconstruction* (1935); Laura Edwards, *Gendered Strife & Confusion: The Political Culture of Reconstruction* (1997); Eric Foner, *Reconstruction: America's Unfinished Revolution, 1863–1877* (1988); John Hope Franklin, *Reconstruction After the Civil War* (1961); Leon Litwack, *Been in the Storm So Long: The Aftermath of Slavery* (1980); James M. McPherson, *Ordeal by Fire: Civil War and Reconstruction*, 3rd ed. (2000).

### National Reconstruction Politics

Richard H. Abbott, *The Republican Party and the South, 1855–1877* (1986); Michael Les Benedict, *A Compromise of Principle: Congressional Republicans and Reconstruction, 1863–1869* (1974); David Donald, *The Politics of Reconstruction* (1965); William Gillette, *Retreat from Reconstruction, 1869–1879* (1979); Ward M. McAfee, *Religion, Race, and Reconstruction: The Public Schools in the Politics of the 1870s* (1998); William McFeeley, *Grant: A Biography* (1981); Brooks D. Simpson, *The Reconstruction Presidents* (1998); Hans L. Trefousse, *Thaddeus Stevens: Nineteenth-Century Egalitarian* (1997); Allen Trelease, *Andrew Johnson: A Biography* (1989).

### The Lives of Freedpeople

Paul Cimbala and Randall M. Miller, eds., *The Freedmen's Bureau and Reconstruction: Reconsiderations* (1999); Paul Cimbala, *Under the Guardianship of the Nation: The Freedmen's Bureau and the Reconstruction of Georgia, 1865–1870* (1997); Eric Foner, *Nothing but Freedom: Emancipation and Its Legacy* (1983); Noralee Frankel, *Freedom's Women: Black Women and Families in Civil War Era Mississippi* (1999); Sharon Ann Holt, *Making Freedom Pay: North Carolina Freedpeople Working for Themselves, 1865–1900* (2000); Tera Hunter, *To 'Joy My Freedom: Southern Black Women's Lives and Labors after the Civil War* (1997); Jacqueline Jones, *Soldiers of Light and Love: Northern Teachers and Georgia Blacks, 1865–1873* (1980); Robert Kenzer, *Enterprising Southerners: Black Economic Success in North Carolina, 1865–1915* (1997); Leon Litwack, *Been in the Storm So Long: The Aftermath of Slavery* (1980); William E. Montgomery, *Under Their Own Vine and Fig Tree: The African-American Church in the South, 1865–1900* (1993); Roger Ransom and Richard Sutch, *One Kind of Freedom: The Economic Consequences of Emancipation* (1977); Edward Royce, *The Origins of Southern Sharecropping* (1993); Julie Saville, *The Work of Reconstruction: From Slave to Wage Laborer in South Carolina, 1860–1870* (1994).

### Reconstruction in the States

W. Fitzhugh Brundage, *Lynching in the New South: Georgia and Virginia, 1880–1930* (1993); Dan T. Carter, *When the War Was Over: The Failure of Self-Reconstruction in the South* (1985); Thomas Holt, *Black over White: Negro Political Leadership in South Carolina During Reconstruction* (1977); Edward A. Miller, *Gullah Statesman: Robert Smalls from Slavery to Congress, 1839–1915* (1995); George C. Rable, *But There Was No Peace: The Role of Violence in the Politics of Reconstruction* (1984); Scott Reynolds, *Iron Confederacies: Southern Railways, Klan Violence, and Reconstruction* (1999); Joel Williamson, *The Crucible of Race* (1984) and *A Rage for Order: Black/White Relations in the American South Since Emancipation* (1986); Richard Zuczek, *State of Rebellion: Reconstruction in South Carolina* (1996).

# CHAPTER 17
# The Realities of Rural America

## CHAPTER OUTLINE

- Modernizing Agriculture
- The Second Great Removal
- The New South

- Farm Protest
- Conclusion: Farming in the Industrial Age

## AMERICAN STORIES
### Realizing Dreams: Life on the Great Plains

In 1873, Milton Leeper, his wife Hattie, and their baby Anna climbed into a wagon piled high with their possessions and set out to homestead in Boone County, Nebraska. Like others, the Leepers believed the opportunities offered by the western plains were vital to continued national health as well as individual well being. Once on the claim, the Leepers dreamed confidently of their future. Wrote Hattie to her sister in Iowa, "I like our place the best of any around here." "When we get a fine house and 100 acres under cultivation," she added, "I wouldn't trade with any one." But Milton had broken in only 13 acres when disaster struck. Hordes of grasshoppers appeared, and the Leepers fled their claim and took refuge in the nearby town of Fremont.

There they stayed for two years. Milton worked first at a store, and then hired out to other farmers. Hattie sewed, kept a boarder, and cared for chickens and a milk cow. The family lived on the brink of poverty, but never gave up hope. "Times are hard and we have had bad luck," Hattie acknowledged, but "I am going to hold that claim . . . there will [be] one gal that won't be out of a home." In 1876, the Leepers triumphantly returned to their claim with $27 to help them start over.

The grasshoppers were gone, there was enough rain, and preaching was only half a mile away. The Leepers, like others, began to prosper. Two more daughters were born. The sod house was "homely" on the outside, but plastered and cozy within. Hattie thought that the homesteaders lived "just as civilized as they would in Chicago."

Their luck did not last. Hattie died in childbirth along with her infant son. Heartbroken, Milton buried his wife and child and left the claim. The last frontier had momentarily defeated him, although he would try farming in at least four other locations before his death in 1905.

The same year that the Leepers established their Boone County homestead, another family tried their luck in a Danish settlement about 200 miles west of Omaha. Rasmus and

Ane Ebbesen and their 8-year-old son, Peter, had arrived in the United States from Denmark in 1868, lured by the promise of an "abundance" of free land "for all willing to cultivate it." By 1870, they had made it as far west as Council Bluffs, Iowa. There they stopped to earn the capital they needed to begin farming. Rasmus dug ditches for the railroad, Ane worked as a cleaning woman in a local boardinghouse, and young Peter brought water to thirsty laborers digging other ditches.

Like the Leepers, the Ebbesens eagerly took up their homestead and began to cultivate the soil. Peter later recalled that the problems that the family had anticipated never materialized. Even the rumors that the Sioux, "flying demons" in the settlers' eyes, were on the rampage proved false. The real obstacles facing the family were unexpected: rattlesnakes, prairie fires, grasshoppers—the latter just as devastating as they had been to the Leeper homestead. But unlike the Leepers, the Ebbesens stayed on the claim. Although the family "barely had enough" to eat, they survived the three years of grasshopper infestation.

In the following years, the Ebbesens thrived. Rasmus had almost all the original 80 acres under cultivation and purchased an additional 80 acres from the railroad. A succession of sod houses rose on the land and finally even a two-story frame house, paid for with money Peter earned teaching school. By their fifties, Rasmus and Ane could look with pride at their "luxurient and promising crop." But once more natural disaster struck, a "violent hailstorm . . . which completely devastated the whole lot."

The Ebbesens were lucky, however. A banker offered to buy them out, for $1,000 under what the family calculated was the farm's "real worth." But it was enough for the purchase of a "modest" house in town. Later, there was even a "dwelling of two stories and nine rooms . . . with adjacent park."

❧ ❧ ❧ ❧

The stories of the Leepers and the Ebbesens, though different in their details and endings, hint at some of the problems confronting rural Americans in the last quarter of the nineteenth century. As a mature industrial economy transformed agriculture and shifted the balance of economic power permanently away from America's farmlands to the country's cities and factories, many farmers found it impossible to realize the traditional dream of rural independence and prosperity. Even bountiful harvests no longer guaranteed success. "We were told two years ago to go to work and raise a big crop; that was all we needed," said one farmer. "We went to work and plowed and planted; the rains fell, the sun shone, nature smiled, and we raised the big crop they told us to; and what came of it? Eight cent corn, ten cent oats, two cent beef and no price at all for butter and eggs—that's what came of it." Native Americans also discovered that changes threatened their values and dreams. As the Sioux leader Red Cloud told railroad surveyors in Wyoming, "We do not want you here. You are scaring away the buffalo."

This chapter explores the agricultural transformation of the late nineteenth century and highlights the ways in which rural Americans—red, white, and black—joined the industrial world and responded to new economic and social conditions. The rise of large-scale agriculture in the West, the exploitation of its natural resources, and the development of the Great Plains form a backdrop for the discussion of the impact of white settlement on western tribes and their reactions to white incursions. In an analysis of the South, the efforts of whites to create a "New South" form a contrast to the underlying realities of race and cotton. Although the chapter shows that discrimination and economic peonage scarred the lives of most black southerners during this period, it also describes the rise of new black protest tactics and ideologies. Finally, the chapter highlights the ways in which agricultural problems of the late nineteenth century, which would continue to characterize much of agricultural life in the twentieth century, led American farmers to become reformers and to form a new political party.

## MODERNIZING AGRICULTURE

Between 1865 and 1900, the nation's farms more than doubled in number as Americans flocked west of the Mississippi. Farmers raised specialized crops with modern machinery and sped them to market over an expanding railroad system. And they became capitalists. Now, as one farmer observed, farmers had to "understand farming as a business; if they do not it will go hard with them."

### Rural Myth and Reality

The number of Americans still farming the land suggested the vigor of the country's rural tradition that pictured the farmer as a central figure for the nation. But this vision obscured the realities of American agriculture. Farmers were slipping from their dominant position in the workforce. In 1860, farmers represented almost 60 percent of the labor force; by 1900, less than 37 percent of employed Americans farmed. Meanwhile farmers' contribution to the nation's wealth declined from a third to a quarter.

Farmers were no longer the independent yeomen celebrated in rural myth, for the industrial and urban world increasingly affected them. Reliable, cheap transportation allowed them to specialize: wheat on the Great Plains, corn in the Midwest. Eastern farmers turned to vegetable, fruit, and dairy farming—or sold out. Cotton, tobacco, wheat, and rice dominated in the South, and grain, fruits, and vegetables in the Far West.

As farmers specialized for national and international markets, they became dependent on outside forces. Bankers provided capital to expand operations; middlemen stored and sometimes sold produce, and railroads carried it to market. A prosperous economy put money into laborers' pockets for food. After 1870, exports of wheat, flour, and animal products rose, with wheat becoming the country's chief cash crop. But when Russian, Argentine, and Canadian farmers began cultivating wheat, American grain growers faced competition in world markets.

As a modern business, farming demanded particular attitudes and skills. "Watch and study the markets," one rural editor advised in 1887. "The work of farming is only half done when the crop is out of the ground."

Like other post–Civil War businesses, farming stimulated technological innovation. "It is no longer necessary for the farmer to cut his wheat with sickle or cradle, nor to rake it and bind it by hand; to cut his cornstalks with a knife and shock the stalks by hand; to thresh his grain with a flail," an expert noted. Such tasks were now performed by animal-drawn mechanized harvesters and binders.

George Inness's *Lackawanna Valley*—with the reclining figure in the foreground, the train, and puffing smokestacks in the background—suggests that there need be no conflict between technology and agriculture. (Inness, George, *The Lackawanna Valley,* Gift of Mrs. Huttleston Rogers, © 2000 Board of Trustees, National Gallery of Art, Washington, c. 1856, oil on canvas, .860 × 1.275 [33⅞ × 50¼])

Machines made work easier and allowed far more land to be farmed. By 1900, more than twice the acreage was under cultivation as in 1860. But machinery was expensive, and many farmers borrowed to buy it. In the 1880s, mortgage indebtedness grew two and a half times faster than agricultural wealth.

## New Farmers, New Farms

Thus American farmers learned to operate much like other nineteenth-century businessmen. Small family farms still typified American agriculture, but vast mechanized operations devoted to the cultivation of one crop appeared, especially west of the Mississippi. "Bonanza" wheat farms of thousands of acres, established in the late 1870s in the Dakotas, foreshadowed the trend to large-scale agriculture. Often owned by corporations, they required capital investment, machinery, hired workers, and efficient managers. Such farms dramatized agricultural changes that were occurring everywhere on a smaller scale.

Only gradually did farmers realize that technology might backfire. Productivity soared 40 percent between 1869 and 1899. But yields for some crops were so large that domestic markets could not absorb them. Prices steadily declined. Corn that sold for 78 cents a bushel in 1867 yielded only 23 cents by 1889.

Falling prices did not necessarily hurt farmers. Deflation meant that farmers received less for crops but also paid less for purchases. But deflation may have encouraged overproduction. To make the same dollar income, many farmers believed they had to produce larger crops, which drove prices even lower and raised the real value of debts. In 1888, it took 174 bushels of wheat to pay interest on a $2,000 mortgage at 8 percent; by 1895, it took 320 bushels. Falling prices hit hardest the newly settled farmers who had borrowed heavily to finance their operations.

## Farming on the Western Plains, 1880s–1890s

Between 1870 and 1900, the last great wave of migration surged into the West bringing many settlers to areas west of the 90th meridian. Prewar emigrants bound for the Far West had scorned the semiarid Plains. Such views changed after the Civil War. Railroads, town boosters, and speculators all needed settlers to make their investments in the Great Plains profitable, and lured them with extravagant claims. "All that is needed is to plow, plant and attend to the crops properly," assured one news article. "The rains are abundant." Above average rainfall in the 1880s bolstered such assertions.

The acreage devoted to farming tripled west of the Mississippi in the last three decades of the century. Late-nineteenth-century industrial innovations helped settlers overcome natural obstacles to farming the Plains. In the 1870s, Joseph Glidden invented barbed wire as a cheap alternative to timber fencing.

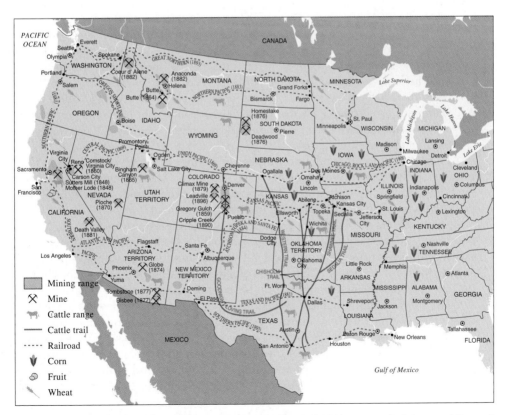

**THE NEW ECONOMY OF THE WEST, 1850–1893** This map shows the importance of mining, ranching, and farming in the western part of the nation. Note the railroad links with the east.

Twine binders speeded up grain harvesting and reduced the threat of losing crops to unpredictable weather. Mail-order steel windmills that pumped water from deep underground relieved water shortages by the 1890s.

In the first boom period of settlement from 1879 to the early 1890s, tens of thousands of eager families like the Leepers and Ebbesens began farming the Great Plains. Some claimed land under the Homestead Act, which granted 160 acres to any family head or adult who lived on the claim for five years or paid $1.25 an acre after six months of residence. Because homestead land was frequently less desirable, however, most settlers bought land from railroads or land companies.

Start-up costs were thus higher than the Homestead Act would suggest. Although western land was cheap compared with farmland in the East, a farmer was lucky to buy a good quarter section for under $500. Machinery would often cost $700. Although some thought it made economic sense to lease rather than buy land, many rented only because they lacked capital. In 1880, some 20 percent of the Plains farmers were tenants, and this percentage rose over time.

Like the Ebbesens, many new settlers were immigrants. The largest numbers came from Germany, the British Isles, and Canada, but Scandinavians, Czechs, and Poles also arrived. Unlike many immigrants to American cities, they came in family groups and intended to stay.

Life on the Plains frontier often proved difficult. Wrote one Kansas homesteader:

> I tell you Auntie no one can depend on farming for a living in this country. Henry is very industrious and this year had in over thirty acres of small grain, 8 acres of corn and about an acre of potatoes. We have sold our small grain . . . and it come to $100; now deduct $27.00 for cutting, $16.00 for threshing, $19.00 for hired help, say nothing of boarding our help, none of the trouble of drawing 25 miles to market and 25 cts on each head for ferriage over the river and where is your profit. I sometimes think this a God forsaken country, the [grass]hopper hurt our corn and we have 1/2 a crop and utterly destroyed our garden. If one wants trials, let them come to Kansas.

This letter highlights the uncertainties of frontier life: high costs, market fluctuations, pests and natural disasters, cash shortages. Many Plains pioneers took up homesteads with only a few dollars in their pockets, and survival often depended on how well families managed during the crucial first years.

Many settlers recoiled from a landscape without trees or human scale. As one New Englander observed, "It has been terrible on settlers, on the women especially, for there is no society and they get doleful and feel almost like committing suicide for want of society." Thousands of letters and diaries that describe church, parties, and social visits, however, provide a more positive picture of farming life.

The Plains required many adjustments. Scarce water and violent weather called for resourcefulness. Without firewood, farmers burned corncobs and straw. The log cabin disappeared as settlers built houses of sod "bricks," frequently with glass windows, wooden shingles, and even plastered interiors. Walls two to three feet thick kept out summer heat and winter cold, winds, and prairie fires. The solidity of the sod house was a welcome contrast to the impersonal power and scale of nature.

The first boom on the Great Plains halted abruptly in the late 1880s and early 1890s. Falling prices cut profits; one wheat farmer reported in 1890 earnings of $41.48 and expenses of $56.00. Then the unusual rainfall that had lured farmers gave way to a devastating drought. The destitute survived on boiled weeds, a few potatoes, and a little bread and butter. Many lost their farms to creditors. Some stayed as tenants. Homesteaders like the Leepers gave up. By 1900, two-thirds of homestead farms had failed. In western Kansas, the population fell by half between 1888 and 1892, and eastward-bound wagons bore a sad epitaph: "In God We Trusted: In Kansas We Busted."

Whether farmers stayed or retreated, their agricultural efforts had a significant long-term impact on the region's environment. The water table level dropped as the steel windmills pumped water from deep underground. When farmers removed sod to build their houses and plowed, they removed the earth's protective covering. Heavy winds, common on the prairies, could lift topsoil and carry it miles away. Deep plowing, essential for dry farming techniques introduced after the drought of the 1880s, worsened the situation. The 1930s dust bowl was the eventual outcome of such agricultural interventions.

## The Early Cattle Frontier, 1860–1890

Although cattle raising dated back to Spanish mission days, the commercial cattle frontier was the by-product of the Civil War when the North had cut Texas off from Confederate cattle markets. By war's end, millions of longhorns roamed the Texas range. The postwar burst of railroad construction made it possible to turn these cattle into dollars. If Texas ranchers drove their steers north to towns like Abilene, Kansas, they could be sent by rail to Chicago and Kansas City packinghouses. In the late 1860s and 1870s, cowboys herded thousands of longhorns north.

Ranchers on the Great Plains, where grasses were ripe for grazing, bought some of the cattle and bred them with Hereford and Angus cows to create animals acclimatized to severe winters. In the late 1870s and early 1880s, huge ranches arose from eastern Colorado to the Dakotas. Such ventures, many owned by eastern or European investors, paid handsomely. Cattle on the public domain cost owners little but commanded good prices. Cowboys (a third of them Mexican and black) who herded the steers made meager wages of $25 to $40 a month, just enough for a fling at the trail's end.

By the mid-1880s, the first phase of the cattle frontier was ending as farmers moved onto the Plains, buying and fencing public lands once used for grazing. But the arrival of farmers was only one factor in the changing cattle frontier. Ranchers overstocked herds in the mid-1880s. Hungry cattle ate everything in sight, then weakened as grass became scarce. Memorable blizzards followed the very hot summer of 1886. By spring, 90 percent of the cattle were dead. Frantic owners dumped their remaining animals on the market, getting $8 or even less per head.

Ranchers who survived the disaster adopted new techniques. Experimenting with new breeds, they began to fence in their herds and feed them grain during the winter. Consumers wanted tender beef rather than tough cuts from free-range animals, and these new methods satisfied the market. Ranching, like farming, was becoming a modern business.

Just as plows and windmills disrupted Plains ecology, so, too, did ranching. Ranchers killed off antelope, elk, wolves, and other wildlife. Cattle on overstocked ranges devoured perennial grasses. Less nutritious annual grasses appeared, which, in turn, sometimes disappeared. Lands once able to support large herds of cattle eventually became deserts of sagebrush, weeds, and dust.

In 1886, Solomon Butcher photographed the Rawding family in Custer County, Nebraska. The family posed with all their prized possessions in front of their sod house. Although the younger Rawdings are barefoot, the women have dressed carefully for the picture. Despite their neat attire, women of farm families like this one worked both in and outside of the house. Although their husbands often had machinery to help them with their tasks, except for the sewing machine and cookstove, farm women did their work without the help of mechanization. (Solomon D. Butcher Collection, Nebraska State Historical Society)

## Cornucopia on the Pacific

When gold was discovered in California, Americans rushed west to find it. But as one father told his son, "Plant your lands; these be your best gold fields." He was right; completion of a national railroad system made farming California's greatest asset. But California farming resembled neither the traditional picture of rural life nor the dreams of homesteaders.

Little of California's land was homesteaded or developed as family farms. When California entered the Union, speculators acquired much of the land held by Mexican ranchers. The prices speculators demanded put land out of the reach of many small farmers. By 1900, farms of 1,000 acres or more made up two-thirds of the state's farmland.

Small farmers and ranchers did exist, but they found it hard to compete with large, mechanized operators using cheap migrant laborers, usually Mexican or Chinese. One San Joaquin Valley wheat farm was so vast that workers started plowing in the morning at one end of the 17-mile field, ate lunch at its halfway point, and camped at its end that night.

The value of much of California's agricultural land, especially the southern half of the Central Valley, depended on water. By the 1870s, water, land, and railroad companies, using the labor and expertise of Chinese workers, were building dams, headgates, and canals—at high costs that they passed on to buyers eager to acquire hitherto barren land and water rights. By 1890, over a quarter of California's farms were irrigated. The irrigation ditches symbolized the importance of both technology and the managerial attitude toward the land characterizing late-nineteenth-century agriculture.

Although grain was initially California's most valuable crop, it faced stiff competition from farmers on the Plains and abroad. Some argued that land capable of raising luscious fruits "in a climate surpassing that of Italy, is too valuable for the cultivation of simple cereals." But high railroad rates and lack of refrigeration limited the volume of fresh produce sent to market. As railroad managers in the 1880s realized the potential profit that California's produce represented, they cut rates and introduced refrigerated cars. Before long, California fruit was sold as far away as London. Some travelers even began to grumble that the railroads treated produce better than people. Perhaps it was true.

## Exploiting Natural Resources

The perspective that led Americans to treat farming as a business also appeared in their attitude toward the country's natural resources. Iron, copper, coal, lead, zinc, tin, and silver strikes lured thousands to Minnesota, Colorado, Montana, Idaho, and Nevada. Popular ideas of hardy forty-niners prospecting for gold bear little resemblance to late-nineteenth-century mining with its machinery, railroads, engineers, and large work forces. Mining was a big business with high costs and a dynamic that encouraged rapid and thorough exploitation of the earth's resources.

Devastation of the nation's forests went hand-in-hand with large-scale mining and the railroads that provided links to markets. Railroads and mines alike depended on wood—for ties, for shaft timber, and for ore reduction. The California State Board of Agriculture estimated in the late 1860s that one-third of the state's forests were already lost. Felling forests affected the flow of streams and destroyed the habitat supporting birds and animals. Like the farmers and cattle owners, the companies that stripped the earth of its forest cover were also contributing to soil erosion.

The idea that the public lands belonging to the federal government ought to be rapidly developed supported such exploitation of resources. Often, in return for royalties, the government leased parts of the public domain to companies planning to extract valuable minerals, not to own land permanently. Or companies bought land, not always legally. In 1878, Congress passed the Timber and Stone Act, which initially applied to Nevada, Oregon, Washington, and California. This legislation allowed the sale of 160-acre parcels of the public domain that were "unfit for cultivation" and "valuable chiefly for timber." Timber companies saw that they could hire men to register for claims and then turn them over to timber interests. By the end of the century, more than 3.5 million acres of the public domain had been sold under the law. Most of it was in corporate hands.

The rapacious exploitation of resources combined with accelerating industrialization made some Americans uneasy. Many believed that forests played a part in the rain cycle and that their destruction would adversely affect the climate. Others, like John Muir, lamented the destruction of the country's great natural beauty. In 1868, Muir came upon the Great Valley of California, "one smooth, continuous bed of honey-bloom." He soon realized, however, that aggressive agriculture and stockraising would destroy this loveliness, and he became a champion of the preservation of natural resources. He helped create Yosemite National Park in 1890 and participated in a successful effort to get President Benjamin Harrison to classify parts of the public domain as forest reserves. In 1892, Muir established the

Sierra Club. Such efforts were more popular in the East, however, than in the West, where people were tempted with seemingly abundant natural resources and driven by the profit motive.

## THE SECOND GREAT REMOVAL

Black Elk, an Oglala Sioux, listened to a story his father had heard from his father.

> A long time ago . . . there was once a Lakota [Sioux] holy man, called Drinks Water, who dreamed what was to be; and this was long before the coming of the Wasichus [white men]. He dreamed . . . that a strange race had woven a spider's web all around the Lakotas. And he said: "When this happens, you shall live in square gray houses, in a barren land, and beside those square gray houses you shall starve."

So great was the wise man's sorrow that he died soon after his strange dream. But Black Elk lived to see it come true.

As farmers settled the western frontier and became entangled in a national economy, they clashed with the Indians who lived on the land. In California, disease and violence killed 90 percent of the Native Americans in the 30 years following the gold rush. Elsewhere, the struggle among Native Americans, white settlers, the U.S. Army, officials, and reformers was prolonged and bitter. Some tribes moved onto government reservations with little protest. But most—including the Nez Percé in the Northwest, the Apache in the Southwest, and the Plains Indians—resisted stubbornly.

## Background to Hostilities

The lives of most Plains Indians revolved around the buffalo. As migration to California and Oregon increased in the 1840s and 1850s, tribal life and animal migration patterns were disrupted. Initially, the federal government tried to persuade the tribes to stay away from white wagon trains and settlements. They did not have much success.

During the Civil War, some of the eastern tribes relocated across the Mississippi sided with the Confederacy; others with the Union. But after the war all were "treated as traitors." The federal government callously nullified pledges and treaties, leaving Indians defenseless against incursions. As settlers pushed into Kansas, tribes there were shunted into Oklahoma.

## The White Perspective

When the Civil War ended, red and white men on the Plains were already at war. In 1864, the Colorado militia massacred a band of friendly Cheyenne at Sand Creek. Cheyenne, Sioux, and Arapaho soon responded in kind. The Plains wars had begun.

Although not all whites condoned this butchery, the congressional commission authorized to make peace viewed Native Americans' future narrowly. The commissioners, including the commander of the army in the West, Civil War hero William T. Sherman, accepted as fact that the West belonged to an "industrious, thrifty, and enlightened population" of whites. Native Americans, the commission believed, must relocate to western South Dakota or Oklahoma to learn white ways. Annuities, food, and clothes would ease their transition to "civilized" life.

At two major conferences in 1867 and 1868, chiefs listened to these drastic proposals spelling the end of traditional native life. Some agreed; others, like a Kiowa chief, insisted, "I don't want to settle. I love to roam over the prairies." In any case, the agreements were not binding because no chief had authority to speak for his tribe. For its part, the U.S. Senate dragged its feet in approving the treaties. Supplies promised to Indians who settled in the arid reserved areas failed to materialize, and wildlife proved too sparse to support them. These Indians soon drifted back to their former hunting grounds.

Sherman warned, "All who cling to their old hunting ground are hostile and will remain so till killed off." When persuasion failed, the U.S. Army went to war. "The more we can kill this year," Sherman remarked, "the less will have to be killed the next war." In 1867, he ordered General Philip Sheridan to deal with the tribes. Sheridan introduced winter campaigning, aimed at seeking out Indians who divided into small groups during the winter and exterminating them.

Completion of the transcontinental railroad in 1869 added yet another pressure for "solving" the Indian question. Transcontinental railroads wanted rights-of-way through tribal lands and needed white settlers to make their operations profitable. Few whites considered Native Americans had any right to lands they wanted.

In his 1872 annual report, the commissioner for Indian affairs, Francis Amasa Walker, addressed two fundamental questions: how to prevent Indians from blocking white migration to the Great Plains, and what to do with them over the long run. Walker suggested buying off the "savages" with promises of food and gifts, luring them onto reservations, and there imposing a "rigid reformatory discipline," necessary because Indians were "unused to manual labor." Though Walker wished to save the Indians from destruction, he offered only one grim choice: "yield or perish."

## The Tribal View

Native Americans defied such attacks on their ancient way of life. Black Elk remembered that in 1863, when he was only three, his father had his leg broken in a fierce battle with white men. "When I was older," he recalled,

> I learned what the fighting was about . . . . Up on the Madison Fork the Wasichus had found much of the yellow metal that they worship and that makes them crazy, and they wanted to have a road up through our country . . . but my people did not want the road. It would scare the bison and make them go away, and also it would let the other Wasichus come in like a river. They told us that they wanted only to use a little land, as much as a wagon would take between the wheels; but our people knew better.

Black Elk's father and many others soon realized fighting was their only recourse. "There was no other way to keep our country."

Broken promises fueled Indian resistance. In 1875, the government allowed gold prospectors into the Black Hills, one of their sacred places and part of the Sioux reservation. Chiefs like Sitting Bull led the angry Sioux on the warpath. At

# Recovering the Past

## Magazines

Weekly and monthly magazines constitute a rich primary source for the historian, offering a vivid picture of the issues of the day and useful insights into popular tastes and values. With advances in the publishing industry and an increasingly literate population, the number of these journals soared in the years following the Civil War. In 1865, only 700 periodicals were published. Twenty years later there were 3,300. As the *National Magazine* grumbled, "Magazines, magazines, magazines! The newsstands are already groaning under the heavy load, and there are still more coming."

Some of these magazines were aimed at the mass market. *Frank Leslie's Illustrated Newspaper*, established in 1855, was one of the most successful. At its height, circulation reached 100,000. Making skillful use of pictures (sometimes as large as two by three feet and folded into the magazine), the weekly covered important news of the day as well as music, drama, sports, and books. Although Leslie relied more heavily on graphics and sensationalism than do modern news weeklies, his publication was a forerunner of *Newsweek* and *Time*.

Another kind of weekly magazine was aimed primarily at middle- and upper-class readers. Editors like Edwin Lawrence Godkin of *The Nation*, with a circulation of about 30,000, hoped to influence those in positions of authority and power by providing a forum for the discussion of reform issues. In contrast, *Scribner's* revealed a more conservative, middle-of-the-road point of view. Both magazines, however, exuded a confident, progressive tone characteristic of middle-class Americans.

*Harper's Weekly* was one of the most important magazines designed primarily for middle- and upper-class readers. Established in 1857, this publication continued in print until 1916. The success of *Harper's Weekly*, which called itself a "family newspaper," rested on a combination of its moderate point of view and an exciting use of illustrations and cartoons touching on contemporary events. The popular cartoons of Thomas Nast appeared in this magazine. In large part because of the use of graphics, in 1872 the circulation of *Harper's Weekly* reached a peak of 160,000.

Illustrated here is a page from the January 16, 1869, issue of *Harper's Weekly*. The layout immediately suggests the importance of graphics. Most of the page is taken up with the three pictures. The top and bottom pictures are wood engravings based on drawings by Theodore R. Davis, one of *Harper's* best-known illustrator-reporters. The center picture was derived from a photograph.

The story featured on this page concerns a victory of General George Custer in the war against the Cheyenne tribe that the U.S. Army was waging that winter. Davis had been a correspondent in the West covering Custer's actions in 1867. But when news of Custer's victory arrived, Davis was back in New York. He thus drew on his imagination for the two scenes reproduced on the next page.

What kind of characterization of Native Americans does Davis give in the picture at the top of the page? What view of American soldiers does he suggest? At the bottom of the page, you can see soldiers slaughtering "worthless" horses while Cheyenne teepees burn in the background. Would the average viewer have any sympathy for the plight of the Cheyenne by looking at this picture? This "victory," in fact, involved the slaughter not only of horses but also of all males over age eight.

**Reflecting on the Past** The editors' decision to insert a picture that had nothing to do with the incident being reported was obviously significant. As you can see, the subject in the center illustration is a white hunter who had been killed and scalped by Indians. What kind of special

*Harper's Weekly* delivered powerful messages about the Native Americans in its choice of illustrations. (The New York Public Library, Astor, Lenox & Tilden Foundations)

relationship were the editors suggesting by placing the picture of one dead white hunter in the center of a page that primarily covered a specific conflict between the Indians and the U.S. Army? How might the reader respond to the group of pictures as a whole? How do you? How does the text contribute to the overall view of the Indian–white relationship that the pictures suggest? By considering the choice of graphics and text, you can begin to discover how magazines provide insight, not only into the events of the day but also into the ways magazines shaped the values and perspectives of nineteenth-century men and women.

the Battle of Little Big Horn in 1876, they vanquished the army's most famous Indian fighter, George Custer. But bravery and skill could not permanently withstand the well-supplied, well-armed, and determined U.S. Army.

The wholesale destruction of the buffalo was an important element in white victory. The animals were central to Indian life. Plains Indians could be wasteful of buffalo where the animals were abundant, but white miners and hunters wiped out the herds. Sportsmen shot the beasts from trains. Railroad crews ate the meat. Ranchers' cattle competed for grass. And demand for buffalo bones for fertilizer and hides for robes and shoes encouraged decimation.

The slaughter of 13 million animals by 1883 appears disgraceful today. Certainly, the Indians considered white men demented. "They just killed and killed because they like to do that," said one, whereas when "we hunted the bison . . . [we] killed only what we needed." But the destruction pleased whites because it helped control the Indians.

## The Dawes Act, 1887

Changing federal policy was aimed at ending Indian power and culture. In 1871, Congress stopped the practice, in effect since the 1790s, of treating the tribes as sovereign nations. Other measures supplemented this attempt to undermine tribal integrity and leaders. Federal authorities extended government jurisdiction to reservations and warned tribes not to gather for religious ceremonies.

The Dawes Severalty Act of 1887 pulled together the strands of federal Indian policy and set its course for the rest of the century. Believing that tribal bonds kept

**INDIAN LANDS AND COMMUNITIES IN THE UNITED STATES**  The map shows a rich variety of Indian groups, state reservations (primarily in the East), and federal reservations in the West.

Indians in savagery, reformers intended to destroy them. Rather than allotting reservation lands to tribal groups, the act allowed the president to distribute these lands to individuals. Holding out the lure of private property, the framers of the bill hoped to destroy communal norms and encourage Indians to settle as farmers. Those who accepted allotments would become citizens and presumably abandon their tribal identity.

The fact that speculators as well as reformers lobbied for the legislation revealed another motive. Even if each Indian family head claimed a typical share of 160 acres, millions of "surplus" acres would remain for sale to whites. Within 20 years of the Dawes Act, Native Americans lost 60 percent of their lands. The federal government held the profits from land sales "in trust" for the "civilizing" mission.

## The Ghost Dance: An Indian Renewal Ritual

By the 1890s, their grim plight prepared many Native Americans for the message of Paiute prophet Wovoka. Wovoka predicted the destruction of the white race through natural disasters, but Indians who performed the Ghost Dance would survive and gain new strength as their ancestors and wild game returned to life. Wovoka's ideas spread rapidly. Believers expressed their hope for change through new rituals of ghost dancing, hypnosis, and meditation.

American settlers were uneasy even though the prophet did not encourage Native Americans to harm whites. Indian agents tried to prevent ghost dances and filed hysterical reports. One agent determined that the Sioux medicine man Sitting Bull, a strenuous opponent of American expansion, was a leading troublemaker and decided to arrest him. In the confusion, Indian police killed Sitting Bull. Bands of Sioux fled the reservation with the army in swift pursuit. In late December 1890, the army caught up with them at Wounded Knee Creek. Although the Sioux had raised a flag of truce and started turning over weapons, a scuffle led to a bloody massacre. Using the most up-to-date machine guns and Hotchkiss cannons, the army killed more than 200 men, women, and children.

With such measures, white Americans defeated the western tribes. Once proud, independent, and strong, Native Americans suffered dependency, poverty, and cultural disorganization on reservations, in Indian schools, or urban slums.

## THE NEW SOUTH

Of all the nation's agricultural regions, the South was the poorest. In 1880, southerners' yearly earnings were half the national average. But despite poverty and backwardness, some late-nineteenth-century southerners dreamed of making the agricultural South the rival of the industrial North.

## Postwar Southerners Face the Future

The vision of a modern, progressive, and self-sufficient South had roots in the 1850s. Then too few southerners were ready to hear the argument that the region must throw off its dependence on the North and on cotton. Now, after war and

Reconstruction, the cry for regional self-sufficiency grew sharper. Publicists of the "New South" movement argued that southern backwardness did not stem from the war, as so many southerners wished to believe, but from southern conditions, especially the cotton-based economy. Defeat only made clearer the reality that power and wealth came from factories, machines, and cities, not cotton.

Pride and self-interest dictated a new course. In hundreds of speeches, editorials, pamphlets, articles, and books, spokesmen for the New South tried to persuade fellow southerners to abandon prewar ideals that glorified leisure and gentility for the ethic of hard work. To lure northern bankers and capitalists, New South advocates held out attractive investment possibilities. Because the South was short of capital, northern assistance was critical.

To attract manufacturers, several southern state governments offered tax exemptions and the cheap labor of leased convicts. Texas and Florida awarded the railroads land grants, and cities like Atlanta and Louisville mounted huge industrial exhibitions. Middle-class southerners increasingly accepted new entrepreneurial values. The most dramatic example of commitment to the New South vision may have come in 1886 when southern railroad companies, in a crash effort, relaid tracks and adjusted rolling stock to fit "standard" northern gauges.

During the late nineteenth century, northern funds flowed south. In the 1880s, northerners increased investments in the cotton industry sevenfold and financed an expansion of southern railroads. Northern capital fuelled southern urban expansion. The percentage of southerners living in cities rose from 7 percent in 1860 to 15 percent in 1900 (as compared to national averages of 20 and 40 percent).

Birmingham, Alabama, symbolized the New South. In 1870 it was a cornfield. The next year, two northern real estate speculators arrived, attracted by rich iron deposits. Despite cholera and the depression of the 1870s, Birmingham rapidly became the center of the southern iron and steel industry. By 1890, a total of 38,414 people lived there. Coke ovens, blast furnaces, rolling mills, iron foundries, and machine shops belched smoke. Mills and factories poured out millions of dollars of finished goods, and eight railroad lines carried them away.

Other southern cities flourished, too. Memphis prospered from its lumber industry and the manufacturing of cottonseed products while Richmond became the country's tobacco capital even as its flour mills and iron and steel foundries continued to produce wealth. Augusta, Georgia, led the emerging textile industry of Georgia, the Carolinas, and Alabama.

## The Other Side of Progress

New South enthusiasts, a small group of merchants, industrialists, and planters, bragged about their iron and textile industries and paraded statistics to prove the success of modernization. But progress was slow, and older values persisted. Even New South spokesmen romanticized the recent past, impeding full acceptance of a new economic order. Despite modernization, southern schools lagged far behind the North's.

Although new industries and signs of progress abounded, two of the new industries depended on tobacco and cotton, crops long at the center of rural life. As they had before the war, commerce and government work drove urban growth. The South's economic achievements, though not insignificant, did not improve its position in relation to the North. While southern industry grew in absolute terms, it declined in relative terms.

Moreover, the South failed to reap many of industrialization's possible benefits. The South remained an economic vassal of the North. Southern businessmen grew in number, but except for the American Tobacco Company, no great southern corporations arose. Instead, southerners worked for northern corporations, which absorbed southern businesses or dominated them financially. Profits and critical decision-making power flowed north. In many cases, southern mills and factories were only allowed to handle the early stages of processing. Northern factories finished the goods.

Individual workers in the new industries may have preferred factory life to sharecropping, but the rewards were meager. The presence of thousands of women and children in factories highlighted their husbands' and fathers' inability to earn a "family wage." As usual, women and children earned less than men. Justifying these policies, one Augusta factory president explained that child labor was "a matter of charity with us; some of them would starve if they were not given employment . . . . The work we give children is very light." Actually, many children at his factory performed adults' work for children's pay.

In general, workers earned less and toiled longer in the South than elsewhere. Per capita income was the same in 1900 as in 1860—and half the national average. In North Carolina in the 1890s, workers averaged 50 cents a day, with a 70-hour week. Black workers, who made up 6 percent of the southern manufacturing force in 1890 (but were excluded from textile mills), usually had the worst jobs and the lowest wages.

## Cotton Still King

Although New South advocates envisioned the South's transformation from a rural to an industrial society, they always recognized the need for agricultural change. "It's time for an agricultural revolution," proclaimed Henry Grady, the New South's most vocal spokesman. Overdependence on "King Cotton" hobbled southern agriculture by making farmers the victims of faraway market forces and an oppressive credit system. Subdivide old cotton plantations into small diversified farms, Grady urged. Raising choice produce for urban markets could result in "simply wonderful profits."

A new agricultural South with new class and economic arrangements did emerge, but not the one Grady envisioned. Despite the breakup of some plantations, large landowners were resourceful in keeping their property and dealing with postwar conditions, as Chapter 16 showed. As they adopted new agricultural arrangements, former slaves sank into peonage.

White farmers on small and medium-size holdings fared only slightly better than black tenants and sharecroppers. Immediately after the war, high cotton prices tempted them to raise as much cotton as they could. Then prices began a disastrous decline, from 11 cents a pound in 1875 to under 5 cents in 1894. Yeoman farmers became entangled in debt. Each year, farmers bought supplies on credit from merchants so they could plant the next year's crop and support their families until harvest. In return, merchants demanded their exclusive business and acquired a lien (claim) on their crops. But when farmers sold their crops at declining prices, they usually discovered that they had not earned enough to settle with the merchant, who had charged dearly for store goods and whose annual interest rates might exceed 100 percent. Each year, thousands of farmers fell farther behind. By 1900, over half the South's white farmers and three-quarters of its black farmers were tenants. Tenancy increased all over rural America, but nowhere faster than in the Deep South.

These patterns had baneful results for individual southerners and for the South as a whole. Caught in a cycle of debt and poverty, few farmers could think of improving techniques or diversifying crops. Desperate to pay debts, they concentrated on cotton despite falling prices. Landowners pressured tenants to raise a market crop. Far from diversifying, farmers increasingly limited their crops. By 1880, the South was not growing enough food to feed its people adequately. Poor nutrition contributed to chronic bad health.

## The Nadir of Black Life

Grady and other New South advocates expected that their region could deal with the race issue without the interference of any "outside power." He had few regrets over the end of slavery, which he thought had contributed to southern economic backwardness. Realizing that black labor would be crucial to the transformation he sought, he advocated racial cooperation. But racial cooperation did not mean equality. Grady assumed that blacks were inferior and therefore supported informal segregation.

By the time of Grady's death in 1889, a much harsher perspective on southern race relations was appearing. Congressional leaders' decision in 1890 to shelve a proposed act protecting black civil rights and the defeat of a bill giving federal assistance for educational institutions rendered black Americans vulnerable. The traditional sponsor of the freedmen rights, the Republican party, left blacks to fend for themselves. The courts also abandoned them. In 1878, the Supreme Court ruled unconstitutional a Louisiana statute banning discrimination in transportation. In 1882, the Court voided the Ku Klux Klan Act of 1871, finding that the civil rights protections of the Fourteenth Amendment applied to states, not to individuals. In 1883, provisions of the Civil Rights Act of 1875 that assured blacks of equal rights in public places were similarly voided.

Rather than opposing these actions, northerners increasingly promoted negative stereotypes of blacks as lazy, ignorant, and childlike. Clearly blacks could hardly enjoy the same rights and freedoms as whites; they needed the paternal protection of the superior white race. Such stereotypes filled magazines and newspapers and were popularized in advertisements, cartoons, and theater.

The *Atlanta Monthly* in 1890 doubted that this "lowly variety of man" could ever be brought up to the intellectual and moral standards of whites. Other magazines opposed black suffrage as wasted on people too "ignorant, weak, lazy and incompetent" to make good use of it. *Forum* magazine suggested that "American Negroes" had "too much liberty." Only lynching and burning would deter "barbarous" rapists and other "sadly degenerated" Negroes corrupted since the Civil War by independence and too much education. Encouraged by northern public opinion, and with the blessing of Congress and the Supreme Court, southern whites sought to make blacks permanently second-class citizens.

In the political sphere, white southerners amended state constitutions to disenfranchise black voters. By various legal devices—poll tax, literacy tests, "good character" and "understanding" clauses administered by white voter registrars, and all-white primary elections—blacks lost the right to vote. The most ingenious method was the "grandfather clause," which specified that only citizens whose grandfathers were registered to vote on January 1, 1867, could cast ballots. This virtually excluded blacks. Although the Supreme Court outlawed such blatantly discriminatory laws, other constitutional changes, beginning in Mississippi in 1890 and spreading to all 11 former Confederate states by 1910, effectively eliminated the black vote.

In a second tactic in the 1890s, southern state and local laws legalized segregation in public facilities. Beginning with railroads and schools, "Jim Crow" laws soon covered libraries, hotels, hospitals, prisons, theaters, parks, cemeteries, toilets, sidewalks, drinking fountains—nearly every place where blacks and whites might mingle. The Supreme Court upheld these laws in 1896 in *Plessy v. Ferguson*, ruling that "separate but equal" facilities did not violate the Fourteenth Amendment's equal protection clause. The decision opened the way for as many forms of legal segregation as southern lawmakers could devise.

Political and social discrimination made it easier to keep blacks permanently confined to agricultural and unskilled labor and dependent on whites. In 1900, nearly 84 percent of black workers nationwide either did some form of agricultural labor or had service jobs, mostly as domestic servants and in laundries. These had been the primary slave occupations. The remaining 16 percent worked in forests, sawmills, mines, and, with northward migration, in northern cities.

At the end of the Civil War, at least half of all skilled craftsmen in the South had been black, but by the 1890s the percentage dropped under 10 percent as whites systematically excluded blacks from the trades. Such factory work as blacks had been doing was also reduced, largely to separate poor blacks from whites and to undercut unionization. Exclusion of blacks from industry prevented them from acquiring the skills and habits that facilitated the entry of European immigrants and their children into the middle class by the mid-twentieth century.

Blacks did not accept their decline passively. In the mid-1880s, they enthusiastically joined the Knights of Labor (discussed in Chapter 18), making up at least a third of the membership in the South. But southern whites feared that the Knights' policies of racial and economic cooperation might lead to social equality. The Charleston *News and Courier* warned darkly about "mongrels and hybrids." As blacks continued to join, whites fled the organization. White violence finished it off.

Lynchings and other violence against blacks increased. On February 21, 1891, the *New York Times* reported that in Texarkana, Arkansas, a mob caught a 32-year-old black man, Ed Coy, charged with raping a white woman, tied him to a stake, and burned him. As Coy pleaded his innocence to a large crowd, his alleged victim somewhat hesitatingly put the torch to his oil-soaked body. The *Times* report concluded that only by the "terrible death such as fire . . . can inflict" could other

IN SELF-DEFENSE

Southern Chiv. [Chivalrous Gentleman]   "Ef I hadn't-er killed
you, you would hev growd up to rule me."

In 1876, *Harper's Weekly* published this print entitled *Self-Defense.* The white man's comment, "Ef I hadn't-er killed you, you would hev growd up to rule me," is witness to the brutal treatment meted out to blacks in the late nineteenth-century South. (Harper's Weekly)

blacks "be deterred from the commission of like crimes." Ed Coy was one of more than 1,400 black men lynched or burned alive during the 1890s. About a third were charged with sex crimes. The rest were accused of a variety of "crimes" related to not knowing their place: marrying or insulting a white woman, testifying in court against whites, or having a "bad reputation." Such violence operated not only to keep blacks but also white women in their "places."

## Diverging Black Responses

White discrimination and exploitation nourished new protest tactics and ideologies among blacks. For years, Frederick Douglass had urged blacks to remain loyal Americans and count on the Republican party. In 1895 his dying words were allegedly "Agitate! Agitate! Agitate!"

Calls for black separatism within white America rang out. Insisting that blacks must join together to fight the rising tide of discrimination, T. Thomas Fortune in 1891 organized the Afro-American League. The League (the precursor of the NAACP) encouraged independent voting, opposed segregation and lynching, and urged the establishment of black institutions like banks to support black businesses. In the 1890s, black leaders lobbied to make the Oklahoma Territory, recently opened to white settlement, an all-black state. Blacks founded 25 towns there, as well as in other states and even Mexico. But these attempts, like earlier ones, were short-lived.

There were more radical black voices, too. Bishop Henry McNeal Turner, a former Union soldier and prominent black leader, despaired of ever securing equal rights for American blacks. The Constitution, he said, was "a dirty rag, a cheat, a libel" that "every Negro in the land" should "spit upon." In 1894, he organized the International Migration Society to return blacks to Africa, arguing that "this country owes us forty billions of dollars" to help. He sent two boatloads of emigrants to Liberia, but this effort worked no more successfully than those earlier in the century.

Douglass had long argued that no matter how important African roots might be, blacks had been in the Americas for generations and would have to win justice and equal rights here. W. E. B. Du Bois, the first black to receive a Ph.D. from Harvard, agreed. Yet in 1900, at the first Pan-African Conference in London, he argued that blacks must lead the struggle for liberation both in Africa and in the United States. It was at this conference that Du Bois first made his prophetic comment that "the problem of the Twentieth Century" would be "the problem of the color line."

Despite such militancy, many blacks worked patiently but persistently within white society for equality and social justice. In 1887, J. C. Price formed the Citizens Equal Rights Association, which supported various petitions and direct-action campaigns to protest segregation. Other blacks boycotted segregated streetcars in southern cities. Most black Americans continued to follow the slow, moderate, self-help program of Booker T. Washington, the best-known black leader in America. Born a slave, Washington had risen through hard work to become the founder (in 1881) and principal of Tuskegee Institute in Alabama, which he made the nation's largest and best-known industrial training school. At Tuskegee, young blacks received a highly disciplined education in scientific agriculture and skilled trades. Washington believed that economic self-help and the familiar Puritan virtues of hard work, frugality, cleanliness, and moderation would help African Americans succeed despite racism. He spent much time traveling through the North to secure philanthropic gifts for Tuskegee, becoming a favorite of the American entrepreneurial elite whose capitalist assumptions he shared.

In 1895, Washington delivered a speech at the Cotton States and International Exposition in Atlanta—his invitation had been a rare honor for a former slave—in which he proclaimed black loyalty to southern economic development while accepting the lowly status of southern blacks. "It is at the bottom of life we must begin, and not at the top," he declared. Although Washington worked behind the scenes for black civil rights, in Atlanta he publicly renounced black interest in the vote, civil rights, or social equality. Whites throughout the country enthusiastically acclaimed Washington's address, but many blacks considered his "Atlanta Compromise" a serious setback.

Washington has often been charged with conceding too quickly that political rights should follow rather than precede economic well-being. In 1903, Du Bois confronted Washington directly in *The Souls of Black Folk*, arguing for the "manly assertion" of a program of equal civil rights, suffrage, and higher education in the ideals of liberal learning. A trip through Dougherty County, Georgia, showed Du Bois the "forlorn and forsaken" condition of southern blacks. Although "here and there a man has raised his head above these murky waters . . . a pall of debt hangs over the beautiful land." The lives of most blacks were still tied to the land of the South. To improve their lives, rural blacks would have to organize.

## FARM PROTEST

During the post–Civil War period, many farmers, black and white, began to realize that only through collective action could they improve rural life. Not all were dissatisfied; midwestern farmers and those near city markets adjusted to changing economic conditions. Southern and western farmers, however, faced new problems that led to the first mass organization of farmers in American history.

## The Grange in the 1860s and 1870s

The earliest effort to organize white farmers came in 1867 when Oliver Kelley founded the Order of the Patrons of Husbandry. Originally a social and cultural organization, it soon was protesting the powerlessness of the "immense helpless mob" of farmers, victims of "human vampires." The depression of the 1870s (discussed in Chapter 18) sharpened discontent. By 1875, an estimated 800,000 had joined Kelley's organization, now known as the National Grange.

The Grangers recognized some, but not all, of the complex changes that had created rural problems. Some of their "reforms" attempted to bypass middlemen by establishing buying and selling cooperatives. Although many cooperatives failed, they indicated that farmers realized the need for unified action. Midwestern farmers also accused grain elevator operators of cheating them, and they pointed to the railroads, America's first big business, as the worst offenders. As Chapter 18 will show, cut-throat competition among railroad companies generally brought lower rates. But even though charges dropped nationwide, railroads often set high rates in rural areas, and their rebates to large shippers discriminated against small operators.

Farmers recognized that confronting the mighty railroads demanded cooperation with others, like western businessmen whose interests railroads also hurt, and political action. Between 1869 and 1874, businessmen and farmers successfully pressed Illinois, Iowa, Wisconsin, and Minnesota to pass so-called Granger laws (an inaccurate name, for the Grangers did not deserve complete credit for them) establishing maximum rates that railroads and grain elevators could charge. Other states set up railroad commissions to regulate railroad rates, or outlawed railroad pools, rebates, passes, and other practices that seemed to represent "unjust discrimination and distortion."

Railroad companies and grain elevators quickly challenged the new laws. In 1877, the Supreme Court upheld them in *Munn* v. *Illinois*. Even so, it soon became apparent that state commissions might control local rates but not long-haul rates. While Granger laws did not control the railroads and raised questions difficult to resolve on the local level, they established an important principle. The Supreme Court had made it clear that state legislatures could regulate businesses of a public nature like the railroads. When the Court reversed its ruling in *Wabash* v. *Illinois* in 1886, pressure increased on Congress to continue the struggle.

## The Interstate Commerce Act, 1887

In 1887, Congress responded with the Interstate Commerce Act, requiring that railroad rates be "reasonable and just," that rate schedules be made public, and that rebates and similar practices be discontinued. The act also created the first federal regulatory agency, the Interstate Commerce Commission (ICC), empowered to investigate and prosecute lawbreakers. But the legislation limited its authority to commerce crossing state lines.

Like state railroad commissions, the ICC found it hard to define a reasonable rate, and thousands of cases overwhelmed its tiny staff. The ICC could only bring offenders into the federal courts for lengthy legal proceedings. Few railroads worried about defying it. When they appeared in court four or five years later, they often won their cases from judges suspicious of new federal authority. Between 1887 and 1906 the Supreme Court decided 15 of 16 such cases in the railroads' favor.

## The Southern Farmers' Alliance in the 1880s and 1890s

The Grange declined in the late 1870s as the nation recovered from depression. But farm protest did not die. Depression struck farmers once again in the late 1880s and worsened in the early 1890s. Official statistics told the familiar, dismal story of falling grain prices on the plains and prairies. The national currency shortage, which usually reached critical proportions at harvest time, helped drive agricultural prices ever lower. Debt and shipping costs, however, climbed. It sometimes cost a farmer as much as one bushel of corn to send another bushel to market. Distraught farmers again tried organization, education, and cooperation.

The Southern Farmers' Alliance became one of the most important reform organizations of the 1880s. Its ambitious organizational drive sent lecturers across the South and onto the Plains. Alliance lecturers proposed programs that would help realize their slogan: "Equal rights to all, special privileges to none."

The Alliance experimented with cooperatives to free farmers from the clutches of supply merchants, banks, and other credit agencies, but they often failed. It also supported legislative efforts to regulate powerful monopolies and corporations that, they believed, gouged farmers. Many Alliance members felt that increasing the money supply was critical to improving the position of farmers and supported a national banking system empowered to issue paper money.

Finally, the Alliance called for a variety of measures to improve the quality of rural life. Better rural public schools, state agricultural colleges, and improvements in the status of women were all on its agenda.

By 1890, rural discontent was sweeping the Plains states and the South. More than a million farmers counted themselves as Alliance members. Never before had there been such a way of organizational activity in rural America.

The Alliance network included black farmers. The Colored Farmers' Alliance, organized in 1888, recognized that black and white farmers had common economic problems and must cooperate. But many southern cotton farmers, depending on black labor, had a different outlook from blacks. In 1891, cotton pickers on plantations near Memphis went on strike. Revealing the racial tensions simmering just below the surface, white posses chased the strikers and lynched 15 of them.

## The Ocala Platform, 1890

In December 1890, the National Alliance gathered in Ocala, Florida, to develop a platform. Most delegates felt that the federal government had failed to address the farmers' problems. They attacked both parties as too subservient to the "will of corporation and money power."

In the context of late-nineteenth-century political life, most of the Alliance's program was radical. It called for the direct election of U.S. senators and supported lowering the tariff (a topic much debated in Congress) with the dangerous-sounding justification that prices must be reduced for the sake of the "poor of our land." Their money plank went far beyond what any national legislator would consider, boldly envisioning a new banking system controlled by the federal government. They demanded that the government take an active economic role by increasing the amount of money in circulation in the form of treasury notes and silver. More money would cause inflation and help debtors pay off loans.

The platform also called for subtreasuries (federal warehouses) in agricultural regions where farmers could store their produce at low interest rates until market prices favored selling. To tide farmers over, the federal government would lend farmers up to 80 percent of the current local price for their produce. Other demands included a graduated income tax and the regulation of transportation and communication networks—or, if regulation failed, their nationalization.

Even though a minority of farmers belonged to the Alliance, many Americans feared it. The New York *Sun* reported that the Alliance had caused a "panic" in the two major parties.

Although the Alliance was not formally in politics, it supported sympathetic candidates in the fall elections of 1890. A surprising number of them won. Alliance victories in the West hurt the Republican party enough to cause President Harrison to refer to "our election disaster."

Before long, many Alliance members were pressing for an independent political party. Legislators elected with Alliance support did not necessarily bring action on issues of interest to farmers, or even respect. On the national level, no one had much interest in the Ocala platform. But among rural spokesmen, the first to realize the necessity of forming an independent third party was Georgia's Tom Watson, who also knew that success in the South would depend on unity between white and black farmers.

## The People's Party, 1892

In February 1892, the People's, or Populist, party was established, with almost 100 black delegates taking part. Leonidas Polk, president of the Alliance, became the party's presidential candidate. "The time has arrived," he thundered, "for the great West, the great South, and the great Northwest, to link their hands and hearts together and march to the ballot box and take possession of the government . . . and run it in the interest of the people." But by the time the party's convention met in Omaha, Polk had died. The party nominated James B. Weaver, a Union army veteran from Iowa, as its standard bearer and James G. Field, a former Confederate soldier, for vice president.

The platform preamble, written by Ignatius Donnelly, a Minnesota farmer, author, and politician, blazed with urgency:

We meet in the midst of a nation brought to the verge of moral, political and material ruin. Corruption dominates the ballot box, the legislatures, the Congress, and touches even the ermine of the bench. The people are demoralized . . . . The

# Timeline

| | | | |
|---|---|---|---|
| **1860s** | Cattle drives from Texas begin | **1887** | Dawes Severalty Act |
| **1865–1867** | Sioux Wars on the Great Plains | | Interstate Commerce Act |
| **1867** | National Grange founded | | Farm prices plummet |
| **1869** | Transcontinental railroad completed | **1888** | Colored Farmers' Alliance founded |
| **1869–1874** | Granger laws | **1890** | Afro-American League founded |
| **1873** | Financial panic triggers economic depression | | Sioux Ghost Dance movement |
| | | | Massacre at Wounded Knee |
| **1874** | Barbed wire patented | | Ocala platform |
| **1875** | Black Hills gold rush incites Sioux War | | Yosemite National Park established |
| **1876** | Custer's last stand at Little Big Horn | **1890s** | Black disenfranchisement in the South |
| **1877** | *Munn v. Illinois* | | Jim Crow laws passed in the South |
| | Bonanza farms in the Great Plains | | Declining farm prices |
| **1878** | Timber and Stone Act | **1891** | Forest Reserve Act |
| **1880s** | "New South" | **1892** | Populist party formed |
| **1881** | Tuskegee Institute founded | | Sierra Club founded |
| **1883–1885** | Depression | **1895** | Booker T. Washington's "Atlanta Compromise" address |
| **1884** | Southern Farmers' Alliance founded | | |
| **1886** | Severe winter ends cattle boom | **1896** | *Plessy v. Ferguson* |
| | *Wabash v. Illinois* | | |

fruits of the toil of millions are boldly stolen to build up colossal fortunes . . . we breed two great classes—paupers and millionaires.

The Omaha demands, drawn from the Ocala platform of 1890, were greatly expanded. They included more direct democracy (popular election of senators, direct primaries, initiative and referendum, and the secret ballot) and several planks intended to enlist support from urban labor. The People's party also endorsed a graduated income tax, the free and unlimited coinage of silver at a ratio of 16 to 1 (meaning that the U.S. Mint would have to buy silver for coinage at one-sixteenth the current official price of the equivalent amount of gold), and government ownership of railroads, telephone, and telegraph.

Populists attempted to widen political debate by promoting a new vision of government activism to resolve farmers' problems. But the obstacles they faced were monumental: weaning the South from the Democrats, encouraging southern whites to work with blacks, and persuading voters of both parties to abandon familiar political ties. Nor were all Alliance members eager to follow their leaders.

The new party nevertheless pressed ahead. Unlike the major-party candidates in 1892, Weaver campaigned actively. In the South, he faced egg- and rock-throwing Democrats. Although he won over a million popular votes (the first third-party candidate to do so), he carried only four western states with 22 electoral votes.

The Populists' support was substantial but regional. Miners and mine owners in Montana, Colorado, and New Mexico Territory favored their demand for silver coinage. Rural Americans in the South and West standing outside the mainstream of American life made up a majority of the party's following. While economic grievances sharpened their political discontent, they were often no poorer or more debt-ridden than other farmers. However, they tended to lead more isolated lives, and they felt powerless.

The People's party failed to break the Democratic stranglehold on the South, defeated by Democratic racial demagogy, violence, and fraud. For example, in Richmond County, Georgia, Democrats won 80 percent in a total vote twice the size of the number of legal voters.

In the North, Weaver failed to appeal to workers, suspicious of the party's anti-urban tone and its desire for higher agricultural prices (which meant higher food prices). Nor did Populism appeal to farmers east of the Mississippi. Their families enjoyed better farming weather, owed fewer debts, and were relatively prosperous. Their disinterest was significant, for the industrial northern states and the agriculturally prosperous Great Lake states formed an electoral majority by the 1890s. Farmers who were better integrated into their world tended to believe they could work through existing political parties. In 1892, when thousands of farmers and others were politically and economically discontented, they voted for the Democrats, not the Populists.

❧ ❧ ❧ ❧

# · CONCLUSION

## Farming in the Industrial Age

The late nineteenth century brought turbulence to rural America. The "Indian problem," which had plagued Americans for 200 years, was tragically solved for a while, but not without resistance and bloodshed. Few whites found these events troubling. Most were caught up in the challenge of responding to a fast-changing world. Believing themselves to be the backbone of the nation, white farmers brought Indian lands into cultivation, modernized their farms, and raised bumper crops. But success and a comfortable competency eluded many who were caught up in a cycle of poverty and debt. Farmers like Milton Leeper never gave up hope or farming. Others, like the Ebbesens, survived grasshopper infestations and prairie fires only to be driven from the land by other natural disasters. The Ebbesons went to a nearby town; others headed for the cities, where they joined the industrial workforce described in the next chapter. Many turned to collective action and politics. Their actions demonstrate that they did not merely react to events but attempted to shape them.

## Discovering U.S. History Online

*"California as I Saw It": First-Person Narratives of California's Early Years, 1849–1900*
http://memory.loc.gov/ammem/cbhtml.cbhome.html
This site is part of the American Memory series and contains texts and illustrations of nearly 200 works, covering the gold rush, the interaction of various groups, and the settling of the region.

*Home on the Range/Cowboy Heritage*   http://history.cc.ukans.edu/heritage/old_west/cowboy.html
This site tells the history of the cattle trails and towns like Dodge City with useful text, links, documents, and maps.

*Kappler's Indian Affairs: Laws and Treaties*   http://www.digital.library.okstate.edu/kappler
This digitized text from Oklahoma State University includes preremoval treaties with the "Five Civilized Tribes" and other tribes.

*The Evolution of the Conservation Movement, 1850–1920*
http://memory.loc.gov/ammem/amrvhtml/conshome.html
A wealth of material about the formation of the conservation movement and the cultural trends that supported its evolution.

*History of the American West, 1860–1920*
http://memory.loc.gov/ammem/award97/codhtml/hawphome.html
Over 30,000 photographs, mostly from the collections of the Denver Public Library. This site includes images of landscapes, towns, Indian tribes, and mining operations.

*Heroes and Villains*   http://www.ukans.edu/carrie/kancoll/galhero.htm
This site is part of the Kansas Collection Gallery, which offers glimpses of books, letters, diaries, photos, and other materials from the past.

*Native American Documents Project*   http://www.csusm.edu/projects/nadp/nadp.htm
California State University at San Marcos has several digital documents relating to Native Americans on this site.

*USA: Geronimo, His Own Story*   http://odur.let.rug.nl/~usa/B/geronimo/geronixx.htm
This site contains biographical and autobiographical information about this famous Native American who resisted European American domination.

## Fiction and Film

Willa Cather's novels *My Antonia* (1918) and *O Pioneers!* (1913) emphasize the energy and determination of those farming in the post–Civil War West as well as the presence of immigrants there. O. E. Rölvaag's *Giants in the Earth* (1927) deals with immigrant families but gives a very grim picture of their adjustment to farming life in the United States. Written in 1885 by Maria Amparo Ruiz de Burton, *The Squatter and the Don* provides insights into the views of Mexican Americans.

The Searchers (1956), *Stagecoach* (1939), and *She Wore a Yellow Ribbon* (1949) come from the heyday of western films and reveal mid-twentieth century (and John Wayne's) views of the late frontier. *Dances with Wolves* (1990) is Kevin Costner's indictment of the white assault on Native American life and culture. His sympathetic depiction of Indian life bears marks of 1990s consciousness. *Ethnic Notions* (1987), an Emmy-winning documentary by Marlon Riggs, traces the evolution of negative stereotypes of African Americans and the ways these stereotypes have been embodied in popular culture.

## Recommended Reading

### Modernizing Agriculture
Rodman W. Paul, with Martin Ridge, *The Far West and the Great Plains in Transition, 1859–1900* (1988); William G. Robbins, *Colony & Empire: The Capitalist Transformation of the American West* (1994); Donald Worster, *Rivers of Empire: Water, Aridity, and the Growth of the American West* (1985) and *An Unsettled Country: Changing Landscapes of the American West* (1994).

## The Second Great Removal

John G. Neihardt, *Black Elk Speaks* (1932); Robert M. Utley, *The Indian Frontier of the American West* (1984) and *The Lance and the Shield: The Life and Times of Sitting Bull* (1993); Richard White, *The Roots of Dependency: Subsistence, Environment, and Social Change Among the Choctaws, Pawnees, and Navajos* (1983).

## The New South

W. Fitzhugh Brundage, *Lynching in the New South; Georgia and Virginia, 1880–1930* (1993); Orville Vernon Burton and Robert C. McMath, Jr., eds., *Toward a New South? Post-Civil War Southern Communities* (1982); Glenda Elizabeth Gilmore, *Gender and Jim Crow: Women and the Politics of White Supremacy in North Carolina, 1896–1920* (1996); Lawrence H. Larsen, *The Rise of the Urban South* (1985); William E. Montgomery, *Under Their Own Vine and Fig Tree: The African-American Church in the South, 1865–1900* (1993); Edward Royce, *The Origins of Southern Sharecropping* (1993).

## Farm Protest

Steven Hahn, *The Roots of Southern Populism: Yeoman Farmers and the Transformation of the Georgia Upcountry, 1850–1890* (1983); Robert W. Larson, *Populism in the Mountain West* (1986); Jeffrey Ostler, *Prairie Populism: The Fate of Agrarian Radicalism in Kansas, Nebraska, and Iowa, 1880–1892* (1993); Bruce Palmer, *"Men over Money:" The Southern Populist Critique of American Capitalism* (1980).

# CHAPTER 18
# The Rise of Smokestack America

## AMERICAN STORIES
### Telling His Story: O'Donnell and the Senators

By 1883, Thomas O'Donnell, an Irish immigrant, had lived in the United States for over a decade. He was 30 years old, married with two young children, and in debt for the funeral of his third child who had died the year before. Money was scarce, for O'Donnell was a textile worker in Fall River, Massachusetts, and not well educated. "I went to work when I was young," he explained, "and have been working ever since." However, O'Donnell worked only sporadically at the mill, whose owners preferred to hire man-and-boy teams. Because O'Donnell's children were only one and three, he often saw others preferred for day work. Once, when he was passed over, he recalled, "I said to the boss . . . what am I to do; I have got two little boys at home . . . how am I to get something for them to eat; I can't get a turn when I come here . . . ." I says, "Have I got to starve; ain't I to have any work?"

O'Donnell and his family were barely getting by. He said that he had earned only $133 the previous year. Rent came to $72. The family spent $2 for a little coal, but depended on driftwood for heat. Clams were a major part of the family diet, but on some days, there was nothing to eat at all.

The children "got along very nicely all summer," but it was now November, and they were beginning to "feel quite sickly." It was hardly surprising. "One has one shoe on, a very poor one, and a slipper, that was picked up somewhere. The other has two odd shoes on, with the heel out." His wife was healthy, but not ready for winter. She had two dresses, one saved for church, and an "undershirt that she got given to her, and . . . an old wrapper, which is about a mile too big for her; somebody gave it to her."

O'Donnell was testifying to a Senate committee, which was gathering testimony in Boston in 1883 on the relations between labor and capital. The senators asked him why he did not go west. "It would not cost you over $1,500," said one. The gap between the worlds of the senator and the worker could not have been more dramatic. O'Donnell replied, "Well, I never saw over a $20 bill . . . if some one would give me $1,500 I will go." Asked by the senator if he had friends who could provide him with the funds, O'Donnell sadly replied no.

The senators, of course, were far better acquainted with the world of comfort and leisure than with the poverty of families like the O'Donnells. For them, the fruits of industrial progress were clear. As the United States became a world industrial leader in the years after the Civil War, its factories poured forth an abundance of ever-cheaper goods ranging from steel rails and farm reapers to mass-produced parlor sets. These were years of tremendous growth and broad economic and social change. Manufacturing replaced agriculture as the leading source of economic growth between 1860 and 1900. By 1890, a majority of the American workforce held nonagricultural jobs; over a third lived in cities. A rural nation of farmers was becoming a nation of industrial workers and city dwellers.

❧ ❧ ❧ ❧

As O'Donnell's appearance before the senatorial committee illustrates, industrial and technological advances profoundly changed American life. For O'Donnell and others like him, the benefits of this transformation were hard to see. Although no nationwide studies of poverty existed, estimates suggest that half the American population was too poor to take advantage of the new goods of the age. Eventually, the disparity between the reality of life for families like the O'Donnells and American ideals would give rise to attempts to improve conditions for working-class Americans, but it is unlikely that O'Donnell ever profited from such efforts.

This chapter examines the new order that resulted from the maturing of the American industrial economy. Focusing on the years between 1865 and 1900, it describes the rise of heavy industry, the organization and character of the new industrial workplace, and the emergence of big business. It then examines the locus of industrial life, the fast-growing city, and its varied people, classes, and social inequities. The chapter's central theme grows out of O'Donnell's story: as the United States built up its railroads, cities, and factories, its production and profit orientation led to a maldistribution of wealth and power. Although many Americans were too exhausted by life's daily struggles to protest new inequalities, strikes and other forms of working-class resistance punctuated the period. The social problems that accompanied the country's industrial development would capture the attention of reformers and politicians for decades to come.

## THE TEXTURE OF INDUSTRIAL PROGRESS

When America went to war in 1861, agriculture was its leading source of economic growth. Forty years later, manufacturing had taken its place. During these years, the production of manufactured goods outpaced population growth. Per capita income increased by over 2 percent a year. But these aggregates disguise the fact that many people won no gains at all.

Big businesses became the characteristic form of economic organization. They could raise the capital to build huge factories, acquire the most efficient machinery, hire hundreds of workers, and use the most up-to-date methods. The result was more goods at lower prices.

New regions grew in industrial importance. From New England to the Midwest lay the country's industrial heartland. New England remained a center of light industry, and the Midwest still processed natural resources. Now, however, the production of iron, steel, and transportation equipment joined older manufacturing operations there. In the Far West, manufacturers concentrated on processing the region's natural resources, but heavy industry made strides as well. In the less industrialized South, the textile industry put down roots by the 1890s.

## The Rise of Heavy Industry, 1880–1900

Although many factors contributed to the dramatic rise in industrial productivity, the changing nature of the industrial sector itself explains many of the gains. Pre-Civil War manufacturers had concentrated either on producing textiles, clothing, and leather goods or on processing agricultural and natural resources like grain, hogs, or lumber. Although these enterprises remained important, heavy industry grew rapidly after the war. The manufacturing of steel, iron, and machinery, meant for other producers rather than consumers, fueled economic growth.

Technological innovations allowed more efficient production that, in turn, helped to generate new needs and further innovation. Developments in the steel industry exemplify this process and highlight the important role of entrepreneurs.

Before the Civil War, skilled workers produced iron in a slow and expensive process. The iron was so soft that trains wore out iron rails within a few years. The need for a harder metal supported the development and introduction of new technology. The Bessemer converter transformed iron into steel by forcing air through the molten iron, thus reducing the carbon. The converter had the added advantage of reducing the need for highly paid skilled workers.

Andrew Carnegie was neither an inventor nor an engineer, but he recognized the possibilities of the new process and the ways to organize industry effectively. Steel companies like Carnegie's acquired access to raw materials and markets and brought all stages of steel manufacturing into one mill. Output soared and prices fell. When Andrew Carnegie introduced the Bessemer process in his plant in the mid-1870s, the price of steel dropped from $100 a ton to $50. By 1890, it cost only $12 a ton.

In turn, the production of a cheaper, stronger, more durable material than iron created new goods, new demands, and new markets, and it stimulated further technological changes. Bessemer furnaces, geared toward making steel rails, did not produce steel appropriate for building. Experimentation with the open-hearth process using high temperatures yielded steel usable by bridge builders, engineers, architects, and even designers of subways. Steel use increased dramatically, from naval vessels to screws.

New power sources facilitated American industry's shift to mass production and also suggest the importance of new ways of organizing research and innovation. In 1869, about half the industrial power came from water. The opening of new anthracite deposits, however, cut the cost of coal, and American industry rapidly converted to steam. By 1900, steam engines generated 80 percent of the nation's industrial energy supply. Then, electricity began to replace steam as a power source. Electricity owed much to Thomas Edison who had decided in 1878 that he would solve the problem of electric lighting. His research lab was based on the idea that successful innovation was fostered by professional collaboration. It had a range of specialists and facilities that included an advanced library, a chemical lab, and eventually a glassblowing lab. From these beginnings eventually came the electric generator.

## Railroads: Pioneers of Big Business

Completion of efficient and speedy national transportation and communications networks encouraged mass production and mass marketing. Beginning in 1862, federal and state governments vigorously promoted railroad construction with land grants from the public domain. Eventually, railroads received lands one and a half times the size of Texas. Local governments gave everything from land for stations to tax breaks.

With such incentives, the first transcontinental railroad was finished in 1869. Four additional transcontinental lines and miles of feeder and branch roads were laid down in the 1870s and 1880s. By 1890, trains rumbled across 165,000 miles of tracks. Telegraph lines arose alongside them.

Railroads were the pioneers of big business and a great modernizing force. After the Civil War, railroad companies expanded in size and complexity. The costs of construction required unprecedented amounts of capital while the numbers of workers and the operation of the business demanded new management techniques. No single person could finance a railroad, supervise its vast operations, or resolve the questions such a large enterprise raised. How should the operations and employees be organized? What were long- and short-term needs? What were proper rates? What share of the profits did workers deserve?

Unlike small businesses, railroads' high costs and heavy indebtedness encouraged aggressive business practices. When several lines competed, railroads often offered lower rates or secret rebates (cheaper fares in exchange for all of a company's business). Rate wars caused freight rates to drop steadily but could also plunge a railroad into bankruptcy. Instability plagued the industry.

In the 1870s, railroad leaders sought to eliminate this ruinous competition. They established "pools," informal agreements that set uniform rates or divided up the traffic. Yet these deals never completely succeeded. Too often, companies broke them, especially during business downturns.

Railroad leaders often tried to control costs and counter late-nineteenth-century falling prices by slashing wages. Owners justified this by reasoning that they had taken all the risks. As a result, railroads faced powerful worker unrest.

The huge scale and complexity of railroads called for innovative management techniques. In 1854, the Erie Railroad hired engineer and inventor Daniel McCallum to discover how to make managers and employees more accountable. McCallum pointed out that large organizations needed to be handled differently than small ones. He worked out a system that divided responsibilities and ensured a regular flow of information. It attracted widespread interest. Other large-scale businesses copied the new procedures that effectively distributed work and separated management from operations. They also learned lessons from the railroads' competitiveness, their efforts to underprice one another, and their drive to cut workers' wages.

## Growth in Other Industries

By the last quarter of the century, the textile, metal, and machinery industries equaled the railroads in size. By 1900, more than 1,000 American factories had giant labor forces ranging between 500 and 1,000, and another 450 employed more than 1,000 workers. Big business had come of age.

Business expansion was accomplished in one of two ways (or a combination of both). Some owners like steel magnate Andrew Carnegie integrated vertically—adding operations either before or after the production process. Even though he had introduced the most up-to-date innovations in his steel mills, Carnegie realized he needed his own sources of pig iron, coal, and coke—"backward" integration—to avoid dependence on suppliers. When Carnegie acquired steamships and railroads to transport his finished products, he was integrating "forward." Companies that integrated vertically frequently achieved economies of scale.

Other companies copied the railroads and integrated horizontally by combining similar businesses. They did not intend to control all stages of production, but rather, by monopolizing the market, hoped to eliminate competition and stabilize prices. While horizontal integration sometimes brought economies and greater profits, monopolistic control over prices did boost earnings.

John D. Rockefeller used horizontal integration to control the oil market. Rockefeller bought or drove out competitors of his Standard Oil of New Jersey. Although his company never achieved a complete monopoly, by 1898 it refined 84 percent of the nation's oil. In the oil business, Rockefeller said, "the day of individual competition . . . is past and gone."

Rockefeller accurately described the new economic climate. As giant businesses competed intensely, often cutting wages and prices, they absorbed smaller, weaker producers. Business ownership became increasingly concentrated. In 1870, some 808 American iron and steel firms competed. By 1900, fewer than 70 were left.

Like the railroads, many big businesses saw the wisdom of incorporation. Corporations had many advantages. By selling stock, they could raise funds for large-scale operations. Limited liability protected investors' personal assets while the corporation's legal identity allowed it to survive the death of original and subsequent shareholders. Longevity suggested a measure of stability that made corporations attractive to investors.

## Financing Postwar Growth

The economic transformations sketched here demanded huge amounts of capital and the willingness to accept financial risks. Building the railroad system cost over $1 billion by 1859 (the prewar canal system's price tag was under $2 million); after the war, another $10 billion went to complete the national railroad network. Foreign investors contributed a third of it.

Americans began to put an increasing percentage of the national income into investment rather than consumption. Although savings and commercial banks continued to invest depositors' capital, investment banking houses like Morgan & Co. played a new and significant role. Because stocks were riskier than bonds, buyers were at first cautious. But when J. Pierpont Morgan, a respected investment banker, began to market stocks, they caught on. The market for industrial securities expanded rapidly in the 1880s and 1890s. Although some Americans feared the power of investment bankers and distrusted the financial market, both were integral to late-nineteenth-century economic expansion.

## The Erratic Economic Cycle

The transformation of the economy was neither smooth nor steady. Rockefeller described his years in the oil business as "hazardous."

Two depressions, from 1873 to 1879 and from 1893 to 1897, surpassed the severity of pre–Civil War downturns. Collapsing land values, unsound banking practices, and changes in the money supply had caused antebellum depressions. In the larger and more interdependent late-nineteenth-century economy, depressions were industrial, intense, and accompanied by widespread unemployment, a phenomenon new to American life.

The business cycle had a regular pattern. First, manufacturers flooded markets with goods. Falling prices and fierce competition encouraged overproduction. When the market was saturated, sales and profits declined and the economy spiraled downward. Owners laid off workers (who lived solely on their wages); and when workers economized on food, farm prices plummeted. Farmers, like wage workers, cut purchases. Business stagnated. Finally the railroads were hurt. Eventually the cycle bottomed out, but millions of workers had lost jobs, thousands of businesses had gone bankrupt, and many Americans had suffered hardship.

## Pollution

The business cycle worried Americans more than did widespread pollution. But by the late nineteenth century, industrial processes were polluting urban air, eastern and midwestern lakes and rivers, and creating acid soil. In Birmingham, Alabama, for example, the production of iron and steel befouled the air with smoke, soot, and ashes. Coal tar, a by-product of the process, was dumped, making the soil so acid that nothing would grow in it.

The intellectual rationale of the times stressed growth, development, and the rapid exploitation of resources. As the last chapter pointed out, some steps were taken to protect the environment. But limited actions like setting aside forest reserves did not touch the problems created by the rise of heavy industry and rapid urban expansion.

## URBAN EXPANSION IN THE INDUSTRIAL AGE

As postwar manufacturers shifted from water to steam power, most favored urban locations that offered workers, specialized services, local markets, and railroad links to raw materials and distant markets. Industry, rather than commerce or finance, fueled urban expansion between 1870 and 1900.

Cities of all sizes grew. New York and Philadelphia doubled and tripled their populations. Smaller cities, especially in the industrial Midwest and the South, shared in the growth; Far Western cities increased explosively. In 1870, some 25 percent of Americans lived in cities; by 1900, fully 40 percent of them did.

## A Growing Population

The American population grew about 2 percent a year, but cities expanded far more rapidly. Why?

Not because of a high birthrate. Although more people were born than died in American cities, births contributed only modestly to the urban explosion. The general pattern of declining family size that had emerged before the Civil War continued. Urban families tended to have fewer children than rural ones, and urban children faced a host of health hazards. The death rate for infants was twice as high in cities as in the countryside. In the 1880s, half the children born in Chicago did not live to celebrate their fifth birthdays.

The real cause of rapid urban growth was the spectacular ability of the cities to attract newcomers. The nation's small town and farm population, as well as foreign immigrants, fed urban expansion. For rural Americans, the "push" came from agricultural modernization: farm machines were replacing human hands. The "pull" was the promise of work. Although urban jobs were often dirty, dangerous, and exhausting, so was farmwork. Furthermore, by 1890 manufacturing workers were earning hundreds of dollars more a year than farm laborers. Higher urban living costs gobbled up some of the differential between rural and urban wages but not all of it.

The "gilded metropolis" offered a collection of "marvels" absent from rural life. Shops, theaters, restaurants, department stores, baseball games, and the crowds amazed and amused young people coming from towns and on farms.

Southern blacks, often single and young, also fed the migratory stream into the cities. In the West and North, blacks formed only a tiny part of the population, but in southern cities they were more numerous. About 44 percent of late-nineteenth-century Atlanta's residents were black, and so were 38 percent of Nashville's. But all cities offered them few rewards as well as many dangers.

## The New Immigration, 1880–1900

In the 40 years before the Civil War, 5 million immigrants poured into the United States; from 1860 to 1900, that volume almost tripled. Three-quarters of them stayed in the Northeast, while many of the rest settled in cities across the nation, where they soon outnumbered native-born whites.

Until 1880, three-quarters of the immigrants, so-called "old immigrants," hailed from the British Isles, Germany, and Scandinavia. Then the pattern slowly changed. By 1890, "old immigrants" composed only 60 percent of the total number of newcomers, and the "new immigrants" from southern and eastern Europe made up most of the rest. Italian Catholics and eastern European Jews were most numerous, followed by Slavs (mostly Russians and Poles).

Better, cheaper transportation facilitated the great tide of migration. Trains reached deep into eastern and southern Europe. Even steerage passengers on transatlantic vessels could expect a bed and communal washroom. But it was dissatisfaction with life at home driving most to America.

The modernization of European economies also stimulated immigration. New agricultural techniques led landlords to consolidate their land, evicting longtime tenants. Some headed to European cities, others to Canada or South America, but the largest group headed to the United States. Artisans, their skills made obsolete by machinery, also pulled up stakes. Especially in Russia, government persecutions and the expansion of military drafts drove millions of Jews and other minorities to emigrate.

Opportunity in "golden" America lured thousands. State commissioners of immigration and American railroad and steamship companies wooed potential immigrants. Friends and relatives wrote optimistic letters promising help in finding work: American cities were great places for "blast frnises and Rolen milles," explained one unskilled worker. Often letters included passage money or pictures of friends in fashionable clothes.

Like rural and small-town Americans, Europeans came primarily to work. Most were young, single men with few skills. Jews, however, came most often in family groups, and women predominated among the Irish. When times were good and American industry needed many unskilled laborers, migration was heavy. In bad times, numbers fell off. Immigrants hoped to earn enough money in America to realize ambitions at home, and as many as a third eventually went back.

Although the greatest influx of Mexicans would come in the twentieth century, Mexican laborers also added to the stream of foreigners migrating to the late-nineteenth-century United States. Like Europe, Mexico was modernizing. Overpopulation and new land policies uprooted many inhabitants, such as Gonzalo

These women and children, photographed as they landed at the Battery in New York City, were part of the new immigration from eastern Europe and Russia. (The Museum of the City of New York)

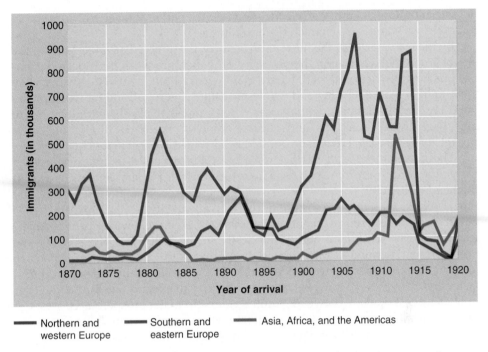

- Northern and western Europe
- Southern and eastern Europe
- Asia, Africa, and the Americas

**IMMIGRATION TO THE UNITED STATES, 1870–1920**   This chart shows the changing pattern of immigration between 1870 and 1920. You can see the growing importance of immigration from southern and eastern Europe as well as a period of intensive immigration from China. Not only did newcomers make the United States more ethnically diverse, but more religiously diverse as well. The new European immigration contained large numbers of Jews and Roman Catholics. (*Source:* U.S. Bureau of the Census.)

Plancarte. In the 1890s, he and his father supported themselves by raising cattle. When the owner of the hacienda decided to switch to producing goods for export, he ended the Plancartes' grazing privileges. After his father died, a desperately poor Gonzalo headed north. In 1895, completion of a 900-mile railroad from central Mexico to the Texas border helped migrants like him find work in the Southwest and West, often on railroads and in mines.

Overpopulation, turmoil, unemployment, and crop failures brought Asians, mostly from south China, to the "Land of the Golden Mountains." Although only 264,000 Chinese came to the United States between 1860 and 1900, they constituted a significant minority on the West Coast. Most were unskilled male contract laborers, away from wives and families for years. They held some of the worst jobs in the West. To serve them, contractors brought in Chinese women to serve as prostitutes.

## THE INDUSTRIAL CITY, 1880–1900

Late-nineteenth-century industrial cities had new physical and social arrangements. To one Scottish visitor, urban "monotony" was "like a nightmare." Slums (nothing new) grew disturbingly, but grand mansions, handsome business and industrial buildings, impressive civic monuments, parks, and acres of substantial middle-class homes also characterized urban life.

By the last quarter of the nineteenth century, the jumbled arrangements of the antebellum city based upon the necessity of walking to work disappeared. Central business districts emerged, where many worked but few lived. Nearby were areas of light manufacturing and wholesale activity with housing for workers. Beyond lay middle-class residential areas. Then came the suburbs with their "pure air, peacefulness, quietude, and natural scenery." Scattered throughout were pockets of industrial activity surrounded by crowded working-class housing.

The new pattern, still characteristic of American cities today, reversed the early nineteenth-century urban form, in which the most desirable housing was in the heart of the city. The new living arrangements were also more segregated by race and class than those in the preindustrial walking city.

Transportation improvements enormously affected the development of American cities. The revolution started modestly in the 1820s and 1830s with slow horse-drawn "omnibuses" accommodating only 10 to 12 passengers. Expensive fares meant most people walked to work. In the 1850s, many cities introduced faster and bigger horse railways, allowing the city to expand outward about four miles. The cost of a fare, however, limited ridership to the prosperous classes. Cable cars, trolleys, and subways after 1880 further extended city boundaries, enabling the middle class to escape grimy industrial districts.

## Neighborhoods and Neighborhood Life

Working-class neighborhoods clustered near the center of most industrial cities. Here lived newcomers from rural America and crowds of foreigners.

Ethnic groups frequently chose to gather in neighborhoods near industries requiring their labor. Although such neighborhoods often had an ethnic flavor, they were not ethnic ghettos. Immigrants and native-born Americans often lived in the same neighborhoods, on the same streets, and even in the same houses.

Working-class neighborhoods were often what would be called slums today. Many workers lived in buildings once occupied by middle- and upper-class residents, now subdivided to accommodate more people than originally intended. Others jammed into tenements, built to house as many families as possible. Outdoor privies, often shared by several families, were the rule. Water came from hydrants, and women had to carry it inside. Such indoor fixtures as existed frequently poured waste directly into unpaved alleys. Refuse piles stank in the summer and froze in the winter. Even when people kept their own living quarters clean, the outside environment was unsanitary. It was no surprise that urban death rates were so high. Not till the turn of the century did the public health movement begin to improve such circumstances.

Working-class living conditions, however, were far from uniform. Skilled workers might rent and furnish comfortable quarters. A few owned their homes. Unskilled and semiskilled workers were not so fortunate. Yet, despite the often drab circumstances, working families succeeded in creating a sense of community. A wide range of institutions and associations came to life. Religious and ethnic associations helped immigrants feel at home. Jews gathered in their synagogues, Hebrew schools, and Hebrew- and Yiddish-speaking literary groups. Germans had their family saloons and their educational and singing societies. Irish associational life focused around the parish church, its Irish priest, clubs, and activities. In Irish nationalist organizations, in ward politics, and in Irish saloons, men met, socialized, drank, and talked politics. These types of organizations provided companionship although they also separated those involved in them from native-born Americans and other ethnic groups.

Black Americans faced the worst living conditions in the city: in segregated black neighborhoods in the North, and in back alleys and small streets in the South. They, too, created a rich religious and associational life. Rapidly growing black churches retained the emotional exuberance of slave religion. Black members of mainline Protestant denominations establish separate branches, and the African Methodist Episcopal Church mushroomed. Some urban blacks rose into the middle class despite heavy odds.

Beyond working-class neighborhoods and pockets of black housing lay streets with the middle-class houses for clerks, shopkeepers, bookkeepers, salesmen, and small tradesmen. Separate spaces for cooking and laundry work kept unpleasant tasks away from other living areas. Many houses boasted new gas lighting and bathrooms. Neighborhoods were cleaner than in the inner city because residents could pay for municipal services.

## Streetcar Suburbs

On the fringes of the city lived the substantial middle class and the rich, who sped between downtown offices and home by public transportation. For example, Robert Work, a modestly successful merchant, moved his family to a $5,500 house in West Philadelphia in 1865 and commuted more than four miles to work. In 1880 his household contained two servants, two boarders, his wife, and their eldest son, who was still in school. The Works' house had running hot and cold water, indoor bathrooms, central heating, and other up-to-date conveniences. Upstairs, comfortable bedrooms provided a maximum of privacy for family members. The live-in servants, who did most of the housework, were mostly restricted to kitchen, pantry, and attic bedrooms.

## The Social Geography of the Cities

Industrial cities sorted people by class, occupation, and race. Physical distances between upper- and middle-class neighborhoods and working-class areas eliminated or distorted firsthand knowledge of other people and bred social disapproval. While middle-class newspapers criticized "crowds of idlers, who, day and night, infect Main Street," often the "idlers" were men unable to find work. A working-class woman's response to visitors who were attacking alcohol captures the critical view from the bottom of society. "When the rich stopped drinking, it would be time to speak to the poor about it."

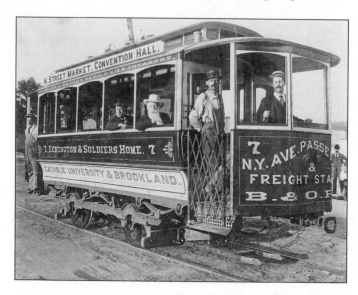

For the middle class, commuting to work from the suburbs became part of the daily routine. (Brown Brothers)

## THE LIFE OF THE MIDDLE CLASS

For middle-class Americans, there was much to value in the new age. Between 1865 and 1890, average middle-class income rose about 30 percent. By 1900, fully 36 percent of urban families owned their homes.

Industrial expansion raised living standards for the increasing numbers of Americans. They were able to purchase dozens of products, manufactured, packaged, and promoted in an explosion of technological inventions and shrewd marketing techniques. Among still familiar products and brands invented or mass-produced for the first time in the 1890s were Jell-O, Wesson oil, the Hershey bar, Aunt Jemima pancake mix, and Coca-Cola.

More leisure time and greater access to consumer goods signaled industrialism's power to transform the lives of middle-class Americans. Plentiful immigrant servant girls relieved urban middle-class wives of many housekeeping chores, and smaller families lightened the burdens of motherhood. New department stores began to appear in the central business districts in the 1870s, feeding women's desire for material possessions and revolutionizing retailing. Shopping for home furnishings and clothes became integral to many middle-class women's lives.

### New Freedoms for Middle-Class Women

As many middle-class women acquired leisure time and enhanced purchasing power, they also won new freedoms. Several states granted women more property rights in marriage, adding to their growing sense of independence. Casting off confining crinolines, they now wore a shirtwaist blouse and ankle-length skirt that was more comfortable for working, school, and sports. The "new woman" was celebrated as *Life* magazine's attractively active, slightly rebellious "Gibson girl."

Using their new freedom, women joined organizations of all kinds—literary societies, charity groups, reform clubs. There they gained organizational experience, awareness of their talents, and contact with people and problems outside their traditional family roles. The depression of 1893 stimulated many women to investigate slum and factory conditions, and some began even earlier. Jane Addams, who told her college classmates in 1881 to lead lives "filled with good works and honest toil," went on to found Hull House, a famous social settlement.

Job opportunities for these educated middle-class women were generally limited to the social services and teaching. Still regarded as a suitable female occupation, teaching was a highly demanding but poorly paying field that grew as urban schools expanded under the pressure of a burgeoning population. By the 1890s, the willingness of middle-class women to work for low pay opened up new forms of employment in office work, nursing, and department stores. But moving up to high-status jobs proved difficult, even for middle-class women.

After the Civil War, educational opportunities for women expanded. New women's colleges offered programs similar to those at competitive men's colleges, while midwestern and western state schools dropped prohibitions against women. In 1890, some 13 percent of all college graduates were women; by 1900, nearly 20 percent were. Higher education prepared middle-class women for conventional female roles as well as for work and public service. A few courageous graduates overcame many barriers to enter the professions. By the early twentieth century, the number of women professionals (including teachers) was increasing at three times the rate for men.

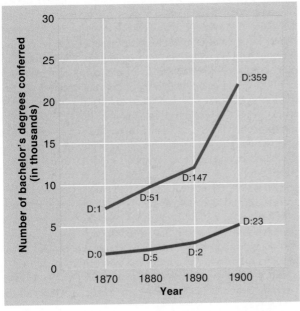

**INCREASE IN HIGHER EDUCATION, 1870–1900** Note the rising pattern of college graduation, which suggests the professionalization of middle-class life. (*Source:* U.S. Department of Commerce.)

# Technology Changes the American People

## The Flush Toilet

In the early nineteenth century, a resident of York, Pennsylvania, described a practice that most of us today regard with horror. Yet the scene he described could happen all too easily in the days before flush toilets. In York's North George Street, a Mr. Day indulged in "a bad practice by pouring out of the upper window his filthiness." Perhaps most of his neighbors were aware of Day's practice of emptying his chamber pot out of his window. But others were not prepared. Certainly, the bride and groom hurrying to their wedding did not know of Day's habits and, to their dismay, they were caught in the odorous discharge that "fouled" the bride's silk dress.

This small incident, surely not so small in the minds of the couple on their way to be married, reminds us of the realities of everyday American life in the first three centuries. For some rural Americans the elimination of waste was no problem. They just gravitated to a convenient spot outdoors when they felt the need. But in crowded places or areas where the weather was problematical, privies and chamber pots were common. Privies, called "necessary houses" or "outhouses," were used during the day. On farms, necessary houses were located in a convenient location, sometimes one connected to the house. In cities, the most common site was in the backyard. No matter where it was placed, the principle of the privy was simple: waste material passed directly into a pit (which might overflow and seep into the yard), or even into a nearby body of water. The most sanitary arrangement was the privy that channeled the waste into a special container that could be emptied from time to time. At night, people used chamber pots located in their bedroom. Sometimes enclosed in a wooden box and called a commode, the chamber pot was convenient. But for the servant or housewife who was responsible for emptying all the bedroom chamber pots, the chore of carrying them to the privy (or perhaps like Mr. Day taking the easy way out) was an unpleasant duty.

In 1849, Catharine Beecher, author of a series of widely read domestic advice books, urged her audience to consider installing an earth closet in their homes. The earth closet, as the name suggests, dumped earth on the waste and allowed it to decompose naturally. It worked without any water supply and saved the householder from the expense of pipes and hardware.

Rapid development of a system depending on water occurred during the final decades of the nineteenth century. Until technological problems were solved, the water closet could threaten health and safety (through poisonous sewer gases or the possibility of contamination, for example), yet it potentially offered the quickest and cleanest way to dispose of human waste. Flush toilets drew upon technological innovations connected with the development of steam power in the mid-eighteenth century. The many improvements that were necessary before flush toilets became a standard feature of American homes, however, resulted from years of experimentation by inventors on both sides of the Atlantic as well as by the unknown plumbers who came up with improvements through a process of trial and error.

Some early luxury hotels had their own water and removal systems and installed working water closets for their guests. But until cities constructed adequate water and sewer systems, real improvements in American sanitary arrangements were slow. By 1875, most large American cities provided municipal water to at least some urban neighborhoods, and a few years later they began building sewer systems. The possibility of a large domestic market stimulated invention and experimentation. By 1900, innovations and the manufacturing of the essential components were common.

A description of some of the stages in the development of the flush toilet will provide an idea of some of the technological advances during the nineteenth century. The pan closet featured an

This elaborate Victorian bathroom shows the importance given to the new room that gathered activities once performed separately into one space. (The Granger Collection, New York)

earthenware bowl sitting on top of a copper pan holding several inches of water. When the user pushed a lever, the copper pan dumped the waste into a cast iron container connected to the drainage system. The siphonic closet, developed by John Randall Mann, in 1870, used water from three pipes. One provided water for the basin's flushing rim, another deposited water into the basin to start the action, while the other brought in new water after the flush. Many others made refinements to the siphonic closet in the last decades of the nineteenth century, while twentieth-century inventors offered improvements like placing the tank on top of the bowl, the arrangement with which we are familiar today.

**Reflecting on the Past**   For much of the nineteenth century, water closets were just that—toilets in closets. Gradually, first in elite and then in middle-class households, the bathtub, sink, and toilet came to be placed in one room. While we take this room for granted, think about the ways the flush toilet, along with the sink and bathtub, changed everyday life. What were the most important consequences of a working flush toilet? How did the toilet affect personal and family habits? Did the innovation influence the patterns and rhythms of each family member's daily routine equally? Do you think that the introduction of the toilet, bathtub, and sink into middle-class and upper-class homes may have contributed to tensions between class? Why or why not?

One reason for the greater independence of American women was that they were having fewer babies. This was especially true of educated women. In 1900, nearly one married woman in five was childless. Advances in birth control technology (the modern diaphragm was developed in 1880) helped make new patterns possible. Decreasing family size and an increase in the divorce rate (1 out of 12 marriages in 1905) fueled male fears. Arguments against the new woman intensified as many men reaffirmed Victorian stereotypes of "woman's sphere." One male orator in 1896 inveighed against the new woman's public role because "a woman's brain involves emotions rather than intellect." Male campaigns against prostitution and for sex hygiene, as well as efforts to reinforce traditional sex roles, reflected deeper fears that female passions might weaken male vigor.

## Male Mobility and the Success Ethic

The postwar economy opened up many new opportunities for middle-class men. As the lower ranks of the white-collar world became more specialized, the number of middle-class jobs increased.

Because these new careers required more education, the educational system expanded. Public high schools increased from 160 in 1870 to 6,000 in 1900. Enrollments in colleges and universities nearly doubled, from 53,000 in 1870 to 101,000 in 1900. Universities gained a new stature in American life. Land-grant state colleges expanded, and philanthropists established research universities like Johns Hopkins, Stanford, and the University of Chicago.

These developments led to greater specialization and professionalism. By the 1890s, government licensing and the rise of professional schools helped to give the word *career* its modern meaning. No longer were tradesmen likely to read up on medicine in their spare time and become doctors. Organizations like the American Medical Association and the American Bar Association were regulating and professionalizing membership.

The need for lawyers, bankers, architects, and insurance agents to serve business and industry expanded opportunities. Large companies required many more managers while the growing public sector provided new positions in social services and government. Young professionals with graduate training in the social sciences filled many of them.

The social ethic of the age stressed that economic rewards were available to anyone who fervently sought them. It was endlessly pointed out, for example, that John D. Rockefeller had raised turkeys as a boy. Horatio Alger's rags-to-riches novels were read by millions. A typical one told the story of a shoeshine-boy-turned-office-boy who decided to "learn the business and grow up 'spectable." Good fortune intervened when he rescued a girl who had tumbled into the harbor. His reward was a position as a clerk in her father's counting house. Virtuous habits were crucial for Alger's heroes, although success often depended as much on luck as on pluck.

Unlimited and equal opportunity for upward advancement in America has never been as easy as the "bootstraps" ethic maintains. But the persistence of the success myth owes something to the fact that many Americans, particularly those who began well, did rise rapidly. Native-born, middle-class whites tended to have the skills, resources, and connections that opened up the most desirable jobs. The typical big businessman was an Anglo-Saxon Protestant from a middle- or upper-class family whose father was most likely in business, banking, or commerce.

## INDUSTRIAL WORK AND THE LABORING CLASS

David Lawlor, an Irish immigrant who came to the United States in 1872, might have agreed with the bootstrap ethic. As a child, he worked in textile mills and read Horatio Alger. Like Alger's heroes, he went to night school and rose in the business world, eventually becoming an advertising executive.

Lawlor's success was exceptional. Most working-class Americans labored long hours, in unpleasant or dangerous conditions, for meager wages. As industrialization transformed work, traditional opportunities for mobility and security eluded many working-class Americans.

### The Impact of Ethnic Diversity

Late-nineteenth-century immigrants formed 20 percent of the labor force and over 40 percent of laborers in the manufacturing and extractive industries. They tended to settle in cities and made up more than half the working-class population.

The fact that more than half the urban industrial class was foreign, unskilled, and often unable to speak English influenced industrial work, urban life, labor protest, and local politics. Immigrants often had little in common with native-born workers or even with one another.

Atop the working-class hierarchy, native-born Protestant whites held most well-paying skilled jobs. Their occupations bore the mark of late-nineteenth-century industrialism: machinists, iron puddlers and rollers, engineers, foremen, conductors, carpenters, plumbers, mechanics, and printers.

Skilled northern European immigrants filled most middle-rank positions. Often they had held similar jobs in their homelands. Jews, who had tailoring experience, became the backbone of the garment industry (where they faced little competition because American male workers considered it unmanly to work on women's clothes). But most "new immigrants" from southern and central Europe had no urban industrial experience. They got the unskilled, dirty jobs near the bottom of the occupational ladder: relining blast furnaces, carrying raw materials or finished products, or cleaning up. Often, they were day laborers on the docks, ditchdiggers, or construction workers. Hiring was often on a daily basis, often arranged through middlemen like the Italian *padrone*. Unskilled work seldom gave much job stability or paid much money.

At the bottom, blacks occupied the most marginal positions as janitors, servants, porters, and laborers. Racial discrimination generally kept them from industrial jobs, even though their occupational background differed little from that of rural white immigrants. There were always plenty of whites eager to work, so it was not necessary to hire blacks except occasionally as scabs during a strike.

# The Changing Nature of Work

Big business and mechanization changed the size and shape of the workforce and the nature of work. More and more Americans were wage earners rather than independent artisans. The number of manufacturing workers doubled between 1880 and 1900, with the fastest expansion in the unskilled and semiskilled ranks.

But skilled workers were still needed. New positions, as in steam fitting and structural ironwork, appeared as industries expanded and changed. Increasingly, though, older skills grew obsolete. And all skilled workers faced the possibility that technical advances would eliminate their favored status or that employers would eat away at their jobs by having unskilled helpers take over parts of them.

# Work Settings and Experiences

A majority of American manufacturing workers now labored not in shops but in factories dominated by the unceasing rhythms of machinery. For those Americans still toiling in small shops and basement, loft, or tenement sweatshops, pressures to produce were almost as relentless as in factories—volume, not hours, determined pay.

The organization of work kept workers apart. Those paid by the piece competed in speed, agility, and output. In large factories, workers were separated into small work groups often defined by ethnicity, and the entire workforce rarely mingled.

All workers shared a very long working day—usually 10 hours a day, six days a week—and often labored in unhealthy, dangerous, and comfortless work places. A few states passed laws to regulate work conditions, but enforcement was spotty, nor did owners concern themselves with health or safety. Women bent over sewing machines developed digestive illnesses and curved spines. In some mines, workers labored in temperatures above 120 degrees, handled dynamite, and died in cave-ins caused by inadequate timber supports. When new drilling machinery was introduced, the air was filled with tiny particles that caused lung disease. Accident rates in the United States far exceeded those of Europe's industrial nations. Nationwide, nearly 25 percent of the men reaching the age of 20 in 1880 would not live to see 44, compared with 7 percent today. The law placed the burden of avoiding accidents on workers, who were expected to quit if they thought conditions unsafe.

Industrial jobs became increasingly specialized and monotonous. Even skilled workers did not produce a complete product, and the range of their skills narrowed.

Still, industrial work provided some personal benefits. New arrangements helped humanize the workplace. Workers who got their jobs through family and friends then worked with them. In most industries, the foreman controlled day-to-day activities. He chose workers from crowds at the gate, fired unsatisfactory ones, selected appropriate materials and equipment, and determined the order and pace of production. Himself a worker, he might sympathize with subordinates. Yet he could also be authoritarian and harsh, especially if his workers were unskilled or belonged to another ethnic group.

# The Worker's Share in Industrial Progress

The huge fortunes accumulated by Andrew Carnegie and John D. Rockefeller during the late nineteenth century dramatized the pattern of wealth concentration that began in the early period of industrialization. In 1890, the top 1 percent of American families possessed over a quarter of the wealth, and the top 10 percent owned about 73 percent. But what of the workers who tended machines that created industrial wealth? Working-class Americans made up the largest segment of the labor force (more than 50 percent), so their experience reveals important facets of the American social and economic system and American values.

Statistics tell an important part of the story. Industry still needed skilled workers and paid them well. Average real wages rose more than 50 percent between 1860 and 1900. Skilled manufacturing workers, about a tenth of the nonagricultural working class in the late nineteenth century, saw their wages rise by about 74 percent. But wages for the unskilled increased by only 31 percent—a substantial differential that widened as the century drew to a close.

On the whole, the working class accrued solid benefits in the late nineteenth century, even if its share of total wealth did not increase. American workers had more material comforts than their European counterparts. But the general picture conceals realities of working-class economic life. A U.S. Bureau of Labor study in 1889 reveals great disparities of income: a young girl in a silk mill made $130 a year; a laborer earned $384 a year; a carpenter took home $686. The carpenter's family lived comfortably in a four-room house, usually breakfasting on meat or eggs, hotcakes, butter, cake, and coffee. The silk worker and the laborer generally ate bread and butter for two of their three daily meals.

For workers without steady employment, rising real wages were meaningless. Workers, especially unskilled ones, often found work only sporadically. When times were slow or conditions depressed, as they were from 1873 to 1879 and 1893 to 1897, employers, especially in small firms, laid off skilled and unskilled workers alike and reduced wages. Even in a good year like 1890, one out of every five men outside of agriculture had been unemployed at least a month.

Unemployment insurance did not exist. One woman grimly recalled, "If the factory shuts down without warning, as it did last year for six weeks, we have a growing expense with nothing to counterbalance." Occasionally, kindhearted employers offered assistance in hard times, but it was rarely enough.

Although nineteenth-century ideology pictured men as breadwinners, many working-class married men could not earn enough to support their families alone. A working-class family's standard of living thus often depended on its number of workers. In the nineteenth century, married women did not usually take outside employment, although they contributed to family income by taking in sewing, laundry, and boarders. In 1890, only 3.3 percent of married women were to be found in the paid labor force.

# The Family Economy

If married women did not work for pay outside their homes, their children did. The laborer whose annual earnings amounted to only $384 depended on his

13-year-old son, not his wife, to earn an extra $196, critical to the family's welfare. In 1880, one-fifth of the nation's children between the ages of 10 and 14 held jobs.

Child labor was closely linked to a father's income, which in turn depended on skill, ethnic background, and occupation. Immigrant families more frequently sent their young children out to work (and also had more children) than native-born families. Middle-class reformers who sentimentalized childhood disapproved of parents who put their children to work. "Father never attended school, and thinks his children will have sufficient schooling before they reach their tenth year, thinks no advantage will be gained from longer attendance at school, so children will be put to work as soon as able." Such a father condemned his children to future poverty, reformers believed. Actually, sending children to work was a means of handling the immediate threat of poverty, of financing the education of one of the children, or even of ensuring that children stayed near their family.

## Women at Work

Many more young people over the age of 14 were working for wages than was the case for children. Half of all Philadelphia's students had quit school by that age. Daughters as well as sons were expected to take jobs, although young women from immigrant families were more likely to work than young American women. By 1900, nearly 20 percent of American women were in the labor force.

Discrimination, present from women's earliest days in the workforce, persisted. An experienced female factory worker might be paid $5 or $6 a week, whereas an unskilled male laborer could make about $8. Still, factory jobs were desirable because they often paid better than other kinds of work open to women.

Employment opportunities for women were limited, and ethnic taboos and cultural traditions helped shape choices. About a quarter of working women secured factory jobs. Italian and Jewish women (whose cultural backgrounds virtually forbade their going into domestic service) clustered in the garment industry, and Poles and Slavs went into textiles, food processing, and meatpacking. In some industries, like textiles, women composed an important segment of the workforce. With the introduction of the typewriter, other sorts of employment opportunities opened up. By 1900 nearly all typists were female. Specialized skills like stenography also meant more office work for working-class young women while big department stores needed scores of clerks to wait on middle-class shoppers. But about 40 percent of working-class women, especially those from Irish, Scandinavian, or black families, were maids, cooks, laundresses, and nurses.

Domestic service was arduous, nor could domestics count on much sympathy from their employers. "Do not think it necessary to give a hired girl as good a room as that used by members of the family," said one lady of the house. "She should sleep near the kitchen and not go up the front stairs or through the front hall to reach her room." A servant received room and board plus $2 to $5 a week. The fact that so many women took such work speaks clearly of their limited opportunities.

The difficult situation facing working women drove some, like Rose Haggerty, into prostitution. Burdened with a widowed and sickly mother and four young brothers and sisters, at 14 Rose started work at a New York paper bag factory. She earned $10 a month, of which $6 went for rent. Her fortunes improved when a friend helped her buy a sewing machine. Rose then sewed shirts at home, often working as much as 14 hours a day to support her family. Suddenly, the piecework rate for shirts was slashed in half. Rose contemplated suicide. But when a sailor offered her money for spending the night with him, she realized that she had an alternative. Prostitution meant food, rent, and heat for her family. "Let God Almighty judge who's to blame most," the 20-year-old Rose reflected, "I that was driven, or them that drove me to the pass I'm in."

Prostitution appears to have increased in the late nineteenth century, although there is no way of knowing the actual numbers of women involved. Probably most single women accepted the respectable jobs open to them. They tolerated discrimination and low wages because their families depended on their contributions. They also knew that when they married, they would probably leave the paid workforce forever.

Marriage hardly ended women's work, however. Like colonial families, late-nineteenth-century working-class families operated as economic units. The unpaid domestic labor of working-class wives was critical to family survival. With husbands away for 10 to 11 hours a day, women bore the burden of caring for children and doing all domestic chores, made more difficult by the lack of conveniences and urban services.

As managers of family resources, married women had significant responsibilities. What American families had once produced for themselves now had to be bought. It was the working-class wife's job to scour secondhand shops for cheap clothes and to practice the small domestic economies that were crucial for survival.

Women also supplemented family income by taking in work. Jewish and Italian women frequently did piecework and sewing at home. In the Northeast and the Midwest, between 10 and 40 percent of all working-class families kept boarders. Immigrant families, in particular, often made ends meet by taking single young countrymen into their homes. The added chores (providing meals and clean laundry), the need to juggle work schedules, and the sacrifice of privacy were disadvantages outweighed by the extra income boarders provided.

Black women's working lives reflected the obstacles African Americans faced in late-nineteenth-century cities. Although few married white women worked outside the home, many black women did, both before and after marriage. In southern cities in 1880, about three-quarters of single black women and one-third of married ones worked outside the home. (For white women the rates were 24 and 7 percent, respectively.) Because industrial employers would not hire black women, most served as domestics or laundresses. The high percentage of married black women in the labor force reflected the marginal wages their husbands earned. But it may also be explained partly by the lesson learned during slavery that children could thrive without the constant attention of their mothers.

## CAPITAL VERSUS LABOR

Class conflict colored late-nineteenth-century industrial life. Although workers welcomed the progress the factory made possible, many rejected their employers' values, which emphasized individual gain at the expense of collective good. While owners reaped most of the profits, workers were becoming wage slaves. Fashioning their arguments from their republican legacy, workers claimed that the degradation of the country's citizen laborers threatened to undermine the republic itself.

## On-the-Job Protests

Workers and employers struggled over who would control the workplace. Many workers staunchly resisted unsatisfactory working conditions. They resented being "like any other piece of machinery, to be made to do the maximum amount of work with the minimum expenditure of fuel." Because skilled workers had indispensable practical knowledge, they were well positioned to direct on-the-job actions. Sometimes they tried to control critical work decisions or to humanize work. Cigar makers clung to their custom of having one worker read to others as they performed their tedious chores.

Workers also sought to control the pace of production. Too many goods meant an inhuman work pace and might result in overproduction, massive layoffs, and a reduction in piecework prices. So an experienced worker might whisper to a new hand, "See here, young fellow, you're working too fast. You'll spoil our job for us if you don't go slower."

Absenteeism, drunkenness at work, and general inefficiency—all widespread—contained elements of protest. In three industrial firms in the late nineteenth century, one-quarter of the workers stayed home at least one day a week. Some lost days were due to layoffs, but not all. The efforts of employers to impose stiff fines on absent workers suggested their frustration with uncooperative employees.

To a surprising extent, workers made the final protest by quitting their jobs altogether. Most employers responded by penalizing workers who left without giving sufficient notice—to little avail. A Massachusetts labor study in 1878 found that although two-thirds of them had been in the same occupation for more than 10 years, only 15 percent of the workers surveyed were in the same job. A similar rate of turnover occurred in the industrial workforce in the early twentieth century. Workers unmistakably and clearly voted with their feet.

## Strike Activity After 1876

The most direct and strenuous attempts to change conditions in the workplace came in the form of thousands of strikes punctuating the late nineteenth century. In 1877, railroad workers staged the first and bloodiest nationwide industrial strike of the nineteenth century. The immediate cause was the railroad owners' decision to reduce wages. But the rapid spread of the strike all over the country, as well as the violence of the strikers who destroyed railroad property and kept trains idle, indicated more fundamental discontent.

An erratic economy, high unemployment, and the lack of job security all fed the conflagration. More than 100 people died before federal troops ended the strike. The frenzied response of the propertied class, which saw the strike as the beginning of revolution and applauded military intervention, forecast the pattern of later conflicts. Time and time again, middle- and upper-class Americans would turn to state power to crush labor activism.

A wave of confrontations followed the strike of 1877. Between 1881 and 1905, there were 36,757 strikes involving over 6 million workers. These numbers indi-

This depiction of working-class unrest appeared in *Harper's Weekly* in 1894. Note the prominence of the destruction wrought by the enraged workers and the artist's decision to place the National Guardsmen in the foreground. Contrast the individualized guardsmen with the faceless mob in the background. The artist's choices convey his sympathy with the forces of order. (The Granger Collection, New York)

cate that far more than the "poorest part" of the workers were involved. Many investigations turned up evidence of widespread working-class discontent. The bitterness exploded into strikes, sabotage, and violence, most often linked to demands for higher wages and shorter hours.

Nineteenth-century strike activity underwent important changes as the consciousness of American workers expanded. In the period of early industrialization, discontented laborers rioted in their neighborhoods rather than at their workplaces. Between 1845 and the Civil War, however, strikes began to replace neighborhood brawls. Although workers expressed anger against their employers by striking for higher wages, they had only a murky sense that the strike might be a weapon to force employers to improve working conditions.

As industrialization transformed work and an increasing percentage of the labor force entered factories, collective actions at the workplace spread. Local and national unions played a more important role in organizing protest, conducting 60 percent of the strikes between 1881 and 1905. Coordination between strikers in different companies improved. Finally, wages among the most highly unionized workers became less of an issue. Workers sought more humane conditions. By the early 1890s, over one-fifth of strikes involved workplace rules.

## Labor Organizing, 1865–1900

Civil War experience colored postwar labor organizing. As one working-class song pointed out, workers had borne the brunt of that struggle. "You gave your son to the war/ The rich man loaned his gold/ And the rich man's son is happy to-day,/ And yours is under the mold." Workers who had fought to save the Union argued that wartime sacrifices justified efforts for justice and equality in the workplace.

Labor leaders quickly realized the need for national as well as local organizations to protect the laboring class against "despotic employers." In 1866, several craft unions and reform groups formed the National Labor Union (NLU). Claiming 300,000 members by the early 1870s, the organization supported a range of causes including temperance, women's rights, and the establishment of cooperatives to bring the "wealth of the land" into "the hands of those who produce it."

The call for an eight-hour day reveals some of the basic assumptions of the organized labor movement. Few workers saw employers as a hostile class or wanted to destroy the economic system. But they did believe bosses were often dangerous tyrants whose demands for their time threatened to turn citizens into slaves. The eight-hour day would curb the power of owners and allow workers the time to cultivate the qualities necessary for republican citizenship.

Many of the NLU's specific goals survived, although the organization did not. An unsuccessful attempt to create a political party and the depression of 1873 decimated the NLU. Survival and job searches took precedence over union causes.

## The Knights of Labor and the AFL

As the depression wound down, a new mass organization, the Noble and Holy Order of the Knights of Labor, rose to prominence. Founded as a secret society in 1869, the order became public and national when Terence V. Powderly was elected Grand Master Workman in 1879. The Knights of Labor sought "to secure to the workers the full enjoyment of the wealth they create." Because the industrial system denied workers their fair share as producers, the Knights of Labor proposed a cooperative system of production paralleling the existing system. Cooperative efforts would give workers the economic independence necessary for citizenship, and an eight-hour day would provide them with the leisure for moral, intellectual, and political pursuits.

The Knights of Labor was open to all American "producers," defined as all contributing members of society—skilled and unskilled, black and white, men and women, even merchants and manufacturers. Only the idle and the corrupt (gamblers, saloonkeepers, speculators, bankers, lawyers) were excluded. Many shopkeepers joined, advertising themselves as a "friend of the workingman."

This inclusive membership policy meant that the Knights potentially had the power of great numbers. The organization grew in spurts, attracting miners between 1874 and 1879, skilled urban tradesmen between 1879 and 1885, and unskilled workers thereafter.

Although Powderly frowned on strikes, the organization reaped the benefit of grass-roots strike activity. Local struggles proliferated after 1883. In 1884, unorganized workers of the Union Pacific Railroad walked off the job when management announced a wage cut. Within two days, the company caved in, and the men joined the Knights. The next year, a successful strike against the Missouri Pacific Railroad brought in another wave of members. Then, in 1886, the Haymarket Riot in Chicago caused such a growth in labor militancy that in that single year the membership of the Knights of Labor ballooned from 100,000 to 700,000.

The "riot" at Haymarket was, in fact, a peaceful protest meeting connected with a lockout at the McCormick Reaper Works. When the Chicago police arrived to disperse the crowd, a bomb exploded. Seven policemen died. Although no one knows who planted the bomb, eight anarchists were tried and convicted. Three were executed, one committed suicide, and the others served prison terms.

Labor agitation and turbulence spilled over into politics. In 1884 and 1885, the Knights lobbied for a national contract labor law that would demand work contracts and state laws outlawing convict labor. The organization also pressed successfully for the creation of a federal Department of Labor. As new members poured in, however, direct political action became increasingly attractive. Despite many local successes, no national labor party emerged. But in the 1890s, the Knights cooperated with the Populists' attempt to reshape American politics and society.

The Knights could not sustain momentum. Alerted by the Haymarket Riot, employers determined to break the organization. A strike against Jay Gould's southwestern railroad system in 1886 failed. Consumer and producer cooperatives fizzled; the policy of accepting both black and white workers led to strife and discord in the South. The two major parties co-opted labor politicians.

National leaders also failed. Powderly could never unify his diverse following, nor control militants opposing him. By 1890, membership had dropped to 100,000, although the Knights continued to play a role well into the 1890s.

The American Federation of Labor (AFL), founded in 1886, became the nation's dominant union in the 1890s. The history of the Knights pointed up the problems of a national union that admitted all who worked for wages, but officially rejected strikes in favor of the ballot box and arbitration. The leader of the AFL, Samuel Gompers, had a different notion of effective worker organization. He was convinced that skilled workers should put their specific occupational interests first, so that they could control the supply of skilled labor and keep wages up.

Gompers organized the AFL as a federation of skilled trades—cigar makers, iron molders, ironworkers, carpenters, and others—each one autonomous, yet linked through an executive council to work together for prolabor national legislation and mutual support during boycott and strike actions. He repudiated dreams of a cooperative commonwealth or of ending the wage system, instead focusing on immediate "bread and butter" issues—higher wages, shorter hours, industrial safety, and the right to organize. Although Gompers rejected direct political action as a means of obtaining labor's goals, he believed in the value of the strike. A shrewd organizer, he knew from bitter experience the importance of dues high enough to sustain a strike fund through a long, tough fight.

Under Gompers's leadership, the AFL grew from 140,000 in 1886 to nearly one million by 1900. Although his notion of a labor organization was elitist, he steered his union through a series of crises, fending off challenges from socialists on his left and corporate opposition to strikes on his right. But there was no room in his organization for the unskilled or for blacks. The AFL did make a brief, halfhearted attempt to unionize women in 1892, but men resented women as coworkers and preferred them to stay in the home. The AFL agreed. In 1900, the International Ladies' Garment Workers Union (ILGWU) was established. Although women were its backbone, men dominated the leadership.

## Working-Class Setbacks

Despite the growth of working-class organizations, workers lost many battles. Some of the more spectacular clashes reveal why working-class activism often failed and why so many workers lived precariously.

In 1892, silver miners in Coeur d'Alene, Idaho, struck when their employers installed machine drills in the mines, reduced skilled workers to shovelmen, and cut wages. The owners, supported by state militiamen and the federal government, successfully broke the strike by using scabs, but not without fighting. Several hundred union men were eventually tried and found guilty of a wide variety of charges. Out of the defeat emerged the Western Federation of Miners (WFM), whose chief goal was an eight-hour law for miners.

The Coeur d'Alene struggle set the pattern for many subsequent strikes. Mine owners fought strikes by shutting off credit to union men, hiring strikebreakers and armed guards, and infiltrating unions with spies. Violence was frequent, usually ending with the arrival of state militia, arrests or intimidation, legal action, and blacklisting. Despite this, the WFM won as many strikes as it lost.

## The Homestead and Pullman Strikes of 1892 and 1894

Labor's worst setback came in 1892 at the Homestead steel mills near Pittsburgh. Carnegie had purchased the Homestead plant and put Henry Clay Frick in charge. Together, they wanted to break the union that threatened to extend its organization of the steel industry. After three months of stalemated negotiations over a new wage contract, Frick issued an ultimatum. Workers must accept wage cuts or be replaced. Frick barricaded the entire plant and hired 300 armed Pinkerton guards. As they arrived on July 6, they and armed steelworkers fought a daylong gun battle. Several men on both sides were killed, and the Pinkertons retreated. Then, at Frick's request, the governor of Pennsylvania sent 8,000 troops to crush the strike and the union. Two and a half weeks later, a New York anarchist tried to assassinate Frick.

The Homestead strike dramatized the lengths to which both labor and capital would go. Eugene Debs, for many years an ardent organizer of railroad workers, wrote, "If the year 1892 taught the workingmen any lesson worthy of heed, it was that the capitalist class, like a devilfish, had grasped them with its tentacles and was dragging them down to fathomless depths of degradation."

Debs saw 1893 as the year in which organized labor would "escape the prehensile clutch of these monsters." Instead, 1893 brought a serious depression and more setbacks for labor. Undaunted, Debs combined several of the separate railroad brotherhoods into a united American Railway Union (ARU). Within a year, over 150,000 railroadmen joined the ARU, and Debs won a strike against the Great Northern Railroad, which had attempted to slash wages.

Debs faced his toughest crisis at the Pullman Palace Car Company in Chicago. The company maintained a model company town near Chicago—naturally, called Pullman—where management controlled all aspects of workers' lives.

Late in 1893, as the depression worsened, the Pullman Company cut wages by one-third and laid off many workers, without reducing rents or prices in its stores. Forced to pay in rent what they could not earn in wages, working families struggled through the winter. Those working experienced speedups, threats, and further wage cuts. Desperate Pullman workers joined the ARU in the spring of 1894 and struck.

In late June, after Pullman refused to submit the dispute to arbitration, Debs led the ARU into a sympathy strike in support of the striking Pullman workers.

Remembering the ill-fated railroad strike of 1877, Debs advised his lieutenants to "use no violence" and "stop no trains." Rather, he sought to boycott trains handling Pullman cars throughout the West. As the boycott spread, the General Managers Association, which ran the 24 railroads centered in Chicago, came to Pullman's support. Hiring 2,500 strikebreakers, the GMA appealed to the state and federal governments for military and judicial support in stopping the strike.

Governor Richard Altgeld of Illinois, sympathizing with the workers and believing that local law enforcement was sufficient, opposed using federal troops. But U.S. Attorney General Richard Olney, a former railroad lawyer, obtained a court injunction on July 2 to end the strike as a "conspiracy in restraint of trade." Two days later, President Cleveland ordered federal troops to crush the strikers.

Violence escalated rapidly. Local and federal officials hired armed guards, and the railroads paid them to help the troops. Within two days, strikers and guards were fighting bitterly. As troops poured into Chicago, the violence worsened, leaving scores of workers dead.

Debs's resources would run out unless he could enlist wider labor support. "We must all stand together or go down in hopeless defeat," he warned other unions. When Gompers refused support, the strike collapsed. Debs and several other leaders were found guilty of contempt of court. Hitherto a lifelong Democrat, Debs became a staunch socialist. His arrest and the defeat of the Pullman strike killed the American Railway Union. In 1895, in *In Re Debs,* the Supreme Court upheld the legality of using an injunction to stop a strike, giving management a powerful weapon against unions. Most unions survived the difficult days of the 1890s, but the labor movement emerged as a distinct underdog in its conflicts with organized capital.

Although in smaller communities strikes against outside owners might win local middle-class support, most labor conflicts encountered the widespread middle- and upper-class conviction that unions were un-American. Many people claimed to accept the idea of worker organizations, but would not concede that unions should participate in making economic or work decisions. Most employers violently resisted union demands as infringements of their right to manage their business. The sharp competition of the late nineteenth century, combined with a pattern of falling prices, stiffened employers' resistance to workers' demands. State and local governments and the courts frequently supported them.

The severe depressions of the 1870s and 1890s further undermined working-class activism. Workers could not focus on union issues when survival itself was in question. Many unions collapsed during hard times.

A fundamental problem was the reluctance of most workers to organize even in favorable times. In 1870, less than one-tenth of the industrial workforce belonged to unions, about the same as on the eve of the Civil War. Thirty years later, despite the expansion of the workforce, only 8.4 percent (mostly skilled workers) were union members.

Why were workers so slow to join unions? Certainly, diverse work settings and ethnic differences made it difficult for workers to recognize common bonds. Many unskilled workers sensed that labor "aristocrats" did not have their interests at heart. Moreover, many native-born American workers still clung to the tradition of individualism or dreamed of entering the middle class.

An Irish woman highlighted another important point. "There should be a law . . . to give a job to every decent man that's out of work," she declared, "and another law to keep all them I-talians from comin' in and takin' the bread out of the mouths of honest people." Ethnic and religious diversity complicated forging a common front. Many foreigners, planning to return to their homeland, had limited interest in changing conditions in the United States—and because their goal was to work, they took jobs as scabs. Much of the violence that accompanied working-class actions erupted when owners brought in strikebreakers. Some Americans blamed immigrants for both low wages and failed worker actions.

Tension within laboring ranks appeared most dramatically in the anti-Chinese campaign of the 1870s and 1880s as white workers in the West began to blame the Chinese for economic hardships. A meeting of San Francisco workers in 1877 in favor of the eight-hour day exploded into a rampage against the Chinese. In 1882 Congress passed the Chinese Exclusion Act with the support of the Knights of Labor, prohibiting the immigration of Chinese workers for a 10-year period. It was extended in 1892 and made permanent in 1902.

Yet many immigrants, especially skilled ones, supported unions and cooperated with native-born Americans. Often ethnic bonds tied members to one another and to the community. For example, in the 1860s and 1870s, as the Molders' Union in Troy, New York, battled with manufacturers, its Irish membership won sympathy and support from the Irish-dominated police force, the Roman Catholic Church, fraternal orders, and public officials.

The importance of workers' organizations lay not so much in their successful struggles and protests as in the implicit criticism they offered of American society. Using the language of republicanism, many workers lashed out at an economic order that robbed them of their dignity and humanity. As producers of wealth, they protested that so little of it was theirs. As members of the working class, they rejected the middle-class belief in individualism and social mobility.

## The Balance Sheet

Except for skilled workers, most laboring people found it impossible to earn much of a share in the material bounty industrialization created. Newly arrived immigrants suffered especially. Long hours on the job and walking to and from work left workers little free time. Family budgets included, at best, only small amounts for recreation.

Yet this harsh view of working-class life partly reflects our standards of what is acceptable today. Because so few working-class men or women recorded their thoughts, it is hard to know how they viewed their experiences. But culture and background influenced perspectives. The family tenement, one Polish immigrant said, "seemed quite advanced when compared with our home" in Poland. Jews found American poverty preferable to Russian pogroms.

Studies of several cities show that nineteenth-century workers achieved some occupational mobility. One worker in five in Los Angeles and Atlanta during the 1890s, for example, managed to climb into the middle class. Most immigrant workers were stuck in ill-paid, insecure jobs, but their children did better.

Mobility, like occupation, was related to background. Native-born whites, Jews, and Germans rose more swiftly and fell less often than Irish, Italians, or

# Timeline

| | | | |
|---|---|---|---|
| **1843–1884** | "Old immigration" | **1879** | Thomas Edison invents incandescent light |
| **1844** | Telegraph invented | | |
| **1850s** | Steam power widely used in manufacturing | **1882** | Chinese Exclusion Act |
| | | **1885–1914** | "New immigration" |
| **1859** | Value of U.S. industrial production exceeds value of agricultural production | **1886** | American Federation of Labor founded |
| | | | Haymarket Riot in Chicago |
| **1866** | National Labor Union founded | **1887** | Interstate Commerce Act |
| **1869** | Transcontinental railroad completed | **1890** | Sherman Anti-Trust Act |
| | Knights of Labor organized | **1892** | Standard Oil of New Jersey formed |
| **1870** | Standard Oil of Ohio formed | | Coeur d'Alene strike |
| **1870s–1880s** | Consolidation of continental railroad network | | Homestead steelworkers strike |
| **1873** | Bethlehem Steel begins using Bessemer process | **1893** | Chicago World's Fair |
| | | **1893–1897** | Depression |
| **1873–1879** | Depression | **1894** | Pullman railroad workers strike |
| **1876** | Alexander G. Bell invents telephone | **1900** | International Ladies' Garment Workers Union founded |
| | Thomas Edison establishes his "invention factory" at Menlo Park, New Jersey | | Corporations responsible for two-thirds of U.S. manufacturing |
| **1877** | Railroad workers hold first nationwide industrial strike | | |

Poles. Cultural attitudes, family size, education, and group leadership all produced different ethnic mobility patterns. Jews, for example, valued education and sacrificed to keep children in school. With an education, they moved upward. Slavs, however, who valued a steady income over mobility and education, took their children out of school and sent them to work young. This not only helped the family, they thought, but also gave the child a head start toward reliable, stable employment. A southern Italian proverb, "Do not make your child better than you are," suggests valuing family success over individual success. Different attitudes led to different aspirations and career patterns.

Two groups found little mobility. African Americans were largely excluded from the industrial occupational structure and were restricted to unskilled jobs. Unlike immigrant industrial workers, they could not move to better jobs as new unskilled workers took the positions at the bottom. Hispanic residents in Los Angeles made minimal gains there and probably elsewhere.

Although occupational mobility was limited for immigrants, other rewards often compensated for the lack of workplace success. Home ownership—all but impossible in their homeland—loomed important for the Irish. Owning a home also meant extra income from boarders and some protection against uncertainties and old age. The Irish proved adept politicians and came to dominate big-city government in the late nineteenth century. They succeeded in the construction industry and dominated the hierarchy of the Catholic Church. Even Irish who did not share this upward mobility could benefit from ethnic connections and take pride in their group's achievements.

Likewise, social clubs and fraternal orders compensated in part for lack of advancement at work. Ethnic associations, parades, and holidays provided a sense of identity and security that offset the limitations of the job world.

A few rags-to-riches stories always encouraged the struggling masses. The family of John Kearney in Poughkeepsie, New York, for example, achieved modest success. After 20 years as a laborer, he started his own business as a junk dealer and even bought a simple house. His sons started off in better jobs than their father. One became a grocery store clerk, later a baker, a policeman, and, finally, at the age of 40, an inspector at the waterworks. Another was an iron molder, and the third son was a post office worker and eventually the superintendent of city streets. If this success paled next to that of industrial giants like Andrew Carnegie and John D. Rockefeller, it was still enough to keep the American dream alive.

⚬⚬⚬ ⚬⚬⚬ ⚬⚬⚬ ⚬⚬⚬

# Conclusion

## *The Complexity of Industrial Capitalism*

The rapid growth of the late nineteenth century made the United States one of the world's industrial giants. Many factors contributed to the "wonderful accomplishments" of the age. They ranged from sympathetic government policies to the rise of big business and the emergence of a cheap industrial workforce. But it was also a turbulent period. Many Americans benefited only marginally from the new wealth. Some of them protested by joining unions, by walking out on strike, or by initiating on-the-job actions. Most lived their lives more quietly without Thomas O'Donnell's opportunity to tell their story. But middle-class Americans began to wonder about the O'Donnells of the country. It is to their concerns, worries, and aspirations that we now turn.

## *Discovering U.S. History Online*

*Alexander Graham Bell Family Papers*    http://memory.loc.gov/ammem/bellhtml/bellhome.html
This Library of Congress site contains papers from 1862 to 1939 and includes a chronology, images, selected documents, and interpretive essays about Bell.

*The American Experience: Andrew Carnegie*    http://www.pbs.org/wgbh/pages/amex/carnegie/
This American Experience/PBS site provides images and text about Carnegie's life and activities.

*African American Pamphlets Home Page*    http://memory.loc.gov/ammem/aap/aaphome.html
This collection includes writings of famous African Americans, including Frederick Douglass, Booker T. Washington, Ida B. Wells-Barnett, Benjamin W. Arnett, Alexander Crummel, and Emanuel Love.

*Anarchy Archives*   http://www.pitzer.edu/~dward/Anarchist_Archives/archivehome.html
This site offers classic anarchist texts, including information and graphics for the Haymarket Riot.

*John D. Rockefeller and the Standard Oil Company*   http://www.micheloud.com/FXM/SO/
This study, with accompanying images by François Micheloud, tells of the rise of Rockefeller and his mammoth company.

*Port of Entry: Immigration*   http://memory.loc.gov/ammen/hdlpedu/activity/port/teacher.html
This site, arranged as an historical mystery, contains photographs and eyewitness narratives focusing on immigrant life.

*American Labor History*   http://www.geocities.com/CollegePark/Quad/6460/AmLabHist/index.html
This site takes a general look at the history of labor in America. It has good links that show living and working conditions.

*ENARCO, The History of the National Refining Company*   http://www.enarco.com/
This positive history of the company reflects the industrial changes of late-nineteenth-century America.

*Samuel Gompers Papers*
http://www.inform.umd.edu/EdRes/Colleges/ARHU/Depts/History/Gompers/web1.html
This site includes information about the papers project and also has a photo gallery, selected documents, and a brief history of the first president of the American Federation of Labor (AFL).

## Fiction and Film

Theodore Dreiser tells the story of a young rural woman who comes to Chicago and violates its social norms to acquire some of the city's offerings in *Sister Carrie* (1900). Stephen Crane's novel *Maggie: A Girl of the Streets* (1893) gives a grim picture of life in urban slums. Thomas Bell follows several generations of the same immigrant family whose American life is entwined with steel in *Out of This Furnace* (1976 ed.).

The *Richest Man in the World: Andrew Carnegie*, a 1997 film made for PBS, analyzes the personal and professional life of Carnegie and makes good use of interviews with business and labor historians. It offers extended treatment of the Homestead strike, for which the film holds Carnegie largely responsible. *The Age of Innocence* (1993), which takes place in 1870s New York, offers a splendid picture of the sumptuous lives of the rich and the norms and values to which they were supposed to adhere. This Martin Scorsese film is based on the novel by the same name by Edith Wharton.

## Recommended Reading

### The Texture of Industrial Progress
Alfred D. Chandler, Jr., *The Visible Hand: The Managerial Revolution in American Business* (1977); Thomas P. Hughes, *American Genius* (1989); Thomas J. Misa, *A Nation of Steel* (1995); James D. Norris, *Advertising and the Transformation of American Society, 1865–1920* (1990); William G. Roy, *Socializing Capitalism: The Rise of the Large Industrial Corporation in America* (1997); Olivier Zunz, *Making America Corporate, 1870–1929* (1990).

### Urban Expansion in the Industrial Age
James Borchert, *Alley Life in Washington: Family, Community, Religion, and Folklife in the City, 1850–1970* (1980); William Cronon, *Nature's Metropolis: Chicago and the Great West* (1991); David Goldfield, *Cotton Fields and Skyscrapers: Southern City and Region* (1989); David Nasaw, *Going Out: The Rise and Fall of Public Amusements* (1993); Carl Smith, *Urban Disorder and the Shape of Belief: The Great Chicago Fire, the Haymarket Bomb, and the Model Town of Pullman* (1993).

## The Industrial City, 1880–1900

Peter C. Baldwin, *Domesticating Space: The Reform of Public Space in Hartford, 1850–1930* (1999); Sam Bass Warner, Jr., *Streetcar Suburbs: The Process of Growth in Boston, 1870–1900* (1962).

## The Life of the Middle Class

Gunther Barth, *The Rise of Modern City Culture in Nineteenth-Century America* (1980); Anne Ruggles Geere, *Intimate Practices: Literacy and Cultural Work in U.S. Women's Clubs, 1880–1992* (1997); Thomas Goebel, *The Children of Athena: Chicago Professionals and the Creation of a Credentialing Society* (1996); Judy Hilkey, *Character in Capital: Success Manuals and Manhood in Gilded Age America* (1997).

## Industrial Work and the Laboring Class

Thomas J. Archdeacon, *Becoming American: An Ethnic History* (1983); Priscilla Ferguson Clement, *Growing Pains: Children in the Industrial Age, 1850–1890* (1997); Kathie Friedman-Kasaba, *Memories of Migration: Gender, Ethnicity* (1996); David M. Gordon, Richard Edwards, and Michael Reich, *Segmented Work, Divided Workers: The Historical Transformation of Labor in the United States* (1982); Herbert G. Gutman, *Work, Culture, and Society in Industrializing America* (1976); Alice Kessler-Harris, *Out to Work: A History of Wage-earning Women in the United States* (1982); Mark Wyman, *Round Trip to America: The Immigrants Return to Europe, 1880–1930* (1993).

## Capital Versus Labor

Leon Fink, *Workingmen's Democracy: The Knights of Labor and American Politics* (1983); David Montgomery, *Workers' Control in America: Studies in the History of Work, Technology, and Labor Struggles* (1970) and *The Fall of the House of Labor: The Workplace, The State, and American Labor Activism, 1865–1925* (1987); Robert W. Weit, *Beyond Labor's Veil: The Culture of the Knights of Labor* (1996); James Whiteside, *Regulating Danger: The Struggle for Mine Safety in the Rocky Mountain Coal Industry* (1990).

# CHAPTER 19
# Politics and Reform

## CHAPTER OUTLINE

## AMERICAN STORIES
### A Utopian Novelist Warns of Two Americas

At the start of his best-seller *Looking Backward* (1888), Edward Bellamy likened the American society of his day to a huge stagecoach. Dragging the coach along sandy roads and over steep hills were the "masses of humanity." While they strained desperately "under the pitiless lashing of hunger," at the top sat the favored few—who, however, constantly feared that they might fall from their seats and have to pull the coach themselves.

Bellamy's famous coach allegory began a utopian novel in which the class divisions and pitiless competition of the nineteenth century were replaced by a classless, caring, cooperative new society. Economic anxieties and hardships were supplanted by satisfying labor and leisure. In place of the coach, all citizens in the year 2000 walked together and shopped in equal comfort and security under a huge umbrella (not unlike modern malls) over the sidewalks of the city.

The novel opens in 1887. The hero, a wealthy Bostonian, falls asleep worrying about the effect local labor struggles might have on his upcoming wedding. When he wakes up, it is the year 2000. Utopia has been achieved peacefully through the development of one gigantic trust, owned and operated by the national government. All citizens between the ages of 21 and 45 work in an industrial army with equalized pay and work difficulty. Retirement after 45 is devoted to hobbies, reading, culture, and the minimal leadership necessary in a society without crime, corruption, poverty, or war.

Bellamy's book was popular with educated middle-class Americans who were attracted by his vision of a society in which humans were both morally good and materially well off— and in which core values of the 1880s survived intact, including individual incentive, private property, and rags-to-riches presidents. Women were relieved of housework by labor-saving gadgets and married for love. Although they worked in the industrial army in "lighter occupations," their primary role was still to supervise domestic affairs, nurture the young, and beautify culture.

Like most middle-class Americans of his day, Bellamy disapproved of European social-ism. Although some features of his utopia were socialistic, he and his admirers called his sys-tem "nationalism." This appealed to a new generation of Americans who had put aside Civil War antagonisms to embrace the greatness of a growing, if now economically divided, na-tion. In the early 1890s, with Americans buying nearly 10,000 copies of Looking Back-ward every week, over 160 Nationalist clubs were formed to crusade for the adoption of Bellamy's ideas.

☙ ☙ ☙ ☙

The inequalities of wealth described in Bellamy's coach scene reflected a political life in which many participated, but only a few benefited. The wealthiest 10 percent, who rode high on the coach, dominated national politics while untutored bosses held sway in govern-ing cities. Except for token expressions of support, national political leaders ignored the cries of factory workers, immigrants, farmers, African Americans, Native Americans, and other victims of the vast transformation of American industrial, urban, and agrarian life in the late nineteenth century. But as the century closed, middle-class Americans like Bellamy, as well as labor, agrarian, and ethnic leaders themselves, proposed various reforms. Their concern was never more appropriate than during the depression of the mid-1890s, a real-life social upheaval that mirrored the worst features and fears of Bellamy's fictional coach.

In this chapter, we will examine American politics at the national and local level from the end of Reconstruction to the 1890s, a period that for the most part bolstered the rich and neglected the corrosive human problems of urban industrial life. Then we will look at the growing social and political involvement of educated middle-class reformers who, despite their distaste for mass politics, now acted to effect change both locally and nationally. We will conclude with an account of the pivotal importance of the 1890s, highlighted by the Populist revolt, the depression of 1893 to 1897, and the election of 1896. In an age of strong national identity and pride, the events of the 1890s shook many comfortable citizens out of their apathy and began the reshaping of American politics.

## POLITICS IN THE GILDED AGE

Co-authoring a satirical book in 1873, Mark Twain coined the expression "Gilded Age" to describe Grant's corrupt presidency. The phrase has come to characterize social and political life in the last quarter of the nineteenth century. Although pol-itics was marred by corruption and politicians avoided fundamental issues in fa-vor of a politics of mass entertainment, voter participation in national elections between 1876 and 1896 hovered at an all-time high of 73 to 82 percent of all regis-tered voters.

Behind the glitter, two gradual changes occurred that would greatly affect twentieth-century politics. First was the development of a professional bureau-cracy. In congressional committees and executive branch offices, elite specialists and experts emerged as a counterfoil to the perceived dangers of majority rule rep-resented by high voter participation. Second, after a period of close elections and party stalemate, new issues and concerns fostered a party realignment in the 1890s.

Although this 1892 painting by John Klir shows the outcome of a "Lost Bet" in the election that year, note the ethnic, racial, and class diversity of the street crowds, momentarily united in enjoyment of the humiliated loser pulling his victorious opponent (and a wagon full of American flags). Will a more diverse America hold together? (Library of Congress)

## Politics, Parties, Patronage, and Presidents

American government in the 1870s and 1880s clearly supported the interests of riders atop Bellamy's coach. Few nineteenth-century Americans would have agreed that the national government should tackle problems of poverty, unemployment, and trusts. They mistrusted organized power and believed that all would benefit from an economic life free of government interference. Political leaders favored governmental passivity that would allow industrial expansion and wealth-creation.

"One might search the whole list of Congress, Judiciary, and Executive during the twenty-five years 1870–95," wrote Henry Adams, "and find little but damaged reputation." Few eras of American government were so corrupt, and Adams was especially sensitive to the low quality of politics compared to the exalted morality of his grandfather John Quincy Adams and great-grandfather John Adams.

During the weak Johnson and Grant presidencies, Congress emerged as the dominant branch of government with power in the committee system. The moral quality of congressional leadership was typified by senators James G. Blaine (Maine) and Roscoe Conkling (New York). Despite lying about having been paid off by railroads, Blaine was probably the most popular Republican politician of the era. Charming, intelligent, witty, and able, he served twice as secretary of state and was a serious contender for the presidency in every election from 1876 to 1892. His foe, Conkling, dispensed lucrative jobs at the New York customhouse and spent most of his career bickering over patronage. In more than two decades in Congress, he never drafted a bill.

In 1879, a disgusted student of legislative politics, Woodrow Wilson, wrote: "No leaders, no principles; no principles, no parties." The two big parties diverged mostly over patronage rather than principles. A British observer, Lord Bryce, concluded that the two parties, like two bottles, bore different labels, yet "each was empty."

Yet these characterizations were not entirely accurate. There were differences, as party professionals solidified their popular base to achieve political ends. Republican votes came from northeastern Yankee industrial interests, New England migrants, and Scandinavian Lutherans across the Upper Midwest. Democrats depended on southern whites, northern workers, and urban immigrants. Affiliation reflected interest in important cultural, religious, and ethnic questions. Because the Republican party had proved its willingness in the past to mobilize the power of the state to reshape society, people who wished to regulate moral and economic life were attracted to it. Catholics and various immigrant groups preferred the Democratic party because it opposed government efforts to regulate morals. Said one Chicago Democrat, "A Republican is a man who wants you t' go t' church every Sunday. A Democrat says if a man wants t' have a glass of beer on Sunday he can have it."

For a few years, Civil War and Reconstruction issues generated party differences. But after 1876, the two parties were evenly matched and they avoided controversial stands on national issues. In three of the five presidential elections between 1876 and 1892, a mere 1 percent of the vote separated the two major candidates. In 1880, James Garfield won by only 7,018 votes; in 1884, Grover Cleveland squeaked by Blaine by a popular vote margin of 48.5 to 48.2 percent. In two elections (1876 and 1888), the electoral vote winner had fewer popular votes. Only twice, each time for only two years, did one party control the White House and both houses of Congress. Although all the presidents in the era except Cleveland were Republicans, Democrats controlled the House of Representatives in eight of ten sessions of Congress between 1875 and 1895.

Gilded Age presidents were undistinguished and played a minor role in national life. None of them—Hayes (1877–1881), Garfield (1881), Chester A. Arthur (1881–1885), Cleveland (1885–1889 and 1893–1897), and Benjamin Harrison (1889–1893)—served two consecutive terms. The only Democrat in the group, Cleveland, differed little from the Republicans. When Cleveland violated the expectation that presidents should not initiate ideas by devoting his entire annual message in 1887 to a call for a lower tariff, Congress did nothing. Voters turned him out of office a year later.

## National Issues

Four issues were important at the national level in the Gilded Age: the tariff, currency, civil service, and government regulation of railroads (see Chapter 18). In confronting these issues, legislators tried to serve both their own self-interest and the national interest of an efficient, productive, growing economy.

The tariff was one issue where party, as well as regional attitudes toward the use of government power, made some difference. Republicans wanted government to support business interests and stood for a high tariff to protect businessmen, wage earners, and farmers from foreign competition. Democrats demanded a low tariff because "the government is best which governs least." But politicians accommodated local interests when it came to tariffs. Democratic senator Daniel Vorhees of Indiana explained: "I am a protectionist for every interest which I am sent here by my constituents to protect."

Tariff revisions were bewilderingly complex as legislators catered to these many special interests. Most tariffs included a jumble of higher and lower rates. The federal government depended on tariffs and excise taxes (primarily on tobacco and liquor) for most of its revenue, so there was little chance that the tariff would be abolished or substantially lowered. Surpluses produced by the tariff during the Gilded Age helped the parties finance patronage jobs and government programs.

The money question was even more complicated. During the Civil War, the federal government had circulated paper money (greenbacks) that could not be exchanged for gold or silver (specie). In the late 1860s and 1870s, politicians debated whether the United States should return to a metallic standard, which would allow paper money to be exchanged for specie. "Hard-money" advocates supported either withdrawing all paper money from circulation or making it convertible to specie. They opposed increasing the volume of money, fearing inflation. "Soft money" Greenbackers argued that there was not enough currency in circulation for an expanding economy and urged increasing the supply of paper money in order to raise farm prices and cut interest rates.

Hard-money interests had more clout. In 1873, Congress demonetized silver. In 1875, it passed the Specie Resumption Act, gradually retiring greenbacks from circulation and putting the nation firmly on the gold standard. But as large supplies of silver were mined in the West, pressure resumed for increasing the money supply by coining silver. Soft-money advocates pushed for the unlimited coinage of silver in addition to gold. In an 1878 compromise, the Treasury was required to buy between $2 and $4 million of silver each month and coin it as silver dollars. Despite this increase in the money supply, the period was not inflationary. Prices fell, disappointing supporters of soft money. They pushed for more silver, continuing the controversy into the 1890s.

The issue of civil service reform was, Henry Adams said, a "subject almost as dangerous in political conversation in Washington as slavery itself in the old days before the war." The worst feature of the spoils system was that parties financed themselves by assessing holders of patronage jobs, often as much as 1 percent of their annual salaries. Reformers, mostly genteel native white Protestants, demanded competitive examinations to create an honest and professional civil service—but also one that would bar immigrants and their urban political machine bosses from the spoils of office.

Most Americans expected their presidents to reward the faithful with government jobs, but Garfield's assassination by a crazed office-seeker created a public backlash. "My God! Chet Arthur in the White House!" someone exclaimed, knowing that the new president was closely identified with Conkling's corrupt machine. Arthur surprised doubters by being a capable and dignified president, responsive to growing demands for civil service reform. Congress found itself forced into passing the Pendleton Act of 1883, mandating merit examinations for about one-tenth of federal offices. Gradually, more bureaucrats fell under its coverage, but parties became no more honest. As campaign contributions from government employees dried up, parties turned to huge corporate contributions, which in 1888 helped elect Benjamin Harrison.

# The Lure of Local Politics

The fact that the major parties did not disagree substantially on issues like money and civil service does not mean that nineteenth-century Americans found politics dull. Far more eligible voters turned out in the late nineteenth century than at any time since. The 78.5 percent average turnout to vote for president in the 1880s contrasts sharply with the near 50 percent of eligible Americans who voted in 1996 and 2000.

American men were drawn to the polls in part by the hoopla, but also by local issues. Iowa farmers turned out to vote for state representatives who favored curbing the railroads. But emotional issues of race, religion, nationality, and alcohol often overrode economic self-interest. Voters expressed strong interest in temperance, anti-Catholicism, compulsory school attendance and Sunday laws, aid to parochial schools, racial issues, immigration restriction, and "bloody shirt" reminders of the Civil War.

The new urban immigrants played a large role in stimulating political participation. As traditional native-born elites left local government for more lucrative and higher-status business careers, city bosses stepped in. Their control rested on their ability to deliver the immigrant vote, which they secured by operating informal welfare systems. Bosses handed out jobs and money for rent, fuel, and bail, and they provided a personal touch in a strange environment.

Party leaders also won votes by making politics exciting. The parades, rallies, and oratory of nineteenth-century campaigns generated excitement as party leaders used hoopla subtly to win voters for substantive issues. In the election of 1884, for example, emotions ran high over the moral lapses of the opposing candidates—Blaine's corruption and Cleveland's illegitimate child. Cleveland won in part because an unwise Republican clergyman called the Democrats the party of "rum, Romanism, and rebellion," ensuring Cleveland an outpouring of Catholic support in crucial New York. But beneath the emotional issues were rational concerns over tariffs, money, and civil service.

Party leaders used local and ethnocultural issues to solidify party affiliation and mobilize voters for their national agendas. Spirited local contests occurred, particularly over prohibition. Many Americans considered drinking a serious social problem. Annual consumption of brewery beer had risen from 2.7 gallons per capita in 1850 to 17.9 in 1880. In one city, saloons outnumbered churches 31 to 1. Such statistics shocked those who believed that drinking would destroy character, corrupt politics, and cause poverty, crime, and unrestrained sexuality. Because they were often the targets of violent drunken men, women especially supported temperance. Rather than try to persuade individuals to give up drink, as the pre–Civil War temperance movement had done, many now sought to ban drinking by putting the question of prohibition on the ballot.

Emotional conflicts boiled in the 1880s at the state level over issues like education. Irish Catholics in New York sought political support for their parochial schools. In Iowa, Illinois, and Wisconsin, however, Republicans sponsored laws mandating that children attend "some public or private day school" where instruction was in English. These laws aimed to undermine parochial schools, which taught in the language of the immigrants. In Iowa, where a state prohibition law also passed, the Republican slogan was "A schoolhouse on every hill, and no saloon in the valley." Local Republicans bragged that "Iowa will go

Democratic when hell goes Methodist," and indeed they won. But in Wisconsin, a law for compulsory school attendance was so strongly anti-Catholic that it backfired. Many voters, disillusioned with Republican moralism, shifted to the Democratic party.

## MIDDLE-CLASS REFORM

Most middle-class Americans avoided reformist politics. But urban corruption and labor violence of the 1880s frightened many out of their aversion to politics.

Frances Willard and the Women's Christian Temperance Union (WCTU) is an example. As president of the WCTU from 1879 until 1898, Willard headed the largest women's organization in the country. Most WCTU members were church-going, white Protestant women who believed drunkenness caused poverty and family violence. But after 1886 the WCTU reversed its position, attributing drunkenness to poverty, unemployment, and bad labor conditions. Willard joined the Knights of Labor in 1887 and by the 1890s influenced the WCTU to extend its programs to alleviate the problems of workers, particularly women and children.

## The Gospel of Wealth

Willard called herself a Christian socialist because she believed in applying the ethical principles of Jesus to economic life. For her and many other educated middle-class reformers, Christianity called for a cooperative social order that would reduce inequalities of wealth. But for most Gilded Age Americans, Christianity supported the competitive individualistic ethic. Philadelphia Baptist preacher Russell Conwell's famous sermon "Acres of Diamonds," delivered 6,000 times to an estimated 13 million listeners, praised riches as a sure sign of "godliness" and stressed the power of money to "do good."

Andrew Carnegie expressed the ethic most clearly. In an article, "The Gospel of Wealth" (1889), Carnegie celebrated competition for producing better goods at lower prices. The concentration of wealth in a few hands, he concluded, was "not only beneficial but essential to the future of the race." The fittest would bring order and efficiency out of the chaos of rapid industrialization. Carnegie's defense of the new economic order found as many supporters as Bellamy's *Looking Backward*. Partly this was because Carnegie insisted that the rich must spend some of their wealth to benefit their "poorer brethren." Carnegie built hundreds of libraries and promoted world peace.

Carnegie's ideas reflected an ideology known as social Darwinism, based on the work of naturalist Charles Darwin, whose *Origin of Species* was published in 1859. Darwin had concluded that plant and animal species evolved through natural selection. Some managed to adapt to their environment and survived; others failed to adapt and perished. Herbert Spencer, an English social philosopher, applied this "survival of the fittest" notion to human society. Progress, Spencer said, resulted from relentless competition in which the weak were eliminated and the strong climbed to the top, as in Bellamy's coach. Spencer warned against any interference in the economic world by tampering with the natural laws of

# Technology Changes the American People

## The Bicycle

At the Centennial Exhibition in Philadelphia in 1876, a Boston merchant, Albert A. Pope, was so intrigued by the display of an English high-wheeled bicycle that he went to England to study its manufacture. Two years later, "the father of the bicycle in America" began making a model called the "Columbia," in Hartford, Connecticut. In 1887, the Pope Manufacturing Company shifted its production to the even more popular "safety" bicycle, a chain-driven model with two wheels of equal size very much like those we ride today. Within a decade, more than 300 companies were producing over a million bicycles a year, and millions of Americans, mostly middle-class but increasingly including working-class riders, were finding a new mobility and freedom.

The bicycle craze peaked in the mid-1890s, but the importance of this innovation in transportation—linking the horse and the automobile—was far-reaching; the bicycle heralded several major technological and marketing developments of the twentieth century. As Joseph Woodworth wrote in *American Tool Making and Interchangeable Manufacturing* in 1907, "The manufacture of the bicycle . . . demonstrated to the world that [the American mechanic] was capable of designing and making special machinery, tools, fixtures, and devices for economic manufacturing in a manner truly marvelous." Woodworth went on to say that the bicycle led to "the installation of the interchangeable system of manufacturing in a thousand and one shops where it was formerly thought to be impractical."

In an 1898 *Atlantic Monthly* article, reviewing 50 years of developments in modern science, W. J. McGee stated that the bicycle was a typical American invention because it not only stimulated inventiveness and new production techniques but also "developed individuality, judgement, and prompt decision on the part of its users." It is revealing that Pope began his manufacture of bicycles in a sewing machine company, which itself had started as a rifle plant, for the manufacturing techniques were virtually identical for all three products. Following the established New England armory principles of machine-produced interchangeable parts, bicycle parts were at first drop-forged, machine-tooled and finished. In a noteworthy innovation, again heralding twentieth-century techniques, a Chicago firm, the Western Wheel Works, developed presses for stamping out parts from large sheets of steel. This technique was superior to drop-forging because it was more precise and required less machine tooling. The development of the pneumatic tire completed the crucial technological improvements.

The social implications of the bicycle were as great as the technological ones. The availability of cheaper bicycles was an economic, gender, and even racial leveler, as bicycle riding became accessible to women and working-class Americans. "The bicycle," McGee wrote, "has broken the pernicious differentiation of the sexes" by making available a model for women that opened up areas of freedom, mobility, sport, and good health practices previously unknown. The bicycle even changed "the bonds of fashion" and was "daily impressing Spartan strength and grace, and more than Spartan intelligence, on the mothers of coming generations."

A 17-year-old African American, Marshall "Major" Taylor, who worked in a bicycle shop in Indianapolis ("a beehive of cycling industry"), shocked the cycling world by winning a 75-mile race in Indiana in 1895. Although the League of American Wheelmen (LAW) had excluded "colored persons" from membership at its annual convention in Louisville in 1894, competitive racing, in the North anyway, was generally open to all. As a debate raged in LAW over exclusion,

The social implications of a new technology—bicycling on Riverside Drive, New York City, 1895. (The Schlesinger Library, Radcliffe Institute, Harvard University)

young "Major" Taylor kept winning races and eventually became the American and world sprint champion in 1899. Taylor made a triumphant tour of Europe in 1901 and broke several world records in an era when bicycle racing was as popular a spectator sport as baseball and boxing.

One of W. J. McGee's insights was that the bicycle was shaping national character by "transforming itself and its rider into a single thing," thus providing autonomy of movement and prefiguring the development of the automobile. In 1895, Albert Pope predicted "the advent of the motor-carriage" and employed Hiram Percy Maxim to begin building experimental automobiles. As Maxim put it later, the bicycle "created a new demand which it was beyond the ability of the railroad to supply." Thus, "the bicycle could not satisfy the demand which it had created. A mechanically propelled vehicle was wanted instead of a foot-propelled one, and we now know that the automobile was the answer." With the principles and practice of mass production, interchangeable parts, sheet metal presswork, and democratic use already established, the bicycle almost literally "paved the road" for Henry Ford.

### Reflecting on the Past

As a result of the availability of bicycle riding to women, African Americans, and working-class Americans, what other social implications do you think were caused by the invention of the bicycle? How has the bicycle influenced gender and family relations, dress, recreation, health, sexuality, and sports? What do you think about McGee's claims that the bicycle not only transformed gender relations but also shaped American national character? What other mass-produced inventions did bicycle manufacturing lead to which made life easier for Americans in the twentieth century?

selection: "The whole effort of nature is to get rid of such as are unfit, to clear the world of them, and make room for better."

Spencer's American followers, like Carnegie and Yale economist William Graham Sumner, insisted that poverty resulted from the struggle for existence. It was "absurd," Sumner wrote, to pass laws permitting society's "worst members" to survive, or to "sit down with a slate and pencil to plan out a new social world."

The scientific vocabulary of social Darwinism injected scientific rationality into what often seemed a baffling economic order. Sumner and Spencer argued that underlying social laws, like those of the natural world, dictated economic affairs. Social Darwinists also believed in the superiority of the Anglo-Saxon race, which they maintained had reached the highest stage of evolution. Their theories were used to justify race supremacy and imperialism, as well as the monopolistic efforts of American businessmen. "The growth of a large business," John D. Rockefeller, Jr., told a YMCA class in Cleveland, "is merely the survival of the fittest."

## Reform Darwinism and Pragmatism

Others questioned social Darwinism. Brooks Adams, Henry's brother, wrote that social philosophers like Spencer and Sumner were "hired by the comfortable classes to prove that everything was all right." Intellectual reformers directly challenged the gloomy social Darwinian notion that nothing could be done to alleviate poverty and injustice. With roots in antebellum abolitionism, women's rights, and other crusades for social justice, men like Wendell Phillips, Frederick Douglass, and Franklin Sanborn and women like Elizabeth Cady Stanton and Susan B. Anthony transferred their reform fervor to postbellum issues. Sanborn, for example, an Emersonian transcendentalist and inspector of charities in Massachusetts, founded the American Social Science Association in 1865 to "treat wisely the great social problems of the day." As the Massachusetts inspector of charities in the 1880s, he became known as the "leading social worker of his day."

Reformer Henry George, who was not a social scientist, nevertheless observed that wherever the highest degree of "material progress" had been realized, "we find the deepest poverty." George's book, *Progress and Poverty* (1879), was an early statement of the contradictions of American life. With Bellamy's *Looking Backward*, it was the most influential book of the age, selling 2 million copies by 1905. George admitted that economic growth had produced wonders, but pointed out the social costs and the loss of Christian values. His remedy was to break up land-holding monopolists who profited from the increasing value of their land, which they rented to those who actually did the work. He proposed a "single tax" on the unearned increases in land value.

George's solution may seem simplistic, but his religious tone and optimistic faith in the capacity of humans to effect change appealed to many middle-class intellectuals. Some went further. Sociologist Lester Frank Ward and economist Richard T. Ely both found examples of cooperation in nature and demonstrated that competition and laissez-faire had proved both wasteful and inhumane. Reform Darwinists urged an economic order marked by cooperation and regulation.

Two pragmatists, John Dewey and William James, established a philosophical foundation for reform. James, a professor at Harvard, argued that while environment was important, so was human will. "What is the 'cash value' of a thought, idea, or belief?" James asked. What was its result? "The ultimate test for us of what a truth means," he suggested, was in the consequences of a particular idea and what kind of moral "conduct it dictates."

James and young social scientists like Ward and Ely gathered statistics documenting social wrongs and rejected social determinism. They argued that the application of intelligence and human will could change the "survival of the fittest" into the "fitting of as many as possible to survive." Their position encouraged educators, economists, and reformers of every stripe, giving them an intellectual justification to struggle against misery and inequalities of wealth.

## Settlements and Social Gospel

Jane Addams saw the gap between progress and poverty in the winter of 1893. She had long been aware that life in big cities for working-class families was bitter and hard. Born in rural Illinois, Addams founded Hull House in Chicago in 1889 "to aid in the solution of the social and industrial problems which are engendered by the modern conditions of life in a great city." Young Wellesley literature professor Vida Scudder and six other Smith graduates formed an organization of college women, also in 1889, to work in settlement houses.

Middle-class activists like Addams and Scudder worried about social conditions, particularly the degradation of life and labor in America's cities, factories, and farms. Most of them drew upon the ethical teachings of Jesus for inspiration in solving social problems. They preferred a society marked by cooperation rather than competition—where, as they liked to say, people were guided by the "golden rule rather than the rule of gold." Some preferred to put their goals in more secular terms; they spoke of radically transforming American society. Most, however, worked within existing institutions. As middle-class intellectuals and professionals, they tended to stress an educational approach to problems. But they were also practical, seeking tangible improvements by running for public office, crusading for legislation, mediating labor disputes, and living among the poor people they helped.

The settlement house movement typified 1890s middle-class reformers' blend of idealism and practicality. The primary purpose of settlement houses was to help immigrant families, especially women, adapt Old World rural styles of child-rearing and housekeeping to American urban life. They launched day nurseries, kindergartens, and boarding rooms for working women; they offered classes in sewing, cooking, nutrition, health care, and English; and they tried to keep young people out of saloons by organizing sports clubs and coffeehouses.

A second purpose of the settlement house movement was to give college-educated women meaningful work at a time when they faced professional barriers and to allow them to preserve the strong feelings of sisterhood they had experienced at college. A third goal was to gather data exposing social misery in order to spur legislative action—developing city building codes for tenements, abolishing child labor, and improving factory safety. Hull House, Addams said, was intended in part "to investigate and improve the conditions in the industrial districts of Chicago."

In the settlement houses, left, immigrant women learned English along with proper cooking, hygiene, child care, and other American domestic practices. (U.S. Government Education Bureau of the National Geographic Image Collection) The settlements also included public health clinics, like this one, right, at Vida Scudder's Denison House in Boston. Settlement house work, Scudder wrote, fulfilled "a biting curiosity about the way the Other Half lived, and a strange hunger for fellowship with them." (Schlesinger Library, Radcliffe Institute, Harvard University)

The settlement house movement, with its dual emphasis on the scientific gathering of facts and spiritual commitment, nourished the new discipline of sociology, first taught in divinity schools. Many organizations were founded to blend Christian belief and academic study in an attempt to change society. One was the American Institute of Christian Sociology, founded in 1893 by Josiah Strong, a Congregational minister, and economist Richard T. Ely.

Traditional Christianity was preached in cities by Dwight Moody, who led hundreds of urban revivals in the 1870s. The revivals appealed to lower-class rural folk who were both drawn to the city by their hopes and pushed there by economic ruin. Supported by businessmen who felt that religion would make workers and immigrants more docile, revivalists battled sin through individual conversion. The revivals helped to nearly double Protestant church membership in the last two decades of the century. Although some urban workers drifted into socialism, most remained conventionally religious.

Unlike Moody, many Protestant ministers embraced the Social Gospel movement of the 1890s, which tied salvation to social betterment. Like the settlement house workers, these religious leaders sought to make Christianity relevant to urban problems. Congregational minister Washington Gladden advocated collective bargaining and corporate profit sharing. A young Baptist minister in the notorious Hell's Kitchen area of New York City, Walter Rauschenbusch, raised an even louder voice. Often called on to conduct funeral services for children killed by the airless, diseased tenements and sweatshops, Rauschenbusch scathingly attacked capitalism and church ignorance of socioeconomic issues. His progressive ideas for social justice and a welfare state were later published in two landmark books, *Christianity and the Social Crisis* (1907) and *Christianizing the Social Order* (1912).

Perhaps the most influential book promoting social Christianity was a best-selling novel *In His Steps*, published in 1897 by Charles Sheldon. The novel portrayed the dramatic changes made possible by a few community leaders who resolved to base all their actions on a single question: "What would Jesus do?" For a minister, this meant seeking to "bridge the chasm between the church and labor." For the idle rich, it meant settlement house work and reforming prostitutes. For landlords and factory owners, it meant improving the living and working conditions of tenants and laborers. Although filled with naive sentimentality characteristic of much of the Social Gospel, Sheldon's novel prepared thousands of influential middle-class Americans for progressive civic leadership after 1900.

## Reforming the City

No late-nineteenth-century institution needed reforming more than urban government, called by the president of Cornell "the worst in Christendom—the most expensive, the most inefficient, and the most corrupt." A Philadelphia committee pointed to years of "inefficiency, waste, badly paved and filthy streets, unwholesome and offensive water, and slovenly and costly management." New York and Chicago were even worse.

Creating a "city beautiful" through environmental remedies was one approach. Urban planners put in water mains and sewers and landscape architects built parks and planted trees along broadened boulevards lined by elegant homes and public buildings—libraries, theaters, music halls. But the transformations of urban space rarely reached the squalid sections of the city inhabited by recent immigrants and rural transplants.

Rapid urban growth swamped city leaders with new demands for service. As city governments struggled, they raised taxes and incurred vast debts, which bred graft and the rise of the boss. Urban bosses awarded utility franchises and construction contracts to local businesses in return for kickbacks while new immigrant voters received jobs and welfare in return for their votes. Bosses tipped off friendly real estate men about projected city improvements and received favors from the owners of saloons, brothels, and gambling clubs in return for help with police protection, bail, and influence with judges. These institutions were vital to the urban economy and played an important role in easing the immigrants' way into American life. For many young women, prostitution meant economic survival. For men, the saloon was the center of social life and a source of cheap meals and job leads.

Bossism deeply offended middle-class urban reformers. "Goo-goos" (as bosses called advocates of "good government") opposed not only graft and vice, but also the perversion of democracy by the exploitation of ignorant immigrants. The immigrants, said one, "follow blindly leaders of their own race, are not moved by discussion, and exercise no judgment of their own"—and so were "not fit for the suffrage."

Urban reformers' programs were similar in most cities. They not only worked for the "Americanization" of immigrants in public schools (and opposed parochial schooling), but also formed voters' leagues to discuss the failings of municipal government. They delighted in spectacularly exposing electoral irregularities and large-scale graft. These discoveries led to strident calls for replacing the mayor, often an Irish Catholic, with an Anglo-Saxon Protestant reformer.

Politics colored every reform issue. Anglo-Saxon men favored prohibition partly to remove ethnic saloon owner influence from politics and supported woman suffrage partly to gain a middle-class political advantage against male immigrant voters. Most urban reformers disdained the "city proletariat mob." They proposed to replace bosses with expert city managers, who would bring honest professionalism to city government. They hoped to make government cheaper and thereby lower taxes. One effect of their emphasis on cost efficiency was to cut services to the poor. Another was to disfranchise working-class and ethnic groups, whose political participation depended on the boss system.

Not all urban reformers were elitist. Samuel Jones, for example, both opposed bossism and passionately advocated political participation by urban immigrants. He himself had begun as a poor immigrant in the Pennsylvania oil fields but worked his way up to the ownership of several oil fields and a factory in Toledo, Ohio. In 1894 he decided to "apply the Golden Rule as a rule of conduct" in his factory, with an eight-hour day, a $2 minimum daily wage (50 to 75 cents higher than the local average for ten hours), cooperative insurance, and a Christmas dividend. He hired social outcasts, offered employees cheap lunches and recreational facilities, and established Golden Rule Hall where social visionaries could speak. In 1897 he was elected to the first of an unprecedented four terms as mayor. A maverick Republican who antagonized prominent citizens, Jones advocated municipal ownership of utilities, public works jobs and housing for the unemployed, more civic parks and playgrounds, and free vocational education and kindergartens (few of which were implemented). A pacifist, he took away policemen's weapons. In police court, he regularly dismissed most cases of petty theft and drunkenness on grounds that the accused were victims of social injustice, and he usually released prostitutes after fining every man in the room 10 cents—and himself a dollar—for condoning prostitution. Crime in notoriously sinful Toledo fell. When "Golden Rule" Jones died in 1904, nearly 55,000 tearful people filed past his coffin.

## The Struggle for Woman Suffrage

Women served, in Jane Addams's phrase, as "urban housekeepers" in the settlement house and good government movements, which reflected the tension many women felt between their public and private lives, between their obligations to self, family, and society. This tension was seldom expressed openly. A few women writers, however, began to vent the frustrations of middle-class domestic life. In her novel *The Awakening* (1899), Kate Chopin told the story of a young woman who, in discovering her own sexuality and life's possibilities beyond being a "mother-woman," defied conventional expectations of a woman's role. Her sexual affair and eventual suicide prompted a St. Louis newspaper to label the novel "poison."

Some middle-class women, Addams and Scudder, for example, avoided marriage, preferring the nurturing relationships found in the female settlement house community. A few women boldly advocated free love or, less openly, formed lesbian relationships. Although most preferred traditional marriages and chose not to work outside the home, the generation of women that came of age in the 1890s married less—and later—than any other in American history.

One way women reconciled the conflicting pressures between their private and public lives, and deflected male criticism, was to see their work as maternal.

Addams called Hull House the "great mother breast of our common humanity." Frances Willard told Susan B. Anthony in 1898 that "government is only housekeeping on the broadest scale," a job men had botched, requiring women's saving participation. One of the leading labor organizers was "Mother" Jones, and the fiery feminist anarchist Emma Goldman titled her monthly journal *Mother Earth*. By using nurturant language to describe their work, women furthered the very arguments used against them. Many remained economically dependent on men, and all women still lacked the essential rights of citizenship. How could they be municipal housekeepers if they could not even vote?

After the Seneca Falls Convention in 1848, women's civil and political rights advanced very slowly. Although several western states gave women the vote in municipal and school board elections, before 1890 only the territory of Wyoming (1869) granted full political equality. Colorado, Utah, and Idaho enfranchised women in the 1890s, but no other states granted suffrage until 1910. This slow pace resulted in part from an antisuffrage movement led by an odd combination of ministers, saloon interests, and men threatened in various ways by women's voting rights. "Equal suffrage," said a Texas senator, "is a repudiation of manhood."

In the 1890s, leading suffragists reexamined their situation. The two wings of the women's rights movement, split since 1869, combined in 1890 as the National American Woman Suffrage Association (NAWSA). Although Elizabeth Cady Stanton and Susan B. Anthony continued to head the association, both were in their seventies. Effective leadership passed to younger, more moderate women who, unlike Stanton and Anthony, concentrated on the single issue of the vote.

Changing leadership meant a shift in the arguments for the suffrage. Since 1848, suffragists had argued primarily from the principle of "our republican idea, individual citizenship." But the younger generation shifted to three expedient arguments. The first was that women needed the vote to pass self-protection laws to guard against rapists and unsafe industrial work. The second argument, Addams's notion of urban housekeeping, pointed out that political enfranchisement would further women's role in cleaning up the immoral cities and their corrupt politics.

The third expedient argument reflected urban middle-class reformers' prejudice against non-Protestant immigrants who voted. Suffragists argued that educated, native-born American women should get the vote to counteract the undesirable influence of male immigrants. In a speech in Iowa in 1894, Carrie Chapman Catt, who would succeed Anthony as president of NAWSA in 1900, argued that the "Government is menaced with great danger . . . in the votes possessed by the males in the slums of the cities," a danger that could be averted only by cutting off that vote and giving it instead to women. In the new century, under the leadership of women like Catt, suffrage would finally be secured.

## THE PIVOTAL 1890s

Americans mistakenly think of the last decade of the nineteenth century as the "gay nineties," symbolized by mustached baseball players and sporty Gibson girls. The 1890s was indeed a decade of sports and leisure, urban electrification,

The contrasts between rich and poor and the threat of social upheaval are dramatically illustrated in this turn-of-the-century work, called "From the Depths." (Culver Pictures)

and the enormous wealth of the few. But for many more Americans, it was also a decade of dark tenements, grinding work and desperate unemployment, and poverty. The early 1890s saw Populism and protesting farmers; Wounded Knee and the "second great removal" of Native Americans; lynchings, disfranchisement, and segregation for blacks; and a changing workplace and devastating labor defeats at Coeur d'Alene, Homestead, and Pullman.

Anticipated by Bellamy, the 1890s were years of contrasts and crises. The Populist Omaha platform proclaimed, "We breed two great classes—paupers and millionaires." Supreme Court Justice John Harlan saw a "deep feeling of unrest" everywhere among people worrying that the nation was in "real danger from . . . the slavery that would result from aggregations of capital in the hands of a few." Populist "Sockless" Jerry Simpson simply saw a struggle between "the robbers and the robbed."

Although Simpson was wrong about the absence of a middle ground, the gap was indeed huge between Kansas orator Mary E. Lease, who in 1890 said, "What you farmers need to do is to raise less corn, and more Hell," and the wealthy Indianapolis woman who told her husband, "I'm going to Europe and spend my money before these crazy people take it." The pivotal nature of the 1890s hinged on this feeling of polarizing unrest and upheaval as the nation underwent the traumas of change from a rural to an urban society. The new immigration from Europe and the internal migrations of African Americans and farmers added to the "great danger" against which Catt warned. The depression of 1893 widened the rich-poor gap and accelerated demands for reform. The bureaucracy slowly began to adapt to the needs of governing a complex specialized society, and Congress purposefully moved to confront national economic problems.

## Republican Legislation in the Early 1890s

Harrison's election in 1888 was accompanied by Republican control of both houses of Congress. The Republicans moved forward in the first six months of 1890 with legislation in five areas: pensions for Civil War veterans and their dependents, trusts, the tariff, the money question, and rights for blacks. A bill providing generous support of $160 million a year for Union veterans and their dependents sailed through Congress.

The Sherman Anti-Trust Act passed with only one nay vote. It declared illegal "every contract, combination . . . or conspiracy in restraint of trade or commerce." Although the Sherman Act was vague and not really intended to break up big corporations, it was an initial attempt to restrain large business combinations. But in *United States* v. *E. C. Knight* (1895), the Supreme Court ruled that the American Sugar Refining Company, which controlled more than 90 percent of the nation's sugar-refining capacity, was not in violation of the Sherman Act.

A tariff bill introduced in 1890 by Ohio Republican William McKinley stirred more controversy. McKinley's bill raised tariffs higher than ever. Despite heated opposition from agrarian interests, whose products were generally not protected, the bill passed the House and, after nearly 500 amendments, also the Senate.

Silver was trickier. Recognizing the appeal of free silver to agrarian debtors and the new Populist party, Republican leaders feared their party might be destroyed by the issue. Senator Sherman proposed a compromise that momentarily satisfied almost everyone. The Sherman Silver Purchase Act ordered the Treasury to buy 4.5 million ounces of silver monthly and to issue Treasury notes for it. Silverites were pleased by the proposed increase in the money supply. Opponents felt they had averted the worst—free coinage of silver. The gold standard still stood.

Republicans were also prepared to confront violations of the voting rights of southern blacks in 1890. Political considerations paralleled moral ones. Since 1877, the South had become a Democratic stronghold, where party victories could be traced to fraud and intimidation of black Republican voters. "To be a Republican . . . in the South," said one Georgian, "is to be a foolish martyr." Republican legislation, then, was intended to honor old commitments to the freedmen and improve party fortunes in the South. An elections bill, proposed by Massachusetts Senator Henry Cabot Lodge, sought to ensure African-American voter registration and fair elections. A storm of Democratic disapproval arose. Ex-president Cleveland called it a "dark blow at the freedom of the ballot," and the Mobile *Daily Register* claimed that it "would deluge the South in blood." Senate Democrats delayed action with a filibuster.

To pass the McKinley Tariff, Republican leaders bargained away the elections bill, ending major-party efforts to protect African-American voting rights in the

South until the 1960s. In a second setback for black southerners, the Senate, fearful of giving the federal government a role in education, defeated a bill to provide federal aid to schools in the South, mostly black, that received a disproportionately small share of local and state funds. "The plain truth is," said the New York *Herald*, "the North has got tired of the negro," foreshadowing a similar abandonment of civil rights legislation 100 years later.

The legislative efforts of the summer of 1890, impressive by nineteenth-century standards, fell far short of solving the nation's problems. Trusts grew more rapidly after the Sherman Act than before. Union veterans were pleased by their pensions, but southerners were incensed that Confederate veterans were left out. Others, seeing the pension measure as extravagant, labeled the 51st Congress the "billion-dollar Congress." Despite efforts to please farmers, many still viewed tariff protection as a benefit primarily for eastern manufacturers. Farm prices continued to slide, and gold and silver advocates were only momentarily silenced. African-American rights were put off to another time. Polarizing inequalities of wealth remained. Nor did Republican legislative activism lead the Republicans to a "permanent tenure of power," as party leaders had hoped. Voters abandoned the GOP in droves in the 1890 congressional elections, dropping the Republican contingent in the House from 168 to 88.

Two years later, Cleveland won a presidential rematch with Harrison. "The lessons of paternalism ought to be unlearned," he said in his inaugural address, "and the better lesson taught that while the people should . . . support their government, its functions do not include the support of the people."

## The Depression of 1893

Cleveland's philosophy soon faced a difficult test. No sooner had he taken office than began one of the worst depressions ever to grip the American economy, lasting from 1893 to 1897. Its severity was heightened by the growth of a national economy and economic interdependence. The depression started in Europe and spread to the United States as overseas buyers cut back on purchases of American products. Shrinking markets abroad soon crippled American manufacturing. Foreign investors, worried about the stability of American currency, dumped some $300 million of their securities in the United States. As gold left the country to pay for these securities, the nation's money supply declined. At the same time, falling prices hurt farmers, who discovered that it cost more to raise their crops and livestock than they could make in the market. Workers fared no better: wages fell faster than the price of food and rent.

The collapse in 1893 was also caused by an over-extension of the domestic economy, especially in railroad construction. Farmers, troubled by falling prices, planted more, hoping that the market would pick up. As the realization of over-extension spread, confidence faltered, and then gave way to financial panic. When Wall Street crashed early in 1893, investors frantically sold their shares, companies plunged into bankruptcy, and disaster spread. People rushed to exchange paper notes for gold, reducing gold reserves and confidence in the economy even further. Banks called in loans, which by the end of the year led to 16,000 business bankruptcies and 500 bank failures.

The depression of 1893 accentuated contrasts between rich and poor. While well-to-do children enjoyed the giant Ferris wheel and other midway attractions at the Chicago World's Columbian Exposition, slum children played in filthy streets nearby. (Library of Congress)

The capital crunch and the diminished buying power of rural and small-town Americans (still half the population) forced massive factory closings. Within a year, an estimated 3 million Americans—20 percent of the workforce—lost jobs. People fearfully watched tramps going from city to city, looking for work.

As in Bellamy's coach image, the misery of the many was not shared by the few, which only increased discontent. While unemployed men foraged in garbage dumps, the wealthy gave lavish parties sometimes costing $100,000. While poor families shivered in poorly heated tenements, the very rich built million-dollar summer resorts at Newport, Rhode Island, or grand mansions on New York's Fifth Avenue. While Lithuanian immigrants walked or rode streetcars, wealthy men luxuriated on huge pleasure yachts.

Nowhere were these inequalities more apparent than in Chicago during the World's Columbian Exposition, which opened on May 1, 1893, five days before a plummeting stock market began the depression. The Chicago World's Fair showcased, as President Cleveland said in an opening-day speech, the "stupendous results of American enterprise." When he pressed an ivory telegraph key, he started electric current that unfurled flags, spouted water through gigantic fountains, lit 10,000 electric lights, and powered huge steam engines. For six months, some 27 million visitors strolled around the White City, admiring its wide lagoons, its neoclassical buildings, and its exhibit halls filled with inventions. Built at a cost of $31 million, the fair celebrated the marvelous accomplishments of American enterprise and of a "City Beautiful" movement to make cities more livable.

But as fairgoers sipped champagne, in immigrant wards less than a mile away people drank contaminated water, crowded into packed tenements, and looked in vain for jobs. "If Christ came to Chicago," British journalist W. T. Stead wrote in 1894, this would be "one of the last precincts into which we should care to take Him." Stead's book showed readers the "ugly sight" of corruption, poverty, and wasted lives in a city with 200 millionaires and 200,000 unemployed men.

## Major Legislative Activity of the Gilded Age

In the table, notice the kinds of issues dealt with at the different levels: mostly money, tariff, immigration, and civil service legislation at the national level and "hot button" emotional, social, and value issues in the states and localities.

| Date | National |
|---|---|
| 1871 | National Civil Service Commission created |
| 1873 | Coinage Act demonetizes silver |
| | "Salary Grab" Act (increased salaries of Congress and top federal officials) partly repealed |
| 1875 | Specie Resumption Act retires greenback dollars |
| 1878 | Bland-Allison Act permits partial coining of silver |
| 1882 | Chinese Exclusion Act |
| | Federal Immigration Law restricts certain categories of immigrants and requires head tax of all immigrants |
| 1883 | Standard time (four time zones) established for the entire country |
| | Pendleton Civil Service Act |
| 1887 | Interstate Commerce Act sets up Interstate Commerce Commission |
| | Dawes Act divides Indian tribal lands into individual allotments |
| 1890 | Dependent Pension Act grants pensions to Union army veterans |
| | Sherman Anti-Trust Act |
| | Sherman Silver Purchase Act has government buy more silver |
| | McKinley Tariff sets high protective tariff |
| | Federal elections bill to protect black voting rights in South fails in Senate |
| | Blair bill to provide support for education defeated |
| 1891 | Immigration law gives federal government control of overseas immigration |
| 1893 | Sherman Silver Purchase Act repealed |
| 1894 | Wilson-Gorman Tariff lowers duties slightly |
| 1900 | Currency Act puts United States on gold standard |

### State and Local

| | |
|---|---|
| 1850s–1880s | State and local laws intended to restrict or prohibit consumption of alcoholic beverages |
| 1871 | Illinois Railroad Act sets up railroad commission to fix rates and prohibit discrimination |
| 1874 | Railroad regulatory laws in Wisconsin and Iowa |
| 1881 | Kansas adopts statewide prohibition |
| 1882 | Iowa passes state prohibition amendment |
| 1880s | Massachusetts, Connecticut, Rhode Island, Montana, Michigan, Ohio, and Missouri all pass local laws prohibiting consumption of alcohol |
| | Santa Fe ring dominates New Mexico politics and land grabbing |
| 1889 | New Jersey repeals a county-option prohibition law of 1888 |
| | Laws in Wisconsin and Illinois mandate compulsory attendance of children at schools in which instruction is in English |
| | Kansas, Maine, Michigan, and Tennessee pass antitrust laws |
| 1889–1890 | Massachusetts debates bill on compulsory schooling in English |
| 1899–1902 | Eleven former Confederate states amend state constitutions and pass statutes restricting the voting rights of blacks |
| 1890–1910 | Eleven former Confederate states pass segregation laws |
| 1891 | Nebraska passes eight-hour workday law |
| 1893 | Colorado adopts woman suffrage |
| 1894–1896 | Woman suffrage referenda defeated in Kansas and California |

Despite the magnitude of despair during the depression, national politicians and leaders were reluctant to respond. Only mass demonstrations forced city authorities to provide soup kitchens and places for the homeless to sleep. When an army of unemployed led by Jacob Coxey marched on Washington in the spring of 1894 to press for public work relief, its leaders were arrested for walking on the Capitol grass. Cleveland's reputation for callousness worsened later that summer when he sent federal troops to Chicago to crush the Pullman strike.

The president focused on tariff reform and repeal of the Silver Purchase Act, which he blamed for the depression. Although repeal was ultimately necessary to establish business confidence, in the short run Cleveland only worsened the financial crisis, highlighted the silver panacea, and hurt conservative Democrats. With workers, farmers, and wealthy silver miners alienated, in the midterm elections of 1894 voters abandoned the Democrats in droves, giving both Populists and Republicans high hopes for 1896.

## The Crucial Election of 1896

The campaign of 1896, waged during the depression and featuring a climactic battle over the currency, was one of the most critical in American history. Although Cleveland was in disgrace for ignoring depression woes, few leaders in either major party thought the federal government was responsible for alleviating the suffering of the people. But the disadvantaged, unskilled, and unemployed everywhere wondered where relief might be found. Would either major party respond to the pressing human needs of the depression? Would the People's party set a new national agenda for politics? These questions were raised and largely resolved in the election of 1896.

As the election approached, Populist leaders emphasized the silver issue and debated whether to fuse with one of the major parties by agreeing on a joint ticket, which meant abandoning much of the Populist platform. Influenced by silver mine owners, many Populists became convinced that they must make a single-issue commitment to the free and unlimited coinage of silver at the ratio of 16 to 1.

In the throes of the depression in the mid-1890s, silver took on enormous importance as the symbol of the many grievances of downtrodden Americans. Popular literature captured the rural, moral dimensions of the silver movement. L. Frank Baum's *The Wonderful Wizard of Oz* (1900) was a free-silver allegory of rural values (Kansas, Auntie Em, the uneducated but wise scarecrow, and the good-hearted tin woodsman) and Populist attitudes and policies (the wicked witch of the East, and the magical silver shoes in harmony with the yellow brick road in "Oz"—ounces).

The Republicans nominated William McKinley. As a congressman and governor of Ohio, McKinley was happily identified with the high protective tariff that bore his name. Citing the familiar argument that prosperity depended on the gold standard and protection, Republicans blamed the depression on Cleveland's attempt to lower the tariff.

The excitement of the Democratic convention in July contrasted with the staid, smoothly organized Republican gathering. With Cleveland already repudiated by his party, state after state elected convention delegates pledged to silver.

Gold Democrats, however, had enough power to wage a close battle for the platform plank on money. The Democrats' surprise nominee was an ardent young silverite, William Jennings Bryan, a 36-year-old congressman from Nebraska. Few saw him as presidential material, but Bryan arranged to give the closing argument for a silver plank himself. His dramatic speech swept the convention for silver and ensured his nomination. Concluding one of the most famous political speeches in American history, Bryan attacked the "goldbugs":

> Having behind us the producing masses of this nation . . . and toilers everywhere, we will answer their demand for a gold standard by saying to them: "You shall not press down upon the brow of labor this crown of thorns, you shall not crucify mankind upon a cross of gold."

Bryan stretched out his arms as if on a cross, and the convention exploded in applause.

Populist strategy lay in shambles when the Democrats named a silver candidate. Some party leaders favored fusion with the Democratic ticket (whose vice-presidential nominee was a goldbug), but anti-fusionists were outraged. Unwisely, the Populists nominated Bryan with Georgia Populist Tom Watson for vice president. Running on competing silver slates damaged Bryan's chances.

During the campaign, McKinley stayed home in Canton, Ohio, where 750,000 admirers came to visit him, brought by low excursion rates offered by the railroads. The Republicans made an unprecedented effort to reach voters through a highly sophisticated media campaign, heavily financed by major corporations. Party leaders hired thousands of speakers and distributed more than 200 million

William Jennings Bryan, surprise nominee at the 1896 Democratic Convention, was a vigorous proponent of the "cause of humanity." His nomination threw the country into a frenzy of fear and the Populist party into a fatal decision over "fusion." (Library of Congress)

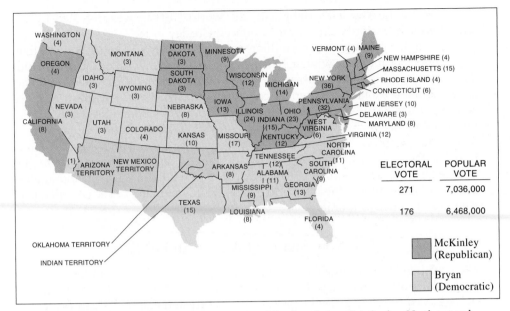

| ELECTORAL VOTE | POPULAR VOTE |
| --- | --- |
| 271 | 7,036,000 |
| 176 | 6,468,000 |

■ McKinley (Republican)

□ Bryan (Democratic)

WASHINGTON (4), MONTANA (3), OREGON (4), IDAHO (3), WYOMING (3), NORTH DAKOTA (3), SOUTH DAKOTA (3), MINNESOTA (9), WISCONSIN (12), MICHIGAN (14), VERMONT (4), MAINE (9), NEW HAMPSHIRE (4), MASSACHUSETTS (15), RHODE ISLAND (4), CONNECTICUT (6), NEW YORK (36), NEW JERSEY (10), DELAWARE (3), MARYLAND (8), VIRGINIA (12), NEVADA (3), CALIFORNIA (8), UTAH (3), COLORADO (4), NEBRASKA (8), IOWA (13), ILLINOIS (24), INDIANA (23), OHIO, PENNSYLVANIA (32), WEST VIRGINIA (6), KANSAS (10), MISSOURI (17), KENTUCKY (12), NORTH CAROLINA (11), ARIZONA TERRITORY, NEW MEXICO TERRITORY, TENNESSEE (12), ARKANSAS (8), ALABAMA (11), SOUTH CAROLINA (9), GEORGIA (13), MISSISSIPPI (9), TEXAS (15), LOUISIANA (8), FLORIDA (4), OKLAHOMA TERRITORY, INDIAN TERRITORY

THE PRESIDENTIAL ELECTION OF 1896   In his sweep of the densely populated urban Northeast and Midwest, McKinley beat Bryan by the largest popular vote margin since 1872. In his cabled congratulations, the first ever by a loser, Bryan, ever the "democrat," said: "We have submitted the issues to the American people and their will is law." Note that California's eight electoral votes (few compared with today) were split. As was then legal, one elector, from the Imperial Valley bordering the Arizona Territory, voted for Bryan and the Democrats.

pamphlets in 14 languages to a voting population of 15 million, all advertising McKinley as the "advance agent of prosperity."

McKinley appealed not only to the business classes but also to unemployed workers, to whom he promised a "full dinner pail." Free silver, he warned, would cause inflation and more economic disaster. Recovery depended not on money, but on tariff reform to stimulate industry and provide jobs.

Bryan took his case to the people. Three million people in 27 states heard him speak as he traveled over 18,000 miles, giving as many as 30 speeches a day. Bryan's message was simple: prosperity required free coinage of silver. Government should attend to the needs of the producing classes rather than the vested interests. But his rhetoric favored rural toilers. "The great cities rest upon our broad and fertile prairies," he had said in the "Cross of Gold" speech. Urban workers were not inspired by this rhetoric, nor were immigrants by Bryan's prairie moralizing.

To influential easterners, the brash young Nebraskan represented a threat. Theodore Roosevelt wrote that "Bryan's election would be a great calamity." One newspaper editor said of Bryan that he was just like Nebraska's Platte River: "six inches deep and six miles wide at the mouth." Theodore Roosevelt wrote, "this silver craze surpasses belief. Bryan's election would be a great calamity."

Voters turned out in record numbers. In key states like Illinois, Indiana, and Ohio, 95 percent of those eligible to vote went to the polls. McKinley won 271 electoral votes to Bryan's 176. Millionaire Mark Hanna jubilantly wired McKinley:

"God's in his heaven, all's right with the world." Bryan was defeated by the largest popular majority since Grant trounced Greeley in 1872.

Although Bryan won over 6 million votes (47 percent of the total), more than any previous Democratic winner, he failed to carry the Midwest or the urban middle classes and industrial masses, who had little confidence that the Democrats could stimulate economic growth or cope with industrialism. McKinley's promise of a "full dinner pail" was more convincing. Northern laborers feared that inflation would leave them even poorer—that prices and rents would rise faster than their wages. Catholic immigrants distrusted Populist Protestantism. In the Great Lakes states, prosperous farmers felt less discontent than farmers elsewhere. But chance also played a part in Bryan's defeat. Bad wheat harvests in India, Australia, and Argentina drove up world grain prices, and many of the complaints of American farmers evaporated.

## The New Shape of American Politics

The landslide Republican victory broke the stalemate in post–Civil War American politics. Republicans dropped their identification with the politics of piety and strengthened their image as the party of prosperity and national greatness, which gave them a party dominance that lasted until the 1930s. The Democrats, under Bryan's leadership until 1912, put on the mantle of populist moralism, but were largely reduced to a sectional party, reflecting narrow southern views on money, race, and national power. The 1896 election demonstrated that the Northeast and Great Lakes states had acquired so many immigrants that they now controlled the nation's political destiny. The demoralized Populists disappeared, yet within the next 20 years many Populist issues were adopted by the two major parties.

Another result of the election of 1896 was a change in political participation. Because the Republicans were so dominant outside of the South and Democrats so powerful in the South, few states had vigorous two-party political battles and less reason to mobilize large numbers of voters. With results so often a foregone conclusion, voters had little motivation to cast a ballot. Many black voters in the South, moreover, were disfranchised, and middle-class good government reformers were not as effective as party bosses in turning out urban voters. The tremendous rate of political participation that had characterized the nineteenth century since the Jackson era gradually declined. In the twentieth century, political involvement among poorer Americans diminished considerably, a phenomenon unique among western industrial countries.

McKinley had promised that Republican rule meant prosperity, and as soon as he took office the economy recovered. Discoveries of gold in the Yukon and the Alaskan Klondike increased the money supply, ending the silver mania until the next great depression in the early 1930s. Industrial production returned to full capacity. Touring the Midwest in 1898, McKinley spoke to cheering crowds about the shift from "industrial depression to industrial activity."

McKinley's election marked not only the return of economic health, but also the emergence of the executive as the preeminent focus of the American political system. Just as McKinley's campaign set the pattern for the extravagant efforts to win office that have dominated modern times, his conduct as president foreshadowed the twentieth-century presidency. McKinley rejected traditional views of

# Timeline

| | | | |
|---|---|---|---|
| **1873** | Congress demonetizes silver | | Sherman Silver Purchase Act |
| **1875** | Specie Resumption Act | | McKinley Tariff |
| **1877** | Rutherford B. Hayes becomes president | | Elections bill defeated |
| **1878** | Bland-Allison Act | **1890s** | Wyoming, Colorado, Utah, and Idaho grant woman suffrage |
| **1879** | Henry George, *Progress and Poverty* | **1892** | Cleveland elected president for the second time |
| **1880** | James A. Garfield elected president | | Populist party wins over a million votes |
| **1881** | Garfield assassinated | | Homestead steel strike |
| | Chester A. Arthur succeeds to presidency | **1893** | World's Columbian Exposition, Chicago |
| **1883** | Pendleton Civil Service Act | **1893–1897** | Financial panic and depression |
| **1884** | Grover Cleveland elected president | **1894** | Pullman strike |
| | W. D. Howells, *The Rise of Silas Lapham* | | Coxey's march on Washington |
| **1887** | College Settlement House Association founded | **1895** | *United States* v. *E. C. Knight* |
| **1888** | Edward Bellamy, *Looking Backward* | **1896** | Charles Sheldon, *In His Steps* |
| | Benjamin Harrison elected president | | Populist party fuses with Democrats |
| **1889** | Jane Addams establishes Hull House | | William McKinley elected president |
| | Andrew Carnegie promulgates "The Gospel of Wealth" | **1897** | "Golden Rule" Jones elected mayor of Toledo, Ohio |
| **1890** | General Federation of Women's Clubs founded | | Economic recovery begins |
| | Sherman Anti-Trust Act | | |

the president as the passive executor of laws, instead playing an active role in dealing with Congress and the press. His frequent trips away from Washington showed an increasing regard for public opinion. Some historians see McKinley as the first modern president for his emphasis on the role of the chief executive in contributing to industrial growth and national power. As we shall see in Chapter 20, he began the transformation of the presidency into a potent force, not only in domestic life, but in world affairs as well.

❧ ❧ ❧ ❧

# CONCLUSION

## *Looking Forward*

This chapter began with Edward Bellamy's imaginary look backward from the year 2000 at the grim economic realities and unresponsive politics of American life in the late nineteenth century. McKinley's triumph in 1896 indicated that in a decade marked by depression, Populist revolt, and cries for action to close the inequalities of wealth—represented by Bellamy's coach—the established order remained intact and politics remained as unresponsive as ever. Calls for change did not necessarily lead to change. But in the areas of personal action and the philosophical bases for social change, intellectual middle-class reformers like Edward Bellamy, Henry George, William James, Jane Addams, "Golden Rule" Jones, and many others were showing the way to progressive reforms in the new century. More Americans were able to look forward to the kind of cooperative, caring, and cleaner world envisioned in Bellamy's utopian novel.

As 1900 approached, people took a predictably intense interest in what the new century would be like. Henry Adams, still the pessimist, saw an ominous future, predicting the explosive and ultimately destructive energy of unrestrained industrial development, symbolized by the "dynamo" and other engines of American power. Such forces, he warned, would overwhelm the gentler, moral forces represented by art, woman, and religious symbols. But others were more optimistic, preferring to place their confidence in America's historic role as an exemplary nation, demonstrating to the world the moral superiority of its economic system, democratic institutions, and middle-class Protestant values. Surely the new century, most thought, would see not only the continued perfection of these values and institutions, but also the spread of American influence throughout the world. Such confidence resulted in foreign expansion by the American people even before the old century had ended. We turn to that next.

## Discovering U.S. History Online

*The Life of William Jennings Bryan*   http://mission.lib.tx.us/exhibits/bryan/bryan.htm
Good links to Bryan's life and the 1896 election.

*The Internet Public Library of Presidents of the United States*
http://www.ipl.org/ref/POTUS/wmckinley.html   http://www.ipl.org/ref/POTUS/gcleveland.html
Grover Cleveland, William McKinley and other Gilded Age presidents, with many related links.

*1896: The Grand Realignment*   http://jefferson.village.virginia.edu/seminar/unit8/home.htm
This fine University of Virginia site contains biographical information, images, great cartoons, and related links about the pivotal election of 1896.

*Edward Bellamy, Christian Socialism and Nationalism*
http://www.vineyard.net/vineyear/history/pdgech3.htm
Text on Bellamy's life and the influence of *Looking Backward* on reform movements in the early 1890s.

*The Era of William McKinley*   http://www.history.ohio-state.edu/projects/mckinley/default.htm
The site contains numerous images from various stages of McKinley's career, along with a brief biographical essay. There is also an excellent collection of cartoons from the era.

*The Gilded (P)Age*   http://www.wm.edu/~srnels/gilded.html
This clever site has links to scores of Gilded Age and progressive era documents and sources.

*World's Columbian Exhibition*   http://www.boondocksnet.com
Part of a larger site, World's Fairs and Expositions: Defining America and the World, 1876–1916, superbly edited by Jim Zwick, this site is full of links to contemporary articles, art, and cartoons about the Columbian Exhibition in Chicago in 1893, with attention to architecture, art and literature, race

relations, religion, social issues, and technology. One can visually visit the fair and experience it through this site.

## Fiction and Film

Mark Twain and Charles D. Warner's *The Gilded Age* (1873) spares no one in its satirical critique of the social, political, and economic life of late nineteenth-century America. Henry Adams's *Democracy: An American Novel* (1880) uses an ironic title to capture the elitist nature of politics and life in Washington in the Gilded Age. Two novels by William Dean Howells, *A Hazard of New Fortunes* (1889) and *The Rise of Silas Lapham* (1885), portray the social life of the new rich in the 1880s. Edward Bellamy's *Looking Backward* (1888) is the utopian novel that began this chapter and that stimulated much late nineteenth-century reform. Kate Chopin's *The Awakening* (1899), set in New Orleans in the 1890s, tells the story of a woman's discovery of self. Theodore Dreiser's *Sister Carrie* (1900), influenced by social Darwinian determinism and set in Chicago and New York, shows the life of a young farm girl who rises to fame and fortune in the city. Frank Norris's immense novel *The Octopus* (1901), set in the San Joaquin Valley of California, shows struggles not only between ranchers and railroads but also between rich and poor, city and country, commercial wheat farmers and sheep herders, and native-born and immigrant Americans.

Anzia Yezierska's *Bread Givers* (1925) reveals the struggles between an Old World Jewish father and his Americanized daughter. *Hester Street* (1975), like the *Bread Givers*, is a wonderfully teachable video about Jewish immigrants in New York City and the process of Americanization. Edgar L. Doctorow's *Ragtime* (1975) is an innovative novel that plays fast and loose with the history and historical figures of turn-of-the-century America; it was also made into a recent Broadway play. Upper-class life in the late nineteenth-century is portrayed in the Hollywood film *The Bostonians* (1998), based on a novel by Henry James. Gore Vidal's *1876: A Novel* (1976) takes a playful, imaginative look at America in its centennial year.

## Recommended Reading

### Politics in the Gilded Age

John Allswang, *Bosses, Machines, and Urban Voters* (1977); Charles W. Calhoun, ed., *The Gilded Age: Essays on the Origins of Modern America* (1996); Sean Dennis Cashman, *America and the Gilded Age: From the Death of Lincoln to the Rise of Theodore Roosevelt* (1984); Morton Keller, *Affairs of State: Public Life in Late Nineteenth-Century America* (1977); Paul Kleppner, *The Third Electoral System, 1853–1892: Parties, Voters, and Political Cultures* (1979); William Riordon, *Plunkitt of Tammany Hall* (1963); Gretchen Ritter, *Goldbugs and Greenbacks* (1997); Richard Schneirov, *Labor and Urban Politics: Class Conflict and the Origins of Modern Liberalism in Chicago, 1864–97* (1998); Mark Wahlgren Summers, *Rum, Romanism and Rebellion: The Making of a President, 1884* (2000); R. Hal Williams, *Years of Decision: American Politics in the 1890s* (1978).

### Middle-Class Reform

Jane Addams, *Twenty Years at Hull House* (1910); Ruth Bordin, *Frances Willard: A Biography* (1986) and *Women and Temperance: The Quest for Power and Liberty, 1873–1900* (1981); Mina Carson, *Settlement Folk: Social Thought and the American Settlement Movement, 1885–1930* (1990); Susan Curtis, *A Consuming Faith: The Social Gospel and Modern American Culture* (1991); Allen F. Davis, *American Heroine: The Life and Legend of Jane Addams* (1973) and *Spearheads for Reform: The Social Settlements and the Progressive Movement, 1890–1914* (1967); Richard Digby-Junger, *The Journalist as Reformer: Henry Demarest Lloyd and Wealth Against Commonwealth* (1996); John P. Diggins, *The Promise of Pragmatism* (1994); Mona Dowash, *Invented Cities: The Creation of Landscape in Nineteenth Century New York & Boston* (1996); Peter J. Frederick, *Knights of the Golden Rule: The Intellectual as Christian Reformer in the 1890s* (1976); Marnie Jones, *Holy Toledo: Religion and Politics in the Life of "Golden Rule" Jones* (1998); Paulette D. Kilmer, *The Fear of*

*Sinking: The American Success Formula in the Gilded Age* (1996); Carol Mattingly, *Well-Tempered Women: Nineteenth-Century Temperance Rhetoric* (1998); Kathryn Kish Sklar, *Florence Kelley and the Nation's Work: The Rise of Women's Political Culture, 1830–1900* (1995); Eleanor J. Stebner, *The Women of Hull House: A Study in Spirituality, Vocation, and Friendship* (1997); Marjorie Spruill Wheeler, ed., *One Woman, One Vote: Rediscovering the Woman Suffrage Movement* (1995).

### The Pivotal 1890s

Peter H. Argersinger, *The Limits of Agrarian Radicalism: Western Populism and American Politics* (1995); H. W. Blands, *The Reckless Decade: America in the 1890s* (1995); Gene Clanton, *Populism: The Humane Preference in America, 1890–1900* (1991); Robert F. Durden, *The Climax of Populism: The Election of 1896* (1965); Paul Glad, *McKinley, Bryan and the People* (1964); Lawrence Goodwyn, *Democratic Promise: The Populist Movement in America* (1976); Charles Hoffman, *The Depression of the Nineties: An Economic History* (1970); Michael Kazin, *The Populist Persuasion* (1994); Robert C. McMath, Jr., *American Populism: A Social History, 1877–1898 (1993)*; Douglas Steeples and David O. Whitten, *Democracy in Desperation: The Depression of 1893* (1998).

# CHAPTER 20
# Becoming a World Power

## CHAPTER OUTLINE

- Steps Toward Empire

- Expansionism in the 1890s

- War in Cuba and the Philippines

- Theodore Roosevelt's Energetic Diplomacy

- Conclusion: The Responsibilities of Power

## AMERICAN STORIES
### Private Grayson Kills a Soldier in the Philippines

In January 1899, the United States Senate was locked in a dramatic debate over whether to ratify the Treaty of Paris concluding the recent war with Spain over Cuban independence. At the same time, American soldiers uneasily faced Filipino rebels across a neutral zone around the outskirts of Manila, capital of the Philippines. Until recent weeks, the Americans and Filipinos had been allies, together defeating the Spanish to liberate the Philippines. The American fleet under Admiral George Dewey had destroyed the Spanish naval squadron in Manila Bay on May 1, 1898. Three weeks later, an American ship brought from exile the native Filipino insurrectionary leader Emilio Aguinaldo, who only represented a small percentage of the population, to lead rebel forces on land while U.S. gunboats patrolled the seas.

At first, the Filipinos looked on the Americans as liberators. Although the intentions of the United States were never clear, Aguinaldo believed that, as in Cuba, the Americans had no territorial ambitions. They would simply drive the Spanish out and then leave. In June, therefore, Aguinaldo declared the independence of the Philippines and began setting up a constitutional government. American officials pointedly ignored the independence ceremonies. When an armistice ended the war in August, American troops denied Aquinaldo's Filipino soldiers an opportunity to liberate their own capital city and shunted them off to the suburbs. The armistice agreement recognized American rights to the "harbor, city, and bay of Manila," while the proposed Treaty of Paris gave the United States the entire Philippine Islands archipelago.

Consequently, tension mounted in the streets of Manila and along 14 miles of trenches separating American and Filipino soldiers. Taunts, obscenities, and racial epithets were shouted across the neutral zone. Barroom skirmishes and knifings filled the nights; American soldiers searched houses without warrants and looted stores. Their behavior was not unlike that of the English soldiers in Boston in the 1770s.

On the night of February 4, 1899, Privates William Grayson and David Miller of Company B, 1st Nebraska Volunteers, were on patrol in Santa Mesa, a Manila suburb surrounded on three sides by insurgent trenches. The Americans had orders to shoot any Filipino soldiers in the neutral area. As the two Americans cautiously worked their way to a bridge over the San Juan River, they heard a Filipino signal whistle, answered by another. Then a red lantern flashed from a nearby blockhouse. The two froze as four Filipinos emerged from the darkness on the road ahead. "Halt!" Grayson shouted. The native lieutenant in charge answered, "Halto!," either mockingly or because he had similar orders. Standing less than 15 feet apart, the two men repeated their commands. After a moment's hesitation, Grayson fired, killing his opponent with one bullet. As the other Filipinos jumped out at them, Grayson and Miller shot two more. Then they turned and ran back to their own lines shouting warnings of attack. A full-scale battle followed.

The next day, Commodore Dewey cabled Washington that the "insurgents have inaugurated general engagement" and promised a hasty suppression of the insurrection. The outbreak of hostilities ended the Senate debates. On February 6, the Senate ratified the Treaty of Paris, thus formally annexing the Philippines and sparking a war between the United States and Filipino nationalists.

In a guerrilla war similar to those fought later in the twentieth century in Eastern Asia and Central America, Aguinaldo's Filipino nationalists tried to undermine the American will by hit-and-run attacks. American soldiers, meanwhile, remained in heavily garrisoned cities and undertook search-and-destroy missions to root out rebels and pacify the countryside. The Filipino-American War lasted until July 1902, three years longer than the Spanish-American War that caused it and involving far more troops, casualties, and monetary and moral costs.

❧❧ ❧❧ ❧❧ ❧❧

How did all this happen? What brought Private Grayson to "shoot my first nigger," as he put it, halfway around the world? For the first time in history, regular American soldiers found themselves fighting outside North America. The "champion of oppressed nations," as Aguinaldo said, had turned into an oppressor nation itself, imposing the American way of life and American institutions on faraway peoples against their will.

The war in the Philippines marked a critical transformation of America's role in the world. Within a few years at the turn of the century, the United States acquired an empire, however small by European standards, and established itself as a world power. In this chapter, we will review the historical dilemmas of America's role in the world, especially those of the expansionist nineteenth century. Then we will examine the motivations for intensified expansionism in the 1890s and how they were manifested in Cuba, the Philippines, and elsewhere. Finally, we will look at how the fundamental patterns of modern American foreign policy were established for Latin America, Asia, and Europe in the early twentieth century. Throughout, we will see that the tension between idealism and self-interest that has permeated America's domestic history has also guided its foreign policy.

## STEPS TOWARD EMPIRE

The circumstances that brought Privates Grayson and Miller from Nebraska to the Philippines originated deep in American history. As early as the seventeenth-century Puritan migration, Americans worried about how to do good in a world that does wrong. John Winthrop sought to set up a "city on a hill" in the New World, a model community of righteous living for the rest of the world to imitate. "Let the eyes of the world be upon us," Winthrop had said. That wish, reaffirmed during the American Revolution, became a permanent goal of American policy toward the outside world.

### America as a Model Society

Nineteenth-century Americans continued to believe in the nation's special mission. The Monroe Doctrine in 1823 warned Europe's monarchies to keep out of the republican New World. In succeeding decades, distinguished European visitors came to observe the "great social revolution." They found widespread democracy, representative and responsive political and legal institutions, a religious commitment to human perfectibility, unlimited energy, and an ability to apply unregulated economic activity and inventive genius to produce more things for more people.

In an evil world, Americans believed that they stood as a transforming force for good. But how could a nation committed to isolationism do the transforming? One way was to encourage other nations to observe and imitate the good example set by the United States. Often, however, other nations preferred their own society or were attracted to competing models of modernization, such as socialism. This implied the need for a more aggressive foreign policy.

Americans have rarely just focused on perfecting the good example at home, waiting for others to copy it. This requires patience and passivity, two traits not characteristic of Americans. Rather, throughout history, the American people have actively and sometimes forcefully imposed their ideas and institutions on others. The international crusades of the United States, well intentioned if not always well received, have usually been motivated by a mixture of idealism and self-interest. Hence, the effort to spread the American model to an imperfect world has been both a blessing and a burden—for others and for the American people.

### Early Expansionism

Persistent expansionism marked the first century of American independence. Jefferson's purchase of Louisiana in 1803, the Jeffersonians' grasping for more territory in 1812, and the mid-century pursuit of "Manifest Destiny" spread the United States across North America. In the 1850s, Americans began to look beyond their own continent as Commodore Perry in 1853 "opened" Japan and southerners sought more cotton lands in the Caribbean. After the Civil War, Secretary of State William Seward spoke of an America that would hold a "commanding sway in the world," destined to exert commercial domination "on the Pacific ocean, and its islands and continents." He purchased Alaska from Russia in 1867 for $7.2 million and acquired a coaling station in the Midway Islands near Hawaii, where missionaries and merchants were already active. He advocated annexing Cuba and other West Indian islands, tried to negotiate a treaty for an American-built canal through Panama, and dreamed of "possession" of the entire North and Central American continent and ultimately "control of the world."

## Expansion After Seward

In 1870, foreshadowing the Philippine debates 30 years later, supporters of President Grant tried to persuade the Senate to annex Santo Domingo on the island of Hispaniola. They cited the strategic importance of the Caribbean and argued forcefully for the economic value that Santo Domingo would bring. Opponents responded that expansionism violated American principles of self-determination and government by the consent of the governed. They claimed that the Caribbean peoples were unassimilable. Expansionism might also involve foreign entanglements, a large and expensive navy, bigger government, and higher taxes. So the Senate rejected the annexation treaty.

Although reluctant to add territory outright, Americans eagerly sought commercial dominance in Latin America and Asia. But American talk of building a canal across Nicaragua produced only Nicaraguan suspicions. In 1881, Secretary of State James G. Blaine sought to convene a conference of American nations to promote hemispheric peace and trade. Latin Americans may have wondered what Blaine intended, for in 1881 he intervened in three separate border disputes in Central and South America, in each case at the cost of goodwill. After an incident and threat of war with Chile in 1889, Blaine's efforts resulted in the first Pan-American Conference to improve economic ties among the nations of the Americas.

American economic influence spread to the Pacific. In the mid-1870s, American sugar-growing interests in the Hawaiian Islands were strong enough to put whites in positions of influence over the monarchy. In 1875, they obtained a treaty admitting Hawaiian sugar duty-free to the United States, and in 1887 the United States also won exclusive rights to build a naval base at Pearl Harbor. Native Hawaiians resented the influence of American sugar interests, especially as they brought in Japanese to replace native people—many of whom died from white diseases—in the sugarcane fields. In 1891, the nationalistic queen Liliuokalani assumed the throne and pursued a policy of "Hawaii for the Hawaiians." So in 1893 white planters staged a coup with the help of U.S. gunboats and marines and imprisoned the queen. An annexation treaty was presented to the Senate by the Harrison administration. But when Grover Cleveland, who opposed imperial expansion, returned to the presidency for his second term, he stopped the move. The white sugar growers waited patiently for a more desirable time for annexation, which came during the war in 1898.

Meanwhile, moving closer to the markets of Eastern Asia, the United States acquired a naval and coaling station in the Samoan Islands in 1878. American and German naval forces almost fought each other there in 1889—before a typhoon ended the crisis by wiping out both navies.

When the United States went to war against Spain in 1898, partly to help the Cubans win their independence from imperial Spanish rule, no one could have imagined the ironic outcomes. Within a year, Americans would impose imperial rule over the Philippines, marching through and burning villages (as the 20th Kansas Volunteers are doing here) and waging war against civilians in a faraway Asian land. (Above, Courtesy of The Newberry Library, Chicago; Right, Keystone-Mast Collection (24039), URL/California Museum of Photography, University of California at Riverside)

Closer to home, the United States sought to replace Great Britain as the most influential nation in Central America and northern South America. In 1895, a boundary dispute between Venezuela and British Guiana threatened to bring British intervention against the Venezuelans. President Cleveland, needing a popular political issue amid the depression, asked Secretary of State Richard Olney to send a message to Great Britain. Invoking the Monroe Doctrine, Olney's note (stronger than Cleveland intended) called the United States "practically sovereign on this continent" and demanded international arbitration to settle the dispute. The British ignored the note, and war loomed. But then both sides realized that war would be an "absurdity." The dispute was settled by agreeing to an impartial American commission to settle the boundary.

Despite these expansionist efforts, the United States in 1895 had neither the means nor a consistent policy for enlarging its role in the world. The diplomatic service was small and unprofessional. No U.S. embassy official in Beijing spoke Chinese. The U.S. Army, with about 28,000 men, was smaller than Bulgaria's. The navy, dismantled after the Civil War and partly rebuilt under President Arthur, ranked no higher than tenth and included dangerously obsolete ships.

## EXPANSIONISM IN THE 1890s

In 1893, historian Frederick Jackson Turner wrote that for three centuries "the dominant fact in American life has been expansion." The "extension of American influence to outlying islands and adjoining countries," he thought, indicated still more expansionism. Turner struck a responsive chord in a country that had always been restless and optimistic. With the western frontier closed, Americans would surely look for new frontiers, for mobility and markets as well as for morality and missionary activity. The motivations for the expansionist impulse of the late 1890s resembled those that had prompted Europeans to settle the New World in the first place: greed, glory, and God. We will examine expansionism as a reflection of profits, patriotism, piety, and politics.

## Profits: Searching for Overseas Markets

Senator Albert Beveridge of Indiana bragged in 1898 that "American factories are making more than the American people can use; American soil is producing more than they can consume. Fate has written our policy for us; the trade of the world must and shall be ours." Americans like Beveridge revived older dreams of an American commercial empire in the Caribbean Sea and the Pacific Ocean. American businessmen saw huge profits beckoning in heavily populated Latin America and Asia, and wanted to get their share of these markets, as well as access to the sugar, coffee, fruits, oil, rubber, and minerals that were abundant in these lands.

Understanding that commercial expansion required a stronger navy and coaling stations and colonies, business interests began to shape diplomatic and military strategy. But not all businessmen in the 1890s liked commercial expansion or a vigorous foreign policy. Some preferred traditional trade with Canada and Europe rather than risky new ventures in Asia and Latin America. Some thought it more important to recover from the depression than annex islands.

But the drop in domestic consumption during the depression also encouraged businessmen to expand into new markets. The tremendous growth of American production in the post–Civil War years made expansionism more attractive than drowning in overproduction, cutting prices, or laying off workers, which would increase social unrest.

Despite the 1890s depression, products spewed from American factories at a staggering rate. The United States moved from fourth place in the world in manufacturing in 1870 to first place in 1900, doubling the number of factories and tripling the value of farm output. Manufactured goods grew nearly fivefold between 1895 and 1914. The total value of American exports tripled, from $434 million in 1866 to nearly $1.5 billion in 1900. By 1914, exports had risen to $2.5 billion, a 67 percent increase over 1900. The increased trade continued to go mainly to Europe rather than Asia. In 1900, for example, only 3 to 4 percent of U.S. exports went to China and Japan. Nevertheless, interest in Asian markets grew, especially as agricultural output continued to increase and prices stayed low.

Investments followed a similar pattern. American direct investments abroad increased from about $634 million to $2.6 billion between 1897 and 1914. Although investments were largest in Britain, Canada, and Mexico, most attention focused on actual and potential investment in Latin America and Eastern Asia. Central American investment increased from $21 million in 1897 to $93 million by 1914, mainly in mines, railroads, and banana and coffee plantations. At the turn of the century came the formation and growth of America's biggest multinational corporations, including the United Fruit Company. Although slow to respond to investment and market opportunities abroad, these companies soon supported an aggressive foreign policy.

## Patriotism: Asserting National Power

In 1898, a State Department memorandum stated that "we can no longer afford to disregard international rivalries now that we ourselves have become a competitor in the world-wide struggle for trade." The national state, then, should support commercial interests.

More Americans, however, saw expansion in terms of national glory and greatness. In the late 1890s, a group centered around Assistant Secretary of the Navy Theodore Roosevelt and Massachusetts Senator Henry Cabot Lodge emerged as highly influential leaders of a changing American foreign policy. These intensely nationalistic young men shifted official policy to what Lodge called the "large policy." Roosevelt agreed that economic interests should take second place to questions of what he called "national honor."

Naval strategist Alfred Thayer Mahan greatly influenced the new foreign policy elite. Mahan's books argued that in a world of Darwinian struggle for survival, national power depended on naval supremacy, control of sea lanes, and vigorous development of domestic resources and foreign markets. He advocated colonies in both the Caribbean and the Pacific, linked by a canal built and controlled by the United States. In a world of constant "strife," he said, it was imperative that Americans begin "to look outward."

## Piety: The Missionary Impulse

As Mahan's and Roosevelt's statements suggest, a strong sense of duty and the missionary ideal of doing good for others also motivated expansionism—and sometimes rationalized the exploitation and oppression of weaker peoples. As a

missionary put it in 1885, "The Christian nations are subduing the world in order to make mankind free." Richard Olney agreed, saying in 1898, "the mission
of this country is . . . to forego no fitting opportunity to further the progress of
civilization."

Josiah Strong, a Congregationalist minister, was another ardent advocate of
American missionary expansionism. He argued that in the struggle for survival
among nations, the United States had emerged as the center of Anglo-Saxonism
and was "divinely commissioned" to spread political liberty, Protestant Christianity, and civilized values over the earth. "This powerful race," he wrote, "will move
down upon Mexico, down upon Central and South America, out upon the islands
of the sea, over upon Africa and beyond." In a cruder statement of the same idea,
Senator Albert Beveridge of Indiana said in 1899 that God had prepared English-
speaking Anglo-Saxons to become "the master organizers of the world to establish
and administer governments among savages and senile peoples."

Missionaries carried Western values to non-Christian lands around the
world, especially China. The number of American Protestant missionaries in
China increased from 436 in 1874 to 5,462 in 1914, and the estimated number of
Christian converts in China jumped from 5,000 in 1870 to nearly 100,000 in 1900.
Although this was much less than missionaries hoped, this tiny fraction of the
Chinese population included young reformist intellectuals who, absorbing Western ideas, in 1912 helped overthrow the Manchu dynasty. Economic relations between China and the United States increased at approximately the same rate as
missionary activity.

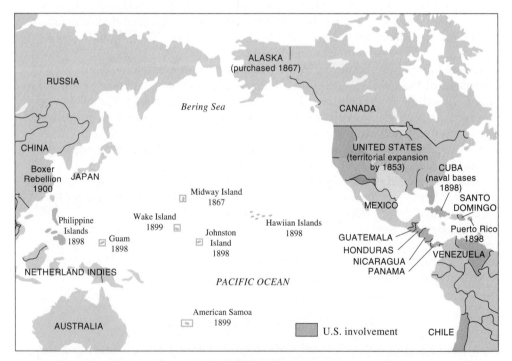

**UNITED STATES TERRITORIAL EXPANSION TO 1900**   By 1900, U.S. involvement expanded beyond North
America to include islands in the Pacific and the Caribbean as well as parts of South America.

# Politics: Manipulating Public Opinion

Although less significant than the other factors, politics also played a role. For the first time in American history, public opinion on international issues helped shape presidential politics. The psychological tensions and economic hardships of the 1890s depression jarred national self-confidence. Foreign adventures provided an emotional release from domestic turmoil and promised to restore patriotic pride—and maybe even win votes.

This process was helped by the growth of a highly competitive popular press, which brought international issues before a mass readership. When New York City newspapers, notably William Randolph Hearst's *Journal* and Joseph Pulitzer's *World,* competed in stirring up public support for the Cuban rebels against Spain, politicians dared not ignore the outcry. Daily reports of Spanish atrocities in 1896 and 1897 kept public moral outrage constantly before President McKinley.

Politics, then, joined profits, patriotism, and piety in motivating the expansionism of the 1890s. These four impulses interacted to produce the Spanish-American War, the annexation of the Philippine Islands and subsequent war, and the energetic foreign policy of President Theodore Roosevelt.

## WAR IN CUBA AND THE PHILIPPINES

Lying 90 miles off Florida, Cuba had been the object of intense American interest for a half century. Spain could not halt the continuing struggle of the Cuban people for a measure of autonomy and relief from exploitive labor in the sugar plantations, even after slavery itself ended. The most recent uprising, which lasted from 1868 to 1878, raised tensions between Spain and the United States, just as it whetted the Cuban appetite for complete independence.

## The Road to War

When the Cuban revolt flared up anew in 1895, the Madrid government again failed to implement reforms. Instead, it sent General Weyler, dubbed the "butcher" by the American press, with 50,000 troops to quell the disturbance. When Weyler began herding rural Cubans into "reconcentration" camps, Americans were outraged. An outpouring of sympathy swept the nation, especially as sensationalist reports of horrible suffering and the deaths of thousands in the camps filled American newspapers.

The Cuban struggle appealed to a country convinced of its role as protector of the weak and defender of the right of self-determination. Motivated in part by genuine humanitarian concern and a sense of duty for the heroic Cuban freedom fighters, many Americans held rallies to raise money and food for famine relief, to call for land reform and, for some, armed intervention. But neither Cleveland nor McKinley wanted war.

Self-interest also played a role. For many years, Americans had noted the profitable resources and strategic location of the island. American companies had invested extensively in Cuban sugar plantations. Appeals for reform had much to do with ensuring a stable environment for further investments and trade ($27 million in 1897), as well as for protecting the sugar fields.

The election of 1896 only temporarily diverted attention from Cuba. A new government in Madrid made halfhearted concessions. Conditions worsened in the reconcentration camps, and the American press kept harping on the plight of the Cuban people. McKinley, eager not to upset recovery from the depression, skillfully resisted war pressures. But he could not control Spanish misrule or Cuban aspirations for freedom.

Events early in 1898 sparked the outbreak of hostilities. Rioting in Havana intensified both Spanish repression and American outrage. A letter from the Spanish minister to the United States, Depuy de Lôme, calling McKinley a "weak," hypocritical politician, was intercepted and made public. Americans fumed.

A second event was more serious. When the rioting broke out, the U.S. battleship *Maine* was sent to Havana harbor to protect American citizens. On February 15, a tremendous explosion blew up the *Maine,* killing 262 men. Newspapers trumpeted slogans like "Remember the *Maine!* To hell with Spain!"

Assistant Secretary of the Navy Theodore Roosevelt had been preparing for war for many years. He said that he believed the *Maine* had been sunk "by an act of dirty treachery on the part of the Spaniards" and would "give anything if President McKinley would order the fleet to Havana tomorrow." When the president did not, Roosevelt privately declared that McKinley had "no more backbone than a chocolate éclair" and continued readying the navy for action. Although a board of inquiry at the time concluded that an external submarine mine caused the disaster, it is probable that a faulty boiler or some other internal problem set off the explosion. Even Roosevelt later conceded this possibility.

After the sinking of the *Maine,* Roosevelt took advantage of Secretary of the Navy John Long's absence from the office one day to cable Commodore George Dewey, commander of the United States' Pacific fleet at Hong Kong. Roosevelt ordered Dewey to fill his ships with coal and, "in the event" of a declaration of war with Spain, to sail to the Philippines and make sure "the Spanish squadron does not leave the Asiatic coast." "The Secretary is away and I am having immense fun running the Navy," Roosevelt wrote in his diary that night.

Roosevelt's act was consistent with policies he had been urging on his more cautious superior for more than a year. As early as 1895, the navy had contingency plans for attacking the Philippines. Influenced by Mahan and Lodge, Roosevelt wanted to enlarge the navy. He also believed that the United States should construct an interoceanic canal, acquire the Danish West Indies (the Virgin Islands), annex Hawaii, and oust Spain from Cuba. As Roosevelt told McKinley late in 1897, he was putting the navy in "the best possible shape" for the day "when war began."

The public outcry over the *Maine* drowned out McKinley's efforts to avoid war. The issues had become highly politicized. McKinley pressured the Madrid government to make concessions. When Spain did, though refusing to grant full independence to the Cubans, McKinley finally acted.

On April 11, 1898, the president sent an ambiguous message to Congress that seemed to call for war. Two weeks later, Congress authorized using troops against Spain and recognized Cuban independence, actions amounting to a declaration of war. In a significant additional resolution, the Teller Amendment, Congress stated that the United States had no intention of annexing Cuba.

## "A Splendid Little War"

As soon as war was declared, Roosevelt resigned from the Navy Department and prepared to lead a cavalry unit. African-American and white regiments headed to Tampa, Florida, to be shipped to Cuba. One black soldier, noting the stark differences in the southern reception of the segregated regiments, commented, "I am sorry that we were not treated with much courtesy while coming through the South." Blacks were especially sympathetic to the Cuban people's struggle against unjust treatment. Blacks and whites alike were greeted warmly by Cubans and Puerto Ricans. As the four-month war neared its end in August, Secretary of State John Hay wrote Roosevelt that "it has been a splendid little war; begun with the highest motives, carried on with magnificent intelligence and spirit."

It was also a short and relatively easy war. Naval battles were won almost without return fire. At both major naval engagements, Manila Bay and Santiago Bay, only two Americans died, one of them from heat prostration while stoking coal. Guam and Puerto Rico were taken virtually without a shot. Only 385 men died from Spanish bullets, but more than 5,000 succumbed to tropical diseases.

The Spanish-American War seemed splendid in other ways, as letters from American soldiers suggest. One young man wrote that his comrades were all "in good spirits" because "every trooper has his canteen full of lemonade all the time." Another wrote his brother that he was having "a lot of fun chasing Spaniards." But the "power of joy in battle" that Theodore Roosevelt felt "when the wolf rises in the heart" was not a feeling all American soldiers shared. One soldier wrote, "Words are inadequate to express the feeling of pain and sickness when one has the fever. For about a week every bone in my body ached and I did not care much whether I lived or not."

Roosevelt's celebrated charge up Kettle Hill near Santiago, his flank protected by African-American troops, made three-inch headlines and propelled him toward the New York governor's mansion. During the war, no one did as much as Roosevelt to advance not only his political career, but also expansionism.

## The Philippines Debates and War

Roosevelt's ordering Dewey to Manila initiated a chain of events that led to the annexation of the Philippines. The most crucial battle of the Spanish-American War occurred on May 1, 1898, when Dewey destroyed the Spanish fleet in Manila Bay and cabled McKinley for additional troops. He sent twice as many troops as Dewey had asked for and began shaping American public opinion to accept the "political, commercial [and] humanitarian" reasons for annexing the Philippines. The Treaty of Paris gave the United States the islands in exchange for a $20 million payment to Spain.

The treaty went to the Senate for ratification during the winter of 1898–1899. Senators hurled arguments across the floor of the Senate as American soldiers hurled oaths and taunts across the neutral zone at Aguinaldo's insurgents near

Manila. Private Grayson's encounter, as we have seen, led to the passage of the treaty in a close Senate vote—and began the Filipino-American War and the debates over what to do with the Philippines.

The entire nation joined the argument. At stake were two very different views of foreign policy and of America's vision of itself. After several months of quietly seeking advice and listening to public opinion, McKinley finally recommended annexation. Many Democrats supported the president out of fear of being labeled disloyal. At a time when openly racist thought flourished in the United States, fellow Republicans confirmed McKinley's arguments for annexation, adding even more insulting ones. Filipinos were described as childlike, dirty, and backward. "The country won't be pacified," a Kansas veteran of the Sioux wars told a reporter, until the Filipinos were "killed off like the Indians."

A small but prominent and vocal Anti-Imperialist League vigorously opposed war and annexation. These dignitaries included ex-presidents Harrison and Cleveland, Samuel Gompers and Andrew Carnegie, Jane Addams, and Mark Twain. The anti-imperialists argued that imperialism in general and annexation in particular contradicted American ideals. First, the annexation of territory without immediate or planned steps toward statehood was unprecedented and unconstitutional. Second, to occupy and govern a foreign people without their consent violated the ideals of the Declaration of Independence. Third, social reforms needed at home demanded American energies and money before foreign expansionism. "Before we attempt to teach house-keeping to the world," one writer put it, we needed "to set our own house in order."

Not all anti-imperialist arguments were so noble. A racist position alleged that Filipinos were nonwhite, Catholic, inferior in size and intelligence, and therefore unassimilable. A practical argument suggested that once in possession of the Philippines, the United States would have to defend them, possibly even acquiring more territories—in turn requiring higher taxes and bigger government, and perhaps demanding that American troops fight distant Asian wars.

The last argument became fact when Private Grayson's encounter started the Filipino-American War. Before it ended in 1902, some 126,500 American troops served in the Philippines, 4,234 died there, and 2,800 more were wounded. The cost was $400 million. Filipino casualties were much worse. In addition to 18,000 killed in combat, perhaps 200,000 Filipinos died of famine and disease as American soldiers burned villages and destroyed crops and livestock. General Jacob H. Smith told his troops that "the more you kill and burn, the better you will please me." Insurgent ineptness, Aguidaldo's inability to extend the fight across ethnic boundaries, and atrocities on both sides increased the frustrations of a lengthening war. The American "water cure" and other tortures were especially brutal.

As U.S. treatment of the Filipinos became more and more like Spanish treatment of the Cubans, the hypocrisy of American behavior became even more evident. This was especially true for black American soldiers who fought in the Philippines. They identified with the dark-skinned insurgents, whom they saw as tied to the land, burdened by debt and pressed by poverty like themselves. "I feel sorry for these people," a sergeant in the 24th Infantry wrote. "You have no idea the way these people are treated by the Americans here."

The war starkly exposed the hypocrisies of shouldering the white man's burden. On reading a report that 8,000 Filipinos had been killed in the first year of the war, Carnegie wrote a letter, dripping with sarcasm, congratulating McKinley for "civilizing the Filipinos . . . . About 8,000 of them have been completely civilized and sent to Heaven. I hope you like it." Another writer penned a devastating one-liner: "Dewey took Manila with the loss of one man—and all our institutions."

The anti-imperialists failed either to prevent annexation or to interfere with the war effort. They were out of tune with the period of exuberant expansionist national pride, prosperity, and promise.

## Expansionism Triumphant

By 1900, Americans had ample reason to be patriotic. Within a year, the United States had acquired several island territories in the Pacific and Caribbean. But several questions arose over what to do with the new territories. Were they colonies? Would they be granted statehood or would they develop gradually from colonies to constitutional parts of the United States? Did Hawaiians, Puerto Ricans, Guamians, and Filipinos have the same rights as American citizens on the mainland? Were they protected by the U.S. Constitution?

Although slightly different governing systems were worked out for each new territory, the solution in each case was to define its status somewhere between a colony and a candidate for statehood. The indigenous people were usually allowed to elect their own legislature, but had governors appointed and other judicial and administrative officials appointed by the president. The first full governor of the Philippines, McKinley appointee William Howard Taft, effectively moved the Filipinos toward self-government. Final independence did not come until 1946.

The question of constitutional rights was resolved by deciding that Hawaiians and Puerto Ricans, for example, would be treated differently from Texans and Oregonians. In the "insular cases" of 1901, the Supreme Court ruled that these people would achieve citizenship and constitutional rights only when Congress said they were ready.

In the election of 1900, Bryan was again the Democratic nominee and tried to make imperialism the "paramount issue" of the campaign. He failed, in part because the country strongly favored annexing the Philippines. In the closing weeks of the campaign, Bryan shied away from imperialism and focused on domestic issues.

That did Bryan no good either. Prosperity returned with the discovery of gold in Alaska, and cries for reform fell on deaf ears. The McKinley forces rightly claimed that four years of Republican rule had brought more money, jobs, thriving factories, and manufactured goods, as well as the tremendous growth in American prestige abroad. As Tom Watson put it, noting the end of the Populist revolt with the war fervor over Cuba, "The blare of the bugle drowned out the voice of the reformer."

He was more right than he knew. Within one year, expansionist Theodore Roosevelt went from assistant secretary of the navy to colonel of the Rough Riders to governor of New York. For some Republican politicos, who thought he was

This 1900 campaign poster for McKinley makes a compelling case that four years of Republican party leadership had brought prosperity and humanity both at home and abroad. Note not only that McKinley and Roosevelt have wrapped themselves in the American flag but also the dramatic contrasts after four years of Republican rule compared with the condition of the United States and Cuba when the Democrats left office in 1896. (From the David J. and Janice L. Frent Collection/CORBIS)

too vigorous and independent, this quick rise as McKinley's potential rival came too fast. One way to eliminate Roosevelt politically, or at least slow him down, was to make him vice president, which they did in 1900. But six months into McKinley's second term, an anarchist killed him, the third presidential assassination in less than 40 years. "Now look," exclaimed party boss Mark Hanna, who had opposed putting Roosevelt on the ticket, "that damned cowboy is President of the United States!"

## THEODORE ROOSEVELT'S ENERGETIC DIPLOMACY

At a White House dinner party in 1905, a guest told a story about visiting the Roosevelt home when "Teedie" was a baby. "You were in your bassinet, making a good deal of fuss and noise," the guest reported, "and your father lifted you out and asked me to hold you." Secretary of State Elihu Root looked up and asked, "Was he hard to hold?" Whether true or not, the story reveals much about President Roosevelt's principles and policies on foreign affairs. As president from 1901 to 1909, and as the most dominating American personality for the 15 years between 1897 and 1912, Roosevelt made much fuss and noise about the activist role he thought the United States should play in the world. As he implemented his policies, he often seemed "hard to hold." Roosevelt's energetic foreign policy in Latin America, Eastern Asia, and Europe paved the way for the vital role of the United States as a world power.

## Foreign Policy as Darwinian Struggle

Roosevelt advocated both individual physical fitness and collective national strength. An undersized boy, he had pursued a rigorous body-building program, and as a young man on his North Dakota ranch he learned to value the "strenuous life." Reading Darwin taught him that life was a constant struggle for survival. As president, his ideal was a "nation of men, not weaklings." Although he believed in Anglo-Saxon superiority, he admired—and feared—Japanese military prowess. Powerful nations, like individuals, Roosevelt believed, had a duty to cultivate vigor, strength, courage, and moral commitment to civilized values. In practical terms, this meant developing natural resources, building large navies, and being ever prepared to fight.

Although famous for saying "speak softly and carry a big stick," Roosevelt often not only wielded a large stick but spoke loudly as well. In a speech in 1897, he used the word *war* 62 times, saying that "no triumph of peace is quite so great as the supreme triumphs of war." But despite his bluster, Roosevelt was usually restrained in exercising force. He won the Nobel Peace Prize in 1906 for helping end the Russo-Japanese War. The big stick and the loud talk were meant to preserve order and peace.

Roosevelt divided the world into civilized and uncivilized nations. The civilized ones had a responsibility to "police" the uncivilized, not only maintaining order but also spreading superior values and institutions. Taking on the "white man's burden," civilized nations sometimes had to wage war on the uncivilized—justly so, because the victors bestowed the blessings of culture and racial superiority on the vanquished. But a war between two civilized nations (for example, Germany and Great Britain) would be foolish. Above all, Roosevelt believed in the balance of power. Strong, advanced nations like the United States had a duty to use their power to preserve order and peace. Americans could no longer "avoid responsibilities." The 1900 census showed that the United States, with 75 million people, was more populous than Great Britain, France, or Germany. It seemed time for Americans to exercise a greater role in world affairs.

Roosevelt developed a highly personal style of diplomacy. Bypassing the State Department, he preferred face-to-face contact and personal exchanges of letters with foreign diplomats and heads of state. A British emissary observed that Roosevelt had a "powerful personality" and a commanding knowledge of the world. Ministries from London to Tokyo respected both the president and the power of the United States.

When threats failed to accomplish his goals, Roosevelt used direct personal intervention. When he wanted Panama, Roosevelt bragged later, "I took the Canal Zone" rather than submitting a long "dignified State Paper" for congressional debate. And while Congress debated, he was fond of pointing out, the building of the canal began. Roosevelt's energetic executive activism in foreign policy set a pattern for nearly every twentieth-century president.

# Recovering the Past

## Political Cartoons

One of the most enjoyable ways of recovering the values and attitudes of the past is through political cartoons. Ralph Waldo Emerson once said, "Caricatures are often the truest history of the times." A deft drawing of a popular or unpopular politician can freeze ideas and events in time, conveying more effectively than columns of print the central issues—and especially the hypocrisies and misbehaviors of an era. Cartoonists are often at their best when they are critical, exaggerating a physical feature of a political figure or capturing public sentiment against the government.

The history of political cartoons in the United States goes back to Benjamin Franklin's "Join or Die" cartoon calling for colonial cooperation against the French in 1754. But political cartoons were rare until Andrew Jackson's presidency. Even after such cartoons as "King Andrew the First" in the 1830s, they did not gain notoriety until the advent of Thomas Nast's cartoons in *Harper's Weekly* in the 1870s. Nast drew scathing cartoons exposing the corruption of William "Boss" Tweed's Tammany Hall, depicting Tweed and his men as vultures and smiling deceivers. "Stop them damn pictures," Tweed ordered. "I don't care so much what the papers write about me. My constituents can't read. But, damn it, they can see pictures." Tweed sent some of his men to Nast with an offer of $100,000 to "study art" in Europe. The $5,000-a-year artist negotiated up to a half million dollars before refusing Tweed's offer. "I made up my mind not long ago to put some of those fellows behind bars," Nast said, "and I'm going to put them there." His cartoons helped to drive Tweed out of office.

The emergence of the United States as a world power and the rise of Theodore Roosevelt gave cartoonists plenty to draw about. At the same time, the rise of cheap newspapers such as William Randolph Hearst's *Journal* and Joseph Pulitzer's *World* provided a rich opportunity for cartoonists, whose clever images attracted more readers. When the Spanish-American War broke out, newspapers whipped up public sentiment by having artists draw fake pictures of fierce Spaniards stripping American women at sea and killing helpless Cubans. Hearst used these tactics to increase his paper's daily circulation to 1 million copies.

By the time of the debates over Philippine annexation, many cartoonists took an anti-imperialist stance, pointing out American hypocrisy. Within a year, cartoonists shifted from depicting "The Spanish Brute Adds Mutilation to Murder" (1898) to "Liberty Halts American Butchery in the Philippines" (1899), both included here. Note the similarities in that both cartoons condemn the "butchery" of native peoples. But the villain has changed. Although Uncle Sam as a killer is not nearly as menacing as the figure of Spain as an ugly gorilla, both cartoons share a similarity of stance, blood-covered swords, and a trail of bodies behind.

To understand and appreciate the meaning of any cartoon, certain facts must be ascertained, such as the date, artist, and source of the cartoon; the particular historical characters, events, and context depicted in it; the significance of the caption; and the master symbols employed by the cartoonist.

**Reflecting on the Past**   What symbols and images do you see in these two cartoons? Who is the woman figure and what does she represent? How would you explain the change of bloodied sword-bearer? In addition to these two cartoons, look at the two others in this chapter. How do the images and symbols used in these reflect the cartoonist's point of view? How are various nationalities depicted in the Theodore Roosevelt cartoon? Check some recent newspapers: Who is criticized today and how do cartoonists reveal their attitudes and political positions?

"The Spanish Brute Adds Mutilation to Murder," by Grant Hamilton, in *Judge*, July 9, 1898. (Culver Pictures)

"Liberty Halts American Butchery in the Philippines," from *Life*, 1899. (TimePix, Inc.)

The "big stick" became a memorable image in American diplomacy as Teddy Roosevelt sought to make the United States a policeman not only of the Caribbean basin, but also of the whole world. "As our modern life goes on," Roosevelt said, "and the nations are drawn closer together for good and for evil, and this nation grows in comparison with friends and rivals, it is impossible to adhere to the policy of isolation." (Culver Pictures)

## Taking the Panama Canal

To justify the intervention of 2,600 American troops in Honduras and Nicaragua in 1906, Philander Knox, later a secretary of state, said, "because of the Monroe Doctrine" the United States is "held responsible for the order of Central America." The closeness of the Canal, he said, "makes the preservation of peace in that neighborhood particularly necessary." The Panama Canal was not yet finished when Knox spoke, but it had already become a cornerstone of United States policy.

Three problems had to be surmounted in order to dig an interoceanic connection. First, an 1850 treaty bound the United States to build a canal jointly with Great Britain, a problem resolved in 1901 when the British canceled the treaty in exchange for an American guarantee that the canal would be open to all nations. A second problem was where to dig it. American engineers rejected a long route through Nicaragua in favor of a shorter, more rugged path across Panama, where a French firm had already begun work. This raised the third problem: Panama was a province of Colombia, which rejected the terms the United States offered. Roosevelt called the Colombians "Dagoes" who tried to "hold us up" like highway robbers.

Aware of Roosevelt's fury, encouraged by hints of American support, and eager for the economic benefits that a canal would bring, Panamanian nationalists in

1903 staged a revolution led by several rich families and Philippe Bunau-Varilla of the French canal company. An American warship deterred Colombian intervention and local troops were separated from their officers, who were bought off. A bloodless revolution occurred on November 3; the next day, Panama declared its independence, and on November 6 the United States recognized it. Although Roosevelt did not directly encourage the revolution, it would not have occurred without American help.

On November 18, Hay and Bunau-Varilla signed a treaty establishing the American right to build and operate a canal through Panama and to exercise "titular sovereignty" over the 10-mile-wide Canal Zone. The Panamanian government protested, and a later government called it the "treaty that no Panamanian signed." Roosevelt, in his later boast that he "took the canal," claimed that his diplomatic and engineering achievement, completed in 1914, would "rank . . . with the Louisiana Purchase and the acquisition of Texas."

## Policeman of the Caribbean

As late as 1901, the Monroe Doctrine was still regarded, according to Roosevelt, as the "equivalent to an open door in South America." To the United States, this meant that although no nation had a right "to get territorial possessions," all nations had equal commercial rights in the Western Hemisphere south of the Rio Grande. But as American investments poured into Central America and the Caribbean, the policy changed to one of asserting U.S. dominance in the Caribbean basin.

This change was demonstrated in 1902 when Germany and Great Britain blockaded Venezuela's ports to force the government to pay defaulted debts. Roosevelt was especially worried that German influence would replace the British. He insisted that the European powers accept arbitration and threatened to "move Dewey's ships" to the Venezuelan coast. The crisis passed, largely for other reasons, but Roosevelt's threat of force made very clear the paramount presence and self-interest of the United States in the Caribbean.

The United States kept liberated Cuba under a military governor until 1902, when the Cubans elected a congress and president. The United States honored Cuban independence, as it had promised to do in the Teller Amendment. But through the Platt Amendment, which Cubans reluctantly added to their constitution in 1901, the United States obtained many economic rights in Cuba, a naval base at Guantanamo Bay, and the right to intervene if Cuban sovereignty were ever threatened.

American policy intended to make Cuba a model of how a newly independent nation could achieve orderly self-government with only minimal guidance. Cuban self-government, however, was shaky. When in 1906 a political crisis threatened to spiral into civil war, Roosevelt expressed his fury with "that infernal little Cuban republic." He sent warships to patrol the coastline and special commissioners and troops "to restore order and peace and public confidence." Along with economic development, which mostly benefited American companies, American political and even military involvement in Cuban affairs would continue throughout the century.

The pattern was repeated throughout the Caribbean. The Dominican Republic, for example, suffered from unstable governments and great poverty. In 1904, as a revolt erupted, European creditors pressured the Dominican government for payment of $40 million in defaulted bonds. Sending its warships to discourage European intervention, the United States took over the collection of customs in the republic. Two years later, the United States intervened in Guatemala and Nicaragua, where American bankers controlled nearly 50 percent of all trade, the first of several twentieth-century interventions in those countries.

Roosevelt clarified his policy that civilized nations should "insist on the proper policing of the world" in his annual message to Congress in 1904. The goal of the United States, he said, was to have "stable, orderly and prosperous neighbors." A country that paid its debts and kept order "need fear no interference from the United States." But "chronic wrong-doing" would require the United States to intervene as an "international police power." This policy became known as the Roosevelt Corollary to the Monroe Doctrine. Whereas the Monroe Doctrine had warned European nations not to intervene in the Western Hemisphere, Roosevelt's corollary justified American intervention. Starting with a desire to protect property, loans, and investments, the United States wound up supporting the

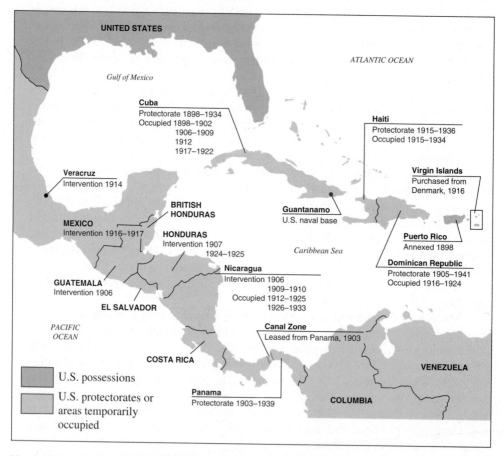

**UNITED STATES INVOLVEMENT IN CENTRAL AMERICA AND THE CARIBBEAN, 1898–1939**  Can you update the location of further interventions in Central America and the Caribbean since the 1950s?

tyrannical regimes of elites who owned most of the land, suppressed the poor, blocked reforms, and acted as American surrogates.

After 1904, the Roosevelt Corollary was invoked in several Caribbean countries. Intervention usually required the landing of U.S. Marines to counter a threat to American property. Occupying the capital and major seaports, Marines, bankers, and customs officials usually remained for several years, until they were satisfied that stability had been reestablished. Roosevelt's successors, William Howard Taft and Woodrow Wilson, pursued the same interventionist policy. So would late-twentieth-century presidents: Ronald Reagan (Grenada and Nicaragua), George Bush (Panama), and Bill Clinton (Haiti).

## Opening the Door to China

Throughout the nineteenth century, American relations with China were restricted to a small but profitable trade. The British, in competition with France, Germany, and Russia, took advantage of the crumbling Manchu dynasty to force treaties on China creating "treaty ports" and granting exclusive trading privileges in various parts of the country. After 1898, Americans with dreams of exploiting the seemingly unlimited markets of China wanted to join the competition and enlarge their share. Those with moral interests, however, including many missionaries, reminded Americans of their revolutionary tradition against European imperialism. They made clear their opposition to crass U.S. commercial exploitation of a weak nation and supported the preservation of China's political integrity as the other imperial powers moved toward partitioning the country.

Although a few Americans admired China's ancient culture, the dominant American attitude viewed the Chinese as heathen, exotic, backward, and immoral. The Exclusion Act of 1882 and riots against Chinese workers in the 1870s and 1880s reflected this negative stereotype. The Chinese, in turn, regarded the United States with a mixture of admiration, curiosity, resentment, suspicion, and disdain.

The annexation of Hawaii and the Philippines in 1898 and 1899 convinced Secretary of State Hay that the United States should announce a China policy. He did so in the Open Door notes of 1899–1900, which became the cornerstone of U.S. policy in Eastern Asia for half a century. The first note demanded an open door for American trade by declaring the principle of equal access to commercial rights in China by all nations. The second note, addressing Russian movement into Manchuria, called on all countries to respect the "territorial and administrative integrity" of China. This second principle announced a larger American role in Asia, offering China protection and preserving the East Asian balance of power.

An early test of this new role came during the Boxer Rebellion in 1900. The Boxers were a society of young traditionalist Chinese in revolt against both the Manchu dynasty and the growing Western presence in China. During the summer of 1900, Boxers killed some 242 missionaries and other foreigners and besieged the western quarter of Peking (Beijing). Eventually an international military force of 19,000 troops, including some 3,000 Americans, marched on Beijing to end the siege.

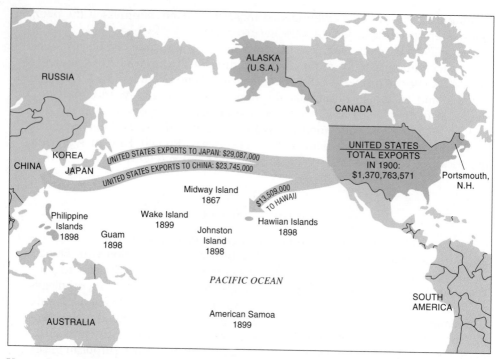

**UNITED STATES INVOLVEMENT IN ASIA, 1898–1909**    What major twentieth-century events have followed the acquisition of territories in the Pacific and the development of intensified trade with East Asian countries?

The relationship with China was plagued by the exclusionist immigration policy of the United States. Despite barriers and riots, Chinese workers kept coming to the United States illegally. In 1905, Chinese nationalists at home boycotted American goods and called for a change in immigration policy. Roosevelt, contemptuous of the "backward" Chinese, bristled and sent troops to the Philippines as a threat. Halfheartedly, he also asked Congress for a modified immigration bill, but nothing came of it.

Despite exclusion and insults, the idea that the United States had a unique guardian relationship with China persisted into the twentieth century. Japan had ambitions in China, so this created a rivalry between Japan and the United States, testing the American commitment to the Open Door in China and the balance of power in Eastern Asia. Economic motives, however, proved to be less significant. Investments there developed very slowly, as did the dream of the "great China market" for American grains and textiles. The China trade always remained larger in imagination than in reality.

## Japan and the Balance of Power

Population pressures, war, and a quest for economic opportunities caused Japanese immigration to the United States to increase dramatically around the turn of the century. Coming first as males working on western railroads and in West

Coast canneries, mines, logging camps, and especially in agriculture, immigrants from Japan increased from 25,000 in the 1890s to 125,000 between 1901 and 1908. Like the earlier Chinese immigrants, they met nativist hostility. In 1906, the San Francisco school board segregated them into separate schools and asked Roosevelt to persuade Japan to stop the emigration. The insulted Japanese agreed to limit the migration of unskilled workers to the United States in a "gentleman's agreement" signed in 1907. In return, the segregation law was repealed, but not without costs in relations between the two nations.

Roosevelt worked hard to maintain the balance of power in East Asia. The Boxer Rebellion of 1900 left Russia with 50,000 troops in Manchuria, making it the strongest regional power. Roosevelt's admiration for the Japanese as a "fighting" people and valuable factor in the "civilization of the future" contrasted with his low respect for the Russians. As Japan moved into Korea and Russia into Manchuria, Roosevelt hoped that each would check the other.

Roosevelt welcomed news in 1904 that Japan had successfully mounted a surprise attack, beginning the Russo-Japanese War. But as Japanese victories continued, many Americans worried that Japan might play the game too well, shutting the United States out of Asian markets. Roosevelt tilted toward Russia. When the Japanese expressed an interest in ending the war, the American president was pleased to exert his influence.

Roosevelt's goal was to achieve peace and leave a balanced situation. Nothing better symbolized the new American presence in the world than the 1905 negotiation and signing of a peace treaty in Portsmouth, New Hampshire, ending a war between Russia and Japan halfway around the globe in Manchuria.

The Treaty of Portsmouth left Japan dominant in Manchuria (as well as in Korea) and established the United States as the major balance to Japan's power. In the Root-Takahira Agreement of 1908, in return for recognizing these developments, Roosevelt got Japan's promise to honor U.S. control in the Philippines and to make no further encroachments into China.

The agreement barely papered over Japanese-American tensions. Some Japanese blamed Roosevelt that the Treaty of Portsmouth had not given them indemnities from Russia. American insensitivity on the immigration issue left bad feelings. In Manchuria, the U.S. consul general aggressively pushed an anti-Japanese program of financing capital investment projects in banking and railroads. This policy, known as "dollar diplomacy" under Roosevelt's successor, William Howard Taft, like the pursuit of markets, was larger in prospect than results. Nevertheless, the United States was in Japan's way, and rumors of war circulated.

It was clearly a moment for Roosevelt's "big stick." In 1907, he told Secretary of State Root that he was "more concerned over the Japanese situation than almost any other. Thank Heaven we have the navy in good shape." Although the naval buildup had begun over a decade earlier, under Roosevelt the U.S. Navy developed into a formidable force. In 1907, to make it clear that "the Pacific was as much our home waters as the Atlantic," Roosevelt sent his "Great White Fleet" on a goodwill world tour. The first stop was Yokohama. Although American sailors were greeted warmly, the act may have stimulated navalism in Japan, which came back to haunt the United States in 1941. But for the time being, the balance of power in Eastern Asia was preserved.

## Preventing War in Europe

The United States had stretched the Monroe Doctrine to justify sending Marines and engineers to Latin America and the Navy and dollars to Eastern Asia. Treaties, agreements, and the protection of territories and interests entangled the United States with foreign nations from Panama and Nicaragua to the Philippines and China. Toward European nations, however, traditional neutrality continued.

Roosevelt believed that the most serious threats to world peace and civilized order lay in the relationships among Germany, Great Britain, and France. He established two fundamental policies toward Europe that would define the U.S. role throughout the century. The first was to make friendship with Great Britain the cornerstone of U.S. policy. Second, the crucial goal of a neutral power like the United States was to prevent a general war in Europe among strong nations. Toward this end, Roosevelt depended on his personal negotiating skills and began the practice of personal diplomacy with the leaders of major nations.

The Venezuelan crisis of 1895 shocked the United States and Britain into an awareness of their mutual interests. Both nations appreciated the neutrality of the other in their respective colonial wars in the Philippines and South Africa. Roosevelt supported British imperialism because he favored the dominance of the "English-speaking race" and believed that Britain was "fighting the battle of civilization." Furthermore, both nations worried about growing German power around the world. As German naval power increased, Britain had to bring its fleet closer to home. Friendly allies were needed to police parts of the world formerly patrolled by the British navy. The United Kingdom therefore concluded a mutual-protection treaty with Japan in 1902 and willingly let the Americans police Central America and the Caribbean Sea.

Language, cultural traditions, and strategic self-interest drew the two countries together. Roosevelt, moreover, was unashamedly pro-British. He knew, as he wrote to Lodge in 1901, that the United States had "not the least particle of danger to fear" from Britain and that German ambitions and militarism represented the major threat to peace in Europe. As Roosevelt left the presidency in 1909, one of his final acts was to proclaim the special American friendship with Great Britain.

German Kaiser Wilhelm II thought that Roosevelt was really pro-German. Roosevelt cultivated the Kaiser's illusion, and Wilhelm sought his support on several diplomatic issues between 1905 and 1909. In each case, Roosevelt flattered the Kaiser while politely rejecting his overtures. The relationship gave Roosevelt a unique advantage in trying to prevent war in Europe, most notably during the Moroccan crisis in 1905 and 1906. When Germany and France threatened to go to war over the control of Morocco, Roosevelt arranged a conference in Algeciras, Spain, to head off conflict. The treaty signed in 1906 peacefully settled the Moroccan issue favorably for the French. Later, at the Hague conference on disarmament in 1907, the Kaiser sought an agreement to reduce British naval supremacy, a superiority Roosevelt thought "quite proper." The German emperor also tried to promote a German-Chinese-American entente to balance the Anglo-Japanese Treaty in Asia. Roosevelt rebuffed all these efforts.

Touring Europe in 1910, the retired American president was warmly entertained by Wilhelm, who continued to misunderstand him. Roosevelt, meanwhile, kept urging his English friends to counter the German naval buildup in order to

# Timeline

| | |
|---|---|
| **1823** | Monroe Doctrine |
| **1857** | Trade opens with Japan |
| **1867** | Alaska purchased from Russia |
| **1870** | Failure to annex Santo Domingo (Hispaniola) |
| **1875** | Sugar reciprocity treaty with Hawaii |
| **1877** | United States acquires naval base at Pearl Harbor |
| **1878** | United States acquires naval station in Samoa |
| **1882** | Chinese Exclusion Act |
| **1889** | First Pan-American Conference |
| **1890** | Alfred Mahan publishes *Influence of Sea Power upon History* |
| **1893** | Hawaiian coup by American sugar growers |
| **1895** | Cuban revolt against Spanish |
| | Venezuelan boundary dispute |
| **1896** | Weyler's reconcentration policy in Cuba |
| | McKinley-Bryan presidential campaign |
| **1897** | Roosevelt's speech at Naval War College |
| **1898** | Sinking of the *Maine* |
| | Spanish-American War |
| | Teller Amendment |
| | Dewey takes Manila Bay |
| | Annexation of Hawaiian Islands |
| | Americans liberate Manila; War ends |
| | Treaty of Paris; Annexation of the Philippines |
| **1899** | Senate ratifies Treaty of Paris |
| | Filipino-American War begins |
| | American Samoa acquired |

| | |
|---|---|
| **1899–1900** | Open Door notes |
| **1900** | Boxer Rebellion in China |
| | William McKinley reelected president |
| **1901** | Supreme Court insular cases |
| | McKinley assassinated; Theodore Roosevelt becomes president |
| **1902** | Filipino-American War ends |
| | U.S. military occupation of Cuba ends |
| | Platt Amendment |
| | Venezuela debt crisis |
| **1903** | Panamanian revolt and independence |
| | Hay-Bunau-Varilla Treaty |
| **1904** | Roosevelt Corollary |
| **1904–1905** | Russo-Japanese War ended by treaty signed at Portsmouth, New Hampshire |
| **1904–1906** | United States intervenes in Nicaragua, Guatemala, and Cuba |
| **1905–1906** | Moroccan crisis |
| **1906** | Roosevelt receives Nobel Peace Prize |
| **1907** | Gentleman's agreement with Japan |
| **1908** | Root-Takahira Agreement |
| **1909** | U.S. Navy ("Great White Fleet") sails around the world |
| **1911** | United States intervenes in Nicaragua |
| **1914** | Opening of the Panama Canal |
| | World War I begins |
| **1916** | Partial home rule granted to the Philippines |

maintain peace in Europe. In 1911, Roosevelt wrote that there would be nothing worse than that "Germany should ever overthrow England and establish the supremacy in Europe she aims at." A German attempt "to try her hand in America," he thought, would surely follow. To avert it, Roosevelt's policy for Europe included cementing friendship with England and, while maintaining official neutrality, using diplomacy to prevent hostilities among European powers. The relationship between Great Britain and Germany continued to deteriorate, however, and by 1914, a new American president, Woodrow Wilson, would face the terrible reality that Roosevelt had skillfully sought to prevent. When World War I finally broke out, no American was more eager to fight on the British side against the Germans than the leader of the Rough Riders.

❦ ❦ ❦ ❦

# CONCLUSION

## *The Responsibilities of Power*

The realities of power in the 1890s brought increasing international responsibilities. Roosevelt said in 1910 that because of "strength and geographical situation," the United States had itself become "more and more, the balance of power of the whole world." This ominous responsibility was also an opportunity to extend American economic, political, and moral influence around the globe.

As president in the first decade of the twentieth century, Roosevelt established aggressive American policies toward the rest of the world. The United States dominated and policed Central America and the Caribbean Sea to maintain order and protect its investments and other economic interests. In Eastern Asia, Americans marched through Hay's Open Door with treaties, troops, navies, and dollars to protect the newly annexed Philippine Islands, to develop markets and investments, and to preserve the balance of power in Asia. In Europe, the United States sought to remain neutral and uninvolved in European affairs and at the same time to cement Anglo-American friendship and prevent "civilized" nations from going to war.

How well these policies worked would be seen later in the twentieth century. Whatever the particular judgment, the fundamental ambivalence of America's sense of itself as a model "city on a hill," an example to others, remained. As questionable actions around the world—Private Grayson's and others' in the Filipino-American War, for example—painfully demonstrated, it was increasingly difficult for the United States to be both responsible and good, both powerful and loved. The American people thus learned to experience both the satisfactions and burdens, the profits and costs, of the missionary role.

## *Discovering U.S. History Online*

William McKinley and the Spanish-American War
http://www.history.ohio-state.edu/projects/mckinley/SpanAmWar.htm
Ohio State University collection of essays and photos about McKinley and the war.

*Images from the Philippine-United States War*
http://www.geocities.com/djmabry/USA/twenty/Filipino.html
An archive of written and visual historical texts.

*Imperialism in the Making of America*   http://www.boondocksnet.com/moa
Nineteenth-century articles about imperialism from archival sites at the University of Michigan and Cornell University.

*Anti-Imperialism in the United States, 1898–1935*   http://www.boondocksnet.com/ail98-35.html
Jim Zwick edits this extensive collection of primary documents about anti-imperialism in America.

*The Age of Imperialism*   http://www.smplanet.com/imperialism/toc.html
An online history of U.S. imperialism with teaching resources and links.

*The Internet Public Library of Presidents of the United States*
http://www.ipl.org/ref/POTUS/wmckinley.html
Good site with many McKinley links.

*The Spanish-American War in Motion Pictures*   http://memory/loc.gov/ammem/sawhome.html
From the Library of Congress American Memory collection.

*The Birth of U.S. Imperialism—An Introduction to the Spanish-American War*
http://www.geocities.com/Athens/Ithaca/9852/usimp.htm
Wonderful site with maps, text, photos, cartoons, essays, primary source documents, bibliographies, and many links to U.S. imperialism.

# Fiction and Film

Ernest Howard Crosby's *Captain Jinks, Hero* (1902), a delight if you can find it, is an anti-imperialist novel set in the Philippines. James Michener's *Hawaii* (1959) is an immense saga of the multicultural history of the islands annexed by the United States in 1898. *The Woman Warrior* by Maxine Hong Kingston (1975) faithfully reflects Chinese culture in the coming-of-age story of a young Chinese-American woman in California. Frank Chinn's *Donald Duk* (1911) is a fanciful story of San Francisco's Chinatown, with flashbacks to the history of Chinese railroad workers in the late nineteenth-century.

See the PBS video *Crucible of Empire: The Spanish-American War* (1999), which uses rare archival materials, photos, motion pictures, newspapers, and popular songs to recreate the war. Two PBS videos from *The American Experience* series depict the history of the era: *Hawaii's Last Queen* (1997) describes the clash between native Hawaiians and U.S. business interests and Marines, and *America, 1900* (1998) focuses on the year 1900, including the second presidential race between McKinley and Bryan. *In Our Image*, a history of America in the Philippines from 1898 to 1946, is a video produced to accompany Stanley Karnow's *In Our Image: America's Empire in the Philippines* (1989). The first tape covers the Filipino-American war.

# Recommended Reading

## Steps Toward Empire and Expansionism in the 1890s

Robert Beisner, *From the Old Diplomacy to the New, 1865–1900* (1975); John Dobson, *Reticent Expansionism: The Foreign Policy of William McKinley* (1988); Ada Ferrer, *Insurgent Cuba: Race, Nation, and Revolution, 1868-1898* (1999); David Healy, *U.S. Expansion: Imperialist Urge in the 1890s* (1970); Walter LaFeber, *The Cambridge History of Foreign Relations: The Search for Opportunity, 1865–1913* (1993); H. Wayne Morgan, *America's Road to Empire: The War with Spain and Overseas Expansion* (1965); Frank Ninkovich, *The United States and Imperialism* (2001); Milton Plesur, *America's Outward Thrust, 1865–1890* (1971).

## War in Cuba and the Philippines

Robert Beisner, *Twelve Against Empire: The Anti-Imperialists, 1898–1900* (1968); James E. Bradford, ed., *Crucible of Empire: The Spanish-American War and Its Aftermath* (1993); Willard Gatewood, Jr., *Black Americans and the White Man's Burden* (1975); Kristen L. Hoganson, *Fighting for American Manhood: How Gender Politics Provoked the Spanish-American and Philippine-American Wars* (1998); Brian Linn, *The Philippine War: 1899–1902* (2000); Stuart Creighton Miller, *"Benevolent Assimilation:" The American Conquest of the Philippines, 1899–1903* (1982); Ivan Musicant, *Empire by Default: The Spanish-American War and the Dawn of the American Century* (1998); John L. Offner, *An Unwanted War: The Diplomacy of the United States and Spain over Cuba, 1895–1898* (1992); Louis A. Perez, Jr., *The War of 1898: The United States and Cuba in History and Historiography* (1998); Angel Smith and Emma Davila-Cox, eds., *The Crisis of 1898: Colonial Redistribution and Nationalist Mobilization* (1999); David Trask, *The War with Spain in 1898* (1981); David Traxel, *1898: The Birth of the American Century* (1998); Richard Welch, *Response to Imperialism: The United States and the Philippine-American War, 1899–1902* (1979).

## Theodore Roosevelt's Energetic Diplomacy

Howard Beale, *Theodore Roosevelt and the Rise of America to World Power* (1956); Richard H. Collin, *Theodore Roosevelt's Caribbean: The Panama Canal, the Monroe Doctrine, and the Latin American Context* (1990); Roger Daniels, *Asian Americans: Chinese and Japanese in the United States Since 1850* (1988); Walter La Feber, *Inevitable Revolutions: The United States in Central America* (1983); Frederick Marks III, *Velvet on Iron: The Diplomacy of Theodore Roosevelt* (1979); David McCollough, *The Path Between the Seas: The Creation of the Panama Canal, 1870–1914* (1977); Edmund Morris, *The Rise of Theodore Roosevelt* (1979) and *Theodore Rex* (2001); Ronald Takaki, *Strangers from a Different Shore: A History of Asian Americans* (1989); Marilyn B. Young, *The Rhetoric of Empire: American China Policy, 1895–1901* (1968).

# CHAPTER 21
# The Progressives Confront Industrial Capitalism

## CHAPTER OUTLINE

- The Social Justice Movement
- The Worker in the Progressive Era
- Reform in the Cities and States
- Theodore Roosevelt and the Square Deal
- Woodrow Wilson and the New Freedom
- Conclusion: The Limits of Progressivism

## AMERICAN STORIES
### A Professional Woman Joins the Progressive Crusade

Frances Kellor, a young woman who grew up in Ohio and Michigan, received her law degree in 1897 from Cornell University and became one of the small but growing group of professionally trained women. Deciding that she was more interested in solving the nation's social problems than in practicing law, she moved to Chicago, studied sociology, and trained herself as a social reformer. Kellor believed passionately that poverty and inequality could be eliminated in America. She also had the progressive faith that if Americans could only hear the truth about the millions of people living in urban slums, they would rise up and make changes. She was one of the experts who provided the evidence to document what was wrong in industrial America.

Like many progressives, Kellor believed that environment was more important than heredity in determining ability, prosperity, and happiness. Better schools and better housing, she thought, would produce better citizens. Even criminals, she argued, were simply victims of environment. Kellor demonstrated that poor health and deprived childhoods explained the only differences between criminals and college students. If it were impossible to define a criminal type, then it must be possible to reduce crime by improving the environment.

Kellor was an efficient professional. Like the majority of the professional women of her generation, she never married but devoted her life to social research and social reform. She lived for a time at Hull House in Chicago and at the College Settlement in New York, centers not only of social research and reform but also of lively community. For many young people the settlement, with its sense of commitment and its exciting conversation around the dinner table, provided an alternative to the nuclear family or the single apartment.

While staying at the College Settlement, Kellor researched and wrote a muckraking study of employment agencies, published in 1904 as *Out of Work*. She revealed how employment agencies exploited immigrants, blacks, and other recent arrivals in the city. Kellor's book, like the writing of most progressives, sizzled with moral outrage. But Kellor went beyond moralism to suggest corrective legislation at the state and national levels. Kellor became one of the leaders of the movement to Americanize the immigrants pouring into the country in unprecedented numbers. Between 1899 and 1920, over 8 million people came to the United States, most from southern and eastern Europe. Many feared that this flood of immigrants threatened the very basis of American democracy. Kellor and her coworkers represented the side of progressivism that sought state and federal laws to protect the new arrivals from exploitation and to establish agencies and facilities to educate and Americanize them. Another group of progressives, often allied with organized labor, tried to pass laws to restrict immigration. Kellor did not entirely escape her generation's ethnocentrism, but she did maintain that all immigrants could be made into useful citizens.

Convinced of the need for a national movement to push for reform legislation, Kellor helped to found the National Committee for Immigrants in America, which tried to promote a national policy "to make all these people Americans," and a federal bureau to organize the campaign. Eventually, she helped establish the Division of Immigrant Education within the Department of Education. A political movement led by Theodore Roosevelt excited her most. More than almost any other single person, Kellor had been responsible for alerting Roosevelt to the problems the immigrants faced in American cities. When Roosevelt formed the new Progressive party in 1912, she was one of the many social workers and social researchers who joined him. She campaigned for Roosevelt and directed the Progressive Service Organization, educating voters in all areas of social justice and welfare after the election. After Roosevelt's defeat and the collapse of the Progressive party, Kellor continued to work for Americanization. She spent the rest of her life promoting justice, order, and efficiency and looking for ways of resolving industrial and international disputes.

❧❧ ❧❧ ❧❧ ❧❧

Frances Kellor's life illustrates two important aspects of progressivism, the first nationwide reform movement of the modern era: first, a commitment to promote social justice, to assure equal opportunity, and to preserve democracy; and second, a search for order and efficiency in a world complicated by rapid industrialization, immigration, and spectacular urban growth. But no one person can represent all facets of so complex a movement. Borrowing from populism and influenced by a number of reformers from the 1890s as well as by social welfare legislation passed in several European countries, progressivism reached a climax in the years from 1900 to 1914. The progressive movement did not plot to overthrow the government; rather, it sought to reform the system in order to ensure the survival of the American way of life.

This chapter traces the important aspects of progressivism. It examines the social justice movement, which sought to promote reform among the poor and to improve life for those who had fallen victim to an urban and industrial civilization. It surveys life among workers, a group the reformers sometimes helped but often misunderstood. Then it describes the reform movements in the cities and states, where countless officials and experts tried to reduce chaos and promote order and democracy. It traces the gradual movement from dependence on voluntary action to solve social problems to the passage of state and federal laws to promote social reform. Finally, it examines progressivism at the national level during the administrations of Theodore Roosevelt and Woodrow Wilson, the first thoroughly modern presidents.

## THE SOCIAL JUSTICE MOVEMENT

Historians write of a "progressive movement." Actually there were a number of movements, some of them contradictory, but all focusing on the problems created by a rapidly expanding urban and industrial world. Some reformers, often from the middle class, sought to humanize the modern city—improving housing and schools, and providing a better life for immigrants. Others focused on working conditions and the rights of labor. Still others sought to make politics responsive to popular interests, including women. Progressivism had roots in the 1890s, when many reformers were shocked by the devastation caused by the depression of 1893, and they were influenced by George's *Progress and Poverty* (1879), Bellamy's *Looking Backward* (1888), and the Social Gospel movement (see Chapter 19).

### The Progressive World View

Intellectually, the progressives were influenced by Darwinism. Believing that the world was in flux, they rebelled against the fixed and the formal. Progressive philosopher John Dewey wrote that ideas could become instruments for change. William James, in his philosophy of pragmatism, denied that there were universal truths; ideas should be judged by their usefulness. Most progressives were convinced that social environment was much more important than heredity in forming character. Building better schools and houses would make better people and a more perfect society. Yet even the more advanced reformers thought in racial and ethnic categories, sure that some groups could be molded more easily than others. Progressivism did not usually mean progress for blacks.

In many ways, progressivism was the first modern reform movement. It sought to bring order and efficiency to a world that had been transformed by rapid growth and new technology. Yet elements of nostalgia infected the movement as reformers tried to preserve pre-industrial handicrafts and to promote small town and farm values in urban settings. Progressive leaders were almost always middle class, and they quite consciously tried to teach middle-class values to immigrants and working people. Often progressives seemed more interested in control than in reform; frequently, they displayed paternalism toward those they tried to help.

The progressives were part of a statistics-minded, realistic generation. They conducted surveys, gathered facts, wrote reports, and usually had faith that all this would lead to change. Their urge to document and to record came out in haunting photographs of young workers taken by Lewis Hine, in the stark and beautiful city paintings by John Sloan, and in the realist novels of Theodore Dreiser and William Dean Howells.

Optimistic about human nature, progressives believed that change was possible. They may seem naive or bigoted, but they wrestled with many social questions, some of them old but fraught with new urgency in an industrialized society. What is the proper relation of government to society? In a world of large corporations and huge cities, how much should the government regulate and control? How much responsibility does society have for its poor and needy? Progressives could not agree on the answers, but for the first time in American history, they struggled with the questions.

## The Muckrakers

Writers who exposed corruption and other social evils were labeled "muckrakers" by Theodore Roosevelt. Not all muckrakers were reformers—some just wrote for the money—but reformers learned from their techniques of exposé.

In part, the muckrakers were a product of the journalistic revolution of the 1890s. Nineteenth-century magazines had elite audiences. The new magazines had slick formats, more advertising, and wider sales. Competing for readers, editors eagerly published articles telling the public what was wrong in American society.

Lincoln Steffens, a young California journalist, wrote articles exposing the connections between respectable businessmen and corrupt politicians. When published as a book in 1904, *The Shame of the Cities* became a battle cry for people determined to clean up city government. Ida Tarbell, a teacher turned journalist, revealed the ruthlessness of John D. Rockefeller's Standard Oil Company. David Graham Phillips uncovered the alliance of politics and business in *The Treason of the Senate* (1906). Robert Hunter, a young settlement worker, shocked Americans in 1904 with his book *Poverty*. Upton Sinclair's novel *The Jungle* (1906) described the horrors of the Chicago meatpacking industry, and Frank Norris dramatized the railroads' stranglehold on farmers in *The Octopus* (1901).

## Working Women and Children

Nothing disturbed the social justice progressives more than the sight of children as young as eight or ten working long hours in dangerous and depressing factories. Florence Kelley was one of the most important leaders in the crusade against child labor. Kelley had grown up in an upper-class Philadelphia family and was a member of the first generation of college women. Refused admission to an American graduate school because of her gender, she went to the University of Zurich in Switzerland and became a socialist. After her marriage failed, Kelley moved into Hull House and poured her energies into the campaign against child labor. When no Chicago attorney would argue child labor cases against prominent corporations, she went to law school, passed the bar exam, and argued the cases herself.

Kelley and other child labor reformers quickly recognized the need for state laws. Marshaling their evidence about the tragic effects on growing children of long working hours in dark and damp factories, they pressured the Illinois legislature into passing an antichild labor law. A few years later, however, the state

Nothing tugged at the heartstrings of the reformers more than the sight of little children, sullen and stunted, working long hours in factory, farm, and mine. These children, breaker boys who spent all day sorting coal in western Pennsylvania, were carefully posed by documentary photographer Lewis Hine while he worked for the National Child Labor Committee in 1911. (Records of the Children's Bureau, The National Archives, Office of the Chief Signal Officer)

supreme court ruled it unconstitutional, showing reformers that national-level action was essential. Kelley led the charge.

The National Child Labor Committee was the brainchild of Edgar Gardner Murphy, a Social Gospel clergyman from Alabama. Headquartered in New York, it drew up a model state child labor law, encouraged state and city campaigns, and coordinated the movement around the country. Although two-thirds of the states passed some form of child labor law between 1905 and 1907, many had loopholes. The committee therefore supported a national bill introduced in Congress by Indiana Senator Albert Beveridge in 1906 "to prevent the employment of children in factories and mines." It went down to defeat, but reformers convinced Congress in 1912 to establish a Children's Bureau in the Department of Labor. Compulsory school attendance laws, however, did more to reduce the number of children who worked than federal and state laws, which proved difficult to pass and even more difficult to enforce.

The crusade against child labor was a typical social justice reform effort. Its origins lay in the moral indignation of middle-class reformers. But reformers went beyond moral outrage; they gathered statistics, took photographs, and used their evidence to push for legislation, first on the local level, then in the states, and eventually in Washington.

Like other progressive reform efforts, the battle against child labor was only partly successful. Too many businessmen profitably employed children. Too many politicians and judges were reluctant to regulate the work of children or adults. And some parents, desperately needing their child's wages, opposed the reformers and broke the law.

Reformers worried over the young people who got into trouble with the law, often for pranks that in rural areas would have seemed harmless. By setting up juvenile courts, the progressives hoped to separate young people from the criminal justice system while preventing them from being turned into hardened criminals by adult prisons. Yet juvenile courts frequently deprived young offenders of all rights of due process, as the Supreme Court finally recognized in 1967.

Closely connected with the anti-child labor movement was the effort to limit the hours of women's work. It seemed inconsistent to protect a girl until she was 16 and then give her the "right to work from 8 A.M. to 10 P.M., 13 hours a day, 78 hours a week for $6." Florence Kelley and the National Consumers League led the campaign. It was foolish and unpatriotic, they argued, to allow the "mothers of future generations" to work long hours in dangerous industries.

The most important court case on women's work came before the U.S. Supreme Court in 1908. Josephine Goldmark, Kelley's friend, wrote the brief for *Muller* v. *Oregon* that her brother-in-law, Louis Brandeis, used when he argued the case. The Court upheld the Oregon 10-hour law largely because Goldmark's sociological argument detailed the danger and disease that factory women faced. Brandeis opposed laissez-faire legal concepts, arguing that the government had a special interest in protecting citizens' health. Most states fell into line with the Supreme Court decision and passed protective legislation for women, though many companies managed to circumvent the laws. But even the 10 hours of work permitted by the law seemed too long for women who had to come home to childcare and housekeeping.

Contending that "women are fundamentally weaker than men in all that makes for endurance . . . ," reformers won some protection for women workers. But their arguments would later be used to reinforce gender segregation at work.

Besides seeking legislation to protect working women, the social justice progressives also campaigned for woman suffrage. Unlike some supporters who argued that middle-class women would offset the ignorant and corrupt votes of immigrant men, these social reformers supported votes for all women. Jane Addams argued that urban women not only could vote intelligently, but also needed the vote to protect their families. The progressive insistence that all women needed the vote helped to push woman suffrage toward victory during World War I.

Much more controversial than either votes for women or protective legislation was the birth control movement. Even many advanced progressives could not imagine themselves teaching immigrant women how to prevent conception (which was also illegal under federal law).

Margaret Sanger, a nurse who had watched poor women suffer from too many births and even die from dangerous, illegal abortions, was one of the founders of the modern American birth control movement. Middle-class Americans had limited family size in the nineteenth century through abstinence, withdrawal, abortion, and primitive birth control devices, but much ignorance remained, even among middle-class women. Sanger obtained the latest medical and scientific European studies and in 1914 explained in her magazine, *The Woman Rebel,* and in a pamphlet, *Family Limitation,* that women could separate sex from procreation. She was indicted for violation of the postal code and fled to Europe to avoid arrest.

Birth control long remained controversial, and in most states illegal. Yet Sanger helped to bring sexuality and contraception out into the open. When she returned to the United States in 1921, she founded the American Birth Control League, which became the Planned Parenthood Federation in 1942.

## Home and School

Reformers believed that better housing and education could transform the lives of the poor and create a better world. Books such as Jacob Riis's *How the Other Half*

*Lives* (1890) horrified them. With vivid language and haunting photographs, Riis had documented the misery of New York's slums.

In the first decade of the twentieth century, the progressives took a new approach to the housing problems. They collected statistics, conducted surveys, organized committees, and constructed exhibits to demonstrate the effect of urban overcrowding. Tenement house laws, passed in several cities, were often ineffectual. In 1910, reformers organized the National Housing Association, and some hoped for federal laws and even government-subsidized housing.

The housing reformers combined a moral sense of what needed to be done to create a more just society with practical ability to stir up the public and get laws passed. But often immigrants' family values differed from those of middle-class reformers'. The immigrants did not mind clutter and lack of privacy, and they hung religious objects rather than "good pictures" on the walls.

Many middle-class women reformers who tried to teach working-class families how to live in their tenements had never organized their own homes. Those who lived in settlement houses never worried about cooking or chores. Some, however, began to realize that domestic tasks kept women of all classes from taking their full place in society. Charlotte Perkins Gilman sketched an alternative to traditional notions of "the woman's sphere," suggesting that entrepreneurs build

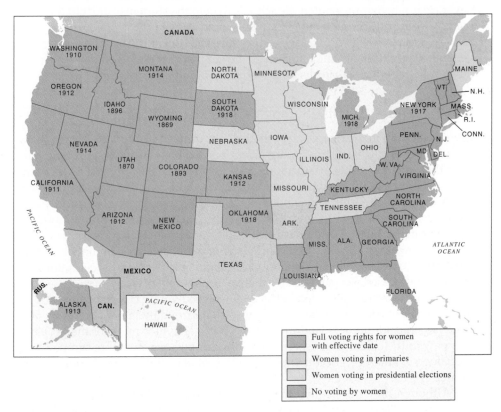

| | Full voting rights for women with effective date |
| | Women voting in primaries |
| | Women voting in presidential elections |
| | No voting by women |

**WOMAN SUFFRAGE BEFORE THE NINETEENTH AMENDMENT** Western states led the battle for women's right to vote, but key victories in New York (1917) and Michigan (1918) and a carefully organized campaign in all parts of the country finally led to the ratification of the Nineteenth Amendment. It was a triumph of progressive reform.

apartment houses in which women could combine motherhood with careers. However, most Americans of all political persuasions continued to view the home as sacred space where the mother ruled supreme and created domestic tranquility for her husband and children.

Next to better housing, the progressives stressed better schools as a way to produce better citizens. Public school systems were often rigid and corrupt, and seemed to reinforce old habits. A Chicago teacher told her students: "Don't stop to think; tell me what you know."

Progressive education, like many other aspects of progressivism, opposed the rigid in favor of flexibility. John Dewey was the key philosopher of progressive education. He tried to create in the city a sense of the small rural community of his native Vermont. He experimented with new educational methods, including seats that could be arranged in small groups rather than bolted down in rows.

Dewey insisted that the schools be child-centered rather than subject-centered, that teachers teach children rather than history or mathematics. He did not mean that history and math should not be taught, but that those subjects should be related to the students' experience. Students should not just learn about democracy; the school itself should operate like a democracy.

Dewey also maintained, somewhat controversially, that the schools should become instruments for social reform. But like most progressives, Dewey was never clear whether he wanted the schools to help the students adjust to the existing world or to turn out graduates who would change the world. Although he wavered, the spirit of progressive education, like the spirit of progressivism in general, was optimistic. The reformers believed that the schools could create more flexible, better-educated adults who would eventually improve society.

## Crusades Against Saloons, Brothels, and Movie Houses

Given their faith in the reforming potential of healthy and educated citizens, it was logical that most social justice progressives opposed the sale of alcohol. Some came from Protestant homes where drinking was considered a sin, but most favored prohibition for pragmatic reasons: to reform the city and conserve human resources.

Americans did drink a lot, and the amount they consumed rose rapidly after 1900, peaking between 1911 and 1915. Only three states still had prohibition laws dating from the 1850s. The modern anti-liquor movement was spearheaded in the 1880s and 1890s by the Women's Christian Temperance Union and after 1900 by the Anti-Saloon League and a coalition of religious leaders and social reformers. Seven states passed temperance laws between 1906 and 1912.

Reformers were often appalled as they watched young children enter saloons to buy a pail of beer for the family. They were horrified by tales of abuse by alcoholic fathers and mothers, and they blamed the saloon for many of the problems they saw in the cities. "Why should the community have any more sympathy for the saloon . . . than . . . for a typhoid-breeding pool of filthy water?" one irate reformer asked.

Although they never quite understood the role alcohol played in the social life of many ethnic groups, Jane Addams and other settlement workers appreciated the saloon's importance as a social center. Addams started a coffeehouse at Hull House to lure people away from the saloon. The progressives never found a substitute for the saloon, but they did work for local and state prohibition laws. As in many other progressive efforts, they joined with diverse groups to push for change, and won. On December 22, 1917, Congress sent to the states for ratification a constitutional amendment prohibiting the sale, manufacturing, or importing of intoxicating liquor within the United States. The spirit of wartime sacrifice facilitated its rapid ratification.

Besides the saloon, progressives saw the urban dance hall and movie theater as threats to youthful morals. The motion picture, invented in 1889, developed as an important form of entertainment only during the first decade of the twentieth century, at first appealing mainly to a lower-class and largely ethnic audience.

Not until World War I, when D. W. Griffith produced long feature films, did the movies begin to attract a middle-class audience. The most popular of these early films was Griffith's *The Birth of a Nation* (1915), a blatantly racist and distorted epic of black debauchery during Reconstruction. Many early films were imported from France, Italy, and Germany; because they were silent, they could be subtitled in any language. But viewers did not need to know the language, or even be able to read, to enjoy the action. That was part of early films' attraction. Many depicted premarital sex, adultery, and violence, and, unlike later films, many attacked authority and had tragic endings. *The Candidate* (1907) showed an upper-class reform candidate who gets dirt thrown at him when he tries to clean up the town. In *Down with Women* (1907), well-dressed men denounced woman suffrage and the incompetence of "the weaker sex," but throughout the film, only strong women were depicted.

Some of the films stressed slapstick humor or romance and adventure; others bordered on pornography. The reformers objected not only to the plots and content of the films, but also to the location of the theaters, near saloons and burlesque houses, and to their dark interiors. "In the dim auditorium which seems to float on the world of dreams . . . an American woman may spend her afternoon alone," one critic wrote. "She can let her fantasies slip through the darkened atmosphere . . . ." This disturbed reformers. But for young immigrant women, who made up the bulk of the audience at most urban movie theaters, the films provided rare exciting moments in their lives.

Saloons, dance halls, and movie theaters all seemed to progressives somehow connected with the worst evil of all: prostitution. Nineteenth-century anti-prostitution campaigns were nothing compared with the progressives' crusade to wipe out the "social evil." All major cities and many smaller ones appointed vice commissions, whose reports, often running to several thick volumes, were typical progressive documents, filled with elaborate statistical studies and moral outrage.

The progressive anti-vice crusade attracted many kinds of people, for often contradictory reasons. Racists and immigration restrictionists claimed that inferior people—blacks and recent immigrants—became prostitutes and pimps. Social hygiene progressives published vivid accounts of prostitution as part of their campaign to fight sexual ignorance. Some women reformers promoted a single moral standard for men and women. Others worried that prostitutes would spread venereal disease to unfaithful husbands, who would pass it on to wives and babies. Most progressives, however, stressed the environmental causes of vice. They believed that prostitution, like child labor and poor housing, could be eliminated through education and reform.

# Recovering the Past

## Documentary Photographs

Photographs are a revealing way of recovering the past visually. But when looking at a photograph, especially an old one, it is easy to assume that it is an accurate representation of the past. Photographers, however, like novelists and historians, have a point of view. They take their pictures for a reason and often to prove a point. As one photographer remarked, "Photographs don't lie, but liars take photographs."

To document the need for reform in the cities, progressives collected statistics, made surveys, described settlement houses, and even wrote novels. But they discovered that the photograph was often more effective than words. Jacob Riis, the Danish-born author of *How the Other Half Lives* (1890), a devastating exposure of conditions in New York City tenement house slums, was also a pioneer in urban photography. Others had taken pictures of dank alleys and street urchins before, but Riis was the first to photograph slum conditions with the express purpose of promoting reform. At first he hired photographers, but then he bought a camera and taught himself how to use it. He even tried a new German flash powder to illuminate dark alleys and tenement rooms in order to record the horror of slum life.

Riis made many of his photographs into lantern slides and used them to illustrate his lectures on the need for housing reform. Although he was a creative and innovative photographer, his pictures were often far from objective. His equipment was awkward, his film slow. He had to set up and prepare carefully before snapping the shutter. His views of tenement ghetto streets and poor children now seem like clichés, but they were designed to make Americans angry, to arouse them to reform.

Another important progressive photographer was Lewis Hine; like Riis, he taught himself photography. Trained as a sociologist, Hine used his camera to illustrate his lectures at the Ethical Culture School in New York. In 1908, he was hired as a full-time investigator by the National Child Labor Committee. His haunting photographs of children in factories helped convince many Americans of the need to abolish child labor. Hine's children were appealing human beings. He showed them eating, running, working, and staring wistfully out factory windows. His photographs avoided the pathos that Riis was so fond of recording, but just as surely they documented the need for reform.

Another technique that the reform photographer used was the before-and-after shot. The two photographs shown here of a one-room apartment in Philadelphia early in the century illustrate how progressive reformers tried to teach immigrants to imitate middle-class manners. The "before" photograph shows a room cluttered with washtubs, laundry, cooking utensils, clothes, tools, even an old Christmas decoration. In the "after" picture, much of the clutter has been cleaned up. A window has been installed to let in light and fresh air. The wallpaper, presumably a haven for hidden bugs and germs, has been torn off. The cooking utensils and laundry have been put away. The woodwork has been stained, and some ceremonial objects have been gathered on a shelf.

What else can you find that has been changed? How well do you think the message of the photographic combinations like this one worked? Would the immigrant family be happy with the new look and condition of their room? Could anyone live in one room and keep it so neat?

**Reflecting on the Past**  As you look at these, or any photographs, ask yourself: What is the photographer's purpose and point of view? Why was this particular angle chosen for the picture? And why center on these particular people or objects? What does the photographer reveal about his or her purpose? What does the photographer reveal unintentionally? How have fast film and new camera styles changed photography? On what subjects do reform-minded photographers train their cameras today?

The reality of one-room tenement apartments (top) contrasted with the tidiness that reformers saw as the ideal (bottom). (Temple University Urban Archives)

Despite all their reports and publicity, the progressives failed to end prostitution and did virtually nothing to address its roots in poverty. "Do you suppose I am going back to earn five or six dollars a week in a factory," one prostitute asked an investigator, "when I can earn that amount any night and often much more?" Reformers wiped out a few red-light districts, closed some brothels, and managed to push a bill through Congress (the Mann Act of 1910) that prohibited the interstate transport of women for immoral purposes. Perhaps more important, in several states, they got the age of consent for women raised, and in 20 states they made the Wassermann test for syphilis mandatory for both men and women before a marriage license could be issued.

## THE WORKER IN THE PROGRESSIVE ERA

Progressive reformers sympathized with industrial workers, who struggled to earn a living for themselves and their families, and sought legislation to protect working women and children. But often they had little understanding of what it was really like to sell one's strength by the hour. For example, they supported labor's right to organize at a time when labor had few friends, yet they often opposed the strike as a weapon against management. And neither organized labor nor the reformers, individually or in shaky partnership, had much power over industry in the years before World War I.

## Adjusting to Industrial Labor

Many workers, whether from Eastern Europe or Michigan, found the factory bewildering. Unlike farm or craft work, the factory was ruled by the clock and the boss. Workers continued to resist the pace of factory work and subtly sabotaged employers' efforts to control them (see Chapters 10 and 18). They stayed home on holidays when they were supposed to work, took unauthorized breaks, and set their own productivity schedules. Often they were fired or quit. In New York needleworker shops in 1912 and 1913, the turnover rate was over 250 percent. Overall, one-third of the workers stayed at their jobs less than a year.

The industrial workforce, still composed largely of immigrants, had a fluid character. Many migrants, especially those from southern and eastern Europe, expected to stay only for a short time. About 40 percent of those who came in the first decade of the twentieth century did return to their native land. In years of economic downturn, more Italians and Austro-Hungarians left the United States than entered. Many men came alone—70 percent in some years—and saved perhaps a third of their money by living in a boardinghouse.

The nature of work continued to change in the early twentieth century as industrialists extended late-nineteenth-century efforts to make their factories and workforces more efficient, productive, and profitable. In some industries, new machines revolutionized work and eliminated highly paid skilled jobs. The moving assembly line, perfected by Henry Ford, transformed the nature of work and turned many laborers into unskilled machine-tenders.

The influence of the machine was uneven, having a greater impact in some industries than in others. Although some skilled weavers and glassblowers were transformed into unskilled operators, the machines themselves created the need for new skilled workers. In the auto industry, for example, the new elite workers were the mechanics and the tool and die men who kept the assembly line running. But the trend toward mechanization was unstoppable, and even the most skilled workers were eventually removed from making decisions about production.

The principles of scientific management were also important in altering industrial work. Here the key figure was Frederick Taylor, the son of a prominent Philadelphia family. Taylor had a nervous breakdown as a youth, and his physicians prescribed manual labor as a cure. Working in a Philadelphia steel plant and studying engineering at night, he became chief engineer in the 1880s. Later he used this experience to rethink the organization of industry.

Taylor was obsessed with efficiency. He emphasized centralized planning, systematic analysis, and detailed instructions. He timed workers with a stopwatch to determine the most efficient way to perform a task. Many owners enthusiastically adopted his concepts of scientific management, seeing an opportunity to increase their profits and their control of the workplace. Not surprisingly, many workers resented "Taylorism."

## Union Organizing

Samuel Gompers, head of the American Federation of Labor, quickly saw that Taylorism would reduce workers to "mere machines." Under his guidance, the AFL prospered during the progressive era. By 1914, the AFL alone had over 2 million members. Gompers's "pure and simple unionism" was most successful among coal miners, railroad workers, and the building trades. As we saw in Chapter 18, Gompers ignored unskilled and immigrant workers and concentrated on raising the wages and improving the working conditions of the skilled craftsmen who were members of unions affiliated with the AFL.

For a time, Gompers's strategy seemed to work. Several industries negotiated with the AFL to avoid disruptive strikes. But cooperation was short-lived. Labor unions were defeated in a number of disastrous strikes, and the National Association of Manufacturers (NAM) launched an aggressive counterattack. The NAM and other employer associations provided strikebreakers, used industrial spies, and blacklisted union members to bar them from other jobs.

The Supreme Court came down squarely on management's side, ruling in the *Danbury Hatters* case in 1908 that trade unions were subject to the Sherman Anti-Trust Act. Thus union members could be held personally liable for money lost by a business during a strike. Courts at all levels often declared strikes illegal and were quick to issue restraining orders.

Working women and their problems aroused more sympathy among progressive reformers than the plight of working men. The number of women working outside the home increased steadily during the progressive era, from over 5 million in 1900 to nearly 8.5 million in 1920. But few belonged to unions, and the percentage had declined by 1910 before increasing a little after that date with aggressive organizing in the textile and clothing trades.

Although the AFL had hired Mary Kenney as an organizer in the 1890s and accepted a few women's unions into affiliation, Gompers and other labor leaders generally opposed organizing women workers (see Chapter 18). "The demand for female labor," one leader announced, "is an insidious assault upon the home."

Of necessity, women continued to work to support themselves and their families. Many well-born women reformers tried to help these working women. Tension and misunderstanding often cropped up between the reformers and the working women, but one organization in which there was genuine cooperation was the Women's Trade Union League. Founded in 1903, the league was organized by Kenney and other progressive reformers and drew leaders from the working class, such as Rose Schneiderman, a Jewish immigrant cap maker. The league established branches in most large eastern and midwestern cities and served for more than a decade as an important force in helping to organize women into unions. It forced the AFL to pay more attention to women, helped out in time of strikes, put up bail money for those arrested, and publicized the plight of working women.

## Garment Workers and the Triangle Fire

Thousands of young women, most of them Jewish and Italian, were employed in the garment industry in New York City. Most were between the ages of 16 and 25. They worked a 56-hour, 6-day week that paid about $6. New York had over 600 shirtwaist (blouse) and dress factories employing more than 30,000 workers.

The Triangle fire shocked the nation, and dramatic photographs, such as this candid shot showing bodies and bystanders waiting for more young women to jump, helped stimulate the investigation that followed. (Brown Brothers)

Like other industries, garment manufacturing had changed. Once conducted in thousands of dark and dingy tenement rooms, all operations were now centralized in large loft buildings in lower Manhattan. Though an improvement over the tenements, many were still overcrowded and had few safety features. Scientific management made life miserable for the workers. Most of the women rented their sewing machines and even paid for their electricity. They were penalized for mistakes or for talking loudly, and were usually supervised by a male contractor who badgered and sometimes sexually harassed them.

In 1909, some of the women went out on strike to protest the working conditions. The International Ladies' Garment Workers Union (ILGWU) and the Women's Trade Union League supported them. But strikers were beaten and sometimes arrested. On November 22, after an impassioned speech in Yiddish by a young shirtwaist worker who had been injured on the picket line, a mass meeting voted for a general strike.

This "uprising of the twenty thousand" startled the nation. Jews and Italians learned a little of each other's language so they could communicate on the picket line. A young state legislator, Fiorello La Guardia, later a congressman and mayor, was one of many public officials who joined clergy and social reformers in aiding the strikers.

The shirtwaist workers won, and in part, the success of the strike made the garment union one of the most powerful in the AFL. But some companies refused to go along, and work conditions remained oppressive and unsafe. That became dramatically obvious on Saturday, March 25, 1911, when a fire broke out on the eighth floor of the ten-story loft building housing the Triangle Shirtwaist Company. Within minutes, the top three floors of the factory were ablaze. The managers had locked many exit doors. The elevators broke down. With no fire escapes, 46 women jumped to their deaths and over 100 died in the flames.

A shocked state legislature appointed a commission to investigate working conditions in the state. One investigator for the commission was a young social worker, Frances Perkins, who in the 1930s would become secretary of labor. She took politicians on a tour through the garment district to show them the miserable conditions under which young women worked. The result was state legislation limiting the work of women to 54 hours a week, prohibiting labor by children under the age of 14, and improving safety regulations in factories. One supporter of the bills was a young state senator named Franklin Delano Roosevelt.

The investigative commission was a favorite progressive tactic, and the Industrial Relations Commission, created in 1912, was one of the most important. The Commission studied the causes of industrial unrest and violence, and investigated a dramatic labor-management conflict in Colorado called the Ludlow Massacre. When the mine workers struck for an eight-hour day, better safety, and the removal of armed guards, the Rockefeller-dominated company refused to negotiate. The strike turned violent, and in the spring of 1914, strikebreakers and national guardsmen fired on the workers, killing eleven children and two women.

The Industrial Relations Commission forced John D. Rockefeller, Jr., to testify and implied that he was personally guilty of murder. Its report concluded that violent class conflict could be avoided only by limiting the use of armed guards and detectives, by restricting monopoly, by protecting workers' right to organize, and, most dramatically, by redistributing wealth through taxation. Not surprisingly, the report fell on deaf ears. Most progressives, like most Americans, denied its conclusion that class conflict was inevitable.

## Radical Labor

Not everyone accepted the progressives' faith in investigations and protective labor legislation. Nor did everyone approve of Samuel Gompers's conservative tactics or his emphasis on getting better pay for skilled workers. About 200 radicals met in Chicago in 1905 to form a new union as an alternative to the AFL. They called it the Industrial Workers of the World (IWW). Like the Knights of Labor in the 1880s, the IWW welcomed all workers, regardless of skill, gender, or race.

Presiding at the Chicago meeting was "Big Bill" Haywood, a colorful, radical worker. "This is the Continental Congress of the working class," he announced. "We are here to confederate the workers of this country into a working-class movement ... for ... the emancipation of the working class from the slave bondage of capitalism."

Eugene Debs attended the organizational meeting. He had become a socialist after the Pullman strike of 1894 and emerged by 1905 as one of the outstanding radical leaders in the country. Also attending was the legendary "Mother" Jones, who dressed like a society matron but attacked labor leaders "who sit on velvet chairs in conferences with labor's oppressors." Now in her sixties, she had been a dressmaker, a Populist, and a member of the Knights of Labor.

The IWW remained small and troubled by internal squabbling. Haywood dominated the movement, which played an important role in organizing the militant strike of textile workers in Lawrence, Massachusetts, in 1912 and the following year in Paterson, New Jersey, and Akron, Ohio. The IWW had its greatest success organizing lumbermen and migrant workers in the Northwest. Elsewhere, especially in times of high unemployment, the "Wobblies" helped the unskilled workers vent their anger against their employers.

But most American workers did not feel, as European workers often did, that they were involved in a class struggle. Some immigrant workers, intent on earning enough money to go home, had no time to join the conflict. Most of those who stayed dreamed the American dream—a better job or moving up into the middle class—and avoided labor militancy. They believed that even if they failed, their sons and daughters would profit from the American way. The AFL, not the IWW, became the dominant American labor organization.

## REFORM IN THE CITIES AND STATES

The reform movements of the progressive era usually started at the local level, moved to the state, and finally reached the nation's capital. Progressivism in the cities and states had roots in the depression and discontent of the 1890s. The reform banners called for more democracy, more power for the people, and legislation regulating railroads and other businesses. Yet often the professional and business classes were the movement's leaders. They intended to bring order out of chaos and to modernize the city and the state during a time of rapid growth.


## Municipal Reformers

American cities grew rapidly in the last part of the nineteenth and the first part of the twentieth centuries. New York, which had a population of 1.2 million in 1880, grew to 3.4 million by 1900 and 5.6 million in 1920. Chicago expanded even more dramatically. Los Angeles, a town of 11,000 in 1880, multiplied ten times by 1900 and then increased another five times, to more than a half million, by 1920.

The spectacular and continuing growth of the cities created a need for housing, transportation, and municipal services. But the kind of people who were filling the cities gave cause for worry. Fully 40 percent of New York's population and 36 percent of Chicago's were foreign-born in 1910; including immigrant children, the percentage approached 80 percent in some cities. "Beaten men from beaten races, representing the worst failures in the struggle for existence," was how the president of MIT described them.

Fear of the city and its new inhabitants motivated progressive municipal reform. Early twentieth-century reformers, mostly middle-class citizens, wanted to regulate the sprawling metropolis, restore democracy, cut corruption, and limit the power of bosses and their immigrant allies. When these reformers talked of restoring power to the people, they usually meant people like themselves.

Municipal reform movements varied from city to city. In Boston, reformers tried to strengthen the power of the mayor, break the hold of the city council, and eliminate council corruption. But in 1910 John Fitzgerald, grandfather of John F. Kennedy and a foe of reform, was elected mayor, defeating the reform candidate. Elsewhere reformers used different tactics, but they almost always conducted elaborate studies and campaigned to reduce corruption.

The most dramatic innovation was the replacement of both mayor and council with a nonpartisan commission of administrators. This innovation began quite accidentally when a hurricane devastated Galveston, Texas, in September 1900—one of the worst natural disasters in the nation's history, killing more than 6,000 people. The existing government was helpless to deal with the crisis, so the state legislature appointed five commissioners to run the city during the emergency.

The idea of government by commission spread rapidly, especially to the small and mid-sized cities in the Midwest and the Pacific Northwest. Dayton, Ohio, went one step further. After a disastrous flood in 1913, the city hired a city manager to run the city and to report to the elected council. Government by experts was the perfect symbol of what most municipal reformers had in mind.

In most large cities, however, the commission and the expert manager did not replace the mayor. One of the most flamboyant and successful of the progressive mayors was Tom Johnson of Cleveland, a wealthy man converted to reform by Henry George's *Progress and Poverty*. Elected mayor of Cleveland in 1901, he cut transit fares and built parks and municipal bath houses throughout the city. He also broke the connection between the police and prostitution by promising "madams" and brothel owners that he would not bother them if they would not steal from customers or pay off the police. His most controversial move was to advocate city ownership of the street railroads and utilities. He was defeated in 1909, in part because he alienated many powerful business interests, but one of his lieutenants, Newton D. Baker, was elected mayor in 1911 and carried on many of his programs. Cleveland was one of many cities that began to regulate municipal utilities or to take them over from the private owners.

## City Beautiful

In Cleveland, Tom Johnson and Newton Baker promoted the arts, music, and adult education, supervised construction of a civic center, and built a library and a museum. Such efforts were typical of progressivism.

The architects of the "city beautiful movement" preferred the impressive and ceremonial architecture of Rome or the Renaissance for libraries, museums, railroad stations, and other public buildings. The huge Pennsylvania Station in New York (now replaced by Madison Square Garden) was modeled after imperial Rome's baths of Caracalla. The city beautiful leaders tried to make the city more attractive for the middle and upper classes. Unfortunately, the museums and libraries were closed on Sundays, the only day the working class could visit them.

The social justice progressives, especially those connected with the social settlements, were more concerned with neighborhood parks and playgrounds. Hull House established the first public playground in Chicago. Jacob Riis and Lillian Wald of the Henry Street Settlement campaigned in New York for small parks and the opening of schoolyards on weekends. Some progressives, remembering their own rural youth, tried to get urban children out of the city to summer camps. But they also tried to make the city more livable and beautiful.

Most progressives both feared and loved the city. Some saw the great urban areas filled with immigrants as a threat, but one of Tom Johnson's young assistants, Frederic C. Howe, wrote a book called *The City: The Hope of Democracy* (1905). Hope or threat, the progressives realized that the United States had become an urban nation and that the problems of the city had to be faced.

## Reform in the States

The progressive movements in the states had many roots and took many forms. In some states, especially in the West, progressive attempts to regulate railroads and utilities were simply an extension of populism. In other states, progressivism bubbled up from urban reform efforts. Most states passed laws designed to extend democracy and give more authority to the people. Initiative and referendum laws allowed citizens to originate legislation and to overturn laws passed by the legislature, and recall laws gave the people a way to remove elected officials. Most of these "democratic" laws worked better in theory than in practice, but they did represent a genuine effort to remove special privilege from government.

Much progressive state legislation concerned order and efficiency, but many states passed social justice measures as well. Maryland enacted the first workers' compensation law in 1902, paying employees for days missed because of job-related injuries. Illinois approved a law aiding mothers with dependent children.

Several states passed anti-child labor bills, and Oregon's 10-hour law restricting women's labor became a model for other states.

States with the most successful reform movements elected strong governors: Charles Evans Hughes in New York, Hokee Smith in Georgia, Woodrow Wilson in New Jersey, and Robert La Follette in Wisconsin. After Wilson, La Follette was the most famous, and in many ways, the model progressive governor. Of small-town origin and an 1879 graduate of the University of Wisconsin, he began his career as a railroad lawyer and became a reformer only after the depression of 1893. Taking advantage of the general mood of discontent, he won the governorship in 1901. Ironically, La Follette owed his victory to his attack on the railroads. But La Follette was a shrewd politician. He used professors from the University of Wisconsin to prepare reports and do statistical studies. Then he worked with the legislature to pass a state primary law and an act regulating the railroads. "Go back to the first principles of democracy; go back to the people" was his battle cry. Journalists touted Wisconsin as the "laboratory of democracy." La Follette became a national figure and was elected to the Senate in 1906.

The progressive movement did improve government and make it more responsible to the people in states like Wisconsin. For example, the railroads were brought under the control of a railroad commission. But by 1910, the railroads no longer complained about the new taxes and restrictions. They had discovered that it was to their advantage to make their operations more efficient, and they often convinced the commission that they should raise rates or abandon unprofitable lines. Progressivism in the states, like progressivism everywhere, had mixed results. But the spirit of reform that swept the country was real, and progressive movements on the local level did eventually have an impact on Washington.

## THEODORE ROOSEVELT AND THE SQUARE DEAL

An anarchist shot President McKinley in Buffalo on September 6, 1901. When McKinley died eight days later, Theodore Roosevelt, at 42, became history's youngest president. As the nation mourned its fallen leader, anarchists and other radicals were rounded up in many cities.

No one knew what to expect from Roosevelt. Some politicians thought he was too radical, but a few social justice progressives remembered his suggestion that the soldiers fire on strikers during the 1894 Pullman strike. Nonetheless, under his leadership, progressivism reshaped the national political agenda. Although early progressive reformers had attacked problems that they saw in their own communities, they gradually understood that some problems could not be solved at the state or local level. The emergence of a national industrial economy had spawned conditions that demanded national solutions.

Progressives at the national level turned their attention to the economic system—the railroads and other large corporations, the state of the natural environment, and the quality of American industrial products. And as they fashioned legislation to remedy economic flaws, they vastly expanded the national government's power.

# A Strong and Controversial President

Roosevelt came to the presidency with considerable experience. He had run unsuccessfully for mayor of New York and served a term in the New York state assembly. He had spent four years as a United States civil service commissioner and two years as New York City's police commissioner. His exploits in the Spanish-American War brought him to the public's attention, but he had also been an effective assistant secretary of the navy and a reform governor of New York. While police commissioner and governor, he had been influenced by progressives like his friend Jacob Riis and a group of New York City settlement workers. They were impressed by his concern for human misery.

But no one was sure how he would act as president. He came from an upper-class family, had associated with the important and the powerful all over the world. He had written books, and was one of the most intellectual presidents since Thomas Jefferson. But none of this ensured that he would be a progressive in office.

Roosevelt loved being president. He called the office a "bully pulpit," and he enjoyed talking to the people and reporters. His appealing personality and sense of humor made him a good subject for the new mass-market press. The public quickly adopted him as their favorite. They called him "Teddy" and named a stuffed bear after him. Sometimes his exuberance got a little out of hand. On one occasion, he took a foreign diplomat on a nude swim in the Potomac River. You have to understand, someone remarked, that "the president is really only six years old."

Roosevelt, however, was more than an exuberant child; he was the strongest president since Lincoln. By revitalizing the executive branch, reorganizing the army command structure, and modernizing the consular service, he made many aspects of the federal government more efficient. He established the Bureau of Corporations, appointed commissions staffed with experts, and enlisted talented men to work for the government. "TR" called a White House conference on the care of dependent children, and in 1905 he even summoned college presidents and coaches to discuss ways to limit violence in football. He angered many social justice progressives by not going far enough. Once Florence Kelley, upset by his moderation, slammed his office door as she left. But he was the first president to listen to the pleas of the progressives and to invite them to the White House. Learning from experts like Frances Kellor, he became more concerned with social justice as time went on.

# Dealing with the Trusts

One of Roosevelt's first actions as president was to attempt to control the large industrial corporations. He took office amid an unprecedented wave of business consolidation. Between 1897 and 1904, some 4,227 companies combined to form 257 large corporations. U.S. Steel, the first billion-dollar corporation, was formed in 1901 by joining Carnegie Steel with its eight main competitors. The new company controlled two-thirds of the market, and J. P. Morgan made $7 million on the deal.

The Sherman Anti-Trust Act of 1890 had been virtually useless in controlling the trusts, but a new outcry from muckrakers and progressives called for regula-

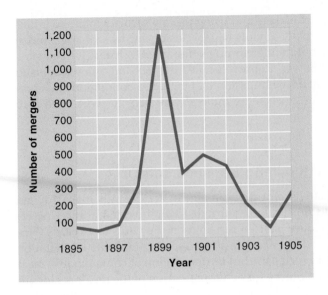

**BUSINESS MERGERS, 1895–1905**
Business mergers did decline during the Roosevelt years, but they did not cease entirely; they even rose again during Roosevelt's second term. (*Source:* U.S. Bureau of the Census)

tion. Some even demanded the return to the age of small business. Roosevelt opposed neither bigness nor the right of businessmen to make money. "We draw the line against misconduct, not against wealth," he said.

To the shock of much of the business community, he directed his attorney general to file suit to dissolve the Northern Securities Company, a giant railroad monopoly put together by Morgan and railroadman James J. Hill. "If we have done anything wrong," Morgan suggested, "send your man to my man and they can fix it up." A furious Roosevelt let Morgan and other businessmen know that the president of the United States was not just another tycoon. The government won its case and proceeded to prosecute some of the largest corporations, including Standard Oil of New Jersey and the American Tobacco Company.

Roosevelt's antitrust policy did not end the power of the giant corporations or even alter their methods of doing business. Nor did it force down the price of kerosene, cigars, or railroad tickets. But it breathed some life into the Sherman Anti-Trust Act and increased the role of the federal government as regulator. It also caused large firms such as U.S. Steel to diversify to avoid antitrust suits.

Roosevelt tried to strengthen the regulatory powers of the federal government in other ways. He steered the Elkins Act through Congress in 1903 and the Hepburn Act in 1906, which together increased the power of the Interstate Commerce Commission (ICC). The first act eliminated the use of rebates by railroads; the second broadened the power of the ICC and gave it the right to investigate and enforce rates. Opponents in Congress weakened both bills, and the legislation neither ended abuses nor satisfied farmers and small businessmen.

Roosevelt firmly believed in corporate capitalism, detested socialism, and was not comfortable around labor leaders. Yet he saw his role as mediator and regulator. His view of the power of the presidency was illustrated in 1902 during the anthracite coal strike. Led by the United Mine Workers, coal miners went on strike to protest low wages, long hours, and dangerous conditions. In 1901, a total of 513 coal miners had died in industrial accidents. The mine owners refused to

talk to the miners, hiring strikebreakers and using private security forces to intim-
idate workers. In the fall of 1902, schools began closing for lack of coal, and it
looked like many citizens would suffer through the winter. Over the managers'
protests about talking to "outlaws," Roosevelt called owners and union leaders to
the White House and appointed a commission that included both union and community representatives. Within weeks, the miners were back at work with a 10
percent raise.

## Meat Inspection and Pure Food and Drugs

Roosevelt's first major legislative reform began almost accidentally in 1904 when
Upton Sinclair, a 26-year-old muckraking journalist who boarded at the University of Chicago Settlement House, started research on the city's stockyards. Sinclair's *The Jungle* was published in 1906. The novel documented labor exploitation
and tried to convert readers to socialism, but its description of contaminated meat
turned stomachs and set off an outcry for better regulation of the meatpacking industry. Roosevelt, who read the book, reportedly could no longer enjoy his break-
fast sausage. He ordered a study of the meatpacking industry and used the report
to pressure Congress and the meatpackers to accept a reform bill.

In the end, the Meat Inspection Act of 1906 was a compromise. It enforced
some federal inspection and mandated sanitary conditions in all companies selling meat in interstate commerce. The meatpackers defeated a provision that
would have required the dating of all meat. Some large companies supported the
compromise bill because it gave them an advantage against smaller firms. But the
bill was a beginning. It illustrates how muckrakers, social justice progressives,
and public outcry eventually led to reform legislation. It also shows how Roosevelt used the public mood and manipulated the political process to get a bill
through Congress. He was always willing to settle for half a loaf rather than none
at all. Ironically, the Meat Inspection Act restored public confidence in the meat
industry and helped it increase profits.

Publicity surrounding *The Jungle* generated legislation to regulate food and
drug sales. Many packaged and canned foods contained dangerous chemicals
and impurities. Americans consumed an enormous quantity of patent medicines;
one popular remedy was revealed to be 44 percent alcohol, and often medicines
were laced with opium. Many people unwittingly became alcoholics or drug ad-
dicts. The Pure Food and Drug Act (1906) was not perfect, but it corrected some of
the worst abuses, including eliminating cocaine from Coca-Cola.

## Conservation versus Preservation

Roosevelt, an outdoorsman and amateur naturalist, considered his conservation
program his most important domestic achievement. Using his executive authority, he more than tripled the land set aside for national forests, bringing the total
to more than 150 million acres.

Roosevelt understood, as few easterners did, the problems created by limited
water in the western states. In 1902, with his enthusiastic support, Congress

passed the Newlands Act, setting aside the proceeds from the sale of public land in 16 western states to pay for the construction of irrigation projects in those states. Although it tended to help big farmers the most, the Newlands Act federalized irrigation for the first time.

More important, Roosevelt raised public consciousness about saving natural resources. He appointed a National Conservation Commission charged with making an inventory of the natural resources in the entire country, chaired by Gifford Pinchot, probably the most important conservationist in the country. An advocate of selective logging, fire control, and limited grazing on public lands, Pinchot became a friend and adviser to Roosevelt.

Pinchot's conservation policies pleased many in the timber and cattle industries and angered those who simply wanted to exploit the land. But the followers of John Muir, a passionate advocate of preserving wilderness, denounced Pinchot's philosophy and policies. Muir had founded the Sierra Club in 1862 and had led a successful campaign to create Yosemite National Park in California. He looked eccentric, but thousands agreed when he argued that to preserve the wilderness was a spiritual and psychological necessity for overcivilized city residents. Muir was one of the leaders in the turn-of-the-century "back-to-nature" movement, which also included the founding of the Boy Scouts (1910) and the Camp Fire Girls (1912).

The conflicting conservation philosophies of Pinchot and Muir were most dramatically demonstrated by the controversy over Hetch-Hetchy, a remote valley deep within Yosemite National Park. It was a pristine wilderness area, and Muir and his followers wanted to keep it that way. But in 1901, the mayor of San Francisco decided the valley would make a perfect place for a dam and reservoir to supply his growing city with water. Muir argued that wilderness soon would be scarcer than water, though more important for the nation's moral strength. Pinchot and other conservationists argued that it was immoral to sacrifice the welfare of the great majority to the aesthetic enjoyment of a tiny group. In the end, Roosevelt and Congress sided with the conservationists, and the valley became (and remains) a lake. The debate between conservationists and preservationists still goes on today.

## Progressivism for Whites Only

Like most whites of his generation, Roosevelt believed that blacks, Indians, and Asians were inferior, and he feared that massive migrations from southern and eastern Europe threatened Anglo-Saxon dominance. But Roosevelt was a politician, so he made gestures of goodwill to most groups. He even invited Booker T. Washington to the White House in 1901, despite vicious southern protests, and appointed several qualified blacks to minor federal posts. But he could also be insensitive to African Americans, as he surely was in his handling of the Brownsville, Texas, riot of 1906. Members of a black army unit who were stationed there rioted, angered by discrimination against them. No one is sure exactly what happened, but one white man was killed and several were wounded. After the midterm elections of 1906, Roosevelt ordered all 167 members of three companies dishonorably discharged—an unjust punishment for an unproven crime. Sixty-six years later,

Tuskegee Institute followed Booker T. Washington's philosophy of black advancement through accommodation to the white status quo. Here students study white American history, but most of their time was spent on more practical subjects. This photo was taken in 1902 by Francis Benjamin Johnson, a pioneer woman photographer. (Library of Congress)

the secretary of the army granted honorable discharges to the men, most of whom were dead by then.

The progressive era coincided with the years of greatest segregation in the South, but even the most advanced progressives seldom included blacks in their reform schemes. Like most settlements, Hull House was segregated, although Addams, more than most progressives, struggled to overcome the racist attitudes of her day. She helped found a settlement that served a black neighborhood in Chicago, and she spoke out repeatedly against lynching. In 1909, Addams supported the founding of the National Association for the Advancement of Colored People (NAACP), the most important organization of the progressive era aimed at promoting equality and justice for blacks.

The founding of the NAACP is the story of cooperation between a group of white social justice progressives and courageous black leaders. Even in the age of segregation and lynching, blacks in all parts of the country—through churches, clubs, and schools—sought to promote a better life for themselves.

The most important black leader who argued for equality and opportunity for his people was W. E. B. Du Bois. As discussed in Chapter 17, Du Bois differed dramatically with Booker T. Washington on the proper position of blacks in American life. Whereas Washington advocated vocational education, Du Bois argued that the "talented tenth" of the black population should get the best education possible. Against Washington's talk of compromise and accommodation to the dominant white society, Du Bois increasingly urged aggressive action for equality.

Denouncing Washington in 1905, Du Bois called a meeting of young and militant blacks across from Niagara Falls in Canada. "We believe in taking what we can get but we don't believe in being satisfied with it and in permitting anybody for a moment to imagine we're satisfied," said the Niagara movement's angry manifesto. Du Bois's small band was soon augmented by white liberals concerned with violence against blacks, including Jane Addams and Oswald Garrison Villard, grandson of abolitionist William Lloyd Garrison. In 1910, it merged with the NAACP, and Du Bois became editor of its journal, *The Crisis*. He toned down his rhetoric but tried to promote equality for all blacks. The NAACP was a typical progressive organization, seeking to work within the American system to promote reform. But Roosevelt and many other progressives thought it dangerously radical.

## William Howard Taft

After two terms as president, Roosevelt decided to step down and go big-game hunting in Africa. But he soon regretted leaving the White House. He was only 50 years old and at the peak of his popularity and power.

William Howard Taft, Roosevelt's choice for the Republican nomination in 1908 and winner over Bryan for the election, was a distinguished lawyer, federal judge, and public servant—the first civil governor of the Philippines and Roosevelt's secretary of war. In some ways, he was more progressive than Roosevelt. His administration instituted more suits against monopolies in one term than Roosevelt had in two. He supported the eight-hour workday and legislation to make mining safer. He supported the Mann-Elkins Act in 1910, which strengthened the ICC. Taft and Congress also authorized the first tax on corporate profits, and he encouraged the process that eventually led to the passage of the federal income tax, which was authorized under the Sixteenth Amendment and was ratified in 1913.

But Taft's presidency quickly ran into difficulties. His biggest problem was his style. He weighed over 300 pounds, wrote ponderously, and spoke with little inspiration. He also lacked Roosevelt's political skills and angered many of the progressives in the Republican party, especially the midwestern insurgents led by La Follette, when he signed the Payne-Aldrich Tariff of 1909. Many progressives thought it favored the eastern industrial interests and left the rates too high.

Even Roosevelt was infuriated when his successor reversed many of his conservation policies and fired Chief Forester Gifford Pinchot, who had attacked Secretary of the Interior Richard A. Ballinger for giving away rich coal lands in Alaska to mining interests. Roosevelt broke with Taft, letting it be known that he was willing to run again for president. This set up one of the most exciting and significant elections in American history.

## The Election of 1912

Woodrow Wilson won the Democratic presidential nomination in 1912. The son and grandson of Presbyterian ministers, he grew up in a comfortable and intellectual southern household. He graduated from Princeton in 1879, got a Ph.D., and published *Congressional Government* (1885), which established his reputation as a shrewd political analyst. He taught history and became a Princeton professor. Less flamboyant than Roosevelt, he was a persuasive speaker. In 1902, he was elected president of Princeton University; during the next few years, he established a national reputation as an educational leader. He eagerly accepted the Democratic machine's offer to run for governor of New Jersey in 1910, but then showed courage by quickly alienating some of the conservatives who had helped elect him. Building a reform coalition, he put through a direct primary law and other progressive reforms. By 1912, Wilson had acquired the reputation of a progressive.

Roosevelt, who had been speaking out on a variety of issues since 1910, competed with Taft for the Republican nomination. As the incumbent president and party leader, Taft won it—but Roosevelt startled the nation by walking out of the convention and forming a new political party, the Progressive party. It appealed to progressives who had become frustrated with the conservative leadership in both major parties. Its platform contained provisions that reformers had been advocating for years: an eight-hour workday; a six-day workweek; abolition of child labor under age 16; federal accident, old age, and unemployment insurance; and—unlike the Democrats—woman suffrage.

Most supporters of the Progressives in 1912 hoped to organize a new political movement that would replace the Republican Party, just as the Republicans had replaced the Whigs after 1856. Progressive leaders, led by Frances Kellor, had plans to apply the principles of social research by educating voters between elections.

The Progressive convention in Chicago seemed like a religious revival or a social work conference. Delegates sang "Onward Christian Soldiers" and "The Battle Hymn of the Republic," and when Jane Addams seconded Roosevelt's nomination, a large group of women marched around the auditorium with a "Votes for Women" banner. The Progressive cause "is based on the eternal principles of righteousness," Roosevelt cried.

But behind the unified facade lurked many disagreements. Roosevelt had become more progressive on many issues since leaving the presidency. He even attacked the financiers "to whom the acquisition of untold millions is the supreme goal of life, and who are too often utterly indifferent as to how these millions are obtained." But he was less committed to social reform than some delegates. A number of social justice progressives fought hard to include a plank in the platform supporting equality for blacks and for seating a black delegation, but Roosevelt hoped to carry several southern states. In the end, no blacks were seated and the platform made no mention of black equality.

The 1912 campaign became a contest primarily between Roosevelt and Wilson, who vigorously debated the proper relationship of government to society in a modern industrial age. Advancing what he called the New Nationalism, Roosevelt argued that in a modern industrial society, large corporations were "inevitable and necessary." What was needed was a strong president and increased power in the hands of the federal government to regulate business and industry for the benefit of the people. He argued for using Hamiltonian means to assure Jeffersonian ends, for using strong central government to guarantee the rights of the people.

Wilson responded with a program and a slogan of his own: the New Freedom. Drawing on the writings of Louis Brandeis, he emphasized the Jeffersonian tradition of limited government with open competition. He spoke of the "curse of bigness" and argued against too much federal power. "What I fear is a government of experts," Wilson declared, implying that Roosevelt's New Nationalism would mean regulated monopoly and even collectivism.

This was one of the few elections in American history in which important ideas were actually discussed. It also marked a watershed for political thought for liberals who rejected Jefferson's distrust of a strong central government. It is easy to exaggerate the differences between Roosevelt and Wilson. Both urged reform within the American system, defended corporate capitalism, and opposed socialism and radical labor organizations. Both wanted more democracy and stronger but conservative labor unions. Both were very different in style and substance from the fourth candidate, Eugene Debs, who ran on the Socialist party ticket in 1912.

Debs, at the time, was the most important socialist leader in the country. Socialism has always been a minority movement in the United States, but it stood at its pinnacle in the first decade of the twentieth century. Thirty-three cities had socialist mayors, and two socialists sat in Congress. The most important socialist periodical increased its circulation from about 30,000 in 1900 to nearly 300,000 in 1906. Its following was quite diverse. In the cities, some who called themselves socialists merely favored municipal ownership of street railways. Some reformers, such as Florence Kelley, joined out of frustration with the slow pace of reform. Many recent immigrants brought to the party a European sense of class and loyalty to socialism.

A tremendously appealing figure and a great orator, Debs had run for president in 1900, 1904, and 1908, but in 1912, he reached much wider audiences in more parts of the country. His message differed radically from that of Wilson or Roosevelt. Unlike the progressives, socialists argued for fundamental change in the American system. The Socialist party is "organized and financed by the workers themselves," Debs announced, "as a means of wresting control of government and industry from the capitalists and making the working class the ruling class of the nation and the world." Debs polled almost 900,000 votes in 1912 (6 percent of the popular vote), the best showing ever for a socialist in the United States. Wilson received 6.3 million votes, Roosevelt a little more than 4 million, and Taft 3.5 million. Wilson garnered 435 electoral votes, Roosevelt 88, and Taft only 8.

## WOODROW WILSON AND THE NEW FREEDOM

Wilson was elected largely because Roosevelt and the Progressive party split the Republican vote. But once elected, Wilson became a vigorous and aggressive chief executive who set out to translate his ideas about progressive government into legislation. He was the first southerner elected president since Zachary Taylor in 1848 and only the second Democrat since the Civil War. Wilson, like Roosevelt, had to work with his party, and that restricted how progressive he could be. He was also constrained by his background and inclinations. Still, like Roosevelt, Wilson became more progressive during his presidency.

# Tariff and Banking Reform

Wilson had a more difficult time than Roosevelt relating to small groups, but he was an excellent public speaker who dominated through the force of his intellect. He probably had an exaggerated belief in his ability to persuade and tended to trust his own intuition too much. His accomplishment in pushing a legislative program through Congress during his first two years in office was matched only by Franklin Roosevelt during the first months of the New Deal and by Lyndon Johnson in 1965. But his early success bred overconfidence, portending trouble.

Within a month of his inauguration, Wilson went before a joint session of Congress to outline his legislative program. He recommended reducing the tariff, freeing the banking system from Wall Street control, and restoring industrial competition. By appearing in person before Congress, he broke a precedent of written presidential messages established by Thomas Jefferson.

First on Wilson's agenda was tariff reform. The Underwood Tariff, passed in 1913, was not a free-trade bill, but it did reduce the schedule for the first time in many years. Attached to the Underwood bill was a provision for a small and slightly graduated income tax, recently allowed by passage of the Sixteenth Amendment. It imposed a modest rate of 1 percent on income over $4,000 (thus exempting a large portion of the population), with a surtax rising to 6 percent on high incomes. The income tax was enacted to replace the money lost from lowering the tariff. Wilson seemed to have no interest in using it to redistribute wealth.

A financial panic in 1907 had revealed the need for a central bank, and much of the private banking system was dominated by a few firms like J. P. Morgan & Co., but few people could agree on what should be done. Progressive Democrats argued for a banking system and currency controlled by the federal government. But talk of banking reform raised the specter among conservative Democrats and the business community of socialism, populism, and the monetary ideas of William Jennings Bryan.

The Federal Reserve System, created by compromise legislation in 1913, was the first reorganization of the banking system since the Civil War. The law gave the federal government some control over the banking system. It also created a flexible currency, based on Federal Reserve notes, that could be expanded or contracted as need required. The Federal Reserve System was not without its flaws, as later developments would show, and it did not end the power of the large eastern banks; but it was an improvement, and it appealed to the part of the progressive movement that sought order and efficiency.

Wilson was not very progressive in some of his early actions. He failed to support a plan for long-term rural credit financed by the federal government. He opposed a woman suffrage amendment and refused to back an anti-child labor bill. And he ordered the segregation of blacks in several federal departments. "I sincerely believe it to be in their [the blacks'] best interest," he said in rejecting the NAACP's protests.

## Moving Closer to a New Nationalism

Wilson and Roosevelt had vigorously debated how to control the great corporations. Wilson's solution was the Clayton Act, which prohibited various unfair

# Timeline

**1901** McKinley assassinated

Theodore Roosevelt becomes president

Robert La Follette elected governor of Wisconsin

Tom Johnson elected mayor of Cleveland

Model tenement house bill passed in New York

U.S. Steel formed

**1902** Anthracite coal strike

**1903** Women's Trade Union League founded

Elkins Act

**1904** Roosevelt reelected

Lincoln Steffens, *The Shame of the Cities*

**1905** Frederic C. Howe, *The City: The Hope of Democracy*

Industrial Workers of the World formed

**1906** Upton Sinclair, *The Jungle*

Hepburn Act

Meat Inspection Act

Pure Food and Drug Act

**1907** Financial panic

**1908** *Muller v. Oregon*

*Danbury Hatters* case

William Howard Taft elected president

**1909** Herbert Croly, *The Promise of American Life*

NAACP founded

**1910** Ballinger-Pinchot controversy

Mann Act

**1911** Frederick Taylor, *The Principles of Scientific Management*

Triangle Shirtwaist Company fire

**1912** Progressive party founded by Theodore Roosevelt

Woodrow Wilson elected president

Children's Bureau established

Industrial Relations Commission founded

**1913** Sixteenth Amendment (income tax) ratified

Underwood Tariff

Federal Reserve System established

Seventeenth Amendment (direct election of senators) passed

**1914** Clayton Act

Federal Trade Commission Act

AFL has over 2 million members

Ludlow Massacre in Colorado

trading practices, outlawed the interlocking directorate, and forbade corporations to purchase stock in other corporations if this tended to reduce competition. But the law was vague and hard to enforce, and the courts interpreted it to mean that labor unions remained subject to court injunctions during strikes.

More important was the creation of the Federal Trade Commission (FTC). Powerful enough to move directly against corporations accused of restricting competition, the FTC was the idea of Louis Brandeis. Wilson accepted it even though it seemed to move him more toward the philosophy of New Nationalism.

The FTC and the Clayton Act did not end monopoly. The success of Wilson's reform agenda appeared minimal in 1914, but the outbreak of war in Europe and the need to win the election of 1916 would force him into becoming more progressive.

Neither Wilson nor Roosevelt satisfied advanced progressives. Most of the efforts of the two progressive presidents were spent trying to regulate economic power rather than promoting social justice. Yet their most important legacy was their attempts to strengthen the office of president and the executive branch of the federal government. The nineteenth-century American presidents after Lincoln had been relatively weak, and much of the federal power had resided with Congress. The progressive presidents reasserted presidential authority, modernized the executive branch, and began the creation of the federal bureaucracy, which has had a major impact on the lives of Americans in the twentieth century.

Both Wilson and Roosevelt used the presidency to advertise and promote their reform agenda. TR called the office a "bully pulpit." He strengthened the Interstate Commerce Commission and Wilson created the Federal Trade Commission, forerunners of many other federal regulatory bodies. By personally delivering his annual message before Congress, Wilson symbolized the new power of the presidency.

More than the increased power of the executive branch changed the nature of politics. The new bureaus, committees, and commissions brought to Washington a new kind of expert, trained in the universities, at the state and local level, and in the voluntary organizations. Julia Lathrop, a coworker of Jane Addams at Hull House, was typical. Appointed by President Taft in 1912 to become chief of the newly created Children's Bureau, she was the first woman ever named to such a position. She used her post not only to work for better child labor laws, but also to train a new generation of women experts who would take their positions in state, federal, and private agencies in the 1920s and 1930s. Other experts emerged in Washington during the progressive era to influence policy in subtle and important ways. The expert, the commission, the statistical survey, and the increased power of the executive branch were all legacies of the progressive era.

ᘓᔆ ᘓᔆ ᘓᔆ ᘓᔆ

# CONCLUSION

## *The Limits of Progressivism*

The progressive era was a time when many Americans set out to promote reform because they saw poverty, despair, and disorder in the country transformed by immigration, urbanism, and industrialism. However, unlike the socialists, the progressives saw nothing fundamentally wrong with the American system. Progressivism was largely a middle-class movement that sought to help the poor, the immigrants, and the working class. Yet the poor were rarely consulted about policy, and many groups, especially African Americans, were almost entirely left out of reform plans. Progressives had an optimistic view of human nature and an exaggerated faith in statistics, commissions, and committees. They talked of the need for more democracy, but they often succeeded in promoting bureaucracy and a government run by experts. Frances Kellor was one of those experts; she represented a growing group of well-educated women who found a role during the progressive era in the new government agencies and private foundations. The progressives believed there was a need to regulate business, promote efficiency, and spread social justice, but these were often contradictory goals. In the end, their regulatory laws tended to aid business and to strengthen corporate capitalism, while social justice and equal opportunity remained difficult to achieve. By contrast, most of the industrialized nations of western Europe, especially Germany, Austria, France, and Great Britain, passed legislation during this period providing for old-age pensions and health and unemployment insurance.

Progressivism was a broad, diverse, and sometimes contradictory movement that had its roots in the 1890s and reached a climax in the early twentieth century. It began with many local movements and voluntary efforts to deal with the problems created by urban industrialism and moved to the state and finally the national level. Women played important roles in organizing reform, and many became experts at gathering statistics and writing reports. Eventually they began to fill positions in the new agencies in the state capitals and in Washington. Neither Theodore Roosevelt nor Woodrow Wilson was an advanced progressive, but during both their administrations, progressivism achieved some success. Both presidents strengthened the power of the presidency, and both promoted the idea that the federal government had the responsibility to regulate and control and to promote social justice. Progressivism would achieve a certain climax during World War I, but during the 1920s, there was a general reaction against most progressive measures. Still the spirit of progressivism survived to influence the New Deal during the 1930s.

## Discovering U.S. History Online

*The American Experience: America 1900*   http://www.pbs.org/wgbh/pages/amex/1900/
This is the companion site to the PBS documentary *America 1900*. It includes audio clips of respected historians on the economics, politics, and culture of 1900; a primary-source database; a timeline of the year; downloadable software to compile your family tree; and other materials.

*The Evolution of the Conservation Movement, 1850–1920*
http://memory.loc.gov/ammem/amrvhtml/conshome.html
This Library of Congress site brings together scores of primary sources and photographs about "the historical formation and cultural foundations of the movement to conserve and protect America's natural heritage."

*Triangle Fire*   http://www.ilr.cornell.edu/trianglefire/
The Kheel Center for Labor-Management Documentation and Archives at Cornell University has put together this excellent site composed of oral histories, cartoons, images, and essays about the shirtwaist factory fire of March 1911.

*Detroit Publishing Company Photographs Home Page*
http://memory.loc.gov/ammem/detroit/dethome.html
This Library of Congress collection has thousands of photographs from turn-of-the-century America.

*The Trial of Bill Haywood*   http://www.law.umkc.edu/faculty/projects/ftrials/haywood/haywood.htm
This site contains images, chronology, and court and official documents maintained by Dr. Doug Linder at the University of Missouri–Kansas City Law School. Bill Haywood was a labor radical accused of ordering the assassination of former governor of Idaho Frank Steunenberg in 1907.

*Westinghouse Works Home Page*   http://emory.loc.gov/ammem/papr/west/westhome.html
Part of the American Memory Project at the Library of Congress, this site provides a glimpse inside a turn-of-the-century factory.

*Theodore Roosevelt Association*   http://www.theodoreroosevelt.org/
This site contains much biographical and research information about this famous American.

*IPL POTUS—Woodrow Wilson*   http://www.ipl.org/ref/POTUS/wwilson.html
This Internet Public Library—Presidents of the United States site contains basic factual data about Wilson's election and presidency, speeches, and online biographies.

## Fiction and Film

Fiction from the period includes Theodore Dreiser's novel, *Sister Carrie* (1900), a classic of social realism; Upton Sinclair's, *The Jungle* (1906), a novel about the meatpacking industry and the failure of the American dream; *Susan Lenox* (1917) by David Graham Phillips, an epic of slum life and political corruption; and Charlotte Perkins Gilman's *Herland* (1915), the story of a feminist utopia.

*Birth of a Nation* (1915) is an important film, not only because of its innovative technique, but also because it is a mirror of the worst racism of the progressive era. *Hester Street* (1975) creates a realistic picture of the urban immigrant experience during the progressive period.

## Recommended Reading

### The Social Justice Movement

Paul Boyer, *Urban Masses and Moral Order in America, 1820–1920* (1978); Susan Curtis, *Consuming Faith: The Social Gospel and Modern American Culture* (1991); Allen F. Davis, *Spearheads for Reform: The Social Settlements and the Progressive Movement* (1967); Steven J. Diner, *A Very Different Age: America in the Progressive Era* (1998); Linda Gordon, *Woman's Body, Woman's Right: A Social History of Birth Control* (1976); Robin Muncy, *Creating a Female Dominion of American Reform* (1991); Daniel T. Rogers, *Atlantic Crossing: Social Politics in a Progressive Age* (1998); Ruth Rosen, *The Lost Sisterhood: Prostitutes in America, 1900–1918* (1982); James H. Timberlake, *Prohibition and the Progressive Movement* (1963).

### The Worker in the Progressive Era

David Brody, *Workers in Industrial America* (1980); Julie Green, *Pure and Simple Politics: The American Federation of Labor and Political Activism* (1998); Alice Kessler-Harris, *Out to Work: A History of Wage Earning Women in America* (1982); David Montgomery, *Worker Control in America* (1979); David Nasaw, *Going Out* (1993).

### Reform in the Cities and States

John D. Buenker, *Urban Liberalism and Progressive Reform* (1973); Melvin G. Holli, *Reform in Detroit* (1969); William A. Link, *The Paradox of Southern Progressivism* (1992); George Mowry, *California Progressives* (1951); Nancy C. Unger, *Fighting Bob La Follette: The Righteous Reformer* (2000); Robert Wiebe, *The Search for Order, 1877–1920* (1967).

### Theodore Roosevelt and the Square Deal

John Milton Cooper, Jr., *The Warrior and the Priest* (1983); Gary Gerstle, *American Crucible: Race and Nation in the Twentieth Century* (2001); Lewis Gould, *The Presidency of Theodore Roosevelt* (1991); Edmund Morris, *Theodore Rex* (2001).

### Woodrow Wilson and the New Freedom

John Morton Blum, *The Progressive Presidents* (1980); Kendrick A. Clements, *The Presidency of Woodrow Wilson* (1992); Paolo E. Coletta, *The Presidency of William Howard Taft* (1973); Phyllis Lee Levin, *Edith and Woodrow: The Wilson White House* (2001); Nick Salvatore, *Eugene V. Debs* (1982).

# CHAPTER 22
# The Great War

## CHAPTER OUTLINE

- The Early War Years
- The United States Enters the War
- The Military Experience

- Domestic Impact of the War
- Planning for Peace
- Conclusion: The Divided Legacy of the War

## AMERICAN STORIES
### A Young Man Enlists in the Great Adventure

On April 7, 1917, the day after the United States declared war on Germany, 22-year-old Edmund P. Arpin, Jr., from Grand Rapids, Wisconsin, enlisted in the Army. The war seemed to provide a solution for his aimless drifting. It was not patriotism but his craving for adventure that led him to join the Army. A month later, he was at Fort Sheridan, Illinois, along with hundreds of other eager young men, preparing to become an Army officer. He felt pride, purpose, and especially comradeship, but the war was far away.

Arpin finally arrived with his unit in Liverpool, England, on December 23, 1917, aboard the *Leviathan*, a German luxury liner that the United States had seized and turned into a troop transport. American troops were not greeted as saviors. English hostility simmered partly because of the previous unit's drunken brawls. Despite the efforts of the United States government to protect soldiers from the sins of Europe, drinking seems to have been a preoccupation of Arpin's outfit. He also learned something about French wine and women, but he spent most of the endless waiting time learning to play contract bridge.

Arpin saw some of the horror of war when he went to the front with a French regiment, but his own unit did not go into combat until October 1918, when the war was almost over. He took part in the bloody Meuse-Argonne offensive, which helped end the war. But he discovered that war was not the heroic struggle of carefully planned campaigns that newspapers and books described. War was filled with misfired weapons, mix-ups, and erroneous attacks. Wounded in the leg in an assault on an unnamed hill and awarded a Distinguished Service Cross for his bravery, Arpin later learned that the order to attack had been recalled, but word had not reached him in time.

When the armistice came, Arpin was in a field hospital. He was disappointed that the war had ended so soon, but he was well enough to go to Paris to take part in the victory celebration and to explore famous restaurants and nightclubs. In many ways, the highlight of his war experiences was not a battle or his medal, but his postwar adventure. With a friend, he went AWOL and explored Germany, making it back without being arrested.

Edmund Arpin was one of 4,791,172 Americans who served in the Army, Navy, or Marines, one of the 2 million who went overseas, and one of the 230,074 who were wounded. Some of his friends were among the 48,909 who were killed. Mustered out in March 1919, he felt confused. Being a civilian was not nearly as exciting as being in the Army and visiting exotic places.

In time, Arpin settled down. He became a successful businessman, married, and reared a family. A member of the American Legion, he periodically went to conventions and reminisced with men from his division about their escapades in France. Although the war changed their lives in many ways, most would never again feel the same sense of common purpose and adventure. "I don't suppose any of us felt, before or since, so necessary to God and man," one veteran recalled.

❧ ❧ ❧ ❧

For Edmund P. Arpin, Jr., the Great War was the most important event of a lifetime. Just as war changed his life, so, too, did it alter the lives of most Americans. The power and influence of the federal government increased. Not only did the war promote woman suffrage, prohibition, and public housing, but it also helped create an administrative bureaucracy that blurred the lines between public and private, between government and business—a trend that continued through the twentieth century.

In this chapter, we examine the complicated circumstances that led the United States into war and share the wartime experiences of American men and women at home and abroad. We will study not only military actions, but also the war's impact on domestic policies and on the lives of ordinary Americans, including the migration of African Americans into northern cities. The war left a legacy of prejudice and hate and raised a basic question: Could the tenets of American democracy, such as freedom of speech, survive participation in a major war? The chapter concludes with a look at the idealistic efforts to promote peace at the end of the war, and the disillusion that followed. The Great War thrust the United States into world leadership, but many Americans were reluctant to accept that role.

## THE EARLY WAR YEARS

Few Americans expected the war that erupted in Europe in the summer of 1914 to affect their lives or to alter their comfortable world. But when a Serbian terrorist shot Archduke Franz Ferdinand of Austria-Hungary in Sarajevo, a place almost no Americans had even heard of, this precipitated a series of events that led to the most destructive war the world had ever known.

### The Causes of War

Despite Theodore Roosevelt's successful peacekeeping attempts (see Chapter 20), intense European rivalries turned minor incidents in Africa, Asia, and the Balkans

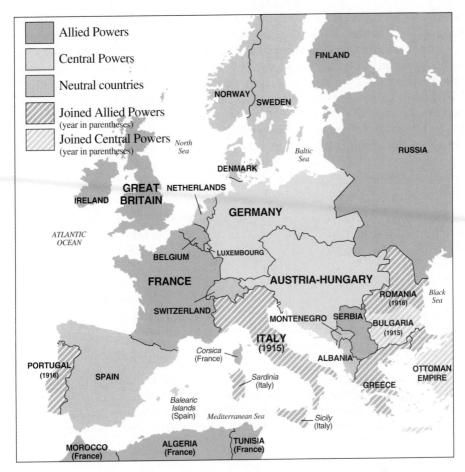

**EUROPEAN ALIGNMENTS, 1914** The Great War had an impact on all of Europe, even on the few countries that managed to remain neutral. Russia left the war in 1917, the same year that the United States joined the fight.

into threats to world peace. Nationalism was fanned by mass newspapers. Anglo-Germany tensions led to a race to build bigger battleships.

As European nations armed, they drew up treaties pitting Austria-Hungary and Germany (the Central Powers) against Britain, France, and Russia (the Allied Powers). Despite peace conferences and international agreements, many promoted by the United States, the European balance of power rested precariously on layers of treaties that barely obscured years of jealousy and distrust.

The incident in Sarajevo destroyed that balance. The leaders of Austria-Hungary wanted to punish Serbia for killing Franz Ferdinand, the heir to the throne. Russia mobilized to aid Serbia. Germany, supporting Austria-Hungary, declared war on Russia and its ally France. When Germany invaded Belgium to attack France, Britain declared war. The slaughter began.

Despite much evidence to the contrary, many intelligent people on both sides of the Atlantic believed that education, science, social reform, and negotiation had replaced war as a way of solving international disputes. But as reports of the first bloody battles began to reach the United States, most Americans felt that madness had replaced reason.

The American sense that the nation would never succumb to the barbarism of war, combined with the knowledge that they were insulated by the Atlantic, brought relief after the first shock wore off. Wilson's official proclamation of neutrality on August 4, 1914, reinforced the belief that the United States had no major stake in the outcome and would stay uninvolved. The president urged Americans to "be neutral in fact as well as in name . . . impartial in thought as well as in action." But it was difficult to stay uninvolved, at least emotionally.

## American Reaction

Although many worked to promote world peace and a few sought to end the war through mediation, others could hardly wait to leap into the adventure. Hundreds of young American men, mostly college students or recent graduates, joined ambulance units. Among the most famous were Ernest Hemingway, John Dos Passos, and e. e. cummings (as he spelled his name), who later turned their wartime adventures into literary masterpieces. Others volunteered for the French Foreign Legion or the Lafayette Escadrille—volunteer American pilots attached to the French army. Many of these young men were inspired by an older generation who pictured war as a romantic and manly adventure.

Many Americans saw war as a test of idealism and manhood because the only conflict they remembered was the "splendid little war" of 1898. Older Americans recalled the Civil War, whose horrors had faded, leaving only the memory of heroic triumphs. But Oliver Wendell Holmes, the Supreme Court justice who had been wounded in the Civil War, remarked, "War, when you are at it, is horrible and dull. It is only when time has passed that you see that its message was divine."

Early reports from the battlefields should have indicated that the message was anything but divine. This would be a modern war in which men died by the thousands, cut down by an improved and efficient technology of killing.

## The New Military Technology

The Germans' plan called for a rapid strike through Belgium to attack Paris and the French army from the rear. However, the French stopped the Germans in September 1914, and the fighting bogged down. Soldiers on both sides dug miles of trenches and strung out barbed wire. Hundreds of thousands died in battles that gained only a few yards or nothing at all. Rapid-firing rifles, improved explosives, incendiary shells, and tracer bullets all added to the destruction. Most devastating of all was the improved artillery that could hit targets miles behind the lines. Machine guns neutralized frontal assaults, but generals on both sides continued to order their men to charge to almost certain death.

The war was the last major conflict in which cavalry was used and the first to employ a new generation of military technologies. By 1918, airplanes were creating terror with their bombs. Tanks made a tentative appearance in 1916, but it was not until the last days of the war that this new offensive weapon began to neutralize the machine gun. Poison gas, first used in 1914, added fear and horror to the battles, but soon both sides developed the gas mask.

## Difficulties of Neutrality

Despite Wilson's efforts to promote neutrality, most Americans favored the Allied cause. About 8 million people of German and Austro-Hungarian descent lived in the United States, and some supported the Central Powers. The anti-British feelings of some Irish Americans led them to side not so much with Germany as against England. A number of American scholars, physicians, and intellectuals fondly remembered studying in Germany and they admired its culture and progressive social planning. For most Americans, however, the ties of language and culture tipped the balance toward the Allies. After all, did not the English-speaking people of the world have special bonds and responsibilities? Memories of Lafayette's role in the American Revolution and France's gift of the Statue of Liberty made many Americans pro-French.

Other reasons made real neutrality nearly impossible. The fact that United States' trade with the Allies was much more important than with the Central Powers caused many American businesses to support the Allies. Wilson's advisers openly supported the French and British. Most newspaper owners and editors had close ethnic, cultural, and sometimes economic ties to the Allies. The newspapers were quick to picture the Germans as barbaric Huns and to accept atrocity stories, some of them planted by British propaganda experts. Gradually for Wilson, and probably for most Americans, the perception that England and France were fighting to preserve civilization from evil Prussians replaced the idea that all Europeans were decadent. But as for going to war to save civilization, let France and England do that.

Wilson sympathized with the Allies for practical and idealistic reasons. He wanted to keep the United States out of the war, but he did not object to using force to promote diplomatic ends. "When men take up arms to set other men free, there is something sacred and holy in the warfare," he had written. Wilson believed that by keeping the United States out of the war, he might control the peace. The war, he hoped, would show the futility of imperialism and would usher in a world of free trade in both products and ideas, a world in which the United States had a special role to play.

Remaining neutral while maintaining trade with the belligerents became increasingly difficult. The need to trade and the desire to control the peace finally led the United States into the Great War.

## World Trade and Neutrality Rights

The United States was part of an international economic community in 1914 in a way that it had not been during the nineteenth century. The outbreak of war in the summer of 1914 caused immediate economic panic in the United States. On July 31, 1914, the Wilson administration closed the stock exchange. It also discouraged loans by American banks to belligerent nations. Most difficult was the matter of neutral trade. Wilson insisted on Americans' right to trade with both sides and with other neutrals, but Great Britain instituted an illegal naval blockade, mined the North Sea, and began seizing American ships. The first crisis that Wilson faced was whether to accept the illicit British blockade. To do so would be to surrender one of the rights he supported most ardently: free trade.

Wilson eventually accepted British control of the sea. His conviction that the destinies of the United States and Great Britain were intertwined outweighed his idealistic belief in free trade and caused him to react more harshly to German than to British violations of international law. Consequently, American trade with the Central Powers declined between 1914 and 1916 from $169 million to just over $1 million, whereas American trade with the Allies increased during the same period from $825 million to over $3 billion. At the same time, the United States government eased restrictions on private loans to belligerents. With dollars as well as sentiments, the United States gradually ceased to be neutral.

Germany retaliated against British control of the seas with submarine warfare. International law obligated a belligerent warship to warn a passenger or merchant ship before attacking, but a submarine rising to the surface to issue a warning would have been blown out of the water by an armed merchant ship.

On February 4, 1915, Germany announced a submarine blockade of the British Isles. Until Britain gave up its campaign to starve the German population, the Germans would sink even neutral ships. Wilson warned Germany that it would be held to "strict accountability" for illegal destruction of American ships or lives.

In March 1915, a German submarine sank a British liner, killing 103 people, including one American. Wilson's advisers could not agree on an appropriate response. Robert Lansing, a legal counsel at the State Department, urged the president to issue a strong protest, charging a breach of international law. William Jennings Bryan, the secretary of state, argued that an American traveling on a British ship was guilty of "contributory negligence" and urged Wilson to ban Americans from belligerent ships in the war zone. Before Wilson could decide what to do, on May 7, 1915, a submarine torpedoed the British luxury liner *Lusitania* off the Irish coast. The unarmed liner, which was carrying war supplies, sank in 18 minutes with a loss of nearly 1,200 lives, including 128 Americans. Suddenly Americans realized that modern war killed civilians as easily as it killed soldiers.

Despite earlier warnings by the Germans in American newspapers that it was dangerous to travel in war zones, the same newspapers denounced the act as "mass murder." Some called for war. Wilson and most Americans had no intention of fighting, but the president rejected Secretary of State Bryan's advice that Americans be prohibited from traveling on ships from the countries at war. Instead, he demanded reparation for the loss of American lives and a German pledge to cease attacking ocean liners without warning. Bryan resigned as secretary of state, charging that the United States was not being truly neutral. The president replaced him with Robert Lansing, who was more eager to oppose Germany, even at the risk of war.

The tense situation eased late in 1915. After a German submarine sank the British steamer *Arabic*, which claimed two American lives, the German ambassador promised that Germany would not attack ocean liners without warning. But the *Lusitania* crisis caused an outpouring of books and articles urging the nation to prepare for war. However, a group of progressive reformers formed the American

Union Against Militarism, fearing that preparedness advocates planned to destroy liberal social reform at home and promote imperialism abroad.

Wilson sympathized with the preparedness groups to the extent of asking Congress on November 4, 1915, for an enlarged and reorganized Army. The bill met great opposition, especially from southern and western congressmen, but the Army Reorganization Bill that Wilson signed in June 1916 increased the regular Army to just over 200,000 and integrated the National Guard into the defense structure. Few Americans expected those young men to go to war. But soon Wilson used the Army and the Marines in Mexico and Central America.

## Intervening in Mexico and Central America

Wilson envisioned a world purged of imperialism, a world of free trade, and a world where American ideas and American products would find their way. Combining the zeal of a Christian missionary with the conviction of a college professor, he spoke of "releasing the intelligence of America for the service of mankind." Along with Secretary of State Bryan, Wilson denounced the "big stick" and "dollar diplomacy" of the Roosevelt and Taft years. Yet Wilson's administration used force more systematically than did Wilson's predecessors. The rhetoric was different, yet like Roosevelt, Wilson tried to maintain stability in the countries to the south in order to promote American economic and strategic interests.

At first, Wilson's foreign policy seemed to reverse the most callous aspects of dollar diplomacy in Central America. Bryan signed a treaty with Colombia in 1913 paying $5 million for the loss of Panama and virtually apologizing for Roosevelt's treatment of Colombia. But the Senate refused to ratify the treaty.

The change in spirit proved illusory. After a disastrous civil war in the Dominican Republic, the United States offered in 1915 to take over the country's finances and police force. When Dominican leaders rejected a treaty making their country virtually an American protectorate, Wilson ordered in the Marines. They took control of the government in May 1916. Although Americans built roads, schools, and hospitals, the Dominican people resented their presence. Americans also intervened in Haiti, with similar results. In Nicaragua, Wilson kept the Marines (sent by Taft in 1912) to prop up a pro-American regime and acquired the right through a treaty to intervene at any time to preserve order and protect American property. Except briefly in the mid-1920s, the Marines remained until 1933.

Wilson's policy of intervention ran into greatest difficulty in Mexico, a country that had been ruled by dictator Porfirio Díaz, who had long welcomed American investors. By 1910, more than 40,000 American citizens lived in Mexico, and more than $1 billion of American money was invested there. In 1911, however, Francisco Madero, a reformer who wanted to destroy the privileges of the upper classes, overthrew Díaz. Two years later, Madero was deposed and murdered by Victoriano Huerta, the head of the army.

To the shock of many diplomats and businessmen, Wilson refused to recognize the Huerta government. Everyone admitted that Huerta was a ruthless dictator, but diplomatic recognition, the exchange of ambassadors, and the regulation of trade and communication had never meant approval. But Wilson set out to remove what he called a "government of butchers."

At first, Wilson applied diplomatic pressure. Then, using a minor incident as an excuse, he asked Congress for power to involve American troops if necessary. Few Mexicans liked Huerta, but they liked North American interference even less, and they rallied around the dictator. The United States landed troops at Veracruz, Mexico. Mobs destroyed American property wherever they could find it. Wilson's action outraged many in Europe, Latin America, and the United States.

Wilson's intervention drove Huerta from power, but a civil war between the forces of Venustiano Carranza and those under General Francisco "Pancho" Villa ensued. The United States sent arms to Carranza, who was considered less radical than Villa, and Carranza's soldiers defeated Villa's. When Villa led what was left of his army in a raid on Columbus, New Mexico, in March 1916, Wilson sent an expedition under Brigadier General John Pershing to track down Villa and his men. An American Army charged 300 miles into Mexico, but it was unable to catch the elusive villain. Mexicans feared that Pershing's army was planning to occupy northern Mexico. Carranza shot off a bitter note to Wilson, but Wilson refused to withdraw. Tensions rose. An American patrol attacked a Mexican garrison. Wilson finally agreed to recall the troops and to recognize the Carranza government. But this was in January 1917, and had it not been for the growing crisis in Europe, war would likely have resulted.

## THE UNITED STATES ENTERS THE WAR

A significant minority of Americans opposed going to war in 1917, and that decision would remain controversial when it was reexamined in the 1930s. But once involved, the government and the American people made the war into a patriotic crusade that influenced all aspects of American life.

## The Election of 1916

American political campaigns do not stop even for international crisis. In 1915 and 1916, Wilson had to think of reelection as well as of preparedness, submarines, and Mexico. His chances seemed poor. If supporters of the Progressives in 1912 returned to the Republican fold, Wilson would probably lose. Because the Progressive party had done very badly in the 1914 congressional elections, Roosevelt seemed ready to seek the Republican nomination.

Wilson knew that he had to win over voters who had favored Roosevelt in 1912. In January 1916, he nominated Louis D. Brandeis to the Supreme Court. Becoming the first Jewish justice, Brandeis was confirmed over strong opposition. His appointment pleased the social justice progressives because he had always championed reform causes. They made it clear to Wilson that the real test for them was whether or not he supported the anti-child labor and workers' compensation bills pending in Congress.

Within a few months, Wilson reversed his earlier New Freedom doctrines, which called for limited government, and aligned the federal government on the side of reform. In August 1916, he pushed through Congress the Workmen's Compensation Bill, which gave some protection to federal employees, and the Keatings-Owen Child Labor Bill, which barred from interstate commerce goods produced by children under the age of 14 and in some cases under the age of 16. This bill, later declared unconstitutional, was a far-reaching proposal that for the first time used federal control over interstate commerce to dictate the conditions under which products could be manufactured. To attract farm support, Wilson backed the Federal Farm Loan Act to extend long-term credit to farmers. Urged on by organized labor as well as by many progressives, he supported the Adamson Act, establishing an eight-hour day for all interstate railway workers.

The flurry of legislation early in 1916 provided a climax to the progressive movement. The strategy seemed to work, for progressives of all kinds enthusiastically endorsed the president.

The election of 1916, however, turned as much on foreign affairs as on domestic policy. Ignoring Roosevelt, Republicans nominated staid Charles Evans Hughes, a former governor of New York and future Supreme Court chief justice. Their platform called for "straight and honest neutrality" and "adequate preparedness." Hughes attacked Wilson for not promoting American rights in Mexico more vigorously and for giving in to what he called labor's unreasonable demands. Wilson implied that electing Hughes would guarantee war with both Mexico and Germany and that his opponents were somehow not "100 percent Americans." As the campaign progressed, the peace issue became more important, and the cry "He kept us out of war" echoed through every Democratic rally. It was a slogan that would soon seem strangely ironic.

The election was extremely close. Wilson went to bed on election night thinking he had lost, and the result was not clear until he took California by less than 4,000 votes. Wilson won by carrying the West as well as the South.

## Deciding for War

Wilson's victory in 1916 seemed to be a mandate for staying out of the European war. But the campaign rhetoric made the president nervous. He had tried to emphasize Americanism, not neutrality.

People who supported Wilson as a peace candidate applauded in January 1917 when he went before the Senate to clarify the American position on a negotiated settlement of the war. The German government had indicated earlier that it might be willing to go to the conference table. Wilson outlined a plan for a negotiated settlement, without indemnities or annexations. The agreement Wilson outlined could have worked only if Germany and the Allies were willing to settle for a draw.

Early in 1917, however, German leaders thought they could win. On January 31, 1917, Berlin announced that any ship, belligerent or neutral, sailing toward Britain or France would be sunk on sight. A few days later, the United States broke diplomatic relations with Germany. An intercepted telegram from the German foreign secretary, Arthur Zimmermann, to the German minister in Mexico increased anti-German feeling. If war broke out, the German minister was to offer Mexico the territory it had lost in Texas, New Mexico, and Arizona. In return, Mexico would join Germany in a war against the United States. When this telegram was released to the press on March 1, 1917, many Americans demanded war against Germany. Wilson still hesitated.

As the country waited on the brink of war, news of revolution in Russia reached Washington. That event would prove as important as the war itself. The

March 1917 revolution in Russia was a spontaneous uprising of workers, house-wives, and soldiers against the tsarist government's inept conduct of the war. The army had suffered staggering losses. Civilian conditions were desperate. Food was scarce, and the railroads and industry had nearly collapsed. At first, Wilson and other Americans were enthusiastic about the new republic led by Alexander Kerensky, who promised to continue the struggle against Germany. But within months, the revolution took a more extreme turn. Vladimir Ilyich Ulyanov, known as Lenin, returned from exile in Switzerland and led the radical Bolshe-viks to victory over the Kerensky regime in November 1917.

Lenin, a brilliant revolutionary tactician, was a follower of Karl Marx (1818–1883). Marx was a German radical philosopher who had described the alienation of the working class under capitalism and predicted a growing split between the proletariat (unpropertied workers) and the capitalists. Lenin ex-tended Marx's ideas and argued that capitalist nations eventually would be forced to go to war over raw materials and markets. Believing that capitalism and imperialism went hand in hand, Lenin argued that the only way to end imperial-ism was to end capitalism. Communism, Lenin predicted, would eventually dominate the globe. The Russian Revolution threatened Wilson's vision of the world and his plan to bring the United States into the war "to make the world safe for democracy."

More disturbing than the first news of revolution in Russia, however, was the situation in the North Atlantic, where German submarines sank five American ships between March 12 and March 21, 1917. On April 2, Wilson urged Congress to declare war. "It is a fearful thing," he concluded, "to lead this great, peaceful people into war, into the most terrible and disastrous of all wars." The war resolu-tion swept the Senate 82 to 6 and the House of Representatives 373 to 50.

Once war was declared, most Americans forgot their doubts. Young men rushed to enlist; women volunteered to become nurses or to serve in other ways.

## A Patriotic Crusade

But not all Americans applauded. Some pacifists, socialists, and others opposed the war, and a black newspaper, *The Messenger,* decried the conflict. "To whom does war bring prosperity?" Senator George Norris of Nebraska asked on the Sen-ate floor.

> Not to the soldier, ... not to the broken hearted widow, ... not to the mother who weeps at the death of her brave boy .... War brings no prosperity to the great mass of common patriotic citizens. We are going into war upon the command of gold .... I feel that we are about to put the dollar sign on the American flag.

For most Americans in the spring of 1917, the war seemed remote. A few days after war was declared, a Senate committee listened to a member of the War De-partment staff list the vast quantities of materials needed to supply an American army in France. One of the senators, jolted awake, exclaimed, "Good Lord! You're not going to send soldiers over there, are you?"

To convince senators and citizens alike that the war was real and that Ameri-can participation was just, Wilson appointed a Committee on Public Information, headed by journalist George Creel. His committee launched a gigantic campaign

GEE !!
I WISH I WERE
A MAN

I'd JOIN
The NAVY

*Howard Chandler Christy, Inc.*

BE A MAN AND DO IT
UNITED STATES NAVY
RECRUITING STATION
34 East 23rd Street, New York

Recruiting posters helped to create a sense of purpose and patriotism, and often used pictures of attractive women to make their point. To be a soldier was to be a real man; to avoid service was to be something less than a man. (The Granger Collection, New York)

to persuade the American public that the United States had gone to war to promote democracy and prevent the "Huns" from overrunning the world.

The patriotic crusade soon became stridently anti-German and anti-immigrant. Most school districts forbade teaching German. Sauerkraut was renamed "liberty cabbage." Many families Americanized German surnames. Several cities banned music by German composers. South Dakota prohibited speaking German on the telephone, and in Iowa, a state official announced, "If their language is disloyal, they should be imprisoned. If their acts are disloyal, they should be shot." The most notorious incident occurred in East St. Louis, Illinois, which had a large German population. In April 1918, a mob seized Robert Prager, a young German American, stripped off his clothes, dressed him in an American flag, marched him through the streets, and lynched him. Brought to trial, the ringleaders were acquitted on the grounds that the lynching was a "patriotic murder."

The Wilson administration did not condone domestic violence and murder, but the heated patriotism fanned by the war led to irrational hatreds and fears. Suspect were not only German Americans, but also radicals, pacifists, and anyone with doubts about the American war efforts or the government's policies. In New York, the black editors of *The Messenger* were given 2 1/2-year jail sentences for the paper's article "Pro-Germanism Among Negroes." The Los Angeles police ignored complaints that Mexicans were being harassed because they believed that all Mexicans were pro-German. Senator La Follette, who had voted against declaring war, was burned in effigy and censured by the University of Wisconsin. At a number of universities, professors were dismissed, sometimes for questioning the morality or necessity of America's participation in the war.

On June 15, 1917, Congress, at Wilson's behest, passed the Espionage Act, providing imprisonment of up to 20 years or a fine of up to $10,000, or both, for people who aided the enemy or who "willfully cause . . . insubordination, disloyalty, mutiny or refusal of duty in the military . . . forces of the United States . . . ." The act also authorized the postmaster general to bar from the mails any matter he thought advocated treason or forcible resistance to United States laws. The act was used to stamp out dissent, even to discipline anyone who questioned the administration's policies.

Congress later added the Trading with the Enemy Act and a Sedition Act. The latter prohibited disloyal, profane, scurrilous, or abusive remarks about the form of government, flag, or uniform of the United States. It even prohibited citizens from opposing the purchase of war bonds. In the most famous case tried under the act, Socialist Eugene Debs was sentenced to 10 years in prison for opposing the war. In 1919, the Supreme Court upheld the conviction, even though Debs had not explicitly urged violating the draft laws. While still in prison, Debs polled close to 1 million votes in the presidential election of 1920. Ultimately, the government prosecuted 2,168 people under the Espionage and Sedition acts and convicted about half of them. These figures do not include the thousands who were persecuted informally.

A group of amateur loyalty enforcers, the American Protective League, cooperated with the Justice Department. League members often reported nonconformists; people they thought were not 100 percent patriotic were arrested for criticizing the Red Cross or a government agency. One woman was sentenced to prison for writing, "I am for the people and the government is for the profiteers." Ricardo Flores Magon, a leading Mexican-American labor organizer and radical in the Southwest, got 20 years in prison for criticizing Wilson's Mexican policy and violating the Neutrality Acts. The attorney general of the United States, speaking of critics, said, "May God have mercy on them for they need expect none from an outraged people and an avenging government."

The Civil Liberties Bureau, an outgrowth of the American Union Against Militarism, protested the blatant abridgment of freedom of speech during the war, but the protests fell on deaf ears at the Justice Department and in the White House. Rights and freedoms have been reduced or suspended during all wars, but the massive disregard for basic rights was greater during World War I than during the Civil War—ironically, because Wilson had often written and spoken of the need to preserve freedom of speech and civil liberties. During the war, however, he tolerated the vigilante tactics of his own Justice Department. Wilson was so convinced his cause was just that he ignored the rights of those who opposed him.

## Raising an Army

The debate over a volunteer army versus the draft had been going on for several years before the United States entered the war. People who favored some form of universal military service argued that college graduates, farmers, and young men from eastern slums could learn from one another as they trained together. Critics pointed out that those making such claims were usually the college graduates, who assumed they would command the boys from the slums. The draft, they argued, was simply the tool of an imperialist power bent on ending dissent. Memories were revived of massive draft riots during the Civil War.

Wilson and his secretary of war, Newton Baker, both initially opposed the draft, but in the end concluded that it was the most efficient way to organize military manpower. Ironically, Theodore Roosevelt tipped Wilson in favor of the draft. With failing health and blind in one eye, the old Rough Rider wanted to recruit a volunteer division and lead it personally against the Germans.

The thought of Roosevelt, whom Wilson considered his enemy, blustering about Europe so frightened Wilson that he supported the Selective Service Act in part, at least, to forestall such volunteer outfits as Roosevelt planned. Yet the House finally insisted that the minimum age for draftees should be 21, not 18. On June 5, 1917, some 9.5 million men between the ages of 21 and 31 registered, with little protest. In August 1918, Congress extended the act to men between the ages of 18 and 45. In all, over 24 million men registered and over 2.8 million were inducted—over 75 percent of soldiers who served in the war.

The draft worked well, but it was not quite the perfect system that Wilson claimed. Most Americans took seriously their obligation of "service" during time of war. But because local draft boards had so much control, favoritism and political influence allowed some to stay at home. Draft protests erupted in a few places, the largest in Oklahoma, where a group of tenant farmers planned a march on Washington to take over the government and end the "rich man's war." A local posse arrested about 900 protesters and took them off to jail.

Some men escaped the draft. Thousands were deferred because of war-related jobs, and others resisted by claiming exemption for reasons of conscience. The Selective Service Act did exempt men who belonged to pacifist religious groups, but religious motivation was often difficult to define, and nonreligious conscientious objection was even more complicated. Thousands of conscientious objectors were inducted. Some served in noncombat positions; others went to prison.

## THE MILITARY EXPERIENCE

For years afterward, men and women who lived through the war (like Edmund Arpin and his friends) remembered nostalgically what it had meant to them. They sang the songs popular during the war, and they carefully preserved their wartime photos. For some, the war was a tragedy in which they saw the horrors of the battlefield firsthand. For others, it was liberating—the most exciting adventure in their lives.

### The American Doughboy

The typical soldier stood 5 feet 7 1/2 inches tall, weighed 141 1/2 pounds, and was about 22 years old. He took a physical exam, an intelligence test, and a psychological test, and he probably watched a movie called *Fit to Fight*, warning

# Recovering the Past

## Government Propaganda

All governments produce propaganda. Especially in time of war, governments try to convince their citizens that the cause is important and worthwhile even if it means sacrifice. Before the United States entered the war, both Great Britain and Germany presented their side of the conflict through stories planted in newspapers, photographs, and other devices. Some historians argue that the British propaganda depicting the Germans as barbaric Huns who killed little boys and Catholic nuns played a large role in convincing Americans of the righteousness of the Allied cause.

When the United States entered the war, a special committee under the direction of George Creel did its best to persuade Americans that the war was a crusade against evil. The committee organized a national network of "four-minute men," local citizens with the proper political views, who could be used to whip up a crowd into a patriotic frenzy. These local rallies, enlivened by bands and parades, urged people of all ages to support the war effort and buy war bonds. The Creel Committee also produced literature for the schools, much of it prepared by college professors who volunteered their services. One pamphlet, titled *Why America Fights Germany*, described in lurid detail a possible German invasion of the United States. The committee also used the new technology of motion pictures, which proved to be the most effective propaganda device of all.

There is a narrow line between education and propaganda. As early as 1910, Thomas Edison made films instructing the public about the dangers of tuberculosis, and others produced movies that demonstrated how to avoid everything from typhoid to tooth decay. However, during the war, the government quickly realized the power of the new medium and adopted it to train soldiers, instill patriotism, and help the troops avoid the temptations of alcohol and sex.

After the United States entered World War I, the Commission of Training Camp Activities made a film called *Fit to Fight* that was shown to almost all male servicemen. It was an hour-long drama following the careers of five young recruits. Four of them, by associating with the wrong people and through lack of willpower, caught venereal disease. The film interspersed a simplistic plot with grotesque shots of men with various kinds of venereal disease. The film also glorified athletics, especially football and boxing, as a substitute for sex. It emphasized the importance of patriotism and purity for America's fighting force. In one scene, Bill Hale, the only soldier in the film to remain pure, breaks up a peace rally and beats up the speaker. "It serves you right," the pacifist's sister remarks, "I'm glad Billy punched you."

*Fit to Fight* was so successful that the government commissioned another film, *The End of the Road*, to be shown to women who lived near military bases. The film is the story of Vera and Mary. Although still reflecting progressive attitudes, the film's message is somewhat different from that of *Fit to Fight*. Vera's strict mother tells her daughter that sex is dirty, leaving Vera to pick up

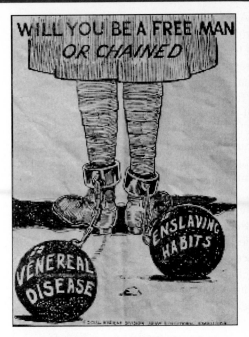

Anti-VD poster issued by the U.S. Commission on Training Camp Activities. (Army Educational Commission/National Archives)

Scene from *Fit to Fight*. (War Department Commission on Training Camps)

"distorted and obscene" information about sex on the street. She falls victim to the first man who comes along and contracts a venereal disease. Mary, in contrast, has an enlightened mother who explains where babies come from. When Mary grows up, she rejects marriage and becomes a professional woman, a nurse. In the end, she falls in love with a doctor and gets married. *The End of the Road* has a number of subplots and many frightening shots of syphilitic sores. Several illustrations show the dangers of indiscriminate sex. Among other things, the film preached the importance of science and sex education and the need for self-control.

**Reflecting on the Past**   What do the anti-VD films tell us about the attitudes, ideas, and prejudices of the World War I period? What images do they project about men, women, and gender roles? Would you find the same kind of moralism, patriotism, and fear of VD today? How have attitudes toward sex changed? Were you shown sex education films in school? Were they like these? Who sponsored them? What can historians learn from such films? Does the government produce propaganda today?

about venereal disease. The majority of American soldiers had not attended high school. The median amount of education for native whites was 6.9 years, and for immigrants 4.7 years, but only 2.6 years for southern blacks. As many as 31 percent of the recruits were declared illiterate, but the tests were so primitive that they probably tested social class more than anything else. Fully 29 percent of the recruits were rejected as physically unfit for service, shocking health experts.

Most World War I soldiers were ill-educated, unsophisticated young men from farms, small towns, and urban neighborhoods. Coming from all classes and ethnic groups, most were transformed into soldiers. In the beginning, they didn't look the part, because uniforms and equipment were in short supply. Many men had to wear their civilian clothes for months, and they often wore out their shoes before they were issued army boots.

The military experience changed the lives and often the attitudes of many young men. Women also contributed to the war effort as telephone operators and clerk-typists in the Navy and the Marines, as nurses, or with organizations like the Red Cross. Yet the military experience was predominantly male. Even going to training camp was new and often frightening. A leave in Paris or London, or even in New York or New Orleans, was an adventure to remember for a lifetime. Many soldiers saw their first movie or their first truck in the army. Men learned to shave with the new safety razor and to wear the new wristwatch. The war also popularized the cigarette, which, unlike a pipe or cigar, could be smoked during a short break.

## The Black Soldier

Blacks had served in all American wars, and many fought valiantly in the Civil War and the Spanish-American War. Yet black soldiers had most often performed menial work in segregated units. Black leaders hoped it would be different this time. W. E. B. Du Bois urged blacks to support the war, predicting that the war experience would cause the "walls of prejudice" to crumble gradually before the "onslaught of common sense." But the walls did not crumble.

The Selective Service Act made no mention of race, and African Americans in most cases registered without protest. Many whites, especially in the South, at first feared having too many blacks trained in the use of arms. In some areas, draft boards exempted single white men, but drafted black fathers. Still, most southern whites found it difficult to imagine a black man in the uniform of the U.S. Army.

White attitudes toward African Americans sometimes led to conflict. In August 1917, violence erupted in Houston, Texas, involving soldiers from the regular Army's all-black 24th Infantry Division. Harassed by the Jim Crow laws, which had been tightened for their benefit, a group of soldiers went on a rampage, killing 17 white civilians. Over 100 soldiers were court-martialed; 13 were condemned to death and hanged three days later before appeals could be filed.

This violence, coming only a month after a race riot in East St. Louis, Illinois, brought on in part by the migration of southern blacks to the area, caused great concern about the handling of African-American soldiers. Secretary of War Baker made it clear that the army had no intention of upsetting the segregated status quo.

Some African Americans were trained as junior officers and were assigned to the all-black 92nd Division, where the high-ranking officers were white. But blacks

World War I, especially on the Western front, was a war of position and defense. Troops on both sides lived in elaborate trenches that turned into a sea of mud when it rained. The men tried to protect themselves with barbed wire and gas masks against new and terrifying technology. But there was little defense against the machine gun that mowed down the troops as they charged from their trenches. Here American soldiers from the New York National Guard, part of the 42nd Division, dig in behind their sandbag-lined trenches in the woods near the Marne River in June 1918. (U.S. Signal Corps., National Archives)

were officially considered unfit to fight. Most of the black soldiers, including about 80 percent of those sent to France, worked as stevedores and common laborers under white noncommissioned officers. Other black soldiers acted as servants, drivers, and porters for the white officers. It was a demeaning and ironic policy for a government that advertised itself as standing for justice, honor, and democracy.

## Over There

The conflict that Wilson called the war "to make the world safe for democracy" had become a contest of stalemate and slaughter. To this ghastly war, Americans made important contributions; without their help, the Allies might have lost. But the American contribution was most significant only in the war's final months.

When the United States went to war in the spring of 1917, the fighting had dragged on for nearly three years. In one battle in 1916, a total of 60,000 British soldiers were killed or wounded in a single day, yet the battle lines did not move an inch. By the spring of 1917, the British and French armies were down to their last reserves. Italy's army had nearly collapsed. In the East, Russia plunged into a bitter internal struggle, and soon Lenin would make a separate peace, freeing German divisions in the East to join in one final assault in the West. The Allies desperately needed fresh American troops, but those troops had to be trained, equipped, and transported to the front.

Token American regiments arrived in France in the summer of 1917 under the command of "Black Jack" Pershing, who had led the Mexican expedition in 1916. When they paraded in Paris on July 4, 1917, the crowd showered them with flowers. But the American commanders worried that many of their soldiers were so inexperienced they did not know how to march, let alone fight. The first American units saw action near Verdun in October 1917. By March 1918, over 300,000 American soldiers had reached France, and by November 1918, that number had risen to more than 2 million.

One reason that the United States forces were slow to see actual combat was Pershing's insistence that they be kept separate from French and British divisions. An exception was made for four regiments of black soldiers who were assigned to the French army. Despite the American warning to the French not to "spoil the Negroes" by allowing them to mix with the French civilian population, these soldiers fought so well that the French later awarded three of the regiments the Croix de Guerre, their highest unit citation.

In the spring of 1918, with Russia out of the war and the British blockade becoming more and more effective, the Germans launched an all-out offensive to win the war before full American military and industrial power became a factor. By late May, the Germans pushed within 50 miles of Paris. American troops helped stem the German advance at Château-Thierry, Belleau Wood, and Cantigny, names that proud survivors would later endow with almost sacred significance. Americans also took part in the Allied offensive in the summer of 1918.

In September, over a half million American troops fought near St. Mihiel, the first battle where large numbers of Americans went into action. One enlisted man "saw a sight which I shall never forget. It was zero hour and in one instant the entire front as far as the eye could reach in either direction was a sheet of flame, while the heavy artillery made the earth quake." The Americans suffered over 7,000 casualties, but they captured more than 16,000 German soldiers. The victory, even if it came against exhausted and retreating German troops, seemed to vindicate Pershing's insistence on a separate American army. The British and French commanders were critical of what they considered the disorganized, inexperienced, and ill-equipped American forces. They especially denounced the quality of the American high-ranking officers.

In the fall of 1918, the combined British, French, and American armies drove the Germans back. Faced with low morale among the German soldiers and finally the mutiny of the German fleet and Austria-Hungary's surrender, Kaiser Wilhelm II abdicated, and the Armistice was signed on November 11. More than a million American soldiers took part in the final Allied offensive. Many were inexperienced, and some "90-day wonders" had never handled a rifle before arriving in France. Edmund Arpin was wounded in an unnecessary battle. There were many other mistakes, some disastrous. The most famous blunder was the "lost battalion," which advanced beyond its support and was cut off and surrounded. It suffered 70 percent casualties.

The performance of the all-black 92nd Division was also controversial. The 92nd had been deliberately dispersed around the United States and had never trained as a unit. Its higher officers were white, and they repeatedly asked to be transferred. Many of its men were partly trained and poorly equipped, and they were continually being called away to work as common laborers. At the last minute during the Meuse-Argonne offensive, the 92nd was assigned to a particularly difficult position on the line, without maps or wire-cutters. Battalion commanders lost contact with their men, and several times the troops ran in the face of enemy fire. The division was withdrawn in disgrace. For years, politicians and military leaders used this incident to claim that black soldiers would never make good fighting men, ignoring the difficulties under which the 92nd fought and the valor shown by black troops assigned to the French army.

The war produced a few American heroes. Joseph Oklahombie, a Choctaw, overran several German machine gun nests and captured more than 100 German soldiers. Sergeant Alvin York, a former conscientious objector from Tennessee, single-handedly killed or captured 160 Germans using only his rifle and pistol. But his heroics were not typical. Artillery, machine guns, and, near the end, tanks, trucks, and airplanes won the war.

With few exceptions, the Americans fought hard and well. Although the French and British criticized the Americans' inexperience and disarray, they admired their exuberance, "pep," and ability to move large numbers of men and equipment efficiently. Sometimes the Americans simply overwhelmed the enemy with their numbers. They suffered over 120,000 casualties in the Meuse-Argonne campaign alone. One officer estimated that he lost 10 soldiers for every German his men killed in the final offensive.

The United States entered the war late, but still lost more than 48,000 service personnel and had many more wounded. Disease claimed 15 of every 1,000 soldiers each year (compared with 65 per 1,000 in the Civil War). But the British lost 900,000 men, the French 1.4 million, and the Russians 1.7 million. The United States contributed huge amounts of men and supplies in the last months of the war, and that finally tipped the balance. But it had entered late and sacrificed little compared with France and England. That would influence the peace settlement.

The end of the Great War brought joy to most Americans, but not to those who came down with the flu. In the fall of 1918 an influenza pandemic swept around the world killing at least 30 million people. There were 675,000 deaths in the United States in a little more than a year. Unlike most epidemics, which were most deadly for children and the elderly, this one hit hardest among young adults. Over 43,000 American servicemen died from the flu, almost as many as died in battle. There were no antibiotics that prevented the disease, and the surgical masks, required in some cities, did no good. The virus that caused the disastrous outbreak has never been identified.

## DOMESTIC IMPACT OF THE WAR

For at least 30 years before the United States entered the Great War, a debate raged over the proper role of the federal government in regulating industry and protecting people who could not protect themselves. Even within the Wilson administration, advisers disagreed on the proper role of the federal government. But the war and the problems it raised increased the power of the federal government. The wartime experience did not end the debate, but the United States emerged from the war a more modern nation, with more power residing in Washington.

## Financing the War

The war, by one calculation, cost the United States over $33 billion, and interest and veterans' benefits brought the total to nearly $112 billion. Early on, when an economist suggested that the war might cost the United States $10 billion, everyone had laughed. Yet many in the Wilson administration knew the war was going to be expensive, and they set out to raise the money by borrowing and by increasing taxes.

Secretary of the Treasury William McAdoo shouldered the task of financing the war. Studying the policies that Treasury Secretary Salmon Chase had followed during the Civil War, he decided that Chase should have appealed to popular emotions. His campaign to sell liberty bonds to ordinary American citizens at a very low interest rate stirred patriotism. "Lick a Stamp and Lick the Kaiser," one poster urged. Celebrities promoted the bonds, Boy Scouts sold them, and McAdoo implied that people who did not buy them were traitors.

The public responded enthusiastically, but they discovered after the war that their bonds had dropped to about 80 percent of face value. Because the interest on the bonds was tax-exempt, well-to-do citizens profited more from buying the bonds than did ordinary people. But the wealthy were not as pleased with McAdoo's other plan to finance the war by raising taxes. The War Revenue Act of 1917 boosted the tax rate sharply, taxed excess profits, and increased estate taxes. The next year, the tax rate on the largest incomes soared to 77 percent. The wealthy protested, but a number of progressives were just as unhappy, for they wanted to confiscate all income over $100,000 a year. Despite taxes and liberty bonds, however, World War I, like the Civil War, was financed in large part by inflation. Food prices, for example, nearly doubled between 1917 and 1919.

## Increasing Federal Power

At first, Wilson tried to work through state agencies to mobilize resources. The need for more central control soon led Wilson to create a series of emergency federal agencies. The first crisis was food. Poor grain crops for two years and an increasing demand for American food in Europe caused shortages. Wilson appointed Herbert Hoover, a young engineer who had won great prestige organizing relief for Belgium, to direct the Food Administration. Hoover set out to meet the crisis not so much through government regulation as through an appeal to the patriotism of farmers and consumers alike. He instituted "wheatless" and "meatless" days and urged housewives to cooperate. Women emerged during the war as the most important group of consumers. The government urged them to save, just as later it would urge them to buy.

The Wilson administration used the authority of the federal government to organize resources for the war effort. The War Industries Board, led by Bernard

Baruch, a shrewd Wall Street broker, used government power to control scarce materials and, on occasion, to set prices and priorities. The government itself went into the shipbuilding business and ran the railroads. When a severe winter and a lack of coordination brought the rail system near collapse in December 1917, Wilson put all the nation's railroads under the control of the United Railway Administration. The government spent more than $500 million to improve the rails and equipment, and in 1918 the railroads did run more efficiently than they had under private control. Some businessmen complained of "war socialism" and regulation. But most agreed with Baruch that a close relationship with government could improve product quality, promote efficiency, and increase profits.

## War Workers

The Wilson administration sought to protect and extend the rights of organized labor during the war, while mobilizing workers to keep the factories running. The National War Labor Board insisted on adequate wages and reduced hours, and it tried to prevent exploitation of working women and children. If a munitions plant refused to accept the board's decision, the government seized it. When workers threatened to strike, the board often ruled that they either had to work or be drafted.

The Wilson administration favored the conservative labor movement of Samuel Gompers and his AFL, and the Justice Department put the radical Industrial Workers of the World "out of business." After September 1917, federal agents conducted massive raids on IWW offices and arrested most of the leaders. Yet the government tolerated ruthless vigilante groups. In Bisbee, Arizona, the sheriff and 2,000 deputies rounded up 1,200 striking workers and sent them by boxcar to New Mexico. They spent two days in the desert without food or water before help came.

Gompers took advantage of the crisis to strengthen the AFL's position. He lent his approval to administration policies by making it clear that he opposed the IWW, Socialists, and Communists. As the AFL won a voice in home-front policy, its membership increased from 2.7 million in 1916 to over 4 million in 1917. Organized labor's wartime gains, however, would prove only temporary.

The war opened up industrial opportunities for black men. With 4 million men in the armed forces and the flow of immigrants ended by the war, factories for the first time hired African Americans in large numbers. Northern labor agents and the railroads actively recruited southern blacks, but the news of jobs in northern cities spread by word of mouth as well. By 1920, more than 300,000 blacks had joined the "great migration" north. This massive movement, which continued into the 1920s, had a permanent impact on the South as well as on the northern cities. As African Americans trekked north, thousands of Mexicans crossed into the United States. Immigration officials relaxed regulations because of the need for labor in the farms and factories of the Southwest.

The war also created new employment opportunities for women. Posters and patriotic speeches urged women to do their duty for the war effort. One poster showed a woman at her typewriter, the shadow of a soldier in the background, with the message: "STENOGRAPHERS, WASHINGTON NEEDS YOU."

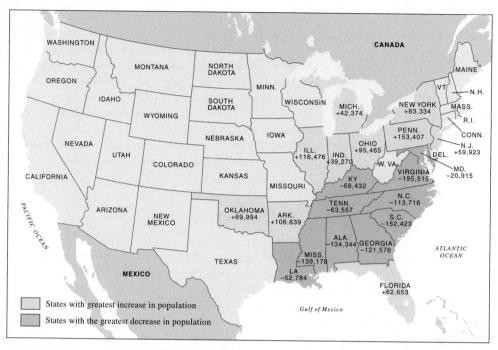

**AFRICAN-AMERICAN MIGRATION, 1910–1920**    This map makes graphic the massive migration of African Americans from the South to the North during the Great War. Most moved to find better jobs, but in the process they changed the dynamics of race relations in the country.

Women responded to these appeals out of both patriotism and a need to increase their earnings and to make up for inflation, which cut real wages. Women went into every kind of industry. They labored in brickyards and factories, as railroad conductors, and in munitions plants. The Woman's Land Army mobilized female labor for the farms. They demonstrated that women could do any kind of job. "It was not until our men were called overseas," one female banking executive reported, "that we made any real onslaught on the realm of finance, and became tellers, managers of departments, and junior and senior officers." Black women left domestic service for textile mills and even stockyards. But racial discrimination, even in the North, kept them from moving very far up the ladder.

Even though women demonstrated that they could do "male" jobs, their wartime progress proved temporary. Only about 5 percent of the women employed during the war, mostly unmarried, were new to the workforce. For most, it meant a shift of occupations or a move up to a better-paying position. Moreover, the war accelerated trends already underway. It increased the need for telephone operators, sales personnel, secretaries, and other white-collar workers, and in these occupations women soon became a majority. Telephone operator became an almost exclusively female job by 1917.

In the end, the war did provide limited opportunities for some women, but it did not change the dominant perception that a woman's place was in the home. After the war was over, the men returned, and women's gains almost disappeared. There were 8 million women in the workforce in 1910 and only 8.5 million in 1920.

Women proved during the war that they could do "men's work." These two young women deliver ice, a backbreaking task, but one that was necessary in the days before electric refrigerators. Despite women like these, the war did not change the American ideal that women's proper place was in the home. (National Archives)

## The Climax of Progressivism

Many progressives, especially the social justice progressives, opposed the entry of the United States into the war until a few months before Congress declared war. But after April 1917, many began to see the "social possibilities of war." They deplored the war's death and destruction, the abridgment of freedom of speech, and the extreme patriotism, but praised the social planning that war stimulated. They approved the Wilson administration's support of collective bargaining, the eight-hour day, and protection for women and children in industry. They welcomed government-owned housing projects, woman suffrage, and prohibition. Many endorsed the government takeover of the railroads and control of business. For many social justice progressives who had fought hard, long, and frustrating battles to humanize the industrial city, it was refreshing that suddenly people in high places were listening and approving.

One of the best examples of the progressives' influence on wartime activities was the Commission on Training Camp Activities, set up early in the war to mobilize, entertain, and protect American servicemen at home and abroad. It organized community singing and baseball, established post exchanges and theaters, and even provided university extension lectures. The overriding assumption was that the military experience would produce citizens ready to vote for social reform.

The Commission on Training Camp Activities also incorporated the progressive crusades against alcohol and prostitution. Laws banned liquor sales to men in uniform and prostitution and alcohol around military bases. "Fit to fight" was the motto. It was a typical progressive effort, combining moral indignation with scientific prophylaxis. The commissioners prided themselves on eliminating all "red-light" districts near the training camps. When the boys go to France, the secretary of war remarked, "I want them to have invisible armour to take with them."

France tested that "invisible armour." Despite hundreds of letters from American mothers, the government decided that it could not stop soldiers from drinking wine, but it did forbid them to buy or accept as gifts anything but light wine and beer. If Edmund Arpin's outfit is typical, troops ignored the rules. Sex was even more difficult to regulate. The British and the French armies tried to control venereal disease by licensing and inspecting prostitutes. French premier Georges Clemenceau accused the Americans of spreading disease throughout the French population and offered to provide the Americans with licensed prostitutes. When Clemenceau's letter reached Baker, the secretary of war said, "For God's sake, . . . don't show this to the President or he'll stop the war." The offer was never accepted.

## Suffrage for Women

In the fall of 1918, Wilson asked the Senate's support of woman suffrage as "vital to the winning of the war." Wilson had earlier opposed the vote for women. His positive statement at this late date was not necessary, but his voice was a welcome addition to a rising chorus of support for an amendment to the Constitution that would permit the female half of the population to vote. Many still argued that voting would make women less feminine and less fit as wives and mothers. The National Association Opposed to Woman Suffrage declared that woman suffrage, socialism, and feminism were "three branches of the same Social Revolution."

Carrie Chapman Catt, an efficient administrator and tireless organizer, devised the strategy that finally secured the vote for women. In 1915, she became president of the National American Woman Suffrage Association (NAWSA), coordinating the state campaigns from the office in Washington and directing a growing army of dedicated workers. The careful planning began to produce results, but a group of more militant reformers, impatient with the slow progress, broke off from NAWSA to form the National Woman's Party (NWP) in 1916. This group was led by Alice Paul, who had participated in suffrage battles in England. Paul and her group picketed the White House, chained themselves to the fence, and blocked the streets. They carried banners that asked, "MR. PRESIDENT, HOW LONG MUST WOMEN WAIT FOR LIBERTY?" In the summer of 1917, the government arrested more than 200 women and charged them with "obstructing the sidewalk." It was just the kind of publicity the militant group sought, and it made the most of it. Wilson, fearing more embarrassment, began to cooperate with moderate reformers.

Careful organizing by the NAWSA and the NWP's more militant tactics both contributed to the final success of the woman suffrage crusade. The war did not cause the passage of the Nineteenth Amendment, but it did accelerate it. In 1917, 14 state legislatures petitioned Congress, urging enactment; an additional 26 states did the same in 1919. Early in 1919, the House of Representatives passed the amendment 304 to 90, and the Senate approved 56 to 25. Fourteen months later, the required 36 states had ratified, and women at last had the vote. But this would not prove the triumph of feminism, nor the signal for the beginning of a new reform movement that the women leaders expected.

## PLANNING FOR PEACE

Wilson turned U.S. participation in the war into a crusade to make the world safe for democracy—and more. On January 8, 1918, partly to counter Bolshevik charges that the war was merely an imperialist struggle, he announced his plan. Called the Fourteen Points, it argued for "open covenants of peace openly arrived at," freedom of the seas, equality of trade, and the self-determination of all peoples. But his most important point, the fourteenth, called for a "league of nations" to preserve peace.

### The Paris Peace Conference

Late in 1918, Wilson announced that he would head the American delegation to Paris to attend the peace conference. Wilson and his entourage of college professors, technical experts, and advisers sailed for France on December 4, 1918. Secretary of State Lansing, Wilson's confidante Edward House, and a number of other advisers were there. Conspicuously missing was Henry Cabot Lodge, the most powerful man in the Senate, or any other Republican senator—a serious blunder, for the Republican-controlled Senate would have to approve the treaty. It is difficult to explain Wilson's lack of political insight, except to say that he hated Lodge and compromise with equal intensity and had supreme confidence in his ability to persuade.

Wilson's self-confidence grew during a triumphant tour through Europe before the conference. He was cheered enthusiastically by ordinary people, but he had greater difficulty convincing the political leaders at the peace conference.

Though Wilson was more naive and idealistic than his European counterparts, he won many concessions at the peace table, sometimes by threatening to go home. The Allied leaders were determined to punish Germany and enlarge their empires. Wilson believed that he could create a new kind of international relations based on his Fourteen Points. He did achieve limited endorsement of self-determination, his dream that each national group could have its own country and that people should decide in what country they wanted to live.

The peacemakers carved Austria, Hungary, and Yugoslavia out of what had been the Austro-Hungarian Empire. They hoped that the new countries of Poland, Czechoslovakia, Finland, Estonia, Latvia, and Lithuania would help contain bolshevism in eastern Europe. France was to occupy Germany's industrial Saar region for 15 years, until a plebiscite determined whether its people wanted to be part of Germany or France. Italy gained the port of Trieste. Dividing up the map of Europe was difficult at best, but perhaps the biggest mistake that Wilson and other major leaders made was to give the small nations little power at the negotiating table and to exclude Soviet Russia entirely.

Wilson had to make major concessions at the peace conference. He was forced to agree that Germany should pay reparations (later set at $56 billion), lose much

of its oil- and coal-rich territory, and admit war guilt. He accepted a mandate system that allowed France and Britain to take over portions of the Middle East and
gave Germany's Pacific colonies to Japan. He acquiesced when the Allies turned
Germany's African colonies into "mandate possessions" because they did not
want to allow self-determination for blacks in areas they had colonized

This was not a "peace without victory," as Wilson had promised; and German feelings of betrayal would later have grave repercussions. Wilson did not
achieve freedom of the seas or the abolition of trade barriers, but he did get the
League of Nations, which he hoped would prevent future wars. The key to collective security was Article 10 of the League covenant, which pledged all members
"to respect and preserve against external aggression the territorial integrity" of
all other members.

## Women for Peace

While the statesmen met at Versailles to make peace and divide up Europe, a
group of prominent and successful women (some from the Central Powers) convened in Zurich, Switzerland. The American delegation was led by Jane Addams
and included Montana Congresswoman Jeannette Rankin, who had voted against
war in 1917. They formed the Women's International League for Peace and Freedom with Addams as president and denounced the one-sided peace terms of the
Versailles treaty that called for disarmament of only one side and exacted gigantic
economic penalties from the Central Powers.

Hate and intolerance were legacies of the war. Clemenceau especially wanted
to humiliate Germany. The peace conference was also haunted by the Bolshevik
success in Russia. This threat seemed so great that the Allies sent American and
Japanese troops to Russia in 1919 to defeat bolshevism and create a moderate republic. By 1920 the mission had failed. The troops withdrew, but the Russians
never forgot, and the threat of Bolshevism remained.

## Wilson's Failed Dream

Probably most Americans supported the concept of the League of Nations in the
summer of 1919, yet the Senate refused to accept American membership. The
League of Nations treaty, one commentator has suggested, was killed by its
friends and not by its enemies.

First there was Lodge, who had earlier endorsed some kind of international
peacekeeping organization. He objected to Article 10, claiming that it would force
Americans to fight the wars of foreigners. Chairman of the Senate Foreign Relations Committee, Lodge (like Wilson) was a lawyer and a scholar as well as a
politician. He disliked all Democrats, especially Wilson, whose missionary zeal
infuriated him.

Then there was Wilson, whose only hope of passage of the treaty in the Senate was a compromise to bring moderate senators to his side. But Wilson refused
to compromise or to modify Article 10. Angry at his opponents, who were exploiting the disagreement for political advantage, he stumped the country to
convince the American people of the rightness of his plan. They did not need to
be convinced. They greeted Wilson much the way the people of France had.

# Timeline

**1914** Archduke Franz Ferdinand assassinated

World War I begins

United States declares neutrality

American troops invade Mexico and occupy Veracruz

**1915** Germany announces submarine blockade of Great Britain

*Lusitania* sunk

*Arabic* pledge

Marines land in Haiti

**1916** Army Reorganization Bill

Expedition into Mexico

Wilson reelected

Workmen's Compensation Bill

Keatings-Owen Child Labor Bill

Federal Farm Loan Act

National Women's Party founded

**1917** Germany resumes unrestricted submarine warfare

United States breaks relations with Germany

Zimmermann telegram

Russian Revolution

United States declares war on Germany

War Revenue Act

Espionage Act

Committee on Public Information established

Trading with the Enemy Act

Selective Service Act

War Industries Board formed

**1918** Sedition Act

Flu epidemic sweeps nation

Wilson's Fourteen Points

American troops intervene in Russian Revolution

**1919** Paris peace conference

Eighteenth Amendment prohibits alcoholic beverages

Senate rejects Treaty of Versailles

**1920** Nineteenth Amendment grants woman suffrage

Traveling by train, he gave 37 speeches in 29 cities in the space of three weeks. When he described the graves of American soldiers in France and announced that American boys would never again die in a foreign war, the people responded with applause.

After one dramatic speech in Pueblo, Colorado, Wilson collapsed. His health had been failing for some months, and the strain of the trip was too much. He was rushed back to Washington, where a few days later he suffered a massive stroke. For the final year and a half of his term, the president was incapable of running the government and could not lead a fight for the League.

The Senate finally killed the League treaty in March of 1920. Had the United States joined the League of Nations, it probably would have made little difference in the international events of the 1920s and 1930s, nor would American participation have prevented World War II. The United States did not resign from the world of diplomacy or trade, nor by that single act become isolated. But the rejection of the League treaty was symbolic of the refusal of many Americans to admit that the world and America's place in it had changed dramatically since 1914.

✤ ✤ ✤ ✤

# CONCLUSION

## The Divided Legacy of the Great War

For Edmund Arpin and many of his friends who left small towns and urban neighborhoods to join the military forces, the war was a great adventure. For the next two decades, at American Legion conventions and Armistice Day parades, they continued to celebrate their days of glory. For others who served, the war's results were more tragic. Many died. Some came home injured, disabled by poison gas, or unable to cope with the complex world that had opened up to them.

In a larger sense, the war was both a triumph and a tragedy for the American people. The war created opportunities for blacks who migrated to the North, for women who found more rewarding jobs, and for farmers who suddenly discovered a demand for their products. But much of the promise and the hope proved temporary.

The war provided a certain climax to the progressive movement. The passage of the woman suffrage and prohibition amendments, and the use of federal power in a variety of ways to promote justice and order pleased reformers, who had been working toward these ends for many decades. But the results were often disappointing. Once the war ended, much federal legislation was dismantled or reduced in effectiveness, and votes for women had little initial impact on social legislation.

The Great War marked the coming of age of the United States as a world power, but the country seemed reluctant to accept the new responsibility. The war stimulated patriotism and pride in the country, but it also increased intolerance. With this mixed legacy from the war, the country entered the new era of the 1920s.

## Discovering U.S. History Online

*World War I Document Archive*   http://www.lib.byu.edu/~rdh/wwi/
This archive contains sources about World War I in general, not just on America's involvement.

*The American Experience: Influenza*   http://www.pbs.org/wgbh/pages/amex/influenza
This PBS site reveals the impact of the great flu epidemic of 1918.

*History of the Suffrage Movement*   http://www.rochester.edu/SBA/hisindx.html
This site includes a chronology, important texts relating to woman suffrage, and biographical information on Susan B. Anthony and Elizabeth Cady Stanton.

*World War I: Trenches on the Web*   http://www.worldwar1.com/index.html
This site provides a mass of data concerning the prosecution of the world's first global war.

*Chicago: Destination for the Great Migration: African-American Mosaic Exhibition*
http://lcweb.loc.gov/exhibits/african/afam011.html
This Library of Congress site looks at the black experience of the great migration through the lens of one prominent destination.

*Explorers Hall @ National Geographic*
http://www.nationalgeographic.com/society/ngo/explorer/titanic/movie.html
This site offers historical perspective and balanced coverage of the sinking of the *Titanic*, including a 14-minute 3-D tour of the ship's wreckage.

## Fiction and Film

Erich Maria Remarque highlights the horror of the war in his classic *All Quiet on the Western Front* (1929); John Dos Passos describes the war as a bitter experience in *Three Soldiers* (1921); and Ernest Hemingway portrays its futility in *A Farewell to Arms* (1929). In *Regeneration* (1991), Pat Barker recreates the nightmare of the western front through British eyes.

*All Quiet on the Western Front* was made into a powerful movie (1930) that became an anti-war classic. *Reds* (1981) is a Hollywood film about socialists, feminists, and communists. It tells the story of John Reed and his radical friends in Greenwich Village before the war and their support of the Russian Revolution after 1917.

## Recommended Reading

### The Early War Years
C. C. Clemenden, *The United States and Pancho Villa* (1961); Niall Ferguson, *The Pity of War* (1998); Paul Fussell, *The Great War and Modern Memory* (1975); Martin Gilbert, *The First World War: A Complete Account* (1994); C. Roland Marchand, *The American Peace Movement and Social Reform* (1973); James Toll, *The Origins of the First World War* (1984); Barbara Tuchman, *The Guns of August* (1962).

### The United States Enters the War
C.C. Adams, *The Great Adventure: Male Desire and the Coming of World War I* (1990); Robert H. Ferrell, *Woodrow Wilson and World War I* (1985); N. Gordon Levin, Jr.,*Woodrow Wilson and World Politics* (1968); Ernest R. May, *The World War and American Isolation* (1966).

### The Military Experience
Arthur D. Barbeau and Florette Henri, *The Unknown Soldiers: Black American Troops in World War I* (1974); Edward M. Coffman,*The War to End All Wars: The American Military Experience in World War I* (1968); John Ellis, *The Social History of the Machine Gun* (1975); Byron Farwell, *Over There* (1999); John Keegan, *The First World War* (1999); Herbert M. Mason, Jr., *The Lafayette Escadrille* (1964); Gary Mead, *The Doughboys* (2000); John Mosier, *The Myth of the Great War* (2000); Russell Weigley, *The American Way of War* (1973).

### Domestic Impact of the War
Nancy K. Bristow, *Making Men Moral: Social Engineering During the Great War* (1996); Alfred W. Crosby, *America's Forgotten Pandemic: The Influenza of 1918* (1989); Eric Foner, *The Story of American Freedom* (1998); Lettie Gavin, *American Women in World War I* (1997); Florette Henri, *Black Migration* (1975); David M. Kennedy, *Over Here* (1980); Ronald Schaffer, *America in the Great War: The Rise of the War Welfare State* (1991).

### Planning For Peace
John Morton Blum, *Woodrow Wilson and the Politics of Morality* (1956); John Milton Cooper, Jr., *Breaking the Heart of the World: Woodrow Wilson and the Fight for the League of Nations* (2001); Peter Filene, *America and the Soviet Experience* (1967): Warren Kuehl, *Seeking World Order (1969)*; Charles L. Mee, Jr., *The End of Order: Versailles, 1919* (1980).

# CHAPTER 23
## Affluence and Anxiety

### AMERICAN STORIES
**A Black Sharecropper and His Family Move North**

John and Lizzie Parker were black sharecroppers living in a "stubborn, ageless hut squatted on a little hill" in central Alabama. They had two daughters, one age six, the other already married. The whole family worked hard in the cotton fields with little to show for it. One day in 1917, Lizzie declared, "I'm through. I've picked my last sack of cotton. I've cleared my last field."

Like many southern African Americans, the Parkers sought a better life in the North. World War I cut off the flow of immigrant workers from Europe. Some companies sent trains into the South to recruit African Americans. John Parker signed up with a mining company in West Virginia. The company offered free transportation for his family. "You will be allowed to get your food at the company store and there are houses awaiting for you," the agent promised.

But it turned out that the houses in the company town in West Virginia were little better than those they left in Alabama. After deducting for rent and for supplies from the company store, almost no money was left at the end of the week. John hated the dirty and dangerous work in the mine and realized that he would never get ahead by staying there. He ran away, leaving his family in West Virginia.

John drifted to Detroit, where he got a job with the American Car and Foundry Company. It was 1918, and the pay was good, more than he had ever made before. After a few weeks, he rented an apartment and sent for his family. For the first time, Lizzie had a gas stove and an indoor toilet, and Sally, now seven, started school. It seemed as if their dream had come true.

Detroit was not quite the dream, however. It was crowded with all kinds of migrants, attracted by the wartime jobs at the Ford Motor Company and other factories. The new arrivals increased racial tensions already present in the city. Sally was beaten up by a gang of white youths at school. Even in their neighborhood, which had been solidly Jewish before their arrival, the shopkeeper and the old residents made it clear that they did not like blacks moving in. The Ku Klux Klan, which gained many new members in Detroit, also made life uncomfortable for the blacks who had moved north to seek jobs and opportunity. Suddenly the war ended, and almost immediately John lost his job. Then the landlord raised the rent, and the Parkers had to leave their apartment for housing in a section just outside the city near Eight Mile Road. The surrounding suburbs had paved streets, wide lawns, and elegant houses, but this black ghetto's dirt streets and shacks reminded the Parkers of the company town in West Virginia. Lizzie had to get along without her bathroom. There was no indoor plumbing and no electricity, only a pump in the yard and an outhouse.

The recession winter of 1921 to 1922 was particularly difficult. The auto industry and the other companies laid off most of their workers. John found only part-time employment, while Lizzie worked as a servant for white families. Because no bus route connected the black community to surrounding suburbs, she often had to trek miles through the snow. Their shack was freezing cold, and it was cramped because their married daughter and her husband had joined them in Detroit.

Lizzie did not give up her dream. With strength, determination, and a sense of humor, she kept the family together. In 1924, Sally entered high school. By the end of the decade, she had graduated from high school, and the Parkers finally had electricity and indoor plumbing, though the streets were still unpaved. Those unpaved streets symbolized their unfulfilled dream. The Parkers, like most African Americans who moved north in the decade after World War I, had improved their lot, but they still lived outside Detroit—and, in many ways, outside America.

❧ ❧ ❧ ❧

Like most Americans in the 1920s, the Parkers pursued the American dream of success. For them, a comfortable house, a steady job, a new bathroom, and an education for their younger daughter constituted that dream. For others during the decade, the symbol of success was a new automobile, a new suburban house, or perhaps making a killing on the stock market. The 1920s, the decade between the end of World War I and the stock market crash, has often been referred to as the "jazz age," a time when the American people had one long party complete with flappers, speakeasies, illegal bathtub gin, and young people doing the Charleston long into the night. This frivolous interpretation has some basis in fact, but most Americans did not share in the party, for they were too busy struggling to make a living.

In this chapter, we will explore some of the conflicting trends of an exciting decade. First, we will examine the intolerance that influenced almost all the events and social movements of the time. We will also look at technological developments, especially the automobile, which changed life for almost everyone during the 1920s and created the illusion of prosperity for all. We will then focus on groups—women, blacks, industrial workers, and farmers—whose hopes were raised but not always fulfilled. We will close by considering how business, politics, and foreign policy intertwined in the era of Harding, Coolidge, and Hoover.

## POSTWAR PROBLEMS

Enthusiasm for social progress evaporated in 1919. The year after the war ended was marked by strikes and violence and by fear that Bolsheviks, blacks, foreigners, and others were destroying the American way of life. Some of the anxiety grew out of wartime patriotism, and some reflected the postwar economic and political turmoil that forced Americans to deal with new and immensely troubling situations.

## Red Scare

Radicals and dissidents have often been feared as threats to the American way of life. In the early twentieth century, anarchists seemed the worst danger, but the Russian Revolution of 1917 suddenly made *Bolshevik* the most dangerous radical, somehow mixed with that other villain, the German. In the spring of 1919, with the Bolsheviks advocating worldwide revolution, many Americans feared that the Communists planned to take over the United States.

Immediately after the war, there were perhaps 25,000 to 40,000 American Communists, but they never threatened the United States. Some were idealists such as John Reed, the son of a wealthy businessman, who had been converted to socialism in New York's Greenwich Village. Appalled by the carnage of the capitalistic war, Reed went to Russia as a journalist in 1917. His eyewitness account of the Bolshevik takeover, *Ten Days That Shook the World*, optimistically predicted a worldwide revolution. Seeing little hope for that revolution in postwar America, he returned to Moscow, where he died in 1920, disillusioned by the new regime's authoritarianism.

## Working-Class Protest

Though small in number, the Communists seemed to be a threat in 1919, especially as a series of devastating strikes erupted across the country. American workers had suffered from wartime inflation, which had almost doubled prices between 1914 and 1919, while most wages remained the same. In 1919, more than 4 million workers staged 4,000 strikes. Few wanted to overthrow the government; they demanded higher wages, shorter hours, and sometimes more control over the workplace.

On January 21, 1919, some 35,000 shipyard workers struck in Seattle. Within a few days, a general strike paralyzed the city. The mayor called for federal troops. Within five days, using strong-arm tactics, he put down the strike and was hailed as a "red-blooded patriot."

Yet other strikes continued. In September 1919, all 343,000 employees of U.S. Steel walked out in an attempt to win an eight-hour day and an "American living wage." Within days, the strike spread to Bethlehem Steel. Owners blamed the steel strikes on Bolsheviks. They imported strikebreakers, provoked riots, broke up union meetings, and used police and soldiers to end the strike. Eighteen strikers were killed. Because most people believed the Communists had inspired the strike, the issue of long hours and poor pay got lost, and eventually the union surrendered.

The Boston police also walked out. Like most other workers, they were struggling to survive on prewar salaries in inflationary times. Again there was talk of Communist influence. College students and army veterans volunteered to replace the police and prevent looting. The government quickly broke the strike and fired the policemen. When Samuel Gompers urged Governor Calvin Coolidge to ask the Boston authorities to reinstate them, Coolidge's answer made him famous: "There is no right to strike against the public safety by anybody, anywhere, anytime."

From the beginning, corporate owners blamed the strikes on Bolsheviks, and the "bomb-throwing radical" became almost a cliché. On April 28, 1919, a bomb was discovered in a small package delivered to the home of the mayor of Seattle. The next day, the maid of a former senator opened a package and had her hands blown off. Other bombings occurred in June; one shattered the front of Attorney General A. Mitchell Palmer's home. The bombings seem to have been the work of a few misguided radicals who thought they might spark a revolution. But their effect was to convince many that revolution was a real and immediate threat.

No one was more convinced than Palmer. In the summer of 1919, he decided to destroy the Red network. He organized a special anti-radical division within the Justice Department and put young J. Edgar Hoover in charge of coordinating information on domestic radical activities. Obsessed by the "Red Menace," Palmer instituted a series of raids to round up radical foreign workers. In December, 249 aliens, including the famous anarchist Emma Goldman, were deported, although very few were Communists and even fewer had any desire to overthrow the government of the United States.

The Palmer raids, probably the most massive violation of civil liberties in America up to then, found few dangerous radicals but did increase fear and intolerance. An Indiana jury quickly acquitted a man who had killed an alien for yelling "To hell with the United States." Palmer briefly became a national hero, though in the end only about 600 aliens were deported, out of more than 5,000 arrested. The worst of the "Red Scare" was over by the end of 1920, but fear of radicalism and emotional patriotism colored almost every aspect of life during the 1920s.

The Red Scare promoted many patriotic organizations and societies determined to purge Communists. These organizations made little distinction between Communists, Socialists, progressives, and liberals, and they saw Bolsheviks everywhere. The best-known of the superpatriot organizations was the American Legion, but all provided a sense of purpose and belonging by attacking radicals and preaching patriotism.

## Ku Klux Klan

Among the superpatriotic organizations claiming to protect the American way of life, the Ku Klux Klan was the most extreme. The Klan was revived in Georgia by William J. Simmons, a lay preacher, salesman, and member of many fraternal organizations. He adopted the name and white-sheet garb of the old anti-black Reconstruction organization that was glorified in 1915 in the immensely popular but racist film *Birth of a Nation*. Simmons appointed himself head ("Imperial Wizard") of the new Klan, which was thoroughly Protestant and anti-foreign, anti-Semitic,

The Ku Klux Klan, with its elaborate rituals and white uniforms, exploited the fear of blacks, Jews, liberals, and Catholics while preaching "traditional" American values. The appeal of the Klan was not limited to the South. This is a photo of a Klan initiation ceremony. (FPG International)

and anti-Catholic. It opposed the teaching of evolution; glorified old-time religion; supported immigration restriction; denounced short skirts, petting, and "demon rum"; and upheld patriotism and the purity of women. The Klan was also militantly anti-black; its members took as their special mission the task of keeping blacks in their "proper place." They often used peaceful measures to accomplish their aim, but if those failed, they resorted to violence, kidnapping, and lynching. The Klan grew slowly until after the war, but added over 100,000 new members in 1920 alone. Postwar fear and confusion, along with aggressive recruiting, explained its explosive growth.

The Klan flourished in the small-town and rural South, but soon it spread throughout the country. The Klan was especially strong in the working-class neighborhoods of Chicago, Detroit, Indianapolis, and Atlanta, where African Americans and other ethnic minorities were settling. At the peak of its power, it had several million members, many of them middle class. The Klan also influenced politics, especially in Indiana, Oregon, Oklahoma, Louisiana, and Texas. The Klan declined after 1924, but widespread fear of everything "un-American" remained.

## The Sacco-Vanzetti Case

The Red Scare and fear of foreign radicalism influenced the conviction and sentencing of two Italian anarchists: Nicola Sacco and Bartolomeo Vanzetti. Arrested in 1920 for allegedly murdering a guard during a robbery in Massachusetts, the two were sentenced to die in 1921 on what many liberals considered flimsy evidence. Indeed, it seemed to many that the two Italians, who spoke in broken English and were admitted anarchists, were punished because of their radical beliefs and foreign appearance.

Even now, it is not clear whether Sacco and Vanzetti were guilty, but the case took on symbolic significance as many intellectuals in Europe and America rallied to their defense. Appeal after appeal failed, but finally the governor of Massachusetts appointed a commission to reexamine the evidence. The commission reaffirmed the verdict, and the two were electrocuted on August 23, 1927 despite massive protests and midnight vigils around the country. But their cause did not die. On the fiftieth anniversary of their deaths in 1977, the governor of Massachusetts exonerated them.

## Religious Intolerance

The Ku Klux Klan and well-publicized cases like Sacco-Vanzetti touched relatively few people, but intolerance affected millions of lives. Henry Ford published anti-Semitic diatribes. Barred from fashionable resorts, Jews built their own hotels in the Catskills in New York State and elsewhere. Many colleges, private academies, and medical schools had Jewish quotas, and many suburbs explicitly limited residents to "Christians." Catholics, too, were prohibited from many organizations, and few even tried to enroll in the elite colleges. Although prejudice and intolerance had always existed, during the 1920s much of that intolerance was made more formal; in some cases, it was translated into law.

## A PROSPERING ECONOMY

The decade after World War I was also a time of industrial expansion and wide prosperity. After recovering from a postwar depression in 1921 and 1922, the economy took off. Fueled by new technology, more efficient management, and innovative advertising, industrial production almost doubled during the decade. The gross national product rose by an astonishing 40 percent. A construction boom created new suburbs around American cities, and new skyscrapers transformed the cities themselves. However, the benefits of this prosperity were not distributed evenly.

## The Rising Standard of Living

Signs of the new prosperity abounded. Millions of homes and apartments were built and equipped with the latest conveniences. Plastics and cellophane altered the habits of millions, and new products, such as cigarette lighters, dry ice, and Pyrex glass, created demands unheard of a decade before.

Perhaps the most tangible sign of the new prosperity was the modern American bathroom. In the early 1920s, the enameled tub, toilet, and washbasin became standard. The bathroom, with unlimited hot water, privacy, and clean white fixtures, symbolized American affluence, but a great many in rural America still used privies.

Americans now had more leisure time. Persistent efforts by labor unions had gradually reduced the 60-hour workweek of the late nineteenth century to a 45-hour week. Paid vacations, unknown in the nineteenth century, became prevalent. The American diet also improved. The consumption of cornmeal and potatoes declined, but the sale of fresh vegetables increased by 45 percent. Health improved and life expectancy lengthened. But not all Americans enjoyed better health and more leisure. A white male born in 1900 had a life expectancy of 48 years and a white female of 51 years. By 1930, these figures had increased to 59 and 63 years. For a black male born in 1900, however, the life expectancy was only 33 years, and for the black female, 35 years. These figures increased to 48 and 47 by 1930, but the discrepancy remained.

Yet almost all Americans benefited to some extent from the new prosperity. Some took advantage of expanding educational opportunities. In 1900, only one in ten young people of high school age was in school. By 1930, that number had increased to six in ten, and much of the improvement came in the 1920s. College enrollment also grew, but only a small percentage went beyond high school during the decade.

## The Rise of the Modern Corporation

The structure and practice of American business were transformed in the 1920s. After the economic downturn of 1920 to 1922, business boomed until the crash of 1929. Mergers increased during the decade at a rate greater than at any time since the end of the 1890s. What emerged was not monopolies but oligopolies (industry domination spread among a few large firms). By 1930, the 200 largest corporations—which were becoming more diversified—controlled almost half the corporate wealth.

Perhaps the most important business trend of the decade was the emergence of a new kind of manager. The prototype was Alfred P. Sloan, Jr., an engineer who reorganized General Motors. He divided the company into components, freeing top managers to concentrate on planning, controlling inventory, and integrating operations. Marketing and advertising became as important as production. The new manager, often a business school graduate, had a large staff but owned no part of the company.

Continuing the trends started by Frederick Taylor (see Chapter 21), the new managers tried to keep employees working efficiently, but they also introduced pensions, recreation facilities, cafeterias, and even paid vacations and profit-sharing plans. This "welfare capitalism" was designed to reduce worker discontent and discourage labor unions. Planning was the key to the new corporate structure, and planning often meant a continuation of the business-government cooperation that had developed during World War I. Even though all the planning failed to prevent the economic collapse in 1929, the modern corporation survived the depression to exert a growing influence on American life in the 1930s and after.

## Electrification

The 1920s also marked the climax of the "second industrial revolution," powered by electricity and producing a growing array of consumer goods. By 1929, electrical generators provided 80 percent of the power used in industry. Less than one of every ten American homes had electricity in 1907; by 1929, more than two-thirds did, and workers were turning out twice as many goods as a similarly sized workforce had 10 years earlier.

Electricity brought dozens of gadgets and labor-saving devices into the home. But the new machines did not reduce the time the average housewife spent doing housework. In many ways, the success of the electric revolution increased the contrast in American life. Urban "Great White Ways" symbolized progress, but they also made slums and rural hamlets seem even darker. For poor women, especially in rural America, the traditional female tasks of carrying water, pushing, pulling, and lifting continued.

## Automobile Culture

Automobile manufacturing, like electrification, grew spectacularly in the 1920s. The automobile was a major factor in the postwar boom. It stimulated and transformed the petroleum, steel, and rubber industries; it forced the construction and upgrading of streets and highways at the cost of millions of dollars for labor and concrete. From the beginning, the United States loved autos. There were nearly 1 million autos in 1912, and in the 1920s, autos came within the reach of the middle class. In 1929, Americans purchased 4.5 million cars, and by the end of that year, nearly 27 million were registered.

The auto created new suburbs and allowed families to live miles from work. Gasoline stations, diners, and tourist courts (forerunners of motels) became familiar landmarks on the American scene. But there was an environmental downside as oil and gasoline contaminated streams, piles of old tires and rusting hulks of discarded cars began to line the highways, and emissions from thousands and then millions of internal combustion engines fouled the air.

The auto transformed American life in other ways. Small crossroads stores and many small churches disappeared as rural families drove into town. Trucks and tractors changed farming. Buses began to eliminate the one-room school, and the tiny rural church began to disappear. Autos also freed young people from chaperoning; and although the car was hardly a "house of prostitution on wheels" as one judge decried, it did change courting habits by allowing young people to escape the watchful eyes of their parents.

Over the decade, the automobile became a sign of status. Advertising made it the symbol of the good life, sex, freedom, and speed. The auto transformed advertising and altered the way products were purchased. By 1926, three-fourths of the cars sold were bought on some kind of deferred-payment plan, and "buy now, pay later" was soon used to sell other consumer products. The auto industry, like most American businesses, consolidated. In 1908, more than 250 companies were making automobiles in the United States. By 1929, only 44 remained. But one name became synonymous with the automobile itself—Henry Ford.

Ford had a reputation as a progressive industrial leader and champion of ordinary people. As with all men and women who become symbols, the truth is less dramatic. For example, his famous assembly line was invented by a team of engineers. Introduced in 1913, it cut production time for a car from 14 hours to an hour and a half. It was the perfect application of Frederick Taylor's system of breaking down each operation into its components, applying careful timing, and integrating the laborer with the machine. The product of this carefully planned system was the Model T, the prototype of the inexpensive family car.

# Technology Changes the American People

## Wireless Communication

On the night of April 14, 1912, the *Titanic,* the largest ship ever built, hit an iceberg in the North Atlantic and sank in just over an hour. When the giant ship went down, it took more than 1,500 passengers to their deaths (651 were saved). While the stricken ship settled in the water, wireless operators on board sent out distress signals that were picked up by at least 10 ships and a wireless station in Newfoundland. Only one of the ships was close enough to rescue passengers, but news of the disaster became headlines in the newspapers of Europe and America the next morning. Thanks to the wireless, millions of people received the news almost simultaneously, and they experienced a shared sense of loss.

Ships had been lost at sea almost from the beginning of history, but until the invention of the wireless, they usually just disappeared. A ship would be missing and then presumed lost, and no one would ever know the exact nature of the tragedy, since communication to other ships or shore was impossible. All types of messages traveled slowly. In the eighteenth century, it often took months for letters to cross the Atlantic, and distant events were reported in newspapers many weeks after they happened. The wireless helped to usher in an era of instant news, and it dramatically changed the way people perceived the world. The *New York Times* for April 21, 1912, commenting on the *Titanic* and the magic of the wireless, observed: "Night and day all the year round the millions upon the earth and the thousands upon the sea now reach out and grasp the thin air and use it as a thing more potent for human aid than any strand of wire or cable that was ever spun or woven."

Guglielmo Marconi invented the wireless in 1894, and less than a decade later, U.S. President Theodore Roosevelt and King Edward VII of Great Britain used it to exchange greetings across the Atlantic. By 1912, the wireless was a common, if not always predictable, form of international communication, linking ships to land in a system of instant communication. It joined the telegraph (1844) and the telephone (1876) in transforming communication and in making it possible to seem to be in two places at the same time. Marconi, who, like all great inventors, built on the work of others, succeeded in sending signals in Morse code over the invisible electromagnetic airwaves. Other experimenters soon successfully transmitted the human voice and music over the same waves. The wireless occupied a midpoint in the rising curve of technology that led to radio, television, the communications satellite, and computers.

The wireless and the radio made ocean travel much safer and war more efficient by improving communications between ships at sea and among army units on the ground. Within a decade after the *Titanic* disaster, technology also transformed American lives in direct and subtle ways. Weather forecasting became more accurate and timely, providing ample warning to farmers and ordinary citizens about approaching storms. News of battles, elections, sporting events, and disasters both domestic and foreign traveled over the airwaves. This instant news could have

Most farmers did not own a radio until the end of the 1930s when they finally got electricity, but for those living in the cities, the radio altered lives and brought a new magic of sound into 2 or 3 million households in the 1920s. This early radio was battery powered and had an antenna wire (seen at left) that connected to an outside aerial antenna. Still, even with antenna and headset, the reception was probably poor. (Bettmann/CORBIS)

very practical ramifications, influencing decisions in everything from business matters to whether or not to wear a coat to work. But in a broader sense, it made all Americans citizens of the world. The news of the end of World War I in 1918, the attack on Pearl Harbor in 1941, and the walk on the moon in 1969 united millions of people worldwide and made them participants in the events. The new communications technology and instant news, symbolized by the wireless and its role in spreading the word about the sinking of the *Titanic*, made twentieth-century Americans very different from those who lived before them.

**Reflecting on the Past** The communication revolution has continued with CNN, e-mail, and the Internet. Can you imagine what life was like before the telegraph, the telephone, and the wireless, let alone e-mail? How has rapid communication and instant news changed the way people live? Has it made your life better or worse than the lives of your great grandparents?

Wireless-telegraphy room of an Atlantic liner, 1912.
(The Granger Collection, New York)

In 1914, Ford startled the country by increasing the minimum pay of the Ford assembly-line worker to $5 a day (almost twice the national average pay for factory workers). Ford was not a humanitarian. He wanted a dependable workforce and knew that skilled workers were less likely to quit if they were well paid. Ford was one of the first to appreciate that workers were also consumers who might buy Model Ts. But despite the high wages, work on the assembly line was numbing, and when the line closed down, workers were released without compensation.

The Model T, which cost $600 in 1912, was reduced gradually in price until it sold for only $290 in 1924. The "Tin Lizzie" was light and easily repaired. Some owners claimed a pair of pliers and some baling wire would keep it running. Except for adding a self-starter, offering a closed model, and making a few minor face-lifts, Ford kept the Model T in 1927 as he had introduced it in 1909. By that time, its popularity had declined as many people traded up to sleeker, more colorful, and, they thought, more prestigious autos put out by Ford's competitors. Ford's new Model A, introduced in 1927, never had the appeal of the Model T.

## The Exploding Metropolis

The automobile both pushed urban areas out into the countryside and brought industry to the suburbs. The great expansion of suburban population came in the 1920s. Shaker Heights, outside Cleveland, was typical. Two businessmen planned and built the new suburb on the site of a former Shaker community. No blacks were allowed. Curving roads and landscape design created a parklike atmosphere. Between 1919 and 1929, the population grew from 1,700 to over 15,000, and the price of lots multiplied by 10. Other suburbs grew just as rapidly—none more than Beverly Hills, California, whose population soared by 2,485 percent. The biggest land boom of all occurred in Florida, where Miami mushroomed from 30,000 people in 1920 to 75,000 in 1925. A plot in West Palm Beach sold for $800,000 in 1923, and two years later was worth $4 million.

The 1920 census indicated that for the first time more than half the American population lived in "urban areas" of more than 2,500. The census designation of an urban area was a little misleading because a town of 5,000 could still be mainly rural. A more significant concept was the metropolitan area of at least 100,000 people. There were only 52 of these areas in 1900; by 1930, there were 115.

The automobile transformed every city, but the growth was most spectacular in two cities that the car virtually created. Detroit grew from 300,000 in 1900 to 1,837,000 in 1930. Los Angeles, held together by a network of roads, expanded from 114,000 in 1900 to 1,778,000 in 1930.

Cities expanded horizontally in the 1920s, sprawling into the countryside, but city centers grew vertically. A building boom that peaked near the end of the decade created new skylines for most urban centers. The most famous skyscraper of all, the 102-story Empire State Building in New York, was finished in 1931 but was not completely occupied until after World War II.

## A Communications Revolution

Changing communications altered the way Americans lived as well as the way they conducted business. The telephone was first demonstrated in 1876, and by

1899, more than a million phones were in operation. During the 1920s, the number of homes with phones increased from 9 to 13 million. Still, by the end of the decade, more than half of American homes lacked telephones.

Even more than the telephone, the radio symbolized the changes of the 1920s. The first station began commercial broadcasting in the summer of 1920, and that fall, election returns were broadcast for the first time. The next year a Newark station transmitted the World Series, beginning a process that would transform American sports. In 1922, a radio station in New York broadcast the first commercial.

Much early broadcasting consisted of classical music, but soon there was news analysis and coverage of important events. Serials and situation comedies made radio a national medium, with millions tuning in to the same program. The record industry grew just as rapidly. By the end of the decade, people everywhere were humming the same popular songs, while actors and announcers became celebrities.

Even more dramatic was the phenomenon of the movies. Forty million viewers a week went to the movies in 1922, and by 1929 that total exceeded 100 million. To countless Americans, the stars were more famous and important than most government officials. Motion pictures before the war had attracted mostly the working class, but now they seemed to appeal to everyone. Many parents feared that they would dictate ideas about sex and life. One young college woman admitted that movies taught her how to smoke, and in some movies "there were some lovely scenes which just got me all hot 'n' bothered."

Sports heroes like Babe Ruth and Jack Dempsey were as famous as the movie stars. The great spectator sports of the decade owed much to the increase of leisure time and to the automobile, the radio, and the mass-circulation newspaper. Thousands drove to college towns to watch football; millions listened for scores or read about the results the next day. The popularity of sports, like the movies and radio, was a product of technology.

The year 1927 seemed to mark the beginning of the new age of mechanization and progress. Henry Ford produced his 15 millionth car and introduced the Model A. Radio-telephone service linked San Francisco and Manila. The first radio network was organized (CBS), and the first sound movie was released (*The Jazz Singer*). The Holland Tunnel, the first underwater vehicular roadway, connected New York and New Jersey, and Charles Lindbergh flew his single-engine plane from New York to Paris and captured the world's imagination. When Americans cheered Lindbergh, they were reaffirming their belief in the American dream and their faith in individual initiative as well as in technology.

## HOPES RAISED, PROMISES DEFERRED

The 1920s was a time when all kinds of hopes seemed realizable. "Don't envy successful salesmen—be one!" one ad screamed. Buy a car. Build a house. Start a career. Invest in land or in stocks. Make a fortune.

Not all Americans, of course, dreamed of making a killing on Wall Street; some merely wished to retain traditional values in a society that seemed to question them. Others wanted a steady job and a little respect. Still others hungered for the new appliances described so alluringly in magazine ads and on the radio. Many discovered, however, that even the most modest hopes lay tantalizingly out of reach.

## Clash of Values

During the 1920s, radio, movies, advertising, and mass-circulation magazines promoted a national, secular culture. But this new culture of consumption, pleasure, upward mobility, and sex clashed with traditional values: hard work, thrift, church, family, home. This was not simply an urban-rural conflict, for many people clinging to old ways had moved into the cities. Still, many Americans feared that familiar ways of life were threatened by new values, scientific breakthroughs, bolshevism, relativism, Freudianism, and biblical criticism. A trial over the teaching of evolutionary ideas in a high school in the little town of Dayton, Tennessee, symbolized (even as it exaggerated) the clash of traditional versus modern, city versus country.

The scientific community and most educated people had long accepted Darwinian evolution. But many evangelical Protestants saw the Bible as literal truth and the dramatic changes of the 1920s as a major spiritual crisis. The theory of evolution epitomized the challenge to traditional faith, and in some states its teaching was outlawed. John Scopes, a young biology teacher, broke the law, and Tennessee put him on trial. The famous lawyer Clarence Darrow defended Scopes, while the World Christian Fundamentalist Association hired former presidential candidate and Secretary of State William Jennings Bryan to assist the prosecution. Bryan was old and tired (he died only a few days after the trial), but he was deeply religious and still eloquent. In cross-examination, Darrow reduced Bryan's statements to intellectual rubble. Nevertheless, the jury declared Scopes guilty.

The national press covered the trial and upheld science and academic freedom. The journalist H. L. Mencken had a field day poking fun at Bryan and the fundamentalists. "Heave an egg out a Pullman window," Mencken wrote, "and you will hit a Fundamentalist almost anywhere in the United States today . . . . They are everywhere where learning is too heavy a burden for mortal minds to carry."

## Religious Fundamentalism

Some, including Mencken, thought that the Scopes trial ended "the fundamentalist menace." Yet fundamentalism continued to survive in an urbanizing, modernizing, and sophisticated world. All fundamentalists believed in the literal interpretation and infallibility of the Bible. They rejected secularism, liberal theology, pluralism, the Social Gospel, and any sense that earthly reform could lead to perfection. They also had an unshakable belief in what they believed was the truth.

Throughout the 1920s and the 1930s, attendance at Christian colleges and the circulation of fundamentalist publications increased dramatically. Evangelical preachers reached large audiences, sometimes using flamboyant performances. One of the most popular of the ministers was Billy Sunday, a former baseball player who jumped about the stage as he pitched his brand of Christianity. Another popular preacher was Aimee Semple McPherson, a glamorous faith healer who became famous for chasing the devil out of her auditorium with a pitchfork.

John Steuart Curry was one of the regionalist painters in the 1920s who found inspiration in the American heartland. In *Baptism in Kansas*, he depicts a religious ritual that underscores the persistence of faith and the importance of religion in creating a sense of community. (John Steuart Curry, "Baptism in Kansas," 1928. Collection of Whitney Museum of American Art, Gift of Gertrude Vanderbilt Whitney.)

Radio extended the reach of the fundamentalist preachers even more dramatically. McPherson was the first woman to hold a radio license, and she had the second most popular radio show in Los Angeles in the late 1920s. For many, the period between the wars was an age of secular humanism, technological marvels, and modernism in all fields, but for many others, it was a time when fundamentalist religion and old-fashioned values prospered.

## Immigration and Migration

Immigrants and anyone else "un-American" seemed to threaten old ways. The fear and intolerance of the war years and the period right after the war resulted in major restrictive legislation.

The first strongly restrictive immigration law passed in 1917 over Wilson's veto. It required a literacy test for the first time and barred radicals. This did not stop the more than 1 million immigrants who poured into the country in 1920 and 1921.

In 1921 and again in 1924, Congress imposed quotas on European immigration. The tighter 1924 quota allowed only 2 percent of those from each country who were in the United States in 1890—before the great flood of newcomers had begun arriving from southern and eastern Europe. All immigrants from Asia were banned. In 1927, a ceiling of 150,000 European immigrants a year was set; more than 60 percent could come from Great Britain and Germany, but fewer than 4 percent were allowed from Italy.

Ethnicity increasingly became a factor in political alignments. Republican-sponsored immigration laws drove Jews, Italians, and Poles to the Democrats. By 1924, the Democratic party was so evenly divided between northern urban Catholics and southern rural Protestants that its convention voted—by a very small margin—to condemn the Klan.

The immigration acts of 1921, 1924, and 1927 cut off the streams of cheap labor that had provided muscle for industrialization since the early nineteenth century. At the same time, by exempting Western Hemisphere immigrants, the new laws opened the country to Mexicans eager to work in the fields and farms of California and the Southwest. Mexicans soon became the country's largest first-generation immigrant group. Mexican farm workers often lived in primitive camps, where conditions were unsanitary and health care nonexistent. "When they have finished harvesting my crops I will kick them out on the country road," one employer announced.

Mexicans also migrated to industrial cities, recruited by northern companies that paid for their transportation. During the 1920s, El Paso became more than half Mexican. The Mexican population in California reached 368,000 in 1929, and Los Angeles was about 20 percent Mexican. Like African Americans, the Mexicans found opportunity by migrating, but they did not escape prejudice or hardship.

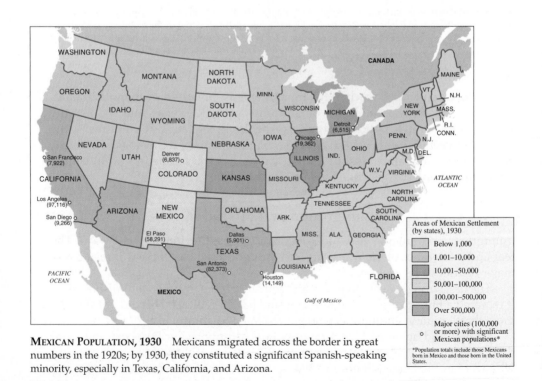

**MEXICAN POPULATION, 1930**   Mexicans migrated across the border in great numbers in the 1920s; by 1930, they constituted a significant Spanish-speaking minority, especially in Texas, California, and Arizona.

African Americans migrated north in great numbers from 1915 to 1920. The black population of Chicago increased from 44,000 in 1910 to 234,000 by 1930. Reduced European immigration and continuing industrial growth caused many northern companies to recruit southern blacks. Trains in small southern depots sometimes picked up hundreds of blacks in a single day. "I don't care where so long as I go where a man is a man," wrote one. It was the young and mostly unskilled who tended to move.

African Americans unquestionably improved their lives by moving north. But for most, like the Parkers, dreams were only partly fulfilled. Most crowded into segregated housing and faced hatred. "Black men stay South," the *Chicago Tribune* advised, and offered to pay the transportation for any who would return.

Often the young black men moved first, and only later brought their wives and children, putting great pressure on many black families. Some young men, like John Parker, restrained their anger, but others, like Richard Wright's fictional Bigger Thomas portrayed movingly in *Native Son* (1940), struck out violently against white society. The concentration of African Americans in northern industrial cities created black ghettos and increased the racial tension that sometimes flared into violence.

One of the worst race riots took place in Chicago in 1919. The riot began on a hot July day when a black youth drowned in a white swimming area—hit by stones, blacks said, but the police refused to arrest any white men. When African Americans attacked the police, a four-day riot was on. Several dozen were killed, and hundreds were wounded. The tension between the races did not die when the riot was over. Nor were other cities exempt.

The wave of violence and racism angered and disillusioned W. E. B. Du Bois, who had urged African Americans to support the American cause during the war. In an angry editorial for *The Crisis*, he called on blacks to "fight a sterner, longer, more unbending battle against the forces of hell in our own land. We return. We return from fighting. We return fighting. Make way for Democracy; we saved it in France, and by the Great Jehovah, we will save it in the United States of America, or know the reason why."

## Marcus Garvey: Black Messiah

Du Bois was not the only postwar militant black leader. Marcus Garvey, a flamboyant Jamaican who arrived in New York at the age of 29, fed black pride. Although he never abandoned Booker T. Washington's self-help philosophy, Garvey thoroughly transformed it. Washington focused on economic betterment; Garvey saw self-help as political empowerment by which African peoples would reclaim their homelands.

In Jamaica, Garvey had founded the Universal Negro Improvement Association. By 1919, he had established 30 branches in the United States and the Caribbean. He also set up a newspaper, the Black Cross Nurses, and chains of stores and restaurants. His biggest project was the Black Star Line, a steamship company that was to be owned and operated by African Americans. Advocating blacks' return to Africa, he declared himself the "provisional president of Africa."

He won converts, mostly among lower-middle-class blacks, through the force of his oratory and powerful personality, but especially through his message of

Marcus Garvey (second from the right),
shown dressed in his favorite uniform,
became a hero for many black
Americans. (Liaison/Getty Images)

black pride. "Up you mighty race, you can accomplish what you will," Garvey
thundered. Thousands of blacks cheered his Universal African Legions, marching in blue and red uniforms and waving a red-black-green flag. Thousands invested in the Black Star Line—which soon collapsed, in part because white
entrepreneurs sold Garvey inferior ships. Garvey was arrested for using the
mails to defraud shareholders and sentenced to five years in prison. Coolidge
commuted the sentence. Ordered deported as an undesirable alien, Garvey left
America in 1927. Despite his failures, he convinced thousands of black Americans, especially the poor and discouraged, that they could unite and feel pride
in their heritage.

## The Harlem Renaissance and the Lost Generation

After the war, a group of black writers, artists, and intellectuals who settled in
Harlem, an uptown neighborhood in New York City, led a movement related in
some ways to Garvey's black nationalism crusade and in the end more important.
They studied anthropology, art, history, and music, and in their novels, poetry,
dance, and music explored the ambivalent role of blacks in America. Like Garvey,
they expressed black pride and sought African and folk roots. Unlike Garvey, they
wanted to be both black and American and had no desire to go back to Africa.

Alain Locke, the first black Rhodes scholar, was the father of the renaissance.
His *The New Negro* (1925) announced the movement to the outside world and outlined black contributions to American culture and civilization. Langston Hughes,
a poet and novelist, wrote bitter but laughing poems, using black vernacular to

describe the pathos and pride of African Americans. In *Weary Blues*, he adapted the rhythms of jazz and the blues.

Jazz was an important force in Harlem in the 1920s, and prosperous whites came to listen to Louis Armstrong, Duke Ellington, and other black musicians. Many brought up in Victorian white America were intrigued by what they saw as Harlem's primitive emotions and erotic atmosphere, as well as its music and illegal sex, drugs, and liquor. Jamaican Claude McKay wrote about the underside of life in Harlem in *Home to Harlem* (1925), one of the most popular "new Negro" novels. McKay portrayed two black men—one, Jake, who finds a life of simple and erotic pleasure in Harlem's cabarets, the other an intellectual unable to make such an easy choice and conscious that "My damned white education has robbed me of . . . primitive vitality."

Many Harlem writers agonized about how to be both black and intellectual. They worried about white patrons who pressured them to conform to the white elite's idea of black authenticity, but they knew that patronage was their only hope to be recognized. Jean Toomer, more self-consciously avant-garde than most other black writers, wrote haunting poems about the difficulty of black identity; in the novel *Cane* (1923), he sketched maladjusted, almost grotesquely alienated characters.

Many African-American writers felt alienated from American society. They tried living in Paris or Greenwich Village, but most felt drawn to Harlem, which in the 1920s was rapidly becoming the center of New York's black population. Over 117,000 whites left during the decade, while over 87,000 blacks moved in. Countee Cullen remarked, "In spite of myself I find that I am activated by a strong sense of race consciousness." So was Zora Neale Hurston, who came to New York to study at Barnard College, earned an advanced degree in anthropology from Columbia University, and used her interest in folklore to write stories of robust and passionate rural blacks. The Harlem writers were read by only a few people, but another generation of young black intellectuals in the 1960s would rediscover it.

Many white intellectuals, writers, and artists also felt estranged from what they saw as the narrow materialism of American life. Some, like F. Scott Fitzgerald, Ernest Hemingway, e. e. cummings, and T. S. Eliot, moved to Europe—where they wrote novels, plays, and poems about America. Like so many American intellectuals in all periods, they had a love-hate relationship with their country.

For many writers, disillusionment began with the war. Hemingway eagerly volunteered to go to Europe as an ambulance driver. But when he was wounded on the Italian front, he reevaluated the meaning of all the slaughter. His novel *The Sun Also Rises* (1926) is the story of the purposeless European wanderings of a group of Americans, as well as the story of Jake Barnes, who was made impotent by a war injury. His "unreasonable wound" symbolized the futility of postwar life.

Fitzgerald, who loved the cafés and parties in Paris, became a celebrity during the 1920s. He epitomized some of the despair of his generation, which had "grown up to find all Gods dead, all wars fought, all faiths in man shaken." His best novel, *The Great Gatsby* (1925), was a critique of the American success myth. But wealth won't buy happiness, and Gatsby's life ends tragically, as so many lives seemed to end in many of the decade's other novels.

It was not necessary to live in France to criticize American society. Sherwood Anderson created a fictional midwestern town in *Winesburg, Ohio* (1919), describing the dull, narrow, warped lives that seemed to provide a metaphor for American culture. Sinclair Lewis, another midwesterner, wrote scathing parodies of middle-class, small-town life in *Main Street* (1920) and *Babbitt* (1922). The "hero" of the latter novel is a salesman from the town of Zenith. He is a "regular guy" who distrusts "red professors," foreign-born people, and anyone from New York. But no one had more fun laughing at the American middle class than Baltimore's H. L. Mencken, whose magazine *The American Mercury* overflowed with his assaults on "the booboisie." Harding's speeches reminded him of "a string of wet sponges, . . . of stale bean soup, of college yells, of dogs barking idiotically through endless nights."

Ironically, while intellectuals despaired over American society and complained that art could not survive in a business-dominated civilization, literature flourished. The 1920s were one of the most creative decades in American literature.

## Women Struggle for Equality

An indelible image of the 1920s is the flapper—a young woman with a short skirt, bobbed hair, and a boyish figure doing the Charleston, smoking, drinking, and being very casual about sex. Fitzgerald's heroines in novels like *This Side of Paradise* (1920) and *The Great Gatsby* (1925) provided role models for young people, and movie stars such as Clara Bow and Gloria Swanson, aggressively seductive on the screen, supplied even more vivid examples of provocative behavior.

Without question, women acquired more sexual freedom in the 1920s. "None of the Victorian mothers had any idea how casually their daughters were accustomed to being kissed," Fitzgerald wrote. However, it is difficult, if not impossible, to know how accustomed those daughters (and their mothers) were to kissing and enjoying other sexual activity. Contraceptives became more readily available, and Margaret Sanger (who had been indicted for sending birth control information through the mail in 1914) organized the first American birth control conference in 1921. Birth control devices and literature, however, were still often illegal.

Family size declined during the decade (from 3.6 children in 1900 to 2.5 in 1930), and young people were apparently more inclined to marry for love than for security. More women expected sexual satisfaction in marriage (nearly 60 percent in one poll) and felt that divorce was the best solution for an unhappy marriage. Nearly 85 percent in another poll approved of sexual intercourse as an expression of love and affection, rather than simply for procreation. But these polls tended to be biased toward urban middle-class attitudes. Despite more freedom for women, the double standard persisted.

Middle-class women lives' were shaped by innovations like electricity, running water, and labor-saving devices. But as standards of cleanliness rose, they spent more time on housework while being bombarded with advertising urging them to make themselves better housekeepers yet still be beautiful. The young adopted new styles quickly, and they also learned to swim, play tennis, and ride bicycles.

More women worked outside the home—22 percent in 1933, compared to 17 percent in 1890. But their share of manufacturing jobs fell from 19 to 16 percent between 1900 and 1930. The greatest expansion of jobs was in white-collar occupations that were being feminized—secretary, bookkeeper, clerk, telephone operator. Although more married women had jobs (an increase of 25 percent during the decade), most held low-paying jobs, and most single women assumed that marriage would end their employment.

For some working women—secretaries and teachers, for example—marriage indeed often led to dismissal. Yet an office was a good place to meet eligible men, and a secretary learned endurance, self-effacement, and obedience—traits that many thought would make her a good wife. Considering these attitudes, it is not surprising that the male-female pay disparity widened. By 1930, women earned only 57 percent of what men were paid.

The image of the flapper in the 1920s promised more freedom and equality for women than they actually achieved. The flapper was young, white, slender, and upper-class, and most women did not fit those categories. Although the proportion of women lawyers and bankers increased slightly, the rate of growth declined. The number of women doctors and scientists dropped.

The promise of prewar feminists and suffrage advocates remained unfulfilled. In some states, women needed their husband's consent in order to hold office, own a business, or sign a contract. Women were usually held responsible for an illegitimate birth, and divorce laws almost always favored men.

Alice Paul, who had led the militant National Woman's Party in 1916, chained herself to the White House fence once again to promote an equal rights amendment to the Constitution. The amendment got support in several states, but many women opposed it, fearing that it would cancel the special legislation to protect women in industry. Feminists disagreed in the 1920s on the proper way to promote equality and rights for women, but the political and social climate was not conducive to feminism.

## Rural America in the 1920s

Most farmers did not share in the decade's prosperity. During the war, farmers had responded to worldwide demand and rising commodity prices by investing in land and equipment. Then prices and farm income tumbled. Many farmers could not make payments on their mortgages, and they lost their farms.

The changing nature of farming was part of the problem. Chemical fertilizers and new hybrid seeds increased yields. Farming became more mechanized and efficient. Production swelled just as worldwide demand for American farm products tumbled.

Few farmers could afford the products of the new technology. Although many middle-class urban families were more prosperous than ever before, only one farm family in ten had electricity in the 1920s. The lot of the farm wife had not changed for centuries.

Farmers tried to act collectively to solve their problems, as they had in the nineteenth century. Most of their effort went into passing the McNary-Haugen Farm Relief Bill, which provided for government support for key agricultural products. The government would buy crops at a "fair exchange value" and then market the excess on the world market at a lower price. The bill passed Congress twice, in 1927 and 1928, and twice was vetoed by President Coolidge. But farm organizations across the country learned how to cooperate and influence Congress, with important future ramifications.

Farmers were particularly vulnerable to the power of nature, and that became apparent in the spring of 1927, when the worst flood in the nation's history devastated the Mississippi River valley. Despite efforts to improve the levies, over 27,000 square miles of land were flooded. Nearly a million people were made homeless. There was over a billion dollars in property damage, and 246 people died. The black sharecroppers, who often lived near the river, bore the brunt of the disaster. President Coolidge appointed Secretary of Commerce Herbert Hoover to coordinate flood relief. Hoover, who believed in voluntary efforts, enlisted the help of the Red Cross, the American Legion, and other groups, but the total relief efforts remained inadequate. The next year, Coolidge signed a flood control bill that for the first time committed the federal government to build levies to control the Mississippi River. But the debate continued about the best way to control nature and how to solve the farmers' problems.

## The Workers' Share of Prosperity

Hundreds of thousands of workers improved their standard of living in the 1920s, yet inequality grew. Between 1923 and 1929, real wages increased 21 percent, but corporate dividends went up by nearly two-thirds. The richest 5 percent of the population increased their share of the wealth from a quarter to a third, and the wealthiest 1 percent controlled a whopping 19 percent of all income. Workers did not profit from the increased production they helped generate.

Even among workers, there was great disparity. For example, those employed on auto assembly lines saw their wages go up and their hours go down. Yet the majority of American working-class families could not move much beyond subsistence. One study suggested that a family needed between $2,000 and $2,400 in 1924 to maintain an "American standard of living." That year, 16 million families earned under $2,000.

Although some workers prospered in the 1920s, organized labor did not. Union membership dropped from about 5 million in 1921 to under 3.5 million in 1929. The National Manufacturing Association carried on a vigorous campaign to restore the open shop, while many businesses added pensions and company unions to lure employees away from unions.

The conservative American Federation of Labor suffered during the 1920s, but so did the more aggressive unions like the United Mine Workers, led by the bombastic John L. Lewis. The union's attempt to organize West Virginia mines had led to violent clashes with imported guards. But internal strife weakened the union, and Lewis had to accept wage reductions in 1927.

Organized labor, like so many other groups, struggled desperately to share in the prosperity of the 1920s. But affluence and a share of the American dream were beyond the reach of most workers.

## THE BUSINESS OF POLITICS

"Among the nations of the earth today America stands for one idea: *Business*," a popular writer announced in 1921. Bruce Barton, the head of the largest advertising firm in the country, published one of the most popular nonfiction books of the decade. In *The Man Nobody Knows* (1925), he depicted Christ as "the founder of modern business." He took 12 men from the bottom of society and forged them into a successful organization.

Business, especially big business, prospered in the 1920s. The government reduced regulation, lowered taxes, and helped aid business expansion at home and abroad. Business and politics, always intertwined, became especially close during the decade. Wealthy financiers played important roles in formulating government policy. Even more significant, a new kind of businessman was elected president in 1928. Herbert Hoover, international engineer and efficiency expert, was the very symbol of modern business techniques and practices.

## Harding and Coolidge

The Republicans, almost assured of victory in 1920 because of bitter reaction against Woodrow Wilson, might have preferred nominating their old standard-bearer, Theodore Roosevelt, but he had died the year before. Warren G. Harding, a former Ohio newspaper editor, captured the nomination after meeting late at night with some of the party's most powerful men in a Chicago hotel room. What was promised in this legendary "smoke-filled room," no one ever discovered. To balance the ticket, the Republicans chose for vice president Calvin Coolidge of police-strike fame. Meanwhile, after 44 roll calls, the Democrats nominated Governor James Cox of Ohio and picked Franklin D. Roosevelt, the assistant secretary of the Navy, for vice president.

Harding won in a landslide. His 60.4 percent of the vote was the widest margin yet-recorded in a presidential election. More significant, fewer than 50 percent of the eligible voters went to the polls. Newly enfranchised women, especially in working-class neighborhoods, avoided the voting booths. So did large numbers of men. Many people did not care who was president.

In contrast to the reform-minded presidents Roosevelt and Wilson, Harding reflected the conservatism of the 1920s. A visitor to the White House found Harding and his cohorts discussing the problems of the day, with "the air heavy with tobacco smoke, trays with bottles containing every imaginable brand of whiskey." A few blocks away, Harry Daugherty, Harding's attorney general and longtime associate, did a brisk business in selling favors, taking bribes, and organizing illegal schemes.

Harding was not personally corrupt, and the nation's leading businessmen approved of his high-tariff, low-tax policies. Nor did Harding spend all his time drinking with his pals. He called a conference on disarmament and another on unemployment. Harding once remarked that he could never be considered a great president, but he thought perhaps he might be "one of the best loved." When he died suddenly in August 1923, the American people genuinely mourned.

Only after Coolidge became president did the full extent of the Harding scandals come out. A Senate committee discovered that Secretary of the Interior Albert Fall had illegally leased government-owned oil reserves in the Teapot Dome section of Wyoming to businessmen for over $300,000 in bribes. Illegal activities were turned up in the Veterans Administration and elsewhere. Harding's attorney general resigned in disgrace, the secretary of the Navy barely avoided prison, two of Harding's advisers committed suicide, and Fall went to jail.

Warren G. Harding (left) and Calvin Coolidge were immensely popular in the 1920s, but later historians have criticized them and rated them among the worst of American presidents. (Corbis/UPI)

Coolidge was dour, taciturn—and honest. Born in a little town in Vermont, he was sworn in as president by his father, a justice of the peace, whom he was visiting when news of Harding's death came. To many, Coolidge represented old-fashioned values, simple religious faith, and personal integrity. But Coolidge felt ill at ease posing for photographers holding a pitchfork, and much more comfortable around corporate executives.

Coolidge ran for reelection in 1924 with the financier Charles Dawes as his running mate. There was little question that he would win. The Democrats were so equally divided between northern urban Catholics and southern rural Protestants that it took 103 ballots to nominate John W. Davis, an affable corporate lawyer.

Dissidents, mostly representing the farmers and laborers dissatisfied with both nominees, formed a new Progressive party. They adopted the name, but little else, from Theodore Roosevelt's party of 1912. Nominating Robert La Follette for president, their platform called for government ownership of railroads and ratification of a child labor amendment. La Follette attacked the "control of government and industry by private monopoly." He received nearly 5 million votes, only 3.5 million short of Davis's total. But Coolidge and prosperity won easily.

Like Harding, Coolidge was immensely popular. Symbolizing his administration was his wealthy secretary of the treasury, Andrew Mellon. In 1922, Congress, with Mellon's endorsement, repealed the wartime excess profits tax. Although it raised some taxes slightly, it exempted most families from any tax by giving everyone a $2,500 exemption, plus $400 for each dependent. In 1926, the rate was lowered to 5 percent and the maximum surtax to 40 percent. Only families with incomes above $3,500 paid any income tax. In 1928, Congress slashed taxes further, removed most excise taxes, and lowered the corporate tax rate. The 200 largest corporations increased their assets during the decade from $43 to $81 billion.

"The chief business of the American people is business," Coolidge said. His idea of the proper role of the federal government was to have as little as possible to do with the functioning of business and the lives of the people. "No other president in my time slept so much," a White House usher remembered. But most Americans approved of their president.

## Herbert Hoover

One bright light in the lackluster Harding and Coolidge administrations was Secretary of Commerce Herbert Hoover. He had made a fortune as a mining engineer before 1914 and earned the reputation of a great humanitarian during the war. Many Progressives supported him as a presidential candidate in 1920.

Hoover was a dynamo. He expanded his department to regulate the airlines, radio, and other new industries. Through the Bureau of Standards, Hoover standardized the size of almost everything manufactured in the United States. He supported zoning codes, the eight-hour day in major industries, better nutrition for children, and conservation. He pushed through the Pollution Act of 1924, the first attempt to control coastal oil pollution.

While secretary of commerce, Hoover used the authority of the federal government to regulate, stimulate, and promote, but he believed first of all in American free enterprise and local volunteer action. In 1921, he convinced Harding of the need to do something about unemployment during the postwar recession. The president's conference on unemployment, convened in September 1921, marked the first time the national government had admitted any responsibility to the unemployed. The conference (the first of many that Hoover was to organize) unleashed a flood of publicity and expert advice. The conference report urged state and local governments and businesses to cooperate voluntarily to solve the problem. The primary responsibility of the federal government, Hoover believed, was to educate and promote, but not to initiate reform.

## Foreign Policy in the 1920s

The 1920s are often called a time of isolation. But the United States remained involved—indeed, increased its involvement—in international affairs. Although the United States never joined the League of Nations, and a few staunch isolationists blocked membership in the World Court, the United States cooperated with many League agencies. And it took the lead in trying to reduce naval armaments and to solve the problems of international finance caused in part by the war.

The seven-fold expansion of American corporate investments overseas turned the United States from a debtor to a creditor nation. Yet the United States took up its role of international power reluctantly and with a number of contradictory and disastrous results.

"We seek no part in directing the destiny of the world," Harding announced in his inaugural address, but he discovered that international problems would not go away. One that required immediate attention was the naval arms race, for which purpose the United States convened the Washington Conference on Naval Disarmament, the first international disarmament conference, in November 1921.

Secretary of State Charles Evans Hughes startled the conference by proposing a 10-year "holiday" on warship construction and offering to sink or scrap 845,000 tons of American ships, including 30 battleships. He urged Britain and Japan to do the same. The delegates cheered Hughes's speech, and they sank more ships than all their admirals had managed to do in a century. The conference ultimately fixed the tonnage of capital ships at a ratio of the United States and Great Britain,

5; Japan, 3; and France and Italy, 1.67. Japan agreed only reluctantly, after the United States promised not to fortify its Pacific islands.

The Washington Conference has often been criticized in the light of Pearl Harbor, but in 1921 it was appropriately hailed as the first time in history that the major nations of the world had agreed to disarm. The conference neither caused nor averted World War II. But it was a creative beginning to reducing tensions and to meeting the challenges of the modern arms race.

American foreign policy in the 1920s tried to reduce the risk of international conflict, resist revolution, and make the world safe for trade and investment. Nobody in the Republican administrations even suggested that the United States remain isolated from Latin America. American diplomats supported an open door to trade in China, but in Latin America, the United States had always assumed a special and distinct role. Throughout the decade, American investment increased in the Western Hemisphere. The United States bought nearly 60 percent of Latin America's exports and sold the region nearly 50 percent of its imports.

By the end of the decade, the United States controlled the financial affairs of 10 Latin American nations. The Dominican Republic remained a virtual protectorate of the United States until 1941. First the Marines—and later the Nicaraguan troops they trained—had a difficult time containing a guerrilla band led by charismatic Augusto Sandino. The Sandinistas, supported by the great majority of peasants, came out of the hills to attack the politicians and their American supporters. "Today we are hated and despised," an American coffee planter announced in 1931. In 1934, Sandino was murdered by the followers of General Anastasio Somoza, a ruthless leader supported by the United States. For more than 40 years, Somoza and his two sons would rule Nicaragua.

Mexico frightened American businessmen in the mid-1920s by beginning to nationalize foreign holdings in oil and mineral rights. Fearing that further military activity would "injure American interests," businessmen and bankers urged Coolidge to negotiate. Coolidge did, and his ambassador's conciliatory attitude led to agreements protecting American investments.

The United States' policy of promoting peace and trade was not always consistent, especially in Europe. The United States was owed more than $10 billion in war loans, three-fourths of it by Britain and France. Both countries, mired in economic problems, suggested that the United States forgive the debts, arguing that they had paid for the war in lives and property destroyed. But the United States, although adjusting the interest and the payment schedule, refused. "They hired the money, didn't they?" Coolidge supposedly asked.

International debt was not the same as money borrowed at the neighborhood bank. The only way European nations could repay the United States was by exports, but Congress supported high tariffs. In 1930, the Hawley-Smoot Tariff raised rates even further, despite the protests of many economists. American policy of high tariffs (a counterproductive policy for a creditor nation) caused retaliation and restrictions on American trade, which American corporations were trying to increase.

Europeans' inability to export to the United States and repay their loans was intertwined with the reparation agreement made with Germany. The postwar German economy was beset by inflation and its industrial plant throttled by the peace treaty. By 1921, Germany was defaulting on reparations payments. Hoping to maintain international stability, the United States introduced the Dawes Plan, under which the German debt would be spread over a longer period while American bankers and the American government lent Germany hundreds of millions of dollars. This enabled Germany to pay reparations to Britain and France so that they could continue debt repayments to the United States.

Although the United States had displaced Great Britain as the dominant force in international finance, it was a reluctant and inconsistent world leader. The United States stayed out of the League of Nations and hesitated to join multinational agreements. But the Kellogg-Briand pact seemed irresistible. French foreign minister Aristide Briand suggested a Franco-American pact, to commemorate long years of friendship between the two countries, but Secretary of State Frank B. Kellogg in 1928 expanded the idea to a multinational treaty outlawing war. Fourteen nations initially signed the treaty and 62 eventually did, but the only power behind it was moral force, and moral force would not prevent World War II.

## The Survival of Progressivism

The decade of the 1920s saw a reaction against reform, but progressivism did not simply die. Progressives interested in efficiency and order were perhaps happier during the 1920s than those who tried to promote social justice, but the fights against poverty and for better housing persisted, as did campaigns to protect children.

The greatest success of the social justice movement was the 1921 Sheppard-Towner Maternity Act, one of the first pieces of federal social welfare legislation and the product of long progressive agitation. The bill, controversial from the beginning, called for a million dollars a year to assist states in providing medical aid, consultation centers, and visiting nurses to teach expectant mothers how to care for themselves and their babies. The American Medical Association attacked it as socialism and the opponents of woman suffrage argued that it was supported by extreme feminists and Communists.

But the bill passed Congress and was signed by President Harding in 1921. The appropriation for the bill was only for six years, and the opposition, still trembling at a feminist-Socialist-Communist plot, got it repealed in 1929. Yet the Sheppard-Towner Act, promoted and fought for by a group of progressive women, indicated that concern for social justice was not dead in the age of Harding and Coolidge.

## Temperance Triumphant

By 1918, over three-fourths of Americans lived in dry states or counties, but the war allowed anti-saloon advocates to link prohibition and patriotism. At first, beer manufacturers supported limited prohibition, but in the end, patriotic fervor prohibited the sale of all alcoholic beverages. "We have German enemies across the water," one prohibitionist announced, "We have German enemies in this country too. And the worst of all our German enemies, the most treacherous, the most menacing are Pabst, Schlitz, Blatz and Miller."

The Volstead Act, passed in 1919, banned the brewing and selling of beverages containing more than 0.5 percent alcohol. The Eighteenth Amendment was ratified in June 1919, but the country had been effectively dry since 1917. A social worker predicted that the Eighteenth Amendment would reduce poverty, nearly wipe out prostitution and crime, improve labor, and "substantially increase our national resources by setting free vast suppressed human potentialities."

The prohibition experiment probably did reduce the total consumption of alcohol in the country, especially in rural areas and urban working-class neighborhoods. Fewer arrests for drunkenness were made, and deaths from alcoholism declined. But prohibition showed the difficulty of using law to promote moral reform. Most people who wanted to drink during the "noble experiment" found a way. Speakeasies replaced saloons, and people consumed many strange and dangerous homemade concoctions. Bartenders invented the cocktail to disguise the poor quality of liquor, and middle- and upper-class women began to drink in public for the first time.

Prohibition also created great bootlegging rings, in many cities tied to organized crime. Chicago's Al Capone was the most famous underworld figure whose power and wealth were based on the sale of illegal alcohol. His organization alone supposedly grossed over $60 million in 1927. Many prohibition supporters slowly came to favor repeal, some because it reduced the power of the states, others because it stimulated too much illegal activity and it did not seem worth the costs.

## The Election of 1928

On August 2, 1927, President Coolidge announced, "I do not choose to run for President in 1928." Hoover immediately became the logical Republican candidate, and he easily got the nomination. Few doubted that the prospering country would elect him. The Democrats nominated Alfred Smith, the colorful, "wet," and Catholic governor of New York who seemed to contrast sharply with Hoover. Anti-Catholicism became a major component of the campaign. But the two candidates differed little. Both were self-made men, and both were progressives. Both sought women voters, favored organized labor, defended capitalism, and were advised by millionaires and corporate executives.

Hoover won in a landslide, receiving 444 electoral votes to Smith's 76. But the campaign revitalized the Democratic party. Smith polled nearly twice as many votes as Davis had in 1924, and for the first time Democrats carried the 12 largest cities.

## Stock Market Crash

Hoover had only six months to apply his progressive, efficient methods to running the country. In the fall of 1929, the seemingly endless prosperity suddenly fizzled.

In 1928 and 1929, rampant speculation made the stock market boom. Money could be made everywhere: in real estate, business ventures, and especially the stock market. "Everybody ought to be Rich," Al Smith's campaign manager proclaimed in an article in the *Ladies' Home Journal* early in 1929. But only a small percentage of the American people invested in the stock market. A large number got into the game in the late 1920s because it seemed a safe and sure way to make money. The *New York Times* index of 25 industrial stocks reached 100 in 1924,

# Timeline

| | | | |
|---|---|---|---|
| **1900–1930** | Electricity powers the "second industrial revolution" | **1924** | Coolidge reelected president |
| | | | Peak of Ku Klux Klan activity |
| **1917** | Race riot in East St. Louis, Illinois | | Immigration Quota Law |
| **1918** | World War I ends | **1925** | Scopes trial in Dayton, Tennessee |
| **1919** | Treaty of Versailles | | F. Scott Fitzgerald, *The Great Gatsby* |
| | Strikes in Seattle, Boston, and elsewhere | | Bruce Barton, *The Man Nobody Knows* |
| | Red Scare and Palmer raids | | Alain Locke, *The New Negro* |
| | Race riots in Chicago and other cities | | Claude McKay, *Home to Harlem* |
| | Marcus Garvey's Universal Negro Improvement Association spreads | | Five million enameled bathroom fixtures produced |
| **1920** | Warren Harding elected president | **1926** | Ernest Hemingway, *The Sun Also Rises* |
| | Women vote in national elections | **1927** | National Origins Act |
| | First commercial radio broadcast | | McNary-Haugen Farm Relief Bill |
| | Sacco and Vanzetti arrested | | Sacco and Vanzetti executed |
| | Sinclair Lewis, *Main Street* | | Lindbergh flies solo, New York to Paris |
| **1921** | Immigration Quota Law | | First talking movie, *The Jazz Singer* |
| | Disarmament Conference | | Henry Ford produces 15 millionth car |
| | First birth control conference | **1928** | Herbert Hoover elected president |
| | Sheppard-Towner Maternity Act | | Kellogg-Briand Treaty |
| **1921–1922** | Postwar depression | | Stock market soars |
| **1922** | Fordney-McCumber Tariff | **1929** | 27 million registered cars in country |
| | Sinclair Lewis, *Babbitt* | | 10 million households own radios |
| **1923** | Harding dies | | 100 million people attend movies |
| | Calvin Coolidge becomes president | | Stock market crash |
| | Teapot Dome scandal | | |

moved up to 181 in 1925, dropped a bit in 1926, and rose again to 245 by the end of 1927.

Then the orgy started. During 1928, the market zoomed to 331. Many investors and speculators began to buy on margin (borrowing to invest). Money went into the market that would ordinarily have gone into houses, cars, and other goods. Yet even at the peak, probably only about 1.5 million Americans owned stock.

In early September 1929, the *New York Times* index peaked at 452 and then began to drift downward. On October 23, the market lost 31 points. The next day ("Black Thursday"), it first seemed that everyone was trying to sell, but at the end of the day, the panic appeared over. It was not. By mid-November, the market had plummeted to 224, about half what it had been two months before—a loss on paper of over $26 billion. Still, a month later, some businessmen got back into the market, thinking that it had reached its low point. But it continued to go down. Tens of thousands of investors lost everything. Those who had bought on margin had to keep coming up with money to pay off their loans as the value of their holdings fell. There was panic and despair, but the legendary stories of executives jumping out of windows were grossly exaggerated.

❦ ❦ ❦ ❦

# CONCLUSION
## A New Era of Prosperity and Problems

The stock market crash ended the decade of prosperity. The crash did not cause the depression, but the stock market debacle revealed the weakness of the economy. The fruits of economic expansion had been unevenly distributed. African-American families, like the Parkers, did not share much of the affluence created during the decade. Many other Americans, including many workers and farmers, could not afford to buy the autos, refrigerators, and other products pouring from American factories. Prosperity had been built on a shaky foundation. When that foundation crumbled in 1929, the nation slid into a major depression.

Looking back from the vantage point of the 1930s or later, the 1920s seemed a golden era—an age of flappers, bootleg gin, constant parties, literary masterpieces, sports heroes, and easy wealth. The truth is much more complicated. More than most decades, the 1920s was a time of paradox and contradictions.

The 1920s was a time of prosperity, yet a great many people, including farmers, blacks, and other ordinary Americans, did not prosper. It was a time of modernization, but only about 10 percent of rural families had electricity. It was a time when women achieved more sexual freedom, but the feminist movement declined. It was a time of prohibition, but many Americans increased their consumption of alcohol. It was a time of reaction against reform, yet progressivism survived. It was a time when intellectuals felt disillusioned with America, yet it was one of the most creative and innovative periods for American writers. It was a time of flamboyant heroes, yet the American people elected the lackluster Harding and Coolidge as their presidents. It was a time of progress, when almost every year saw a new technological breakthrough, but it was also a decade of hate and intolerance. The complex and contradictory legacy of the 1920s continued to fascinate and to influence Americans in the 1930s and after.

## Discovering U.S. History Online

*Automotive History*   http://mel.lib.mi.us/business/autos-history.html
This site, from the Michigan Electronic Library, has several links to sites about automotive history in America.

*National Arts & Crafts Archives*   http://arts-crafts.com/archive/archive.shtml
This site serves as a guide to materials on the arts & crafts movement, which lasted roughly from 1890 to 1929.

*Harlem 1900–1940: An African-American Community*   http://www.si.umich.edu./CHICO/Harlem
The New York Public Library's Schomburg Center for Research in Black Culture hosts this site, which includes a database, a timeline, and an exhibit.

*Photographs from the Golden Age of Jazz*   http://memory.loc/gov/ammem/wghtml/wghome.html
The Music Division of the Library of Congress offers numerous images, audio elements, and scanned articles from the 1940s.

*Negro League Baseball*   http://www.negroleaguebaseball.com/
Essays about desegregation, baseball, and Jim Crow, as well as images of teams and players, constitute much of this site.

*American Temperance and Prohibition*   http://www.cohms.ohio-state.edu/history/projects/prohibition/
This site looks at the temperance movement over time and contains many informative links.

*Flapper Culture & Style*   http://www.geocities.com/flapper_culture/
This site contains many links to information about the popular culture of the 1920s with special reference to the flapper.

## Fiction and Film

Ernest Hemingway's novel *The Sun Also Rises* (1926) is a classic tale of disillusionment and despair in the 1920s; F. Scott Fitzgerald gives a picture of the life of the rich in *The Great Gatsby* (1925); and Claude McKay's novel *Home to Harlem* (1928) is one of the best to come out of the Harlem Renaissance.

*Front Page* (1931) is a movie that depicts the world of corrupt politicians and cynical newspapermen in Chicago during the Roaring Twenties. The 1974 film version of *The Great Gatsby*, starring Robert Redford, is not entirely faithful to the novel, but it still captures some of the opulence and pathos of the very rich in the 1920s.

## Recommended Reading

### Postwar Problems
David M. Chalmers, *Hooded Americanism: The History of the Ku Klux Klan* (1965); Roberta Strauss Feurlicht, *Justice Crucified: The Story of Sacco and Vanzetti* (1977); David J. Goldberg, *Discontented America: The United States in the 1920s* (1998); Kenneth Jackson, *The Ku Klux Klan in the City* (1967); Robert K. Murray, *Red Scare* (1965).

### A Prospering Economy
Lendal Calder, *Financing the American Dream: A Cultural History of Consumer Credit* (1999); Lizabeth Cohen, *Making a New Deal: Industrial Workers in Chicago, 1919–1939* (1990); James K. Flink, *The Car Culture* (1975); Gerald Leinwand, *1927: High Tide of the 1920s* (2001); Tom Lewis, *Empire of the Air: The Men Who Made Radio* (1991); David Nye, *Electrifying America* (1991); Rokand Marchand, *Advertising the American Dream* (1985); Susan Strasser, *Satisfaction Guaranteed: The Making of the American Mass Market* (1989).

### Hopes Raised, Promises Deferred
John M. Barry, *Rising Tide: The Great Mississippi Flood of 1927 and How It Changed America* (1997); William H. Chafe, *The American Woman: Her Changing Social and Political Worlds* (1992); Ellen Chesler, *Woman of Valor: Margaret Sanger and the Birth Control Movement* (1992); Lyle W. Dorsett, *Billy Sunday and the Redemption of Urban America* (1991); Lynn Dumenil, *Modern Temper: American Culture and Society in the 1920s* (1995); Paula Fass, *The Damned and the Beautiful: American Youth in the 1920s* (1977); Alice Kessler-Harris, *Out to Work: A History of Wage Earning Women in America* (1982); John Higham, *Strangers in the Land: Patterns of American Nativism* (1955); Frederick Hoffman, *The Twenties* (1949); Nathan I. Huggins, *Harlem Renaissance* (1971); J. Stanley Lemons, *The Woman Citizen: Social Feminism in*

*the 1920s* (1973); George M. Marsden, *Fundamentalism and American Culture* (1980); Theodore Vincent, *Black Power and the Garvey Movement* (1979).

## The Business of Politics

David Burner, *The Politics of Provincialism* (1967); Warren I. Cohen, *Empire Without Tears* (1987); Robert H. Ferrell, *The Presidency of Calvin Coolidge* (1998); John Kenneth Galbraith, *The Great Crash* (1954); K. Austin Kerr, *Organized For Prohibition* (1985); David Wilson, *The Presidency of Warren G. Harding* (1977); Robert A. Slayton, *Empire Statesman: The Rise and Redemption of Al Smith* (2000); William Appleman Williams, *The Tragedy of American Diplomacy* (1962); Joan Hoff Wilson, *Herbert Hoover: Forgotten Progressive* (1975).

# CHAPTER 24
# The Great Depression and the New Deal

## CHAPTER OUTLINE

### AMERICAN STORIES
**A "Southern Belle" Suffers During the Depression**

Diana Morgan grew up in a small North Carolina town, the daughter of a prosperous cotton merchant. She lived the life of a "southern belle," oblivious to national problems. But the Great Depression changed that. She came home from college one Christmas to discover that the telephone had been disconnected. Her world suddenly fell apart. Her father's business had failed, her family didn't have a cook or a cleaning woman anymore, and their house was being sold for back taxes. Sometimes the little things were the hardest. Out-of-town friends would come, and there would be no ice because her family did not own an electric refrigerator and could not afford ice. "There were those frantic arrangements of running out to the drugstore to get Coca-Cola with crushed ice, and there'd be this embarrassing delay, and I can remember how hot my face was."

Like many Americans, Diana Morgan and her family blamed themselves for what happened during the Great Depression. Americans had been taught to believe that if they worked hard, saved their money, and lived upright and moral lives, they could succeed. Success was an individual matter for Americans. When so many failed during the Depression, they blamed themselves, not society or larger forces. Shame and guilt affected people at all levels. The businessman who lost his business, the farmer who watched his farm being sold at auction, the worker who was suddenly unemployed and felt his manhood stripped away because he could not provide for his family were all devastated by the Depression.

Diana Morgan had never intended to get a job; she expected to get married and let her husband support her. But the failure of her father's business forced her to join the growing number of women who worked outside the home in the 1930s. She finally found a position with the Civil Works Administration, a New Deal agency, where at first she had to ask humiliating questions of people applying for assistance to make sure they were destitute. "Do you own a car?" "Does anyone in the family work?" Diana was appalled at the conditions she saw when she traveled around the county to corroborate their stories: dilapidated houses, a dirty, "almost paralyzed-looking mother," a drunken father, malnourished children. She felt helpless. One day, a woman who had formerly cooked for her family came in to apply for help. Each was embarrassed to see the other in changed circumstances.

Diana had to defend the New Deal programs to many of her friends, who accused her of being sentimental and told her that the poor, especially poor blacks, did not know any better. "If you give them coal, they'd put it in the bathtub," was a charge she often heard. But she knew "they didn't have bathtubs to put coal in. So how did anybody know that's what they'd do with coal if they had it?"

Diana Morgan's experience working for a New Deal agency influenced her life and her attitudes; it made her more of a social activist. Her Depression experience gave her a greater appreciation for the struggles of the country's poor and unlucky. Although she prospered in the years after the Depression, the sense of guilt and the fear that the telephone might again be cut off never left her.

❧ ❧ ❧ ❧

The Great Depression changed the lives of all Americans and haunted that generation. An exaggerated need for security, the fear of failure, a nagging sense of guilt, and a real sense that it might happen again divided the Depression generation from everyone born after 1940. Like Diana Morgan, most Americans never forgot those bleak years.

This chapter explores the causes and consequences of the Great Depression. We will look at Herbert Hoover's efforts to combat it and then turn to Franklin Roosevelt, the dominant personality of the 1930s. We will examine the New Deal and Roosevelt's program of relief, recovery, and reform. But we will not ignore the other side of the 1930s, for the decade did not just mean unemployment and New Deal agencies. It was also a time that saw great strides in technology, and innovations in radio, movies, and a time when the automobile affected the lives of most Americans.

## THE GREAT DEPRESSION

There had been recessions and depressions in American history, notably in the 1830s, 1870s, and 1890s, but nothing compared to the devastating economic collapse of the 1930s. The Great Depression was all the more shocking because it came after a decade of unprecedented prosperity, when most experts assumed that the United States was immune to a business-cycle downturn. The Great Depression affected all areas of American life; perhaps most important, it destroyed American confidence in the future.

# The Depression Begins

Few people anticipated the stock market crash in the fall of 1929. But even after the collapse of the stock market, no one expected the entire economy to go into a tailspin. General Electric stock, selling for $396 in 1929, fell to $34 in 1932. By 1932, the median income had plunged to half what it had been in 1929. Construction spending fell to one-sixth of the 1929 level. By 1932, at least one of every four American breadwinners was out of work, and industrial production ground almost to a halt.

Why did the country sink deeper and deeper into depression? After all, only about 2 percent of the population owned stock. The answer is complex, but the prosperity of the 1920s, it appears in retrospect, was superficial. Farmers and coal and textile workers had suffered all through the 1920s from low prices, and the farmers were the first group in the 1930s to plunge into depression. But other economic sectors also lurched out of balance. Two percent of the population received about 28 percent of the national income, but the lower 60 percent got only 24 percent. Businesses increased profits while holding down wages and the prices of raw materials. This pattern depressed consumer purchasing power. Workers, like farmers, did not have the money to buy the goods they helped to produce. There was a relative decline in purchasing power in the late 1920s, unemployment was high in some industries, and the housing and automobile industries were already slackening before the crash.

Well-to-do Americans were speculating a significant portion of their money in the stock market. Their illusion of permanent prosperity helped fire the boom of the 1920s, just as their pessimism and lack of confidence helped exaggerate the depression in 1931 and 1932.

But there were other factors. The stock market crash revealed serious structural weaknesses in the financial and banking systems. The Federal Reserve Board, fearing inflation, tightened credit—the opposite of what it should have done. High American tariffs during the 1920s had reduced trade, and when American investment in Europe slackened in 1928 and 1929, European economies declined. As the European financial situation worsened, the American economy spiraled downward.

The federal government might have prevented the Wall Street crash and the Depression by more careful regulation of business and the stock market. Central planning might have ensured a more equitable distribution of income. But that kind of policy would have taken more foresight than most people had in the 1920s. It certainly would have required different people in power, and it is unlikely that the Democrats, had they been in control, would have altered the government's policies in fundamental ways.

# Hoover and the Great Depression

Initial business and government reactions to the stock market crash were optimistic. "All the evidence indicates that the worst effects of the crash upon unemployment will have been passed during the next sixty days," Herbert Hoover reported, tailoring his upbeat first statements to prevent further panic.

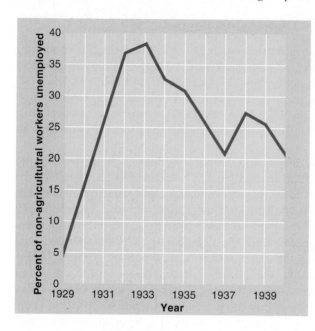

**UNEMPLOYMENT RATE, 1929–1940** Although the unemployment rate declined during the New Deal years, the number still unemployed remained tragically high until World War II brought full employment. (*Source:* U.S. Bureau of the Census)

The Agricultural Marketing Act of 1929 set up a $500 million revolving fund to help farmers organize cooperative marketing associations and to establish minimum prices. But as agricultural prices plummeted and banks foreclosed on farm mortgages, the available funds proved inadequate. The Farm Board was helpless to aid the farmer who could not meet mortgage payments because the price of grain had fallen so rapidly, nor the Arkansas woman who stood weeping as her possessions were sold one by one.

Hoover acted aggressively. More than any president before him, he used the power of the federal government and the office of the president to deal with a crisis that seemed much like earlier cyclic recessions. Hoover called conferences of businessmen and labor leaders. He encouraged mayors and governors to speed up public works projects. He created agencies and boards, such as the National Credit Corporation and the Emergency Committee for Employment, to obtain voluntary action to solve the problem. Hoover also supported the tax cut that Congress enacted in December 1929, but it did little to stimulate spending. Hoover also went on the radio to assure the American people that the fundamental structure of the economy was sound.

## The Collapsing Economy

Voluntary action and psychological campaigns could not stop the Depression. The stock market, after appearing to bottom out in the winter of 1930 and 1931, continued its decline, responding in part to the European economic collapse that threatened international finance and trade. Of course, not everyone lost money. Joseph Kennedy, film magnate, entrepreneur, and father of a future president, and a few others made millions by selling short as the market went down.

More than a collapsing market afflicted the economy. Over 1,300 banks failed in 1930. Despite Hoover's pleas, many factories cut production, and some simply closed. More than 4 million Americans were out of work in 1930, and that number increased to at least 12 million by 1932. Foreclosures and evictions created thousands of personal tragedies. While the middle class watched in horror as life savings and dreams disappeared, the rich worried increasingly as the price of government bonds (the symbol of safety and security) dropped. They began to hoard gold and fear revolution.

There was never any real danger of revolution. Some farmers organized to dump their milk to protest low prices, and when a neighbor's farm was sold, they gathered to hold a penny auction, bidding only a few cents for equipment and returning it to their dispossessed neighbor. But everywhere people despaired as the Depression deepened in 1931 and 1932. For unemployed blacks and many tenant farmers, the Depression had little immediate effect because their lives were already so depressed. The 98 percent of Americans who did not own stock hardly noticed the crash; for them, the Depression meant a lost job or a foreclosure. For Diana Morgan, it was the discovery that the telephone had been cut off; for some farmers, it was burning corn rather than coal because the price of corn had fallen so low that it was not worth marketing. For some in the cities, the Depression meant not having enough money to feed the children. In Chicago, children fought with men and women over the garbage dumped by the city trucks.

Not everyone went hungry, stood in breadlines, or lost jobs, but almost everyone suffered, and many tended to blame themselves. A businessman who lost his job and had to stand in a relief line remembered years later how he would bend his head low so nobody would recognize him.

The Depression probably disrupted women's lives less than men's. When men lost their jobs, their identity and sense of purpose as the family breadwinner generally collapsed. Some men helped out with family chores, usually with bitterness. For women, however, even when money was short, there were still chores, and they were still in command of their households. Yet many women had to do extra work: taking in laundry, renting a room to a boarder, and making clothes they formerly would have bought. They also bore the psychological burden of unemployed husbands, hungry children, and unpaid bills. Many families moved in with relatives. The marriage rate, the divorce rate, and the birthrate all dropped during the decade, creating tensions that statistics cannot capture.

Hoover kept urging more voluntary action. "We are going through a period," he announced in February 1931, "when character and courage are on trial." He insisted on maintaining the gold standard and a balanced budget, but so did almost everyone else. New York Governor Franklin Roosevelt accused him of spending too much. Hoover increasingly blamed the Depression on international economic problems, and he was not entirely wrong. But Americans began to blame Hoover. The president became isolated and bitter. The shanties that grew near all the large cities were called "Hoovervilles." Unable to admit mistakes and take a new tack, he could not communicate personal empathy for the poor and the unemployed.

Hoover did try innovative schemes. More public works projects were built during his administration than in the previous 30 years. In the summer of 1931, he organized a pool of private money to rescue banks and businesses that were near failure. When that private effort failed, he turned reluctantly to Congress,

The worst result of the Depression was hopelessness and despair. Those emotions are captured in this painting of an unemployment office by Isaac Soyer. (Isaac Soyer, "Employment Agency," 1937. Collection of Whitney Museum of American Art Purchase.)

which in 1932 authorized the Reconstruction Finance Corporation. The RFC was capitalized at $500 million and soon increased to $3 billion. It lent to banks, insurance companies, farm mortgage companies, and railroads. Some critics charged that it was simply a trickle-down measure while the unemployed were ignored. Hoover, however, understood the immense costs to individuals and communities when a bank or mortgage company failed. The RFC helped shore up shaky financial institutions and remained the major government finance agency until World War II. But it became much more effective under Roosevelt because it lent directly to industry.

Hoover also asked Congress for a Home Financing Corporation to make mortgages more readily available. The Federal Home Loan Bank Act of 1932 became the basis for the Federal Housing Administration of the New Deal years. He also pushed the passage of the Glass-Steagall Banking Act of 1932, which expanded credit in order to make more loans available to businesses and individuals.

But Hoover rejected calls for the federal government to restrict production in hopes of raising farm prices—that, he believed, was too much federal intervention. He firmly believed in loans, not direct subsidies, and he thought it was the responsibility of state and local governments, as well as private charity, to provide direct relief to the unemployed and the needy.

## The Bonus Army

Many World War I veterans lost their jobs during the Great Depression; beginning in 1930, they lobbied for immediate payment of their veterans' bonuses that were due in 1945. In May 1932, about 17,000 veterans marched on Washington. Some took up residence in a shantytown, called Bonus City, outside town.

In mid-June, the Senate defeated the bonus bill, and most of the disappointed veterans accepted a free railroad ticket home. Several thousand remained, however, along with some wives and children, in the unsanitary shacks during the steaming summer heat. Among them were a few Communists and other radicals. Hoover, who exaggerated the subversive elements among those still camped out in Bonus City, refused to talk to the leaders, and finally called out the U.S. Army.

General Douglas MacArthur, the Army chief of staff, ordered troops to disperse the veterans, "a mob," he said, ". . . animated by the essence of revolution." With tanks, guns, and tear gas, troops routed men who 15 years before had worn the same uniform. Two Bonus marchers died. Far from attacking revolutionaries in the streets of Washington, the Army was routing bewildered, confused, unemployed men whose American dream had collapsed.

The Bonus army fiasco, breadlines, and shanty towns called Hoovervilles became the symbols of Hoover's presidency. He deserved better because he tried to use the power of the federal government to solve growing and increasingly complex economic problems. But his personality and background limited him. He could not understand why veterans marched on Washington to ask for a handout when they should be back home working hard, practicing self-reliance, and cooperating. He believed that the greatest problem besetting Americans was a lack of confidence. He could not communicate with these people or inspire their confidence. Willing to give federal support to business, he could not accept giving federal aid to the unemployed. He feared an unbalanced budget and a large federal bureaucracy that would interfere with the "American way." Ironically, his actions and inactions soon led to a massive increase in federal power and in federal bureaucracy.

## ROOSEVELT AND THE FIRST NEW DEAL

The first New Deal, from 1933 to early 1935, focused mainly on recovery and relief for the poor and unemployed. Some of its programs were borrowed from the Hoover administration or from the progressive period. Others were inspired by the nation's experiences in mobilizing for World War I. No single ideological position united all the programs, for Roosevelt was a pragmatist who was willing to try different programs. More than Hoover, however, he believed in economic planning and in government spending to help the poor.

Roosevelt's caution and conservatism shaped the first New Deal. He did not promote socialism. The basic assumption of the New Deal was that a just society could be created by superimposing a welfare state on the capitalist system, leaving the profit motive in place. Roosevelt believed he could achieve this through cooperation with the business community. Later he would move toward reform, but at first his concern was primarily relief and recovery.

## The Election of 1932

In the summer of 1932, the Republicans nominated Hoover for a second term, but the Depression and Hoover's unpopularity opened the way for the Democrats.

Franklin D. Roosevelt won the nomination. Distantly related to Theodore Roosevelt, he had served as assistant secretary of the Navy during World War I and was the Democratic vice presidential candidate in 1920. Crippled by polio not long after, he had recovered enough to serve as governor of New York for two terms. Despite his considerable experience, he was not especially well-known by the general public in 1932.

As governor, Roosevelt had promoted cheaper electric power, conservation, and old-age pensions, and he became the first governor to support state aid for the unemployed. But it was difficult to tell during the campaign exactly what he stood for. Ambiguity was probably the best strategy in 1932, but Roosevelt had no master plan to save the country. Yet he won overwhelmingly, carrying more than 57 percent of the popular vote.

During the campaign, Roosevelt had promised a "new deal for the American people." But the New Deal had to wait for four months, because the Constitution provided for presidents to be inaugurated on March 4. (This was changed to January 20 by the Twentieth Amendment, ratified in 1933.) During the long interregnum, the state of the nation deteriorated badly. The banking system was near collapse and hardship increased. Despite his bitter defeat, Hoover tried to cooperate with the president-elect and a hostile Congress. But he could accomplish little. Everyone waited for the new president to take office.

In his inaugural address, Roosevelt announced confidently, "The only thing we have to fear is fear itself." This, of course, was not true: The country faced the worst crisis since the Civil War. But Roosevelt's confidence and ability to communicate with ordinary Americans were obvious early in his presidency. He had clever speech writers, a sense of pace and rhythm in his speeches, and an ability, in his "fireside chats" on the radio, to convince listeners that he was speaking directly to them. When he said "my friends," millions believed that he meant it.

## The Cabinet and the "Brain Trust"

During the interregnum, Roosevelt surrounded himself with intelligent and innovative advisers. His cabinet consisted of a mixture of people from different backgrounds who often did not agree with one another. Harold Ickes, the secretary of the interior, was a Republican lawyer from Chicago and onetime supporter of Theodore Roosevelt. Another Republican, Henry Wallace of Iowa, a plant geneticist and agricultural statistician, became the secretary of agriculture. Frances Perkins, the first woman ever appointed to a cabinet post, became the secretary of labor. A disciple of Jane Addams and Florence Kelley, she had been a settlement resident, the secretary of the New York Consumers League, and an adviser to Al Smith.

Besides the formal cabinet, Roosevelt had an informal "Brain Trust," including Adolph Berle, Jr., a young expert on corporation law, and Rexford Tugwell, a Columbia University authority on agricultural economics and a committed national planner. Roosevelt also listened to Raymond Moley, another Columbia professor who later became one of the president's severest critics, and to Harry Hopkins, a nervous, energetic man who loved to bet on horse races and was passionately concerned for the poor and unemployed.

Eleanor Roosevelt was a controversial first lady. She wrote a newspaper column, made radio broadcasts, traveled widely, and was constantly giving speeches and listening to the concerns of women, minorities, and ordinary Americans. Attacked by critics who thought she had too much power, she took courageous stands for social justice and civil rights, pushing the president toward social reform.

Roosevelt was an adept politician. He was not well-read, especially on economic matters, but he demonstrated that he could learn from his advisers and yet not be dominated by them. He took ideas, plans, and suggestions from conflicting sources and combined them. An improviser who once likened himself to a quarterback who called one play and if it did not work called a different one, Roosevelt was an optimist by nature. And he believed in action.

## ONE HUNDRED DAYS

Congress was ready to pass almost any legislation that Roosevelt put before it. In three months, a bewildering number of bills were rushed through. Some were not well thought out, and some contradicted other bills. But many of these laws would have far-reaching implications for the relationship of government to society. Roosevelt was an opportunist, but unlike Hoover, he was willing to use direct government action against depression and unemployment. None of the bills passed during the first 100 days cured the Depression, but taken together, the "Hundred Days" were one of the most innovative periods in American political history.

## The Banking Crisis

The most immediate problem Roosevelt faced was the banking crisis. Many banks had closed, and citizens were hoarding money and gold. Roosevelt immediately declared a four-day bank holiday. Three days later, an emergency session of Congress approved his action and within hours gave the president broad powers over financial transactions, prohibited the hoarding of gold, and allowed for the reopening of sound banks, sometimes with RFC loans.

Over the next few years, Congress gave the federal government more regulatory power over the stock market and over the process by which corporations issued stock. The Banking Act of 1933 strengthened the Federal Reserve System, established the Federal Deposit Insurance Corporation (FDIC), and insured individual deposits up to $5,000. Although the American Bankers Association opposed the plan, banks were soon attracting depositors by advertising that they were protected by government insurance.

The Democratic platform in 1932 called for reduced government spending and an end to prohibition. Roosevelt moved quickly on both. The Economy Act, which passed easily, called for a 15 percent reduction in government salaries and a reorganization of federal agencies to save money. The bill also cut veterans' pensions, despite the protests of veteran's organizations. But other bills called for additional spending. The Beer-Wine Revenue Act legalized 3.2 beer and light wines and levied a tax on both. The Twenty-first Amendment, ratified on December 5, 1933, repealed the Eighteenth Amendment and officially ended prohibition.

Despite some opposition, Congress gave the president broad power to devalue the dollar and induce inflation. Some members revived the old Populist solution of free and unlimited silver coinage, while others called for issuing billions of dollars in paper currency. Bankers and businessmen feared inflation, but farmers and debtors favored some inflation to put more dollars in their pockets. Roosevelt rejected the more extreme inflationary plans of many congressmen from agricultural states, but he did take the country off the gold standard. No longer would paper currency be redeemable in gold. The action terrified some conservative businessmen, and even Roosevelt's director of the budget announced solemnly that it "meant the end of Western Civilization."

Devaluation neither ended Western civilization nor produced instant recovery. Roosevelt and his advisers fixed the price at $35 an ounce in January 1934 (against the old price of $20.63), inflating the dollar by about 40 percent. Soon the country settled down to a slightly inflated currency and a dollar based on both gold and silver. Some experts still believed that gold represented fiscal responsibility, even morality, while others still cried for more inflation.

## Relief Measures

Roosevelt believed in economy in government and in a balanced budget, but he also wanted to help the unemployed and the homeless. One survey estimated that in 1933 1.5 million Americans were homeless. A man with a wife and six children who was being evicted wrote, "I have 10 days to get another house, no job, no means of paying rent, can you advise me as to which would be the most humane way to dispose of myself and family, as this is about the only thing that I see left to do."

Roosevelt's answer was the Federal Emergency Relief Administration (FERA), which Congress authorized with an appropriation of $500 million in direct grants to cities and states. A few months later, Roosevelt created a Civil Works Administration (CWA) to put more than 4 million people to work on various state, municipal, and federal projects. Hopkins, who ran both agencies, believed it was much better to pay people to work than to give them charity. So did most people in need. An accountant working on a road project said, "I'd rather stay out here in that ditch the rest of my life than take one cent of direct relief."

The CWA was not always effective, but in just over a year, it built or restored a half-million miles of roads and constructed 40,000 schools and 1,000 airports. It hired 50,000 teachers to keep rural schools open and others to teach adult education courses in the cities. The CWA helped millions of people get through the bitterly cold winter of 1933 to 1934. It also put over a billion dollars of purchasing power into the economy. Roosevelt, who later would be accused of deficit spending, feared that the program was costing too much and might create a permanent class of relief recipients. In the spring of 1934, he ordered the CWA closed down.

The Public Works Administration (PWA), directed by Harold Ickes, lasted longer. Between 1933 and 1939, the PWA built hospitals, courthouses, and school

Margaret Bourke-White, one of the outstanding documentary photographers of the 1930s, captured the disjunction between the ideal and the real in the Depression era. This photograph, depicting African-American flood victims lining up for food in Louisville, Kentucky, underneath a propaganda billboard erected by the National Association of Manufacturers, contrasts the American Dream with the reality of racism and poverty. (Margaret Bourke-White, "The Louisville Flood," 1937. Photograph © Whitney Museum of American Art, New York, Gift of Sean Callahan. LIFE Magazine, © TimePix.)

buildings. Its projects included the port of Brownsville, Texas, two aircraft carriers, and low-cost slum housing.

One purpose of the PWA was economic pump priming—to stimulate the economy through government outlays. Afraid of scandals, Ickes spent money slowly and carefully. Thus during the first years, PWA projects, worthwhile as most of them were, provided little economic stimulus.

## Agricultural Adjustment Act

By 1933, most farmers were desperate, caught between mounting surpluses and falling prices. Some in the Midwest even talked of revolution. But most observers saw only despair in farmers who had worked hard but were still losing their farms.

Congress passed a number of bills in 1933 and 1934 to deal with the agricultural crisis, including foreclosures and evictions. But the New Deal's principal solution was the Agricultural Adjustment Act (AAA), which sought to control the overproduction of basic commodities so that farmers might regain their pre-World War I purchasing power. To guarantee these "parity prices" (the average

For many people, the Depression meant homeless despair. Here an Oklahoma family who has lost their farm walk with all their possessions along the highway. This compelling photograph was taken by Dorothea Lange, one of several accomplished photographers who documented the impact of the Depression for the Farm Security Administration. (Photograph © 1966: Whitney Museum of American Art, New York, Gift of Sean Callahan)

prices in the years 1909 to 1914), the production of major agricultural staples—wheat, cotton, corn, hogs, rice, tobacco, and milk—would be controlled by paying the farmers to reduce their acreage under cultivation. The AAA levied a tax at the processing stage to pay for the program.

The act caused great disagreement among farm leaders and economists, but the controversy was nothing compared with the public outcry in the summer of 1933, when, to boost prices, the AAA ordered 10 million acres of cotton plowed up and 6 million young pigs slaughtered. It seemed immoral to kill pigs and plow up cotton when millions of people were hungry and ill-clothed.

The Agricultural Adjustment Act did raise the prices of some agricultural products. But it helped the larger farmers more than the small operators, and it was often disastrous for the tenant farmers and sharecroppers, made expendable by crop reduction. When they reduced their acreage, landowners often discharged tenant families. Many were simply cast out on the road with nowhere to go. Large farmers cultivated their fewer acres more intensely, so that the total crop was little reduced. In the end, the prolonged drought that hit the Southwest in 1934 did more than the AAA to limit production and raise agricultural prices. But the long-range significance of the AAA, which was later declared unconstitutional, was to entrench the idea that the government should subsidize farmers for limiting production.

## Industrial Recovery

The legislation during the first days of the Roosevelt administration contained something for almost every group. The National Industrial Recovery Act (NIRA) was designed to help business, raise prices, control production, and put people back to work. Its goal was to restrict competition, restrain profits, and produce la-bor-management harmony. The act established the National Recovery Adminis-tration (NRA) with the power to set fair competition codes in all industries. For a time, everyone forgot about antitrust laws and talked of cooperation.

To run the NRA, Roosevelt appointed Hugh Johnson, who used his wartime administrative experiences (he had run the draft) and the enthusiasm of bond drives to rally the country around the NRA and, implicitly, around the New Deal. There were parades and rallies, a postage stamp, and "We Do Our Part" posters for cooperating industries. But the results were somewhat less than the promise.

Section 7a of the NIRA, included at labor unions' insistence, guaranteed la-bor's right to organize and to bargain collectively and established the National Labor Board to see that unions' rights were respected. But the board, usually dominated by businessmen, often interpreted the labor provisions of the contracts loosely. In addition, small businessmen complained that the NIRA was unfair to their interests. Any attempt to set prices led to controversy.

Many consumers suspected that the codes and contracts were raising prices, while others feared the return of monopoly. Johnson's campaign backfired be-cause anyone with a complaint about the New Deal seemed to take it out on the NIRA's blue eagle symbol. When the Supreme Court declared the NIRA unconsti-tutional in 1935, few complained. Still, the NIRA was an ambitious attempt to bring some order into a confused business situation, and its labor provisions were picked up later by the National Labor Relations Act.

## Civilian Conservation Corps

One of the most popular and successful New Deal programs, the Civilian Conser-vation Corps (CCC), combined work relief with the preservation of natural re-sources. It put young, unemployed men between the ages of 18 and 25—2.5 mil-lion of them—to work on reforestation, road and park construction, flood control, and other projects. The men lived in work camps and earned $30 a month, $25 of which had to be sent home to their families.

The CCC ran separate camps for young black men and a few camps were or-ganized for unemployed young women, but the program was designed to help unemployed, young men. Some complained that the camps were too military in their organization. Despite complaints, the CCC was one of the most successful and least controversial of all the New Deal programs.

## Tennessee Valley Authority

FDR, like TR, believed in conservation. He promoted flood-control projects and added millions of acres to the country's national forests, wildlife refuges, and fish and game sanctuaries. But the most important New Deal conservation project, the Tennessee Valley Authority (TVA), owed more to Republican George Norris, a progressive senator from Nebraska, than to Roosevelt.

During World War I, the federal government had built a hydroelectric plant and two munitions factories at Muscle Shoals, on the Tennessee River in Alabama. The government tried unsuccessfully to sell these facilities to private industry, but all through the 1920s, Norris campaigned to have the federal government operate

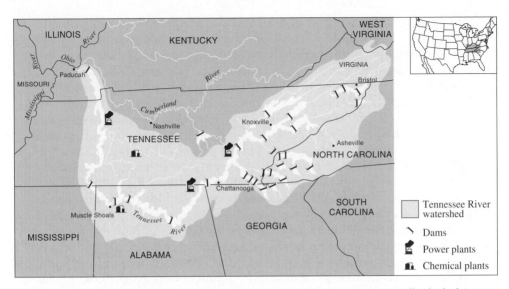

**THE TENNESSEE VALLEY AUTHORITY**   The TVA transformed the way the Tennessee valley looked; it replaced a wild river with a series of flood-control and hydroelectric dams and created a series of lakes behind the dams. It stopped short of the coordinated regional planning that some people wanted, but it was one of the most important New Deal projects, as it had an impact on portions of seven states.

them for the benefit of the valley's residents. Twice Republican presidents vetoed bills providing for federal operation, but Roosevelt endorsed Norris's idea and expanded it into a regional development plan.

Congress authorized the TVA as an independent public corporation to sell electricity and fertilizer and to promote flood control and land reclamation. The TVA built nine major dams and many minor ones between 1933 and 1944, affecting parts of Virginia, North Carolina, Georgia, Alabama, Mississippi, Tennessee, and Kentucky. Some private utility companies claimed that the TVA unfairly competed with private industry, but it was an imaginative experiment in regional planning. For residents of the valley, it meant cheaper electricity and changed lifestyles. The largest federal construction project ever launched, it also created jobs for many thousands who helped build the dams. But government officials and businessmen who feared that the experiment would lead to socialism always curbed the regional planning possibilities of the TVA.

## Critics of the New Deal

The furious legislative activity during the first 100 days of the New Deal helped alleviate the country's pessimism and despair. The stock market rose slightly, and industrial production was up 11 percent at the end of 1933. Still, the country remained locked in depression, and nearly 12 million Americans lacked jobs.

Roosevelt captured the imagination of ordinary Americans everywhere, but conservatives became increasingly angry. Many businessmen, after being impressed with Roosevelt's early economy measures and approving programs such as the NIRA, began to fear that the president was leading the country toward socialism.

The conservative revolt against Roosevelt surfaced in the summer of 1934 as the congressional elections approached. A group of disgruntled politicians and businessmen formed the Liberty League. Led by Alfred E. Smith and John W. Davis, the league supported conservative or at least anti-New Deal candidates for Congress, but it had little influence. In the election of 1934, the Democrats increased their majority from 310 to 319 in the House and from 60 to 69 in the Senate (only the second time in the twentieth century that the party in power had increased its control of Congress in the mid-term election). A few people were learning to hate "that man in the White House," but most Americans approved of what he was doing.

But what Roosevelt and his advisers found much more disturbing in 1934 and 1935 than people who thought the New Deal too radical were those on the left who maintained that the government had not done enough to help the poor. The Communist party increased its membership from 7,500 in 1930 to 75,000 in 1938. Communists organized protest marches and tried to reach out to the oppressed and unemployed. While a majority who joined the party came from the working class, Communism had a special appeal to writers, intellectuals, and some college students during a decade when the American dream had turned into a nightmare.

More Americans, however, were influenced by other movements promising easy solutions. In Minnesota, Governor Floyd Olson accused capitalism of causing the Depression and thundered, "I hope the present system of government goes right to hell." In California, Upton Sinclair, the muckraking socialist and author of *The Jungle,* ran for governor on the EPIC platform ("End Poverty in California"). He promised to pay everyone over 60 years of age a pension of $50 a month, financed by higher income and inheritance taxes. He won the primary but lost the election, and his movement collapsed.

California also produced Dr. Francis E. Townsend, who claimed a national following of over 5 million. His supporters backed a scheme that promised $200 a month to all unemployed citizens over age 60 on the condition that they spend it in the same month they received it. Economists laughed, but followers organized thousands of Townsend Pension Clubs across the country.

More threatening to Roosevelt and the New Deal were the protest movements led by Father Charles E. Coughlin and Senator Huey P. Long. Father Coughlin, a Roman Catholic priest from a Detroit suburb, attracted an audience of 30 to 45 million to his national radio show. At first he supported Roosevelt's policies, but later he savagely attacked the New Deal as excessively pro-business. Mixing religious commentary with visions of a society without bankers and big businessmen, he roused his audience with blatantly anti-Semitic tirades. Anti-Semitism reached a peak in the 1930s, as Jews bore the brunt of nativist fury.

Like Coughlin, Huey Long had a charisma that won support from the millions still trying to survive in a country where the continuing Depression made day-to-day existence a struggle. Elected governor of Louisiana in 1928, Long called his program "Share the Wealth." He taxed the oil refineries and built hospitals, schools, and thousands of miles of new highways. By 1934, he was the virtual dictator of his state, personally controlling the police and the courts. Long talked about a guaranteed $2,000 to $3,000 income for all American families (18.3 million families earned less than $1,000 per year in 1936) and promised pensions for the elderly and college educations for the young, all to be paid for by soaking the rich. Had an assassin not killed Long in September 1935, he might have mounted a third-party challenge to Roosevelt.

## THE SECOND NEW DEAL

Responding in part to lower-middle-class discontent but also to head off utopian schemes, Roosevelt moved his programs in 1935 toward the goals of social reform and social justice. At the same time, he ceased trying to cooperate with the business community. "In spite of our efforts and in spite of our talk, we have not weeded out the overprivileged and we have not effectively lifted up the underprivileged," Roosevelt announced in his annual message to Congress in January 1935.

## Work Relief and Social Security

The Works Progress Administration (WPA), authorized by Congress in April 1935, was the first massive attempt to deal with unemployment and its demoralizing effect on millions of Americans. The WPA employed about 3 million people a year (at wages below what private industry paid) on projects ranging from bridges to libraries. It built nearly 6,000 schools, more than 2,500 hospitals, and 13,000 playgrounds. Nearly 85 percent of its funds went directly to workers. A minor but important part of its funding supported writers, artists, actors, and musicians.

Only one member of a family could get a WPA job—always a man unless a woman headed the household. But eventually more than 13 percent of the people who worked for the WPA were women, usually making over old clothes. "For unskilled men we have the shovel. For unskilled women we have only the needle," one official explained.

The WPA was controversial from the beginning. Its initials, critics said, stood for "We Putter Around." Yet the WPA not only did useful work but also gave millions of unemployed Americans a sense that they were working and supporting their families.

The National Youth Administration (NYA) supplemented the work of the WPA and assisted young men and women between the ages of 16 and 25 (including a young law student at Duke University named Richard Nixon). Lyndon Johnson began his political career as director of the Texas NYA.

By far the most enduring reform was the passage of the Social Security Act of 1935. Since the progressive period, reformers had argued for national health and unemployment insurance and old-age pensions. By the 1930s, the United States was the only major industrial country without them. Secretary of Labor Perkins argued most strongly for social insurance, but Roosevelt also wanted to head off popular schemes like the Townsend Plan.

The Social Security Act of 1935 was a compromise. To appease the medical profession, Congress quickly dropped a plan for federal health insurance. The act's central provision was old-age and survivor insurance, paid for by a tax of 1 percent on both employers and employees. The act also established a cooperative federal-state system of unemployment compensation, gave federal grants to the states for the disabled and the blind, and provided aid to dependent children—the provision that years later expanded to become the largest federal welfare program.

Conservatives denounced Social Security for regimenting people and destroying self-reliance. But in no other country was social insurance paid for in part by a regressive tax on the workers' wages. "With those taxes in there, no damn politician can ever scrap my Social Security program," Roosevelt later explained, insisting that by paying the taxes wage earners won a moral claim on their benefits. But farm laborers and domestic servants were not covered. The system discriminated against married women wage earners and failed to protect against sickness. Still, it was one of the most important New Deal measures, and it marked the beginning of the welfare state that would expand greatly after World War II.

## Aiding the Farmers

The Social Security Act and the Works Progress Administration were only two signs of Roosevelt's greater concern for social reform. The flurry of legislation in 1935 and early 1936, often called the "second New Deal," also included an effort to help American farmers. The Resettlement Administration (RA), motivated in part by a Jeffersonian ideal of yeoman farmers working their own land, tried to relocate tenant farmers to land purchased by the government. But it failed to accomplish much, a victim of underfunding and of scare talk about Soviet-style collective farms.

Much more important in improving the lives of farm families was the Rural Electrification Administration (REA), which was authorized in 1935 to lend money to cooperatives to generate and distribute electricity in isolated rural areas not served by private utilities. Only 10 percent of the nation's farms had electricity in 1936. When the REA's lines were finally attached, they dramatically changed the lives of millions of farm families who had only been able to dream about the radios, washing machines, and farm equipment advertised in magazines.

## The Dust Bowl: An Ecological Disaster

Those who tried to farm on the Great Plains fell victim to years of drought and dust storms, as record heat waves and below-average rainfall in the 1930s turned the Oklahoma panhandle and western Kansas into a giant dust bowl. Thousands died of "dust pneumonia." By the end of the decade, 10,000 farm homes were abandoned, 9 million acres of farmland were reduced to wasteland, and 3.5 million people had joined a massive migration to find a better life. Many tenant farmers and hired hands were evicted, their plight immortalized by John Steinbeck in his novel *The Grapes of Wrath* (1939).

The dust bowl was a natural disaster, aided and exaggerated by human actions and inactions. The semiarid plains west of the 98th meridian were not suitable for intensive agriculture, and 60 years of improper land use had exposed the thin soil to the elements. When the winds came, much of the land simply blew away. In the end, it was a matter of too little government planning and regulation and too many farmers using new technology to exploit nature.

Whatever the administration tried to do was too little and too late. Even worse, according to some authorities, government measures applied after the disaster of 1930 encouraged farmers to return to raising wheat and other inappropriate crops, leading to more dust bowl crises in the 1950s and 1970s.

## The New Deal and the West

The New Deal probably aided the West more than any other region. The CCC, the AAA, drought relief measures, and various federal agencies helped the region out of proportion to the number of people who lived there. Most important were the large-scale water projects, such as Boulder Dam (later renamed Hoover Dam) on the Colorado River and (the largest of all) Grand Coulee Dam on the Columbia River. These dams produced massive amounts of hydroelectric power, poured millions of dollars into the economy, and provided enormous amounts of water for cities and irrigation.

Despite all the federal aid to the region, many westerners bitterly criticized the regulation and the bureaucracy that came with the grants. The cattlemen in Wyoming, Colorado, and Montana desperately needed the help of the federal government, but even as they accepted the aid, they denounced the New Deal.

## Controlling Corporate Power and Taxing the Wealthy

In the summer of 1935, Roosevelt also moved to control the large corporations, and he even toyed with radical plans to tax the well-to-do heavily and redistribute wealth in the United States. The Public Utility Holding Company Act, passed in 1935, attempted to restrict the power of the giant utility companies, the 12 largest of which controlled more than half the country's power. It gave each company five years to demonstrate that its services were efficient or face being dissolved. This was one of the most radical attempts to control corporate power in American history.

In the same year, Roosevelt urged higher taxes on the rich and a heavy inheritance tax. When Congress dropped the inheritance tax provision, however, Roosevelt did not fight for it. Even the weakened bill angered many in the business community who thought that FDR had sold out to Huey Long's "Share the Wealth" scheme.

## The New Deal for Labor

Like many progressive reformers, Roosevelt was more interested in helping working people by social legislation than by strengthening unions. Yet he saw labor as an important balance to the power of industry, and he listened to his advisers, especially to Frances Perkins and to Senator Robert Wagner of New York, who persistently brought up the needs of organized labor.

After a series of strikes, Roosevelt supported the 1935 Wagner Act (officially the National Labor Relations Act), which outlawed blacklisting and a number of other practices and reasserted labor's right to organize and to bargain collectively. The act also established a Labor Relations Board with the power to certify a properly elected bargaining unit. The act did not require workers to join unions, but it

made the federal government a regulator, or at least a neutral force, in manage-
ment-labor relations. That alone made the National Labor Relations Act one of the
most important New Deal reform measures.

The Roosevelt administration's friendly attitude helped increase union membership from under 3 million in 1933 to 4.5 million by 1935. Many groups, however, were left out, including farm laborers, unskilled workers, and women. Only
about 3 percent of working women belonged to unions, and they earned only
about 60 percent of wages paid to men for equivalent work. Still, many resented
the women being employed at all. One writer had a perfect solution for unemployment: "Simply fire the women, who shouldn't be working anyway, and hire
the men."

The AFL had never organized unskilled workers, but a new group of committed and militant labor leaders emerged in the 1930s to take up that task: John L.
Lewis of the United Mine Workers, David Dubinsky of the International Ladies'
Garment Workers, and Sidney Hillman of the Amalgamated Clothing Workers.
The latter two were socialists who believed in economic planning and had
worked closely with social justice progressives. These new progressive labor leaders formed the Committee of Industrial Organization (CIO) within the AFL and
set out to organize workers in the steel, auto, and rubber industries. Rather than
separating workers by skill or craft as the AFL preferred, they organized industry-
wide unions. They also used aggressive new tactics, such as declaring a spontaneous strike when management made unwanted demands. This "brass knuckle
unionism" worked especially well in the auto and rubber industries.

In 1936, the workers at three rubber plants in Akron, Ohio, went on unauthorized strikes. Instead of picketing, they took over the buildings. The "sit-down
strike" became a new protest technique, disorderly but largely nonviolent (as
would be civil rights demonstrations in the 1960s). After several such strikes,

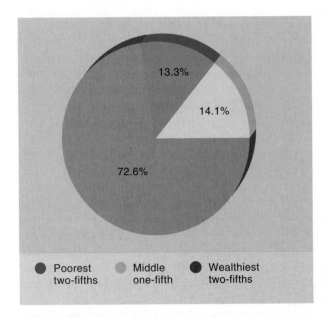

13.3%

14.1%

72.6%

● Poorest
two-fifths
● Middle
one-fifth
● Wealthiest
two-fifths

**DISTRIBUTION OF INCOME,
1935–1936** Roosevelt and the
New Deal never sought
consistently to redistribute
wealth in America, and a great
disparity in income and assets
remained. (*Source:* U.S. Bureau of the
Census)

General Motors finally accepted the United Auto Workers (UAW) as their employees' bargaining agent. The GM strike was the most important event in a critical period of labor upheaval. Labor's voice now began to be heard in the decision-making process in major industries where labor had long been denied any role, raising the status of organized labor in the eyes of many Americans.

Violence spread along with the sit-down strikes. Chrysler capitulated, but Ford fought back with armed guards, and it took a bloody struggle before the UAW was accepted as the bargaining agent. Militantly anti-union U.S. Steel agreed to a 40-hour week and an eight-hour day, but other steel companies refused to go along. In the "Memorial Day Massacre" in 1937, police fired into a crowd of workers and their families peacefully picketing the Republic Steel plant in Chicago. All 10 who died were shot in the back.

The CIO's aggressive tactics gained many members, to the horror of AFL leaders. They expelled the CIO leaders, only to see them form a separate Congress of Industrial Organization (the initials stayed the same). Accepting unskilled workers, African Americans, and others who had never belonged to a union before, the CIO won increased pay, better working conditions, and the right to bargain collectively in most basic industries, and infused the labor movement with a new spirit.

## America's Minorities in the 1930s

A half-million African Americans joined unions through the CIO, and New Deal agencies aided many blacks. Yet familiar patterns of poverty, discrimination, and violence persisted. Lynchings in the South also increased in the New Deal years.

Throughout the decade, the nation was gripped by the "Scottsboro Boys" case in Alabama, which began in 1931 when two young white women accused nine black youths of rape. Convicted and condemned to death by an all-white jury, the blacks were given a new trial in 1933 by order of the Supreme Court on the grounds that they had not received proper legal counsel. Liberals and radicals (including the Communist party) mobilized in defense of the youths' civil rights, while many from the South saw the honor of white women at stake. Evidence supporting the alleged rapes was never presented, and eventually one of the women recanted. Yet in new trials, five of the young men were convicted and given long prison terms. Charges against the other four were dropped in 1937. Four of the remaining five were paroled in 1944, and the fifth escaped to Michigan.

The migration of blacks to northern cities, which had accelerated during World War I, continued during the 1930s. The collapse of cotton prices forced black farmers and farm laborers to flee north for survival. But since most were poorly educated, they soon became trapped in northern ghettos, where they got only the most menial jobs. The black unemployment rate was triple that of whites, and blacks often received less per person in welfare payments.

Black leaders attacked the Roosevelt administration for supporting or allowing segregation in government-sponsored facilities. Roosevelt, dependent on the vote of the South and afraid to antagonize powerful southern congressmen, refused to support the two major civil rights bills of the era: an anti-lynching bill and a bill to abolish the poll tax. Yet Ickes and Hopkins worked to ensure that blacks were given opportunities in New Deal agencies. By 1941, black federal employees totaled 150,000, more than three times the number during the Hoover administration. Most worked in the lower ranks, but some were lawyers, architects, office managers, and engineers.

Partly responsible for the presence of more black employees was the "black cabinet," a group of more than 50 young blacks working in various New Deal agencies and led by Mary McLeod Bethune, the daughter of a sharecropper and organizer of the National Council of Negro Women. She had a large impact on New Deal policy—speaking out forcefully, picketing and protesting, and intervening shrewdly to obtain civil rights and more jobs for African Americans.

Although FDR appointed some blacks to government positions, he was never particularly committed to civil rights. That was not true of Eleanor Roosevelt, who was educated in part by Bethune. In 1939, when the Daughters of the American Revolution denied black concert singer Marian Anderson their stage, Mrs. Roosevelt protested by resigning her DAR membership and arranged for Anderson to sing from the steps of the Lincoln Memorial before an audience of 75,000.

Hundreds of thousands of Mexicans, brought to the United States for work in the 1920s, lost their jobs in the Depression. Drifting to the Southwest or settling in urban *barrios*, they met signs like "No Niggers, Mexicans, or Dogs Allowed." Some New Deal agencies helped destitute Mexicans, but as aliens and migrants, most could not qualify for relief. The preferred solution was to ship them back to Mexico, often after illegal roundups. One estimate placed the number sent back in 1932 at 200,000, which included some American citizens. But some who remained adopted militant tactics to obtain fair treatment.

By the 1930s, Native American hunger, disease, and despair had been compounded by years of exploitation. Native Americans had lost over 60 percent of the 138 million acres allocated to them under the Dawes Act in 1887 (see Chapter 17), and many who remained on the reservations were not even citizens. In 1924, Congress granted citizenship to all Indians born in the United States, but that did not end their suffering.

FDR brought a new spirit to Indian policy by appointing John Collier as commissioner of Indian affairs. Collier was primarily responsible for passage of the Indian Reorganization Act of 1934, which sought to restore tribes' political independence, to end the Dawes Act's allotment policy, and to promote the "study of Indian civilization." Not all Indians agreed with the new policies. Some Americans charged that the act was inspired by Communism or would increase government bureaucracy, while missionaries claimed that the government was promoting paganism.

The paradox of United States policy toward the Indians can be illustrated by Collier's attempt to solve the Navajo problem. Genuinely sympathetic to Native Americans, he also believed in soil conservation, science, and progress. The Navajo lands, like most of the West, were overgrazed, and soil erosion threatened to fill the new lake behind Hoover Dam with silt. By supporting a policy of reducing the herds of sheep and goats on Indian land and by promoting soil conservation, Collier contributed to the change in the Navajo lifestyle and to the end of their self-sufficiency, something his other policies supported.

## Women and the New Deal

Women made some gains during the 1930s, and more women occupied high government positions than in any previous administration. Some of these women had collaborated as social workers and now joined government bureaus to continue the fight for social justice. But they were usually in offices where they did not threaten male prerogatives. Despite some gains, the early New Deal programs did nothing for an estimated 140,000 homeless women. Married women were often fired from their jobs on the grounds that they should be home caring for their families rather than depriving men of employment.

Despite the number of women working for the government, feminism declined in the 1930s. The older feminists died or retired, and younger women did not replace them. Despite some dramatic exceptions, the image of a woman's proper role in the 1930s continued to be that of a housewife and mother.

## THE LAST YEARS OF THE NEW DEAL

The New Deal was not a consistent or well-organized effort to end the Depression and restructure society. A pragmatic politician, Roosevelt was unconcerned about ideological or programmatic consistency. The first New Deal in 1933 and 1934 had concentrated on relief and recovery; the legislation of 1935 and 1936 stressed social reform. In many ways, the election of 1936 marked the high point of Roosevelt's power and influence. After 1937, in part because of the growing threat of war but also because of increasing opposition in Congress, the pace of social legislation slowed. Yet several measures passed in 1937 and 1938 had such far-reaching significance that some historians refer to a third New Deal.

## The Election of 1936

The Republicans in 1936 nominated a moderate, Governor Alfred Landon of Kansas. Although he attacked the New Deal, charging it with waste and too much bureaucracy, Landon promised to do the same thing more efficiently. The *Literary Digest* magazine predicted his victory on the basis of its "scientific" telephone poll.

Roosevelt, helped by signs of economic recovery and supported by a coalition of the Democratic South, organized labor, farmers, and urban voters, won easily. For the first time, a majority of African Americans deserted the GOP—"the party of Lincoln"—out of appreciation for New Deal relief programs. No viable candidate to the left of the New Deal materialized. Winning by over 10 million votes and carrying every state except Maine and Vermont, Roosevelt now had a mandate to continue his New Deal reforms. As Roosevelt announced in his acceptance speech, "To some generations much is given, of other generations much is expected. This generation has a rendezvous with destiny."

## The Battle of the Supreme Court

"I see one-third of a nation ill-housed, ill-clad, ill-nourished," Roosevelt declared in his second inaugural address, and he vowed to alter it. But the president's first action in 1937 was a plan to reform the federal judiciary and the Supreme Court, whose "nine old men" had struck down various important New Deal measures.

To create a more sympathetic Court, FDR asked for power to appoint an extra justice for each of the six justices over 70 years of age. He also called for modernizing the court system at all levels, but that plan got lost in the public outcry over "court-packing."

Roosevelt's plan foundered. Republicans accused him of subverting the Constitution. Many congressmen from his own party refused to support him. Led by Vice President John Nance Garner of Texas, a number of southern Democrats broke with the president and formed a coalition with conservative Republicans that lasted for more than 30 years. Finally Roosevelt admitted defeat. He had perhaps misunderstood his mandate, and he certainly underestimated the respect, even reverence, that most Americans felt for the Supreme Court. Even amid economic catastrophe, Americans proved themselves fundamentally conservative toward their institutions.

Ironically, though he lost the battle of the Supreme Court, Roosevelt won the war. By the spring of 1937, the Court began to reverse its position and in a 5–4 decision upheld the National Labor Relations Act. When a conservative justice retired, Roosevelt made his first Supreme Court appointment, thus ensuring at least a shaky liberal majority on the Court. But Roosevelt triumphed at great cost. His attempt to reorganize the Court slowed the momentum of his legislative program. The most unpopular action he took as president, it made him vulnerable to criticism from New Deal opponents, and even some of his supporters were dismayed by what they regarded as an attack on the separation of powers.

In late 1936 and early 1937, recovery from the Depression seemed real: Employment was up, and even the stock market had recovered some of its losses. But in August, the fragile prosperity collapsed. Unemployment shot back up nearly to the peak levels of 1934, industrial production fell, and Wall Street plummeted. Roosevelt had probably helped cause the recession by assuming that the prosperity of 1936 was permanent. A believer in balanced budgets, he had cut federal spending and reduced outlays for relief. Now, facing an embarrassing economic slump and charges that the New Deal had failed, he gave in to those of his advisers who were followers of British economist John Maynard Keynes.

Keynes argued that to get out of a depression, the government must spend massively on goods and services. This would spur demand and revive production. By increasing appropriations for the WPA and other agencies, the Roosevelt administration consciously incurred a deficit for the first time in order to stimulate consumption and production. But the economy responded slowly, never fully recovering until wartime expenditures, beginning in 1940, eliminated unemployment and ended the Depression.

## The Third New Deal

Despite increasing hostility, Congress passed a number of important bills in 1937 and 1938 that completed the New Deal reform legislation. The Bankhead-Jones Farm Tenancy Act of 1937 created the Farm Security Administration (FSA) to aid tenant farmers, sharecroppers, and owners who had lost their farms. The

FSA, which provided loans to grain collectives, also set up camps for migratory workers. But the FSA never had enough money to make a real difference.

Congress passed a new Agricultural Adjustment Act in 1938 that tried to solve the problem of farm surpluses by controlling production. Under the new act, the federal treasury made direct payments to farmers. It introduced a soil conservation program and tried to market surplus crops. But only the outbreak of World War II would end the problem of farm surplus—temporarily.

A shortage of urban housing continued to be a problem. Reformers who had worked in the first experiment with federal housing during World War I convinced FDR that federal low-cost housing should be part of New Deal reform. The National Housing Act of 1937 provided federal funds for slum clearance projects and the construction of low-cost housing. By 1939, however, only 117,000 units had been built—mostly bleak, boxlike structures that soon became a problem rather than a solution.

New Deal housing legislation had a greater impact on middle-class housing policies and patterns. During the first 100 days of the New Deal, Congress created the Home Owners Loan Corporation (HOLC) at Roosevelt's urging, which over the next two years made more than $3 billion in low-interest loans and helped over a million people save their homes from foreclosure. The HOLC also had a strong impact on housing policy by introducing the first long-term fixed-rate mortgages. (Formerly, mortgages ran no longer than five years and were subject to frequent renegotiation.) The HOLC also introduced a uniform system of real estate appraisal that tended to undervalue urban property, especially in old, crowded, and ethnically mixed neighborhoods. The system gave the highest ratings to suburban developments in which the HOLC determined there had been no "infiltration of Jews"—the beginning of the practice later called "redlining" that made it nearly impossible for certain prospective homeowners to obtain a mortgage.

The Federal Housing Administration (FHA), created in 1934 by the National Housing Act, expanded and extended many HOLC policies. The FHA-insured mortgages, many of them for 25 or 30 years, reduced the minimum down payment from 30 percent to under 10 percent and allowed over 11 million families to buy homes between 1934 and 1972. It also tended to favor purchasing new suburban homes rather than repairing older urban residences.

An equally important reform measure was the Fair Labor Standards Act, passed in June 1938. Roosevelt's bill proposed for all industries engaged in interstate commerce a minimum wage of 25 cents an hour and a maximum work week of 44 hours. Despite congressional watering down, when the act went into effect, 750,000 workers immediately got raises, and by 1940, some 12 million had them. The law also barred child labor in interstate commerce, making it the first permanent federal law to prohibit youngsters under 16 from working. And the law made no distinction between men and women, thus diminishing the need for special legislation for women.

The New Deal had many weaknesses, but it did dramatically increase government support for the needy. In 1913, local, state, and federal government spent $21 million on public assistance. By 1932, that had risen to $218 million; by 1939, it was $4.9 billion.

## THE OTHER SIDE OF THE 1930s

The Great Depression and the New Deal so dominate the history of the 1930s that it is easy to conclude that there were only breadlines and relief agencies. But there is another side of the decade. A communications revolution changed the lives of middle-class Americans. The sale of radios and attendance at movies increased during the 1930s, and literature flourished. Americans were fascinated by technology, especially automobiles. Many people traveled and looked ahead to a brighter future of streamlined appliances and gadgets that would mean a better life.

## Taking to the Road

"People give up everything in the world but their car," a banker in Muncie, Indiana, remarked during the Depression, and that seems to have been true all over the country. Although automobile production dropped off after 1929 and did not recover until the end of the 1930s, the number of motor vehicles registered, which declined from 26.7 million in 1930 to just over 24 million in 1933, increased to over 32 million by 1940. Even the "Okies" fled the dust bowl of the Southwest in cars—secondhand, run-down ones, to be sure.

The American middle class traveled at an increasing rate after the low point of 1932 and 1933. In 1938, the tourist industry was the third largest in the United States, behind only steel and automobile production.

## The Electric Home

If the 1920s was the age of the bathroom, the 1930s was the era of the modern kitchen. In 1930, the number of electric refrigerators that were produced exceeded the number of iceboxes for the first time, and refrigerator production peaked at 2.3 million in 1937. At first, the refrigerator looked like an icebox with a motor on top. In 1935, however, the refrigerator, like most other appliances, became streamlined. The Sears Coldspot, which quickly influenced the look of all other models, was designed by Raymond Loewy. He was one of a group of industrial designers who emphasized sweeping horizontal lines and rounded corners.

Replacing an icebox with an electrical refrigerator, as many middle-class families did in the 1930s, altered more than the appearance of the kitchen. Unlike the constant tending demanded by the icebox, the refrigerator required only an occasional defrosting.

Streamlining became the symbol of modern civilization in the 1930s. At the end of the decade, in 1939, the World's Fair in New York glorified the streamlined, planned, technologized future. This reverence for progress contrasted with the economic despair in the 1930s, but people adapted to it selectively. For example, the electric washing machine and electric iron revolutionized washday—although Monday continued to be washday and Tuesday ironing day.

Ironically, despite these new conveniences, a great many middle-class families maintained their standard of living during the 1930s only because the women in the family learned to stretch and save and make do, and most wives spent as much time on housework as before. Some also took jobs outside the home to maintain their level of consumption. The number of married women who worked increased substantially during the decade.

## The Age of Leisure

During the Depression, many middle-class people found themselves with time on their hands. The 1920s had been a time of spectator sports watched by huge crowds. Those sports continued during the Depression decade, although attendance suffered. Cheap forms of entertainment like softball and miniature golf also became popular. But leisure in the 1930s actually grew into something on which professionals published some 450 new books.

Many popular games of the period had elaborate rules. Contract bridge swept the country. Monopoly was the most popular game of all, as Americans became fascinated by a game of building real estate and utility monopolies and bankrupting their opponents.

## Literary Reflections of the 1930s

Though much of the literature of the 1930s reflected the decade's troubled currents, reading continued to be a popular and cheap entertainment. John Steinbeck described the plight of Mexican migrant workers in *Tortilla Flat* (1935) and in his 1939 novel *The Grapes of Wrath* followed the deteriorating fortunes of an Okie family. His novels expressed his belief that there was in American life a "crime . . . that goes beyond denunciation"—the crime being the toleration of suffering and injustice.

Other writers also questioned the American dream. John Dos Passos's trilogy *U.S.A.* (1930–1936) conveyed a deep pessimism about American capitalism that many intellectuals shared. Less political were the novels of Thomas Wolfe and William Faulkner, who more sympathetically portrayed Americans caught up in the web of local life and facing modern complexities. Faulkner's fictional Yoknapatawpha County, brought to life in *The Sound and the Fury, As I Lay Dying, Sanctuary*, and *Light in August* (1929–1932), documented the South's racial problems, poverty, and stubborn pride. But a far more optimistic and far less complex book about the South became one of the decade's best-sellers—Margaret Mitchell's Civil War novel *Gone with the Wind* (1936). Its success showed that most Americans read to escape, not to explore their problems.

## Radio's Finest Hour

The number of radios purchased increased steadily during the 1930s. In 1929, slightly more than 10 million households owned a radio; by 1939, the number had increased to 27.5 million. In Chicago's working-class neighborhoods in 1930, there was one radio for every two or three households, but often families and friends gathered to listen to the radio. The radio became a focal point of the living room. Families gathered around it at night to laugh at Jack Benny and during the day to listen to soap operas. "Between thick slices of advertising," wrote James Thurber, "spread twelve minutes of dialogue, add predicament, villainy, and female suffering in equal measure, throw in a dash of nobility, sprinkle with tears, season with organ music, cover with a rich announcer sauce and serve five times a week."

# Timeline

| | |
|---|---|
| **1929** Stock market crashes | **1935** Second New Deal begins |
| Agricultural Marketing Act | Works Progress Administration established |
| **1930** Depression worsens | Social Security Act |
| Hawley-Smoot Tariff | Rural Electrification Act |
| **1932** Reconstruction Finance Corporation established | National Labor Relations Act |
| | Public Utility Holding Company Act |
| Federal Home Loan Bank Act | Committee for Industrial Organization (CIO) formed |
| Glass-Steagall Banking Act | |
| Federal Emergency Relief Act | **1936** United Auto Workers hold sit-down strikes against General Motors |
| Bonus march on Washington | Roosevelt reelected president |
| Franklin D. Roosevelt elected president | Economy begins to rebound |
| **1933** Emergency Banking Relief Act | **1937** Attempt to expand the Supreme Court |
| Home Owners Loan Corporation | Economic collapse |
| Twenty-first Amendment repeals Eighteenth Amendment, ending prohibition | Farm Security Administration established |
| | National Housing Act |
| Agricultural Adjustment Act | **1938** Fair Labor Standards Act |
| National Industrial Recovery Act | Agricultural Adjustment Act |
| Civilian Conservation Corps | **1939** John Steinbeck, *The Grapes of Wrath* |
| Tennessee Valley Authority established | Margaret Mitchell, *Gone with the Wind* |
| Public Works Administration established | |
| **1934** Unemployment peaks | |
| Federal Housing Administration established | |
| Indian Reorganization Act | |

Radio allowed many people to feel connected to distant places and to believe they knew the performers personally. Radio was also responsible for one of the most widespread episodes of mass hysteria of all time. Orson Welles's Halloween 1938 broadcast of "The War of the Worlds" was so realistic that thousands actually believed that Martians had just landed in New Jersey. If anyone needed proof, that single program demonstrated the power of the radio.

## The Silver Screen

The 1930s were the golden decade of the movies. Between 60 and 90 million Americans went to the movies every week. The medium was not entirely Depression-proof, but even in the depth of the Depression, movie money was almost as important as food money for many families.

City residents could go to an elaborate movie palace and live in a fantasy world far removed from the reality of Depression America. In small towns across the country, for a quarter (a dime for those under age 12) people could see at least four

# Recovering the Past

## The Movies

Just as some historians have used fiction to help define the cultural history of a decade, others in the twentieth century have turned to film to describe the "spirit of an age." On an elementary level, the movies help us appreciate changing styles in dress, furniture, and automobiles. We can even get some sense of how a particular time defined a beautiful woman or a handsome man, and we can learn about ethnic and racial stereotypes and assumptions about gender and class.

The decade of the 1930s is sometimes called the "golden age of the movies." Careful selection among the 500 or so feature films Hollywood produced each year during the decade—ranging from gangster and cowboy movies to Marx brothers comedies, from historical romances to Busby Berkeley musical extravaganzas—could support a number of interpretations about the special myths and assumptions of the Depression era. But one historian has argued that especially after 1934, "Not only did the movies amuse and entertain the nation through its most severe economic and social disorder, holding it together by their capacity to create unifying myths and dreams, but movie culture in the 1930s became a dominant culture for many Americans, providing new values and social ideas to replace shattered old traditions."

The year 1934 was a dividing line for two reasons. The motion picture industry, like all other industries, had suffered during the Depression; 1933 marked the low point in attendance, with more than a third of the theaters in the country shut down. The next year, however, attendance picked up, heralding a revival that lasted until 1946. Also in 1934, the movie industry adopted a code for which the Catholic Legion of Decency and other religious groups had lobbied. The new code prohibited the depiction of "sex perversion, interracial sex, abortion, incest, drugs and profanity." Even married couples could not be shown together in a double bed. Although a movie could depict immoral behavior, sin always had to be punished. "Evil and good should never be confused," the code announced.

Before the code, Hollywood had indeed produced graphic films, such as *The Public Enemy* (1931) and *Scarface* (1932), with a considerable amount of violence; musicals, such as *Gold Diggers of 1933* (1933), filled with scantily clad young women; films featuring prostitutes, such as Jean Harlow in *Red Dust* (1932) and Marlene Dietrich in *Blond Venus* (1930); and other films that confronted the problems of real life. But after 1934, Hollywood concentrated on movies that created a mythical world where evil was always punished, family moral values won out in the end, and patriotism and American democracy were never questioned. Although the code was modified from time to time, it was not abandoned until 1966, when it was replaced by a rating system.

*It Happened One Night* (1934) and *Drums Along the Mohawk* (1939), two films out of thousands, illustrate some of the myths the movies created and sustained. Frank Capra, one of Hollywood's masters at entertaining without disturbing, directed *It Happened One Night*, a comedy-romance. A rich girl played by Claudette Colbert dives from her father's yacht off the coast of Florida and takes a bus for New York. She meets a newspaper reporter played by Clark Gable, and they have a series of madcap adventures and fall in love. But mix-ups and misunderstandings make it appear that she will marry her old boyfriend. In the end, however, they are reunited and marry in an elaborate outdoor ceremony. Afterward, they presumably live happily ever after. The movie is funny and entertaining and presents a variation on the poor-boy-marries-

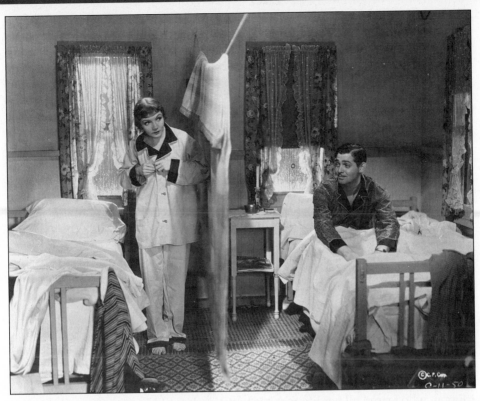

A scene from *It Happened One Night*, 1934. (The MOMA Film Stills Archive)

rich-girl theme. Like so many movies of the time, this one suggests that life is fulfilled for a woman only if she can find the right man to marry.

Claudette Colbert also stars in *Drums Along the Mohawk*, this time with Henry Fonda. Based on a 1936 novel by Walter Edmonds, *Drums* is a sentimental story about a man who builds a house in the wilderness, marries a pretty girl, fights off the Indians, and works with the simple country folk to create a satisfying life in the very year the American colonies rebel against Great Britain. *Drums* was one of a number of films based on historical themes that Hollywood released just before World War II. *The Howards of Virginia* (1940), *Northwest Passage* (1939), and most popular of all, *Gone with the Wind* (1939) were others in the same genre. Historical themes had been popular before, but with the world on the brink of war, the story of men and women in the wilderness struggling for family and country against the Indians (stereotyped as savages) proved comforting as well as entertaining.

**Reflecting on the Past** Can a historian use movies to describe the values and myths of a particular time, or are the complexities and exaggerations too great? Are the most popular or most critically acclaimed films more useful than others in getting at the "spirit of an age"? What films popular today tell us most about our time and culture? Is there too much sex and violence in movies today? Should the government control the language, themes, and values depicted in movies? Are movies as important today as they were in the 1930s in defining and influencing the country's myths and values?

movies during the week. There was a Sunday–Monday feature film (except in communities where the churches forbade Sunday movies), a different feature of somewhat lesser prominence on Tuesday–Wednesday, and another on Thursday–Friday.
On Saturday there was a cowboy or detective movie. Sometimes a double feature
played, and always there were short subjects, a cartoon, and a newsreel. The Saturday serial would leave the heroine or hero in such a dire predicament that patrons
just had to come back the next week.

The animated cartoons of Walt Disney, one of the true geniuses of the movie
industry, were so popular that Mickey Mouse was more famous and familiar than
most politicians. In May 1933, halfway into Roosevelt's first 100 days, Disney released *The Three Little Pigs*, whose theme song "Who's Afraid of the Big Bad
Wolf?" became a national hit overnight. One critic suggested that the moral of the
Disney film was that the little pig survived because he was conservative, diligent,
and hard-working; others felt that it was the pig who used modern tools and
planned ahead who won out.

ᏜᏜ ᏜᏜ ᏜᏜ ᏜᏜ

# CONCLUSION

## *The Ambivalence of the Great Depression*

The New Deal, despite its great variety of legislation, did not end the Depression,
nor did it solve the problem of unemployment. For many Americans, like Diana
Morgan who feared all her life that her telephone would be cut off, the most vivid
memory was the shame and guilt of being unemployed, the despair and fear that
came from losing a business or being evicted from a home or an apartment. Parents who lived through the decade urged their children to find a secure job, get
married, and settle down. "Every time I've encountered the Depression it has
been used as a barrier and a club," one daughter of Depression parents remembered; "older people use it to explain to me that I can't understand anything: I
didn't live through the Depression."

New Deal legislation did not solve the country's problems, but it did
strengthen the federal government, especially the executive branch. Federal agencies like the Federal Deposit Insurance Corporation and programs like Social Security influenced the daily lives of most Americans, and rural electrification, the
WPA, and the CCC changed the lives of millions. The New Deal also established
the principle of federal responsibility for the health of the economy, initiated the
concept of the welfare state, and dramatically increased government spending to
help the poor. Federally subsidized housing, minimum-wage laws, and a policy
for paying farmers to limit production, all aspects of these principles, had far-
reaching implications.

The New Deal was as important for what it did not do as for what it did. It did
not promote socialism and it did not redistribute income. It promoted social justice and social reform, but it provided little for people at the bottom of American
society. In the long run, it probably strengthened corporate capitalism.

With his colorful personality and dramatic response to the nation's crisis,
FDR dominated his times in a way few presidents have done. And his legacy has

remained controversial. For all of the twentieth century, and even into the twenty-first, much of American politics has centered around preserving and extending or trying to abolish or revise legislation passed during the Depression decade.

## Discovering U.S. History Online

*Voices from the Dust Bowl*  http://memory.loc.gov/ammem/afctshtml/tshome.html
Farm Security Administration (FSA) studies of migrant work camps in central California in 1940 and 1941 compose the bulk of this site. The collection includes audio recordings, photographs, manuscript materials, and publications.

*New Deal Network*  http://newdeal.feri.org/
This database includes photographs, political cartoons, and texts—including speeches, letters, and other historic documents—from the New Deal period.

*IPL POTUS—Franklin Delano Roosevelt*  http://www.ipl.org/ref/POTUS/fdroosevelt.html
This Internet Public Library—Presidents of the United States site provides information about FDR, the only president to serve more than two terms.

*A New Deal for the Arts*  http://www.nara.gov/exhall/newdeal/newdeal.html
Artwork, documents, and photographs recount the federal government's efforts to fund artists in the 1930s in this National Archives site.

*The Price of Civilization*  http://www.taxhistory.org/civilization
This site is part of the Tax History Project at Tax Analysts, an online tax information resource. It includes thousands of searchable pages of documents and analysis on tax issues during the Depression and WWII and is part of a larger site that contains a cartoon gallery and WWII-era posters.

## Fiction and Film

James Farrell describes growing up in Depression Chicago in *Studs Lonigan* (1932–1935); John Steinbeck shows Okies trying to escape the dust bowl in his novel *The Grapes of Wrath* (1939); Richard Wright details the trials of a young black man in *Native Son* (1940).

    *Modern Times* (1936) is a classic film that features Charlie Chaplin at his best as he depicts the impersonality of industrial civilization where machines dominate people. *Grapes of Wrath* (1940) is another classic film. Although it doesn't exhibit the despair and anger of the book on which it is based, it is still a powerful film that explores the human cost of the dust bowl and the Depression.

## Recommended Reading

### The Great Depression
David M. Kennedy, *Freedom From Fear: The American People in Depression and War* (1999); Robert S. McElvain, *The Great Depression* (1984); William Mullins, *The Depression and the Urban West Coast* (1991); Arthur M. Schlesinger, Jr., *The Crisis of the Old Order* (1957); Studs Terkel, *Hard Times* (1970); T. H. Watkins, *The Hungry Years* (1999); Donald Worster, *Dust Bowl* (1979).

### Roosevelt and the First New Deal
James MacGregor Burns, *Roosevelt: The Lion and the Fox* (1956); Paul Conkin, *The New Deal* (1967); Blanch Wiesen Cook, *Eleanor Roosevelt, Vol. 2* (1999); Frank Freidel, *Franklin D. Roosevelt* (1990); William E. Leuchtenburg, *Franklin Roosevelt and The New Deal* (1963); James J. Patterson, *America's Struggle Against Poverty* (1981); Eliot Rosen, *Hoover, Roosevelt on the Brain Trust* (1977).

## One Hundred Days

Anthony Badger, *The New Deal* (1989); Alan Brinkley, *Voices of Protest: Huey Long, Father Coughlin and the Great Depression* (1982); Thomas K. McGraw, *TVA and the Power Fight* (1970); Arthur M. Schlesinger, Jr., *The Coming of the New Deal* (1959).

## The Second New Deal

Irving Bernstein, *The Turbulent Years: A History of the American Worker, 1933–1941* (1970); Dan T. Carter, *Scottsboro* (1969); Lisabeth Cohen, *Making a New Deal: Industrial Workers in Chicago, 1919–1939* (1990); Abraham Hoffman, *Unwanted: Mexican Americans and the Great Depression* (1974); Richard Lowitt, *The New Deal and the West* (1984); Roy Lubove, *The Struggle For Social Security* (1968); Kenneth R. Philip, *John Collier's Crusade for Indian Reform* (1977); Vicki L. Ruiz, *From Out of the Shadows: Mexican Women in Twentieth Century America* (1998); Harvard Sitkoff, *A New Deal for Blacks* (1978); Susan Ware, *Holding Their Own: American Women in the 1930s* (1982).

## The Last Years of the New Deal

Alan Brinkley, *The End of Reform: New Deal Liberalism, Recession and War* (1995); Barry Cushman, *Rethinking the New Deal Court* (1998); Steve Fraser and Gary Gertstle, eds., *The Rise and Fall of the New Deal Order* (1989); William E. Leuchtenburg, *The Supreme Court Reborn: The Constitutional Revolution in the Age of Roosevelt* (1995); James T. Patterson, *The New Deal and the States* (1969).

## The Other Side of the 1930s

Andrew Bergman, *We're in the Money: Depression America and Its Films* (1971); Terry A. Cooney, *Balancing Acts: American Thought and Culture in the 1930s* (1995); Jeffrey L. Meikle, *Twentieth Century Limited: Industrial Design in America, 1925–1939* (1979); Robert Sklar, *Movie Made America* (1975); William Stott, *Documentary Expression and Thirties America* (1973).

# CHAPTER 25
# World War II

## CHAPTER OUTLINE

- The Twisting Road to War
- The Home Front
- The Social Impact of the War

- A War of Diplomats and Generals
- Conclusion: Peace, Prosperity, and International Responsibilities

## AMERICAN STORIES
### A Native-American Boy Plays at War

N. Scott Momaday, a Kiowa Indian born in Lawton, Oklahoma, in 1934, grew up on reservations. He was only 11 years old when World War II ended, yet the war changed his life. Shortly after the United States entered the war, Momaday's parents moved to New Mexico, where his father got a job with an oil company and his mother worked in the civilian personnel office at an Army Air Force base. Like many couples, they had struggled through the hard times of the Depression. The war meant jobs.

Momaday's best friend was Billy Don Johnson. Together they played war, digging trenches and dragging themselves through imaginary minefields. They hurled grenades and fired endless rounds from their imaginary machine guns, pausing only to drink Kool-Aid from their canteens. At school, they were taught how to hate the enemy and be proud of America. They recited the Pledge of Allegiance to the flag and sang "God Bless America," "The Star-Spangled Banner," and "Remember Pearl Harbor." Like most Americans, they believed that World War II was a good war fought against evil empires. The United States was always right, the enemy always wrong. It was an attitude that would influence Momaday and his generation for the rest of their lives.

Momaday's only difficulty was that his Native-American face was often mistaken for that of an Asian. Almost every day on the playground, someone would yell, "Hi ya, Jap," and a fight was on. Billy Don always came to his friend's defense, but it was disconcerting to be taken for the enemy. His father read old Kiowa tales to Momaday, who was proud to be an Indian but prouder still to be an American. On Saturday, he and his friends would cheer at the movies as they watched a Japanese Zero or a German ME-109 go down.

Near the end of the war, Momaday's family moved again, as so many families did, so that his father might get a better job. This time they lived right next door to an Air Force base, and Momaday fell in love with the B-17 "Flying Fortress," the bomber that military strategists thought would win the war in the Pacific and in Europe.

Looking back, Momaday reflected on the importance of the war in his growing up. "I see now that one experiences easily the ordinary things of life," he decided, "the things which cast familiar shadows upon the sheer, transparent panels of time, and he perceives his experience in the only way he can, according to his age." Though Momaday's life during the war differed from the lives of boys old enough to join the armed forces, the war was no less real for him.

The Momadays fared better than most Native Americans. Although they had been made U.S. citizens by an act of Congress in 1924, the Momadays, like all Native Americans living in Arizona and New Mexico, were denied the right to vote by state law. Jobs, even in wartime, were hard to find. Native-American servicemen returning from the war discovered that as "Indians" they still faced blatant discrimination in many states. Still, Momaday thought of himself not so much as an Indian but as an American, and that too was a product of his generation. But as he grew to maturity, he became a successful writer and spokesman for his people. In 1969, he won the Pulitzer Prize for his novel *House Made of Dawn*. In his writing, he stresses the Indian's close identification with the land. Writing about his grandmother, he says: "The immense landscape of the continental interior lay like memory in her blood."

⚭ ⚭ ⚭ ⚭

No American cities were bombed and the country was never invaded, but World War II still influenced almost every aspect of American life. The war ended the Depression. Industrial jobs were plentiful, and even though prejudice and discrimination did not disappear, blacks, Hispanics, women, and other minorities had new opportunities. Like World War I, this second global war expanded cooperation between government and industry and increased the influence of government in all areas of American life. The war also ended the last remnants of American isolationism. The United States emerged from the war in 1945 as the most powerful and most prosperous nation in the world.

This chapter traces the gradual involvement of the United States in the international events during the 1930s that finally led to participation in the most devastating war the world had seen. It traces the diplomatic and military struggles of the war and the search for a secure peace. It also explores the war's impact on ordinary people and on American attitudes about the world, on patriotism and the American way of life. Even those, like Momaday, who grew up during the war and were too young to fight, were influenced by the war—and the sense of moral certainty that the war inspired—for the rest of their lives. The war brought prosperity to some, death to others. It left Americans the world's richest people and the United States its most powerful nation.

## THE TWISTING ROAD TO WAR

Looking back on the events between 1933 and 1941 that eventually led America into World War II, it is easy to criticize decisions made or actions not taken, or else to see everything as inevitable. But historical events are never inevitable, and leaders who must make decisions never have the advantage of hindsight. They must deal with situations as they find them, and they never have all the facts.

## Foreign Policy in the 1930s

In March 1933, Roosevelt faced not only overwhelming domestic difficulties but also an international crisis. The worldwide depression had caused near financial disaster in Europe.

Roosevelt had no master plan in foreign policy, just as he had none in the domestic sphere. In the first days of his administration, he gave conflicting signals about the international situation. First it seemed that FDR would cooperate in some kind of international economic agreement on tariffs and currency, which was to be negotiated in London. But then he refused to go along with any such agreement. In 1933, Roosevelt believed it was more important to solve the domestic economic crisis than to achieve international economic cooperation. His actions signaled a decision to "go it alone" in foreign policy.

Roosevelt did, however, alter some of the foreign policy decisions of previous administrations. For example, he recognized the Soviet government. In reversing the 1920s non-recognition policy (which rested largely on anti-Communist sentiments), Roosevelt hoped to gain a market for surplus American grain—a trade bonanza that never materialized. But diplomatic recognition opened communications between two emerging world powers.

The administration also reversed earlier interventionist policies in Latin America. The United States continued to support dictators, especially in Central America, because they promised to promote stability and preserve U. S. economic interests. But Roosevelt, extending the Good Neighbor policy Hoover had initiated, completed the removal of American military forces from Haiti and Nicaragua in 1934. In a series of pan-American conferences, he joined in pledging that no country in the hemisphere would intervene in the "internal or external affairs" of any other.

The new policy's first test came in Cuba, where a revolution threatened American investments of more than a billion dollars. But the United States did not send troops. Instead, Roosevelt dispatched envoys to work out a conciliatory agreement. A short time later, when a coup led by Fulgencio Batista overthrew the revolutionary government, the United States not only recognized the Batista government but also offered a large loan. The United States agreed to abrogate the Platt Amendment (which made Cuba a virtual protectorate of the United States) in return for continued rights to the Guantanamo naval base.

The Trade Agreements Act of 1934 empowered the president to lower tariff rates by as much as 50 percent and took the tariff away from the pressure of special-interest groups in Congress. Secretary of State Cordell Hull negotiated a series of pacts that improved trade. By 1935, half of American cotton exports and a large proportion of other products were going to Latin America. So the Good Neighbor policy was also good business for the United States. But increased trade did not solve the economic problems for either the United States or Latin America.

Another test for Latin American policy came in 1938 when Mexico nationalized the property of American oil companies. Instead of intervening, as many businessmen urged, the State Department patiently worked out an agreement

FIFTEEN CENTS                              April 13, 1936

# TIME
*The Weekly Newsmagazine*

Volume XXVII              ADOLF HITLER              Number 15
                          *by*
                          *(See Foreign News)*

Newsreels and popular magazines such as *Life, Look,* and *Time* made Hitler's image and mannerisms familiar to all Americans. Hitler's picture appeared on the cover of *Time* at least six times between 1931 and 1935. In this 1936 cover, he strikes a characteristic pose. (© 1936/Time Inc.)

that included some compensation for the companies. Washington might have acted differently had not the threat of war in Europe in 1938 created a sense that all the Western Hemisphere nations should cooperate. At a pan-American conference held that year, the United States and most Latin American countries agreed to resist all foreign intervention in the hemisphere.

## Neutrality in Europe

On January 30, 1933, about two months before Roosevelt's inauguration, Nazi leader Adolf Hitler became German chancellor. Born in Austria in 1889, he served in the army during World War I. Like so many other Germans, he was angered by the harsh terms of the Treaty of Versailles. But Hitler blamed the German defeat in the war on Jews and Communists. He had a charismatic style and a plan that attracted many followers. Shortly after he became chancellor, he suspended the constitution and made himself Fuehrer (leader) and dictator and set out to conquer Europe. As the first step, in 1934 he announced German rearmament, violating the Versailles Treaty. That same year, Italy's Fascist dictator Benito Mussolini (who had come to power a decade earlier) threatened to invade the East African country of Ethiopia. These ominous rumblings frightened Americans at the very time they were reexamining the history of American entry into the Great War and vowing that it would never happen again.

Senator Gerald P. Nye of North Dakota launched an investigation into the connection between corporate profits and American participation in World War I. His committee's public hearings revealed that many American businessmen had close relationships with the War Department. Although no conspiracy was proved, it was easy to conclude that the United States had been tricked into going to war by the people who profited heavily from it.

On many campuses, students demonstrated against war. They joined organizations like the Veterans of Future Wars and protested Reserve Officer Training Corps programs on their campuses. They were determined never again to support a foreign war. But in Europe, Asia, and Africa, there were already rumblings of another great international conflict.

## Ethiopia and Spain

In May 1935, Italy invaded Ethiopia after rejecting the League of Nations' offer to mediate disputes between the two countries. The remote Ethiopian war frightened Congress into passing the Neutrality Act, which authorized the president to prohibit all arms shipments to nations at war and to advise all United States citizens not to travel on belligerents' ships except at their own risk. Congress was determined to prevent America from entering another world war.

Although he would have preferred a more flexible bill, Roosevelt used the authority of the Neutrality Act of 1935 to impose an arms embargo. The League of Nations condemned Italy as the aggressor. But neither Britain nor the United States wanted to stop oil shipments to Italy or join the fight. The embargo had little impact on Italy but was disastrous for the poor African nation. Having conquered Ethiopia, Mussolini made an alliance with Germany, the Rome-Berlin Axis, in 1936.

"We shun political commitments which might entangle us in foreign war," Roosevelt announced in 1936. But isolation became more difficult when General Francisco Franco, supported by the Catholic Church, large landowners, and reactionary politicians, revolted against the republican government of Spain. Germany and Italy aided Franco, sending planes and other weapons, while the Soviet Union supplied the Spanish republican Loyalists.

The Spanish Civil War polarized the United States. Most Catholics and many anti-Communists sided with Franco. But many American liberals and radicals— even those who said they opposed all war—found the republican cause worth fighting for. Over 3,000 Americans joined the Abraham Lincoln Brigade, and hundreds died fighting fascism. "If this were a Spanish matter, I'd let it alone," wrote Sam Levenger, an Ohio State student. "But the rebellion would not last a week if it weren't for the Germans and the Italians." Levenger was killed in Spain in 1937 at the age of 20.

The U.S. government took neutrality seriously. The Neutrality Act, extended in 1936, did not apply to civil wars. However, when an American businessman tried to send 400 used airplane engines to the Loyalists, Roosevelt asked Congress to extend the arms embargo to Spain. While the United States, Britain, and France carefully stayed neutral, Franco consolidated his dictatorship with German and Italian help. Meanwhile, Congress in 1937 passed another Neutrality Act, this time forbidding American citizens to travel on belligerents' ships. The embargo on arms was tightened, and belligerents could buy nonmilitary items only on a cash-and-carry basis.

So the United States tried to avoid repeating the mistakes that had led it into World War I. Unfortunately, World War II, which moved closer each day, would be a different kind of war, and the lessons of the first war would be of little use.

## War in Europe

Roosevelt had no careful strategy to deal with the rising tide of troubles in Europe in the late 1930s. He was no isolationist, but he wanted to keep the United States out of any European conflict. When he publicly announced, "I hate war," he meant it. Unlike his distant cousin Theodore Roosevelt, he did not view war as a test of manhood. In foreign policy, as in domestic affairs, he responded to events, but he moved reluctantly toward greater American involvement.

In March 1938, Hitler annexed Austria, and in September he occupied the Sudetenland, a part of Czechoslovakia. Within six months, Hitler seized the rest of that country. Little protest came from the United States. Most Americans sympathized with the victims of Hitler's aggression, and eventually some were horrified by rumors of the murder of hundreds of thousands of Jews. But because newspapers avoided intensive coverage of these well-documented but unpleasant stories, many Americans did not learn of the Holocaust until near the end of the war.

At first, almost everyone hoped that Europeans could work out compromises. But that notion was destroyed on August 23, 1939, by the news of a Nazi-Soviet pact. Many Americans had secretly hoped that Nazi Germany and Soviet Russia would destroy each other. Now these ideological enemies had signed a nonaggression pact. A week later, Hitler's army attacked Poland, marking the onset of World War II. Britain and France came to Poland's defense. "This nation will remain a neutral nation," Roosevelt said, "but I cannot ask that every American remain neutral in thought as well."

Roosevelt asked for repeal of the embargo section of the Neutrality Act and for approval of cash-and-carry arms sales to France and Britain. And he took some risks. In August 1939, physicist Albert Einstein, a Jewish refugee from Nazi Germany, warned him that German scientists were working on an atomic bomb. The president feared the consequences of Hitler being the first to possess such a weapon, and authorized secret exploratory work. The top-secret Manhattan Project—known only to a few advisers and key members of Congress—was officially launched in 1941. Ultimately it would change the course of human history.

There was a lull in the war after Germany and the Soviet Union crushed Poland in September 1939. A number of Americans, including the American ambassador to Great Britain, Joseph Kennedy, who feared Communist Russia more than Fascist Germany, urged the United States to take the lead in negotiating a peace settlement that would recognize the German and Russian occupation of Poland. The British and French were not interested, and neither was Roosevelt. Great Britain sent several divisions to aid the French against the expected German attack, but for months nothing happened.

The "phony war" dramatically ended on April 9, 1940, when Germany attacked Norway and Denmark. At the beginning of May, the German *Blitzkrieg* ("lightning war") swept into the Low Countries. A week later, mechanized German forces stormed into France, sweeping around fortifications known as the Maginot line. France surrendered in June as the British army fled across the English Channel.

How should the United States respond to this desperate situation? Some concerned citizens organized the Committee to Defend America by Aiding the Allies, but others, including Charles Lindbergh, supported a group called America First. They argued that the United States should forget England and concentrate on defending America. Roosevelt steered a cautious course. He sent Britain 50 old American destroyers. In return, the United States received the right to establish naval and air bases from Newfoundland to Bermuda and British Guiana. British Prime Minister Winston Churchill asked for much more.

But Roosevelt hesitated and emphasized U.S. preparedness. In July 1940, he authorized $4 billion for more American warships. In September, Congress passed the Selective Service Act, providing for America's first peacetime draft. Over 1 million men were to serve for one year, but only in the Western Hemisphere.

## The Election of 1940

Part of Roosevelt's reluctance to aid Great Britain more aggressively came from his genuine desire to keep the United States out of the war, but it also reflected the presidential campaign of 1940. Roosevelt broke tradition by seeking a third term. The increasing support he was drawing from the liberal wing of the Democratic party led him to select liberal farm economist Henry Wallace from Iowa as his running mate.

The Republicans nominated energetic Wendell Willkie of Indiana. Despite his big-business ties, Willkie approved of most New Deal legislation and supported aid to Great Britain. Willkie was the most exciting Republican candidate since Theodore Roosevelt. Yet amid the international crisis, the voters stayed with FDR—27 million to 22 million. Roosevelt carried 38 of the 48 states.

## Lend-Lease

After the election, Roosevelt invented a "lend-lease" scheme for sending aid to Britain without demanding payment. He compared this to lending a garden hose to a neighbor whose house was on fire. Republican Senator Robert Taft thought it was more like lending chewing gum: "Once it had been used you did not want it back." Others were even more critical.

The Lend-Lease Act, which Congress passed in March 1941, destroyed the fiction of neutrality. By then, U-boats were sinking a half-million tons of Atlantic shipping each month. In June, Roosevelt proclaimed a national emergency. Then, on June 22, Germany attacked Russia.

When Roosevelt extended lend-lease aid to Russia, the former Communist enemy, in November 1941, many Americans were shocked. But most quickly shifted from viewing the Soviet Union as an enemy to treating it like a friend.

By the autumn of 1941, the United States was virtually at war with Germany in the Atlantic. On September 11, Roosevelt issued a "shoot on sight" order for all American ships operating in the Atlantic, and on October 30, a German submarine sank an American destroyer. The war in the Atlantic was undeclared, and many Americans opposed it. However, it was not Germany but Japan that dragged the United States into World War II.

## The Path to Pearl Harbor

Japan, controlled by ambitious military leaders, was the aggressor in the Far East as Hitler's Germany was in Europe. Intent on becoming a major world power and desperate for natural resources, especially oil, Japan was willing to risk war to get them. It invaded Manchuria in 1931 and launched an all-out assault on China in 1937. But Japanese leaders wanted to put off attacking the Philippines. For its part, the United States feared a two-front war and was willing to delay a confrontation with Japan until it had dealt with the German threat. Thus between 1938 and 1941, the United States and Japan engaged in diplomatic shadow boxing.

America exerted economic pressure on Japan in July 1939, giving the required six months' notice for cancellation of the 1911 commercial agreement between the two countries. In September 1940, the administration forbade shipping aircraft fuel and scrap metal to Japan. Other items were added to the embargo until by the spring of 1941 only oil could be shipped to Japan; the administration hoped that the threat of cutting off that important resource would force negotiations and avert a crisis. Japan opened negotiations with the United States, but there was little to discuss. Japan would not withdraw from China and from 1940 to 1941 occupied French Indochina. In July 1941, Roosevelt froze all Japanese assets in the United States, effectively embargoing trade with Japan.

Roosevelt had an advantage in negotiating with Japan, for Americans had broken the Japanese secret diplomatic code. But Japanese intentions were hard to decipher from the intercepted messages. American leaders knew that Japan planned to attack, but they didn't know where. In September 1941, the Japanese decided to strike sometime after November unless the United States offered real concessions.

On the morning of December 7, 1941, Japanese airplanes launched from aircraft carriers attacked the United States fleet at Pearl Harbor, in Hawaii. The surprise attack destroyed or disabled 19 ships (including five battleships) and 150 planes and killed 2,335 soldiers and sailors and 68 civilians. On the same day, Japan invaded the Philippines, Guam, Midway, and British Hong Kong and Malaya. The next day, Congress declared war on Japan.

December 7, 1941, was a day that "would live in infamy," Franklin Roosevelt told Congress and the nation as he asked for the declaration of war. It was also a day that would have far-reaching implications for American foreign policy and for American attitudes toward the world. The surprise attack united the country—even isolationists and "America Firsters"—as nothing else could have.

After the shock and anger subsided, Americans searched for a villain. The myth still persists that the villain was Roosevelt, who supposedly knew of the Japanese attack but failed to warn the military so that the American people might unite behind the war against Germany. But Roosevelt did not know. There was no warning that the attack was coming against Pearl Harbor, and the American ability to read Japanese coded messages was no help because the fleet kept radio silence.

The Americans underestimated the Japanese, partly because of racial prejudice. They ignored many warning signals because they simply did not believe the

This photo shows an exploding American destroyer at Pearl Harbor on December 7, 1941. The attack on Pearl Harbor united the country and came to symbolize Japanese treachery and American lack of preparedness. Photographs such as this were published throughout the war to inspire Americans to work harder. (Official U.S. Navy Photo/The National Archives)

Japanese capable of attacking a target as far away as Hawaii. Roosevelt and most experts expected the Japanese to attack the Philippines or Thailand. Many people blundered, but there was no conspiracy.

Even more important in the long run was the Japanese attack's effect on a generation of military and political leaders. Pearl Harbor became the symbol of unpreparedness. For a generation that had been stunned by an unscrupulous enemy attack, the lesson was to be ready to stop an aggressor before it struck. That lesson would influence American policy in Korea, Vietnam, and beyond.

## THE HOME FRONT

Too often wars are described in terms of leaders, grand strategy, and elaborate campaigns. But wars affect all people—the soldiers who fight and the women and children and men who stay home. World War II especially had an impact on all aspects of society: the economy, entertainment, even attitudes toward women and blacks. For many people, the war represented opportunity and the end of the Depression. On others, it left lasting scars.

## Mobilizing for War

Converting American industry to war production was a complex task. Shortly after Pearl Harbor, Roosevelt created the War Production Board (WPB) and appointed Donald Nelson, executive vice-president of Sears, Roebuck, to mobilize resources for an all-out war effort. The WPB offered businesses "cost-plus" contracts, guaranteeing a generous profit. Often the government also financed new plants and equipment. Secretary of War Henry Stimson explained: "If you . . . go to war . . . in a capitalist country, you have to let business make money out of the process or business won't work."

The Roosevelt administration leaned over backward to gain the cooperation of businessmen, many of them alienated by New Deal policies. The president appointed many business executives to key positions and abandoned antitrust actions in any industry that was remotely war-related.

The policy worked. Industrial production and net corporate profits nearly doubled during the war. Large commercial farmers also profited. The war years accelerated the mechanization of the farm and dramatically increased the use of fertilizer, but between 1940 and 1945, the farm population declined by 17 percent.

Many government agencies besides the War Production Board helped run the war effort efficiently. The Office of Price Administration (OPA) set prices to control inflation and rationed products—and because it affected so many lives so disagreeably, many Americans regarded it as oppressive. The National War Labor Board (NWLB) had the authority to set wages and hours and to monitor working conditions, and it could seize plants whose owners refused to cooperate.

Union membership grew rapidly, aided by government policy. In return for a "no-strike pledge," the NWLB allowed agreements that required workers to retain their union membership through the life of a contract. Responding to labor leaders' protests, the NWLB finally allowed a 15 percent cost-of-living increase on some contracts, but that did not apply to overtime pay, which helped drive up wages in some industries during the war by about 70 percent. Believing that the miners were still underpaid, John L. Lewis broke the no-strike pledge by calling a nationwide coal strike in 1943. When Roosevelt ordered a government seizure of the mines, Lewis called off the strike. But his bold protest did help raise miners' wages.

Besides imposing wage and price controls and rationing, the government fought inflation by selling war bonds and increasing taxes. The Revenue Act of 1942 raised tax rates, broadened the tax base, boosted corporate taxes to 40 percent, and set the excess-profits tax at 90 percent. In addition, the government initiated payroll deductions, making the income tax a reality for most Americans for the first time.

Despite some unfairness and much confusion, the American economy turned out the equipment and supplies that eventually won the war. American industries built 300,000 airplanes, 88,140 tanks, and 3,000 merchant ships. In 1944 alone, American factories produced 800,000 tons of synthetic rubber to replace natural rubber, cut off by the Japanese. By the war's end, the American economy was turning out an astonishing 50 percent of all the world's goods.

Although the national debt grew from about $143 billion in 1943 to $260 billion in 1945, taxes paid for about 40 percent of the war's cost. At the same time, full employment and the increase in two-income families, together with forced savings, helped amass capital for postwar expansion. In a limited way, the tax policy also tended to redistribute wealth, which the New Deal had failed to do. The top 5 percent income bracket, which controlled 23 percent of the disposable income in 1939, accounted for only 17 percent in 1945.

The war stimulated the growth of the federal bureaucracy and accelerated the trend, begun during World War I and extended in the 1920s and 1930s, toward a federal government role in the economy. The war also increased the cooperation between industry and government, creating what would later be called a military-industrial complex. But for most Americans, despite their anger at the OPA and the income tax, the war meant the end of the Depression.

## Patriotic Fervor

The war, so horrible elsewhere, was remote in the United States—except for the thousands of families that received the official telegram telling of a loved one killed in action. The government tried to keep the conflict alive in Americans' minds, and the country united behind the war effort. The Office of War Information, staffed by writers and advertising executives, controlled the news that the public received about the war, presenting things in the best possible light. The government also sold war bonds, not only to help pay for the war and reduce inflation but also to sell the war to the American people. As during World War I, celebrities appeared at bond rallies. Schoolchildren purchased war stamps and pasted them in an album until they had accumulated stamps worth $18.75, enough to buy a $25 bond (redeemable 10 years later). Their bonds, they were told, would purchase bullets or an airplane part to kill "Japs" and Germans. Working men and women purchased bonds through payroll deduction plans and looked forward to spending the money on consumer goods after the war. In the end, the government sold over $135 billion in war bonds. While the bond drives did help control inflation, they were most important in making millions of Americans feel that they were contributing to the war effort.

Those too old or too young to join the armed forces served as air raid wardens or civilian defense and Red Cross volunteers. They raised victory gardens, contributed to scrap drives, and did without. "Hoarders are the same as spies," one ad announced.

## Internment of Japanese Americans

Cooperating with the war effort fostered pride and a feeling of community—but also hate for the enemy. The Nazis, especially Hitler and his Gestapo, were synonymous with evil before 1941. Later, most Americans ceased making distinctions between Germans and Nazis, although the anti-German hysteria that had swept the country during World War I never returned.

The Japanese were easier to hate. The attack on Pearl Harbor created a special animosity toward them, but depicting them as warlike and subhuman owed something to an old American distrust of all Asians. Two weeks after Pearl Harbor, *Time* magazine told Americans how to distinguish the friendly Chinese from "the Japs." "Chinese . . . have an easy gait. The Chinese expression is likely to be more kindly, placid, open; the Japanese more positive, dogmatic, arrogant."

Racial stereotypes played a role in the treatment of Japanese Americans during the war. They were the only group confined in concentration camps, in the greatest mass abridgment of civil liberties in American history.

At the time of Pearl Harbor, about 127,000 Japanese Americans lived in the United States, most on the West Coast. About 80,000 were *nisei* (Japanese born in the United States and holding American citizenship) and *sansei* (the sons and daughters of *nisei*); the rest were *issei* (aliens born in Japan who were ineligible for U.S. citizenship). They had long suffered from prejudice—barred, for example, from intermarriage with other groups and excluded from many clubs, restaurants, and recreation facilities. Many worked as tenant farmers, fishermen, or

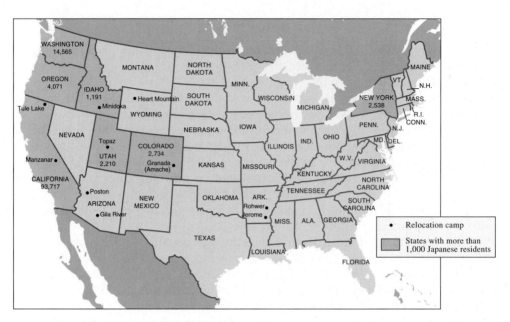

**RELOCATION CAMPS**   Early in 1942, responding to the hysterical fear that Japanese Americans living on the West Coast might engage in sabotage, the government ordered over 100,000 Japanese Americans (many of them citizens) into relocation camps. A larger group of Japanese Americans living in Hawaii did not have their lives disrupted or their property confiscated.

small businessmen, or were land-owning farmers, but some belonged to a small professional class of lawyers, teachers, and doctors.

Although many retained cultural ties to Japan and spoke Japanese, these people posed no more threat to the country than did the much larger groups of Italian Americans and German Americans. But their physical characteristics made them stand out. After Pearl Harbor, an anti-Japanese panic seized the West Coast. Rumors suggested that Japanese fishermen were preparing to mine harbors, blow up tunnels, and poison water supplies.

West Coast politicians and citizens urged the War Department to remove the Japanese. The president capitulated and issued Executive Order 9066, authorizing the evacuation in February 1942. "The continued pressure of a largely unassimilated, tightly knit racial group, bound to an enemy nation by strong ties of race, culture, custom and religion, constituted a menace which had to be dealt with," General John De Witt argued, justifying the removal on military grounds. But racial fear and hatred, not military necessity, stood behind the order.

"The Japs live like rats, breed like rats, and act like rats. We don't want them," the governor of Idaho announced. So it was in remote, often arid, sections of the West that eventually the government built the primitive "relocation centers." "When I first entered our room, I became sick to my stomach," a Japanese-American woman remembered.

The government evacuated about 110,000 Japanese, who lost almost all of their property. Farmers left their crops to be harvested by their American neighbors. Store owners sold out for a small percentage of what their goods were

In this photo, Japanese-American children are on their way to a "relocation center." For many Japanese Americans, but especially for the children, the nightmare of the relocation camp experience would stay with them all their lives. (Library of Congress)

worth. Japanese Americans lost all of their personal possessions, and something more—their pride and respect.

The evacuation appears unjustified in retrospect. In Hawaii, with its much larger Japanese-American population, authorities attempted no evacuation, and no sabotage and little disloyalty occurred. Late in the war, the government allowed Japanese-American men to volunteer for military service, and many served bravely in the European theater. The 442nd Infantry Combat Team, made up entirely of *nisei,* became the most decorated unit in all the military service—another indication of the loyalty and patriotism of the Japanese Americans. In 1988, Congress belatedly apologized and voted limited compensation for Japanese Americans relocated during World War II.

## African Americans and Hispanic Americans at War

Black Americans profited little from the wartime revival of prosperity and the expansion of jobs early in the war. Those who joined the military were usually assigned to menial jobs, always in segregated units with whites as the high-ranking officers. The myth persisted that black soldiers had failed to perform well in World War I.

Some black leaders found it especially ironic that as the country prepared to fight Hitler and his racist policies, the United States kept its own brand of racism. A black labor leader, A. Philip Randolph, decided to act. Randolph had worked

Even before the United States entered the war, black families like this one moved north to look for work and a better life. This massive migration would change the racial mix in northern cities. (Library of Congress)

with the first wave of African Americans migrating from the South to the northern cities during and just after World War I. Afterwards he organized and led the Brotherhood of Sleeping Car Porters and in 1937 finally won grudging recognition of the union from the Pullman Company.

Admired by black leaders of all political persuasions, Randolph convinced many of them in 1941 to join him in a march on Washington to demand equal rights. The thought of as many as 100,000 African Americans marching in protest in the nation's capital alarmed Roosevelt. At first, he sent his assistants and his wife Eleanor, who was greatly admired in the black community, to dissuade Randolph. Finally, he talked to Randolph in person on June 18, 1941, and they struck a bargain. Roosevelt refused to desegregate the armed forces, but in return for Randolph's calling off the march, the president issued Executive Order 8802, which stated that it was government policy that "there shall be no discrimination in the employment of workers in defense industries or government because of race, creed, color or national origin." To enforce the order, he established the Fair Employment Practices Commission (FEPC).

By threatening militant action, the black leaders wrested a major concession from the president. But the executive order did not end prejudice, and the FEPC (which its chairman described as the "most hated agency in Washington") had limited success in erasing the color line. Many black soldiers were angered and humiliated throughout the war by being made to sit in the back of buses and being barred from hotels and restaurants. A former black soldier recalled being refused service in a restaurant in Salina, Kansas, while the same restaurant served

German prisoners from a camp nearby. "We continued to stare," he recalled. "This was really happening . . . . The people of Salina would serve these enemy soldiers and turn away black American G.I.'s."

Jobs in war industries helped many African Americans improve their economic conditions. Continuing the migration that had begun during World War I, about 750,000 southern blacks moved to northern and western cities. Some became skilled workers, and a few became professionals. The new arrivals increased pressure on overcrowded housing and other facilities, accentuating tension among all hard-pressed groups. In Detroit, a major race riot broke out in the summer of 1943 after Polish Americans protested a public housing development that promised to bring blacks into their neighborhood. A series of incidents led to fights between black and white young people and then to looting in the black community. Before federal and state troops restored order, 25 blacks and 9 whites had been killed and more than $2 million worth of property was destroyed. Groups of whites roamed the city attacking blacks, overturning cars, setting fires, and sometimes killing wantonly. Other riots broke out in Mobile, Los Angeles, New York, and Beaumont, Texas. In all these cities, and in many others where the tension did not lead to open violence, the legacy of hate lasted long after the war.

Mexican Americans, like most minority groups, benefited from wartime job opportunities, but they, too, faced prejudice. In California and in many parts of the Southwest, Mexicans could not use public swimming pools and certain restaurants. Usually they were limited to menial jobs and were constantly harassed by the police. In Los Angeles, anti-Mexican prejudice got violent. Most of the anger focused on Mexican gang members wearing zoot suits—long, loose coats with padded shoulders, ballooned pants, and wide-brimmed hats.

Zoot-suiters especially angered soldiers and sailors in Los Angeles. After many provocative incidents, the violence peaked on June 7, 1943, when gangs of servicemen attacked all the young zoot-suiters they could find or anyone who looked Mexican. The servicemen, joined by others, beat up the Mexicans, stripped off their offensive clothes, and cut the long, duck-tailed hair that was part of the look. The police usually looked the other way or arrested the victims. The local press and the chamber of commerce hotly denied that race was a factor, but *Time* magazine was probably closer to the truth when it called the riots the "ugliest brand of mob action since the coolie race riots of the 1870s."

## THE SOCIAL IMPACT OF THE WAR

Modern wars have been incredibly destructive of lives and property, but they have had social consequences as well. World War II altered patterns of work, leisure, education, and family life; caused a massive migration of people; created jobs; and changed lifestyles. It is difficult to overemphasize the war's social impact.

### Wartime Opportunities

More than 15 million American civilians moved during the war. Like the Momadays, many left home seeking better jobs. For Native Americans, wartime opportunities caused a migration into the cities—as it did for countless other Americans

# Technology Changes the American People

## Plastics

When Nylon stockings were put on sale in February 1946, 30,000 people, "including many brave men," mobbed Gimbel's department store in New York eager to buy an advertised 26,000 pairs of the hose "that would not run." Dupont had introduced the Nylon stocking in 1940, but few were able to buy them because the government appropriated the entire supply of the synthetic fiber for use in making parachutes and even tires during the war.

Nylon was only one of many forms of plastic that transformed the way Americans lived in the twentieth century. Plastics, usually defined as synthetic materials composed of organic molecules that can be shaped and hardened, have a relatively long history. One of the early pioneers was John Wesley Hyatt, a young printer from Albany, New York, who tried in 1868 to devise a substitute for the ivory billiard ball to win a $10,000 prize. He never succeeded, but he did produce a "transparent slab" as hard as wood, which he called "Celluloid." The new product was used to imitate amber and semiprecious stones. In 1888, George Eastman used a form of Celluloid to produce a flexible film for his Kodak box camera; in the process, he revolutionized photography. One problem with Celluloid was that it had a tendency to burst into flames. A young Belgian chemist who immigrated to the United States solved that problem in 1908 by developing Bakelite, a hard plastic that would not burn, melt, or dissolve. In the 1920s and 1930s, the Bakelite Corporation produced door handles, telephones, cases for radios, colorful handles for cooking utensils, and billiard balls superior to those made of ivory.

The plastics industry had to overcome the public's perception that plastics, often used to produce buttons, combs, and knickknacks, were flimsy. The fact that plastics, most often made from petroleum by-products and coal tar, could be made into sheets or poured, shaped, and molded made it a natural product for the streamlined, modern era. The radio industry discovered plastics in the 1930s. A plastic radio case looked bright and colorful, as well as sleek and modern. Just as important, a plastic radio was cheaper to produce than the elaborately carved wooden models. Probably without even recognizing it, many Americans accepted plastics when they bought a table-model radio in the 1930s.

The Bakelite Corporation was not the only promoter of plastics. Du Pont, known as a manufacturer of explosives, moved into plastics in the 1920s and advertised its products with the slogan: "Better Things for Better Living Through Chemistry." It was in the Du Pont laboratories where a group of young chemists, after many failures, finally produced a synthetic fiber that could be stretched and woven. At first they called it "Fiber 6," then "Exton," and finally "Nylon." The new miracle plastic not only made wonderful stockings but also soon replaced pig bristles in the manufacture of toothbrushes. The same Du Pont laboratories produced Cellophane, a transparent and moisture-resistant plastic that revolutionized the marketing of food and tobacco. Cellophane promised purity and freshness, and soon everything from meat to cookies to cigars were wrapped in the new, magic material.

Plastics were important in the 1930s, but it was during World War II and the postwar years that they became commonplace. From disposable pens to Formica tabletops, from Barbie dolls to Styrofoam cups, plastics transformed American life. Yet by the 1960s, for all their innovative uses, plastics had come to seem shoddy and cheap, not modern and sleek. Some called for a return to the use of natural products, such as wool, cotton, and wood, while others worried about the garbage dumps filling up with plastic bottles and bags. Du Pont, perhaps influenced by the bad publicity that chemical companies had received during the Vietnam War for producing Agent Orange and other defoliants, dropped the word *chemistry* from its slogan. The company bragged about how it produced "Better Things for Better Living."

A woman proudly tries on her new Nylon stockings after waiting in line to purchase them when they were first released to the stores in 1945. (Hagley Museum and Library)

In 1971, ecologist Barry Commoner charged in a crusading book, *The Closing Circle,* that plastics, especially polyvinyl chloride (popularly known as vinyl), were dangerous to the environment. He claimed that plastics contaminated the soil and the water supply and would cause cancer and create problems for generations unborn. But the American people were probably more disturbed by the news that thousands of seals and other wildlife were dying from becoming entangled with discarded plastic. A photograph of a dead wild duck, strangled on a discarded six-pack holder, summed up the potential evil of plastic. Commoner's book and other reports and articles helped create a series of protests that persuaded McDonald's and other corporations to replace plastic packages with paper or cardboard.

Still, Americans continued to buy Nylons, use plastic computers, and accept plastic products as a natural part of their world. In 1979, the global production of plastics surpassed that of steel. Vinyl, polyester, teflon, silicone, acrylic, and polyurethane have entered our vocabulary and altered our lives. Every day we encounter plastic bottles and bags and plastic wrappings for food, six-packs, and frozen dinners. We wear plastic glasses and use plastic skis, running shoes, backpacks, and surfboards. Automobiles and airplanes, even missiles, are made, at least in part, of plastics. And credit cards, so much a part of modern life, are often called simply "plastic." The development of plastics, like so many advances in science and technology, has been both a benefit and a menace.

**Reflecting on the Past**   How would your life be different without plastics? How many plastic objects or materials do you use in a day? Can you imagine standing in line to buy nylons? Do you have a different attitude toward plastics than your parents? Have plastics made the world better or worse?

who left farms and small towns for urban defense jobs. California alone gained more than 2 million people during the war. But Americans also moved from the rural South into northern cities, and a smaller number moved from the North to the South. Two hundred thousand came to the Detroit area, nearly a half-million to Los Angeles, and about 100,000 to Mobile, Alabama. They put pressure on the schools, housing, and other services. In Los Angeles, Mrs. Colin Kelley, the widow of a war hero, could find no place to live until a newspaper publicized her plight.

Nowhere was the change more dramatic than in the West, which the wartime boom transformed more dramatically than any development since the nineteenth-century economic revolution created by the railroads and mining. The federal government spent over $70 billion in California (one-tenth of the total for the entire country) on army bases, shipyards, supply depots, and testing sites. Private industry built so many facilities that the region became the center of a growing military-industrial complex. This spectacular growth created housing shortages and overwhelmed schools, hospitals, and municipal services. Crime, prostitution, and racial tension all increased.

For the first time in years, many families had money to spend, but they had nothing to spend it on. The last new car rolled off the assembly line in February 1942. There were no washing machines, refrigerators, or radios in the stores, little gasoline, and few tires. Even when people had time off, they tended to stay home, go to the movies, or listen to the radio.

The war required major adjustments in American family life. With several million men in the service or working at faraway defense jobs, the number of households headed by a woman increased dramatically. The number of marriages also rose sharply. Early in the war, a young man could be deferred if he had a dependent, including a wife. Later, many servicemen got married, often to women they barely knew, because they wanted a little excitement and perhaps someone to come home to. Reversing a decline that extended back to the colonial period, the birthrate also began to rise in 1940, as young couples started families as fast as they could. Since birthrates had been especially low during the Depression, the shift marked a significant change. Some children—"good-bye babies"—were conceived just before the husband joined the military or went overseas. Illegitimacy and divorce rates also went up sharply. Yet most wartime marriages survived, and many of the women left behind looked ahead to a normal life after the war.

## Women Work for Victory

Thousands of women took jobs in heavy industry that once would have been considered unladylike. They built tanks, airplanes, and ships, but they still earned less than men. At first, women were rarely taken on because, as the war in Europe pulled American industry out of its long slump, unemployed men snapped up the newly available positions.

But by 1943, with many men drafted and male unemployment virtually non-existent, the government was quick to suggest that it was women's patriotic duty to join the assembly line. A popular song was "Rosie the Riveter," who helped her marine boyfriend by "working overtime on the riveting machine."

At the end of the war, the labor force included 19.5 million women, but three-fourths of them had been working before the conflict, and some of the new ones might have sought work in normal times. The new women war workers tended to be older, and they were more often married than single. Some worked for patriotic reasons. "Every time I test a batch of rubber, I know it's going to help bring my three sons home quicker," said a female worker in a rubber plant. But others worked for the money or to have something useful to do. Yet in 1944, women's weekly wages averaged $31.21, compared with $54.65 for men, reflecting women's menial tasks and low seniority as well as outright discrimination. Married women with young children found it difficult to obtain jobs. There were few day-care facilities, and women were often told that they should be home with their children. Women workers often had to endure overt sexual harassment. Still, most persisted, and they tried to look feminine despite work clothes.

Black women faced the most difficult situation. Often, when they applied for work, they were told something like "We have not yet installed separate toilet facilities." Not until 1944 did the telephone company in New York City hire a black operator. Still, some black women moved during the war from domestic jobs to higher-paying factory work.

Many women war workers quickly left their jobs after the war ended. Some left by choice, but dismissals ran twice as high for women as for men. Some women who learned what an extra paycheck meant for the family's standard of living would have preferred to keep working. But most women, and even more men, agreed at the war's end that women did not deserve an "equal chance with men" for jobs.

## Entertaining the People

According to one survey, Americans listened to the radio an average of four and a half hours a day during the war. The major networks increased their news programs from less than 4 percent of broadcasting time to nearly 30 percent. Americans heard Edward R. Murrow broadcasting from London during the German air blitz with air-raid sirens in the background. Often static made listening difficult, but the live broadcasts had an authenticity never before possible. Commentators became celebrities on whom millions depended for war news.

The war intruded on almost all programming. Ads reminded listeners of the fighting. Lucky Strikes, whose package color changed from green to white because there was a shortage of green pigment, made "Lucky Strike Green Has Gone to War" almost as famous as "Remember Pearl Harbor." Serials, the standard fare of daytime radio, adopted wartime themes. Popular music, which occupied a large share of radio programming, mirrored the war. There was "Goodbye, Mama (I'm Off to Yokohama)," but more numerous were songs of romance, love, separation, and hope for a better time after the war. The danceable tunes of Glenn Miller and Tommy Dorsey became just as much a part of wartime memories as ration books and far-off battlefields.

For many Americans, the motion picture became the most important leisure activity. Movie attendance averaged about 100 million viewers a week. There might not be gasoline for Sunday drives, but the whole family could go to the movies. Even those in the military could watch American movies on-board ship or at a remote outpost. "Pinups" of Hollywood stars decorated barracks, tanks, and planes wherever American troops went.

The war engulfed Hollywood. Newsreels offering a visual synopsis of war news, always with an upbeat message and a touch of human interest, preceded most movies. Their theme was that the Americans were winning, even if early on there was little evidence of it. Many feature films also had a wartime theme, picturing the Pacific war complete with grinning Japanese villains (usually played by Chinese or Korean actors). Movies set in Europe differed somewhat from those depicting the Pacific war. British and Americans heroes behind enemy lines outwitted Nazis at every turn, sabotaged installations, and made daring escapes from prison camps. Many wartime movies featured a multicultural platoon led by a veteran sergeant with a Protestant, a Catholic, a Jew, a farmer, and a city resident. The message was that we could all get along and join forces to defeat the enemy. Missing from the movies, and from the real army units, were blacks. They served in segregated platoons.

A number of Hollywood actors went into the service, and some even became heroes. Most, like Ronald Reagan, were employed to produce, narrate, or act in government films. The Office of War Information produced short subjects and documentaries, some of them distinguished, like John Huston's *Battle of San Pietro*, a realistic depiction of war on the Italian front. More typical were propaganda films aimed at American soldiers. *Letter from Bataan* (1942) portrayed a wounded GI who wrote home asking his brother-in-law to save his razor blades because "it takes twelve thousand razor blades to make a one-thousand-pound bomb." The film ended by announcing that the soldier had died in the hospital.

## The GIs' War

GI, short for *government issue,* became the affectionate designation for the ordinary soldier in World War II. The GIs came from every background and ethnic group. Some served reluctantly, some eagerly. A few became genuine heroes, and all were turned into heroes by the press and the public, who seemed to believe that one American could easily defeat at least 20 Japanese or Germans. Ernie Pyle, a war correspondent who chronicled the authentic story of the ordinary GI, wrote of soldiers "just toiling from day to day in a world full of insecurity, discomfort, homesickness, and a dulled sense of danger."

In the midst of battle, the war was no fun, but only one soldier in eight ever saw combat, and even for many of them the war was a great adventure (just as World War I had been). "When World War II broke out I was delighted," Mario Puzo, author of *The Godfather*, remembered. "My country called."

Mexican Americans were drafted and volunteered in great numbers. A third of a million served in all branches of the military, a larger percentage than for many other ethnic groups. Although they encountered prejudice, they probably found less in the armed forces than at home, and many returned to civilian life with new ambitions and self-esteem.

Many Native Americans also served, often recruited for special service in the Marine Signal Corps. One group of Navajo completely befuddled the Japanese with a code based on their native language. But the Navajo code talkers and all other Indians who chose to return to reservations after the war were ineligible for benefits like veterans' loans and hospitalization. (They lived on federal land, and that, by law, canceled the advantages that other veterans enjoyed.)

For African Americans, who served throughout the war in segregated units and faced prejudice everywhere, the military experience also had much to teach. Fewer blacks were sent overseas (about 79,000 out of 504,000 blacks in the service in 1943), and fewer were in combat outfits, so the percentage of black soldiers killed and wounded was low. Many illiterate blacks, especially from the South, learned to read and write. Blacks who went overseas began to realize that not everyone viewed them as inferior. Most realized the paradox of fighting for freedom when they themselves had little freedom; they hoped things would improve after the war.

Because the war lasted longer than World War I, its impact was greater. In all, over 16 million men and women served in the military. About 322,000 were killed, and more than 800,000 were wounded. The 12,000 listed as missing just disappeared. The war claimed many more lives than World War I and was the nation's costliest after the Civil War. But penicillin, blood plasma, sulfa drugs, and rapid battlefield evacuation made it twice as likely for the wounded in World War II to survive as in World War I. Penicillin also minimized the threat of venereal disease, but all men who served still saw an anti-VD film.

## Women in Uniform

Women have served in all American wars as nurses and cooks and in other support capacities, and during World War II many continued in these roles. A few nurses landed in France just days after the Normandy invasion. Nurses with the Army and the Marines in the Pacific dug their own foxholes and treated men under fire. Sixty-six nurses spent the entire war in the Philippines as prisoners of the Japanese. Most nurses, however, were far behind the lines.

Although nobody objected to women nurses, not until April 1943 did women physicians win the right to join the Army and Navy Medical Corps. Despite some objections, Congress authorized full military participation (except combat duty) for women because they would free men for combat. World War II thus became the first U.S. war in which women received regular military status. About 350,000 women joined up, most in the Women's Army Corps (WACS) and the women's branch of the Navy (WAVES).

Many recruiting posters suggested that the services needed women "for the precision work at which women are so adept" or to attend to the wounded "as only women can do." Still, men and women were not treated equally. Women were explicitly kept out of combat situations and were often underused by male officers who found it difficult to view women in nontraditional roles. Army nurses with officer rank were forbidden to date enlisted men.

Men were informed about contraceptives and encouraged to use them, but information about birth control was explicitly prohibited for women. Rumors charged many servicewomen with promiscuity, spread apparently by men uncomfortable with women's invasion of the male military domain. Pregnancy brought instant dismissal; yet the pregnancy rate for both married and unmarried women remained low.

Thus, despite difficulties, women played important roles during the war, and when they left the service, they had the same rights as male veterans. The women in the service did not permanently alter the military or the public's perception of women's proper role, but they did change a few minds, and many of these women had their lives altered and their horizons broadened.

## A WAR OF DIPLOMATS AND GENERALS

Pearl Harbor thrust the country into war with Japan. On December 11, 1941, Hitler declared war on the United States. The reason why has never been fully explained. He was not required by his treaty with Japan to go to war with the United States, and without his action, the United States might have concentrated on fighting Japan. Hitler forced the United States into war against the Axis powers in both Europe and Asia.

### War Aims

What did the United States hope to accomplish? Roosevelt and other American leaders never really decided. In a speech before Congress in January 1941, Roosevelt had mentioned the four freedoms: freedom of speech and expression, freedom of worship, freedom from want, and freedom from fear. For many Americans, this was what they were fighting for. Roosevelt spoke vaguely of extending democracy and establishing a peacekeeping organization, but in direct contrast to Woodrow Wilson, he never spelled out in any detail the political purposes for fighting. The only American policy was to end the war as quickly as possible and to solve the political problems it created when the time came.

Roosevelt and his advisers decided on a holding action in the Pacific while concentrating efforts against Hitler in Europe. But the United States was not fighting alone. It joined the Soviet Union and Great Britain in a difficult, but ultimately effective, anti-Nazi alliance. Churchill and Roosevelt got along well, although they often disagreed on strategy. Roosevelt's relationship with Stalin was much more strained, but often he agreed with the Soviet leader about the way to fight the war. Stalin, who had murdered hundreds of thousands of potential or actual opponents, distrusted both the British and the Americans, but he needed them, just as they depended on him. Without the tremendous Russian sacrifices in 1941 and 1942, Germany would have won the war before the vast American military and industrial might could be mobilized.

### Year of Disaster, 1942

The first half of 1942 was disastrous for the Allies. The Japanese captured the resource-rich Dutch East Indies, swept into Burma, took Wake and Guam, and invaded Alaska's Aleutian Islands. They pushed American forces in the Philippines onto the Bataan peninsula and finally onto the tiny island of Corregidor, where General Jonathan Wainwright surrendered more than 11,000 men to the Japanese. American reporters tried to play down the disasters, concentrating on tales of American heroism against overwhelming odds.

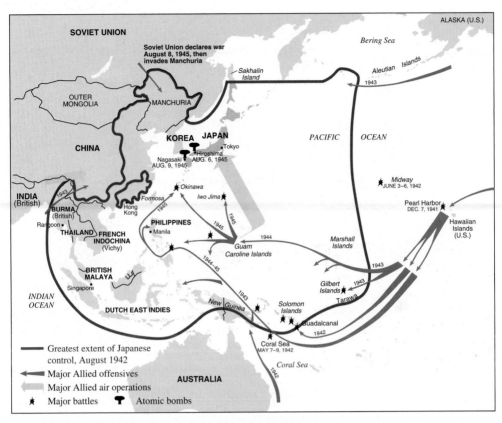

**WORLD WAR II: PACIFIC THEATER**    After the surprise attack on Pearl Harbor, the Japanese extended their control in the Pacific from Burma to the Aleutian Islands and almost to Australia. But after American naval and air victories at Coral Sea and Midway in 1942, the Japanese were increasingly on the defensive.

In Europe, the Germans pushed deep into Russia, threatening to take all the industrial centers, the valuable oil fields, and even Moscow. In North Africa, General Erwin Rommel's mechanized Afrika Korps neared the Suez Canal. U-boats sank British and American ships faster than they could be replaced. For a few dark months in 1942, it seemed that the Axis would win before the United States got prepared for war.

The Allies could not agree on a military strategy in Europe. Churchill advocated tightening the ring around Germany, using bombing raids to weaken the enemy and encouraging resistance among the occupied countries. He wanted to avoid any direct assault on the continent until success was assured. Stalin, on the other hand, demanded a second front, an invasion of Europe in 1942 to relieve the pressure on the Red Army, which faced 200 German divisions along a 2,000-mile front. Roosevelt agreed to an offensive in 1942. But the invasion in 1942 was not in France but in North Africa. The decision was probably right from a military point of view, but it taught Russia to distrust Britain and the United States.

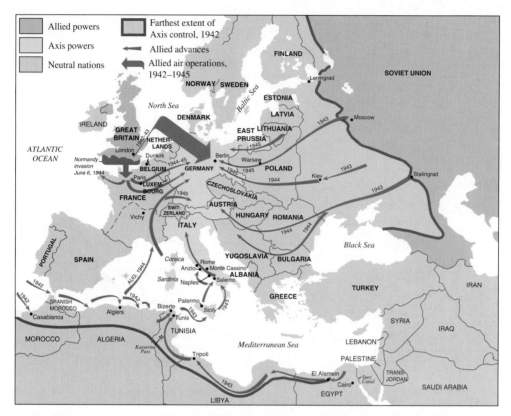

**WORLD WAR II: EUROPEAN AND NORTH AFRICAN THEATERS**    The German war machine swept across Europe and North Africa and almost captured Cairo and Moscow, but after major defeats at Stalingrad and El Alamein in 1943, the Axis powers were in retreat. Many lives were lost on both sides before the Allied victory in 1945.

Landing in North Africa in November 1942, American and British troops tried to link up with a beleaguered British army fighting westward from Egypt. The American army, enthusiastic but inexperienced, met little resistance until, at Kasserine Pass in Tunisia, the Germans counterattacked and destroyed a large American force, inflicting 5,000 casualties. Roosevelt, who launched the invasion in part to give the American people a victory to relieve dreary news from the Far East, learned that victories often came with long casualty lists.

Conquering French North Africa drew Roosevelt into unpleasant political compromises. To gain a cease-fire, the United States recognized a provisional government under Admiral Jean Darlan, a former Nazi collaborator. Did this mean that the United States would negotiate with Mussolini? Or with Hitler? The Darlan deal reinforced Soviet distrust of the Americans and angered many Americans.

Roosevelt never made a deal with Hitler, but he did aid Fascist Spain in return for safe passage of American shipping into the Mediterranean. But the United States did not aid only right-wing dictators like Franco. It also supplied arms to the left-wing resistance in France, to the Communist guerrilla Tito in Yugoslavia, and to Ho Chi Minh, the anti-French resistance leader in Indochina. Roosevelt

ATROCITIES — CAPTURE OF THE GERMAN CONCENTRATION CAMPS PILES UP EVIDENCE OF BARBARISM THAT REACHES THE LOW POINT OF HUMAN DEGRADATION

Only at the end of the war did most Americans learn of the horrors of Nazi concentration camps and the gas chambers. These photographs, which appeared in *Life* magazine, were taken of the dead and dying at Buchenwald in May 1945. They emphasized, more than any words could, the horrors of Nazi Germany. (George Rodger/Margaret Bourke-White/LIFE Magazine © Time, Inc.)

also authorized large-scale, lend-lease aid to the Soviet Union. Although liberals criticized his support of dictators, Roosevelt was willing to do almost anything to win the war. Military expediency often dictated his political decisions.

Even on the issue of the plight of the Jews in Nazi-occupied Europe, Roosevelt's solution was to win the war as quickly as possible. By November 1942, confirmed information reached the United States that the Nazis were systematically exterminating Jews. Yet the administration did nothing for more than a year, and even then it did scandalously little. Only 21,000 refugees were allowed to enter the United States over a period of three and a half years, just 10 percent of those who could have been admitted under immigration quotas. The War Department refused to bomb the Auschwitz gas chambers, and officials turned down many rescue schemes. Widespread anti-Semitism in the United States in the 1940s and fears of massive Jewish immigration partly explain the administration's policy. The failure of the media, Christian leaders, and even American Jews to bring effective pressure on the government does not excuse the president for his shameful indifference to the systematic murder of millions of people. Roosevelt could not have prevented the Holocaust, but vigorous action by him could have saved many thousands of lives. Roosevelt was not always right, nor even consistent. People who assumed he had a master strategy or a fixed ideological position misunderstood him.

## A Strategy for Ending the War

The commanding general of the Allied armies in the North African campaign emerged as a genuine leader. Born in Texas, Dwight D. Eisenhower spent his boyhood in Abilene, Kansas. His small-town background made it easy for the media to make him an American hero. Eisenhower, however, had not come to hero status easily. In World War I, he trained soldiers in Texas. He was only a lieutenant colonel when World War II erupted. But George Marshall, who became the Army's top general in September 1939, had discovered Eisenhower's talents even before the war began. He was quickly promoted to general and achieved a reputation as an expert planner and organizer. Gregarious and outgoing, "Ike" had a broad smile that made most people like him instantly. He was not a brilliant field commander and made many mistakes in the African campaign, but he could get diverse people working together, which was crucial where British and American units had to cooperate.

The American army moved slowly across North Africa, linked up with the British, invaded Sicily in July 1943, and finally stormed ashore in Italy in September. The Italian campaign proved long and bitter. After the overthrow of Mussolini and Italy's surrender in September 1943, the Germans occupied the country and the American army bogged down. The Allies did not reach Rome until June 1944, and they never controlled all of Italy.

Despite the decision to make the war in Europe the first priority, American ships and planes halted the Japanese advance in the spring of 1942. In the Battle of Coral Sea in May 1942, American carrier-based planes inflicted heavy damage on the Japanese fleet and probably prevented the invasion of Australia. It was the first naval battle in history in which surface ships did not fire on each other; airplanes did all the damage. In World War II, aircraft carriers were more important than battleships. A month later, at the Battle of Midway, American planes sank four Japanese carriers and destroyed nearly 300 planes. This first major Japanese defeat restored some balance of power in the Pacific and ended the threat to Hawaii.

In 1943, the American sea and land forces leapfrogged from island to island, retaking territory and building bases to attack the Philippines and eventually Japan. Progress often had terrible costs. In November 1943, about 5,000 Marines landed on the coral beaches of the tiny island of Tarawa. Despite heavy naval bombardment and the support of hundreds of planes, they met massive resistance. The four-day battle killed more than 1,000 Americans and wounded over 3,000. One general thought it was all wasted effort—that the island should have been bypassed. Others disagreed. No one asked the Marines who hit the beaches. Less than half of the first wave survived.

## D-Day: The Invasion of France

Operation Overlord, the code name for the largest amphibious invasion in history, the invasion Stalin had wanted in 1942, finally began on June 6, 1944. It was, according to Churchill, "the most difficult and complicated operation that has ever taken place." The initial assault along a 60-mile stretch of the Normandy coast was conducted with 175,000 men supported by 600 warships and 11,000 planes. Within a month, over 1 million troops and more than 170,000 vehicles had landed.

Eisenhower coordinated and planned the operation. During the first hours of the invasion, there seemed to be too many supplies. It cost 2,245 killed and 1,670 wounded to secure the beachhead. "It was much lighter than anybody expected," one observer remarked. "But if you saw faces instead of numbers on the casualty list, it wasn't light at all."

The Allies dropped more than 1.5 million tons of bombs on Europe. Evidence gathered after the war suggests that this bombardment disrupted German war production less than Allied strategists expected. Often a plant or a rail center would be back in operation days or hours after an attack, and the bombing of the cities may have strengthened the German people's resolve to fight to the bitter end. Nor did the destruction of German cities come cheaply. German fighter planes and anti-aircraft guns shot down thousands of American and British planes.

The most destructive bombing raid of the war, against Dresden on the night of February 13–14, 1945, had no strategic purpose. The British and Americans launched the raid to help demonstrate to Stalin that they were aiding the Russian offensive. Dresden, a city of 630,000, was a communications center. Three waves of planes dropped 650,000 incendiary bombs, causing a firestorm that swept over eight square miles, destroying everything in its path, and killing an estimated 100,000 civilians.

With eccentric General George Patton leading the charge and staid General Omar Bradley in command, the American army broke out of the Normandy beachhead in July 1944 and swept across France. American productive capacity and the ability to supply a mobile and motorized army eventually brought victory. But not all American equipment was superior. The American fighter plane, the P-40, could not compete early in the war with the German ME-109. The United States was far behind Germany in the development of rockets, but that was not as important as the American inability, until the end of the war, to develop a tank that could compete in armament or firepower with the German tanks. The American army partly made up for the deficiency of its tanks by having superior artillery. Perhaps even more important, most American soldiers had grown up tinkering with cars and radios. Children of the machine age, they managed to keep tanks, trucks, and guns functioning under difficult circumstances, which gave the American army superior mobility.

By late 1944, the American and British armies had driven across France, while the Russians had pushed far into Eastern Europe. The war seemed nearly over. However, just before Christmas in 1944, the Germans launched a massive counterattack on the western front against thinly dispersed and inexperienced American troops. The Germans drove 50 miles inside the American lines before they were checked. During this so-called Battle of the Bulge, Eisenhower was so desperate for additional troops that he offered to pardon any military prisoners in Europe who would go into battle. Most declined. Eisenhower also promised any black soldiers in the service and supply outfits an opportunity to become infantrymen in the white units, though usually with a lower rank. However, his chief of staff pointed out that this was the "most dangerous thing I have seen in regard to race relations." Eisenhower recanted, not wishing to start a social revolution.

## The Politics of Victory

As American and British armies assaulted Germany in the winter and spring of 1945, the political and diplomatic aspects of the war began to overshadow military concerns. Relations between the Soviet Union and the other Allies had been badly strained at times during the war; with victory in sight, the tension grew worse. Although the American press idealized Stalin and the Russian people, a number of high-level American diplomats and presidential advisers distrusted the Russians and anticipated a postwar confrontation. They urged Roosevelt to make military decisions with the postwar political situation in mind.

The main issue in the spring of 1945 was who would capture Berlin. The British wanted to beat the Russians to the capital city. Eisenhower, however, fearing that the Germans might hold out indefinitely in the Alps, ordered the armies south rather than toward Berlin. He also wanted to avoid unnecessary American casualties, and he planned to meet the Russian army at an easily marked spot to avoid any unfortunate incidents. British and American forces could probably not have arrived in Berlin before the Russians, but Eisenhower's decision generated controversy after the war. Russian and American troops met on April 25, 1945, at the Elbe River. On May 2, the Russians took Berlin. Hitler committed suicide. The long war in Europe finally ended on May 8, 1945.

Meanwhile, throughout 1944, the United States had tightened the noose on Japan. Long-range B-29 bombers began sustained strikes on the Japanese mainland in June 1944, and by November, they were firebombing Tokyo. In a series of naval and air engagements, especially at the Battle of Leyte Gulf, American planes destroyed most of the remaining Japanese navy. By the end of 1944, an American victory in the Pacific was all but assured. American forces recaptured the Philippines early the next year. Yet it might take years to conquer the Japanese home islands.

While the military campaigns reached a critical stage, Roosevelt ran for a fourth term. He dropped Vice President Henry Wallace from the ticket because some thought him too radical and impetuous. To replace him, the Democratic convention selected a relatively unknown senator from Missouri. Harry S Truman's only fame had come from leading a Senate investigation of war contracts.

The Republicans nominated Thomas Dewey, the colorless and moderate governor of New York, who had a difficult time criticizing Roosevelt without appearing unpatriotic. Roosevelt seemed haggard and ill during much of the campaign, but he won easily. He would need all his strength to deal with the difficult problems of ending the war and constructing a peace settlement.

## The Big Three at Yalta

Roosevelt, Churchill, and Stalin met at the Soviet resort city of Yalta in February 1945 to discuss the peace settlements. Most of the Yalta agreements were secret, and during the subsequent Cold War they would become controversial. Roosevelt wanted Soviet help in ending the Pacific war, to avoid the slaughter of American men in an invasion of Japan. In return for a promise to enter the war within three months after the war in Europe was over, the Soviet Union was granted the Kurile Islands, the southern half of Sakhalin Island, and railroads and port facilities in

Korea, Manchuria, and Mongolia. That later seemed like a heavy price to pay, but realistically the Soviet Union controlled most of this territory and could not have been dislodged without going to war.

When the provisions of the secret treaties were revealed much later, many people would accuse Roosevelt of trusting Stalin too much. But Roosevelt wanted to retain a working relationship with Moscow to preserve the peace, and he hoped to get Soviet agreement to cooperate with the new international organization, The United Nations.

The European section of the Yalta agreement proved even more controversial. The diplomats decided to partition Germany and to divide Berlin. The Polish agreements were even more difficult to swallow. The Polish government-in-exile in London was militantly anti-Communist and looked forward to returning home after the war. Stalin demanded that eastern Poland be given to the Soviet Union. Churchill and Roosevelt finally agreed to the Russian demands with the proviso that Poland be compensated with German territory on its western border. Stalin agreed to include some London Poles in the pro-Soviet Polish government and to "free and unfettered elections as soon as possible."

The Polish settlement would prove divisive after the war, for it quickly became clear that what the British and Americans wanted in eastern Europe contrasted with what the Soviet Union intended. Yet at the time it seemed imperative that Russia enter the war in the Pacific, and the reality was that in 1945 the Soviet army occupied most of eastern Europe.

The most potentially valuable accomplishment at Yalta was Stalin's agreement to join Roosevelt and Churchill in calling a conference in San Francisco in April 1945 to draft a United Nations charter. The charter gave primary responsibility for keeping global peace to the Security Council, composed of five permanent members (the United States, the Soviet Union, Great Britain, France, and China) and six other nations elected for two-year terms.

## The Atomic Age Begins

Two months after Yalta, on April 12, 1945, Roosevelt died suddenly. Hated and loved to the end, he was replaced by Harry Truman, who was more difficult to hate and harder to love. In the beginning, Truman seemed tentative and unsure. Yet it fell to him to make some of history's most difficult decisions.

The Manhattan Project, organized in 1941, was one of the best-kept secrets of the war. A distinguished group of scientists, headquartered at Los Alamos, New Mexico, had orders to build an atomic bomb before Germany did. But by the time the bomb was successfully tested in the New Mexico desert on July 16, 1945, the war in Europe had ended.

The scientists working on the bomb assumed they were perfecting a military weapon. Yet when they first saw its ghastly power, remembered J. Robert Oppenheimer, a leading scientist on the project, "some wept, a few cheered. Most stood silently." Some opposed using the bomb. They realized its revolutionary power and worried about the future reputation of the United States if it unleashed this new force. But a presidential committee made up of scientists, military leaders, and politicians recommended that it be dropped on a military target in Japan as soon as possible.

# *Timeline*

| | |
|---|---|
| **1931–1932** Japan seizes Manchuria | Germany attacks Russia |
| **1933** Hitler becomes German chancellor | Japanese assets in United States frozen |
| United States recognizes the Soviet Union | Japanese attack Pearl Harbor |
| Roosevelt extends Good Neighbor policy | United States declares war on Japan |
| **1934** Germany begins rearmament | Germany declares war on United States |
| **1935** Italy invades Ethiopia | **1942** Internment of Japanese Americans |
| First Neutrality Act | Second Allied front in Africa launched |
| **1936** Spanish civil war begins | **1943** Invasion of Sicily |
| Second Neutrality Act | Italian campaign |
| Roosevelt reelected | Italy surrenders |
| **1937** Third Neutrality Act | United Mine Workers strike |
| **1938** Hitler annexes Austria, occupies Sudetenland | Race riots in Detroit and other cities |
| German persecution of Jews intensifies | **1944** Normandy invasion (Operation Overlord) |
| **1939** Nazi-Soviet Pact | Congress passes GI Bill |
| German invasion of Poland | Roosevelt elected for a fourth term |
| World War II begins | **1945** Yalta Conference |
| **1940** Roosevelt elected for a third term | Roosevelt dies |
| Selective Service Act | Harry Truman becomes president |
| **1941** FDR's "Four Freedoms" speech | Germany surrenders |
| Proposed black march on Washington | Successful test of atomic bomb |
| Executive order outlaws discrimination in defense industries | Hiroshima and Nagasaki bombed |
| | Japan surrenders |
| Lend-Lease Act | |

"The final decision of where and when to use the atomic bomb was up to me," Truman later remembered. "Let there be no doubt about it. I regarded the bomb as a military weapon and never had any doubt that it should be used." But the decision had military and political ramifications. Even though Japan had lost most of its empire by the summer of 1945, it still had several million troops and thousands of kamikaze planes, whose pilots gave their lives by crashing, heavily laden with bombs, into an American ship. There was little defense against them.

Even with the Russian promise to enter the war, it appeared that an amphibious landing on the Japanese mainland would be necessary. The month-long battle for Iwo Jima, 750 miles from Tokyo, had killed over 4,000 Americans and wounded 15,000, and the battle for Okinawa was even more costly. Invading the Japanese mainland would presumably be far worse. The bomb, many thought, could end the war without an invasion. Some people involved in the decision wanted to avenge Pearl Harbor, and still others felt they needed to justify spending over $2 billion on the project in the first place. To some historians, the timing of the first bomb indicates that the decision was intended to impress the Russians and ensure that they had little to do with the peace settlement in the Far East.

Historians debate whether the use of the atomic bomb on Japanese cities was necessary to end the war, but for the hundreds of thousands of American troops waiting to invade Japan, there was no question about the rightness of the decision. They believed that it saved their lives. On August 6, 1945, two days before the Soviet Union had promised to enter the war against Japan, a B29 bomber, the "Enola Gay," dropped a single atomic bomb over Hiroshima. It killed or severely wounded 140,000 civilians and destroyed four square miles of the city. One of the men on the plane thought that they had missed the target: "I didn't see any sign of the city." The Soviet Union entered the war on August 8. When Japan refused to surrender, a second bomb destroyed Nagasaki on August 9. The Japanese surrendered five days later. The war was over, but the problems of the atomic age and the postwar world were only beginning.

❧ ❧ ❧ ❧

# CONCLUSION

## *Peace, Prosperity, and International Responsibilities*

The United States emerged from World War II with an enhanced reputation as the world's most powerful industrial and military nation. The demands of the war had finally ended the Great Depression and brought prosperity to most Americans. Even N. Scott Momaday's family found better jobs because of the war, but like many Americans, they had to relocate in order to take those jobs. The war had also increased the power of the federal government. The payroll deduction of federal income taxes, begun during the war, symbolized the growth of a federal bureaucracy that affected the lives of all Americans. The war had also ended American isolationism and made the United States into the dominant international power. Of all the nations that fought in the war, the United States had suffered the least. No bombs were dropped on American factories, and no cities were destroyed. Although more than 300,000 Americans lost their lives, even this carnage seemed minimal when compared with the more than 20 million Russian soldiers and civilians who died or the 6 million Jews and millions of others systematically exterminated by Hitler.

Americans greeted the end of the war with joy and relief. They looked forward to the peace and prosperity for which they had fought. Yet within two years, the peace would be jeopardized by the Cold War, and the United States would be rearming its former enemies, Japan and Germany, to oppose its former friend, the Soviet Union. The irony of that situation reduced the joy of the hard-won peace and made the American people more suspicious of their government and its foreign policy. Yet the memory of World War II and the perception that the country was united against evil enemies, indeed that World War II was a "good war," would have an impact on American foreign policy, and even on Americans' perception of themselves, for decades to come.

## Discovering U.S. History Online

*World War II Exhibit: A People at War*    http://www.nara.gov/exhall/people/people.html
This National Archives exhibit takes a close look at the contributions millions of Americans made to the war effort.

*Powers of Persuasion—Poster Art of World War II*
http://www.nara.gov/education/teaching/posters/poster.html
These powerful posters at the National Archives were part of the battle for the hearts and minds of the American people during WWII.

*A-Bomb WWW Museum*    http://www.csi.ad.jp/ABOMB/
This site offers information about the impact of the first atomic bomb as well as the background and context of weapons of total destruction.

*United States Holocaust Memorial Museum*    http://www.ushmm.org
This is the official Web site of the Holocaust Museum in Washington, D.C.

*Tuskegee Airmen*    http://www.wpafb.af.mil/museum/history/prewwii/ta.htm
The Air Force Museum at Wright-Patterson Air Force Base maintains this site about the African-American pilots of Word War II.

*Resource Listing for WWII*    http://www.sunsite.unc.edu/pha/index.html
This site has a large number of searchable primary texts from all aspects of World War II.

*Japanese Internment*    http://www.lib.washington.edu/exhibits/harmony
The Japanese American Exhibit and Access Project at the University of Washington deals with all aspects of the Japanese wartime internment, relocation centers, and the human stories behind the massive removal of Japanese Americans from the West Coast.

## Fiction and Film

In the *Dollmaker* (1954), Harriette Arnow tells the story of a young woman from Kentucky who finds herself in wartime Detroit. Two powerful novels that tell the story of the battlefield experience are Norman Mailer, *The Naked and the Dead* (1948), and Irwin Shaw, *The Young Lions* (1948).

*Pearl Harbor* (2001) is a blockbuster film worth seeing for the special effects, but more interesting is *Tora! Tora! Tora!* (1970), a film that tells the story of the attack on Pearl Harbor from both the American and Japanese point of view. It is compelling even as it oversimplifies history. *Saving Private Ryan* (1998), a film about one platoon's adventures on D-Day and after, is sentimental and romantic in spots but contains some graphic scenes from the invasion of Normandy.

## Recommended Reading

### The Twisting Road to War

Robert Dalleck, *Franklin Roosevelt and American Foreign Policy, 1932–1945* (1979); Waldo Heinrichs, *Threshold of War* (1988); Akira Iiriye, *The Origins of the Second World War in Asia and the Pacific* (1988); Gordon W. Prange, *At Dawn We Slept* (1981); Gerhard Weinberg, *A Global History of World War II* (1994).

## The Home Front

Amy Bently, *Eating For Victory: Food Rationing and the Politics of Domesticity* (1997); Alison Bernstein, *American Indians and World War II* (1991); John Morton Blum, *V Was for Victory* (1976); D'Ann Campbell, *Women at War with America* (1984); Thomas Fleming, *The New Dealers War: FDR and the World Within World War II* (2001); Doris Kearns Goodwin, *No Ordinary Time: Franklin and Eleanor Roosevelt, The Home Front in World War II* (1994); Susan M. Hartman, *The Homefront and Beyond: Women in the 1940s* (1982); Nicholas Lemann, *The Promised Land: The Great Black Migration and How It Changed America* (1991); Ruth Milkman, *Gender at Work* (1987); Gerald D. Nash, *The American West Transformed: The Impact of the Second World War* (1985); Richard Polenberg, *War and Society* (1972); William Tuttle, *"Daddy's Gone to War"* (1993); Allan M. Winkler, *The Politics of Propaganda: The Office of War Information, 1942–1945* (1978).

## Social Impact of the War

Richard Dalffiume, *Desegregation of the Armed Forces* (1975); Sherna B. Gluck, *Rosie the Riveter Revisited* (1987); David M. Kennedy, *Freedom From Fear: The American People in Depression and War* (1999); George H. Roseder, *The Censored War* (1993); Ronald Takaki, *Double Victory: A Multicultural History of America in World War II* (2000).

## A War of Diplomats and Generals

Gar Alperovitz, *Atomic Diplomacy* (1965); Stephen Ambrose, *Citizen Soldiers* (1997) and *D-Day* (1994); John Dower, *War Without Mercy* (1986); Paul Fussell, *Wartime* (1989); John Keegan, *The Battle For History: Re-fighting World War II* (1995); Gerald F. Linderman, *The World Within War: America's Combat Experience in World War II* (1997); Williamson Murray and Alan R. Millet, *A War to Be Won: Fighting The Second World War* (2000); Russell Weigley, *Eisenhower's Lieutenants: The Campaign of France and Germany, 1944–1945* (1981); David S. Wyman, *The Abandonment of the Jews: America and the Holocaust, 1941–1945* (1984).

# CHAPTER 26
# Postwar Growth and Social Change

## CHAPTER OUTLINE

## AMERICAN STORIES
### An Entrepreneur Franchises the American Dream

Ray Kroc, an ambitious salesman, headed toward San Bernardino, California, on a business trip in 1954. For more than a decade he had been selling "multimixers"—stainless steel machines that could make six milkshakes at once—to restaurants and soda shops around the United States. On this trip, he was particularly interested in checking out a hamburger stand run by Richard and Maurice McDonald, who had bought eight of his "contraptions" and could therefore make 48 shakes at the same time.

Always eager to increase sales, Kroc wanted to see the McDonalds' operation for himself. The 52-year-old son of Bohemian parents had sold everything from real estate to paper cups before peddling the multimixers, but had enjoyed no stunning success. Yet he was still on the alert for the key to the fortune that was part of the American dream. As he watched the lines of people at the San Bernardino McDonald's, the answer seemed at hand.

The McDonald brothers sold only standard hamburgers and french fries, but they had developed a system that was fast, efficient, and clean. It drew on the heavy automobile traffic of Route 66. And it was profitable indeed. Sensing the possibilities, Kroc proposed that the two owners open other establishments as well. When they balked, he negotiated a 99-year contract that allowed him to sell the fast-food idea and the name—and their golden arches design—wherever he could.

On April 15, 1955, Kroc opened his first McDonald's in Des Plaines, a suburb of Chicago. Three months later, he sold his first franchise in Fresno, California. Others soon followed. Kroc scouted out new locations, almost always on highway "strips," persuaded people to put up the capital, and provided them with specifications guaranteed to ensure future success. For his efforts, he received a percentage of the gross take.

From the start, Kroc insisted on standardization. Every McDonald's was the same—from the two functional arches supporting the glass enclosure that housed the kitchen and take-out window to the single arch near the road bearing a sign indicating how many 15-cent hamburgers had already been sold. All menus and prices were exactly the same, and Kroc demanded that everything from hamburger size to cooking time be constant. He insisted, too, that the establishments be clean. No pinball games or cigarette machines were permitted; the premium was on a good, inexpensive hamburger, quickly served, at a nice place.

McDonald's, of course, was an enormous success. In 1962, total sales exceeded $76 million. In 1964, before the company had been in operation 10 years, it had sold over 400 million hamburgers and 120 million pounds of french fries. By the end of the next year, there were 710 McDonald's stands in 44 states. In 1974, only 20 years after Kroc's vision of the hamburger's future, McDonald's did $2 billion worth of business. When Kroc died in 1984, a total of 45 billion burgers had been sold at 7,500 outlets in 32 countries. Ronald McDonald, the clown who came to represent the company, became known to children around the globe after his Washington, D.C., debut in November 1963. When McDonald's began to advertise, it became the country's first restaurant to buy TV time. Musical slogans like "You deserve a break today" and "We do it all for you" became better known than some popular songs.

❧ ❧ ❧ ❧

The success of McDonald's provides an example of the development of new trends in the United States in the post–World War II years. Kroc capitalized on the changes of the automobile age. He understood that a restaurant had a better chance of succeeding if it was located along the highway than in a city. His drive-in design, catering to a new and ever-growing clientele, soon became common.

He understood, too, that the franchise notion provided the key to rapid growth. Not prepared to open up thousands of stands himself, he sold the idea to entrepreneurs who stood to make sizable profits as long as they remained a part of the larger whole. In numerous other product areas as well as the hamburger business, franchises helped create a nationwide web of firms.

Finally, Kroc sensed the importance of standardization and uniformity. He understood the mood of the time, the quiet conformity of Americans searching for success. The very monotony of McDonald's image was part of its appeal. Customers always knew what they would get at the golden arches. If the atmosphere was "bland," that, too, was deliberate. As Kroc said, "Our theme is kind of synonymous with Sunday school, the Girl Scouts and the YMCA. McDonald's is clean and wholesome." It was a symbol of the age.

This chapter describes the structural changes in American society in the 25 years following World War II. Even as the nation became involved in the Cold War with the Soviet Union (a story we will take up in Chapter 27), Americans were preoccupied with the shifts in social and economic patterns that were taking place. This chapter examines how economic growth, spurred by technological advances, transformed the patterns of work and daily life in the United States and provided the context for the development of the liberal state described in Chapter 28. Self-interest triumphed over idealism as most people gained a level of material comfort previously unknown. Working-class Americans shared in the gains, as the union movement pressed its claims more successfully than it had ever done in the past, and workers entered into a new equilibrium with the world of management. With standardization and conformity the norm, life for most Americans was more comfortable than it had ever been before. For many, this period promised to deliver the American dream.

But even as the nation prospered, it experienced serious social and economic divisions. This chapter also shows the enormous gaps that existed between rich and poor, even in the best of times. It shows the continuing presence of what one critic eloquently called "the other America" and documents the considerable income disparity and persistent prejudice that most minority groups encountered in their effort to share in the postwar prosperity. Their frustrations led to the reform movements described in Chapter 29 and highlighted the limits of the postwar American dream.

## ECONOMIC BOOM

Despite Cold War anxieties, most Americans were optimistic after 1945. As servicemen came home, their very presence changed family patterns. A baby boom brought unprecedented population growth. The simultaneous and unexpected economic boom had an even greater impact. Large corporations increasingly dominated the business world, but unions grew as well, and most workers improved their lives. Technology appeared triumphant, with new products flooding the market and finding their way into most American homes. Prosperity convinced the growing middle class that all was well.

McDonald's provided a model for other franchisers in the 1950s and the years that followed. The Golden Arches, shown here in an early version, were virtually the same wherever they appeared. Initially found along highways around the country, they were later built within cities and towns as well. (Used with permission from McDonald's Corporation)

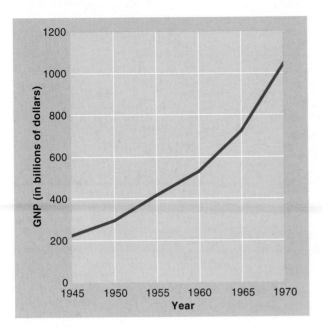

**INCREASE IN GNP, 1945–1970**
This graph shows the steady rise in gross national product in the post-World War II years. Note the continued increase in the 1960s. (*Source:* National Income and Product Accounts, 1929–1994.)

## The Thriving Peacetime Economy

The return of prosperity during World War II continued in the postwar years, relieving fears of another depression. The next several decades saw one of the longest sustained economic expansions the country had ever known. The United States solidified its position as the richest nation in the world.

The statistical evidence was impressive. The gross national product (GNP) jumped dramatically between 1945 and 1970 while per capita personal income likewise rose—from $1,223 in 1945 to $3,945 in 1970. Almost 60 percent of all families in the country were now part of the middle class, a dramatic change from the class structure in the nineteenth and early twentieth centuries.

Personal resources fueled economic growth. During World War II, with factories concentrating on military needs, American consumers could not spend all they earned, so at war's end they were ready to spend savings of $140 billion. Equally important, between 1946 and 1960 real purchasing power rose by 22 percent, which meant that families now had far more discretionary income—money to satisfy wants as well as needs—than before. At the end of the Great Depression, fewer than one-quarter of all households had any discretionary income; in 1960, three of every five did.

The United States, which produced half the world's goods, was providing new products that average Americans, unlike their parents, could afford. Higher real wages allowed people of all classes to buy consumer goods. That consumer power, unlike the underconsumption of the 1920s and 1930s, spurred the economy.

The automobile industry, which expanded dramatically after the war, played a key part in the boom. Two million cars were made in 1946; eight million were built in 1955, and more than nine million were built in 1965. Customers now chose

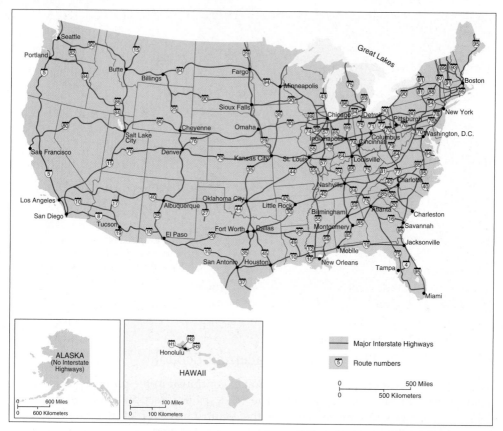

**U.S. Interstate Highway System**   The interstate highway system, established by legislative action in 1956, created an extensive network of roads that changed the landscape and living patterns of people throughout the United States. While the network was most extensive in the East, it extended throughout the entire country.

from a wide variety of engines, colors, and options. Grills and tail fins distinguished each year's models. A fancy car could signal solid middle-class achievement. Younger people, especially from the working class, valued speed more.

Both the automobile culture and national prosperity got massive boosts from the interstate highway system launched by the Eisenhower administration in 1956. The Interstate Highway Act poured $26 billion—the largest public works expenditure in American history—into the construction of more than 40,000 miles of federal highways, linking all parts of the United States. Eisenhower was right when he proudly said that "more than any single action by the government since the end of the war, this one would change the face of America." But there were costs. Money was not invested in mass transit. Highways spawned pollution, triggered urban flight, and helped increase national dependence on a constant flow of cheap oil.

A housing boom also fed economic growth. In 1940, 43 percent of all American families owned their own homes; by 1970, 63 percent did. Much of the stimulus came from the GI Bill of 1944. In addition to giving returning servicemen priority for many jobs and providing educational benefits, it offered low-interest home mortgages. Millions of former servicemen from all social classes eagerly purchased their share of the American dream.

The government's increasingly active economic role both stimulated and sustained the expansion. Businesses were allowed to buy almost 80 percent of the factories built by the government during the war for much less than they cost. Even more important was the dramatic rise in defense spending as the Cold War escalated. In 1947, Congress created the Department of Defense with an initial budget of $13 billion. With the onset of the Korean War, the defense budget rose to about $47 billion by 1953. Approximately half the total federal budget went to the armed forces, stimulating the aircraft and electronic industries. The close business-government ties of World War II grew stronger.

Most citizens welcomed these huge expenditures, not only because they supported a strong stand against communism (see Chapter 27), but also because they understood the economic impact of military spending. As columnist David Lawrence noted in 1950, "Cold war is an automatic pump primer. Turn a spigot, and the public clamors for more arms spending."

Postwar American growth avoided some of the major problems that often bedevil periods of economic expansion—inflation and the enrichment of a few at the expense of the many. During the late 1940s inflation was indeed a problem, running at an annual average of 7 percent, but in the 1950s and 1960s it slowed to a gentle 2 to 3 percent annually. And though the concentration of income remained the same—the bottom half of the population still earned less than the top tenth—middle-class ranks grew. Despite occasional recessions—in 1953–1954, 1957–1958, and 1960–1961—the economy continued to grow, and most Americans prospered. A tax cut in the mid-1960s promoted even greater growth.

A major economic transformation had occurred in the United States. Peaceful, prosperous, and productive, the nation had become what a prominent economist called "the affluent society." Charles Lehman, a veteran from Missouri, later recalled: "I was a twenty-one-year-old lieutenant with a high school education, and my only prewar experience was as a stock boy in a grocery store. But on V-J day, I knew it was only a matter of time before I was rich—or well-off, anyway."

## The Corporate Impact on American Life

After 1945, the major corporations tightened their hold on the American economy. Government policy in World War II had produced tremendous industrial concentration. Antitrust actions were suspended in the interest of wartime production, while government contracts spurred expansion of the big corporations at the expense of smaller firms.

Industrial concentration continued after the war, making oligopoly—domination of a given industry by a few firms—a feature of American capitalism. At the same time, the booming economy encouraged the development of conglomerates—firms with holdings in a variety of industries to protect themselves against instability in one particular area. It also led to the further development of finance capitalism to help put the deals together.

Expansion took other forms as well. Even as the major corporations expanded, so did franchise operations like Ray Kroc's pioneering McDonald's and emulators like Kentucky Fried Chicken and Burger King.

While expanding at home, large corporations also moved increasingly into foreign markets, as they had in the 1890s. At the same time, they began to build plants overseas, where labor costs were cheaper. In the decade after 1957, General Electric built 61 plants abroad. So did many other corporations. Corporate planning, meanwhile, developed rapidly, as firms sought managers who could assess information, weigh marketing trends, and make rational decisions to maximize profit.

## Changing Work Patterns

As corporations changed, so did the world of work. Reversing a 150-year trend, in the years after World War II the United States became less of a goods producer and more of a service provider. Between 1947 and 1957, the number of factory workers fell by 4 percent, while the number of clerical workers increased by 23 percent and the number of salaried middle-class employees rose by 61 percent. By 1956, a majority of American workers held white-collar jobs, and that percentage rose in the years that followed. People lived comfortably, enjoying an abundance of leisure time. Experts predicted a four-day work week.

Yet white-collar employees paid a price. Work in the huge corporations became ever more impersonal and bureaucratic. Just as product standardization became increasingly important, individual acceptance of company norms became necessary. Social critic C. Wright Mills observed that "when white-collar people get jobs, they sell not only their time and energy but their personalities as well."

But not all Americans held white-collar jobs. Many were still workers on assembly lines. They, too, dreamed of owning a suburban home and more than one car and providing more for their children than they had enjoyed while growing up. Their lives were now more comfortable than ever before, as the union movement brought substantial gains (see the next section). These were the more fortunate members of the working class.

Millions of others, perhaps 40 percent of the workforce, held less appealing and poorer-paying positions as taxi drivers or farm laborers or dime-store sales clerks. Casual employment had involved manual labor in the past; now it consisted of service work, and much of this was done by minorities, teenagers, and women gradually returning to the labor force.

## The Union Movement at High Tide

The union movement had come of age during the New Deal (see Chapter 24), and the end of World War II found it even stronger. There were more union members—14.5 million—than ever before. Having taken a wartime no-strike pledge and given the war effort their full support, they now looked forward to better pay and a greater voice in workplace management.

The immediate postwar period was difficult. Cancellations of defense orders laid off war workers and prompted fears of a depression. Even workers who held their jobs lost the overtime pay of the war years. Many responded by striking. In 1946 alone, 4.6 million workers went out on strike—more than ever before in the history of the United States. These disruptions annoyed middle-class Americans in general and outraged conservative Republicans, who felt that unionization had gone too far.

In the late 1940s, a new equilibrium emerged. In most industries, big business at last accepted the basic rights of industrial workers, and unions in turn acknowledged the prerogatives of management and accepted the principle of fair profit. Corporations in the same industry agreed to cooperate rather than compete with one another over labor costs. This meant that once a leading firm reached agreement with the union, the other firms in that sector would adopt similar terms, and the costs of the new contract would be met by a general increase in prices.

At the same time, companies made material concessions to workers, for example protecting them against inflation. In 1948, General Motors offered the United Automobile Workers a contract that included a cost-of-living adjustment (COLA) and a 2 percent "annual improvement factor" wage increase intended to share GM's productivity gains with workers and, in 1950, added a pension plan. Five years later, automobile workers won a guaranteed annual wage. By the end of the decade, COLAs were built into most union contracts.

The union movement made peace with itself, too. The rivalry of trade and industrial unions, so bitter in the 1930s and with a history running back to the late-nineteenth century (see Chapter 18), largely ended in 1955 with the merger of the AFL and CIO. The new organization represented more than 90 percent of the country's now larger group of 17.5 million union members.

Union gains, like middle-class affluence, came at a price. With higher, more predictable incomes, workers were more willing to limit strikes and surrender the last vestiges of workplace autonomy. Co-opted by the materialistic benefits big business provided, workers fell increasingly under the control of middle-level managers and watched anxiously as companies automated at home or expanded abroad, where labor was cheaper. But the agreements they had reached often precluded any response.

The union movement stalled in the 1960s. Stagnation began to afflict the heavy industries whose workers dominated the union movement. The unionized percentage of the nonfarm workforce remained stable in the decade and a half following World War II but then began to fall. Unions tried to expand their base by reaching out to new groups—less skilled minority workers and white-collar, service-oriented employees—but these groups proved difficult to organize.

## Agricultural Workers in Trouble

The agricultural world changed even more than the industrial world in the postwar United States. Prior to World War II, agriculture had supported one of every five Americans. Now, in one generation, mechanization and consolidation forced that figure down to one in twenty.

New technology revolutionized farming. Improved planting and harvesting machines and better fertilizers and pesticides brought massive gains in productivity. Increasing profitability led to agricultural consolidation. In the 25 years after 1945, average farm size almost doubled. Farms specialized more in cash crops like corn or soybeans, which could be used to feed animals. Demanding large-scale investment, farming became a big business—often called "agribusiness."

More and more small farmers left the land. Some were midwestern whites, who generally found jobs in local offices and factories. In the South, however, the upheaval was more disruptive. Many of the uprooted agricultural workers were

African Americans, who became part of the huge migration that had been going north since World War I. Overall, from 1910 to 1970 more than 6.5 million African Americans left the South; of these, 5 million went north after 1940. Most of them gravitated to cities, where they faced difficulties described later in this chapter.

## DEMOGRAPHIC AND TECHNOLOGICAL TRENDS

The postwar economic boom intertwined with a series of demographic changes. The population grew dramatically and continued moving west. At the same time, millions of white Americans left the cities for the suburbs, which began to grow exponentially in the postwar years. New patterns, revolving around television and other gadgets pouring from modern technology's cornucopia, came to characterize the consumer culture of suburban life.

## Population Shifts

In post–World War II America, a growing population marked prosperity's return. The birthrate soared in the postwar years as millions of Americans started families. The "baby boom" peaked in 1957, with a rate of more than 25 births per 1,000. In that year, 4.3 million babies were born, one every seven seconds. While the population growth of 19 million in the 1940s was double that of the decade before, the latter increase paled against the increase in the 1950s, which totaled 29 million.

The death rate was also declining. Miracle drugs made a difference. Federal sponsorship of medical research during World War II had spurred the develop-

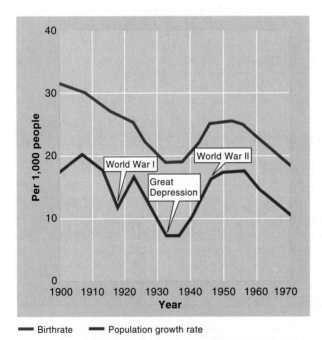

**BIRTH AND POPULATION RATES, 1900–1970**  Both birth and population rates increased dramatically after the difficult years of the Great Depression. Note the baby boom that began at the end of World War II and continued for the next several decades. (*Sources:* U.S. Bureau of the Census and *Statistical Abstract of the United States.*)

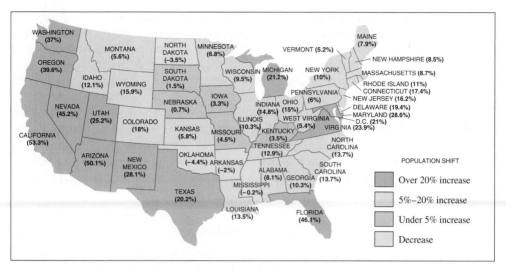

**POPULATION SHIFTS, 1940–1950**   This map reveals the huge growth of population in the West and the sizable, though less extensive, increase in the Northeast and Southeast between 1940 and 1950.

ment of penicillin and streptomycin, now widely available in the United States. They helped cure strep throat and other bacterial infections, intestinal ailments, and more serious illnesses such as tuberculosis. A polio vaccine introduced a decade after the war virtually eliminated that dreaded disease. Life expectancy rose: midway through the 1950s, the average life expectancy was 70 years for whites and 64 for blacks; in 1920 it was 55 for whites and 45 for blacks.

The baby boom shaped family patterns and material needs. Many women now did housework instead of paid wartime work. Demand grew for diaper services and baby foods. Entering school, the baby boom generation strained the educational system. Since school construction had slowed during the Depression and had virtually halted during the Second World War, classrooms were needed. Teachers, too, were in short supply.

As the population grew, Americans became more mobile. For many generations, working-class Americans had been the most likely to move; now geographic mobility spread to the middle class. Each year in the 1950s, over a million farmers left their farms. Other Americans picked up stakes and headed on as well. Some moved to look for better jobs. Others simply wandered a while after returning home from the war and then settled down.

The war had produced increasing movement, most of it westward. Although the scarcity of water in the West required massive water projects to support population growth, war workers and their families streamed to western cities. After the war, this migration pattern persisted. The Sun Belt—the region stretching along the southern tier of the United States from Florida to California—attracted new arrivals. Cities there expanded phenomenally. In the 1950s, Los Angeles pulled ahead of Philadelphia as the third-largest city in the United States. One-fifth of all the growth in the period took place in California. By 1963, California passed New York as the nation's most populous state.

Fueling the West's growth was the booming Cold War defense industry. As the Korean War sparked increased military expenditures, California's economic growth outpaced that of the country as a whole. Aircraft production in the state accounted for more than 40 percent of the total increase in manufacturing employment there between 1949 and 1953. By 1962, the Pacific Coast as a whole held almost half of all Defense Department research and development contracts.

The West also benefited from the boom in the service economy. Many western workers in postwar America belonged to the service sector. The percentage of workers in such jobs was higher in virtually all western states than in eastern counterparts. Denver became a major regional center of the federal bureaucracy, with more people on the federal payroll in 1975 than any other city except Washington, D.C.

## The New Suburbs

As the population shifted westward after World War II, another form of movement was taking place. Millions of white Americans fled the inner city to suburban fringes. Fourteen of the nation's largest cities lost population in the 1950s. As central cities became places where poor nonwhites clustered, new urban and racial problems emerged.

For people of means, cities were places to work but leave at five o'clock. In Manhattan south of City Hall, the noontime population of 1.5 million dropped to 2,000 overnight. "It was becoming a part-time city," according to writer John Brooks, "tidally swamped with bustling humanity every weekday morning when the cars and commuter trains arrived, and abandoned again at nightfall when the wave sucked back—left pretty much to thieves, policemen, and rats." By the end of the 1950s, a third of all Americans resided in suburbs; in 1970 nearly 38 percent did.

Often rapidly constructed and overpriced, suburban tract houses provided the appearance of comfort and space and the chance to have at least one part of the American dream, a place of one's own. They seemed protected from the growing troubles of the cities, insulated from the difficulties of the world outside.

The pioneer of postwar suburbanization was William J. Levitt, a builder who had recognized the advantages of mass production during World War II, when his firm constructed housing for war workers. Aware that the GI Bill made mortgage money readily available, he saw the possibilities of suburban development. But to cash in, Levitt had to use new construction methods.

Mass production was the key. "The reason we have it so good in this country," he said, "is that we can produce lots of things at low prices through mass production." Houses were among them. Working on a careful schedule, Levitt's team brought precut and preassembled materials to each site, put them together, and moved on. As on an assembly line, tasks were broken down into individual steps. Groups of workers performed a single job on each tract.

Levitt proved that his system worked. Construction costs at Levittown, New York, a new community of 17,000 homes built in the late 1940s, were only $10 per square foot, compared with the $12 to $15 common elsewhere. The next Levittown appeared in Bucks County, Pennsylvania, several years after the first, and

Step-by-step mass production, with units completed in assembly-line fashion, was the key to William Levitt's approach to housing. But the suburban developments he and others created were marked by street after street of houses that all looked the same. The Levittown in this picture was built on 1,200 acres of potato fields on Long Island in New York. (Cornell Capa/Magnum Photos, Inc.)

another went up in Willingboro, New Jersey, at the end of the 1950s. Levitt's success provided a model for other developers.

Levitt argued that his homes helped underscore American values. "No man who owns his own house and lot can be a Communist," he once said. "He has too much to do." Levitt also helped perpetuate segregation by refusing to sell homes to blacks. "We can solve a housing problem, or we can try to solve a racial problem but we cannot combine the two," he declared in the early 1950s.

Government-insured mortgages, especially for veterans, fueled the housing boom. So did fairly low postwar interest rates. With many American families vividly remembering the Depression and saving significant parts of their paychecks, the nation had a pool of savings large enough to keep mortgage interest rates in the affordable 5 percent range.

Suburbanization transformed the American landscape in the 1950s. Huge tracts of former fields, pastures, and forests were now divided into standardized squares, each with a house, a two-car garage, and a manicured lawn. It was cheaper to cut trees down than to work around them.

As suburbs flourished, businesses followed their customers out of the cities. At the end of World War II, there were eight shopping centers, but the number multiplied rapidly in the 1950s. Shopping centers catered to suburbanites and transformed consumer patterns. If they wished, suburb dwellers could avoid the city entirely. Downtown department stores declined, further eroding urban health.

# Technology Changes the American People

## Air Conditioning

For much of their history, Americans had little relief from hot weather and heat waves. Before the invention of air conditioning, the federal government sent workers in Washington, D.C., home whenever the temperature/humidity index rose above 90 degrees. People drove their cars with the windows open, hoping for a cooling breeze even if the noise made it difficult to carry on a conversation. Over the course of the twentieth century, the development of successful air conditioning systems changed residential patterns, altered cultural behavior, and improved the health of the American people. At the same time, technological improvements led to often acrimonious debate about the consequences of the new developments.

Early attempts at controlling the climate in the United States involved forcing air over ice. By the 1890s, a number of American cities had central refrigeration systems patterned after those providing electricity, water, and gas, but these were expensive and failed to catch on.

During the early years of the twentieth century, several breakthroughs occurred. Engineer Alfred R. Wolfe installed a system in the New York Stock Exchange that worked by chilling a calcium chloride brine and circulating it through a cooling coil over which air was circulated by fans. Stuart Cramer, another engineer, found a way to help textile manufacturers moderate the humidity to keep fibers soft by forcing air from outside through a fine water spray and a cloth filter and then releasing it inside. He called his procedure "air conditioning," and the name stuck.

Willis H. Carrier, in this same period, devised an even better system for a printing plant using chilled coils that managed to cool air and reduce humidity with remarkable precision. Carrier continued to improve his process in the decades that followed, figuring out ways to push air through the ever-larger buildings that were constructed in the 1920s and 1930s.

Industries affected by the heat were among the first to install air conditioning. Chocolate factories, tobacco factories, bakeries, and printing plants could now maintain continuous production in the summer. An occasional hospital introduced air conditioning to make doctors and patients more comfortable. The government implemented air conditioning too, starting in 1928. First the House of Representatives was centrally air conditioned, then the Senate, the White House, and the Supreme Court.

More and more movie theaters were air conditioned in the 1920s. A theater in Montgomery, Alabama, had installed a system in 1917, but the real breakthrough came at the Rivoli on Broadway in New York City in 1925. For a dime, Americans could get relief from the hot weather and forget about the mundane patterns of their daily existence.

A major shift in the patterns of air conditioning occurred with the advent of smaller, less expensive units that could be used in homes. The first home units, such as the Weathermaker in the 1920s, cost about $3,000, a huge amount of money, and followed the centralized structure used in industry. The Great Depression of the 1930s encouraged manufacturers to experiment with smaller room coolers. By the late1930s, Frigidaire, Kelvinator, and General Electric were designing less expensive air conditioners that could cool just one room. Window units came next, and mass production drove costs down still further and made them almost universally accessible in the years following World War II. From 74,000 window units in 1948, the number sold reached 1,045,000 in 1953. In the 1960s, more than 3 million units were being made each year.

Air conditioning had an enormous impact. It allowed government employees to work through the hot summer. It was responsible for the tremendous growth of the Sun Belt—that region stretching across the lower tier of the country from east to west—as people discovered they could moderate

THE NEW SILHOUETTE *Carrier* ROOM AIR CONDITIONER

BUILT BY THE PEOPLE WHO KNOW AIR CONDITIONING BEST. CARRIER CORPORATION, SYRACUSE, NEW YORK

Window units not only cooled the air but made everything inside more glamorous. (Courtesy of Carrier)

Air-conditioning made movie theaters even more popular than before. (Corbis)

the effects of the heat. Porches on houses disappeared as people became accustomed to living in the air-conditioned indoors. American culture became more homogenized, as increasingly the patterns of life in one part of the country resembled the patterns in other parts.

Americans moved from one air-conditioned location to another in air-conditioned cars. They shopped in air-conditioned malls, entertained themselves in air-conditioned theme parks, and then returned to their air-conditioned homes. With the construction of the Houston Sports Astrodome in 1965, they could now watch a baseball or football game in an entirely enclosed arena, with temperature and humidity carefully controlled.

As the country became air conditioned, some Americans complained about sealed rooms in what they considered sterile buildings, where they lost any sense of the world outside. Others objected to the huge amounts of electricity expended in cooling and worried about the environmental impact of the coolants used. Yet air conditioning remained an inextricable component of American life.

**Reflecting on the Past**   Historians often debate the impact of social change. They attempt to weigh the benefits of development against the consequences of such progress. One recent historian, reflecting on changes in the South and referring back to the Civil War, has written, "General Electric has proved a more devastating invader than General Sherman." Do you agree? How do you weigh the benefits and consequences of air conditioning? What advantages do you see in the window units that helped spread air conditioning? What are some of the disadvantages of such units? What patterns of ordinary life have changed with the advent of air conditioning? How extensive do you think the impact has been?

# The Environmental Impact

Suburbanization had environmental consequences. Rapid development often took place without extensive planning and encroached on some of the nation's most attractive rural areas. Before long, virtually every American city was ringed by an ugly highway sporting garish neon signs. Billboards filled whatever space was not yet developed.

Despite occasional protests against the spreading ugliness, there was little real consciousness of environmental issues in the early post–World War II years. The term *environment* itself was hardly used prior to the war. Americans had been concerned with conservation earlier in the century, focusing on efficient use and development of water and forests. Later they turned their attention to preservation.

The very prosperity that created dismal highway strips was leading more and more Americans to appreciate natural environments as treasured parts of their rising standard of living. The shorter workweek provided more free time, and many Americans now had the means for longer vacations. They began to explore mountains and rivers and ocean shores—and began to consider how to protect them. In 1958, Congress established the National Outdoor Recreation Review Commission, a first step toward consideration of environmental issues that became far more common in the next decade. In 1964, Congress went further, passing a National Wilderness Preservation Act, followed by a Wild and Scenic Rivers Act and a National Trails Act in 1968. Americans also began to recognize the need for open space in their communities to compensate for urban overdevelopment. With the 1962 publication of Rachel Carson's *Silent Spring* attacking chemical pesticides (see Chapter 29), they became more aware of their own impact on the environment.

# Technology Supreme

A technological revolution transformed postwar America. Some developments—the use of atomic energy, for example—flowed directly from wartime research. Federal support for scientific activity increased dramatically as the pattern of wartime collaboration continued. The government established the National Institutes of Health in 1948 to coordinate medical research and the National Science Foundation in 1950 to fund basic scientific research. The Cold War brought constantly increasing government research and development ("R & D") funding through the Atomic Energy Commission (1946) and the Department of Defense (1947). Money went to large research universities, which grew enormously. Basic and applied research developed not only nuclear weapons, jet planes, and satellites, but also the consumer goods that were often the spinoffs of military projects. Big business had its own research and development activities as well.

Computers both reflected and assisted technological development. Prior to World War II, Vannevar Bush, an electrical engineer at the Massachusetts Institute of Technology, had built a machine filled with gears and shafts to solve differential equations. A major contribution was using electronic tubes that could be turned on and off in place of some mechanical parts to make the machine manipulate numbers.

Wartime advances resulted in large but workable calculators, such as the Mark I electromechanical computer developed by engineer Howard Aiken and installed by IBM at Harvard in 1944. It was huge—55 feet long and 8 feet high—and had a million components.

Even more complicated was the Electronic Numerical Integrator and Calculator, called ENIAC, built in 1946 at the University of Pennsylvania. Like the Mark I, it was huge, containing 18,000 electronic tubes and requiring tremendous amounts of electricity and special cooling procedures. In a widely publicized test, a reporter pushed the button, and in less than half a second it multiplied 97,367 by itself 5,000 times.

A key breakthrough in making computers faster and more reliable was the development of the transistor by three scientists at Bell Laboratories in 1948. Computers were now on the way to transforming twentieth-century American society as radically as industrialization had revolutionized the nineteenth century. Computers were essential for space exploration. Airlines, hotels, and other businesses computerized their reservation systems. Business accounting and inventory control began to depend on computers. Computer programmers and operators were in increasing demand as computers contributed dramatically to the centralization and interdependence of the components of American life.

Computers allowed scientists to venture beyond the confines of the earth itself. In the postwar years, increasingly sophisticated forms of space exploration became possible. Rocketry had developed during World War II but really came of age in the postwar years. Rockets could deliver nuclear weapons but could also launch satellites and provide the means to venture millions of miles into outer space.

An ominous technological trend was automation. Mechanization was not new, but now it became far more widespread, threatening both skilled and unskilled workers. The implications of falling purchasing power as machines replaced workers were serious for an economy dependent on consumer demand.

## The Consumer Culture

Americans fell in love with appliances and gadgets. By the end of the 1950s, most families had at least one automobile, as well as the staple appliances they had begun to purchase before—the refrigerator, washing machine, television, and vacuum cleaner. Dozens of less essential items caught on, from electric can openers to aerosol sprays.

The greatest gadget of all was the TV. Developed in the 1930s, it became a major influence on American life after World War II. There were fewer than 17,000 sets in 1946, but by 1949 Americans were buying them at a rate of 250,000 a month. By 1960, three-quarters of all families owned at least one set. Youngsters grew up with "Howdy Doody" and their parents followed "I Love Lucy." In 1955, the average family tuned in four to five hours each day.

Consumption, so vital to the American economy, required a vast expansion of consumer credit. Installment plans facilitated buying a new car. For smaller purchases, the credit card became essential. Diner's Club, the first of the consumer credit cards, appeared in 1950, and by the end of the decade came the American Express card and the BankAmericard (later renamed VISA). By the end of the 1960s, about 50 million credit cards of all kinds were in use in the United States. Consumer credit—total private indebtedness—increased astronomically. It went from $8.4 billion in 1946 to nearly $45 billion in 1958, and reached $113.2 billion in 1968.

For consumers momentarily unsure about new purchases, a revitalized advertising industry was ready to convince them to go ahead. Advertising had come of age in the 1920s, as businesses persuaded customers that buying new products brought status and satisfaction. It had faltered when the economy collapsed in the 1930s but began to revive during the war. With the postwar boom, admen were hawking wares more persuasively than ever before.

Motivational research discovered new ways of persuading people to buy. Unlike radio, which could only talk about new wonders, television could show them. Ads bombarded TV viewers with everything they needed to know about the luxuries indispensable to the good life. "The Price Is Right" went to the heart of the matter: contestants won goods by guessing their correct retail price.

Having experienced poverty in the 1930s and sacrifice during the war, most Americans now regarded abundance and leisure as their due. A small minority of cultural critics, however, scolded them. The decade of the 1950s, journalist William Shannon wrote, was a time of "self-satisfaction and gross materialism . . . . The loudest sound in the land has been the oink and grunt of private hoggishness . . . . It has been the age of the slob."

## CONSENSUS AND CONFORMITY

As the economy expanded, an increasing sense of sameness pervaded American society. Some believed this was the great age of conformity, when members of all social groups learned to emulate those around them rather than strike out on their own. Third- and fourth-generation ethnic Americans became much more alike. As immigration slowed to a trickle after 1924, old-country ties weakened, assimilation speeded up, and inter-ethnic marriage increased. Television gave young and old a shared, visually seductive experience. Escaping the homogenizing tendencies was difficult.

## Conformity in School and Religious Life

The willingness to conform to group norms affected students at all levels. Elementary school children watched the same television shows and coveted the same toys. High school students, always concerned with group norms, dressed similarly and shared a vocabulary based on television programs and advertising jingles. College students seemed most concerned with security. They joined fraternities and sororities that engaged in panty raids and other pranks, but usually took little interest in world affairs.

Postwar Americans discovered a shared religious sense and returned to their churches in record numbers. By the end of the 1950s, fully 95 percent of all Americans identified with some religious denomination. Church membership doubled between 1945 and 1970.

Part of this upsurge of church attendance grew out of anxieties about "godless Communism" and the threat of nuclear annihilation (see Chapter 27). Evangelist Billy Graham was in the forefront of the anti-Communist campaign in the 1950s and 1960s. "The greatest and most effective weapon against Communism today is to be born again Christian," he thundered in a widely read article. In "Hour of Decision," his radio ministry in the 1950s, he tried to convert sinners and so save the nation. "When you make your decision for Jesus Christ," Graham said, "it is America making her decision through you."

The religious resurgence had other roots as well. Ecumenical activities—worldwide efforts on the part of different Christian churches—became more common following a first World Council of Churches meeting in 1948. These helped draw attention to the place of religion in modern life. In the early 1960s Pope John XXIII convened the Vatican Ecumenical Council to make the Catholic Church's traditions and practices more accessible, for example substituting modern languages for Latin in the liturgy. Judaism, likewise, went through important shifts in the postwar years. Second- and third-generation Jews became increasingly affluent, and between 1945 and 1965 a third of all American Jews left cities for the suburbs. There they built new synagogues, most of which adhered to the easier-to-follow patterns of Reform or Conservative, rather than Orthodox, Judaism. In part, this shift reflected an effort by Jews to seek greater acceptance in mainstream American society.

The religious revival resulted to some degree, as well, from the power of suggestion that led Americans to do what others did. According to one slogan, "The family that prays together stays together." The renewal of interest in religion also offered an acceptable means of escape from the anxieties of a middle-class executive's life. In the 1950s, the Full Gospel Businessmen's Fellowship not only provided religious camaraderie but also enjoyed access to the White House.

President Dwight Eisenhower reflected the national mood when he observed that "our government makes no sense unless it is founded in a deeply felt religious faith—and I don't care what it is." In 1954, Congress added the words "under God" to the pledge to the flag, and the next year voted to require the phrase "In God We Trust" on all U.S. currency. Yet the revival sometimes seemed to rest on a shallow base of religious knowledge. In one public opinion poll, 80 percent of the respondents avowed that the Bible was God's revealed word, but only 35 percent could name the four Gospels. Over half were unable to name even one.

## Traditional Roles for Women

World War II had interrupted traditional patterns of behavior for both men and women. As servicemen went overseas, women went to work. After 1945, there was a period of adjustment as the men returned and many working women were told that they were no longer needed in their jobs. In the 1950s, women faced tremendous pressure to conform to accepted prewar gender patterns, even though, paradoxically, more women entered the workforce than ever before.

Men and women had different postwar expectations. Most men planned to go to school and then find jobs to support a family. Viewing themselves as the primary breadwinners, they wanted their jobs back after the war. For women, the situation was more complex. While they wanted to resume disrupted patterns of family life, many had enjoyed working in the plants and were reluctant to retreat to the home, despite pressure to do so.

In 1947, *Life* magazine ran a long photo essay called "The American Woman's Dilemma." Women, it observed, were caught in a conflict between the traditional expectation to stay home and a new desire to have a paid job. The dilemma affected white, well-educated, middle-class women most intensely; black and lower-class white women usually had to continue working outside the home whether they liked it or not.

By the 1950s, middle-class doubts had largely receded. The baby boom increased average family size and made the decision to remain home easier. The flight to the suburbs gave women more to do, and they settled into the routines of redecorating their homes and gardens and transporting children to and from activities and schools.

In 1956, when *Life* produced a special issue on women, the message had changed strikingly from that of nine years before. Profiling Marjorie Sutton, the magazine spoke of the "Busy Wife's Achievements" as "Home Manager, Mother, Hostess, and Useful Civic Worker." Married at the age of 16, Marjorie was now involved with the PTA, Campfire Girls, and charity causes. She cooked and sewed for her family, which included four children, supported her husband by entertaining 1,500 guests a year, and worked out on the trampoline "to keep her size 12 figure."

Marjorie Sutton typified the widespread social emphasis on marriage and home. Many women went to college to find husbands—and dropped out if they succeeded. Almost two-thirds of the women in college, but less than half the men, left before completing a degree. Women were expected to marry young, have children early, and support their husbands' careers. An article in *Esquire* magazine in 1954 called working wives a "menace." Adlai Stevenson, Democratic presidential candidate in 1952 and 1956, defined the female role in politics, telling a group of women that "the assignment for you, as wives and mothers, you can do in the living room with a baby in your lap or in the kitchen with a can opener in your hand." As in much of the nineteenth century, a woman was "to influence man and boy" in her "humble role of housewife" and mother.

Pediatrician Benjamin Spock agreed. In 1946 he published the first edition of *Baby and Child Care,* the book most responsible for the child-rearing patterns of the postwar generation. He advised mothers to stay at home if they wanted to raise stable and secure youngsters. Working outside the home might jeopardize their children's mental and emotional health.

Popular culture highlighted the stereotype of the woman concerned only about marriage and family. Author Betty Friedan described these patterns in her explosive 1963 critique, *The Feminine Mystique.* Shifting her attention away from working class and union issues that had concerned her before, she examined women's magazines and other publications and put together a profile of women in the 1950s and early 1960s. They "could desire no greater destiny than to glory in their own femininity . . . . All they had to do was to devote their lives from earliest girlhood to finding a husband and bearing children." Their role was clear. "It was unquestioned gospel," she wrote, "that women could identify with *nothing* beyond the home—not politics, not art, not science, not events large or small, war or peace, in the United States or the world, unless it could be approached through female experience as a wife or mother or translated into domestic detail."

Movies reinforced conventional images. Doris Day, charming and wholesome, was a favorite heroine. In film after film, she showed how an attractive woman who played her cards right could land her man.

The family was all-important in this scenario. Fewer than 10 percent of all Americans felt that an unmarried person could be happy. A healthy family strengthened the nation in its Cold War struggle. In the pattern endlessly reiterated by popular television programs, the family was meant to provide all satisfaction and contentment. The single-story ranch house that became so popular in this period reflected the focus on the family as the source of recreation and fun.

Sexuality was a troublesome if compelling postwar concern. In 1948, Alfred C. Kinsey published *Sexual Behavior in the Human Male*. Kinsey was an Indiana University zoologist who had been asked to teach a course on marriage problems but found little published material about human sexual activity. Collecting his own, he compiled case histories of 5,300 white males and recorded patterns of sexual behavior.

Kinsey shocked the country. Among males who went to college, he concluded, 67 percent had engaged in sexual intercourse before marriage, as had 84 percent of those who went to high school but not beyond. Thirty-seven percent of the total male population had experienced some kind of overt homosexual activity. Five years later, Kinsey published *Sexual Behavior in the Human Female*, detailing many of the same patterns. Although critics denounced Kinsey for his methodology and his results, both of his books sold widely, for they opened the door to a subject that had previously been considered taboo.

Interest in sexuality was reflected in the fascination with sex goddesses like Marilyn Monroe. With her blonde hair, breathy voice, and raw sexuality, she personified the forbidden side of the good life and became one of Hollywood's most popular stars. The images of such film goddesses corresponded to male fantasies of women, displayed in *Playboy* magazine, which first appeared in 1953 and soon achieved a huge readership. These men's wives were expected to manage their suburban homes and to be cheerful and willing objects of their husbands' desire.

Despite reaffirming the old ideology that a woman's place was in the home, the 1950s were years of unnoticed but important change. Because the supply of single women workers was diminished by the low birthrate of the Depression years and by increased schooling and early marriage, older married women continued the pattern begun during the war and entered the labor force in larger numbers than before. In 1940, only 15 percent of American wives had jobs. By 1950, 21 percent were employed, and 10 years later, the figure had risen to 30 percent. Moreover, married women now accounted for more than half of all working women, a dramatic reversal of pre–World War II patterns. Although the media hailed those women who primarily tended to their families, some magazine articles, in fact, did stress the achievements of women outside the home.

While many working women were poor, divorced, or widowed, many others worked to acquire the desirable new products that were badges of middle-class status. They stepped into the new jobs created by economic expansion, clustering in office, sales, and service positions, occupations already defined as female. They and their employers considered their work subordinate to their primary role as wives and mothers. The conviction that a woman's main role was homemaking justified low wages and the denial of promotions. Comparatively few women entered professions where they would have challenged traditional notions of a woman's place. In 1956, *Life* magazine reflected on the typical female employee: "Household skills take her into the garment trades; neat and personable, she becomes office worker and sales lady; patient and dexterous, she does well on competitive, detailed factory work; compassionate, she becomes teacher and nurse."

African-American women worked as always but often lost the jobs they had held during the war. As the percentage of women in the Detroit automobile industry, for example, dropped from 25 to 7.5 in the immediate postwar period, black women who had held some of the jobs were the first to go. Bernice McCannon, an African-American employee at a Virginia military base, observed, "I have always done domestic work for families. When war came, I made the same move many domestics did. I took a higher paying job in a government cafeteria as a junior baker. If domestic work offers a good living, I see no reason why most of us will not return to our old jobs. We will have no alternative." These jobs, however, did not pay as well as others. In the 1950s, the employment picture improved somewhat. African-American women succeeded both in moving into white-collar positions and in increasing their income. By 1960, more than a third of all black women held clerical, sales, service, or professional jobs. The income gap between white women and black women holding similar jobs dropped from about 50 percent in 1940 to about 30 percent in 1960.

Some of the patterns of the 1950s persisted in the next decade. By the middle of the 1960s, however, the roots of what became a powerful women's movement were visible. Women challenged stereotypical patterns of behavior and patterns of dress. They demanded and seized greater control over their own lives, in a story we will take up in much greater detail in Chapter 29.

## Cultural Rebels

Not all Americans fit the 1950s stereotypes. As young people struggled to meet the standards and expectations of their peers, they often contemplated Holden Caulfield, the central character in J. D. Salinger's novel *The Catcher in the Rye* (1951). Holden, a boarding school misfit, rebelled against the "phonies" around him who threatened his individuality and independence, and his ill-fated effort to preserve his integrity in the face of pressures to conform struck a resonant chord.

Writers of the so-called "beat generation" espoused unconventional values. Stressing spontaneity and spirituality, they proclaimed intuition superior to reason and Eastern mysticism more satisfying than Western faith. The "beats" deliberately challenged respectability by sneering at materialism, flaunting unconventional sex lives, and smoking marijuana. Dispensing with punctuation and paragraphing, Jack Kerouac used a single 250-foot roll of paper to type his best-selling novel *On the Road* (1957), a saga of freewheeling trips across the country that glorified the beat lifestyle. Allen Ginsberg became equally well-known for his poem "Howl." Written during a wild weekend in 1955 while Ginsberg was under the influence of drugs, "Howl" was a scathing critique of modern, mechanized culture. Ginsberg became a celebrity when the poem appeared in print in 1956, particularly after it survived a court test on obscenity charges. Ginsberg, Kerouac, and the other beats would be models for countercultural rebellion in the 1960s, described in Chapter 29.

The popularity of Salinger, Kerouac, and Ginsberg owed much to a revolution in book publishing and to the democratization of education that accompanied the program of GI educational benefits. More Americans than ever before acquired a taste for literature, which they could satisfy with the huge numbers of inexpensive books made available by the "paperback revolution." The paperback, introduced in 1939, dominated the book market after World War II. By 1965, readers could choose among some 25,000 titles sold in bookstores, supermarkets, drugstores, and airplane terminals. They purchased nearly 7 million copies per week.

The signs of cultural rebellion also appeared in popular music. Parents recoiled as their children flocked to hear Elvis Presley belt out rock-and-roll songs. Presley's sexy voice, gyrating hips, and other techniques borrowed from black singers made him the undisputed "king of rock-and-roll." A multimedia blitz of movies, television, and radio helped make songs like "Heartbreak Hotel," "Don't Be Cruel," and "Hound Dog" smash singles, and his black leather jacket and ducktail haircut became a virtual uniform for rebellious male teenagers.

American painters, shucking off European influences that had shaped American artists for two centuries, also became a part of the cultural rebellion. Led by Jackson Pollock and the "New York school," some artists discarded the easel, laid gigantic canvases on the floor, and then used trowels, putty knives, and sticks to apply paint, glass shards, sand, and other materials in wild explosions of color. Known as abstract expressionists, these painters regarded the unconscious as the source of their artistic creations. "I am not aware of what is taking place [as I paint]," Pollock explained; "it is only after that I see what I have done." Like much of the literature of rebellion, abstract expressionism reflected the artist's alienation from a world increasingly filled with nuclear threats, computers, and materialistic patterns.

## THE OTHER AMERICA

Not all Americans shared postwar middle-class affluence. Poverty persisted in inner cities and rural areas. African Americans, uprooted from rural roots and crowded into urban slums, were among the dispossessed. But other minorities and disadvantaged whites suffered similar dislocations, unknown to the middle class.

### Poverty Amid Affluence

Economic growth favored the upper and middle classes. Although the popular "trickle-down" theory argued that economic expansion benefited all classes, little wealth actually reached people at the bottom. In 1960, according to the Federal Bureau of Labor Statistics, a yearly subsistence-level income for a family of four was $3,000 and for a family of six, $4,000. The Bureau reported that 40 million people (almost a quarter of the population) lived below those levels, with nearly the same number only marginally above the line. Two million migrant workers labored long hours for a subsistence wage. According to the 1960 census, 27 percent of the residential units in the United States were substandard, and even acceptable dwellings were often hopelessly overcrowded in some slums.

Michael Harrington, socialist author and critic, shocked the country with his 1962 book *The Other America*. The poor, Harrington showed, were everywhere. He described New York City's "economic underworld," where "Puerto Ricans and Negroes, alcoholics, drifters, and disturbed people" haunted employment agencies for temporary positions as "dishwashers and day workers, the fly-by-night jobs." In rural America, Appalachian mountain folk, Mississippi tenant farmers, and migrant farm workers everywhere suffered in the same relentless cycle of poverty.

## Hard Times for African Americans

African Americans were among the postwar nation's least prosperous citizens. They had always known poverty. Now, however, most of them were concentrated in cities, driven from rural life by mechanization and the collapse of tenant farming. Millions of blacks moved to southern cities where they found better jobs, better schooling, and freedom from landlords. Some reached middle-class status; many more did not. They remained poor, with even less of a support system than they had before.

The millions of African Americans who headed for northern cities after 1940 usually wound up in slums, where the growth of facilities and social services lagged behind population growth. At one point in the 1950s, Chicago's black population rose by more than 2,200 people each week.

The black ghetto that had begun to develop earlier in the twentieth century became a permanent fixture in the post–World War II years. African Americans attempting to move elsewhere often found the way blocked, sometimes violently. In 1951, a black couple purchasing a home in Cicero, Illinois, was driven away when an angry white crowd broke the house's windows, defaced the walls, and shouted vile insults. Even passage in 1968 of the Fair Housing Act barring racial discrimination in housing failed to end such residential segregation.

Black author James Baldwin eloquently described slum conditions and their corrosive effect on African Americans in his 1961 book *Nobody Knows My Name:*

> They work in the white man's world all day and come home in the evening to this fetid block. They struggle to instill in their children some private sense of honor or dignity, which will help the child to survive. This means, of course, that they must struggle, stolidly, incessantly, to keep this sense live in themselves, in spite of the insults, the indifference, and the cruelty they are certain to encounter in their working day. They patiently browbeat the landlord into fixing the heat, the plaster, the plumbing; this demands prodigious patience, nor is patience usually enough . . . . Such frustration, so long endured, is driving many strong and admirable men and women whose only crime is color to the very gates of paranoia.

Such conditions, and the constant slights that accompanied segregation in both the North and the South, took a toll. African Americans learned how, in the words of a turn-of-the-century poem by Paul Laurence Dunbar, to "wear the mask." Employment opportunities had improved during World War II and later improved still further in the 1960s with the expansion of public programs that were part of the Great Society (see Chapter 28), but cutbacks in the 1970s, when the economy faltered, had a corrosive effect on the stability of African-American family life. While the black family managed to hold together until the 1960s, with 70 percent of all units including both husband and wife, in the years that followed, this pattern changed. As a still-smoldering racism erupted into more violent confrontations and drugs became increasingly available, more black men found themselves in trouble with the law. Family stability began to crumble, until by 1983, 50 percent of all black children under 18 lived in households headed by women, and many of these suffered from oppressive poverty from which there appeared to be no escape.

Still, the larger black community remained intact. Chicago's South Side neighborhood was a vibrant place, replacing New York's Harlem as black America's cultural capital in the 1950s. Here and elsewhere, the black church played an important role in sustaining African-American life. Blacks moving into the cities retained churchgoing habits and commitment to religious institutions from their rural days. Older, established churches assisted newcomers in the transition to urban America, while new religious groups began to form, creating a sense of community for recent arrivals. The churches offered more than just religious sustenance. Many provided day-care facilities, ran Scout troops, and sponsored other social services. These activities gave them a crucial place in the civil rights movement that began to flourish in these years (see Chapter 29).

The growth of the black urban population fostered businesses catering to the African-American community. Black newspapers now provided a more regional, rather than a national, focus, but magazines such as *Jet*, a pocket-size weekly with a large countrywide circulation, filled the void. Black-owned or black-operated banks and other financial institutions proliferated.

Yet most African Americans remained second-class citizens. Escape from the slums was difficult for many, impossible for most. Persistent poverty was a dismal fact of life, even as the rest of the United States enjoyed prosperous times.

## Minorities on the Fringe

Other groups had similar difficulties in the postwar United States. Latino immigrants from Cuba, Puerto Rico, Mexico, and Central America, often unskilled and illiterate, followed other less fortunate Americans to the cities. The conditions they encountered there were similar to those faced by blacks. Author Piri Thomas, born of Puerto Rican and Cuban parents in New York City's Spanish Harlem, described his neighborhood in his memoir *Down These Mean Streets:*

> Man! How many times have I stood on the rooftop of my broken-down building at night and watched the bulb-lit world below.
>
> Like somehow it's different at night, this my Harlem.
>
> There ain't no bright sunlight to reveal the start naked truth of garbage-lepered streets.
>
> Gone is the drabness and hurt, covered by a friendly night.
>
> It makes clean the dirty-faced kids.

In the face of recurring discrimination, these Spanish-speaking groups maintained strong group identities in their *barrios,* even in the midst of pervasive poverty. The ties fostered in these communities provided a strong base on which a growing political consciousness could rest as it emerged in the next decade (see Chapter 29).

Chicanos, or Mexican Americans, were the most numerous of the newcomers and faced special difficulties. During World War II, faced with a labor shortage, American farmers had sought Mexican *braceros* (helping hands) to harvest their crops. A U.S.-Mexican program to encourage the seasonal immigration of farm workers continued after the war. Between 1948 and 1964, some 4.5 million Mexicans were brought to the United States for temporary work. *Braceros* were expected to return to Mexico at the end of their contract, but often they stayed. Millions more entered the country illegally.

Conditions were harsh for *braceros* in the best of times, but in periods of economic difficulty, troubles worsened. During a serious recession from 1953 to 1954, the federal government mounted a massive attempt to round up and deport illegal Mexican immigrants. Some 1.1 million were expelled. As immigration officials searched out illegal workers, all Chicanos found themselves vulnerable. They bitterly protested the violations of their rights, to little effect.

Reliance on poor Mexican farm laborers continued despite the deportations. A coalition of southern Democrats and conservative Republicans, mostly representing farm states, wanted to continue to take advantage of cheap labor. Two years after the massive deportations of 1954, a record 445,000 *braceros* crossed the border.

Puerto Ricans were numerous in other parts of the country. A steady stream of immigrants had been coming to New York from Puerto Rico since the 1920s. As the island's sugarcane economy became more mechanized, nearly 40 percent of the inhabitants left their homeland. By the end of the 1960s, New York City had more Puerto Ricans than San Juan, the island's capital. El Barrio, in East Harlem, became the center of Puerto Rican immigrant life. Author Guillermo Cotto-Thorner described the place fondly in his autobiographical novel *Trópico en Manhattan* through the words of Antonio, an older resident.

> This . . . is our neighborhood, El Barrio . . . . It's said that we Latins run things here. And that's how we see ourselves. While the American take most of the money that circulates around here, we consider this part of the city to be ours . . . .
> The stores, barbershops, restaurants, butcher shops, churches, funeral parlors, greasy spoons, pool halls, everything is all Latino. Every now and then you see a business run by a Jew or an Irishman or an Italian, but you'll also see that even these people know a little Spanish.

Puerto Ricans, like many other immigrants, hoped to earn money in America and then return home. Some did; others stayed. Like countless Latinos, most failed to enjoy the promise of the American dream.

Native Americans likewise remained outsiders. They faced the consequences of the same technological developments affecting other Americans, but often had greater difficulty coping with the changes they faced, given their long history of persistent discrimination. As power lines reached their reservations, Indians purchased televisions, refrigerators, washing machines, and automobiles. As they joined the consumer culture, reservation life lost its cohesiveness and alcohol became a major problem. With good jobs unavailable on the reservations, Indians gravitated to the cities. Bennie Bearskin, a Winnebago, left home for Chicago in 1947, explaining: "The most important reason was that I could at least feel confident that [I could get] perhaps fifty paychecks a year here . . . . Even though it might be more pleasant to be back home, for instance, Nebraska." But Indians

# Timeline

| | | | |
|---|---|---|---|
| **1946** | 4.6 million workers on strike | **1955** | First McDonald's opens in Illinois |
| | ENIAC computer built | | Merger of AFL and CIO |
| | Benjamin Spock, *Baby and Child Care* | | Congress adds "In God We Trust" to currency |
| **1947** | Defense budget of $13 billion | **1956** | Interstate Highway Act |
| **1948** | GM offers UAW cost-of-living adjustment | | Majority of U.S. workers hold white-collar jobs |
| | Transistor developed at Bell Laboratories | | Allen Ginsberg, "Howl" |
| | Kinsey report on male sexuality | **1957** | Baby boom peaks |
| **1950s** | Each year a million farmers leave farms | | Jack Kerouac, *On the Road* |
| | | **1960** | Three-quarters of all Americans own a TV set |
| **1950** | Diner's Card inaugurated | | |
| **1951** | J. D. Salinger, *The Catcher in the Rye* | **1962** | Michael Harrington, *The Other America* |
| **1953** | Defense budget of $47 billion | **1963** | California passes New York as most populous state |
| | Operation Wetback begins | | Betty Friedan, *The Feminine Mystique* |
| **1954** | Congress adds "under God" to pledge to flag | **1970** | 38 percent of all Americans live in suburbs |

who moved to the cities often had difficulty adjusting to urban life and faced white hostility, much as did Latinos and blacks. They, too, began to protest in a movement that gained strength in succeeding years (see Chapter 29).

❧ ❧ ❧ ❧

# CONCLUSION

## *Qualms Amid Affluence*

In general, the United States during the decade and a half after World War II was stable and secure. Structural adjustments caused occasional moments of friction but were seldom visible in prosperous times. Recessions occurred periodically, but the economy righted itself after short downturns. For the most part, business boomed. The standard of living for many of the nation's citizens reached new heights, especially compared with standards in other parts of the world. Millions of middle-class Americans joined the ranks of suburban property owners, enjoying the benefits of shopping centers and fast-food establishments and other material manifestations of what they considered the good life. Workers found themselves savoring the materialistic advantages of the era.

Some Americans did not share in the prosperity, but they were not visible in the affluent suburbs. Many African Americans and members of other minority groups were seriously disadvantaged, yet most still believed they could share in the American dream and remained confident that deeply rooted patterns of discrimination could be changed. Even when they began to mobilize, their protest was peaceful at first.

Beneath the calm surface, though, there were signs of discontent. The seeds for the protest movements of the 1960s had already been sown. Disquieting signs were likewise evident on other fronts. The divorce rate increased, as a third of all marriages in the 1950s broke apart. Americans increasingly used newly developed tranquilizers in an effort to cope with problems in their lives. Some Americans began to criticize the materialism that seemed to undermine American efforts in the Cold War. Such criticisms in turn legitimized challenges by other groups, in the continuing struggle to make the realities of American life match the nation's ideals.

Criticisms and anxieties notwithstanding, the United States—for most whites and some people of color—continued to develop according to Ray Kroc's dreams as he first envisioned McDonald's establishments across the land. Healthy and comfortable, upper- and middle-class Americans expected prosperity and growth to continue and were surprised by the challenges and protests of the years ahead.

## Discovering U.S. History Online

*Fifties Website Home Page*   http://www.fiftiesweb.com/
This entertaining site tells about and samples music and television from the 1950s. It also includes a related links page.

*Levittown: Documents of an Ideal American Suburb*   http://www.uic.edu/~pbhales/Levittown/
The postwar housing boom made suburban living the cultural norm in America and shaped a generation. This story of the classic suburb, Levittown, is told on this site in pictures and text.

*Virtual Museum of Computing*   http://vmoc.museophile.com/
This site relates the history of computing through a series of online exhibits.

*Harry S Truman*   http://www.ipl.org/ref/POTUS/hstruman.html
This site contains basic factual data about Truman's election and presidency, speeches, and online biographies.

*Harry S Truman Library & Museum*   http://www.trumanlibrary.org
This presidential library site has numerous photos and various important primary documents relating to Truman.

*Dwight David Eisenhower*   http://www.ipl.org/ref/POTUS/ddeisenhower.html
This site contains basic factual data about Eisenhower's election and presidency, including speeches and other materials.

*The Dwight D. Eisenhower Library and Museum*   http://www.eisenhower.utexas.edu/
This site contains mainly photos of the presidents.

## Fiction and Film

Guillermo Cotto-Thorner, *Trópico en Manhattan* (1967) is an autobiographical novel about the Puerto Rican community in New York City; Ralph Ellison's *Invisible Man* (1952) is a powerful fictional account of an African American's journey through the 1950s; Allen Ginsberg, *Howl and Other Poems* (1956) is a collection of iconoclastic poetry challenging the materialism of contemporary life; Jack Kerouac, *On the*

Road (1957) is a stream of consciousness novel that questioned the values of the 1950s; Arthur Miller, *Death of a Salesman* (1949) is the Pulitzer Prize-winning play about the shallow values of postwar American culture; J. D. Salinger, *The Catcher in the Rye* (1951) is the story of Holden Caulfield, a troubled adolescent, who is overwhelmed by the phoniness of contemporary life; Sloan Wilson, *The Man in the Gray Flannel Suit* (1955) is a novel challenging the conformity of corporate America in the 1950s.

The Best Years of Our Lives (1946) is the Academy Award-winning story of three servicemen returning home after World War II that captures the values of the immediate postwar era; *The Seven Year Itch* (1955) featured Marilyn Monroe as the beautiful and enticing girl next door; *The Man in the Gray Flannel Suit* (1956) is the film made from the novel of the same name, critiquing the lifestyle of corporate America in the 1950s.

## Recommended Reading

### Economic Boom

American Social History Project, *Who Built America? Working People & the Nation's Economy, Politics, Culture, and Society* (1992); David Brody, Workers in Industrial America (1980); James R. Green, *The World of the Worker* (1980); Jacqueline Jones, *American Work: Four Centuries of Black and White Labor* (1998); James T. Patterson, *Grand Expectations: Postwar America, 1945–1974* (1996); Juliet B. Schor, *The Overworked American: The Unexpected Decline of Leisure* (1991); Robert H. Zieger, *American Workers, American Unions*, 2d ed. (1994) and *The CIO, 1935–1955* (1995).

### Demographic and Technological Trends

Peter Blake, *God's Own Junkyard: The Planned Deterioration of America's Landscape* (1964); Paul A. Carter, *Another Part of the Fifties* (1983); David Halberstam, *The Fifties* (1993); Samuel P. Hays, *Beauty, Health, and Permanence: Environmental Politics in the United States, 1955–1985* (1987); Daniel Horowitz, ed., *American Social Classes in the 1950s: Selections from Vance Packard's The Status Seekers* (1995); Kenneth T. Jackson, *Crabgrass Frontier: The Suburbanization of the United States* (1985); Zane L. Miller, *The Urbanization of Modern America* (1973); Richard Polenberg, *One Nation Divisible: Class, Race, and Ethnicity in the United States Since 1938* (1980); Richard White, *"It's Your Misfortune and None of My Own": A History of the American West* (1991).

### Consensus and Conformity

Erik Barnouw, *Tube of Plenty: The Evolution of American Television* (1975); Joel Foreman, ed., *The Other Fifties: Interrogating Midcentury American Icons* (1997); James Howard Jones, *Alfred C. Kinsey: A Public/Private Life* (1997); C. Wright Mills, *White Collar: The American Middle Classes* (1951); David Riesman, *The Lonely Crowd: A Study of the Changing American Character* (1950).

David Chidester, *Patterns of Power: Religion and Politics in American Culture* (1988); Erling Jorstad, *Holding Fast/Pressing On: Religion in America in the 1980s* (1990); R. Laurence Moore, *Selling God: American Religion in the Marketplace of Culture* (1994); Peter W. Williams, *Popular Religion in America: Symbolic Change and the Modernization Process in Historical Perspective* (1980); Garry Wills, *Under God: Religion and American Politics* (1990).

Beth L. Bailey, *From Front Porch to Back Seat: Courtship in Twentieth-Century America* (1988); William H. Chafe, *The American Woman: Her Changing Social, Economic, and Political Roles, 1920–1970* (1972); Stephanie Coontz, *The Way We Never Were: American Families and the Nostalgia Trap* (1992); John D'Emilio and Estelle B. Freedman, *Intimate Matters: A History of Sexuality in America* (1988); Betty Friedan, *The Feminine Mystique* (1963); Susan M. Hartmann, *The Home Front and Beyond: American Women in the 1940s* (1982); Judith A. Hennessee, *Betty Friedan: Her Life* (1999); Daniel Horowitz, *Betty Friedan and the Making of The Feminine Mystique: The American Left, the Cold War and Modern Feminism* (1998); Eugenia Kaledin, *Mothers and More: American Women in the 1950s* (1984); Elaine Tyler May, *Homeward Bound: American Families in the Cold War Era* (1988); Joanne Meyerowitz, ed., *Not June Cleaver: Women and Gender in Postwar America, 1945–1960* (1994); Gloria Steinem, *Outrageous Acts and Everyday Rebellions*, 2nd ed. (1995).

**The Other America**

Michael Harrington, *The Other America: Poverty in the United States* (1962); James T. Patterson, *America's Struggle Against Poverty, 1900–1994* (1994).

James Baldwin, *Nobody Knows My Name* (1961); Darlene Clark Hine and Kathleen Thompson, *A Shining Thread of Hope: The History of Black Women in America* (1998); Jacqueline Jones, *Labor of Love, Labor of Sorrow: Black Women, Work, and the Family from Slavery to the Present* (1985); Robin D. G. Kelley and Earl Lewis, eds., *To Make Our World Anew: A History of African Americans* (2000); Nicholas Lemann, *The Promised Land: The Great Black Migration and How It Changed America* (1991); Carole Marks, *Farewell, We're Good and Gone: The Great Black Migration* (1989).

Rodolfo Acuña, *Occupied America: A History of Chicanos* , 4th ed. (2000); George J. Sánchez, *Becoming Mexican American: Ethnicity, Culture and Identity in Chicano Los Angeles, 1900–1945* (1993); Peter Skerry, *Mexican Americans: The Ambivalent Minority* (1993); Ronald Takaki, *A Different Mirror: A History of Multicultural America* (1993) and *A Larger Memory: A History of Our Diversity, With Voices* (1998); Piri Thomas, *Down These Mean Streets* (1967).

Frederick E. Hoxie, ed., *Indians in American History* (1988); Peter Iverson, *"We Are Still Here": American Indians in the Twentieth Century* (1998); Alvin M. Josephy, Jr., *Now That the Buffalo's Gone* (1982); James S. Olson and Raymond Wilson, *Native Americans in the Twentieth Century* (1986).

# CHAPTER 27
# Chills and Fever During the Cold War

## CHAPTER OUTLINE

- Origins of the Cold War
- Containing the Soviet Union
- Containment in Asia, the Middle East, and Latin America
- Atomic Weapons and the Cold War

- The Cold War at Home
- Continuing Confrontations with Communists
- The Quagmire of Vietnam
- Conclusion: The Cold War in Perspective

## AMERICAN STORIES
### A Government Employee Confronts the Anti-Communist Crusade

Val Lorwin was in France in November 1950 when he learned of the charges against him. A State Department employee on leave of absence after 16 years of government service, he was in Paris working on a book. Now he had to return home to face an accusation that, as a Communist party member, he was a loyalty and security risk. It seemed to him a tasteless joke. Yet Communism was no laughing matter in the United States. Suspicions of the Soviet Union had escalated after 1945, and a wave of paranoia swept through the United States.

Lorwin had an unblemished record of government service. In 1935 he had begun working in a series of New Deal agencies. Before being drafted during World War II, he served on the War Production Board. While in the Army, he was assigned to the Office of Strategic Services, an early intelligence agency, and had frequently received security clearances in the United States and abroad.

Lorwin, however, did have a left-wing past. In the 1930s, his social life had revolved around various Socialist party causes, particularly unionizing southern tenant farmers and aiding the unemployed. But that work had been open and legal, and Lorwin had always been aggressively anti-Communist.

Suddenly Lorwin, like others at that time, faced a nightmare. An unnamed accuser had identified him as a Communist. The burden of proof was entirely on him, and the chance of clearing his name was slim. He could undergo a hearing, or resign.

Lorwin requested a hearing, which was held late in 1950. Still struck by the absurdity of the situation, he refuted all accusations but made little effort to cite his own positive achievements. After the hearing, he learned that the government no longer doubted his loyalty but still considered him a security risk—likewise grounds for dismissal from his job. Appealing the ruling, Lorwin still was not told who had accused him.

At the appeal hearing, Lorwin produced 97 sworn witnesses who testified to his good character and meritorious service. The accuser, it came out, had once lived with Lorwin and his wife in Washington, D.C., and claimed that in 1935 Lorwin had revealed that he was holding a Communist party meeting in his home, even showing him a red party card. But Lorwin proved that in 1935 the *Socialist* party card was red, while the *Communist* party card was black. In March 1952, Lorwin was finally cleared for both loyalty and security.

Lorwin's troubles were not yet over. His name appeared on one of the lists produced by Senator Joseph McCarthy of Wisconsin, the most aggressive anti-Communist of the era. In 1953, Lorwin was indicted for making false statements to the State Department Loyalty Security Board. Again the charges proved specious. Finally, in May 1954, admitting that its special prosecutor had lied to the grand jury and had no legitimate case, the Justice Department asked for dismissal of the indictment. Cleared at last, Lorwin went on to become a distinguished labor historian.

⚜ ⚜ ⚜ ⚜

Lorwin was more fortunate than some victims of the anti-Communist crusade. People rallied around him and gave him valuable support. Despite considerable emotional cost, he survived the witch hunt of the early 1950s, but his case still reflected vividly the ugly domestic consequences of the breakdown in relations between the Soviet Union and the United States.

The Cold War, which unfolded soon after the end of World War II and lasted for nearly 50 years, powerfully affected all aspects of American life. Rejecting for good the isolationist impulse that had governed foreign policy in the 1920s and 1930s, the United States began to play a major role in the world in the postwar years. Doubts about intervention in other lands faded as the nation acknowledged its dominant international position and resolved to do whatever was necessary to maintain it. The same sense of mission that had infused the United States in the Spanish-American War, World War I, and World War II now committed most Americans to the struggle against Communism at home and abroad.

This chapter explores that continuing sense of mission and its consequences. It examines the roots of the Cold War both in the idealistic aim to keep the world safe for democracy and in the pursuit of economic self-interest that had long fueled American capitalism. It records how the determination to prevent the spread of Communism led American policy makers to consider vast parts of the world as pivotal to American security and to act accordingly, particularly in Korea and Vietnam. It notes the impact on economic development, especially in the West, where the mighty defense industry flourished. And it considers the tragic consequences of the effort to promote ideological unity within the United States, where excesses threatened the principles of democracy itself.

## ORIGINS OF THE COLD WAR

The two strongest powers after World War II—the United States and the Soviet Union—differed profoundly over the shape of the postwar world. European colonial empires were crumbling in Asia, Africa, and the Middle East. The United

States was intent on spreading political freedom and free trade around the world to maintain its economic hegemony. The Soviet Union demanded politically sympathetic neighbors on its borders to preserve its security. Suppressed during World War II, these differences now led to Soviet-American conflict.

## The American Stance

The United States emerged from World War II as the most powerful nation in history, and it sought to use that might to achieve a world order that could sustain American aims. American policy makers, following in Woodrow Wilson's footsteps, hoped to spread the values—liberty, equality, and democracy—underpinning the American dream. They also wanted to create a world where economic enterprise could thrive and to forestall another depression. This meant promoting worldwide recovery from wartime devastation, supporting economic enterprise abroad, and opening markets for the industrial and agricultural products that poured out of the American economy, operating at full capacity as a result of the war. In 1947, the United States was the largest source of goods for world markets with exports totaling $14 billion. To sustain economic growth, American officials reasoned, global trade barriers imposed by the Soviet Union and other nations had to fall. Americans assumed that their prosperity would benefit the rest of the world, even when other nations disagreed.

## Soviet Aims

Historically, Russian governments had been strongly centralized autocracies. That authoritarian tradition—as much as Communist ideology, with its stress on class struggle and the inevitable triumph of a proletarian state—shaped Soviet goals after World War II.

During the war, the Russians had played down talk of world revolution, which they knew their allies found threatening, and had mobilized domestic support with nationalistic appeals. As the struggle drew to a close, the Soviets said little about world conquest and emphasized socialism within the nation itself.

Rebuilding was the first priority. Devastated by the war, Soviet agriculture and industry lay in shambles. But revival required internal security. At the same time, the Russians felt vulnerable along their western border, from which Napoleon in the nineteenth century and the Germans twice in the twentieth century had penetrated deep into Russia. Haunted by fears of a quick German recovery, the Soviets demanded defensible borders and sympathetic neighbors.

## Early Cold War Leadership

Both the United States and the Soviet Union had strong leadership in the early years of the Cold War. On the American side, presidents Harry Truman and Dwight Eisenhower accepted the centralization of authority that Franklin Roosevelt had begun, as the executive branch became increasingly powerful in guiding foreign policy. In the Soviet Union, first Joseph Stalin and then Nikita Khrushchev provided equally forceful direction.

America's first postwar president, Democrat Harry S Truman, was an unpretentious man who took a straightforward approach to public affairs. But he was ill-prepared for the office he assumed in the final months of World War II. During Truman's three months as vice-president, Franklin Roosevelt had never confided in him, and Truman had been told nothing of the complexity of postwar issues. "I'm not big enough for this job," he groaned to a former Senate colleague.

Yet Truman matured quickly. Impulsive and aggressive, he made a virtue out of rapid response. At his first press conference, reporters could not keep up with his quick replies. A sign on his desk read "The Buck Stops Here," underscoring his determination to make speedy decisions—even though associates sometimes wondered whether he understood all the implications. His rapid-fire decisions had important consequences for the Cold War.

War hero Dwight Eisenhower, elected president in 1952 (the first Republican in 20 years), stood in stark contrast to Truman. His easy manner and warm smile made him widely popular. As British Field Marshall Bernard Montgomery observed, "He has the power of drawing the hearts of men towards him as a magnet attracts bits of metal." Sometimes he made convoluted comments at press conferences. Yet beneath his casual approach lay real shrewdness. "Don't worry," he once reassured officials briefing him for a press conference. "If that question comes up, I'll just confuse them."

Although his ambitions for high office grew during World War II, Eisenhower did not take the typical route to the presidency. After the war he served successively as army chief of staff, president of Columbia University, and head of the North Atlantic Treaty Organization (NATO), but he made no bid for the White House before 1952. Despite his apolitical background, he had a knack for getting people to compromise and cooperate. Whereas Truman loved political infighting and wanted to take charge, Eisenhower saw things differently. "You do not lead by hitting people over the head. Any damn fool can do that," he said, "but it's usually called 'assault,' not leadership." Even so, Ike knew exactly where he wanted to go and worked behind the scenes to get there.

Both presidents subscribed to traditional American attitudes about self-determination and the superiority of American political institutions and values. Viewing collaboration with the Soviet Union as a wartime necessity, Truman grew increasingly hostile to Soviet moves as the war neared its end. Like Truman, Eisenhower saw Communism as a monolithic force struggling for world supremacy and believed that the men in the Kremlin were orchestrating subversion around the globe. Truman would have agreed with his denunciation of the Soviet system as "a tyranny that has brought thousands, millions of people into slave camps and is attempting to make all mankind its chattel." Yet Eisenhower was more willing than Truman to practice accommodation when it served his purposes.

The Soviet leader at the war's end, Joseph Stalin, possessed almost absolute power. He had presided over ruthless purges against his opponents in the 1930s. Now he was determined to rebuild Soviet society, if possible with Western assistance, and to keep eastern Europe within the Soviet sphere of influence.

Stalin's death in March 1953 left a power vacuum that was eventually filled by Nikita Khrushchev, who by 1958 held the offices of both premier and party secretary. Known for his rude behavior, Khrushchev once pounded a table at the United Nations with his shoe and did his best to bully opponents whenever he could.

## Disillusionment with the USSR

American support for the Soviet Union faded quickly after the war. In September 1945, a national poll revealed that 54 percent of the American public trusted the Russians to cooperate with the United States in the postwar years. Two months later, the figure had dropped to 44 percent, and by February 1946, to 35 percent.

As Americans soured on Russia, they began to equate the Nazi and Soviet systems. Just as they had in the 1930s, authors, journalists, and public officials pointed—sometimes legitimately—to similarities between the two regimes. Both states, they contended, maintained total control over communications and could eliminate political opposition whenever they chose. Both used terror and concentration camps to silence dissidents. After the U.S. publication in 1949 of British writer George Orwell's frightening novel *1984*, an editorial in *Life* magazine noted that Orwell's ominous fictional figure "Big Brother" was but a "mating" of Hitler and Stalin. Truman spoke for many Americans when he said in 1950 that "there isn't any difference between the totalitarian Russian government and the Hitler government . . . . They are all alike. They are . . . police state governments."

A lingering sense that the nation had not been quick enough to resist totalitarian aggression in the 1930s heightened American fears. Had the United States stopped the Germans, Italians, or Japanese, it might have prevented the long, devastating war. The free world had not responded quickly enough before; postwar Americans were determined not to repeat that mistake.

## The Troublesome Polish Question

The first East-West clash came, even before the war ended, over Poland. Soviet demands for a friendly Polish government collided with American hopes for a democratic one. The Yalta Conference of February 1945 had attempted to settle the question (see Chapter 25), with a loosely worded and imprecise agreement. When Truman assumed office, the Polish situation remained unresolved.

Truman assumed an unbending stance toward the Soviet Union over Poland. Meeting Soviet Foreign Minister Vyacheslav Molotov in April 1945, he insisted that the Russians were breaking the Yalta agreements and demanded a new democratic government for Poland. As Truman recalled in his memoirs, Molotov protested that "I have never been talked to like that in my life." "Carry out your agreements," Truman retorted bluntly, "and you won't get talked to like that."

Truman and Stalin met face-to-face for the first (and last) time at the Potsdam Conference, the final wartime Big Three meeting. There, outside devastated Berlin, the two leaders sized each other up as they considered the Soviet-Polish boundary, the fate of Germany, and the American desire to obtain Japan's unconditional surrender. It was Truman's first exposure to international diplomacy at the highest level, and it left him confident of his abilities. When he learned during the meeting of the first successful atomic bomb test in New Mexico, he became even more determined to get his way.

## Economic Pressure on the USSR

One major source of controversy in the last stages of World War II was the question of U.S. aid to its allies. Responding to congressional pressure to limit foreign assistance as hostilities ended, Truman acted impulsively. Six days after Germany's surrender on V-E Day in May 1945, he issued an executive order cutting off lend-lease supplies to the Allies. Though the policy hurt all nations receiving aid, it hurt the Soviet Union most of all.

The United States intended to use economic pressure in other ways as well. The USSR desperately needed financial assistance to rebuild after the war and, in January 1945, had requested a $6 billion loan. Roosevelt hedged, hoping to win concessions in return. In August 1945 the Soviets renewed their application, this time for only $1 billion. Truman dragged his heels, seeking to use the loan as a lever to gain access to new markets in areas traditionally dominated by the Soviet Union. Stalin refused the offer of a loan with such conditions and launched his own five-year plan instead.

## Declaring the Cold War

As Soviet-American relations deteriorated, both sides stepped up their rhetorical attacks. In 1946, Stalin spoke out first, publicly asserting that capitalism and Communism were on a collision course, that a series of cataclysmic disturbances would tear the capitalist world apart, and that the Soviet system would triumph. Stalin's speech, said Supreme Court Justice William O. Douglas, was "the declaration of World War III."

Long suspicious of the Soviet Union, former British prime minister Winston Churchill provided a Western response. Speaking in Fulton, Missouri, in 1946, with Truman listening on the platform, Churchill warned that a vigilant association of English-speaking peoples must contain Soviet designs. "From Stettin in the Baltic to Trieste in the Adriatic," he declared, "an iron curtain has descended across the Continent."

## CONTAINING THE SOVIET UNION

"Containment" formed the basis of postwar American policy. Both Democrats and Republicans were determined to check Soviet expansion. In an increasingly contentious world, the American government formulated rigid anti-Soviet policies and the Soviet Union responded in an equally uncompromising way.

## Containment Defined

George F. Kennan, the chargé d'affaires at the American embassy in the Soviet Union and an expert on Soviet matters, was primarily responsible for defining the new policy. After Stalin's ominous speech in February 1946, Kennan sent an 8,000-word telegram to the State Department. In it he argued that Soviet hostility stemmed from "the Kremlin's neurotic view of world affairs," which in turn came from "the traditional and instinctive Russian sense of insecurity." Soviet fanaticism would not soften, regardless of how accommodating American policy became. Therefore, it had to be opposed at every turn.

Kennan's "Long Telegram" struck a resonant chord in Washington. It made his diplomatic reputation and brought him into an important State Department position. Soon he published an extended analysis in the influential journal *Foreign Affairs* under the pseudonym "Mr. X." "The whole Soviet governmental machine, including the mechanism of diplomacy," he wrote, "moves inexorably along the prescribed path, like a persistent toy automobile wound up and headed in a given direction, stopping only when it meets with some unanswerable force." Many Americans agreed with Kennan that Soviet pressure must "be contained by the adroit and vigilant application of counter-force at a series of constantly shifting geographical and political points."

The concept of containment provided the philosophical justification for the hard-line stance that Americans, both in and out of government, adopted. Containment created the framework for military and economic assistance around the globe.

## The First Step: The Truman Doctrine

The Truman Doctrine was the first major application of containment policy. In February 1947, the British ambassador to the United States informed the State Department that his exhausted country could no longer give the Greek and Turkish governments economic and military aid. The Soviet Union was demanding that Turkey agree to joint control of the Dardanelles, the passage between the Black Sea and the Mediterranean. Meanwhile Communist-led forces were winning a civil war against a right-wing monarchy in Greece. Would the United States fill the void and help the two pro-Western governments resist Communist pressure? The State Department was willing to act in the eastern Mediterranean, which the United States had never before considered vital to national security, but it knew that a conservative, economy-minded Congress would likely object. A key Republican, Senator Arthur Vandenberg of Michigan, warned the top policy makers that they would have to begin "scaring hell out of the country" if they wanted to embark on a bold new containment policy.

Truman took Vandenberg's advice to heart. On March 12, 1947, he told Congress, in a statement that became known as the Truman Doctrine, "I believe that it must be the policy of the United States to support free peoples who are resisting subjugation by armed minorities or by outside pressures." Unless the United States acted, the free world might not survive. To avert that calamity, he urged Congress to appropriate $400 million for military and economic aid to Turkey and Greece. Not everyone agreed with Truman's overblown description of the situation, but Congress nonetheless passed his foreign aid bill.

In assuming that Americans could police the globe, the Truman Doctrine was a major step in the advent of the Cold War. Truman's address, observed financier Bernard Baruch, "was tantamount to a declaration of an ideological or religious war." Journalist Walter Lippmann was more critical. He termed the new containment policy a "strategic monstrosity" that could embroil the United States in disputes around the world. In the succeeding two decades, Lippmann proved correct.

An American and British airlift in 1948 brought badly needed supplies to West Berliners isolated behind a Soviet blockade of the city. By refusing to allow the Western powers to reach the city, located within the Soviet zone, the Russians hoped to drive them from Berlin, but the airlift broke the blockade. (Corbis-Bettmann)

## The Marshall Plan, NATO, and NSC-68

The next step for American policy makers involved sending extensive economic aid for the postwar recovery of western Europe. To forestall Communist movements in an area that was economically and politically unstable, decisive American action was necessary. "The patient is sinking while the doctors deliberate," declared the new secretary of state, George C. Marshall. Another motive for action was to bolster the European economy to provide markets for American goods.

Marshall revealed the administration's willingness to assist European recovery in a speech in June 1947. He asked all troubled European nations to draw up an aid program that the United States could support, a program "directed not against any country or doctrine but against hunger, poverty, desperation, and chaos." Communist states were welcome to participate if they ceased being secretive about their economic affairs, a condition that Marshall knew they were not likely to accept. The proposed program would assist the ravaged nations, provide the United States with needed markets, and advance the nation's ideological aims. American aid, Marshall pointed out, would permit the "emergence of political and social conditions in which free institutions can exist." The Marshall Plan and the Truman Doctrine, Truman noted, were "two halves of the same walnut."

In early 1948, Congress agreed to provide $17 billion over a period of four years to 16 cooperating nations. Not all Americans supported the Marshall Plan.

Former vice president Henry A. Wallace, who had broken with the administration, criticized the "Martial Plan" as another step toward war. Some legislators objected that the scheme spread U.S. resources too thin. Still, the nation accepted the commitment to fund European recovery and moved the containment policy forward another step.

Closely related to the Marshall Plan was a concerted Western effort to integrate a rebuilt Germany into a reviving Europe. Roosevelt, Churchill, and Stalin had agreed at Yalta to divide Germany into four occupation zones (Soviet, American, British, and French) and to force Germany to pay reparations. A year after the war ended, however, the balance of power in Europe had shifted. With the Soviets threatening to dominate eastern Europe, the West moved to fill the vacuum in central Europe. In late 1946, the Americans and British merged their zones economically and began assigning administrative duties to Germans. By mid-1947, despite French worries, the process of rebuilding West German industry was under way.

In mid-1948 a crisis erupted when the Soviets attempted to force the Western powers out of Berlin. The former German capital, deep in the Soviet occupation zone, was itself divided into four occupation zones. When the Soviets refused to allow their former allies land access to West Berlin, the U.S. Air Force and the Royal Air Force responded by airlifting more than 2 million tons of supplies to the beleaguered West Berliners. The airlift broke the Soviet blockade.

The next major link in the containment strategy was the creation of a military alliance in Europe in 1949 to complement the Marshall Plan. After the Soviets tightened their control of Hungary and Czechoslovakia, the United States took the lead in establishing the North Atlantic Treaty Organization (NATO). This alliance of 12 nations, including the United States, vowed that an attack against one would be considered an attack against all, to be met with appropriate armed force. The U.S. Senate ratified the pact, which was the United States' first military alliance since the American Revolution. Congress also voted military aid for the NATO allies. The Cold War had softened long-standing American reluctance to become closely involved in European affairs.

Two dramatic events in 1949—the Communist victory in the Chinese civil war and the Russian detonation of an atomic device—jolted the United States into sharpening its strategy. Responding to Truman's request for a full-fledged review of U.S. policies, the National Security Council (an agency established in 1947 to advise the president) produced the document called NSC-68, which shaped U.S. policy for the next 20 years.

NSC-68 built on the inflammatory Cold War rhetoric of the Truman Doctrine. It assumed that East-West conflict was unavoidable and that negotiation with Soviets—who could never be trusted to bargain in good faith—was useless. Instead, it called for a massive increase in defense spending, from the $13 billion set for 1950 to as much as $50 billion per year. These huge costs, the document argued, were necessary for the free world to survive.

## Containment in the 1950s

When the Republicans took over the White House in 1953, containment, the keystone of American policy throughout the Truman years, came under attack by

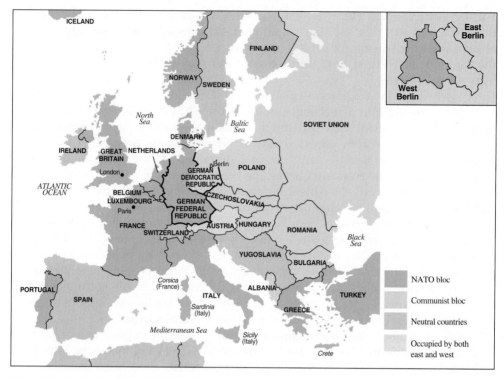

**COLD WAR EUROPE IN 1950**   This map shows the rigid demarcation between East and West during the Cold War. Although there were a number of neutral countries in Europe, the other nations found themselves in a standoff, as each side tried to contain the possible advances of the other. The small insert map in the upper-right-hand corner shows the division of Berlin itself after World War II.

high officials of the Eisenhower administration. To them, containment seemed too cautious a response to the threat of Communism.

Leading the charge was John Foster Dulles, secretary of state for most of Eisenhower's two terms. A devout Presbyterian who hated atheistic Communism, Dulles sought to move beyond containment and mount a holy crusade to promote democracy and liberate Soviet-dominated countries.

Though Eisenhower, too, argued that "freedom is pitted against slavery, lightness against dark," he was more conciliatory and realistic than Dulles. He recognized the impossibility of changing the governments of Russia's satellites. He also understood the need for caution. In mid-1953, as East Germans mounted anti-Soviet demonstrations, the United States kept its distance. In 1956, when Hungarian "freedom fighters" rose up against Soviet domination, the United States again stood back as Soviet tanks smashed the rebels. Because Western action could have precipitated a more general conflict, Eisenhower refused to translate rhetoric into action. Throughout the 1950s the policy of containment, largely as it had been defined earlier, remained in effect.

In the 1950s, however, the government depended increasingly on the Central Intelligence Agency (CIA). Established along with the National Security Council in 1947, the CIA conducted espionage abroad and analyzed the information it gathered. Some of its work was open; some was secret. Eisenhower appointed

John Foster Dulles's brother Allen to head the agency. With presidential approval, the CIA rearranged its priorities, so that by 1957 it was spending 80 percent of its budget on covert activities. Eisenhower used clandestine CIA actions to undermine unfriendly foreign governments, to subsidize sympathetic newspapers abroad, and to assist pro-American figures around the world.

## CONTAINMENT IN ASIA, THE MIDDLE EAST, AND LATIN AMERICA

The containment policy in Europe represented an unprecedented American effort to promote continental stability. Soon the United States departed even further from its traditions by extending its commitments in a policy of global containment. As European colonial empires disintegrated, Americans recognized that Communism exerted a tremendous appeal in newly emerging nations. Even greater efforts were required to advance American aims.

### The Shock of the Chinese Revolution

America's commitment to global containment became stronger with the Communist victory in the Chinese civil war in 1949. An ally during World War II, China had struggled against the Japanese while simultaneously fighting a domestic conflict rooted deeply in the Chinese past—in widespread poverty, disease, oppression by the landlord class, and national humiliation at the hands of foreign powers. Mao Zedong (Mao Tse-tung),* founder of the Chinese Communist Party, wished to reshape China in a distinctive Marxist mold. Opposing the Communists were the Nationalists, led by Jiang Jieshi (Chiang Kai-shek). By the early 1940s, Jiang's regime was exhausted, inefficient, and corrupt. Mao's movement, meanwhile, grew stronger during World War II as it opposed the Japanese invaders and won the loyalty of the peasantry. When Mao prevailed in 1949, Jiang fled to the island of Taiwan (Formosa). There he nursed the improbable belief that he was still the rightful ruler of all China and would one day return to the mainland.

The United States failed to understand what had happened in China or to appreciate the immense popular support that Mao generated. As the Communist army moved toward victory, the *New York Times* dismissed it as a "nauseous force." Secretary of State Dean Acheson considered granting diplomatic recognition to the new regime but backed off after the Communists seized American property, harassed American citizens, and openly allied China with the USSR. Acheson and other American leaders mistakenly considered Mao a Soviet puppet.

Chinese-American tension increased during the Korean War and again in 1954, when Mao's government began shelling Nationalist positions on the tiny offshore islands of Quemoy and Matsu. But Eisenhower was unwilling to respond forcefully. Cautiously, he committed America only to defending the Nationalists on Taiwan.

---

*Chinese names are rendered in their modern *pinyin* spelling. At first occurrence, the older but perhaps more familiar spelling (usually Wade-Giles) is given in parentheses.

## Stalemate in the Korean War

The Korean War, on the other hand, highlighted growing U.S. intervention in Asia. Concern about China and determination to contain Communism led the United States into a bloody foreign struggle. But the sometimes ambiguous American objectives remained largely unrealized after three years of war.

The conflict in Korea stemmed from tensions lingering after World War II. Korea, long under Japanese control, hoped for independence after Japan's defeat. But the Allies temporarily divided Korea along the 38th parallel when the rapid end to the Pacific struggle allowed Soviet troops to accept the Japanese surrender in the north while American forces did the same in the south. Initially intended as a matter of military convenience, the Soviet-American line hardened after 1945, just as a similar division became rigid in Germany. In time, the Soviets set up one Korean government in the north and the Americans another government in the south. Each Korean government hoped to reunify the country on its own terms.

North Korea moved first. On June 25, 1950, North Korean forces crossed the 38th parallel to invade South Korea. Though the North Koreans followed Soviet-built tanks, they operated on their own initiative. Kim Il Sung, the North Korean leader, had visited Moscow earlier and may have gained Soviet acquiescence to the idea of an attack, but both the planning and implementation occurred in Korea.

The United States had earlier seemed reluctant to defend South Korea but, taken by surprise, Truman responded vigorously to the invasion. "If this is allowed to go unchallenged," he declared, "it would mean a third world war, just as similar incidents had brought on the second world war." Truman directed General Douglas MacArthur, who headed the American occupation of Japan, to supply South Korea. Because Moscow was boycotting the UN to protest China's exclusion from it, the United States was able to get the Security Council to brand North Korea an aggressor and obtained another resolution calling on members of the organization to assist the South in repelling aggression and restoring peace.

American forces, fighting on behalf of the United Nations, went into battle south of the 38th parallel. First naval and air units, then American ground forces, resisted the invasion. Following a daring amphibious landing in September that pushed the North Koreans back to the former dividing line, the UN forces crossed the 38th parallel and sought to reunify Korea under an American-backed government. Chinese warnings that this movement threatened their security were ignored. After briefly appearing in battle in October, the Chinese mounted a full-fledged counterattack in November 1950, which drove the UN forces below the dividing line.

In the stalemate that followed, the brilliant but arrogant MacArthur clashed openly with Truman, his commander-in-chief. MacArthur demanded retaliatory air strikes against China; Truman, trying to conduct a limited war, refused. MacArthur's public statements, issued from the field, finally went too far. In April 1951, he argued that the American approach to Korea was wrong—that "there is no substitute for victory." Truman had no choice but to relieve him for insubordination. An outraged public, remembering the stunning American victories of World War II, largely supported MacArthur and reviled Truman.

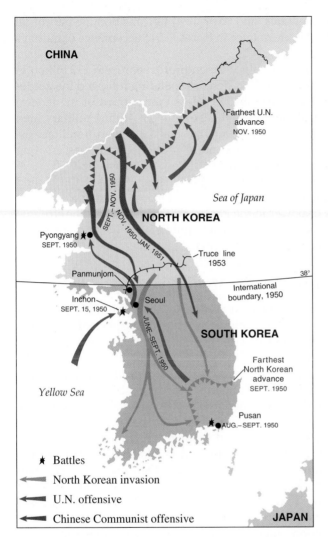

CHINA

Farthest U.N.
advance
NOV. 1950

Sea of Japan

SEPT.-NOV. 1950

NOV. 1950-JAN. 1951

NORTH KOREA

Pyongyang ★●
SEPT. 1950

Truce line
1953

Panmunjom

38°

Inchon
SEPT. 15, 1950 ★

Seoul

International
boundary, 1950

JUNE-SEPT. 1950

SOUTH KOREA

Farthest
North Korean
advance
SEPT. 1950

Yellow Sea

Pusan
★●AUG.–SEPT. 1950

★ Battles

◄▬▬ North Korean invasion

◄▬▬ U.N. offensive

◄▬▬ Chinese Communist offensive

JAPAN

**THE KOREAN WAR**  This map
shows the ebb and flow of the
Korean War. North Korea
crossed the 38th parallel first,
then the UN offensive drove the
North Koreans close to the
Chinese border, and finally the
Chinese Communists entered
the war and drove the UN forces
back below the 38th parallel. The
armistice signed at Panmunjom
in 1953 provided a dividing line
very close to the prewar line.

The Korean War dragged on into Eisenhower's presidency. Campaigning in
1952, Ike promised to go to Korea, and made the trip three weeks after he was
elected. When truce talks bogged down again in May 1953, the new administration privately threatened China with atomic weapons. Peace negotiations resumed, and on July 27, 1953, an armistice was signed. The Republican administration had succeeded where the preceding Democratic administration had failed.
After three long years, the unpopular war was over.

The Korean War carried a heavy price: 34,000 Americans dead and many
more wounded. These figures paled beside as many as 2 million Koreans dead
and countless others maimed.

The war significantly changed American attitudes and institutions. For the
first time, American forces fought in racially integrated units. As commander-in-
chief, President Truman had ordered the integration of the armed forces in 1948,

over the opposition of many generals, and African Americans became part of all military units. Their successful performance in Korea led to acceptance of military integration.

The Korean War years also saw military expenditures soar from $13 billion in 1950 to about $47 billion three years later as defense spending followed the guidelines of NSC-68. Whereas the military absorbed less than a third of the federal budget in 1950, a decade later it took one-half. More than a million military men were stationed around the world. At home, an increasingly powerful military establishment became closely tied to corporate and scientific communities, creating a military-industrial complex that employed 3.5 million Americans by 1960.

The Korean War had important political effects as well. It led the United States to sign a peace treaty with Japan in September 1951 and to rely on that nation to maintain the balance of power in the Pacific. At the same time, the struggle poisoned America's relations with the People's Republic of China and ensured a diplomatic standoff that lasted more than 20 years.

## Turbulence in the Middle East

Cold War attitudes also influenced American diplomacy in the Middle East, a part of the world with tremendous strategic importance as the supplier of oil for the industrialized nations. During World War II, the major Allied powers had occupied Iran, agreeing that they would withdraw six months after the war's end. As of early 1946, both Great Britain and the United States had withdrawn, but the Soviet Union, which bordered on Iran, continued its occupation. Stalin claimed that earlier security agreements had not been honored and demanded oil concessions. Only a threat of vigorous American action forced the Soviets out.

The Eisenhower administration maintained its interest in Iran. In 1953, the CIA helped the Iranian army overthrow the government of Mohammed Mossadegh, which had nationalized oil wells formerly held by the British, and placed the shah of Iran securely on the Peacock Throne. After the coup, British and American companies regained control of the wells, and thereafter the United States government provided military assistance to the shah.

A far more serious situation emerged in Palestine, which since the end of World War I had been under British rule. With British control set to end in 1948, the United Nations attempted to partition Palestine into an Arab state and a Jewish state. Truman officially recognized the new state of Israel 15 minutes after it was proclaimed. But American recognition could not end bitter animosities between Arabs, who felt they had been robbed of their territory, and Jews, who felt that they had finally regained a homeland after the horrors of the Holocaust. As Americans looked on, Arab forces from Egypt, Trans-Jordan, Syria, Lebanon, and Iraq invaded Israel, but the Israelis won the war and added territory to what the UN had given them.

The United States cultivated close ties with Israel but could not afford to alienate oil-rich Arab states or allow them to fall into the Soviet orbit. In Egypt, Arab nationalist Gamal Abdel Nasser planned a great dam on the Nile River to produce electricity—and proclaimed his country neutral in the Cold War. Dulles offered American financial support for the Aswan Dam project, but when Nasser also began discussions with the Soviet Union, the secretary of state furi-

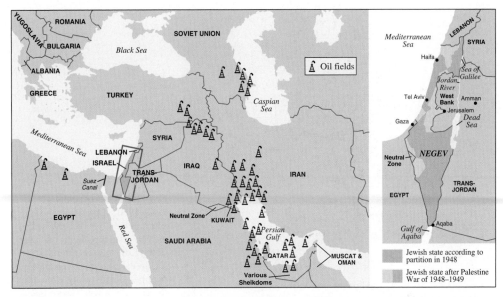

**THE MIDDLE EAST IN 1949**  This map shows the extensive oil resources that made the Middle East such an important region, and the shifting boundaries of Israel as a result of the war following its independence in 1948. Notice how its size increased after its victory in the first of a series of Middle Eastern conflicts.

ously withdrew the American offer. Left without funds for the dam, Nasser nationalized the British-controlled Suez Canal in July 1956 and closed it to Israeli ships. All of Europe feared that Nasser would disrupt the flow of oil from the Middle East.

In the fall of 1956, Israeli, British, and French troops invaded Egypt. Eisenhower, who had not been consulted, was irate. Realizing that the attack might push Nasser into Moscow's arms, the United States sponsored a UN resolution condemning the attack and cut off oil from Britain and France. These actions persuaded them, and the Israelis, to withdraw.

In 1958, the United States again intervened in the Middle East to block perceived Communist aggression. Eisenhower landed 14,000 soldiers in Lebanon to prop up a right-wing government challenged from within.

The Middle East remained a battleground. In 1967, Israeli forces defeated an Arab coalition in the Six Day War and seized the West Bank and Jerusalem, the Golan Heights, and the Sinai Peninsula. Egypt struck again in 1973 in the Yom Kippur War, but Israel again prevailed. In both cases, the United States used its influence to halt the fighting in order to maintain regional stability and uninterrupted supplies of oil.

## Restricting Revolt in Latin America

The Cold War also led to intervention in Latin America, the United States' traditional sphere of influence. In 1954, Dulles sniffed Communist activity in Guatemala, and Eisenhower ordered CIA support for a right-wing coup to oust the legitimate elected government of Colonel Jacobo Arbenz Guzmán. The property of the United

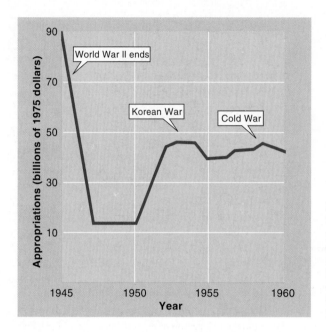

**DEFENSE EXPENDITURES,**
**1945–1960**   Defense spending
plummeted after World War II,
only to quadruple with the onset
of the Korean War. After that
increase, spending levels never
dropped dramatically, even after
the end of the war. (*Source:* U.S.
Bureau of the Census)

Fruit Company that the Guatemalan government had seized was restored, but at the cost of aborting needed reform. Interference in Guatemala fed anti-American feeling throughout Latin America.

In 1959, when Fidel Castro overthrew the dictatorship of Fulgencio Batista in Cuba, the shortsightedness of American policy became even clearer. Nationalism and the thrust for social reform were powerful forces in Latin America and in other parts of the developing world. When Castro confiscated American property in Cuba, the Eisenhower administration cut off exports and severed diplomatic ties. Castro turned to Russia for support.

## ATOMIC WEAPONS AND THE COLD WAR

Throughout the Cold War, the atomic bomb was a crucial factor that hung over all diplomatic discussions and military initiatives. Atomic bombs were destructive enough, but when the United States and the Soviet Union both developed hydrogen bombs, an age of overkill began.

### Sharing the Secret of the Bomb

The United States, with British aid, had built the atomic bomb in secrecy. Soviet spies, however, had discovered that the Americans were at work on the bomb. Before the war's end, a program to create a Soviet atomic bomb was under way.

The question of sharing the atomic secret was considered in the immediate postwar years. Secretary of War Henry L. Stimson favored cooperating with the Soviet Union. Recognizing the futility of trying to cajole the Soviets while "having this weapon ostentatiously on our hip," he warned that "their suspicions and their distrust of our purposes and motives will increase." Only mutual accommodation, he argued, could bring international cooperation.

But the United States failed to follow Stimson's advice. Realizing by early 1946 that mere possession of the bomb by the United States did not make the Russians more malleable, Truman decided to offer the United Nations a proposal for an international agency to control atomic energy. The Russians balked at a plan they argued favored the United States and negotiations collapsed.

Instead of sharing atomic secrets, Truman now became intent on retaining the technological advantage until the creation of a "foolproof method of control." He endorsed the Atomic Energy Act, passed by Congress in 1946, which established the Atomic Energy Commission to supervise all atomic energy development in the United States. It also opened the way to a nuclear arms race once the USSR developed its own bomb.

## Nuclear Proliferation

As the atomic bomb found its way into popular culture, Americans at first showed more excitement than fear. In Los Angeles the "Atombomb Dancers" wiggled at the Burbank Burlesque Theater. Even so, anxiety lurked beneath the exuberance, though it did not surface while the United States held a nuclear monopoly. Then, in September 1949, reporters called to the White House were told: "We have evidence that within recent weeks an atomic explosion occurred in the U.S.S.R." Over the Labor Day weekend, a U.S. Air Force weather reconnaissance plane on a routine mission had picked up air samples showing higher than normal radiation counts. Scientists soon concluded that the Soviets had conducted a nuclear test.

The American public was stunned. Suddenly the security of being the world's only atomic power vanished. Harold C. Urey, a Nobel Prize-winning scientist, summed up the feelings of many Americans: "There is only one thing worse than one nation having the atomic bomb—that's two nations having it."

In early 1950, Truman authorized the development of a new hydrogen superbomb, potentially far more devastating than the atomic bomb. Edward Teller, a physicist on the Manhattan Project, had theorized that nuclear fusion might release energy in even greater amounts than nuclear fission, which had powered the atomic bomb. Now he had the chance to prove it.

By 1953, both the United States and the Soviet Union had unlocked the secret of the hydrogen bomb. Rumors circulated that the first test of a hydrogen device in the Pacific Ocean had blasted a hole in the ocean floor 175 feet deep and a mile wide. Later, after the 1954 BRAVO test, Lewis Strauss, Atomic Energy Commission chairman, admitted that "an H-bomb can be made . . . large enough to take out a city." Then, in 1957, shortly after the news that the Soviets had successfully tested their first intercontinental ballistic missile (ICBM), Americans learned that the Soviets had fired the first satellite, *Sputnik,* into outer space—with a rocket that could also deliver a hydrogen bomb on the United States. The apparent inferiority of American rocketry and the vulnerability of the country to attack shocked the nation.

There was another dimension to the nuclear dilemma as well. The world learned about fallout when the BRAVO blast showered Japanese fishermen

85 miles away with radioactive dust. They became ill with radiation sickness, and several months later, one died. The Japanese, who had been the first to feel the effects of atomic weapons, were outraged and alarmed. Everywhere people began to realize the terrible consequences of the new weapons.

Authors in both the scientific and the popular press focused attention on radioactive fallout. Radiation, physicist Ralph Lapp observed, "cannot be felt and possesses all the terror of the unknown." Nevil Shute's best-selling 1957 novel *On the Beach*, and the film that followed, described a war that released so much radioactive waste that all life in the Northern Hemisphere perished, while the Southern Hemisphere waited for the residue to bring the same deadly end. In 1959, when *Consumer Reports* warned of the contamination of milk with strontium-90 from nuclear fallout, public alarm grew.

The discovery of fallout provoked a bomb shelter craze. Companies advertised prefabricated shelters to panicky customers. A firm in Miami reported many inquiries about shelters costing between $1,795 and $3,895, depending on capacity, and planned 900 franchises. By the end of 1960, some 1 million family shelters had been installed.

## The Nuclear West

The nuclear arms race sparked an enormous increase in defense spending and created a huge nuclear industry, particularly in the West. Contractors liked the region because of its anti-union attitudes, arguing that labor stability would facilitate meeting government deadlines.

Several key facilities of the Manhattan Project had been located in the West. The plant at Hanford, Washington, was one of the important producers of fissionable material, and the bomb had been assembled at Los Alamos, New Mexico. Such activities continued after the war: Hanford produced plutonium; a facility at Rocky Flats outside Denver made plutonium triggers for thermonuclear bombs; and the Los Alamos laboratory remained a major research center. In 1951, the Nevada Test Site opened 65 miles north of Las Vegas. The local chamber of commerce published schedules of test shots, which people liked to watch.

Defense spending brought prosperity to these and other communities. Naval commands maintained headquarters in Seattle, San Francisco, San Diego, and Honolulu. Radar sites to track incoming missiles stretched all the way to Alaska. The Boeing Company, then headquartered in Seattle, stimulated tremendous development in that city as it produced the B-47s and B-52s that were the Air Force's main delivery vehicles for nuclear bombs.

## "Massive Retaliation"

As Americans grappled with the consequences of nuclear weapons, government policy came to depend increasingly on an atomic shield. Truman authorized the development of a nuclear arsenal but also stressed conventional forms of defense. President Eisenhower, however, decided to rely on atomic weapons rather than combat forces as the key to American defense. Dulles developed a policy of threatening "massive retaliation," whereby the United States proclaimed that it was ready and willing to use nuclear weapons against Communist aggression "at places of our own choosing." The policy allowed troop cutbacks and promised to be cost-effective by giving "more bang for the buck."

Massive retaliation provided for an all-or-nothing response, leaving no middle course, no alternative between nuclear war and surrender. Critics called Dulles's foreign policy "brinksmanship" and wondered what would happen if the line was crossed in the new nuclear age. Eisenhower himself was horrified when he saw reports indicating that a coordinated atomic attack could leave a nation "a smoking, radiating ruin at the end of two hours," and with characteristic caution he did his best to ensure that the rhetoric of massive retaliation did not lead to war.

## Atomic Protest

As the arms race escalated, critics demanded that it end. In 1956, Democratic presidential candidate Adlai Stevenson called for a halt to nuclear tests that were "poisoning the atmosphere." Eisenhower did not respond, but Dulles minimized the hazards by claiming that "from a health standpoint, there is greater danger from wearing a wrist watch with a luminous dial."

Unimpressed, in 1957 anti-nuclear activists organized SANE, the National Committee for a Sane Nuclear Policy. One of its most effective advertisements featured the internationally known pediatrician Dr. Spock pondering a little girl with a frown on his face. "Dr. Spock is worried," the caption read, and the text below amplified on his concern. "I *am* worried," he said, "not so much about the effect of past tests but at the prospect of endless future ones. As the tests multiply, so will the damage to children here and around the world."

Several years later, women who had worked with SANE took the protest movement a step further. Concerned about radiation in the milk they served their children, they called on women all over the country to suspend normal activities for a day and strike for peace. An estimated 50,000 women marched in 60 communities around the nation.

Pressure from many groups produced a political breakthrough and sustained it for a time. The superpowers began a voluntary test moratorium in the fall of 1958, which lasted until the Soviet Union broke it in September 1961. The United States resumed tests the following March.

## THE COLD WAR AT HOME

The Cold War deeply affected domestic fears and led to the creation of an internal loyalty program that seriously violated civil liberties. As Americans began to suspect infiltration at home, some determined that they needed to root out any traces of Communism inside the United States.

## Truman's Loyalty Program

As the Truman administration mobilized support for containment, its rhetoric became increasingly shrill. Attorney General J. Howard McGrath spoke of "many Communists in America," each bearing "the germ of death for society." When officials uncovered an internal threat to security after the discovery of classified

# Recovering the Past

## Public Opinion Polls

In recent years, historians have used a new source of evidence, the public opinion poll. People have always been concerned with what others think, and leaders have often sought to frame their behavior according to the preferences of the populace. As techniques of assessing the mind of the public have become more sophisticated, the poll has emerged as an integral part of the analysis of social and political life. Polls now measure opinion on many questions—social, cultural, intellectual, political, and diplomatic. Because of their increasing importance, it is useful to know how to use the polls in an effort to understand and recover the past.

The principle of polling is not new. In 1824 the *Harrisburg Pennsylvanian* sought to predict the winner of that year's presidential race, and in the 1880s, the *Boston Globe* sent reporters to selected precincts on election night to forecast final returns. In 1916, *Literary Digest* began conducting postcard polls to predict political results. By the 1930s, Elmo Roper and George Gallup had further developed the field of market research and public opinion polling. Notwithstanding an embarrassing mistake by *Literary Digest* in predicting a Landon victory over FDR in 1936, polling had by World War II become a scientific enterprise.

According to Gallup, a poll is not magic but "merely an instrument for gauging public opinion," especially the views of those often unheard. As Elmo Roper said, the poll is "one of the few ways through which the so-called common man can be articulate." Polling, therefore, is a valuable way to recover the attitudes, beliefs, and voices of ordinary people.

Yet certain cautions should be observed. Like all instruments of human activity, polls are imperfect and may even be dangerous. Historians using information from polls need to be aware of how large the samples were, when the interviewing was done, and how opinions might have been molded by the form of the poll itself. Questions can be poorly phrased. Some hint at the desirable answer or plant ideas in the minds of those interviewed. Polls sometimes provide ambiguous responses that can be interpreted many ways. More seriously, some critics worry that human freedom itself is threatened by the pollsters' manipulative and increasingly accurate predictive techniques.

Despite these limitations, polls have become an ever-present part of American life. In the late 1940s and early 1950s, Americans were polled frequently about topics ranging from foreign aid, the United Nations, and the occupation of Germany and Japan to labor legislation, child punishment, and whether women should wear slacks in public (39 percent of men said no, as did 49 percent of women). Such topics as the first use of nuclear arms, presidential popularity, national defense, and U.S. troop intervention in a troubled area of the world remain as pertinent today as they were then.

**Reflecting on the Past**   A number of the polls included here deal with foreign policy during the Cold War in the early 1950s. How did people respond to Soviet nuclear capability? How did they regard Russian intentions and the appropriate American response? How do you analyze the results of these polls? What do you think is the significance of rating responses by levels of education? In what ways are the questions "loaded"? How might the results of these polls influence American foreign policy? These polls show the challenge-and-response nature of the Cold War. How do you think Americans would respond today to these questions?

Polls also shed light on domestic issues. Consider the poll on professions for young men and women taken in 1950. What does it tell us about the attitudes of the pollster on appropriate careers for men and women? Why do you think both men and women had nearly identical views on this subject? How do you think people today would answer these questions? Would they be presented in the same way? Also observe the poll on women in politics. To what extent have attitudes on this issue changed in the intervening years?

## Foreign Policy Polls

### December 2, 1949—
### Atom Bomb

*Now that Russia has the atom bomb, do you think another war is more likely or less likely?*

| | |
|---|---|
| More likely | 45% |
| Less likely | 28% |
| Will make no difference | 17% |
| No opinion | 10% |

#### By Education
*College*

| | |
|---|---|
| More likely | 36% |
| Will make no difference | 23% |
| Less likely | 35% |
| No opinion | 6% |

*High School*

| | |
|---|---|
| More likely | 44% |
| Will make no difference | 19% |
| Less likely | 28% |
| No opinion | 9% |

*Grade School*

| | |
|---|---|
| More likely | 50% |
| Will make no difference | 12% |
| Less likely | 26% |
| No opinion | 12% |

### January 11, 1950—
### Russia

*As you hear and read about Russia these days, do you believe Russia is trying to build herself up to be the ruling power of the world, or is Russia just building up protection against being attacked in another war?*

| | |
|---|---|
| Rule the world | 70% |
| Protect herself | 18% |
| No opinion | 12% |

#### By Education
*College*

| | |
|---|---|
| Rule the world | 73% |
| Protect herself | 21% |
| No opinion | 6% |

*High School*

| | |
|---|---|
| Rule the world | 72% |
| Protect herself | 18% |
| No opinion | 10% |

*Grade School*

| | |
|---|---|
| Rule the world | 67% |
| Protect herself | 17% |
| No opinion | 16% |

### February 12, 1951—
### Atomic Warfare

*If the United States gets into an all-out war with Russia, do you think we should drop atom bombs on Russia first, or do you think we should use the atom bomb only if it is used on us?*

| | |
|---|---|
| Drop A-bomb first | 66% |
| Only if used on us | 19% |
| No opinion | 15% |

The greatest difference was between men and women—72% of the men questioned favored our dropping the bomb first, compared to 61% of the women.

*Source:* George H. Gallup, *The Gallup Poll: Public Opinion, 1935–1971*, vol. 2 (New York: Random House, 1972). © American Institute of Public Opinion.

## Domestic Policy Polls

### October 29, 1949—
### Women in Politics

*If the party whose candidate you most often support nominated a woman for president of the United States, would you vote for her if she seemed qualified for the job?*

| | | | |
|---|---|---|---|
| Yes | 48% | No | 48% |
| No opinion | | | 4% |

#### By Sex
*Men*

| | | | |
|---|---|---|---|
| Yes | 45% | No | 50% |
| No opinion | | | 5% |

*Women*

| | | | |
|---|---|---|---|
| Yes | 51% | No | 46% |
| No opinion | 3% | | |

#### By Political Affiliation
*Democrats*

| | | | |
|---|---|---|---|
| Yes | 50% | No | 48% |
| No opinion | | | 2% |

*Republicans*

| | | | |
|---|---|---|---|
| Yes | 46% | No | 50% |
| No opinion | | | 4% |

*Would you vote for a woman for vice-president of the United States if she seemed qualified for the job?*

| | | | |
|---|---|---|---|
| Yes | 53% | No | 43% |
| No opinion | | | 4% |

### July 12, 1950—Professions

*Suppose a young man came to you and asked your advice about taking up a profession. Assuming that he was qualified to enter any of these professions, which one of them would you first recommend to him?*

| | |
|---|---|
| Doctor of medicine | 29% |
| Government worker | 6% |
| Engineer, builder | 16% |
| Professor, teacher | 5% |
| Business executive | 8% |
| Banker | 4% |
| Clergyman | 8% |
| Dentist | 4% |
| Lawyer | 8% |
| Veterinarian | 3% |
| None, don't know | 9% |

*Source:* George H. Gallup, *The Gallup Poll: Public Opinion, 1935–1971*, vol. 2 (New York: Random House, 1972). © American Institute of Public Opinion.

### July 15, 1950—Professions

*Suppose a young girl came to you and asked your advice about taking up a profession. Assuming that she was qualified to enter any of these professions, which one of them would you first recommend?*

#### Choice Of Women

| | |
|---|---|
| Nurse | 33% |
| Actress | 3% |
| Teacher | 15% |
| Journalist | 2% |
| Secretary | 8% |
| Musician | 2% |
| Social service worker | 8% |
| Model | 2% |
| Librarian | 2% |
| Dietician | 7% |
| Medical, dental technician | 1% |
| Dressmaker | 4% |
| Beautician | 4% |
| Others | 2% |
| Airline stewardess | 3% |
| Don't know | 4% |

The views of men on this subject were nearly identical with those of women.

documents in the offices of the allegedly pro-Communist *Amerasia* magazine, Truman appointed a Temporary Commission on Employee Loyalty—partly because he feared disloyalty and partly to undercut Republican charges that the Democrats were "soft on Communism."

In 1947, after receiving the report of his temporary commission, Truman established a new Federal Employee Loyalty Program by executive order. As he articulated his containment policy, the president ordered the FBI to check its files for evidence of subversive activity and to bring suspects before a new Civil Service Commission Loyalty Review Board. Initially, the program contained safeguards and assumed that a challenged employee was innocent until proved guilty. But as the Loyalty Review Board assumed more power, it ignored individual rights. Employees under suspicion had little chance to fight back. Val Lorwin, discussed at the start of the chapter, was one of many victims. Although the Truman loyalty program investigated several million government employees, it found grounds to dismiss only a few hundred. Nonetheless, it bred unwarranted fears of subversion and legitimated investigatory tactics that were used irresponsibly to harm many innocent people.

## The Congressional Loyalty Program

While Truman's loyalty probe investigated government employees, Congress launched its own program. The Smith Act of 1940 had made it a crime to advocate or teach the forcible overthrow of the U.S. government. The McCarran Internal Security Act of 1950, passed over Truman's veto, further circumscribed Communist activity by declaring that it was illegal to conspire to act in a way that would "substantially contribute" to establishing a totalitarian dictatorship in America and by requiring members of Communist organizations to register with the attorney general. The American Communist party, which had never been large, even in the Depression, declined still further. Membership, numbering about 80,000 in 1947, fell to 55,000 in 1950 and 25,000 in 1954.

The investigations of the House Committee on Un-American Activities (HUAC) contributed to that decline. Intent on rooting out subversion, HUAC probed the motion picture industry in 1947, claiming that left-wing sympathies were corrupting the American public. A frequent refrain in congressional hearings was "Are you now or have you ever been a member of the Communist Party?" When 10 Hollywood figures called to testify refused to answer such questions by invoking their constitutional right to remain silent, Congress issued contempt citations and they went to prison and served sentences ranging from six months to one year. At that point, Hollywood knuckled under and blacklisted anyone with even a marginally questionable past. No one on these lists could find jobs at the studios anymore.

Congress made a greater splash with the Hiss-Chambers case. Whittaker Chambers, a former Communist who had broken with the party in 1938 and had become a successful *Time* magazine editor, charged that Alger Hiss had been a Communist in the 1930s. Hiss was a distinguished New Dealer who had served in the Agriculture Department before becoming assistant secretary of state. Now out of the government, he was president of the Carnegie Endowment for International Peace. He denied Chambers's charge, and the matter might have died there had not freshman congressman Richard Nixon taken up the case. Nixon finally extracted Hiss's admission that he had once known Chambers. When Hiss sued Chambers for libel, Chambers changed his story and charged that Hiss was a Soviet spy.

Hiss was indicted for perjury—for lying under oath about his former relationship with Chambers. As the case unfolded, Chambers appeared unstable and changed his story several times. Yet Hiss, too, seemed contradictory in his testimony and never adequately explained how he had such close ties with members of the Communist party or how copies of stolen State Department documents had been typed on a typewriter he had once owned. The first trial ended in a hung jury; the second trial, in January 1950, sent Hiss to prison for almost four years. While Hiss maintained his innocence until his death, recently disclosed evidence seems to underscore his guilt.

The case had powerful political implications. Republicans attacked the approach of Truman and the Democratic Party's to the apparent Communist threat, and used the episode to justify the even worse witch hunt that followed.

## The Second Red Scare

The key anti-Communist warrior in the 1950s was Joseph R. McCarthy. He had not distinguished himself since being elected to the Senate as a Republican from Wisconsin in 1946; now, facing reelection in a state Harry Truman had carried in 1948, McCarthy needed an issue. Speaking before a women's club in Wheeling, West Virginia, in February 1950, not long after Hiss's conviction, McCarthy brandished what he said was a list of 205 known Communists in the State Department. Pressed for details, he first said that he would give his list only to the president and then reduced the number to 57.

McCarthy drew mixed early reactions. A subcommittee of the Senate Foreign Relations Committee, after looking into his charges, found them "a fraud and a hoax." Working-class ethnic groups liked his attacks on established elites, and conservative Republicans admired him for lambasting liberals. As his public support grew, Republican senators realized his partisan value and egged him on.

He selected assorted targets. In the elections of 1950, he attacked Millard Tydings, the Democrat from Maryland who chaired the subcommittee that had dismissed McCarthy's first accusations. A doctored photograph, supposedly showing Tydings with deposed American Communist leader Earl Browder, helped bring about the defeat of Tydings. McCarthy also blasted Secretary of State Dean Acheson as the "Red Dean of the State Department" and slandered George C. Marshall, the architect of victory in World War II and a powerful figure in formulating Far Eastern policy, as "a man steeped in falsehood."

A veteran demagogue, McCarthy liked to play tough in press coverage. He did not mind appearing disheveled, unshaven, and half sober. He used obscenity and vulgarity freely. His tactics worked because the public feared the Communist threat. The arrest in 1950 of Julius and Ethel Rosenberg fueled hysteria. The Rosenbergs, a seemingly ordinary American couple with two small children, were charged with stealing and transmitting atomic secrets to the Russians. To many Americans, only treachery from within could explain how the backward Russians had built an atomic bomb. When the Rosenbergs were convicted and, in

COMMUNIST PARTY ORGANIZATION U.S.A-FEB. 9, 1950

Senator Joseph McCarthy's spurious charges inflamed anticommunist sentiment in the 1950s. Here he uses a chart of Communist Party organization in the United States to suggest that the nation was at risk until subversives were rooted out. (Bettmann/CORBIS)

1953, executed, the nation made clear its commitment to respond to the Communist threat. While some continued to argue their innocence, documents released at the end of the Cold War affirmed Julius's guilt, though left Ethel's involvement in question.

McCarthy's power grew when the Republicans captured the Senate in 1952. He became chairman of the Government Operations Committee and head of its Permanent Investigations Subcommittee. He now had a stronger base and two dedicated assistants, Roy Cohn and G. David Schine. Eisenhower, who disliked McCarthy, grew uneasy but, recognizing his popularity, was reluctant to challenge him.

Finally, McCarthy, Cohn, and Schine pushed too hard. In 1953 the Army drafted Schine and refused him preferential treatment. Angered, McCarthy began to investigate Army security and even top-level military leaders. When the Army charged that McCarthy was going too far, the Senate investigated the complaint. In April 1954 the Army-McCarthy hearings began and soon demonstrated the power of TV to shape people's opinions. For 36 days Americans watched McCarthy's savage tactics and finally judged him irresponsible and destructive, particularly in contrast to the quiet eloquence of the Army's lawyer, Boston attorney Joseph Welch, who at one point asked him, "Have you no sense of decency, sir, at long last? Have you left no sense of decency?" McCarthy's ruthless methods discredited him, and the Senate finally summoned the courage to condemn him. Conservatives then turned against him because by attacking Eisenhower and the Army, he was no longer venting his venom on liberals and Democrats. Although

McCarthy remained in the Senate, his influence disappeared. Three years later, at the age of 48, he died a broken man.

## The Casualties of Fear

The anti-Communist crusade kindled pervasive suspicion in American society. In the late 1940s and early 1950s, dissent no longer seemed safe. Civil servants, government workers, academics, and actors all came under attack and found that the right of due process often evaporated amid the Cold War Red Scare. Seasoned China experts lost their diplomatic jobs, and social justice legislation faltered.

The paranoia affected American life in countless ways. New York subway workers were fired for refusing to answer questions about their political beliefs. Arizona and New Mexico Navajos, facing starvation in the bitter winter of 1947–1948, were denied government relief because their communal way of life seemed "communistic." A Senate report branded homosexuals as unfit for government service, claiming they were subject to blackmail and thus a threat to national security. Black actor Paul Robeson, who, along with the aged African-American intellectual W. E. B. Du Bois, criticized American foreign policy, was accused of Communist leanings and found few opportunities to perform. Eventually both Robeson and Du Bois (who joined the Communist party) lost their passports. Latino laborers faced deportation for belonging to left-wing unions. In 1949, the Congress of Industrial Organizations (CIO) expelled 11 unions with a total membership of more than a million members for alleged Communist domination. Many individual victims of the witch hunts were less lucky than Val Lorwin, met at the start of this chapter. They were the unfortunate victims as the United States became consumed by the passions of the Cold War.

## CONTINUING CONFRONTATIONS WITH COMMUNISTS

The Cold War continued into the 1960s and 1970s. Presidents John F. Kennedy and Lyndon B. Johnson were both aggressive cold warriors who subscribed to their predecessors' policies. Their anti-Communist commitments kept the nation locked in the same bitter conflict that had dominated foreign policy in the 1950s and led to continuing global confrontations.

## John F. Kennedy and the Bay of Pigs Fiasco

Kennedy, who won the presidency in 1960, was an activist eager to provide bold executive leadership. At 43, he was the youngest man ever elected president, and he was impatient to get the country moving again after the Eisenhower years. He also intended to stand up to the Russians. The United States, he proclaimed in his inaugural address, would "pay any price, bear any burden, meet any hardship, support any friend, oppose any foe, to assure the survival and success of liberty."

Kennedy first clashed with Communism in the spring of 1961. Fidel Castro's radical regime in Cuba not only leaned toward the Soviet Union but also provided a model for anti-American uprisings elsewhere in Latin America. Just before Kennedy took office, the United States broke diplomatic relations with Cuba.

Meanwhile the CIA began training anti-Castro exiles to storm the Cuban coast and provoke the uprising that American planners assumed would follow. Told of the plan, Kennedy approved it.

The invasion, which took place at the Bay of Pigs on April 17, 1961, was an unmitigated disaster. Cuban forces stopped the invaders on the beach, and there was no popular uprising. The United States stood exposed of clumsily and unsuccessfully trying to overthrow a sovereign government and of breaking promises not to interfere in the internal affairs of hemispheric neighbors.

Chastened, Kennedy nevertheless remained determined to deal sternly with the perceived Communist threat. Following a hostile meeting with Soviet leader Nikita Khrushchev in Vienna in June 1961, where tense discussions focused on Soviet demands for a permanent settlement of West Berlin's status that would close the city as an escape hatch from East Germany, Kennedy reacted aggressively. He asked Congress for $3 billion more in defense spending, for more men in the armed services, and for funds for a civil defense fallout shelter program, as if to warn of the threat of nuclear war. The crisis eased only when the USSR erected a wall to seal off West Berlin permanently from East Germany.

## The Cuban Missile Face-off

In 1962 a new crisis arose. Understandably fearful of the American threat after the Bay of Pigs invasion, Castro sought and secured Soviet assistance. American aerial photographs taken in October 1962 revealed that the USSR had begun to place what Kennedy considered offensive missiles on Cuban soil, although Cuba insisted they were defensive. The missiles did not change the strategic balance significantly; the Soviets could still wreak immense damage on American targets from more distant bases. But with Russian weapons installed just 90 miles from American shores, appearance was more important than reality. Kennedy was determined to confront the Soviet Union in Cuba and this time to win.

Kennedy went on nationwide TV to tell the American people about the missiles and to demand their removal. He declared that the United States would not shrink from the risk of nuclear war and announced a blockade around Cuba to prevent Soviet ships from bringing in additional missiles. He called the move a quarantine, for a blockade was an act of war.

As Soviet ships steamed toward the island and the nations stood "eyeball to eyeball" at the brink, people around the world held their breath. After several days, the tension broke, but only because Khrushchev called the Soviet ships back. Khrushchev then sent Kennedy a long letter pledging to remove the missiles if the United States lifted the quarantine and promised to stay out of Cuba altogether. A second letter demanded that America remove its missiles from Turkey, as well. The United States agreed to the first letter, ignored the second, and said nothing about its intention, already voiced, of removing its own missiles from Turkey. With that, the crisis ended.

The Cuban missile crisis was the most terrifying confrontation of the Cold War. Yet the president emerged from it as a hero who had stood firm, and his party benefited a few weeks later in the congressional elections. As the relief began to fade, however, critics charged that what Kennedy saw as his finest hour was in fact an unnecessary crisis. One consequence of the crisis was the installation of a Soviet-American hot line to avoid similar episodes in the future. Another consequence was the USSR's determination to increase its nuclear arsenal so that it would never again be exposed as inferior to the United States.

## Confrontation and Containment Under Johnson

After Kennedy's brutal assassination in 1963, Vice President Lyndon Johnson assumed the presidency. An extraordinarily effective legislative leader (see Chapter 28), he had considerably less experience in foreign affairs. Yet he shared many of Kennedy's assumptions, including the conviction, born of World War II, that aggressors had to be stopped before their actions led to further aggression. Like Eisenhower and Kennedy, he also believed in the domino theory, which held that if one country in a region fell, the others would follow. He was determined to preserve American power and contain the Communist menace. He assumed he could treat foreign adversaries just as he treated political opponents at home.

In 1965, believing that "Castro-type elements" might win a civil war in the Dominican Republic, he dispatched more than 20,000 American troops to that Caribbean nation. In fact, the so-called Communist group was led by a former president, Juan Bosch, who had been overthrown by a military junta. The rueful Bosch complained that "this was a democratic revolution smashed by the leading democracy of the world." Johnson's credibility suffered from the episode.

## THE QUAGMIRE OF VIETNAM

The commitment to stopping the spread of Communism led to the massive U.S. involvement in Vietnam. That struggle tore the United States apart, wrought enormous damage in Southeast Asia, and finally forced a reexamination of America's Cold War policies.

## Roots of the Conflict

Indochina, including Vietnam, had been under French control since the mid-nineteenth century. During World War II, Japan occupied the area but allowed French collaborators to administer internal affairs. An independence movement, led by the Communist organizer and revolutionary Ho Chi Minh, sought to expel the Japanese.

In 1945, the Allies faced the question of how to deal with Ho's nationalistic movement. Franklin Roosevelt, like Woodrow Wilson, believed in self-determination and wanted to end colonialism. But France was determined to regain its colony, and by the time of his death, Roosevelt had backed down. Meanwhile Ho had proclaimed the Democratic Republic of Vietnam in 1945. Although the new government enjoyed widespread internal support, the United States refused to recognize it. A long, bitter struggle broke out between French and Vietnamese forces and became entangled with the larger Cold War.

President Truman was less concerned about ending colonialism than with checking Soviet power. He needed France to balance the Soviets in Europe, and that meant cooperating with France in Vietnam. Although Ho did not have close ties to the Soviets and was committed to his independent nationalist crusade, Truman and his advisers were fixated on the notion of monolithic Communism. They wrongly assumed that Ho took orders from Moscow. Hence, in 1950 the United States recognized a French puppet government in Vietnam, and by 1954 Washington was paying over three-quarters of the cost of France's Indochina War.

After Eisenhower took office, France's position in Southeast Asia deteriorated. Secretary of State Dulles was eager to assist the French, and the chairman of the Joint Chiefs of Staff even contemplated using nuclear weapons, but Eisenhower refused to intervene directly. After the French fortress of Dien Bien Phu fell to Ho's forces, an international conference in Geneva divided Vietnam along the 17th parallel. Elections were promised in 1956 that would unify the country and determine its political fate.

## The Start of U.S. Involvement in Vietnam

The elections were never held, and two Vietnamese states emerged. Ho Chi Minh held power in the north, while in the south a fierce anti-Communist, Ngo Dinh Diem, formed a separate government. Intent on securing stability in Southeast Asia, the United States supported Diem and refused to sign the Geneva pact. In the next few years, American aid increased and U.S. military advisers began assisting the South Vietnamese. The United States had taken the first steps toward direct involvement in a ruinous war halfway around the world that would later escalate out of control.

John Kennedy's commitment to Cold War victory led him to expand the U.S. role in Vietnam, a country he once called the "cornerstone of the free world in Southeast Asia." He and his closest associates were confident of success. As Secretary of Defense Robert McNamara observed, "North Vietnam will never beat us. They can't even make ice cubes."

Despite American backing, Diem was losing support in his country. Buddhist priests burned themselves alive in the capital, Saigon, to dramatize his unpopularity. After receiving assurances that the United States would not object to a coup, South Vietnamese military leaders killed Diem and seized the government. Kennedy understood the importance of having a South Vietnamese government with popular support, but he was reluctant to withdraw and let the Vietnamese solve their own problems.

Lyndon Johnson shared the same reservations. After an early briefing he said that he felt like a catfish that had "grabbed a big juicy worm with a right sharp hook in the middle of it." But soon after becoming president, Johnson made a fundamental decision that guided policy for the next four years. With North Vietnamese aid, the Viet Cong and its political arm, the National Liberation Front, slowly gained ground. "I am not going to be the President who saw Southeast Asia go the way of China," Johnson vowed. He posed as a man of peace in the 1964 election campaign, promising that "We are not going to send American boys nine or ten thousand miles away from home to do what Asian boys ought to be doing for themselves." All the while, however, he was secretly planning to escalate the American role.

## Escalation

In August 1964, Johnson cleverly obtained congressional authorization for war by announcing that North Vietnamese torpedo boats had made unprovoked attacks on American destroyers in the international waters of the Gulf of Tonkin. Congress handed Johnson what he sought: a resolution which, he said, was "like grandma's nightshirt—it covered everything." The Tonkin Gulf Resolution gave him authority to "take all necessary measures to repel any armed attack against the forces of the United States and to prevent further aggression." Only later did it become clear that the incident resulted from American vessels violating North Vietnamese territorial waters by assisting South Vietnamese commando raids.

Military escalation began in earnest in February 1965. Retaliating for a guerrilla attack on an American base, Johnson ordered North Vietnam bombed to cut off the Viet Cong's supplies. Johnson personally authorized every raid, boasting that the Air Force "can't even bomb an outhouse without my approval." Saturation bombing, using both fragmentation bombs and napalm (which seared off human flesh), brought enormous destruction to both North and South Vietnam. A few months later, Johnson sent American ground forces into action, a crucial turning point in Americanizing the war. Only 25,000 Americans were in Vietnam at the beginning of 1965; there were 184,000 by the end of the year, 385,000 in 1966, 485,000 in 1967, and 543,000 in 1968. American forces had become direct participants in a struggle to prop up a faraway dictatorial regime.

## Protesting the War

A protest movement developed in the United States. As escalation began, 82 percent of the public told pollsters that American forces should stay in Vietnam until the Communist elements withdrew. Then students began to question basic Cold War assumptions about battling Communism around the globe. The first teach-in took place in March 1965, and as such campus gatherings became more frequent, they tended to turn into antiwar rallies. Draft resistance also grew, legitimated by boxing champion Muhammad Ali who declared, "I ain't got no quarrel with them Viet Cong," and refused military induction. Soon activists were attacking the draft, ROTC programs, and firms that produced the destructive tools of war. (See Chapter 29 for a full discussion of student activism.)

The antiwar movement expanded. Women Strike for Peace, the most forceful women's antiwar organization, marched under such placards as "Stop! Don't drench the jungles of Asia with the blood of our sons." Students chanted, "Hey, hey, LBJ, how many kids did you kill today?" In 1967, some 300,000 people marched in New York while 100,000 tried to close down the Pentagon.

Working-class and middle-class Americans began to sour on the war in early 1968, at the time of the Tet offensive, celebrating the lunar new year. The North

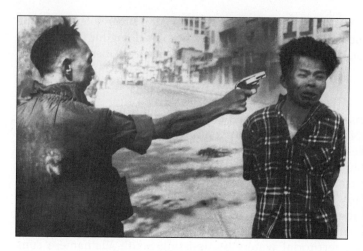

In this picture, General Loan, the chief of the South Vietnamese National Police, looks at a Viet Cong prisoner, lifts his gun, and calmly blows out the captive's brains. This prize-winning photograph captured the horror of the war for many Americans. (AP/Wide World Photos)

Vietnamese launched massive attacks throughout South Vietnam, including an assault on the U.S. embassy in Saigon. The Tet offensive was a psychological victory for the Communists, although militarily they were beaten back. American audiences now saw on television horrific images of the war (including the photograph on this page) and began to wonder about their nation's purposes and actions—indeed, about whether the war could be won at all.

When Richard Nixon assumed office in 1969, he understood the need to heal the rifts that split American society. Wanting to extricate the United States while avoiding defeat, he devised a strategy called Vietnamization. Under it, American forces were withdrawn and replaced by South Vietnamese ones, while American air attacks on the North were stepped up. Between 1968 and 1972, American troop strength in South Vietnam fell from 543,000 to 39,000, winning Nixon political support at home. Yet as the transition occurred, South Vietnamese forces steadily lost ground. Realizing that Communist forces relied on supplies channeled through Cambodia, Nixon in 1970 sent American and South Vietnamese forces into that neutral country to clear out enemy bases there.

Antiwar demonstrations did not stop; indeed, they multiplied in 1969 and 1970. In November 1969, as a massive protest took place in Washington, D.C., stories surfaced about a horrifying massacre of civilians in Vietnam the year before. The small South Vietnamese village of My Lai allegedly had been harboring 250 Viet Cong guerrillas. American troops sent to clear the guerrillas out of My Lai lost control when they found only civilians in the village. One GI confessed:

> We huddled them up. We made them squat down . . . . I poured about four clips into the group . . . . The mothers was hugging their children . . . . Well, we kept right on firing. They was waving their arms and begging . . . . I still dream about it. About the women and children in my sleep. Some days . . . some nights, I can't even sleep.

Nixon's 1970 invasion of Cambodia brought renewed campus demonstrations, some with tragic consequences. At Kent State University in Ohio, the antiwar response was fierce. After students burned down the ROTC building, the

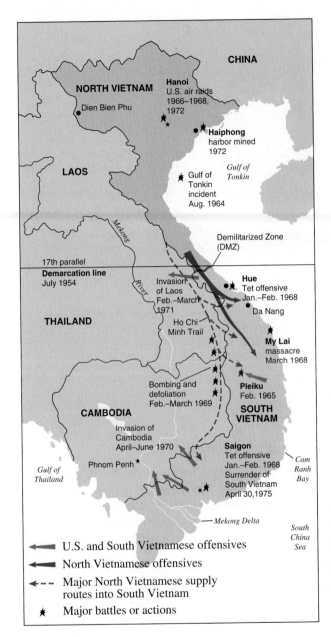

**THE VIETNAM WAR** This map shows the major campaigns of the Vietnam War. The North Vietnamese Tet offensive of early 1968 turned the tide against U.S. participation in the war and led to peace talks. The American invasion of Cambodia in 1970 provoked serious opposition.

governor of Ohio ordered the National Guard to the campus, and without provocation the soldiers fired on a gathering crowd. Two demonstrators, who were more than 250 feet away, were killed; so were two bystanders, almost 400 feet from the troops. Nine other students were wounded. Somewhat less media attention focused on a similar incident at a black institution, Jackson State College in Mississippi, where two black students were killed and two wounded, also by automatic weapons fired from National Guardsmen.

When Ohio National Guardsmen fired on a crowd of antiwar demonstrators and killed four students, even prowar Americans were shocked. This photograph shows the grief and outrage of others who survived the savage shooting of innocent bystanders. (John Filo)

In 1971, the Vietnam War made major headlines once more when the *New York Times* began publishing a secret Defense Department account of American involvement. The so-called Pentagon Papers, leaked by defense analyst Daniel Ellsberg, gave Americans a firsthand look at the fabrications and faulty assumptions that had guided the steady expansion of the struggle. Even though the study stopped with the Johnson years, the Nixon administration was furious and tried, unsuccessfully, to block publication.

## Peace and Its Consequences

Vietnam remained a political football as Nixon ran for reelection in 1972. Just days before the vote, Nixon's chief foreign policy adviser, Henry Kissinger, announced that "peace is at hand." But Kissinger would not come to terms with the North Vietnamese until after the election, and the administration unleashed the war's most intensive bombing campaign, hitting the North Vietnamese capital of Hanoi and mining the nation's principal harbors.

Although American forces were withdrawn after the peace settlement was signed in January 1973, the war went on. In 1975, as the North Vietnamese forces were about to win and South Vietnamese units were disintegrating, Nixon's successor in the White House, Gerald Ford, called for another $1 billion in aid to stave off defeat. But Congress refused, leaving South Vietnam's crumbling government to fend for itself.

The long conflict had enormous consequences. Disillusionment with the war undermined assumptions about America's role in world affairs. In the longest war in its history, the United States lost almost 58,000 men, with far more wounded or maimed. Blacks and Chicanos suffered more than whites, since they were disproportionately represented in combat units. Financially, the nation spent more than $150 billion on the unsuccessful war. Domestic reform slowed, then stopped. Cynicism about government increased. American society was deeply divided. Only time would heal the wounds.

## Post-Vietnam Détente

If the Republicans' Vietnam policy was a questionable success, accomplishments were impressive in other areas. Nixon, the consummate Red-baiter of the past, dealt imaginatively and successfully with the major Communist powers, reversing the direction of American policy since World War II.

Opening formal relations with the People's Republic of China was his most dramatic initiative. Ever since 1949 the United States had refused to recognize the Communist government on the mainland, insisting that Jiang Jieshi's rump regime on Taiwan was the legitimate representative of the Chinese people. In 1971, with an eye on upcoming elections, Nixon began softening his rigidity toward China and then announced that he would visit the People's Republic in 1972. Acknowledging what most nations already knew—that Communism was not monolithic—he suspected that Chinese-American friendship could serve as leverage on the Soviet Union. Having long ago established his anti-Communist credentials, he realized, he could open a dialogue with Beijing without political harm. Finally, undertaking so dramatic a trip could boost his image.

Seeking to play one Communist state against another, Nixon also traveled to the Soviet Union in 1972 and likewise got a warm welcome. At a cordial summit meeting, the president and the Soviet leader, Leonid Brezhnev, signed the first Strategic Arms Limitation Treaty (SALT I). In addition to this agreement to limit missile stockpiles, the two nations also promised to cooperate in space and to ease long-standing trade restrictions. Business applauded the new approach, and most Americans approved of this relaxation of tension known as détente.

Nixon shifted the course of U.S.–China relations by his dramatic visit to the People's Republic. He met Chinese officials for the first time, visited the Great Wall, shown in this picture, and then reported back enthusiastically to the American people. (Corbis)

# *Timeline*

| | |
|---|---|
| **1945** | Yalta Conference |
| | Roosevelt dies; Harry Truman becomes president |
| | Potsdam Conference |
| **1946** | American plan for control of atomic energy fails |
| | Atomic Energy Act |
| | Iran crisis |
| | Churchill's "Iron Curtain" speech |
| **1947** | Truman Doctrine |
| | Federal Employee Loyalty Program |
| | House Un-American Activities Committee (HUAC) investigates the movie industry |
| **1948** | Marshall Plan launched |
| | Berlin airlift |
| | Israel created by United Nations |
| | Hiss-Chambers case |
| | Truman elected president |
| **1949** | Soviet Union tests atomic bomb |
| | North Atlantic Treaty Organization (NATO) established |
| | George Orwell, *1984* |
| | Mao Zedong's forces win Chinese civil war; Jiang Jieshi flees to Taiwan |

| | |
|---|---|
| **1950** | Truman authorizes development of the hydrogen bomb |
| | Alger Hiss convicted |
| | Joseph McCarthy's Wheeling (W. Va.) speech on subversion |
| | NSC-68 |
| | McCarran Internal Security Act |
| **1950–1953** | Korean War |
| **1951** | Japanese-American treaty |
| **1952** | Dwight D. Eisenhower elected president |
| | McCarthy heads Senate Permanent Investigations Subcommittee |
| **1953** | Stalin dies; Khrushchev consolidates power |
| | East Germans stage anti-Soviet demonstrations |
| | Shah of Iran returns to power in CIA-supported coup |
| **1954** | Fall of Dien Bien Phu ends French control of Indochina |
| | Geneva Conference |
| | Guatemalan government overthrown with CIA help |
| | Mao's forces shell Quemoy and Matsu |
| | Army-McCarthy hearings |

When Gerald Ford assumed office in 1974 after Nixon's resignation, he followed Nixon's policies, even if he ceased calling the approach détente. He continued the strategic arms limitation talks that provided hope for eventual nuclear disarmament and culminated in the even more comprehensive SALT II agreement—signed but never ratified during Jimmy Carter's administration.

❧ ❧ ❧ ❧

# CONCLUSION

## *The Cold War In Perspective*

The Cold War had a powerful impact on American society in the post–World War II decades. The Soviet-American standoff dominated international relations for nearly 50 years.

| | | | |
|---|---|---|---|
| **1956** | Suez incident | **1967–1968** | Antiwar demonstrations |
| | Hungarian "freedom fighters" suppressed | **1968** | Tet offensive in Vietnam |
| | | | Richard Nixon elected president |
| | Eisenhower reelected | | My Lai incident |
| **1957** | Russians launch *Sputnik* satellite | **1969** | Nixon Doctrine announced |
| **1958** | U.S. troops sent to support Lebanese government | | Moratorium against the Vietnam War |
| | | | SALT talks begin |
| **1959** | Castro deposes Batista in Cuba | **1970** | U.S. invasion of Cambodia |
| **1960** | John F. Kennedy elected president | | Shootings at Kent State and Jackson State universities |
| **1961** | Bay of Pigs invasion fails | | |
| | Khrushchev and Kennedy meet in Berlin | **1971** | *New York Times* publishes Pentagon Papers |
| | Berlin Wall constructed | **1972** | Nixon visits People's Republic of China and Soviet Union |
| **1962** | Cuban missile crisis | | Nixon reelected |
| **1963** | Buddhist demonstrations in Vietnam | | SALT I treaty on nuclear arms |
| | President Diem assassinated in Vietnam | **1973** | Vietnam cease-fire agreement |
| | | **1975** | South Vietnam falls to the Communists |
| | Kennedy assassinated; Lyndon B. Johnson becomes president | | End of the Vietnam War |
| **1964** | Gulf of Tonkin resolution | | |
| | Johnson reelected | | |
| **1965** | Vietnam conflict escalates | | |
| | Marines sent to Dominican Republic | | |

Historians have long differed over which side caused the Cold War. In the early postwar years, policy makers and commentators justified the American stance as a bold and courageous effort to meet the Communist threat. Later, particularly during the 1960s when the war in Vietnam was eroding confidence in American foreign policy, historians began to argue that American actions were misguided, insensitive to Soviet needs, and at least partially responsible for escalating friction. As with most historical questions, there are no easy answers, but both sides must be weighed.

The Cold War grew out of the two great world powers' competition for international influence. After World War II, the U.S. goal was to exercise economic and political leadership in the world and thus encourage capitalist economies and democratic political institutions throughout Europe and in nations emerging from colonialism. But these goals put the United States on a collision course with nations, such as the Soviet Union, that had a different vision of what the postwar world should be like, as well as with anticolonial movements around the globe.

Perceiving threats from the Soviet Union, China, and other Communist countries, the United States clung to its deep-rooted sense of mission and embarked on an increasingly aggressive policy of containment, culminating in the ill-fated war in Vietnam. Here, as elsewhere, policy makers followed the advice of George Kennan as they sought to preserve and extend America's influence. The Cold War, with its profound impact on innocent people like Val Lorwin, met at the start of this chapter, was the unfortunate result.

## Discovering U.S. History Online

*Cold War*   http://www.cnn.com/SPECIALS/cold.war/
This is the companion site to the CNN series on the Cold War. It contains a good deal of information about a wide variety of issues.

*Korean War Project*   http://www.koreanwar.org
This site has information about the Korean War and is a guide to resources on the struggle.

*NATO at 50*   http://www.cnn.com/SPECIALS/1999/nato/
This site from CNN has an excellent timeline and images telling the history of the North Atlantic Treaty Organization.

*Senator Joe McCarthy*   http://webcorp.com/mccarthy/
This site includes audio and visual clips of McCarthy's speeches.

*Fourteen Days in October: The Cuban Missile Crisis*   http://library.thinkquest.org/11046/
This creative site allows the viewer to explore the Cuban missile crisis.

*Vietnam Online*   http://www.pbs.org/wgbh/amex/vietnam/
From PBS and the American Experience, this site contains a detailed, interactive timeline of the war, interpretive essays, and autobiographical reflections.

*Investigating the Vietnam War*   http://www.spartacus.schoolnet.co.uk/vietintro.htm
This site contains narratives, personal accounts, and an excellent list of annotated links to the best Vietnam-related sites.

*The My Lai Courts Martial (1970)*   http://www.law.umkc.edu/faculty/projects/ftrials/mylai/mylai.htm
This site contains chronology, images, and court documents describing the massacre of Vietnamese civilians at My Lai.

*May 4, 1970*   http://www.library.kent.edu/exhibits/4may95/index.html
This site commemorates the 25th anniversary of the shootings at Kent State University with a detailed chronology and other information.

## Fiction and Film

*The Bridges at Toko-ri* (1953) by James A. Michener is a novel about the frustrations of fighting the Korean War when people at home do not seem to care; Walter M. Miller, Jr., *A Canticle for Leibowitz* (1959) is about the devastation following a nuclear war that reduces civilization to a primitive state; Tim O'Brien, *Going After Cacciato* (1978) is a novel about Vietnam in which one soldier simply decides to lay down his gun and walk home; Nevil Shute, *On the Beach* (1957) is a novel about a nuclear war that wiped out most life and created a radioactive cloud that is killing the rest.

    *Born on the Fourth of July* (1989) is the film made from Ron Kovic's story about being wounded in Vietnam and then returning home; *Dr. Strangelove or: How I Learned to Stop Worrying and Love the Bomb*

(1964) is a movie made by Stanley Kubrick about the absurdity of nuclear war; *On the Beach* (1959) is the film from the novel of the same name about a nuclear war that ended all life on earth; *Platoon* (1986) is a film about the soldiers' war in Vietnam; *Thirteen Days* (2000) is a movie about the Kennedy administration and the Cuban Missile Crisis.

## *Recommended Reading*

### Origins of the Cold War
Stephen E. Ambrose and Douglas G. Brinkley, *Rise to Globalism: American Foreign Policy Since 1938*, 8th rev. ed. (1997); John Lewis Gaddis, *The Long Peace: Inquiries into the History of the Cold War* (1987), *The United States and the Origins of the Cold War, 1941–1947* (1972), and *We Now Know: Rethinking Cold War History* (1997); Walter LaFeber, *America, Russia, and the Cold War, 1945–1996*, 8th ed. (1996); Ralph B. Levering, *The Cold War: A Post-Cold War History* (1994); Thomas J. McCormick, *America's Half Century: United States Foreign Policy in the Cold War* (1992); Ronald A. Powaski, *The Cold War: The United States and the Soviet Union, 1917–1991* (1997); Allan M. Winkler, *The Cold War: A History in Documents* (2000); Daniel Yergin, *Shattered Peace: The Origins of the Cold War and the National Security State* (1977).

### Containing the Soviet Union
H. W. Brands, Jr., *Cold Warriors: Eisenhower's Generation and American Foreign Policy* (1988); Robert A. Divine, *Eisenhower and the Cold War* (1981) and *The Sputnik Challenge: Eisenhower's Response to the Soviet Satellite* (1993); Michael J. Hogan, *The Marshall Plan: America, Britain, and the Reconstruction of Western Europe* (1987) and *A Cross of Iron: Harry S Truman and the Origins of the National Security State, 1945–1954* (1998); Townsend Hoopes, *The Devil and John Foster Dulles* (1973); Melvyn P. Leffler, *A Preponderance of Power: National Security, the Truman Administration, and the Cold War* (1992); Thomas G. Patterson, *Meeting the Communist Threat: Truman to Reagan* (1988).

### Containment in Asia, the Middle East, and Latin America
Joseph C. Goulden, *Korea: The Untold Story of the War* (1982); Chaim Herzog, *The Arab-Israeli Wars: War and Peace in the Middle East*, rev. ed. (1984); Burton I. Kaufman, *The Korean War: Challenges in Crisis, Credibility, and Command* (1986); Walter LaFeber, *Inevitable Revolutions: The United States in Central America*, 2nd ed. (1993).

### Atomic Weapons and the Cold War
Paul Boyer, *By the Bomb's Early Light: American Thought and Culture at the Dawn of the Atomic Age* (1985); McGeorge Bundy, *Danger and Survival: Choices About the Bomb in the First Fifty Years* (1988); Gregg Herken, *Counsels of War* (1985); Richard G. Hewlett and Francis Duncan, *Atomic Shield: Volume II: A History of the United States Atomic Energy Commission, 1947–1952* (1972); Richard G. Hewlett and Jack M. Holl, *Atoms for Peace and War: Eisenhower and the Atomic Energy Commission, 1953–1961* (1989); John Newhouse, *War and Peace in the Nuclear Age* (1989); Spencer R. Weart, *Nuclear Fear: A History of Images* (1988); Allan M. Winkler, *Life Under a Cloud: American Anxiety About the Atom* (1993).

### The Cold War at Home
John D'Emilio, "The Homosexual Menace: The Politics of Sexuality in Cold War America," *Making Trouble: Essays on Gay History, Politics, and the University* (1992); Robert Griffith, *The Politics of Fear: Joseph R. McCarthy and the Senate* (1970); John Earl Haynes and Harvey Klehr, *Venona: Decoding Soviet Espionage in America* (1999); David M. Oshinsky, *A Conspiracy So Immense: The World of Joe McCarthy* (1983); Ronald Radash and Joyce Milton, *The Rosenberg File: A Search for Truth* (1984); Thomas C. Reeves, *The Life and Times of Joe McCarthy: A Biography* (1982); Lisle A. Rose, *The Cold War Comes to Main Street: America in 1950* (1999); Richard H. Rovere, *Senator Joe McCarthy* (1960); Ellen W. Schrecker, *No Ivory Tower: McCarthyism and the Universities* (1986), *The Age of McCarthyism: A Brief History with Documents* (1994), and *Many Are the Crimes: McCarthyism in America* (1998); Allen Weinstein, *Perjury: The*

*Hiss-Chambers Case*, rev. ed. (1997); Allen Weinstein and Alexander Vassiliev, *The Haunted Wood: Soviet Espionage in America—The Stalin Era* (1999).

### Continuing Confrontations with Communists

Laurence Chang and Peter Kornbluh, eds., *The Cuban Missile Crisis, 1962: A National Security Archive Documents Reader* (1998); Aleksandr Fursenko and Timothy Naftali, *One Hell of a Gamble: Khrushchev, Castro, and Kennedy* (1997); Ernest R. May and Philip D. Zelikow, eds., *The Kennedy Tapes: Inside the White House During the Cuban Missile Crisis* (1997); Richard J. Walton, *Cold War and Counterrevolution: The Foreign Policy of John F. Kennedy* (1972).

### The Quagmire of Vietnam

Christian G. Appy, *Working-Class War: American Combat Soldiers and Vietnam* (1993); Frances FitzGerald, *Fire in the Lake: The Vietnamese and the Americans in Vietnam* (1972); David Halberstam, *The Best and the Brightest* (1972); Le Ly Hayslip, *When Heaven and Earth Changed Places* (1989); George C. Herring, *America's Longest War: The United States and Vietnam, 1950–1975*, 3rd ed. (1996) and *LBJ and Vietnam: A Different Kind of War* (1994); Stanley Karnow, *Vietnam: A History: The First Complete Account of Vietnam at War* (1983); Jeffrey P. Kimball, *Nixon's Vietnam War* (1998); Ron Kovic, *Born on the Fourth of July* (1976); Robert S. McNamara, *In Retrospect* (1995); Al Santoli, *Everything We Had: An Oral History of the Vietnam War by Thirty-three American Soldiers Who Fought It* (1981); Neil Sheehan, *A Bright Shining Lie: John Paul Vann and America in Vietnam* (1988).

# CHAPTER 28

# High Water and Ebb Tide of the Liberal State

## CHAPTER OUTLINE

- The Origins of the Welfare State
- The High-Water Mark of Liberalism

- The Decline of Liberalism
- Conclusion: Political Readjustment

## AMERICAN STORIES
### A Young Liberal Questions the Welfare State

Paul Cowan was an idealist in the 1960s. Like many students who came of age during that time, he believed in the possibility of social change and plunged into the struggle for liberal reform. He shared the hopes and dreams of other members of his generation who felt that their government could make a difference in people's lives.

Cowan's commitment had developed slowly. He was a child of the 1950s, when most Americans were caught up in the consumer culture and paid little attention to the problems of less fortunate people. His grandfather had sold used cement bags in Chicago, but his father had become an executive at CBS television, and Cowan grew up in comfortable surroundings. He graduated from the Choate School (where John Kennedy had gone) in 1958, and then from Harvard University (where Kennedy had also been a student) in 1963.

When he entered college, Cowan was interested in politically conscious writers like John Dos Passos, John Steinbeck, and James Agee, and folk singers like Pete Seeger and Woody Guthrie. They offered him entrance, he later recalled, into a "nation that seemed to be filled with energy and decency," one that lurked "beneath the dull, conformist facade of the Eisenhower years." While at Harvard, he was excited by antinuclear campaigns in New England and civil rights demonstrations in the South.

After college, he made good on his commitment to civil rights by going to Mississippi to work in the Freedom Summer project of 1964. He was inspired by the example of John Kennedy, the liberal president whose administration promised "a new kind of politics" that could make the nation, and the world, a better place. During that summer, he wrote, "it was possible to believe that by changing ourselves we could change, and redeem, our America."

The Peace Corps came next. Paul and his wife Rachel were convinced that this organization, the idea of the young president, "really was a unique government agency, permanently protected by the lingering magic of John F. Kennedy's name." They were sent to the South American city of Guayaquil, Ecuador. Their task was to serve as mediators between administrators of the city hall and residents of the slums. They wanted to try to raise the standard of living by encouraging local governments to provide basic services such as garbage disposal and clean water.

But the work proved more frustrating than they had imagined. They bristled at restrictions imposed by the Peace Corps bureaucracy. They despaired at the inadequate resources local government officials had to accomplish their aims. They wondered if they were just new imperialists, trying to impose their values on others who had priorities of their own. "From the day we moved into the barrio," Cowan later recalled, "the question we were most frequently asked by the people we were supposed to be organizing was whether we would leave them our clothes when we returned to the States."

Cowan came home disillusioned. "I saw that even the liberals I had wanted to emulate, men who seemed to be devoting their lives to fighting injustice, were unable to accept people from alien cultures on any terms but their own." He called his account of his own odyssey *The Making of an Un-American.*

❦ ❦ ❦ ❦

Paul Cowan's passage through the 1960s mirrored the passage of American society as a whole. Millions of Americans shared his views as the period began. Mostly comfortable and confident, they supported the liberal agenda advanced by the Democratic party of John Kennedy and Lyndon Johnson. They endorsed the idea that the government had responsibility for the welfare of all its citizens and accepted the need for a more active governmental role to help those who were unable to help themselves. That commitment lay behind the legislative achievements of the "Great Society," the last wave of twentieth-century reform that built upon the gains of the Progressive era and the New Deal years before.

Then political reaction set in, as the nation was torn apart by the ravages of the Vietnam War. Liberal assumptions eroded as conservatives argued that an activist approach was responsible for the chaos consuming the country. Republicans who assumed power at the end of the 1960s accepted the basic outlines of the welfare state but rejected many of the liberal initiatives of Democratic administrations as expensive failures. Under Richard Nixon and Gerald Ford, Republicans capitalized on disillusionment with federal policy and crafted a new consensus that kept them in the White House for most of the next decade and a half. The presidency of Democrat Jimmy Carter failed to reverse the conservative shift. Liberals despaired as they watched the destruction of their dreams.

This chapter describes the climax of twentieth-century liberalism and its subsequent decline. It focuses on the effort of the government, begun in Franklin Roosevelt's New Deal, to help those left behind by the advances of industrial capitalism. It examines first the initiatives in the 1940s and 1950s and early 1960s to provide necessary assistance to the less fortunate members of American society, then the efforts in the late 1960s and 1970s to limit such aid. In pondering the possibilities of reform, this chapter outlines the various attempts to devise an effective political response to the major structural changes in the post–World

War II economy outlined in Chapter 26. It explores the debates that took place and the shifts that occurred as the political system struggled to cope with the problems of wholesale economic transformation and to maintain the promise of American life.

## THE ORIGINS OF THE WELFARE STATE

The modern American welfare state originated in the New Deal. Franklin Roosevelt's efforts to combat the Great Depression and protect Americans from problems stemming from industrial capitalism (see Chapter 24) provided the basis for subsequent reform. Harry Truman's Fair Deal built on Roosevelt's New Deal, though Truman often found himself curbed by a conservative Congress. His Republican successor, Dwight Eisenhower, tried to scale down spending but made no effort to roll back the most important initiatives of the welfare state. Actions taken in the post–World War II years provided the groundwork for the major reforms of the 1960s.

## Truman's Approach

Like FDR, Harry Truman believed that the federal government had the responsibility for ensuring the social welfare of all Americans. He shared his predecessor's commitment to assisting less prosperous inhabitants of the country in a systematic, rational way. Truman wanted his administration to embrace and act upon a series of carefully defined social and economic goals that would extend New Deal initiatives even further. Immediate problems of reconversion—demands for the return of servicemen, fears of inflation, and labor unrest—had to be resolved first, to be sure. But even as he worked (not always successfully) to handle these issues, Truman outlined his vision of the welfare state.

As he articulated his goals, Truman took the same feisty approach to public policy that characterized his conduct of foreign affairs (see Chapter 27). He stated his position clearly and simply, often in black and white terms, and seldom hesitated to let others know exactly where he stood. He attacked his political enemies vigorously and often took his case to the American people. He was, in many ways, an old-style Democratic machine politician who hoped to use his authority to benefit his political base of middle-class and working-class Americans.

Less than a week after the end of World War II, Truman called on Congress to pass a 21-point program that would produce postwar stability and security. He wanted housing assistance, a higher minimum wage, more unemployment compensation, and a national commitment to maintain full employment. During the next 10 weeks, Truman sent blueprints of further proposals to Congress, including health insurance and atomic energy legislation. But this liberal program soon ran into fierce opposition.

The debate surrounding the Employment Act of 1946 hinted at the fate of Truman's proposals. This measure was a deliberate effort to apply the theory of English economist John Maynard Keynes to preserve economic equilibrium and prevent depression. Keynes had argued a decade earlier that massive spending was necessary to overcome a depression (see Chapter 24). The money spent during World War II caused the economy to respond precisely as Keynes had predicted.

Now economists wanted to institutionalize his ideas to forestall problems. The initial bill, which enjoyed the strong support of labor, would have committed the government to maintaining full employment by monitoring the economy and taking remedial action in case of decline. Responses to a downturn included tax cuts and spending programs to stimulate the economy and reduce unemployment.

While liberals and labor leaders hailed the measure, business groups condemned it. They claimed that government intervention would move the United States closer to socialism. Responding to the business community, Congress cut the proposal to bits. As finally passed, the act created a Council of Economic Advisers to make recommendations to the president, who was to report annually to Congress and the nation on the state of the economy. But it stopped short of committing the government to using fiscal tools to maintain full employment when economic indicators turned downward.

## Truman's Struggle with a Conservative Congress

As the midterm elections of 1946 approached, Truman and his supporters knew they were vulnerable. Many Democrats still pined for FDR. Truman appeared to be a petty bungler, the butt of countless jokes. His support dropped from 87 percent of those polled after he assumed the presidency to 32 percent in November 1946. Gleeful Republicans asked the voters, "Had enough?"

They had. Republicans won majorities in both houses of Congress for the first time since the 1928 elections, and gained a majority of the governorships as well. Truman now faced an unsympathetic 80th Congress in which Republicans and conservative Democrats planned to reverse the liberal policies of the Roosevelt years. Hoping to reestablish congressional authority and cut the power of the executive branch, they insisted on less government intervention in business and private life. They demanded tax cuts and a curtailment of the privileged position they felt labor had come to enjoy.

When the new Congress met, it moved to slash spending and reduce taxes. In 1947, Congress twice passed tax-cut measures. Both times Truman vetoed them, but in 1948, another election year, Congress overrode the veto.

Congress also struck at Democratic labor policies. Angry at the gains won by labor in the 1930s and 1940s, Republicans wanted to curtail unions' right to call disruptive strikes such as those that had occurred after the war, when more workers than ever before in the nation's history stayed away from their jobs. Early in Truman's presidency, Congress had passed a bill requiring prior notice for strikes, as well as a cooling-off period if a strike occurred. Truman vetoed it. But in 1947, commanding more votes, the Republicans passed the Taft-Hartley Act, which intended to limit the power of unions by restricting the weapons they could deploy. Revising the Wagner Act of 1935, the legislation spelled out unfair labor practices (such as preventing nonunion workers from working if they wished) and outlawed the closed shop, in which an employee had to join a union before getting a job. The law likewise allowed states to prohibit the union shop, which forced workers to join the union after they had been hired. It also gave the president the right to call for an 80-day cooling-off period in strikes affecting national security and required union officials to sign non-Communist oaths.

Union leaders and members were furious. They called the measure a "slave-labor law" and argued vigorously that it eliminated many of their hard-won rights and set labor-management relations back to the way they were in pre–New Deal days. Vetoing the measure, Truman went on nationwide radio to seek public approval. This regained him some of the labor support he had earlier lost when he tried to force strikers back to work immediately after the war. But Congress passed Taft-Hartley over his veto.

## The Fair Deal and Its Fate

In 1948, Truman wanted to consolidate a liberal program and to win the presidency in his own right. He knew that some Democrats wanted to replace him with Dwight Eisenhower or Supreme Court Justice William O. Douglas or anyone else. That effort failed, but Truman was left with what most people thought was a worthless nomination. Not only was his own popularity waning, but the Democratic party seemed to be falling apart.

The civil rights issue, aimed at securing political rights for African Americans, split the Democrats. Truman hoped to straddle it, at least until after the election, to avoid alienating the South. When liberals defeated a moderate platform proposal and pressed for a stronger stand on black civil rights, angry delegates from Mississippi and Alabama stormed out of the convention. They later formed the States' Rights, or Dixiecrat, party, which nominated Governor J. Strom Thurmond of South Carolina for the presidency and affirmed support for segregation.

Meanwhile, Henry A. Wallace, who had held the positions of secretary of agriculture, vice president, and secretary of commerce under FDR, mounted his own challenge. Truman had fired Wallace from his cabinet for supporting a more temperate approach to the Soviet Union. Now Wallace became the presidential candidate of the Progressive party. Initially, he attracted widespread liberal interest because of his moderate position on Soviet-American affairs, his promotion of desegregation, and his promise to nationalize the railroads and major industries. But as Communists and "fellow travelers" surfaced in his organization, other support dropped off.

Once again the GOP nominated New York Governor Dewey, its unsuccessful candidate in 1944. Although Dewey was stiff and egocentric, the polls uniformly indicated a Republican victory. Dewey saw little value in brawling with his opponent and campaigned, according to one commentator, "with the humorless calculation of a Certified Public Accountant in pursuit of the Holy Grail."

Truman, the underdog, ran a two-fisted campaign. He appealed to ordinary Americans as an unpretentious man in an uphill fight. He addressed Americans in familiar language, calling the Republicans a "bunch of old mossbacks" out to destroy the New Deal, and attacked the "do nothing" 80th Congress. Speaking without a prepared text in his choppy, aggressive style, he warmed to crowds, and they warmed to him. "Give 'em hell, Harry," they yelled. He did.

The pollsters were wrong. On election day, despite the early headline "Dewey Defeats Truman" in the *Chicago Daily Tribune,* the incumbent president scored one of the most unexpected political upsets in American history, winning 303–189 in the Electoral College. Democrats also swept both houses of Congress.

In one of the nation's most extraordinary political upsets, Harry Truman beat Thomas E. Dewey in 1948. Here an exuberant Truman holds a newspaper headline printed while he slept, before the vote turned his way. (Bettmann/CORBIS)

Truman won primarily because he was able to revive the major elements of the Democratic coalition that FDR had constructed more than a decade before. Despite the rocky days of 1946, Truman managed to keep labor, farm, and black votes. Labor's support made a big difference. Working men and women had been buoyed by his veto, even though unsuccessful, of the Taft-Hartley Act. Union leaders, less happy with Truman, backed him because they were afraid of being tarnished with the Communist label if they supported Wallace.

With the election behind him, Truman pursued his liberal program. In his 1949 State of the Union message, he declared, "Every segment of our population and every individual has a right to expect from our Government a fair deal." The Fair Deal became the name for his domestic program, which included the measures he had proposed over and over since 1945.

Parts of the Fair Deal passed; others did not. Lawmakers raised the minimum wage and expanded Social Security. A housing program brought modest gains but did not really meet housing needs. A farm program, aimed at providing income support to farmers if prices fell, never made it through Congress. Although he desegregated the military, other parts of his civil rights program failed to win congressional support (see Chapter 29). The American Medical Association successfully opposed national health insurance, and Congress rejected federal aid to education.

The mixed record was not entirely Truman's fault. Conservative legislators repeatedly sabotaged his efforts. But critics charged correctly that Truman was often unpragmatic and shrill. He sometimes seemed to provoke the confrontations that became a hallmark of his presidency. Seeking bipartisan support for checking the perceived Soviet threat (see Chapter 27), he allowed his domestic program to suffer. As defense expenditures mounted, correspondingly less money was available for projects at home.

Still, Truman kept the liberal vision alive. The Fair Deal ratified many of the New Deal's initiatives and led Americans to take programs like Social Security for granted. Truman had not come close to achieving everything he wanted, but the nation had taken another step toward endorsing liberal goals.

## The Election of Eisenhower

Acceptance of the liberal state continued in the 1950s, even as the Republicans took control. By 1952, Truman's popularity had plummeted to only 23 percent of the American people, and all indicators pointed to a political shift. The Democrats nominated Adlai Stevenson, Illinois's able, articulate, and moderately liberal governor. The Republicans turned to Dwight Eisenhower, the World War II hero known as Ike.

Stevenson approached political issues in intellectual terms. "Let's talk sense to the American people," he said. While liberals loved his approach, Stevenson himself anticipated the outcome. How, he wondered, could a man named Adlai beat a soldier called Ike?

The Republicans focused on Communism, corruption, and Korea as major issues. They called the Democrats "soft on Communism" and demanded a more aggressive approach at home and abroad. They criticized assorted scandals involving Truman's cronies and friends. The president himself was blameless, but some of the people near him were not. The Republicans also promised to end the unpopular Korean War.

Eisenhower proved to be a great campaigner. Though this was his first effort to win political office, he had a natural talent for taking his case to the American people. He spoke in simple, reassuring terms. He struck a grandfatherly pose, unified his party, and won with 55 percent of the vote and 41 states. He took office with a Republican Congress and had little difficulty gaining a second term four years later.

## "Modern Republicanism"

Eisenhower believed firmly in limiting the presidential role. He was uncomfortable with the growth of the executive office over the past 20 years. Like the Congressional Republicans with whom Truman had tangled, he wanted to restore the balance between the branches of government and to reduce the authority of the national government. He recognized, however, that it was impossible to scale back federal power to the levels of the 1920s, and he wanted to preserve social gains that even Republicans now accepted. Eisenhower sometimes called his approach "dynamic conservatism" or "modern Republicanism," which, he explained, meant "conservative when it comes to money, liberal when it comes to human beings." Liberals quipped that this meant endorsing social projects but failing to authorize the funds.

Economic concerns dominated the Eisenhower years. The president and his chief aides wanted desperately to preserve the value of the dollar, pare down levels of funding, cut taxes, and balance the budget after years of deficit spending. To achieve those aims, the president appointed George Humphrey, a fiscal conservative, as secretary of the treasury. In times of economic stagnation, Humphrey and other Republicans were willing to risk unemployment to control inflation.

Charles E. Wilson, the secretary of defense and former GM president, epitomized the administration's pro-business stance: "What is good for our country is good for General Motors," he declared, "and vice versa."

Eisenhower fulfilled his promise to reduce government's economic role. After Republicans received financial support from oil companies during the campaign, the new Congress, with a presidential strong endorsement, transferred control of about $40 billion worth of federal oil lands to the states. Speaking about the Tennessee Valley Authority and the public generation of electric power, Eisenhower noted privately, "I'd like to see us sell the whole thing, but I suppose we can't go that far." He opposed a TVA proposal for expansion to provide power to the Atomic Energy Commission and authorized a private group to build a plant for that purpose. Later, when charges of scandal arose, the administration canceled the agreement, but the basic preference for private development remained.

Committed to supporting business interests, the administration sometimes saw its program backfire. As a result of its reluctance to stimulate the economy too much, the annual rate of economic growth declined from 4.3 percent between 1947 and 1952 to 2.5 percent between 1953 and 1960. The country also suffered three recessions in Eisenhower's eight years, during which tax revenues fell and deficits increased. Liberal economists argued that Keynesian tools were available to avoid such troubles but were not being used.

Eisenhower's understated approach led to a legislative stalemate, particularly when the Democrats regained control of Congress in 1954. Opponents laughed about limited White House leadership and spoke of the Eisenhower doll—you wound it up, and it did nothing for eight years.

Yet Eisenhower understood just what he was doing and had a better grasp of public policy than his critics realized. He worked quietly to create the consensus that he believed was necessary to make legislative progress and often pushed his favorite programs from behind the scenes. He believed in what later scholars called a "hidden hand" presidency.

Eisenhower was the first president to make extensive use of the new medium of television. Though he took a low-key approach to his office, his intent gaze and wide smile gave Americans a sense of confidence that the country was in good hands, and they listened carefully when he spoke to the nation, as in this televised report on civil defense in 1955.
(AP/Wide World Photos)

Even more important was his role in ratifying the welfare state. By 1960, the government had become a major factor in ordinary people's lives. It had grown enormously, employing close to 2.5 million people throughout the 1950s. Federal expenditures, which had stood at $3.1 billion in 1929, rose to $75 billion in 1953 and passed $150 million in the 1960s. The White House now took the lead in initiating legislation and steering bills through Congress. Individuals had come to expect old-age pensions, unemployment payments, and a minimum wage. By accepting the fundamental features of the national state the Democrats had created, Eisenhower ensured its survival. Now the debate about social policy broadened, as issues such as educational assistance, federal health care, and increased welfare benefits became part of the political agenda of the 1960s.

For all the jokes about him, Eisenhower remained popular. He accomplished most of the things he had wanted to do. He was one of the few presidents to leave office as highly regarded by the people as when he entered it. He was the kind of leader Americans wanted in prosperous times.

## THE HIGH-WATER MARK OF LIBERALISM

The commitment to a welfare state grew stronger in the 1960s. The Democrats who won office in these years wanted to broaden the role of government even further. Dismayed at the problems of poverty, unemployment, and racism, John F. Kennedy and Lyndon B. Johnson sought to manage the economy more effectively, eradicate poverty, and protect the civil rights of all Americans. Midway through the decade they came close to achieving their goals.

## The Election of 1960

In the 1960 campaign, Kennedy argued that the government in general, and the president in particular, had to play an even more active role than they had in the Eisenhower years. He charged that the country had become lazy as it reveled in the prosperity of the 1950s. There were, he said, problems that needed to be addressed.

Kennedy squared off against Richard Nixon, the Republican nominee, in the first televised presidential debates. Seventy million Americans saw the two men in the first contest. The debates made a major difference in the campaign (see the Recovering the Past section of this chapter). From now on, television would play a major role in politics and reshape its character.

Kennedy overcame seemingly insuperable odds to become the first Catholic in the White House. Yet his victory was razor-thin. The electoral margin of 303 to 219 concealed the close popular tally, in which he triumphed by fewer than 120,000 of 68 million votes cast. If a few thousand people had voted differently in Illinois and Texas, the election would have gone to Nixon. While Kennedy had Democratic majorities in Congress, many members of his party came from the South and were unsympathetic to liberal causes.

The new president had a charismatic presence. He was able to voice his aims in eloquent yet understandable language that motivated his followers. During the campaign, he pointed to "uncharted areas of science and space, unsolved problems of peace and war, unconquered pockets of ignorance and prejudice, unanswered questions of poverty and surplus" that Americans must confront, for

# Recovering the Past

## Television

In the last 50 years, television has played an increasingly important part in American life, providing historians with another source of evidence about American culture and society in the recent past.

Television's popularity by the 1950s was the result of decades of experimentation dating back to the nineteenth century. In the 1930s, NBC installed a television station in the new Empire State Building in New York. With green makeup and purple lipstick to provide better visual contrast, actors began to perform before live cameras in studios. At the end of the decade, "Amos 'n' Andy," a popular radio show, was telecast, and as the 1940s began, Franklin D. Roosevelt became the first president to appear on television. World War II interrupted the development of television, as Americans relied on radio to bring them news. After the war, however, the commercial development of television quickly resumed. Assembly lines that had made electronic implements of war were now converted to consumer production, and thousands of new sets appeared on the market. The opening of Congress could be seen live in 1947; baseball coverage improved that same year owing to the zoom lens; children's shows like "Howdy Doody" made their debut; and "Meet the Press," a radio interview program, made the transition to television.

Although sports programs, variety shows hosted by Ed Sullivan and Milton Berle, TV dramas, and episodic series ("I Love Lucy" and "Gunsmoke," for example) dominated TV broadcasting in the 1950s, television soon became entwined with politics and public affairs. Americans saw Senator Joseph McCarthy for themselves in the televised Army-McCarthy hearings in 1954; his malevolent behavior on camera contributed to his downfall. The 1948 presidential nominating conventions were the first to be televised, but the use of TV to enhance the public image of politicians was most thoroughly developed by the fatherly Dwight D. Eisenhower and the charismatic John F. Kennedy.

In November 1963, people throughout the United States shared the tragedy of John Kennedy's assassination, sitting stunned before their sets trying to understand the events of his fateful Texas trip. The shock and sorrow of the American people were repeated in the spring of 1968 as they gazed in disbelief at the funerals of Martin Luther King, Jr., and Robert Kennedy. A year later, a quarter of the world's population watched as Neil Armstrong became the first man to set foot on the moon. In that same era, television played an important part in shaping impressions of the war in Vietnam. More and more Americans began to understand the nature and impact of the conflict from what they saw on TV.

This combination of visual entertainment and enlightenment made owning a television set virtually a necessity. By 1970, fully 95 percent of American households owned a TV set, a staggering increase from the 9 percent only 20 years earlier. Fewer families owned refrigerators or indoor toilets.

**Reflecting on the Past** The implications of the impact of television on American society are of obvious interest to historians. How has television affected other communications and entertainment industries, such as radio, newspapers, and movies? What do popular TV shows tell us about the values, interests, and tastes of the American people?

Perhaps most significant, what impact has TV had on the course of historical events like presidential campaigns, human relations, and wars? The pictures you see here come from the Kennedy-Nixon debates in the presidential campaign of 1960. The first picture shows the two candidates in the studio. The second picture shows a relaxed and energetic Kennedy staring directly into the TV camera. The third picture shows a taut and tense Nixon challenging the points made by his opponent. Which candidate seems to be speaking directly to the American people? Which candidate makes the better impression? Why? Polls of radio listeners taken after the first debate showed Nixon the winner; surveys of television viewers placed Kennedy in front. How do you account for this discrepancy?

The candidates squaring off in their debate. (AP/Wide World Photos)

John Kennedy (left) and Richard Nixon (right). (AP/Wide World Photos)

John Kennedy's energy and enthusiasm captured the imagination of Americans and people around the world, though few were aware of the physical ailments that affected him. He was fond of using this rocking chair in the White House, which he found comfortable for his ailing back. (Corbis)

"the New Frontier is here whether we seek it or not." He made the same point even more movingly in his inaugural address: "The torch has been passed to a new generation of Americans—born in this century, tempered by war, disciplined by a hard and bitter peace, proud of our ancient heritage." Many, like Paul Cowan whom we met at the start of the chapter, were inspired by Kennedy's concluding call to action: "And so, my fellow Americans: Ask not what your country can do for you—ask what you can do for your country."

For Kennedy, strong leadership was all-important. The president, he believed, "must serve as a catalyst, an energizer." Viewing himself as "tough-minded," he was determined to provide firm direction and play a leading role in creating the national agenda, just as Franklin Roosevelt had done.

Kennedy had talented assistants. On his staff were 15 Rhodes scholars and several famous authors. The secretary of state was Dean Rusk, a former member of the State Department who had then served as president of the Rockefeller Foundation. The secretary of defense was Robert S. McNamara, the highly successful president of the Ford Motor Company, who had used computer analysis to turn the company around.

Further contributing to Kennedy's attractive image were his glamorous wife Jacqueline and the glittering dinners the couple hosted for Nobel Prize winners, musicians, and artists. Energy, exuberance, and excitement filled the air. It seemed like King Arthur's Camelot, popularized in a Broadway musical in 1960.

## The New Frontier

Kennedy was committed to extending the welfare state by expanding the economy and enlarging social welfare programs. Regarding civil rights, Kennedy espoused liberal goals and social justice although his policies were limited (see Chapter 29). On the economic front, he tried to end the lingering recession by working with the business community, while controlling inflation at the same time.

These two goals conflicted when, in the spring of 1962, the large steel companies decided on a major price increase after steel unions had accepted a modest wage package. The angry president termed the price increases unjustifiable and on television charged that the firms pursued "private power and profit" rather than the public interest. Determined to force the steel companies to their knees, Kennedy pressed for executive and congressional action. In the end, the large companies capitulated, but they disliked Kennedy's heavy-handed approach and decided that this Democratic administration, like all the others, was anti-business. Six weeks after the steel crisis, the stock market plunged in the biggest drop since the Great Crash of 1929. Kennedy got the blame.

It now seemed doubly urgent to end the recession. Earlier a proponent of a balanced budget, Kennedy began to listen to liberal advisers who proposed a Keynesian approach. Budget deficits had promoted prosperity during World War II and might work in the same way in peacetime. By the summer of 1962, the president was convinced. In early 1963, he called for a $13.5 billion cut in corporate taxes over the next three years. That cut would cause a large deficit, but it would also provide capital that business leaders could spend to stimulate the economy and ultimately increase tax revenues.

Opposition mounted. Conservatives refused to accept the basic premise that deficits would stimulate economic growth. Some liberals claimed that it would be better to stimulate the economy by spending money to improve society rather than by cutting taxes and putting money in people's pockets. What good would it do, economist John Kenneth Galbraith wondered, to have "a few more dollars to spend if the air is too dirty to breathe, the water is too polluted to drink, the commuters are losing out in the struggle to get in and out of cities, the streets are filthy, and the schools are so bad that the young, perhaps wisely, stay away?" In Congress, where Democrats had thin majorities but still had to contend with conservative Southerners within the party, opponents pigeonholed the proposal in committee, and there it remained.

On other issues on the liberal agenda, Kennedy met similar resistance. He proposed an increased minimum wage, federal aid for education, medical care for the elderly, housing subsidies, and urban renewal, but the results were meager. While a scaled-down minimum wage hike passed, his call for federal aid to education foundered amid debates about bureaucratic control and the funding of segregated and parochial schools.

Kennedy was more successful in securing funds for space exploration. As first Alan Shepard and then John Glenn flew in space, Kennedy proposed that the United States commit itself to landing a man on the moon and returning him to earth before the end of the decade. Congress, caught up in the glamour of the proposal and worried about Soviet achievements in space, assented and increased funding of the National Aeronautics and Space Administration (NASA).

Kennedy also established the Peace Corps, which sent men and women to assist developing countries. Paul Cowan, introduced at the start of this chapter, was one of thousands of volunteers who hoped that they could share their liberal dreams.

If Kennedy's successes were modest, he had at least made commitments that could be broadened later. He had reaffirmed the importance of executive leadership in extending the boundaries of the welfare state. And he had committed himself to using modern economics to maintain fiscal stability. The nation was poised to achieve liberal goals.

# Change of Command

Facing reelection in 1964, Kennedy wanted not only to win the presidency for a second term but also to increase liberal Democratic strength in Congress. In November 1963, he went to Texas, hoping to unite the state's Democratic party for the upcoming election. Dallas, one of the stops on the trip, was reputed to be hostile to the administration. Now, on November 22, Kennedy had a chance to feel the pulse of the city for himself. Arriving at the airport, Henry González, a congressman accompanying the president in Texas, remarked jokingly, "Well, I'm taking my risks. I haven't got my steel vest yet." As the party entered the city in an open car, the president encountered friendly crowds. Suddenly shots rang out, and Kennedy slumped forward as bullets ripped through his head and throat. Mortally wounded, he died a short time later. Lee Harvey Oswald, the accused assassin, was himself killed a few days later by a minor underworld figure as he was being moved within the jail.

Americans were stunned. For days people stayed at home and watched endless television replays of the assassination and its aftermath. United around the event, members of an entire generation remembered where they had been when Kennedy was shot, just as an earlier generation recalled Pearl Harbor.

Vice President Lyndon Johnson became president. Less polished, Johnson was a more effective political leader than Kennedy and brought his own special skills and vision to the presidency.

Johnson was a man of elemental force. Always manipulative, he reminded people of a riverboat gambler, according to one White House aide. Though he desperately wanted to be loved, he was, as former secretary of state Dean Acheson once told him, "not a very likable man." A streak of vulgarity contributed to his earthy appeal but offended some of his associates. Asked once why he had not responded more sympathetically to a suggestion from Richard Nixon, he said to his friends in Congress, "Boys, I may not know much, but I know the difference between chicken shit and chicken salad."

Those qualities notwithstanding, he was successful in the passion of his life—politics. Schooled in Congress and influenced by FDR, Johnson was the most able legislator of the postwar years. As Senate majority leader, he became famous for his ability to get things done. Ceaseless in his search for information, tireless in his attention to detail, he knew the strengths and weaknesses of everyone he faced. The "Johnson treatment" became famous. He zeroed in, according to columnists Rowland Evans, Jr., and Robert Novak, "his face a scant millimeter from his target, his eyes widening and narrowing, his eyebrows rising and falling." He grabbed people by the lapels, made them listen, and usually got his way.

Johnson ran the Senate with tight control and established a credible record for himself and his party during the Eisenhower years. He was the Democrat most responsible for keeping liberal goals alive in a conservative time, as he tried to broaden his own appeal in a quest for the presidency. Unsuccessful in his bid for the White House in 1960, he took the second spot under JFK and helped Kennedy win the election. But then he went into eclipse. He felt useless and stifled in his new role and agreed with John Nance Garner, FDR's first vice president, who once observed that the office "wasn't worth a pitcher of warm spit."

Despite his own ambivalence about Kennedy, Johnson sensed the profound shock that gripped the United States after the assassination and was determined to utilize Kennedy's memory to achieve legislative success. Even more than Kennedy, he was willing to wield presidential power aggressively and to exploit the media to shape public opinion in pursuit of his vision of a society in which the comforts of life would be more widely shared and poverty would be eliminated once and for all.

## The Great Society in Action

Johnson had an expansive vision of the possibilities of reform. He began to develop the support he needed the day he took office. In his first public address, delivered to Congress and televised nationwide, he embraced Kennedy's liberal program. "All I have," he began in a measured tone, "I would have given gladly not to be standing here today." "Let us continue" was his theme.

Johnson resolved to secure what Kennedy had been unable to extract from Congress. Bills to reduce taxes and ensure civil rights were his most pressing priorities, but he was interested, too, in aiding public education, providing medical care for the aged, and eliminating poverty. By the spring of 1964, he had begun to use the phrase "Great Society" to describe his reform program.

Successful even before the election of 1964, his landslide victory over conservative Republican challenger Barry Goldwater of Arizona validated his approach. LBJ received 61 percent of the popular vote and an electoral tally of 486 to 52 and gained Democratic congressional majorities of 68–32 in the Senate and 295–140 in the House. Despite his defeat, Goldwater's candidacy reflected a growing conservatism within the Republican party and the ability of a grassroots group to organize a successful campaign in party primaries. It also drove moderate Republicans to vote Democratic and gave Johnson a far more impressive mandate than Kennedy had ever enjoyed.

Johnson knew how to get laws passed. He appointed task forces (which included legislators) to study problems and suggest solutions, worked with them to draft bills, and maintained close contact with congressional leaders through a sophisticated liaison staff. Not since the FDR years had there been such a coordinated effort.

Civil rights reform was LBJ's first legislative priority and an integral part of the Great Society program (see Chapter 29), but other measures were equally important in extending the boundaries of government action and bolstering the welfare state. Accepting the Keynesian theory that managed deficits could promote prosperity, Johnson pressed for a tax cut to stimulate the economy. If people had more money to spend, their purchases could have a significant impact. To gain conservative support, he agreed to hold down government spending. On one occasion, he applied such pressure that the author of an amendment ended up voting against his own proposal. Soon the tax bill passed.

With the tax cut in hand, the president pressed for the anti-poverty program that Kennedy had begun to plan. Such an effort was bold and unprecedented. In the Progressive era, at the turn of the century, some legislation had attempted to alleviate conditions associated with poverty. During the New Deal, FDR had proposed assisting the one-third of the nation that could not help itself. Now Johnson took a step that no president had taken before; in his 1964 State of the Union message, he declared "unconditional war on poverty in America."

The centerpiece of this utopian effort to eradicate poverty was the Economic Opportunity Act of 1964. It created an Office of Economic Opportunity (OEO) to provide education and training through programs such as the Job Corps for unskilled young people. VISTA (Volunteers in Service to America), patterned after the Peace Corps, offered assistance to America's poor, while Head Start tried to give disadvantaged children a chance to succeed in school. Assorted community action programs gave the poor a voice in improving their lot.

Aware of escalating medical-care costs, Johnson also proposed a medical assistance plan, which Truman and Kennedy had sought. Johnson succeeded where they had failed. To head off conservative attacks, the administration tied the Medicare measure to the Social Security system and limited the program to the elderly; Medicaid was for those on welfare and certain others who could not afford private insurance. The Medicare-Medicaid program was the most important extension of federally directed social benefits since the Social Security Act of 1935. By 1976 the two programs were paying for the medical costs of 20 percent of the American people.

Johnson was similarly successful in his effort to provide aid for elementary and secondary schools. Kennedy had met defeat when Catholics had insisted on assistance to parochial schools. Johnson, a Protestant, was able to deal with the ticklish religious question without charges of favoritism. His legislation allocated education money to the states based on the number of children from low-income families, which could then be used to assist deprived children in public as well as private schools.

In LBJ's expansive vision, the federal government would ensure that everyone shared in the promise of American life. As a result of his prodding, Congress created a Department of Housing and Urban Development in the Cabinet, gave rent supplements to the poor, and provided legal assistance for those who could not afford it. The scope of funding for higher education expanded, and artists and scholars were subsidized through the National Endowments for the Arts and Humanities—the first such government aid programs since the New Deal's WPA.

Johnson's administration also provided much-needed immigration reform. The Immigration Act of 1965 replaced the restrictive immigration policy, in place since 1924, limiting immigration severely and favoring northern Europeans. It raised the ceiling on immigration and opened the door to immigrants from Asia and Latin America, while exempting from the quotas family members of U.S. citizens and political refugees, including first Cuban and later Indochinese immigrants. This new and growing stream of immigration—largely from Asia and Latin America—created a population more diverse than it had been since the early decades of the twentieth century. The consequences of this new diversity were far-ranging and affected many areas of American life, from politics to public school classrooms to street signs.

The Great Society also reflected the stirring of the environmental movement. In 1962, naturalist Rachel Carson alerted the public to the dangers of pesticide poisoning and environmental pollution in her book *Silent Spring* (see Chapter 29). Though the chemical industry fought Carson, a special presidential advisory committee warned against widespread pesticide use. Johnson recognized the need to go further, dealing with caustic fumes in the air, lethal sludge in rivers and streams, and the steady disappearance of wildlife. The National Wilderness Preservation Act of 1964 set aside 9.1 million acres of wilderness. Lady Bird Johnson, the president's wife, led a beautification campaign to eliminate billboards and junkyards along highways, and Congress passed other measures to combat air and water pollution.

## A Sympathetic Supreme Court

With the addition of four new liberal justices appointed by Kennedy and Johnson, the Supreme Court promoted the liberal agenda. Under the leadership of Chief Justice Earl Warren, the Court followed the lead it had taken in the 1954 landmark civil rights case *Brown* v. *Board of Education* (see Chapter 29). Several decisions reaffirmed the Court's support of black rights, by moving against Jim Crow practices in other public establishments.

The Court also supported civil liberties. Where earlier judicial decisions had affirmed restrictions on members of the Communist party and radical groups, now the Court began to defend the rights of individuals with radical political views. Similarly, the Court sought to protect accused suspects from police harassment. In *Gideon* v. *Wainwright* (1963), the justices decided that poor defendants in serious cases had the right to free legal counsel. In *Escobedo* v. *Illinois* (1964), they ruled that a suspect had to be given access to an attorney during questioning. In *Miranda* v. *Arizona* (1966), they ordered that people in custody had to be warned that statements extracted by the police could be used against them and that they could remain silent.

Other decisions similarly broke new ground. *Baker* v. *Carr* (1962) opened the way to reapportionment of state legislative bodies, according to the standard, defined a year later by Justice William O. Douglas, as "one person, one vote." This crucial ruling helped break the political control of lightly populated rural districts in many state assemblies and made the U.S. House of Representatives much more responsive to urban and suburban issues. And the Court outraged conservatives by ruling against prayer in the public schools and holding that obscenity laws could no longer restrict allegedly pornographic material if it had "redeeming social value."

## The Great Society Under Attack

Supported by healthy economic growth, the Great Society worked for a few years as Johnson had hoped. After the tax cut's passage, the gross national product (GNP) rose steadily—7.1 percent in 1964, 8.1 percent in 1965, and 9.5 percent in 1966—while the budget deficit shrank, unemployment fell, and inflation remained under control. Medical programs provided basic security for the old and the poor. Schools were built and teachers' salaries increased.

Yet Johnson's Great Society dream proved illusory. Some programs promised too much, and the administration's rhetorical oversell led to disillusionment when problems failed to disappear. Other programs, planned in haste, simply did not work. Never were the massive sums allocated to these programs that some argued were necessary to make them successful.

Factionalism also plagued the Great Society. Johnson had reconstituted the old Democratic coalition in his triumph in 1964. But diverse interests within the coalition soon clashed. Conservative white southerners and blue-collar white northerners felt threatened by the government's support of civil rights. Urban bosses, long the backbone of the Democratic party, objected to grassroots participation of the urban poor, which threatened their own control.

From across the political spectrum came criticisms of the Great Society, which had never generated widespread enthusiasm. Conservatives attacked the centralization of authority and the government's increased role in defining the national welfare. They also questioned whether the poor, lacking a broad vision of national needs, should be involved in shaping reform programs. Even middle-class Americans, generally supportive of liberal goals, sometimes grumbled that the government neglected them in favor of the underprivileged. Meanwhile the radical left attacked the Great Society as a warmed-over New Deal whose real intent was to indoctrinate the working-class poor with middle-class values, while making no serious effort to redistribute income.

The Vietnam War (discussed in Chapter 27) dealt the Great Society a fatal blow. LBJ wanted both to fight the war and to pursue his domestic reform programs, but pursuing these goals simultaneously produced serious inflation. The economy was already booming as a result of the tax cut and the spending for reform. As military expenditures increased, the productive system of the country could not keep up with demand. When Johnson refused to raise taxes, trying to hide the costs of the war, inflation spiraled out of control. Congress finally got into the act and slashed Great Society programs. As hard economic choices became increasingly necessary, many decided the country could no longer afford social reform on the scale Johnson had proposed.

## THE DECLINE OF LIBERALISM

After eight years of Democratic rule, many Americans became frustrated with liberalism. They questioned the liberal agenda and the government's ability to solve social problems. The war in Vietnam had polarized the country and fragmented the Democratic party. Capitalizing on the alienation sparked by the war, Republicans resolved to scale down the commitment to social change. Like Eisenhower,

## Roots of Selected Great Society Programs

| Progressive Period | New Deal | Great Society |
|---|---|---|
| Settlement house activity of Jane Addams and others | Relief efforts to ease unemployment (FERA, WPA) | Poverty programs (OEO) |
| Efforts to clean up slums (tenement house laws) | Housing program | Rehabilitation of slums through Model Cities program |
| Progressive party platform calling for federal accident, old-age, and unemployment insurance | Social security system providing unemployment compensation and old-age pensions | Medical care for the aged through social security (Medicare) |
| Activity to break up monopolies and regulate business | Regulation of utility companies | Regulation of highway safety and transportation |
| Efforts to regulate working conditions and benefits | Establishment of standards for working conditions and minimum wage | Raising of minimum wage |
| Efforts to increase literacy and spread education at all levels | Efforts to keep college students in school through NYA | Assistance to elementary, secondary, and higher education |
| Theodore Roosevelt's efforts at wilderness preservation | Conservation efforts (CCC, TVA planning) | Safeguarding of wilderness lands |
| Establishment of federal income tax | Tax reform to close loopholes and increase taxes for the wealthy | Tax cut to stimulate business activity |
| Theodore Roosevelt's overtures to Booker T. Washington | Discussion (but not passage) of antilynching legislation | Civil rights measures to ban discrimination in public accommodations and to guarantee right to vote |

they accepted some social programs as necessary for the well-being of modern America, but they were determined to cut spending and the federal bureaucracy. And they were intent on paying more attention to white, middle-class Americans, who disliked the mounting social disorder they saw as a consequence of rapid social change and resented the government's perceived favoritism toward the poor and dispossessed.

## The Election of 1968

Richard Nixon had pursued his dream of the White House ever since his days as Eisenhower's vice president. He had failed in his first bid in 1960, and two years later his loss in a race for governor of California seemed to kill his political career. But after the Goldwater disaster of 1964 he made a comeback. By 1968 he had a good shot at the presidency again.

In the election, Nixon faced Vice President Hubert H. Humphrey. The war in Vietnam had fractured the Democratic party and made Johnson so unpopular that he chose not to run for reelection. The turbulent Democratic convention in Chicago, where police ran amok on nationwide TV, clubbing demonstrators, reporters, and bystanders alike, helped Nixon. But he faced a serious threat from

Policemen attacked demonstrators and bystanders alike at the turbulent Democratic convention of 1968. The senseless violence, pictured in graphic detail on national television, undermined the Democratic party and helped Nixon win the election. (Bettmann/CORBIS)

Governor George C. Wallace of Alabama, the third-party candidate adept at exploiting social and racial tensions. Appealing to northern working-class voters as well as southern whites, Wallace characterized those who wanted to reform American life as "left-wing theoreticians, briefcase-totin' bureaucrats, ivory-tower guideline writers, bearded anarchists, smart-aleck editorial writers and pointy-headed professors."

Nixon addressed the same constituency, calling it the "silent majority." Capitalizing on the dismay these Americans felt over campus disruptions and inner-city riots and appealing to latent racism, he promised law and order and called the Great Society a costly mistake. Yet he avoided shrill criticism himself, and left the sharpest attacks to his running-mate, Governor Spiro Agnew of Maryland, who sounded like the Nixon of old.

Nixon received 43 percent of the popular vote, not quite 1 percent more than Humphrey, with Wallace capturing the rest. But it was enough to give the Republicans a majority in the electoral college and Nixon the presidency at last. Sixty-two percent of all white voters (but only 12 percent of black voters) cast their votes for either Nixon or Wallace, suggesting the covert racial appeal had worked. But the Democrats won both houses of Congress.

A complex, remote man, Nixon was careful to conceal his private self. There was, one of his aides noted, "a mean side to his nature" that he sought to keep from public view. Awkward and humorless, he was most comfortable alone or with a few wealthy friends.

Nixon understood the psychology of politics in the electronic age. "In the modern presidency," he believed, "concern for image must rank with concern for substance." In public he posed as the defender of American morality, but in private he was frequently coarse and profane. Earlier in his career he had been labeled "Tricky Dick" for his apparent willingness to do anything to advance his career. In subsequent years he had tried to create the appearance of a "new Nixon," but to many he still appeared to be a mechanical man, always calculating his next step.

Philosophically, Nixon disagreed with the liberal faith in federal planning and wanted to decentralize social policy. But he agreed with his liberal predecessors that the presidency ought to be the engine of the political system. Faced with a Congress dominated by Democrats who allocated money for programs he opposed, he impounded—refused to spend—funds Congress had authorized. Later commentators would see the Nixon years as the height of what they came to call the "imperial presidency."

Nixon's cabinet appointees were white, male Republicans. For the most part, however, the president relied on other White House staff members to make policy. In domestic affairs, one of his most important advisers was Daniel Patrick Moynihan, a Harvard professor of government (and a Democrat). In foreign affairs, the talented and ambitious Henry A. Kissinger, another Harvard government professor, was his chief adviser and later secretary of state.

Another tier of White House officials—none with policy-making experience but all intensely loyal to him—insulated Nixon from the outside world and carried out his commands. Advertising executive H. R. Haldeman became chief of staff and lawyer John Ehrlichman soon rose to the post of chief domestic adviser. John Mitchell, a tough attorney from Nixon's law office, became his fast friend, daily confidante, and attorney general.

## The Republican Agenda

Accepting the basic contours of the welfare state, Nixon sought to scale it back. His goal was "to reverse the flow of power and resources" away from the federal government and back toward state and local governments.

Despite initial reservations, Nixon proved willing to use economic tools to maintain stability. When he assumed office the economy was faltering, beset by inflation that largely resulted from the Vietnam War. Nixon responded by reducing government spending and pressing the Federal Reserve Board to raise interest rates. Although parts of the conservative plan worked, a mild recession struck in 1969 and 1970, and inflation continued to rise. Realizing the political dangers of pursuing this policy, Nixon shifted course, imposing wage and price controls to stop inflation and using monetary and fiscal policies to stimulate the economy. After his reelection in 1972, however, he lifted the controls and inflation resumed.

A number of factors besides the Vietnam War contributed to the troubling price spiral. Eager to court the farm vote, the administration made a large wheat sale to the Soviet Union in 1972—a major miscalculation, because with insufficient wheat left for the American market, grain prices soared. Between 1971 and 1974, farm prices rose 66 percent. The most critical factor in disrupting the economy, though, was an Arab oil embargo. American economic expansion had rested on cheap energy just as American patterns of life had depended on inexpensive gasoline. Although the Organization of Petroleum Exporting Countries (OPEC) had slowly raised oil prices in the early 1970s, the 1973 Arab-Israeli war led Saudi Arabia to end oil shipments to Israel's ally, the United States. Other OPEC nations continued to supply oil but quadrupled their prices. Dependent on imports for one-third of their energy needs, Americans faced shortages and skyrocketing prices. When the embargo ended in 1974, prices remained high.

The oil crisis affected all aspects of American economic life. A loaf of bread that had cost 28 cents in the early 1970s jumped to 89 cents, and automobiles cost 72 percent more in 1978 than they had in 1973. Accustomed to filling up their gas

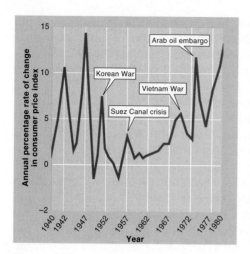

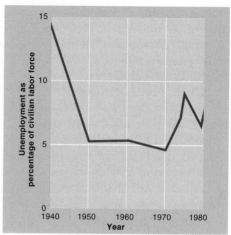

RATE OF INFLATION, 1940–1980   Inflation often accompanied military spending in the postwar years. In the early 1970s, the Arab oil embargo contributed to an even higher rate. (*Source:* U.S. Bureau of the Census.)

UNEMPLOYMENT RATE, 1940–1980   The unemployment rate, which had fallen dramatically during World War II and remained relatively constant in the 1950s and 1960s, rose at the same time inflation increased in the 1970s. (*Source:* U.S. Bureau of Labor Statistics.)

tanks for only a few dollars, Americans were shocked at paying 65 cents a gallon. In 1974, inflation reached 11 percent. Then, as higher energy prices drove consumers to cut back on purchases, the nation entered a recession. Unemployment climbed to 9 percent, the highest level since the 1930s.

As economic growth and stability eluded him, Nixon tried to overhaul the rapidly expanding and expensive welfare programs. Critics claimed that welfare was inefficient and that benefits discouraged people from seeking work. Nixon recognized the conservative tide growing in the Sun Belt, where many voters wanted cutbacks in what they viewed as excessive government programs. But he also wanted to create a new Republican coalition by winning over traditionally Democratic blue-collar workers with reassurances that the Republicans would not dismantle the parts of the welfare state on which they relied.

At the urging of domestic adviser Daniel Moynihan, Nixon endorsed an expensive but feasible new program. The Family Assistance Plan would have guaranteed a minimum yearly stipend of $1,600 to a family of four, with food stamps providing about $800 more. To crack down on "welfare cheaters" and encourage welfare recipients to work, all participants would have to register for job training and accept employment when found. But the plan was attacked by liberals as too little and by conservatives as too much. It died in the Senate.

As he struggled with the economy and what many called the "welfare mess," Nixon irritated liberals with his pursuit of "law and order." Political protest, rising crime rates, increased drug use, and permissive attitudes toward sex all created a growing backlash among the working class and many middle-class Americans (see Chapter 29). Nixon decided to use government power to silence disruption and strengthen his conservative constituency.

Part of the administration's campaign involved denouncing disruptive elements. Nixon lashed out at demonstrators, at one point calling student activists "bums." But he generally relied on his vice president as the hatchet man. And Agnew had a sure eye for the jugular, branding opponents (students in particular) "ideological eunuchs" who made up an "effete corps of impudent snobs."

Nixon also attacked liberalism by lambasting the communications industry. Well aware of the power of radio and television and able to use it effectively, Nixon believed the media represented the "Eastern establishment," which he felt hated him. He challenged the television networks, with Agnew spearheading the attack.

The third and strongest part of Nixon's plan was Attorney General John Mitchell's effort to demonstrate administration support for the values of citizens upset by domestic upheavals. Mitchell sought enhanced powers for a war against crime, sometimes at the expense of constitutional liberties. This included reshaping the Supreme Court, which Republican leaders accused of being excessively concerned with the rights of lawbreakers. During his first term, Nixon had the opportunity to fill four Court vacancies, and he nominated men who shared his views. His first choice—the moderate Warren E. Burger as chief justice to replace the retiring liberal Earl Warren—was confirmed quickly. His next nominations, however, reflected Nixon's aggressively conservative approach. Appealing to white southerners, he selected two judges with racial biases so strong or limitations so great that the Senate refused to confirm them. Nixon then appointed Harry Blackmun, Lewis F. Powell, Jr., and William Rehnquist, all able and qualified—and all inclined to tilt the Court in a more conservative direction.

Not surprisingly, the Court gradually shifted to the right. It narrowed defendants' rights and slowed the process of liberalization by upholding pornography laws if they reflected community standards. It supported Nixon's assault on the media by ruling that journalists did not have the right to refuse to answer questions for a grand jury, even if they had promised their sources confidentiality. On other

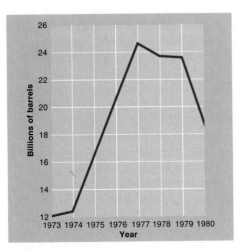

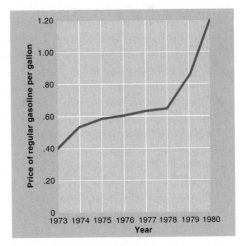

**OIL IMPORTS, 1973–1980**  American reliance on foreign oil increased in the mid-1970s, until the United States tried to respond to price increases by reducing reliance on imports. (*Source:* U.S. Energy Information Administration.)

**GASOLINE PRICES, 1973–1980**  Gasoline prices rose steadily in the years following the Arab oil embargo and affected the entire American economy. (*Source:* U.S. Energy Information Administration.)

questions, however, the Court did not always act as the president had hoped. In the controversial 1973 *Roe* v. *Wade* decision, the Court legalized abortion, stating that women's rights included the right to control their own bodies. This decision was one that feminists, a group hardly supported by the president, had ardently sought.

## The Watergate Affair

A solidly Democratic Congress blocked the administration's legislative initiatives. Nixon sought to end the stalemate by winning a second term and sweeping Republican majorities into both houses of Congress. But his efforts to gain a decisive victory at the polls led to excesses that brought his demise.

Nixon's reelection campaign was even better organized than the effort four years earlier. His fiercely loyal aides were prepared to do anything to win. Special counsel Charles W. Colson described himself as a "flag-waving, kick-'em-in-the-nuts, anti-press, anti-liberal Nixon fanatic" and had earlier drawn up an "enemies list" of prominent anti-administration figures. White House counsel John Dean defined his job as finding a way to "use the available federal machinery to screw our political enemies." Commands were carried out by such men as E. Howard Hunt, a former CIA agent and specialist in "dirty tricks," and G. Gordon Liddy, a onetime member of the FBI who prided himself on a willingness to do anything without flinching.

The Committee to Re-elect the President (CREEP) was led by John Mitchell, who had resigned as attorney general. Its massive fund-raising drive tried to collect as much money as possible before contributions had to be reported under a new campaign-finance law. That money could be used for any purpose, including dirty tricks to disrupt the opposition's campaign. Other funds financed an intelligence branch within CREEP, headed by Liddy and including Hunt.

Early in 1972, Liddy proposed an elaborate scheme to wiretap the phones of various Democrats and disrupt their convention. Twice Mitchell refused to go along with what he saw as too risky and expensive an idea. Finally he approved a less ambitious plan to tap phones at the Democratic National Committee's headquarters in the Watergate apartment complex in Washington, D.C. Mitchell, formerly the nation's top law enforcement official, had authorized breaking the law.

The wiretapping attempt took place on the evening of June 16, 1972, and ended with the arrest of those involved. Their connection to the Republican party could incriminate the reelection campaign. Top officials of the Nixon reelection team had to decide quickly what to do.

Reelection remained the most pressing priority, so Nixon's aides played down the matter and used federal resources to stifle an investigation. When the FBI traced the money carried by the burglars to CREEP, the president authorized the CIA to call off the FBI on the grounds that national security was at stake. Though not privy to planning the break-in, the president was now party to the cover-up. In the succeeding months, he authorized payment of hush money to silence the burglars. Members of the administration, including Mitchell, perjured themselves to shield the top officials who were involved.

Nixon trounced Democrat George McGovern in the election of 1972, receiving 61 percent of the popular vote. In a clear sign of the collapse of the Democra-

Although Nixon steadfastly denied his complicity in the Watergate affair, his tape recordings of White House conversations told a different story. In this classic "Doonesbury" cartoon from September 17, 1973, Garry Trudeau notes Nixon's efforts to head off the investigation. (Doonesbury © 1973 G. B. Trudeau. Reprinted with permission of Universal Press Syndicate. All rights reserved.)

tic coalition, 70 percent of southern voters cast their ballots for Nixon. The president, however, failed to gain the congressional majorities necessary to support his programs.

When the Watergate burglars were brought to trial after the election, they pleaded guilty and were sentenced to jail, but the case refused to die. Judge John Sirica was not satisfied that justice had yet been done. Meanwhile, two zealous reporters, Bob Woodward and Carl Bernstein of the *Washington Post*, were following a trail of leads on their own. Slowly they recognized who else was involved.

The unraveling continued. The Senate Select Committee on Presidential Campaign Activities undertook an investigation, and one of the convicted burglars testified to White House involvement. Newspaper stories generated further leads, and the Senate hearings in turn provided new material for the press. Eventually Nixon decided that Haldeman and Ehrlichman, his two closest aides, must be sacrificed to save his own neck.

In May 1973, the Senate committee began televised public hearings, watched by millions of Americans. John Dean, to save himself, testified that Nixon knew about the cover-up, and other staffers revealed a host of illegal activities at the White House: money paid to the burglars; State Department documents forged to smear a previous administration; wiretaps used to stop top-level leaks. The most electrifying disclosure was that the president had installed a secret taping system that recorded all conversations in his office. Tapes could verify or disprove the growing rumors that Nixon had been party to the cover-up.

In an effort to demonstrate his own honesty, Nixon appointed Harvard law professor Archibald Cox as a special prosecutor. But when Cox tried to gain access to the tapes, Nixon first resisted and finally fired him. Nixon's popularity plummeted, and even the appointment of another special prosecutor, Leon Jaworski, did not help. More and more Americans now believed that the president had played at least some part in the cover-up. Congress began considering impeachment.

The first steps, in accordance with constitutional mandate, took place in the House of Representatives. The House Judiciary Committee, made up of 21 Democrats and 17 Republicans, began to debate the impeachment case in late July

1974. By sizable tallies, it voted to impeach the president on the grounds of obstruction of justice, abuse of power, and refusal to obey a congressional subpoena to turn over his tapes. A full House of Representatives vote still had to occur, and the Senate would have to conduct a trial and convict the president before removal could take place. But Nixon saw the handwriting on the wall.

After a brief delay, on August 5 Nixon obeyed a Supreme Court ruling and released the tapes. Besides a suspicious 18 1/2-minute gap, they contained the "smoking gun"—clear evidence of his complicity in the cover-up. Four days later, on August 9, 1974, the extraordinary episode came to an end, as Nixon became the first American president ever to resign.

The Watergate affair seemed disturbing evidence that the balance of power in the federal government had disappeared. As the scandal wound down, many questioned the centralization of power in the American political system and cited the "imperial presidency" as the cause of recent abuses. Others simply lost faith in the presidency. On the heels of Lyndon Johnson's lying to the American people about Vietnam, the Watergate affair contributed to the cumulative disillusionment with politics in Washington and to the steady decrease in political participation. Barely half of those eligible to vote bothered to go to the polls in the presidential elections of 1976, 1980, and 1984. Even fewer cast ballots in nonpresidential contests.

## Gerald Ford: Caretaker President

When Nixon resigned in disgrace, he was succeeded by Gerald Ford. An unpretentious middle-American Republican who believed in traditional virtues, Ford became vice president in 1973 when Spiro Agnew resigned in disgrace for accepting bribes. The new president acknowledged that "I am a Ford, not a Lincoln."

More important were his views about public policy. Throughout his tenure in Congress, Ford had voted according to the Republican convictions he shared with his Michigan constituents. Over the years he had opposed federal aid to education, the poverty program, and mass transit. He had voted for civil rights measures only when the weaker substitutes he favored had gone down to defeat. Like his predecessor, he was determined to stop the liberal advances promoted by the Democrats in the 1960s.

Ford faced a daunting task. After Watergate, Washington was in turmoil. Americans wondered whether any politician could be trusted. The new president had to use his authority to restore national confidence at a time when the misuse of presidential power itself had precipitated the crisis.

Ford worked quickly to restore trust in the government. He emphasized conciliation and compromise, and he promised to cooperate both with Congress and with American citizens. The nation responded gratefully.

But the new feeling did not last long. Ford weakened his base of support by pardoning Nixon barely a month after his resignation. His decidedly conservative bent often threw him into confrontation with a Democratic Congress. Economic problems proved most pressing in 1974, as inflation, fueled by oil price increases, hit 11 percent a year, unemployment stood at 7.2 percent, and GNP declined. Home construction slackened and interest rates rose while stock prices fell. Nixon, preoccupied with the Watergate crisis, had been unable to curb rising inflation and unemployment. Not since Franklin Roosevelt took office in the depths of the Great Depression had a new president faced economic difficulties so severe.

Like Hoover 45 years before, Ford hoped to restore confidence and persuade the public that conditions would improve with patience and goodwill. But his campaign to cajole Americans to "Whip Inflation Now" voluntarily failed dismally. At last convinced of the need for strong governmental action, the administration introduced a tight-money policy to halt inflation. The result was the worst recession since the Depression, with unemployment peaking at 9 percent in 1975. In response, Congress pushed for an anti-recession spending program. Recognizing political reality, Ford endorsed a multibillion-dollar tax cut coupled with higher unemployment benefits. The economy made a modest recovery, although inflation and unemployment remained high, and federal deficits soared.

Ford's dilemma was that his belief in limited presidential involvement set him against liberals who argued for strong executive leadership to make the welfare state work. When he failed to take the initiative, Congress intervened, and the two branches of government clashed. Ford vetoed numerous bills, including those creating a consumer protection agency and expanding programs in education, housing, and health. Congress overrode a higher percentage of vetoes than at any time since the presidency of Franklin Pierce more than a century before.

## The Carter Interlude

In the election of 1976, the nation's bicentennial year, Ford faced Jimmy Carter, former governor of Georgia. Appealing to voters distrustful of political leadership, Carter portrayed himself as an outsider. He made a virtue of not being from Washington and of not being a lawyer. Carter's quest for the Democratic nomination benefited from reforms that increased the significance of primary elections in selecting a presidential candidate and decreased the influence of party professionals. Assisted by public relations experts, he effectively used the media, especially television, to bypass party machines and establish a direct electronic relationship with voters.

Most elements of the old Democratic coalition came together once again, as the Democrats profited from the fallout of the Watergate affair. Carter won a 50 to 48 percent majority of the popular vote and a 297 to 240 tally in the Electoral College. He did well with members of the working class, African Americans, and Catholics. He won most of the South, heartening to the Democrats after Nixon's gains there. Racial voting differences continued, however, as Carter attracted less than half of all white voters but an overwhelming majority of black voters.

Carter stood in stark contrast to recent occupants of the White House. He was a peanut farmer who shared the rural South's values. He was also a graduate of the Naval Academy, trained as a manager and an engineer. A modest man, he was uncomfortable with the pomp and incessant political activity in Washington. He hoped to diminish the presidency's imperial trappings.

Initially, voters saw Carter as a reform Democrat committed to his party's liberal goals. When he had accepted the Democratic nomination, he had called for an end to race and sex discrimination. He had challenged the "political and

# Timeline

| | |
|---|---|
| **1946** Employment Act | **1968** Robert F. Kennedy assassinated |
| **1947** Taft-Hartley Act | Police and protesters clash at Democratic national convention |
| **1948** "Dixiecrat" party formed | Richard Nixon elected president |
| Truman defeats Dewey | **1972** Nixon reelected |
| **1949** Truman launches Fair Deal | **1973** Watergate hearings in Congress |
| **1952** Dwight D. Eisenhower elected president | Spiro Agnew resigns as vice president |
| **1956** Eisenhower reelected | **1974** OPEC price increases |
| **1960** John F. Kennedy elected president | Inflation hits 11 percent |
| **1962** JFK confronts steel companies | Unemployment reaches 7.2 percent |
| **1963** Kennedy assassinated; Lyndon B. Johnson becomes president | Nixon resigns; Gerald Ford becomes president |
| **1964** Economic Opportunity Act initiates War on Poverty | Ford pardons Nixon |
| Johnson reelected president | **1975** Unemployment reaches 9 percent |
| **1965** Department of Housing and Urban Development established | **1976** Jimmy Carter elected president |
| Elementary and Secondary Education Act | **1977** Carter energy program |

economic elite" in America and sought a new approach to providing for the poor, old, and weak.

But Carter was hardly the old-line liberal for whom some Democrats had hoped. Though he called himself a populist, his political philosophy and priorities were never clear. Critics charged that he had no legislative strategy. Rather, they said with some truth, he responded to problems haphazardly and failed to provide firm direction. His stance as an outsider, touted during the campaign, led him to ignore traditional political channels when he assumed power. He became mired in detail, losing sight of larger issues. Like Herbert Hoover, he was a technocrat when liberals wanted a visionary to lead the country out of hard times.

Carter gave liberals some hope at first as he accepted deficit spending, only to disappoint them when the economy failed to improve. As the Federal Reserve increased the money supply to help meet mounting deficits, which reached peacetime records in these years, inflation rose to about 10 percent a year. Seeking to reduce inflation in 1979, Carter slowed down the economy by reducing spending, and cut the deficit slightly. Contraction of the money supply led to greater unemployment and many small-business failures. Budget cuts fell largely on social programs and distanced Carter from reform-minded Democrats who had supported him three years before. Yet even that effort to arrest growing deficits was not enough. When the budget released in early 1980 still showed high spending levels, the financial community reacted strongly. Bond prices fell, and interest rates rose dramatically.

Similarly, Carter disappointed liberals by failing to construct an effective energy policy. OPEC had been boosting oil prices rapidly since 1973. Americans began to resent their dependence on foreign oil—over 40 percent was being imported by the end of the decade—and clamored for energy self-sufficiency. Carter responded in April 1977 with a comprehensive energy program, which he called the "moral equivalent of war," only to see critics ridicule it by using the acronym MEOW. Never an effective leader in working with the legislative branch, Carter watched his proposals bog down in Congress for 26 months. Eventually, the program committed the nation to move from oil dependence to reliance on coal, possibly even on sun and wind, and established a new synthetic-fuel corporation. Nuclear power, another alternative, seemed less attractive as costs rose and accidents, like the frightening one at Three Mile Island, occurred.

Carter further upset liberals by beginning deregulation—the removal of governmental controls in economic life. Arguing that restrictions established over the past century stifled competition and increased consumer costs, he supported decontrol of oil and natural gas prices to spur production. He also deregulated the railroad, trucking, and airline industries.

Liberals were disappointed as the 1970s ended. Their hopes for a stronger commitment to a welfare state had been dashed and conservatives had the upper hand. Despite a tenuous Democratic hold on the presidency, liberalism was in decline.

❧ ❧ ❧ ❧

# CONCLUSION

## *Political Readjustment*

The course of public policy shifted significantly in the post–World War II years. In the late 1940s and 1950s, American leaders took the first steps toward consolidating the welfare state that Franklin Roosevelt had begun to create in the decade before. In the 1960s, liberal Democrats went even further, as they pressed for large-scale government intervention to meet the social and economic problems that accompanied the modern industrial age. They were inspired by John Kennedy's rhetoric and saw the triumph of their approach in Lyndon Johnson's Great Society, as the nation strengthened its commitment to a capitalist welfare state. When the Democratic party became impaled on the Vietnam War and lost the presidency, the Republicans began dismantling the Great Society programs. While accepting some provisions of the modern welfare state, they objected to the aggressive liberal effort to make the government the major player in the political game and took exception to many of the programs aimed at the poor.

Most Americans, like Paul Cowan, whom we met at the start of this chapter, embraced the message of John Kennedy and the New Frontier in the 1960s and endorsed the liberal approach. But over time, they began to question the tenets of liberalism as the economy faltered, as hard economic choices had to be made, and as the country became mired in Vietnam. Republicans challenging Democratic priorities gained the upper hand and disillusioned liberals like Cowan wondered if their approach could ever succeed.

## Discovering U.S. History Online

*John Fitzgerald Kennedy*   http://www.ipl.org/ref/POTUS/jfkennedy.html
This site contains basic factual data about Kennedy's election and presidency, speeches, and online biographies.

*The Kennedy Assassination*   http://mcadams.posc.mu.edu/home.htm
This well-organized site has images, essays, and photos on the assassination.

*Lyndon Baines Johnson*   http://www.ipl.org/ref/POTUS/lbjohnson.html
This site contains basic factual data about Johnson's election and presidency, speeches, and online biographies.

*Richard Milhous Nixon*   http://www.ipl.org/ref/POTUS/rmnixon.html
This site contains basic factual data about Nixon's election and presidency, speeches, and online biographies.

*Watergate 25*   http://www.washingtonpost.com/wp-srv/national/longterm/watergate/front.htm
This site features a chronology, images, searchable articles, and a good deal of background information about the burglary and its consequences.

*Constitutional Issues: Watergate and the Constitution*
http://www.nara.gov/education/teaching/watergate/watergat.html
From the National Archives teaching materials, this site has a good chronology of Watergate and documents the pros and cons of seeking an indictment against former president Richard Nixon.

*Gerald Rudolph Ford*   http://www.ipl.org/ref/POTUS/grford.html
This site contains basic factual data about Ford's presidency, speeches, and online biographies.

*James Earl Carter, Jr.*   http://www.ipl.org/ref/POTUS/jecarter.html
This site contains basic factual data about Carter's election and presidency, speeches, and online biographies.

*Giant Leap*   http://www.cnn.com/TECH/specials/apollo/
This CNN site commemorates the 30th anniversary of the 1969 moonwalk and tells the story of NASA and the ongoing space program.

## Fiction and Film

Allen Drury, *Advise and Consent* (1959) is a novel about Washington politics, complete with blackmail and demagoguery; Barbara Garson, *MacBird* (1966) is a play, patterned loosely after *Macbeth*, that pokes fun at the overarching ambitions of Lyndon Johnson.

*All the President's Men* (1976) is the film (based on the book of the same name) of the effort by *Washington Post* reporters Bob Woodward and Carl Bernstein to find the truth about the Watergate scandal; *Network* (1976) is a film about the problems and abuses of television journalism.

## Recommended Reading

### The Origins of the Welfare State
Edward D. Berkowitz and Kim McQuaid, *Creating the Welfare State: The Political Economy of 20th Century Reform* (1994); Jacqueline Jones, *The Dispossessed: America's Underclasses from the Civil War to the Present* (1992); Michael B. Katz, *In the Shadow of the Poorhouse: A Social History of Welfare in America*, 10th anniv. ed. (1997) and *The Undeserving Poor: From the War on Poverty to the War on Welfare* (1990); Charles

Murray, *Losing Ground: American Social Policy, 1950–1980*, 10th anniv. ed. (1995); James T. Patterson, *America's Struggle Against Poverty: 1900–1994* (1995); Frances F. Piven and Richard A. Cloward, eds., *Regulating the Poor: The Functions of Public Welfare*, 2nd ed. (1993); Margaret Weir, Ann Shola Orloff, and Theda Skocpol, *The Politics of Social Policy in the United States* (1988).

Erik Barnouw, *Tube of Plenty: The Evolution of American Television*, 2nd rev. ed. (1990); James L. Baughman, *The Republic of Mass Culture* (1992); Todd Gitlin, *The Whole World Is Watching: Mass Media in the Making and Unmaking of the New Left* (1980); Cecelia Tichi, *Electronic Hearth; Creating an American Television Culture* (1991).

Robert J. Donovan, *Conflict and Crisis: The Presidency of Harry S Truman, 1945–1948* (1977) and *Tumultuous Years: The Presidency of Harry S. Truman* (1982); Robert H. Ferrell, *Harry S. Truman and the Modern American Presidency* (1998); Alonzo L. Hamby, *Man of the People: A Life of Harry S. Truman* (1995); David McCullough, *Truman* (1992); Harry S. Truman, *Memoirs*, 2 vols. (1955, 1956).

Craig Allen, *Eisenhower and the Mass Media: Peace, Prosperity, and Prime-Time TV* (1993); Stephen E. Ambrose, *Eisenhower: The President* (1984) and *Eisenhower: Soldier and President* (1990); Dwight D. Eisenhower, *Mandate for Change, 1953–1956* (1963) and *Waging Peace* (1965); Fred I. Greenstein, *The Hidden-Hand Presidency: Eisenhower as Leader* (1982); Chester J. Pach, Jr., and Elmo Richardson, *The Presidency of Dwight D. Eisenhower* (1991).

### The High-Water Mark of Liberalism

Terry H. Anderson, *The Movement and the Sixties: Protest in America from Greensboro to Wounded Knee* (1995); David Farber, *The Age of Great Dreams: America in the 1960s* (1994); Todd Gitlin, *The Sixties: Years of Hope, Days of Rage* (1987); Godfrey Hodgson, *America in Our Time* (1976); James L. Sundquist, *Politics and Policy: The Eisenhower, Kennedy, and Johnson Years* (1968).

James N. Giglio, *The Presidency of John F. Kennedy* (1991); Nigel Hamilton, *JFK: Reckless Youth* (1992); Seymour M. Hersh, *The Dark Side of Camelot* (1997); Herbert S. Parmet, *Jack: The Struggles of John F. Kennedy* (1980) and *JFK: The Presidency of John F. Kennedy* (1983); Richard Reeves, *President Kennedy: Profile of Power* (1993); Thomas C. Reeves, *A Question of Character: A Life of John F. Kennedy* (1991); Arthur M. Schlesinger, Jr., *A Thousand Days: John F. Kennedy in the White House* (1965); Theodore C. Sorensen, *Kennedy* (1965).

Michael R. Bechloss, ed., *Taking Charge: The Johnson White House Tapes, 1963–1964* (1997); Robert Dallek, *Lone Star Rising: Lyndon Johnson and His Times* (1990) and *Flawed Giant: Lyndon Johnson and His Times, 1961–1973* (1998); Robert A. Divine, ed., *Exploring the Johnson Years* (1981), *The Johnson Years, Volume Two: Vietnam, the Environment, and Science* (1984), and *The Johnson Years: LBJ at Home and Abroad* (1994); Lyndon Johnson, *The Vantage Point: Perspectives of the Presidency* (1971).

### The Decline of Liberalism

Mary C. Brennan, *Turning Right in the Sixties: The Conservative Capture of the GOP* (1995); Paul Cowan, *The Making of an Un-American: A Dialogue with Experience* (1970); Godfrey Hodgson, *The World Turned Right Side Up: A History of the Conservative Ascendency in America* (1996); Allen J. Matusow, *The Unraveling of America: A History of Liberalism in the 1960s* (1984).

Rowland Evans, Jr., and Robert D. Novak, *Nixon in the White House* (1972); Stanley I. Kutler, *The Wars of Watergate: The Last Crisis of Richard Nixon* (1990); Stanley I. Kutler, ed., *Abuse of Power: The New Nixon Tapes* (1997); J. Anthony Lukas, *Nightmare: The Underside of the Nixon Years* (1976); Allen J. Matusow, *Nixon's Economy: Booms, Busts, Dollars, and Votes* (1998); Richard Nixon, *RN: The Memoirs of Richard Nixon* (1978); Bob Woodward and Carl Bernstein, *All the President's Men* (1974) and *The Final Days* (1976).

John Robert Greene, *The Limits of Power: The Nixon and Ford Administrations* (1992) and *The Presidency of Gerald R. Ford* (1995); John Hersey, *The President* (1975); Richard Reeves, *A Ford, Not a Lincoln* (1975).

Jimmy Carter, *Keeping Faith: Memories of a President* (1982); Gary M. Fink and Hugh Davis Graham, eds., *The Carter Presidency: Policy Choices in the Post-New Deal Era* (1998); Burton I. Kaufman, *The Presidency of James Earl Carter, Jr.* (1993); Kenneth A. Morris, *Jimmy Carter: American Moralist* (1996).

# CHAPTER 29
# The Struggle for Social Reform

## CHAPTER OUTLINE

- The Black Struggle for Equality
- Pressure from the Women's Movement
- Latino Mobilization

- Native American Protest
- Social and Cultural Protest
- Conclusion: Extending the American Dream

## AMERICAN STORIES
### An Older Woman Returns to School

Ann Clarke—as she chooses to call herself now—always wanted to go to college. But girls from Italian families rarely did when she was growing up. Her mother, a widowed Sicilian immigrant, asked her brother for advice: "Should Antonina go to college?" "What's the point?" he replied. "She's just going to get married."

Life had not been easy for Antonina Rose Rumore. As a child in the 1920s, her Italian-speaking grandmother cared for her while her mother supported the family, first in the sweat-shops, then as a seamstress. Even as she dreamed about the future, Ann accommodated her culture's demands for dutiful daughters. Responsive to family needs, Ann finished the high school commercial course in three years. She struggled with ethnic prejudice as a legal sec-retary on Wall Street but still believed in the American dream and the Puritan work ethic. She was proud of her ability to bring money home to her family.

When World War II began, Ann wanted to join the WACS. "Better you should be a prostitute," her mother said. Ann went off to California instead, where she worked at a number of resorts. When she left California, she vowed to return to that land of freedom and opportunity.

After the war, Ann married Gerard Clarke, a college man with an English background. Her children would grow up accepted with Anglo-Saxon names. Over the next 15 years, Ann devoted herself to her family. She was a mother first and foremost, and that took all her time. But she still waited for her own chance. "I had this hunger to learn, this curiosity," she later recalled. By the early 1960s, her three children were all in school. Promising her hus-band to have dinner on the table every night at six, she enrolled at Pasadena City College. It was not easy, for family still came first, but Ann proved creative in finding time to study. When doing dishes or cleaning house, she memorized lists of facts and dates for school.

Holidays, however, complicated her efforts to complete assignments. Ann occasionally felt compelled to give everything up "to make Christmas." Forgetting about a whole semester's work two weeks before finals one year, she sewed nightgowns instead of writing her art history paper.

Her conflict over her studies was intensified by her position as one of the first older women to go back to college. "Sometimes I felt like I wanted to hide in the woodwork," she admitted. Often her teachers were younger than she was. It took four years to complete the two-year program. But she was not yet done, for she really wanted a bachelor's degree. Back she went, this time to California State College at Los Angeles.

As the years passed and the credits piled up, Ann became an honors student. Her children, now in college themselves, were proud and supportive; dinners became arguments over Faulkner and foreign policy. Even so, Ann still felt caught between her world at home and outside. Since she was at the top of her class, graduation should have been a special occasion. But she was only embarrassed when a letter from the school invited her parents to attend the final ceremonies. Ann could not bring herself to go.

With a college degree in hand, Ann returned to school for a teaching credential. Receiving her certificate at age 50, she faced the irony of social change. Once denied opportunities, Italians had assimilated into American society. Now she was just another Anglo in Los Angeles, caught in a changing immigration wave; now the city sought Latinos and other minorities to teach in the schools. Jobs in education were scarce, and she was close to "retirement age," so she became a substitute in Mexican-American areas for the next 10 years, specializing in bilingual education.

Meanwhile, Ann was troubled by the Vietnam War. "For every boy that died, one of us should lie down," she told fellow workers. She was not an activist, but rather one of the millions of quieter Americans who ultimately helped bring about change. The social adjustments caused by the war affected her. Her son grew long hair and a beard and attended protest rallies. She worried that he would antagonize the women in Pasadena. Her daughter came home from college in boots and a leather miniskirt designed to shock. Ann accepted her children's changes as relatively superficial, confident in their fundamental values. She trusted them, even as she worried about them.

❧ ❧ ❧ ❧

Ann Clarke's experience paralleled that of millions of women in the post–World War II years. Caught up in traditional patterns of family life, these women began to recognize their need for something more. Like blacks, Latinos, Native Americans, and members of other groups, American women struggled to transform the conditions of their lives and the rights they enjoyed within American society. In the process, they changed the nation itself.

This chapter describes the reform impulse that accompanied the effort to define the government's responsibility for economic and social stability described in Chapter 28. Like earlier reform efforts, particularly those during the Progressive era and the New Deal, this modern struggle sought to fulfill the promise of the American past and to provide liberty and equality in racial, gender, and social relations. The third reform cycle of the twentieth century, however, drew more from the militancy of those on the mudsills of society than from the pleas of middle-class activists. It reflected the attempt of often marginalized Americans to make the nation live up to its professed values. This chapter highlights the voices of such "outsiders" as it describes their efforts to square the ideals of American life with the realities many Americans faced. The chapter records the continuing frustrations of integrating diverse groups into American society while acknowledging their integrity and identity. And it notes the still-present tension accompanying the sharp debate over power and its distribution in the United States.

## THE BLACK STRUGGLE FOR EQUALITY

African Americans' quest for equality influenced the postwar struggle for civil rights by all other groups in the United States. Stemming from an effort dating back to the Civil War and Reconstruction, the black movement gained momentum by the mid-twentieth century. African Americans continued to press for reform through peaceful protest and political pressure. But change came slowly. Despite some major victories in the 1950s, the Jim Crow system of rigid segregation remained the rule in the South. In the North, urban ghettos grew with the continuing influx of southern blacks. Crowded public housing, poor schools, and limited economic opportunities bred serious discontent.

### Mid-Twentieth Century Roots

Stepping up their demands for change in the 1930s and 1940s, African Americans made significant gains during World War II (see Chapter 25). Black servicemen returning from the war vowed to reject second-class citizenship and helped mobilize a grass-roots movement to counter discrimination. In the postwar years, African struggles for independence, such as the Kenyan Mau Mau revolt against the British, inspired African-American leaders who now saw the quest for black equality in a broader context. As Adam Clayton Powell, a Harlem preacher (and later congressman), warned, the black man "walks conscious of the fact that he is no longer alone—no longer a minority."

The racial question was dramatized in 1947 when Jackie Robinson broke the color line and began playing major league baseball with the Brooklyn Dodgers. Sometimes teammates were hostile, sometimes runners slid into him with spikes high, but Robinson kept his frustrations to himself. A splendid first season helped ease the way, and after Robinson's trailblazing effort, other blacks, formerly confined to the old Negro leagues, started to move into the major leagues. Next came professional football and basketball.

The nation's racial problems became entangled with Cold War politics. As leader of the "free world," the United States sought support in Africa and Asia. Discrimination at home was an obvious embarrassment in the struggle to gain new friends.

Somewhat reluctantly, Truman supported the civil rights movement. A moderate who believed in political, not social, equality, he responded to the growing strength of the African-American vote. In 1946, he appointed a Committee on

Civil Rights to investigate lynching and other brutalities against blacks and recommend remedies. The committee's report, released in October 1947, showed
that black Americans remained second-class citizens in every area of American
life. The report set a civil rights agenda for the next two decades.

Though Truman hedged at first, in February 1948, he sent a 10-point civil
rights program to Congress—the first presidential civil rights plan since Reconstruction. When the southern wing of the Democratic party bolted later that year
(see Chapter 28), he moved forward even more aggressively. First he issued an executive order barring discrimination in the federal establishment. Then he ordered equality of treatment in the military services. Manpower needs in the Korean War broke down the last restrictions, particularly when the army found that
integrated units performed well.

Elsewhere the administration pushed other reforms. The Justice Department,
not previously supportive of civil rights litigation from the National Association
for the Advancement of Colored People (NAACP), now filed briefs challenging
discrimination in housing, education, and interstate transportation. These actions
helped build the pressure for change that influenced the Supreme Court. Congress, however, took little action.

## Integrating the Schools

As the civil rights struggle gained momentum during the 1950s, the judicial system played a crucial role. The NAACP was determined to overturn the 1896
Supreme Court decision *Plessy* v. *Ferguson,* in which the Court had approved of
segregation if the facilities used by each race were "separate but equal." The de-
cree had been used for generations to sanction rigid segregation, primarily in the
South, though the separate facilities were seldom, if ever, equal.

In 1951, Oliver Brown sued the school board of Topeka, Kansas, to allow his
eight-year-old daughter Linda to attend a school for white children that she
passed while walking to the bus that carried her to a black school farther away.
The case reached the Supreme Court, which added other school segregation cases
to this one.

On May 17, 1954, the Supreme Court released its bombshell ruling in *Brown* v.
*Board of Education.* For more than a decade, Supreme Court decisions had gradually expanded black civil rights. Now the Court unanimously decreed that "separate facilities are inherently unequal" and concluded that the "separate but equal"
doctrine had no place in public education. A year later, the Court declared that local school boards, acting with the guidance of lower courts, should move "with all
deliberate speed" to desegregate facilities.

President Eisenhower privately disagreed with the *Brown* ruling, but he knew
that it was his constitutional duty to see that the law was carried out. Even while
urging sympathy for the South in its period of transition, he acted immediately to
desegregate the Washington, D.C., schools as a model for the rest of the country.
He also ordered desegregation in navy yards and veterans' hospitals.

The South resisted. In district after district, vicious scenes occurred. The crucial confrontation came in Little Rock, Arkansas, in 1957. A desegregation plan,
beginning with the token admission of a few black students to Central High

Federal officials and local law enforcement authorities frequently had to assist African-American children attending integrated schools in the sometimes turbulent aftermath of the *Brown* v. *Board of Education* decision of 1954. (Norman Rockwell Family Trust)

School, was ready. Just before the school year began, Governor Orval Faubus declared on television that it would not be possible to maintain order if integration took place. National Guardsmen, posted by the governor and armed with bayonets, turned away nine black students as they tried to enter the school. After three weeks, a federal court ordered the troops to leave. When the black children entered the building, the white students, spurred on by their elders, belligerently opposed them, chanting such slogans as "Two, four, six, eight, we ain't gonna integrate." In the face of hostile mobs, the black children left the school.

With the lines drawn, attention focused on the moderate man in the White House, who faced a situation in which Little Rock whites were clearly defying the law. As a military officer, Ike knew that such resistance could not be tolerated, and he finally took the one action he had earlier called unthinkable. For the first time since the end of Reconstruction, an American president called out federal troops to protect the rights of black citizens. Eisenhower ordered paratroopers to Little Rock and placed National Guardsmen under federal command. The black children entered the school and attended classes with the military protecting their rights.

## Black Gains on Other Fronts

Meanwhile, African Americans themselves began organizing to take direct action. In the 1930s and 1940s, some had joined demonstrations protesting job discrimination and segregation. Now they were ready for an even more dramatic confrontation.

The crucial event occurred in Montgomery, Alabama. In December 1955, Rosa Parks, a 42-year-old black seamstress who was also secretary of the Alabama NAACP, sat down in the whites-only front section of a bus. When ordered to move back, the longtime activist refused to budge. The bus driver called the police at the next stop, and Parks was arrested and ordered to stand trial for violating the segregation laws. Her calculated decision to resist the law marked a new phase in the civil rights struggle. Like Rosa Parks, ordinary black men and women would challenge the racial status quo and force both white and black leaders to respond.

In Montgomery, black civil rights officials seized the issue. Fifty black leaders met and decided to organize a massive boycott of the bus system.

Martin Luther King, Jr., the 27-year-old minister of the Baptist church where the meeting was held, soon emerged as the preeminent spokesman of the protest. King was an impressive figure and an inspiring speaker. "There comes a time when people get tired . . . of being kicked about by the brutal feet of oppression," he declared.

Although King, like others, was arrested on a trumped-up speeding charge and jailed, grass-roots support bubbled up. In Montgomery, 50,000 African Americans walked or formed car pools to avoid the transit system. Their actions cut gross revenue on city buses by 65 percent. Almost a year later, the Supreme Court ruled that bus segregation, like school segregation, violated the Constitution, and the boycott ended. But the mood it fostered continued, and for many blacks peaceful protest became a way of life.

Meanwhile, a concerted effort developed to guarantee black voting rights. Notwithstanding the Fifteenth Amendment (see Chapter 16), many states had

Baptist minister Martin Luther King, Jr., emerged as the black spokesman in the Montgomery, Alabama, bus boycott and soon became the most eloquent African-American leader of the entire civil rights movement. He was often jailed for his efforts, as shown in this picture of him sharing a cell with Ralph Abernathy, another civil rights leader. (Corbis)

disfranchised blacks for decades with a poll tax, a literacy test, or an examination of constitutional understanding.

Largely because of the legislative genius of Senate majority leader Lyndon Johnson, the first civil rights bill since Reconstruction moved toward passage. With his eye on the presidency, Johnson wanted to establish his credentials as a man who could look beyond narrow southern interests. Paring the bill down to provisions he felt would pass, Johnson pushed the measure through.

The Civil Rights Act of 1957 created a Civil Rights Commission and empowered the Justice Department to go to court in cases where blacks were denied the right to vote. Though a compromise measure, it was the first successful effort to protect civil rights in 82 years. A few years later, Congress passed the Civil Rights Act of 1960, which set stiffer penalties for people who interfered with the right to vote. But, like its predecessor, it stopped short of authorizing federal registrars to register blacks to vote and so was generally ineffective.

The civil rights movement made important strides during the Eisenhower years. Yet presidential leadership had little to do with the progress. Rather, Supreme Court rulings and blacks' own efforts brought the most significant changes.

## Confrontation Continues

A spectrum of organizations—some old, some new—carried the fight forward. The NAACP, founded in 1910, remained committed to overturning the legal bases for segregation. The Congress of Racial Equality (CORE), an interracial group established in 1942, promoted change through peaceful confrontation. In 1957, after their victory in Montgomery, Martin Luther King, Jr., and others formed the Southern Christian Leadership Conference (SCLC), an organization of southern black clergy. Far more militant was the Student Nonviolent Coordinating Committee (SNCC, pronounced "snick"), which began to operate in 1960 and recruited young Americans who had not been involved in the civil rights struggle.

Confrontations continued in the 1960s. On January 31, 1960, four black college students from the Agricultural and Technical College in Greensboro, North Carolina, sat down at a segregated Woolworth's lunch counter and deliberately violated segregation laws by refusing to leave despite often brutal responses. The sit-ins captured media attention and soon involved thousands of African Americans.

The next year, 1961, freedom rides began, aimed at testing southern transportation facilities, recently desegregated by a Supreme Court decision. Organized initially by CORE and aided by SNCC, the program sent groups of blacks and whites on buses heading south and stopping at terminals along the way. The riders, peaceful themselves, wanted to publicize their cause and generate political support. They anticipated violent confrontations—and got them. In Anniston, Alabama, a white mob attacked and firebombed the bus. In Birmingham the police gave the Ku Klux Klan 15 minutes alone to beat the Freedom Riders. The FBI knew about the plan, but did nothing to stop it.

In North and South alike, consciousness of the need to combat racial discrimination grew. The civil rights movement became the most powerful moral campaign since the abolitionist crusade before the Civil War. Often working together closely, blacks and whites vowed to eliminate racial barriers.

In violation of southern law, black college students refused to leave a lunch counter, launching a new campaign in the struggle. Here the students wait patiently for service, or forcible eviction, as a way of dramatizing their determination to end segregation. (Bruce Roberts/Photo Researchers, Inc.)

Anne Moody, who grew up in a small town in Mississippi, personified the black awakening. As a child, she had seen friends and acquaintances killed for transgressing the limits set for blacks. Overcoming enormous hardships, she became the first member of her family to go to college, and at all-black Tougaloo College, near Jackson, where she joined the civil rights movement. Slowly, she noted, "I could feel myself beginning to change. For the first time I began to think something would be done about whites killing, beating, and misusing Negroes. I knew I was going to be a part of whatever happened." Participating in sit-ins where she was thrashed and jailed, she remained deeply involved in the movement.

Many whites also joined the movement in the South. Mimi Feingold, a white student at Swarthmore College, helped picket a Chester, Pennsylvania, Woolworths and worked to unionize Swarthmore's black dining hall workers. In 1961, after her sophomore year, she headed south to join CORE's freedom rides. There she, too, found herself in the midst of often-violent confrontations and went to jail as an act of conscience. In Jackson, Mississippi, she spent a month behind bars.

In 1962, the civil rights movement accelerated. James Meredith, a black air force veteran and student at Jackson State College, applied to the all-white University of Mississippi, only to be rejected on racial grounds. Suing for admission, he won his case in the U.S. Supreme Court. Then Governor Ross Barnett, an adamant racist, announced defiantly that Meredith would not be admitted, whatever the Court decision. A major riot followed. Tear gas covered the university grounds, and two men were killed and hundreds were hurt.

Other governors were equally aggressive. In his 1963 inaugural address, George C. Wallace of Alabama declared boldly, "Segregation now! Segregation tomorrow! Segregation forever!" as he voiced his opposition to integration.

Alabama became a national focus that year as a violent confrontation unfolded in Birmingham. Local black leaders encouraged Martin Luther King, Jr., to launch another attack on southern segregation in the city, 40 percent black, which remained rigidly segregated along racial and class lines. "We believed that while a campaign in Birmingham would surely be the toughest fight of our civil rights careers," King later explained, "it could, if successful, break the back of segregation all over the nation."

Though the demonstrations were nonviolent, the responses were not. Over a five-week period, city officials arrested 2,200 blacks, some of them schoolchildren, for parading without licenses. Police Commissioner Eugene "Bull" Connor used high-pressure fire hoses, electric cattle prods, and snarling police dogs to force the protesters back. As the media recorded the events, Americans watching television and reading newspapers were horrified. The images of violence created mass sympathy for black Americans' civil rights struggle.

## Kennedy's Response

John F. Kennedy claimed to be sickened by the pictures from Birmingham but insisted that he could do nothing, even though he had sought and won black support in 1960. The narrowness of his electoral victory made him reluctant to press white southerners on civil rights when he needed their votes on other issues. Kennedy initially failed to propose any civil rights legislation and likewise ignored a campaign promise to use his presidential power to end housing discrimination with the "stroke of a pen," despite gifts of numerous bottles of ink. Not until November 1962, after the midterm elections, did he take a modest action—an executive order ending segregation in federally financed housing.

Events finally forced the president to act more boldly. In the confrontation at the University of Mississippi, Kennedy, like Eisenhower at Little Rock, had to send federal troops to restore control and enforce the Supreme Court's order allowing Meredith to attend. The administration also forced the desegregation of the University of Alabama and helped arrange a compromise providing for desegregation of Birmingham's municipal facilities. And when white bombings aimed at black leaders in Birmingham caused thousands of blacks to abandon nonviolence and rampage through the streets, Kennedy readied federal troops to intervene.

He also spoke out more forcefully than before. On national television, he called the quest for equal rights a "moral issue." Just hours after Kennedy spoke, assassins killed Medgar Evers, a black NAACP official, in Jackson, Mississippi.

Kennedy finally sent Congress a new and stronger civil rights bill, outlawing segregation in public places, banning discrimination in federally funded programs, and promoting school integration. Polls showed that 63 percent of the nation supported his stand.

To lobby for passage of this measure, civil rights leaders, pressed from below by black activists, arranged a massive march on Washington in August 1963. More than 200,000 people and numerous celebrities gathered, and popular folk singers led the crowd in "Blowin' in the Wind" and "We Shall Overcome."

The high point of the day was the address by Martin Luther King, Jr. With all the power of a southern preacher, he implored his audience to share his faith in decency and equality. "I have a dream," King cried, "that one day this nation will rise up and live out the true meaning of its creed: 'We hold these truths to be self-evident, that all men are created equal.' I have a dream that one day on the red hills of Georgia, the sons of former slaves and the sons of former slave-owners will be able to sit together at the table of brotherhood." It was a fervent appeal, and one to which the crowd responded. Each time King used the refrain "I have a dream," thousands of blacks and whites roared together. King concluded by quoting from an old hymn: "Free at last! Free at last! Thank God almighty, we are free at last!"

Not all were moved. Anne Moody, who had come up from her activist work in Mississippi to attend the event, sat on the grass by the Lincoln Memorial. "Martin Luther King went on and on talking about his dream," she said. "I sat there thinking that . . . we never had time to sleep, much less dream." Nor was Congress prompted to do much. Despite Democratic majorities, strong white southern resistance to civil rights continued, and when Kennedy was assassinated in November 1963, his bill was still bottled up in committee.

## Legislative Success in the Johnson Years

Lyndon Johnson was more successful than Kennedy in advancing the cause of civil rights. "No memorial oration or eulogy could more eloquently honor President Kennedy's memory than the earliest possible passage of the civil rights bill," he told Congress—and the nation—in his first address after becoming president. He pushed the bill through Congress, heading off a Senate filibuster by persuading his old colleague, Republican minority leader Everett Dirksen of Illinois, to work for cloture—a two-thirds vote to cut off debate. In June 1964, the Senate for the first time imposed cloture to advance a civil rights measure, and passage soon followed. "No army can withstand the strength of an idea whose time has come," said Dirksen.

The Civil Rights Act of 1964 outlawed racial discrimination in all public accommodations and authorized the Justice Department to act with greater authority in school and voting matters. In addition, an equal opportunity provision prohibited discriminatory hiring on grounds of race, gender, religion, or national origin in firms with more than 25 employees.

Though the law was one of the great achievements of the 1960s, Johnson realized that it was only a starting point because widespread discrimination still existed in American society. African Americans still found it difficult to vote in large areas of the South. Freedom Summer, sponsored by SNCC and other civil rights groups in 1964, sent black and white students to Mississippi to work for black rights. Early in the summer, two whites, Michael Schwerner and Andrew Goodman, and one black, James Chaney, were murdered. By the end of the summer, 80 workers had been beaten, 1,000 had been arrested, and 37 churches had been bombed. Early in 1965 there was another confrontation in the national headlines when Alabama police clubbed and tear-gassed demonstrators trying to march from Selma to Montgomery, the state capital. Sending the National Guard to protect another march to Montgomery, Johnson asked Congress for a voting bill to close loopholes in earlier civil rights laws.

The Voting Rights Act of 1965, perhaps the most important law of the decade, authorized the U.S. attorney general to appoint federal examiners to register

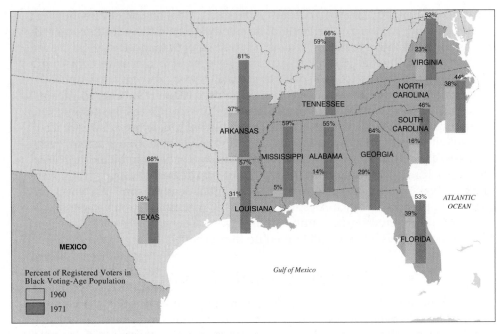

**IMPACT OF THE VOTING RIGHTS ACT OF 1965**   The Voting Rights Act of 1965 greatly increased the African-American vote throughout the South but also sparked a reaction on the part of whites who feared the enhanced power of the larger black electorate.

voters where local officials were obstructing the registration of blacks. In the year after passage of the act, 400,000 blacks registered to vote in the Deep South; by 1968, the number reached a million.

## Black Power Challenges Liberal Reform

Despite legislative success, racial discrimination persisted in both North and South. Still-segregated schools, wretched housing, and inadequate job opportunities were continuing problems. As the struggle for civil rights progressed, divisions within the movement emerged. Initially, the civil rights campaign had been integrated and nonviolent. Martin Luther King, Jr., had become its acknowledged leader. But now black-white tensions flared within organizations, and younger black leaders began to challenge King's nonviolent approach. They were tired of beatings, jailings, church bombings, and the slow pace of change that was dependent on white liberal support and government action. Anne Moody, the stalwart activist in Mississippi, voiced the doubts so many blacks harbored about the possibility of real change. Discouraged after months of struggle, she boarded a bus taking civil rights workers north to testify about abuses. As "We Shall Overcome" reverberated around her, all she could think was, "I wonder. I really wonder."

One episode that contributed to many blacks' suspicion of white liberals occurred at the Democratic national convention of 1964 in Atlantic City. In Mississippi's Freedom Summer campaign, SNCC had founded the Freedom Democratic party as an alternative to the all-white regular state delegation. Testifying before the credentials committee, black activist Fannie Lou Hamer reported that she had been beaten, jailed, and denied the right to vote. Yet the committee's final compromise—pressed by President Johnson, who worried about losing southern support in the upcoming election—was to seat the white delegation while offering the protest organization two at-large seats. That response hardly satisfied those who had risked their lives and families to try to vote in Mississippi. As civil rights leader James Forman observed, "Atlantic City was a powerful lesson . . . . No longer was there any hope . . . that the federal government would change the situation in the Deep South." SNCC, once a religious and integrated organization, began to turn into an all-black cadre dedicated to mobilizing poor blacks for militant action. "Liberation" replaced civil rights as a goal.

Increasingly, angry blacks argued that the nation must no longer withhold the rights pledged in its founding credo. Black author James Baldwin wrote in one of his eloquent essays that unless change came soon, the worst could be expected: "If we do not now dare everything, the fulfillment of that prophecy, recreated from the Bible in song by a slave, is upon us: God gave Noah the rainbow sign, No more water, the fire next time!"

Even more responsible for channeling black frustration into a new set of goals and tactics was Malcolm X. Born Malcolm Little and reared in northern ghettos, he was a petty criminal. In prison, he became a convert to the Nation of Islam and a disciple of black leader Elijah Muhammad. He began to preach that the white man was responsible for the black man's condition and that blacks had to help themselves.

Malcolm was impatient with the moderate civil rights movement. He grew tired of hearing "all of this non-violent, begging-the-white-man kind of dying . . . all of this sitting-in, sliding-in, wading-in, eating-in, diving-in, and all the rest." Espousing black separatism and black nationalism for most of his public career, he argued for black control of black communities, preached an international perspective embracing African peoples in diaspora, and appealed to blacks to fight racism "by any means necessary."

Malcolm X became the most dynamic spokesman for poor northern blacks since Marcus Garvey in the 1920s. Though he was assassinated by black antagonists in 1965, his African-centered, uncompromising perspective helped shape the struggle against racism.

One man influenced by Malcolm's message was Stokely Carmichael. Born in Trinidad, he came to the United States at the age of 11 and grew up with an interest in politics and black protest. While at Howard University, he picketed and demonstrated and was beaten and jailed. Frustrated with civil disobedience as he became active in SNCC, he urged field workers to arm for self-defense. It was time for blacks to cease depending on whites, he argued, and to make SNCC a black organization. His election as its head reflected SNCC's growing radicalism.

The split in the black movement was dramatized in June 1966 during a march in Mississippi. Carmichael's followers challenged those of Martin Luther King, Jr., the advocate of nonviolence and interracial cooperation. Carmichael, just out of jail after arrest for his protest activities, shouted to the crowd: "This is the twenty-seventh time I have been arrested—and I ain't going to jail no more! The only way we gonna stop them white men from whippin' us is to take over. We been saying freedom for six years and we ain't got nothing. What we gonna start saying now is Black Power!" Carmichael had the audience with him as he repeated, and the crowd shouted back, "We . . . want . . . Black . . . Power!"

Black Power was a call for a broad-based campaign to build independent institutions in the African-American community. It drew on growing demands for an end to the physical and sexual abuse of black women and fostered a powerful sense of black pride. Its most enduring legacy was political and cultural mobilization at the grassroots level, even if it only partially realized its goals.

Black Power led to demands for more drastic action. The Black Panthers, radical activists who organized first in Oakland, California, militantly vowed to eradicate not only racial discrimination but capitalism as well. H. Rap Brown, who succeeded Carmichael as head of SNCC, became famous for saying that "violence is as American as cherry pie."

Violence accompanied the more militant calls for reform and showed that racial injustice was not a southern problem but an American one. Riots erupted in Rochester, New York City, and several New Jersey cities in 1964. In 1965, in the Watts neighborhood of Los Angeles, a massive uprising lasted five days and left 34 dead, more than 1,000 injured, and hundreds of buildings burned to the ground. Other cities experienced similar riots in 1966 and 1967. When Martin Luther King, Jr., fell to a white assassin's bullet in April 1968, angry blacks went on rampages in cities throughout the country.

## "Southern Strategy" and Showdown on Civil Rights

Richard Nixon, elected president in 1968, was less sympathetic to the civil rights cause than his immediate predecessors. He had won only 12 percent of the black vote and concluded that trying to woo the black electorate would endanger his white southern support.

From the start, the Nixon administration sought to scale back federal commitments to civil rights. It moved to reduce appropriations for fair-housing enforcement and tried to block an extension of the Voting Rights Act of 1965. When southern politicians sought to get federal school desegregation guidelines suspended, the Justice Department supported them, and Nixon publicly criticized a unanimous Supreme Court rejection of the effort.

Nixon also faced the growing controversy over busing as a means of desegregation, a highly charged issue in the 1970s. Transporting students from one area to another to attend school was nothing new. In the South, busing had long been used to maintain segregated schools. Yet when busing was used to break down racial barriers, it inflamed passions.

The issue came to a head in North Carolina's Charlotte-Mecklenburg school system. A desegregation plan involving voluntary transfer was in effect, but many blacks still attended largely segregated schools. In 1971, the Supreme Court ruled that district courts had broad authority to order the desegregation of school systems—by busing, if necessary.

Nixon opposed busing, and went on television to denounce it. Although Congress did not grant his request for a moratorium, southerners knew where he stood. So did northerners, for the issue became a national one. Many of the nation's largest northern cities had school segregation as rigid as in the South, largely because of residential patterns. This segregation was called *de facto* to differentiate it from the *de jure,* or legal, segregation that had existed in the South. Mississippi Senator John C. Stennis, a bitter foe of busing, hoped to stir up the North by subjecting it to the same busing standards as the South. Court decisions subsequently ordered many northern cities to desegregate their schools.

Northern resistance to integration was fiercest in Boston. In 1973, more than half of the African-American students were in schools that were 90 percent black. In June 1974, a federal judge ordered busing to begin. The effort went smoothly enough for many younger students, but whites boycotted South Boston High and stoned buses bringing in black students, injuring some children. White working-class South Bostonians felt that they were being asked to carry the burden of middle-class liberals' racial views. Often white families either enrolled their children in private schools or fled the city.

The Republicans managed to slow down the school desegregation movement. Nixon openly catered to his conservative constituents. His successor, Gerald Ford, never came out squarely against civil rights, but his lukewarm approach to desegregation demonstrated a further weakening of the federal commitment.

The situation was less inflamed at the college level, but the same pattern held. Blacks made significant progress until the Republican administrations in the late 1960s and 1970s slowed the movement for civil rights. Integration at the postsecondary level came easier as federal affirmative-action guidelines brought more blacks into colleges and universities. In 1950, only 83,000 black students were enrolled in institutions of higher education; in 1960, there were about one million. Black enrollment in colleges peaked at 9.3 percent of the college population in 1976, before falling back slightly.

Some whites protested "reverse discrimination." Allan Bakke, who was white, was twice rejected by the medical school at the University of California, Davis. He sued on the grounds that a racial quota reserving 16 of 100 places for minority-group applicants was discriminatory, violating the Civil Rights Act of 1964. In 1978, the Supreme Court ordered Bakke's admission in a complex ruling that allowed consideration of race but not quotas in admissions policies.

Jimmy Carter, president when the *Bakke* decision was handed down, was more supportive of civil rights than his Republican predecessors. He brought a large number of qualified blacks, some of them highly visible, into his administration. But Carter's lack of support for increased social programs for the poor hurt the majority of black citizens and strained their loyalty to the Democratic party.

The civil rights movement underscored the democratic values on which the nation was based, but the gap between rhetoric and reality remained. Most black families remained poor, with African-American income substantially below white income. After early optimism in the years when the movement made its greatest strides, blacks and sympathetic whites were troubled by the direction of public policy. Given a wavering national commitment to reform in the 1970s, only pressures from reform groups kept the faltering civil rights movement alive.

## PRESSURE FROM THE WOMEN'S MOVEMENT

The black struggle in the 1960s and 1970s was accompanied by a women's movement that grew out of the agitation for civil rights but soon developed a life of its own. This struggle, like those of Latinos and Native Americans, employed the confrontational approach and the vocabulary of the civil rights movement to create pressure for change. Using proven strategies, it sometimes proceeded even faster than the black effort.

### Attacking the Feminine Mystique

Many white women joined the civil rights movement only to find themselves second-class citizens. Men, black and white, held the top positions and relegated women to menial chores when not actually involved in demonstrations or voter drives. Many women also felt sexually exploited. Stokely Carmichael only underscored their point when he declared, "The only position for women in SNCC is prone."

Although the civil rights movement helped spark the women's movement, broad social changes provided the preconditions. During the 1950s and 1960s, increasing numbers of married women entered the labor force (see Chapter 26). Equally important, many more young women were attending college. By 1970, women earned 41 percent of all B.A. degrees awarded, in comparison with only 25 percent in 1950. These educated young women had high hopes for themselves, even if they still earned substantially less than men.

Just as in the civil rights movement, reform legislation played a part in ending sexual discrimination. Title 7 of the 1964 civil rights bill, as originally drafted, prohibited discrimination on the grounds of race. Conservatives opposed to black civil rights introduced an amendment also banning discrimination on the basis of gender, hoping to guarantee the entire bill's failure. But both the amendment and the full measure were approved, giving women a legal tool for attacking discrimination. They discovered, however, that the Equal Employment Opportunity Commission regarded women's complaints as far less important than those of blacks.

In 1966, a group of 28 professional women, including author Betty Friedan, established the National Organization for Women (NOW) "to take action to bring American women into full participation in the mainstream of American society now." By full participation the founders meant not only fair pay and equal opportunity but also a more egalitarian form of marriage. NOW also attacked the "false image of women . . . in the media." By 1967, some 1,000 women had joined the organization, and four years later, its membership reached 15,000.

NOW was a pressure group, dedicated to reforming American society by promoting equal opportunity for women. But radical feminists, who had come up through the civil rights movement, found NOW's agenda an inadequate answer to gender discrimination. "Women's liberation does not mean equality with men," said Jo Freeman, a radical activist, because "equality in an unjust society is meaningless." Through consciousness-raising, these feminists wanted to educate millions of discontented but unpoliticized women about their oppression—to demonstrate, in their phrase, that the personal was political.

The radicals attracted mass-media attention at the Miss America pageant in September 1968. On the Atlantic City boardwalk, a hundred women nominated a sheep as their candidate for Miss America and filled a "freedom trash can" with "instruments of torture": bras, girdles, hair curlers, high heels, and copies of *Playboy* and *Cosmopolitan* magazines. In the pageant hall, they unfurled banners reading "Women's Liberation."

## Feminism at High Tide

Real changes were under way. A 1970 survey of first-year college students showed that men interested in such fields as business, medicine, engineering, and law outnumbered women eight to one; by 1975, the ratio dropped to three to one. The proportion of women beginning law school quadrupled between 1969 and 1973. Women gained access to the military academies and entered senior officer ranks, although they were still kept out of combat command positions. According to the Census Bureau, 45 percent of mothers with preschool children held jobs outside the home in 1980—four times more than 30 years before. To be sure, many employers systematically excluded women from certain positions, and women usually held "female" jobs in the clerical, sales, and service sectors, but the progress was still unmistakable.

Legal changes brought women more benefits and opportunities. For example, Title 9 of the Education Amendments of 1972 broadened the Civil Rights Act of 1964 by barring gender bias in federally assisted educational activities and programs— which included sports teams, greatly boosting the visibility of women's sports.

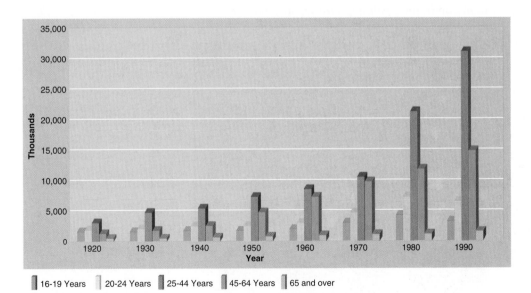

**WOMEN IN THE WORK FORCE, 1920–1990**  This graph shows the dramatic increase in the number of women in the work force. Note particularly the rise in the number of working women 25 to 44 years old. (*Source:* U.S. Bureau of the Census)

A flurry of publications spread the principles of the women's movement. In 1972, journalist Gloria Steinem and several other women founded a new magazine, *Ms.*, which succeeded beyond their wildest dreams. By 1973, there were almost 200,000 subscribers. *Our Bodies, Ourselves,* a handbook published by a women's health collective, encouraged women to understand and control their bodies; it sold 850,000 copies between 1971 and 1976.

These new books and magazines differed radically from older women's magazines like *Ladies' Home Journal,* which focused on domestic interests and needs. *Ms.* dealt with abortion, employment, discrimination, and other feminist issues such as the Equal Rights Amendment.

Women both in and out of NOW worked for congressional passage, then ratification, of the Equal Rights Amendment (ERA) to the Constitution. Passed by Congress in 1972, with ratification seemingly assured, it stated simply, "Equality of rights under the law shall not be denied or abridged by the United States or by any State on account of sex."

More radical feminists insisted that legal changes were not enough. Traditional gender and family roles would have to be discarded to end social exploitation. Socialist feminists claimed that it was not enough to strike out at male domination, for capitalist society itself was responsible for women's plight. Only through revolution could women be free.

Black women frequently viewed the women's movement with ambivalence. Some, like attorney Pauli Murray, became feminists. She worked closely with bureaucrats and legislators in Washington on legal measures to end sex discrimination. Others insisted that race, more than gender, was the source of their oppression, and were suspicious of the middle-class orientation of many white feminists. Members of NOW and similar organizations, they claimed, "suffered little more than boredom, gentle repression, and dishpan hands."

Women marched to mobilize support for ratification of the Equal Rights Amendment, but the campaign failed as opponents aroused public fears and blocked support in a number of key states. A decade after passage in Congress, the ERA was dead. (J. T. Alan/Corbis/Sygma)

## The Struggle for Equal Rights

| Year | Event | Effect |
|------|-------|--------|
| 1947 | Report of Truman's Committee on Civil Rights | Showed that African Americans remained second-class citizens in the United States |
| 1948 | Truman's executive order integrating the armed services | Opened the way for equal opportunity in the armed forces |
| 1954 | *Brown v. Board of Education* decision | Supreme Court ruled that "separate but equal" schools were unconstitutional; first step in ending school segregation |
| 1955 | Montgomery bus boycott | Black solidarity tested local petty segregation laws and customs |
| 1957 | Little Rock school integration crisis | White resistance to integration of Little Rock's Central High School resulted in Eisenhower's calling in federal troops |
|  | Civil Rights Act | Created Civil Rights Commission and empowered Justice Department to go to court to guarantee blacks the right to vote |
| 1960 | Civil Rights Act | Plugged loopholes in Civil Rights Act of 1957 |
|  | Sit-in demonstrations | Gained support for desegregation of public facilities |
| 1961 | Freedom rides | Dramatized struggle to desegregate transportation facilities |
| 1962 | James Meredith's attempt to attend University of Mississippi | Required federal intervention to uphold blacks' right to attend public institutions |
| 1963 | Effort to desegregate Birmingham, Alabama | Brutal response of police televised, sensitizing entire nation to plight of blacks |
|  | March on Washington | Gathered support and inspiration for the civil rights movement; scene of Rev. Martin Luther King, Jr.,'s "I Have a Dream" speech |
| 1964 | Civil Rights Act | Outlawed racial discrimination in public accommodations |
| 1965 | Voting Rights Act | Allowed federal examiners to register black voters where necessary |
| 1971 | Busing decision | Supreme Court ruled that court-ordered desegregation was constitutional, even if it employed busing |
| 1978 | *Bakke* decision | Supreme Court ruled that affirmative action was constitutional but that firm racial quotas were not |

Not all women were feminists. Many felt the women's movement was contemptuous of women who stayed at home to perform traditional tasks. Marabel Morgan, the wife of a Florida attorney, was one who still insisted that the woman had a place at home by her husband's side. Political activist Phyllis Schlafly headed a nationwide campaign to block ratification of the ERA. "It won't do anything to help women," she said, "and it will take away from women the rights they already have, such as the right of a wife to be supported by her husband, the right of a woman to be exempted from military combat, and the right, if you wanted it, to go to a single-sex college." The ERA, she predicted, would lead to the establishment of coed bathrooms, the elimination of alimony, and the legalization of homosexual marriage.

Schlafly and her allies had their way. Within a few years after passage of the ERA, 35 states had agreed to the measure, but then the momentum disappeared. Even with an extension in the deadline granted in 1979, the amendment could not win support of the necessary 38 states. By mid-1982, the ERA was dead.

Despite the counterattacks, the women's movement flourished in the 1960s and 1970s. In the tenth anniversary issue of *Ms.* magazine, in 1982, founding editor Gloria Steinem noted the differences a decade had made. "Now, we have words like 'sexual harassment' and 'battered women,'" she wrote. "Ten years ago, it was just called 'life.'"

## LATINO MOBILIZATION

Latinos, like women, profited from the example of blacks in the struggle for equality. They became more vocal and confrontational as their numbers increased dramatically in the postwar years. In 1970, some 9 million residents of the United States declared they were of Spanish origin; in 1980, the figure was 14.6 million. But median household income remained less than three-fourths that of Anglos and inferior education and political weakness reinforced social and cultural separation. Latinos included Puerto Ricans in the Northeast, Cubans in Florida, Chicanos in California, and Tejanos in Texas. Chicanos took the lead, though all developed a heightened sense of solidarity and group pride as they began to assert their rights.

### Early Efforts for Equality

The roots of the Latino struggle dated back to the World War II years. Chicanos established the American GI Forum because a Texas funeral home refused to bury a Mexican-American casualty of World War II. When the group's protest led to a burial in Arlington National Cemetery, the possibilities of concerted action became clear. In the waning months of the war, a court case challenged Mexican-American segregation in the schools. In Orange County, California, Gonzalo Méndez, a U.S. citizen, sued to permit his children to attend the school reserved for Anglo-Americans rather than an inferior Mexican one. The federal courts backed him, opening the way for integration elsewhere. Meanwhile, Mexican Americans returning from the military, where they had often been racially invisible, chafed at the discrimination they still met at home.

New organizations arose to struggle for equal rights. The Community Service Organization mobilized Chicanos against discrimination, as did the more radical Asociación Nacional México-Americana, while the League of United Latin American Citizens continued efforts to promote educational reform.

Advances, however, came slowly. In the late 1940s, many Chicanos sought official classification as Caucasian, hoping that the change would lead to better treatment. But even when the designation changed, their status did not. They still faced discrimination and police brutality, particularly in the cities with the largest Chicano populations. Los Angeles, with its large number of Chicanos, saw incidents such as the 1951 "Bloody Christmas" case in which officers took seven Mexican Americans from jail cells and beat them severely.

César Chávez organized the United Farm Workers to give migrant Mexican workers representation in their struggle for better wages and working conditions. Here he works with laborers in his tireless campaign for their support. (Bob Fitch/Black Star)

Protests continued, yet in the 1950s Chicano activism was fragmented. Some Mexican Americans considered their situation hopeless. While new and aggressive challenges appeared, fully effective mobilization had to wait for another day.

## César Chávez and the Politics of Confrontation

In the 1960s and 1970s, Mexican-Americans became more active politically. In 1960, Chicanos supported Kennedy, helping him win Texas, and started seeing the benefits of such support. In the next few years, Chicanos began to get elected to Congress.

Direct action was more immediately effective than political action. César Chávez, founder of the United Farm Workers, provided an example of its potential by organizing one of the most exploited and ignored groups of laboring people in the country, the western migrant farm workers. Chávez, who came from an activist family, concentrated on migrant Mexican field hands, who worked long hours for meager pay. By 1965, his organization had recruited 1,700 people and was beginning to attract volunteer help.

Chávez first took on the grape growers of California. His union struck for better pay and working conditions, and union recognition. Chávez skillfully appealed to middle-class consumers nationwide to support his struggle by boycotting grapes. Some employers came to terms, but others held out or rigged the results of union elections. When California governor Edmund G. Brown, Sr., launched an investigation of such tactics, he became the first major political leader to support the long-powerless Chicano field hands. In a new election, Chávez's

United Farm Workers won. Later they were equally successful in boycotts of lettuce and other products harvested by exploited labor. In 1975, the long struggle on behalf of farm workers culminated with the enactment in California of a measure requiring growers to bargain collectively with the elected representatives of the workers. Farm workers had never been covered by the National Labor Relations Board. Now they had achieved the legal basis for representation that could help bring higher wages and improved working conditions. And Chávez had become a national figure.

Meanwhile, Mexican Americans pressed for reform in other areas. In the West and Southwest, Mexican-American studies programs flourished. They offered degrees, built library collections, and gave Chicanos access to their own past. Campuses also provided a network linking students together and mobilizing them for political action. Protests spread to the secondary-school level, where educational conditions were often deplorable. Walkouts in a number of western states brought about the hiring of more Latino teachers and better facilities.

Militant new Chicano organizations emerged. In East Los Angeles, Young Citizens for Community Action began as a neighborhood service club but then adopted a paramilitary stance, trying to protect local residents. Its members became identified as the Brown Berets and formed chapters throughout the Midwest and Southwest.

Other Latinos followed a more political path. In Texas, José Angel Gutiérrez formed a citizens' organization which developed into the La Raza Unida political party and successfully promoted Mexican-American candidates for political offices. This organization gained strength in the West and Southwest throughout the 1970s. In New Mexico, the charismatic preacher Reis López Tijerina, or "El Tigre," took up the land-grant cause and argued that the United States government had fraudulently deprived Chicanos of village lands. His organization, La Alianza Federal de Mercedes (the Federal Alliance of Land Grants), marched on the New Mexico state capitol and occupied a number of national forests. Arrested, he stood trial and eventually served time in prison, where he became a symbol of political repression.

Latinos made a particular point of protesting the Vietnam War. Because the draft drew most heavily from the poorer segments of society, the Latino casualty rate was far higher than that of the population at large. In 1969, the Brown Berets organized the National Chicano Moratorium Committee and demonstrated against what they argued was a racial war. Some of the rallies ended in confrontations with the police. News reporter Rubén Salazar, active in exposing questionable police activity, was killed in one such episode in 1970, and his death brought renewed charges of police brutality.

Aware of the growing numbers and growing demands of Latinos, the Nixon administration sought to defuse their anger and win their support. Cuban-American refugees, strongly opposed to Communism, shifted toward the Republican party, which they saw as more vigorously anti-Castro than the Democratic party. Nixon courted Chicanos by dangling political positions, government jobs, and promises of better programs for Mexican Americans. The effort paid off; Nixon received 31 percent of the Latino vote in 1972. But then the president moved to cut back the poverty program, begun under Johnson, that assisted many Latinos.

Despite occasional gains, all Latinos faced continuing problems. Discrimination persisted in housing, education, and employment. Activists had laid the groundwork for a campaign for equal rights, but the struggle had just begun.

## NATIVE AMERICAN PROTEST

Like Latinos, Native Americans continued to suffer second-class status as the 1960s began. But, partly inspired by the confrontational tactics of other groups, they mounted more aggressive efforts to claim their rights and to improve living and working conditions. As their numbers soared—from 550,000 in 1960 to 1,480,000 in 1980—American Indians became increasingly determined to improve their own lot.

## Origins of the Struggle

Native Americans began the struggle for equality well before the 1960s. They achieved an important victory just after the end of World War II when Congress established the Indian Claims Commission. The commission was mandated to review tribal cases arguing that ancestral lands had been illegally seized and federal treaties violated. Hundreds of tribal suits against the government in federal courts

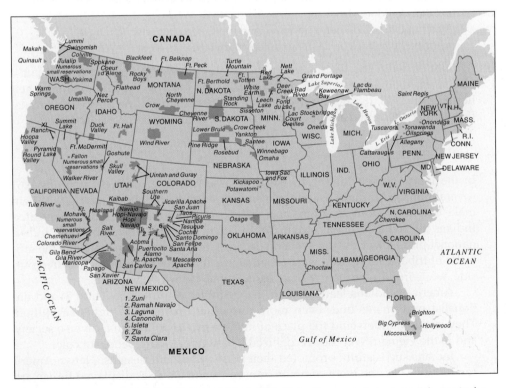

**INDIAN RESERVATIONS IN THE MID-1970S** While Indian reservations occupied substantial areas in the West in the mid-1970s, they still included far less territory than in past years.

were now possible. Many of them would lead to large cash settlements—a form of reparation for past injustices—and sometimes the return of long-lost lands.

In the 1950s, federal Indian policy shifted course. Hoping to limit the role of the national government, the Eisenhower administration turned away from the New Deal policy of government support for tribal autonomy. In the Indian Reorganization Act of 1934, the government had stepped in to restore lands to tribal ownership and end their loss or sale to outsiders. In 1953, instead of trying to encourage Native American self-government, the administration adopted a new "termination" policy. The government proposed settling all outstanding claims and eliminating reservations as legitimate political entities. To encourage their assimilation into mainstream society, the government offered small subsidies to families willing to leave the reservations and relocate in the cities.

The new policy infuriated American Indians. With their lands no longer federally protected and their members deprived of treaty rights, many tribes became unwitting victims of people who wanted to seize their land. Though promising more freedom, the new policy caused great disruption as the government terminated a number of tribes.

An unintended consequence of the policy was increased Indian activism. The National Congress of American Indians mobilized opposition to the federal program. A Seminole petition to the president in 1954 summed up a general view:

> We do not say that we are superior or inferior to the White Man and we do not say that the White Man is superior or inferior to us. We do say that we are not White Men but Indians, do not wish to become White Men but wish to remain Indians, and have an outlook on all things different from the outlook of the White Man.

Not only did the termination policy foster a sense of Indian identity, but it also sparked an awareness among whites of the Indians' right to maintain their heritage. In 1958, the Eisenhower administration changed the policy of termination so that it required a tribe's consent. Implementation of the policy ceased.

## Tribal Voices

In the 1960s, Native Americans began to assert themselves even more. In 1961 several hundred Indians asked the Kennedy administration for the right to help make decisions about programs and budgets for the tribes, and college-educated Indians formed a National Indian Youth Council aimed at reestablishing Indian national pride. Over the next several decades, the council helped change the attitudes of tribal leaders, who were called Uncle Tomahawks and "apples" (red outside, white inside) for their willingness to submit to white demands.

American Indians learned from the examples of protest in Third World nationalist movements and, even more important, in the civil rights revolution. They came to understand the place of interest-group politics in a diverse society, and in the Vietnam War they recognized a pattern of killing people of color.

Indians successfully promoted their own values and designs. Native-American fashions became more common, museums and galleries displayed Indian art, and Indian jewelry found a new market. The larger culture came to appreciate important work by Native Americans. In 1968, N. Scott Momaday won the Pulitzer Prize for his book *House Made of Dawn*. Vine Deloria, Jr.'s *Custer Died for Your Sins*

(1969) had even wider readership. Popular films such as *Little Big Man* (1970) sympathetically portrayed Indian history. Indian studies programs developed at universities. Organizations like the American Indian Historical Society protested traditional textbook treatment of Indians.

## Confrontational Tactics

At the same time, Native Americans became more confrontational. Like other groups, they worked through the courts but also challenged authority more aggressively when necessary.

Led by a new generation of leaders, American Indians tried to protect their remaining tribal lands. Intrusion had to cease. "Everything is tied to our homeland," D'Arcy McNickle, a Flathead anthropologist, told other Indians in 1961.

The protest spirit was apparent on the Seneca Nation's Allegany reservation in New York State. Although a 1794 treaty had established the Seneca right to the land, since 1928 the federal government had wanted to build a flood control dam there. In 1956, after hearings to which the Indians were not invited and about which they were not informed, Congress appropriated funds for the project, and the dam was eventually built. Belated reparations of $15 million did not compensate for the loss of sacred sites, hunting and fishing grounds, and homes.

The Seneca did somewhat better in the 1970s. When New York State tried to build a superhighway through part of the same reservation, the Indians blocked it in court, and eventually negotiated an exchange: state land, plus a cash settlement, in return for an easement through the reservation. That decision encouraged tribal efforts elsewhere to resist similar incursions.

Native-American leaders launched lawsuits charging violations of treaty rights in other areas as well. In 1967, in the first of many decisions upholding the Indian side, the U.S. Court of Claims ruled that in 1823 the government had forced the Seminole in Florida to cede their land for an unreasonably low price, and now 144 years later, the government had to pay additional funds. In the 1970s, a number of tribes fought back when corporations, responding to the international oil shortage, tried to extend western coal strip-mining operations on a vast scale, infringing on Indian water rights. In a landmark 1973 case, a federal court ruled that the government must carry out its obligation as trustee to protect Indian property. The courts also upheld various Indian nations' rights to fish without state regulatory intrusion, as guaranteed by nineteenth-century treaties.

Urban Indian activism became highly visible in 1968, when George Mitchell and Dennis Banks, Chippewa living in Minneapolis, founded the American Indian Movement (AIM). It secured Office of Economic Opportunity funds for Indian-controlled organizations and established patrols to protect drunken Indians from police harassment. Chapters formed in other cities.

There were several well-publicized instances of Native American militancy. In 1969, a landing party of 78 Indians seized Alcatraz Island in San Francisco Bay. By converting the island and its defunct federal prison into a cultural and educational center, the protesters hoped, according to author Vine Deloria, Jr., "to see what we could do toward developing answers to modern social problems . . . . It just seems to a lot of Indians that this continent was a lot better off when we were running it." In 1971 federal officials removed the Indians. Then, in 1972, other

The American Indian Movement's armed occupation of Wounded Knee, South Dakota, site of a late-nineteenth-century massacre of the Sioux, resulted in bloodshed that dramatized unfair government treatment of Native Americans. (AP/Wide World Photos)

militants occupied the Bureau of Indian Affairs in Washington for six days. Finally, in 1973, AIM took over the South Dakota village of Wounded Knee, the site of the 1890 Sioux massacre, to dramatize the desperate impoverishment, alcoholism, and hopelessness of the people on the surrounding reservation and to draw attention to the 371 treaties AIM leaders claimed the government had broken. Federal officials encircled the area and, when AIM tried to bring in supplies, killed one Indian and wounded another. The confrontation ended with a government agreement to reexamine the treaty rights of the Indians, although little of substance was subsequently done.

Gaining education and legal skills became important for Native Americans. The number of Indians in college increased from a few hundred in the early 1960s to tens of thousands by 1980. Because roughly half the Indian population lived on reservations, many tribal communities founded their own colleges. Indians studied law and acted as advocates for their own people in the court cases they filed. In 1968, funding from the Office of Economic Opportunity helped the University of New Mexico Law School start a Native American scholarship program. Since 1971, that program has graduated 35 to 40 Indian lawyers each year. They have worked for tribes directly and have successfully argued for tribal jurisdiction in conflicts between whites and Indians on the reservations.

## Government Response

Indian protest brought results. The outcry against termination in the 1960s led the Kennedy and Johnson administrations to steer a middle course, neither endorsing nor disavowing the policy. Instead they tried to bolster reservation economies and raise standards of living by persuading private industries to locate on reservations and by promoting the leasing of reservation lands to energy and development corporations. In the 1970s, the Navajo, Northern Cheyenne, Crow, and other tribes tried to cancel or renegotiate such leases, fearing "termination by corporation."

In the mid-1960s, the Native-American cry for self-determination brought Indian involvement in the Great Society's poverty program. Two agencies, the Area Redevelopment Administration (later the Economic Development Administration) and the Office of Economic Opportunity, responded to pressure by letting Indians devise programs and budgets and to administer programs themselves. Indians were similarly involved with Great Society housing, health, and education initiatives.

Finally, in 1975, Congress passed Indian Self-determination and Education Assistance Acts. Five years earlier, Nixon had declared that self-determination had replaced termination as American policy. The self-determination act was a largely rhetorical statement of that position, while the education act involved subcontracting federal services to tribal groups. Though both laws were limited, they nonetheless reflected the government's decision to respond to Indian pressure and created a framework to guide federal policy in the decades ahead.

## SOCIAL AND CULTURAL PROTEST

As blacks, Latinos, and American Indians agitated, white middle-class American society experienced an unprecedented upheaval. Young people in particular rejected the stable patterns of affluent life their parents had forged. Some embraced radical political activity; many more renounced old standards of sexual behavior and adopted new kinds of music and dress. In time their actions spawned still other protests as Americans tried to make the political and social world more responsive.

## Student Activism

Post–World War II demographic patterns lay behind youthful activism and help explain the generation gap. Members of the baby boom generation came of age in the 1960s. Between 1950 and 1964, the number of students in college more than doubled. By the end of the 1960s, college enrollment stood more than four times above the 1940s level. In college, some students joined the struggle for civil rights. Hopeful at first, they gradually became discouraged by the gap between Kennedy's New Frontier rhetoric and the government's actual commitment.

Out of that disillusionment arose the radical spirit of the New Left. Civil rights activists were among those who in 1960 organized Students for a Democratic Society (SDS). In 1962, SDS issued a manifesto, the Port Huron Statement, written largely by Tom Hayden of the University of Michigan. "We are people of this generation, bred in at least modest comfort, housed now in universities, looking uncomfortably at the world we inherit," it began. It went on to deplore the vast social and economic distances separating people from each other and to condemn the isolation and estrangement of modern life. The document called for a better system, a "democracy of individual participation."

The first blow of the growing student rebellion came at the University of California in Berkeley. There, civil rights activists became involved in a confrontation soon known as the Free Speech Movement. It began in September 1964 when the university refused to allow students to distribute protest material outside the main campus gate. When police arrested one of the leaders, students surrounded the police car and kept it from moving all night.

The university brought charges against the student leaders, and when the regents refused to drop the charges, students occupied the administration building. Mario Savio, one of the arrested, denounced the university as an impersonal machine: "It becomes odious, so we must put our bodies against the gears, against the wheels . . . and make the machine stop until we're free." Folk singer Joan Baez sang "We Shall Overcome," the marching song of the civil rights movement. Then police stormed in and arrested the students in the building. A student strike, with faculty aid, mobilized wider support for the right to free speech.

The Free Speech Movement at Berkeley was basically a plea for traditional liberal reform. Students sought only the reaffirmation of the long-standing right to express themselves, and they aimed their attacks at the university, not at society. Later, in other institutions, the attack broadened. Students sought greater involvement in university affairs, argued for curricular reform, and demanded admission of more minority students. Their success in gaining their demands changed the governance of American higher education.

The mounting protest against the escalation of the Vietnam War fueled and refocused the youth movement. Confrontation became the new tactic of radical students, and protest became a way of life. Between January 1 and June 15, 1968, hundreds of thousands of students staged 221 major demonstrations at more than 100 educational institutions.

One of the most dramatic uprisings, intertwining the antiwar and civil rights protests, came in April 1968 at Columbia University. A strong SDS chapter urged the university to break ties with military research projects. The Students' Afro-American Society tried to stop the building of a new gymnasium, which it claimed encroached on the Harlem community. Whites occupied one building, blacks another. Finally, the university president called in the police. Hundreds of students were arrested; many were hurt. A student sympathy strike followed, and Columbia closed for the summer several weeks early.

The next year, in October 1969, the Weathermen, a militant fringe group of SDS, sought to show that the revolution had arrived by making a frontal attack on Chicago. Weathermen rampaged through the streets with clubs, pipes, chains, and rocks, smashing whatever was in reach. "The status quo meant to us war, poverty, inequality, ignorance, famine and disease in most of the world," Bo Burlingham, a

Weatherman from Ohio, reflected. "To accept it was to condone and help perpetuate it. We felt like miners trapped in a terrible poisonous shaft with no light to guide us out. We resolved to destroy the tunnel even if we risked destroying ourselves in the process." Few other Americans were convinced by such logic.

The New Left was, briefly, a powerful force. Although activists never composed a majority, radicals attracted students and other sympathizers to their cause until the movement fragmented. But while it was healthy, the movement focused opposition to the Vietnam War and challenged inequities in American society in a more pointed way than ever before.

## The Counterculture

Cultural change accompanied political upheaval. In the 1960s, many Americans, particularly young people, lost faith in the sanctity of the American system. "There was a general feeling that the platitudes of Americanism were horseshit," observed Joseph Heller, the irreverent author of the 1961 novel *Catch-22*. Protests exposed the emptiness of some old patterns, and many Americans—some politically active, some not—found new ways to assert individuality and independence. The young led the way, often inspired by the beats of the 1950s as they sought new means of self-gratification and self-expression.

Surface appearances were most visible and, to older Americans, most troubling. The "hippies" of the 1960s carried themselves in different ways. Men grew long hair and sprouted beards; men and women both donned jeans, muslin shirts, and other simple garments. Stressing spontaneity above all else, some rejected traditional marital customs and gravitated to communal living groups. Their example, shocking to some, soon found its way into the culture at large.

A revolution in sexual norms occurred. A generation of young women came of age with access to "the pill"—an oral contraceptive that was effortless to use and freed sexual experimentation from the threat of pregnancy. The first tests took place in the 1950s, and then in 1960, the Food and Drug Administration approved Enovid, the first oral contraceptive available on the market. Within three years of its introduction, more than 2 million women were on the pill, and as the cost dropped, millions more began to use it. Americans of all social classes became more open to exploring, and enjoying, their sexuality. Scholarly findings supported natural inclinations. In 1966, William H. Masters and Virginia E. Johnson published *Human Sexual Response*, based on intensive laboratory observation of couples engaged in sexual activities and destroyed the myth of the sexually passive woman.

Nora Ephron, author and editor, summed up the sexual changes in the 1960s as she reflected on her own experiences. Initially she had "a hangover from the whole Fifties virgin thing," she recalled. "The first man I went to bed with, I was in love with and wanted to marry. The second one I was in love with, but I didn't have to marry him. With the third one, I thought I might fall in love."

The arts reflected the sexual revolution. Federal courts ruled that books like D. H. Lawrence's *Lady Chatterley's Lover,* earlier considered obscene, could not be banned. Nudity became more common on stage and screen.

Paintings reflected both the mood of dissent and the urge to innovate apparent in the larger society. "Op" artists painted geometric figures in vibrant colors, starkly

# Recovering the Past

## Popular Music

One way to recover the past is through music. Popular songs not only provide insight into attitudes and beliefs but also quickly convey the mood and feelings of an era. As the United States confronted the challenges of the counterculture and the crosscurrents of political and social reform, new kinds of music reflected the changes taking place.

Folk music took off at the start of the period. Bob Dylan, a disheveled and gravelly-voiced singer from Minnesota, wrote a number of remarkable protest songs like "Blowin' in the Wind" that were soon sung by other artists like Peter, Paul and Mary as well. His song "The Times They Are A-Changin'" (included here) captured the inexorable force of the student protest movement.

But the 1960s were marked by far more than folk music alone. In early 1964, an English group from Liverpool called the Beatles released "I Want to Hold Your Hand" in the United States and took the country by storm. With *Sergeant Pepper's Lonely Hearts Club Band* a few years later, the Beatles branched out in new musical directions and reflected the influence of the counterculture with songs like "Lucy in the Sky with Diamonds" (which some people said referred to the hallucinogenic drug LSD). Another English group, the Rolling Stones, played a blues-based rock music that proclaimed a commitment to drugs, sex, and a decadent life of social upheaval.

Meanwhile, on the pop scene, Motown Records in Detroit popularized a new kind of black rhythm and blues. By 1960, the gospel-pop-soul fusion was gaining followers. Stevie Wonder, the Temptations, and the Supremes were among the groups who became enormously popular. The Supremes, led by Diana Ross, epitomized the Motown sound with such hits as "Where Did Our Love Go."

The Beatles. (Liaison/Getty Images)

The Supremes. (Brown Brothers)

**Reflecting on the Past**  What songs come to your mind when you think of the 1960s? How is the music different from that of the 1950s? What do the lyrics tell you about the period?

Look at the lyrics for "The Times They Are A-Changin'" reprinted here. What do they tell you about the social upheaval of the 1960s? What, if anything, does the song imply can be done about the changes in the air?

## The Times They Are A-Changin'

Come gather 'round people
Wherever you roam
And admit that the waters
Around you have grown
And accept it that soon
You'll be drenched to the bone.
If your time to you
Is worth savin'
Then you better start swimmin'
Or you'll sink like a stone
For the times they are a-changin'.

Come writers and critics
Who prophesize with your pen
And keep your eyes wide
The chance won't come again
And don't speak too soon
For the wheel's still in spin
And there's no tellin' who
That it's namin'
For the loser now
Will be later to win
For the times they are a-changin'.

Come senators, congressmen
Please heed the call
Don't stand in the doorway
Don't block up the hall
For he that gets hurt
Will be he who has stalled
There's a battle outside
And it is ragin'.
It'll soon shake your windows
And rattle your walls
For the times they are a-changin'.

Come mothers and fathers
Throughout the land
And don't criticize
What you can't understand
Your sons and your daughters
Are beyond your command
Your old road is
Rapidly agin'.
Please get out of the new one
If you can't lend your hand
for the times they are a-changin'.

The line it is drawn
The curse it is cast
The slow one now
Will later be fast
As the present now
Will later be past
The order is
Rapidly fadin'.
And the first one now
Will later be last
For the times they are a-changin'.

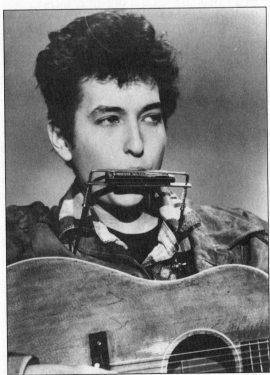

Bob Dylan. (AP/Wide World Photos)

different from the flowing work of the abstract expressionists. "Pop" artists such as Andy Warhol, Roy Lichtenstein, and Jasper Johns made ironic comments on American materialism and taste with their representations of soup cans, comic strips, or Marilyn Monroe.

Hallucinogenic drugs also became a part of the counterculture. Timothy Leary, a Harvard researcher experimenting with LSD, was fired for violating a pledge not to use undergraduates as subjects. Aggressively asserting that drugs were necessary to free the mind, he preached "Tune in, turn on, drop out." Novelist Ken Kesey used the profits from his first book, *One Flew Over the Cuckoo's Nest,* to establish a commune of "Merry Pranksters" in California. In 1964, the group headed east in a converted school bus painted in psychedelic Day-Glo colors, wired for sound, and stocked with enough orange juice and "acid" (LSD) to sustain the Pranksters across the continent.

Drug use was no longer confined to urban subcultures. Soldiers brought experience with drugs back from Vietnam. Young professionals began trying cocaine, and a "tab" of LSD became part of the coming-of-age ritual for many middle-class college students. Marijuana became phenomenally popular in the 1960s.

Music was intimately connected with these cultural changes. The rock and roll of the 1950s and the gentle strains of folk music gave way to a new kind of rock that swept the country—and the world (see the Recovering the Past section of this chapter for a discussion of the music of the 1960s). Festivals at Woodstock and Altamont drew hundreds of thousands of young people.

But there was a disturbing underside to the counterculture, most visible in the Haight-Ashbury section of San Francisco, where runaway "flower children" mingled with "burned-out" drug users and radical activists. "Adolescents drifted from city to torn city, sloughing off both the past and the future as snakes shed their skins, children who were never taught and would never now learn the games that had held the society together," essayist Joan Didion observed in 1967. For all the spontaneity and exuberance, the counterculture's darker side could not be ignored.

## Gay and Lesbian Rights

Closely tied to the revolution in sexual norms was a fast-growing and increasingly militant gay liberation movement. There had always been people who accepted the "gay" lifestyle, but American society as a whole was unsympathetic, and many homosexuals kept their preferences private. The spirit of the times encouraged gays to "come out of the closet." In response to a police raid in 1969 on the Stonewall Inn, a homosexual bar in Greenwich Village in New York, a nightlong riot helped spark a new consciousness and a movement for gay rights. Throughout the 1970s, homosexuals gained partial relief from some of the most blatant forms of discrimination against them. In 1973, the American Psychiatric Association ruled that homosexuality should no longer be classified as a mental illness, and that decision was overwhelmingly supported in a vote by the membership the next year. In 1975, the U.S. Civil Service Commission lifted its ban on the employment of homosexuals.

In this new climate, many gay men who had hidden or suppressed their sexuality revealed their secret. Homosexual women, too, became more open and a lesbian movement developed, sometimes involving more radical feminists. But many Americans and some churches remained unsympathetic—sometimes vehemently so—to those who challenged traditional sexual norms.

## Environmental and Consumer Agitation

Although many of the social movements of the 1960s were defined by race, gender, and sexual preference, one cut across all boundaries. Beginning in the early 1960s, Americans concerned with the environment revived issues dating back to the Progressive era and pushed them further. In the mid-1960s, a Gallup poll revealed that only 17 percent of the public included pollution among the three major problems of the day. By 1970, that figure had risen to 53 percent.

The modern environmental movement stemmed in part from post–World War II yearnings for a better "quality of life." Clear air, unpolluted waters, and unspoiled wilderness became, for many, indispensable to a decent existence (see Chapter 26). And threats to natural surroundings began to worry the public, particularly after naturalist Rachel Carson published her brilliant book *Silent Spring* in 1962. She took aim at chemical pesticides, especially DDT, which had increased crop yields with disastrous side effects. Earth Day in 1970 celebrated the world's natural resources and warned of continuing threats.

Public concern focused on a variety of targets. Americans were troubled in 1969 to learn how thermal pollution from nuclear power plants was killing fish in both eastern and western rivers. An article in *Sports Illustrated* aroused fishermen, sailors, and other previously unconcerned recreational enthusiasts. A massive oil spill off the coast of southern California turned white beaches black and wiped out much of the marine life in the immediate area. In 1978, the public became alarmed about the lethal effects of toxic chemicals dumped in the Love Canal neighborhood of Niagara Falls, New York. A few years later, attention focused on dioxin, one of the poisons in the Love Canal and one of the deadliest substances ever made, which surfaced in a number of locations in concentrated form.

Equally frightening was the potential environmental damage from a nuclear accident. That possibility became more real as a result of a mishap at one of the reactors at Three Mile Island near Harrisburg, Pennsylvania, in 1979. A faulty pressure relief valve led to a loss of coolant. Initially, plant operators refused to believe indicators showing a serious malfunction. Part of the nuclear core became uncovered, part began to disintegrate, and the surrounding steam and water became highly radioactive. There was danger of an explosion releasing radioactivity into the atmosphere, and thousands of area residents fled. The scenario for nuclear disaster depicted in a current film, *The China Syndrome,* suddenly seemed frighteningly real. The worst never occurred, but the plant remained shut down and filled with radioactive debris, a monument to a form of energy once hailed as the wave of the future.

The threat of a nuclear catastrophe underscored the arguments of grassroots environmental activists who campaigned aggressively against licensing new nuclear plants. While they did not always succeed, they mobilized opinion sufficiently that no new plants were authorized after 1978.

Western environmentalists were particularly worried about excessive use of water. The American West, one critic observed, was "the greatest hydraulic society ever built in history." Massive irrigation systems had boosted the nation's use of water from 40 billion gallons a day in 1900 to 393 billion gallons a day by 1975, though the population had only tripled. Americans used three times as much water per capita as the world's average, and far more than other industrialized societies.

One serious source of concern was the Ogallala aquifer in the Great Plains. The drawing of enormous amounts of water in the 1950s and 1960s to make arid areas productive for farming had, by the mid-1970s, dramatically depleted the water stored in the aquifer. Conservation measures might delay, but not prevent, the day of reckoning.

The situation was similar in California. Naturally dry, the state's prosperity rested on massive irrigation projects. In the late 1970s, the state had 1,251 major reservoirs. Virtually every large river had at least one dam. Almost as much water was pumped from the ground, with little natural replenishment and even less regulation. Pointing to the destruction of the nation's rivers and streams and the severe lowering of the water table in many areas, environmentalists argued that something needed to be done before it was too late. Slowly, they attracted a following.

Environmental agitation produced legislative results in the 1960s and 1970s. Lyndon Johnson, whose vision of the Great Society included an "environment that is pleasing to the senses and healthy to live in," won basic legislation to halt the depletion of the country's natural resources (see Chapter 28). In the next few years, environmentalists went further, pressuring legislative and administrative bodies to regulate polluters. Under Richard Nixon, Congress passed the Clean Air Act, the Water Quality Improvement Act, and the Resource Recovery Act and mandated a new Environmental Protection Agency (EPA) to spearhead the effort to control abuses. Initially, these measures aimed at controlling the toxic by-products of the modern industrial order. In subsequent years, environmentalists broadened the effort to include occupational health and social-justice issues.

One such effort developed into an extraordinarily bitter economic and ecological debate. The Endangered Species Act of 1973 prohibited the federal government from supporting any projects that might jeopardize species threatened with extinction. It ran into direct conflict with commercial imperatives in the Pacific Northwest. Loggers in the Olympic Peninsula had long exploited the land by clearcutting (cutting down all trees in a region). Environmentalists claimed that the forests they cut provided the last refuge for the spotted owl. Scientists and members of the U.S. Forest Service pushed to set aside timberland so that the owl could survive. Loggers protested that this action jeopardized their livelihood. As the issue wound its way through the courts, logging fell off drastically.

Another protest against regulation in the late 1970s and early 1980s came to be called the Sagebrush Rebellion. Critics argued that large federal landholdings in the West put that region at a disadvantage in economic competition with the East. They demanded that the national government cede the lands to states, which could sell or lease them for local gain. Conservative state legislatures in the Rocky Mountain states supported the scheme, and ranchers applauded. In the end, it went nowhere, though the agitation did persuade federal authorities to endorse a less restrictive policy on grazing.

# Timeline

| | | | |
|---|---|---|---|
| **1947** | Jackie Robinson breaks the color line in major league baseball | **1966** | Stokely Carmichael becomes head of SNCC and calls for "Black Power" |
| **1950** | Asociación Nacional México-Americana formed | | Black Panthers founded |
| | | | NOW founded |
| **1954** | Brown v. Board of Education | | William H. Masters and Virginia E. Johnson, Human Sexual Response |
| **1955** | Montgomery, Alabama, bus boycott begins | **1967** | Urban riots in 22 cities |
| **1957** | Little Rock, Arkansas, school integration crisis | **1968** | Martin Luther King, Jr., assassinated |
| | Civil Rights Act | | Student demonstrations at Columbia University and elsewhere |
| **1960** | Civil Rights Act | | Chicano student walkouts |
| | Birth control pill becomes available | | American Indian Movement (AIM) founded |
| | Sit-ins begin | **1969** | Woodstock and Altamont rock festivals |
| | Students for a Democratic Society (SDS) founded | | Weathermen's "Days of Rage" in Chicago |
| **1961** | Freedom rides | | Native Americans seize Alcatraz |
| | Joseph Heller, Catch-22 | | La Raza Unida founded |
| | Ken Kesey, One Flew Over the Cuckoo's Nest | **1971–1975** | School busing controversies in North and South |
| **1962** | James Meredith crisis at the University of Mississippi | **1972** | Ms. magazine founded |
| | SDS's Port Huron Statement | | Congress passes Equal Rights Amendment |
| | Rachel Carson, Silent Spring | **1973** | AIM occupies Wounded Knee, South Dakota |
| **1963** | Birmingham demonstration | **1975** | Farmworkers win right to bargain collectively with growers |
| | Civil rights march on Washington | | Indian Self-determination and Education Assistance Acts |
| | Betty Friedan, The Feminine Mystique | **1978** | Bakke v. Regents of the University of California |
| **1964** | Civil Rights Act | **1979** | Accident at Three Mile Island nuclear power plant |
| | Free speech movement, Berkeley | **1982** | Ratification of ERA fails |
| **1965** | Martin Luther King, Jr., leads march from Selma to Montgomery | | |
| | Voting Rights Act | | |
| | United Farm Workers grape strike | | |
| | Malcolm X assassinated | | |
| | Riot in Watts section of Los Angeles | | |
| | Ralph Nader, Unsafe at Any Speed | | |

The consumer movement was related to the environmental movement. As in the Progressive era, Americans worried about unscrupulous sellers. In the 1970s, a stronger consumer movement developed, aimed at protecting the public and making business more responsible to consumers.

Ralph Nader led the movement. His book *Unsafe at Any Speed: The Designed-in Dangers of the American Automobile* (1965) argued that many cars were coffins on wheels. His efforts paved the way for the National Traffic and Motor Vehicle Safety Act of 1966, which set minimum safety standards for vehicles on public highways, provided for inspection to ensure compliance, and created a National Motor Vehicle Safety Advisory Council.

Nader's efforts attracted scores of volunteers, called "Nader's Raiders." They turned out critiques and reports and, more important, inspired consumer activists at all levels of government—city, state, and national. Consumer protection offices began to monitor a flood of complaints as ordinary citizens became more vocal in defending their rights.

◌ᛉ◌ ◌ᛉ◌ ◌ᛉ◌ ◌ᛉ◌

# CONCLUSION

## *Extending the American Dream*

The 1960s and 1970s were turbulent years. Yet this third major reform era of the twentieth century accomplished a good deal for the groups fighting to expand the meaning of equality. African Americans now enjoyed greater access to the rights and privileges enjoyed by mainstream American society, despite the backlash the movement brought. Women like Ann Clarke, introduced at the start of the chapter, returned to school in ever-increasing numbers and found jobs and sometimes independence after years of being told that their place was at home. Native Americans and Latinos mobilized, too, and could see the stirrings of change. Environmentalists created a new awareness of the global dangers the nation and the world faced. Slowly reformers succeeded in pressuring the government to help the nation fulfill its promise and ensure the realization of the ideals of American life.

But the course of change was ragged. The reform effort reached its high-water mark during Lyndon Johnson's Great Society and in the years immediately following, then faltered with the rise of conservatism and disillusionment with liberalism, as noted in Chapter 28. Some movements were circumscribed by the changing political climate; others simply ran out of steam. Still, the various efforts left a legacy of ferment which could help spark further change in future years.

## *Discovering U.S. History Online*

*Timeline of the American Civil Rights Movement*   http://www.wmich.edu/politics/mlk/
This site contains a timeline of events in the 1950s and 1960s with pictures and documents.

*Historical Audio Archives: Voices of the Civil Rights Era*   http://webcorp.com/civilrights/index.htm
This site provides audio clips about the civil rights movement from Martin Luther King, Jr., and Malcolm X.

*Martin Luther King, Jr., Papers Project at Stanford University*
http://www.stanford.edu/group/king/
This site has links and selected digital documents by and about Martin Luther King, Jr.

*American Identities*   http://xroads.virginia.edu/~yp/ethnic.html
This site suggests resources for studying America's multiple ethnic identities.

*Free Speech Movement: Student Protest—U.C. Berkeley, 1964–65*
http://bancroft.berkeley.edu/FSM/
This site describes student protest through oral histories, documents, and a chronology.

*The Sixties Project*   http://lists.village.virginia.edu/sixties/
This site has extensive exhibits, documents, and personal narratives from the 1960s.

*The Digger Archives*   http://www.diggers.org
This site provides information about the San Francisco Diggers, who became one of the legendary groups in Haight-Ashbury during the years 1966–1968.

*1969 Woodstock Festival and Concert*   http://www.woodstock69.com/index.htm
This site provides pictures and lists of songs from the famous rock festival.

*Meltdown at Three Mile Island*   http://www.pbs.org/wgbh/amex/three/
This site provides a chronology and description of the frightening nuclear accident in 1979.

## Fiction and Film

Sara Davidson, *Loose Change* (1977) is a novel about the lives of three young women at the University of California at Berkeley; Richard Fariña, *Been Down So Long It Looks Like Up to Me* (1966) is a novel about hallucinatory life in the 1960s; Marilyn French, *The Women's Room* (1977) is a novel about the impact of the women's movement on a circle of women; N. Scott Momaday, *House Made of Dawn* (1968) is the Pulitzer Prize-winning novel about a young Indian living in two worlds; Alix Kates Shulman, *Memoirs of an Ex-Prom Queen* (1972) is the story of a young midwestern woman and her awakening during and after college.

*Annie Hall* (1977) is Woody Allen's film about the problems of relationships; *Easy Rider* (1969) is a low-budget movie about two motorcyclists looking for freedom in a world of conformity; *The Graduate* (1967) became a cult film as it challenged the values of the 1950s and mocked the priorities of the world in which "plastics" were most important; *In the Heat of the Night* (1967) is a movie about a black man in Mississippi accused of murder solely because of his color; *To Kill a Mockingbird* (1962) is a film about children learning about racism—and how to deal with it—in the South.

## Recommended Reading

### The Black Struggle for Equality
James Baldwin, *The Fire Next Time* (1962); Taylor Branch, *Parting the Waters: America in the King Years, 1954–1963* (1988) and *Pillar of Fire: America in the King Years, 1963–1965* (1998); Clayborne Carson, *In Struggle: SNCC and the Black Awakening of the 1960s* (1981); William H. Chafe, *Civilities and Civil Rights: Greensboro, North Carolina, and the Black Struggle for Freedom* (1980); John Dittmer, *Local People: The Struggle for Civil Rights in Mississippi* (1994); Eric Foner, *The Story of American Freedom* (1998); David J. Garrow, *Bearing the Cross: Martin Luther King, Jr., and the Southern Christian Leadership Conference* (1986); Joanne Grant and Ella Baker: *Freedom Bound* (1998); Martin Luther King, Jr., *Why We Can't Wait*, reissue ed. (1991); John Lewis with Michael D'Orso, *Walking with the Wind: A Memoir of the Movement* (1998); Malcolm X with Alex Haley, *The Autobiography of Malcolm X* (1966); Anne Moody,

*Coming of Age in Mississippi* (1968); Arnold Rampersad, *Jackie Robinson: A Biography* (1997); Harvard Sitkoff, *The Struggle for Black Equality, 1954–1992,* revised ed. (1993).


## Pressure from the Women's Movement

William H. Chafe, *The American Woman: Her Changing Social, Political, and Economic Roles, 1920–1970* (1972); Sara Evans, *Personal Politics: The Roots of Women's Liberation in the Civil Rights Movements and the New Left* (1979); Peter Gabriel Filene, *Him/Her/Self: Sex Roles in Modern America,* 2nd ed. (1986); Jacqueline Jones, *Labor of Love, Labor of Sorrow: Black Women, Work, and the Family from Slavery to the Present* (1985); Alice Kessler-Harris, *Out to Work: A History of Wage-earning Women in the United States* (1982); Susan M. Hartmann, *The Other Feminists: Activists in the Liberal Establishment* (1998); Blanche Linden-Ward, *Changing the Future: American Women in the 1960s* (1993); Gloria Steinem, *Outrageous Acts and Everyday Rebellions,* 2nd ed. (1995); Winifred D. Wandersee, *On the Move: American Women in the 1970s* (1988).


## Latino Mobilization

Rodolfo Acuña, *Occupied America: A History of Chicanos,* 4th ed. (2000); Mario T. García, *Memories of Chicano History: The Life and Narrative of Bert Corona* (1994) and *Mexican Americans: Leadership, Ideology, and Identity, 1930–1960* (1989); Ed Ludwig and James Santibañez, eds., *The Chicanos: Mexican American Voices* (1971); Beatrice Rodriguez Owsley, *The Hispanic-American Entrepreneur: An Oral History of the American Dream* (1992); Peter Skerry, *Mexican Americans: The Ambivalent Minority* (1993).


## Native American Protest

Dee Brown, *Bury My Heart at Wounded Knee: An Indian History of the American West* (1971); Stephen Cornell, *The Return of the Native: American Indian Political Resurgence* (1988); Vine Deloria, Jr., *Custer Died for Your Sins: An Indian Manifesto* (1969); Frederick E. Hoxie, ed., *Indians in American History* (1988); Peter Iverson, *"We Are Still Here": American Indians in the Twentieth Century* (1998); Alvin M. Josephy, Jr., *Now That the Buffalo's Gone* (1982); James S. Olson and Raymond Wilson, *Native Americans in the Twentieth Century* (1984).


## Social and Cultural Protest

Terry H. Anderson, *The Movement and the Sixties: Protest in America from Greensboro to Wounded Knee* (1995) and *The Sixties* (1999); David Burner, *Making Peace with the Sixties* (1996); David Chalmers, *And the Crooked Places Made Straight: The Struggle for Social Change in the 1960s* (1991); Joan Didion, *Slouching Towards Bethlehem* (1968); Barbara Epstein, *Political Protest and Cultural Revolution: Nonviolent Direct Action in the 1970s and 1980s* (1991); David Farber, *The Age of Great Dreams: America in the 1960s* (1994); Todd Gitlin, *The Sixties: Years of Hope, Days of Rage* (1987); Neil A. Hamilton, *The ABC-CLIO Companion to The 1960s Counterculture in America* (1997); W. J. Rorabaugh, *Berkeley at War: The 1960s* (1989); Theodore Roszak, *The Making of a Counter Culture* (1969); Jules Witcover, *The Year the Dream Died: Revisiting 1968 in America* (1998); Tom Wolfe, *The Electric Kool-Aid Acid Test* (1968).

Beth L. Bailey, *From Front Porch to Back Seat: Courtship in Twentieth Century America* (1988); Dudley Clendinen and Adam Nagourney, *Out for Good: The Struggle to Build a Gay Rights Movement in America* (1999); John D'Emilio and Estelle B. Freedman, *Intimate Matters: A History of Sexuality in America* (1988); John Loughery, *The Other Side of Silence: Men's Lives and Gay Identities: A Twentieth Century History* (1998).

Rachel Carson, *Silent Spring* (1962); William Dietrich, *The Final Forest: The Battle for the Last Great Trees of the Pacific Northwest* (1992); Robert Gottlieb, *Forcing the Spring: The Transformation of the American Environmental Movement* (1993); Samuel P. Hays, *Beauty, Health, and Permanence: Environmental Politics in the United States, 1955–1985* (1987); Patricia Nelson Limerick, *The Legacy of Conquest: The Unbroken Past of the American West* (1987); Marc Reisner, *Cadillac Desert: The American West and Its Disappearing Water,* revised and updated ed. (1993); Kirkpatrick Sale, *The Green Revolution: The American Environmental Movement, 1962–1992* (1993); Charles F. Wilkinson, *Crossing the Next Meridian: Land, Water, and the Future of the West* (1992); Donald Worster, *Rivers of Empire: Water, Aridity and the Growth of the American West* (1985).

# CHAPTER 30

# The Revival of Conservatism

## CHAPTER OUTLINE

- The Conservative Transformation
- An End to Social Reform
- Economic and Demographic Change

- Foreign Policy and the End of the Cold War
- Conclusion: Conservative Transformation

## AMERICAN STORIES
### Two Workers Wonder About the American Dream

After 11 years as a baggage handler, Andy Hjelmeland of Maple Plain, Minnesota, found himself out of work in December 1980. Hjelmeland was not immediately concerned, for he had never failed to find employment in the past. Like Hjelmeland, Jerry Espinoza of Los Angeles, California, also lost his job in the early 1980s. He had worked at the Bethlehem Steel Plant for 23 years. Now it closed its doors, and he too faced finding a new job.

Both Hjelmeland and Espinoza, in their mid-40s, discovered that conditions had changed since they had last sought work. The unemployment rate, which stood at 3.5 percent in 1969, was now almost three times as high. Old industries could not compete with more vital firms abroad whose labor costs were much lower, and many workers were let go.

Millions of unemployed Americans pursued every lead for the few jobs available in the early 1980s. Responding to a local newspaper for a "handyman," Hjelmeland found himself up against 300 applicants. Although he had a happy marriage and two healthy sons, he found the strains difficult to bear. He continued to fill out applications and to answer ads, but the repeated rejections filled him with dismay. "It was a new experience for me to confront an impenetrable wall," he observed. "I began to feel like a person on a blacklist." After years of paying bills on time, he now faced a growing stack of unpaid bills. A parking ticket lost in the pile was followed by an arrest warrant that made him feel worse.

With five children to support and mortgage payments due, Espinoza felt similar strains. Unemployment benefits and his wife's paychecks kept the family going, but his problems, like Hjelmeland's, mounted. After his two decades at Bethlehem, he had hearing problems, a result

905

of running noisy machines without ear protection. His left hand was scarred, and two fingers were numb from an accident on the job. A back injury from work still troubled him. "When I go looking for a job, no one is hiring," Espinoza said. "Or maybe they are hiring but they look at me and maybe I'm too old or maybe it's my nationality, because they still discriminate." The discrimination rankled most of all. Latinos had a jobless rate of 13.8 percent in 1982, far higher than the Anglo rate of 8.6 percent. It was hard to subscribe to the American dream when the doors of opportunity were closed.

For both Hjelmeland and Espinoza, old attitudes gave way as the months of unemployment grew. Hjelmeland had previously viewed food stamp recipients as "freeloaders," but now he had to apply for food stamps himself. "My wavering self-esteem plummeted," he confessed. "By my own lights I had officially become a loser." Espinoza was similarly glum. "One day you're OK, the next day you're depressed," he said. "We're just lost souls now, that's what we are, lost souls."

Both Hjelmeland and Espinoza found the Republican administration in Washington insensitive to their fate. When President Ronald Reagan, who took office in early 1981, lashed out at television officials for harping on continuing economic troubles and asked, "Is it news that some fellow out in South Succotash someplace has just been laid off [and] . . . should be interviewed nationwide?" Hjelmeland was irate. "I wish," he said, "the President could be that unemployed guy in South Succotash for just one month." The conservative administration had an economic recovery program, but to the unemployed it often seemed slow and unworkable.

❧ ❧ ❧ ❧

The difficulties of Hjelmeland and Espinoza mirrored those of countless Americans in the 1980s who could not understand what had gone wrong. At a time when people were recovering from the shocks of the Vietnam War and the disillusionment of the Watergate affair, they found their nation mired in the worst economic recession since the dismal days of the Great Depression half a century before. Over the next few years the economy improved, but as more affluent Americans prospered from the policies of the Reagan administration, the poor found conditions unchanged. Gaps between rich and poor grew larger; poverty became more widespread; members of minority groups encountered continued difficulty finding jobs; the national debt skyrocketed; and finally, the stock market crashed. Meanwhile, harsh Cold War rhetoric led to fears that the continuing confrontation between the Soviet Union and the United States might end in nuclear war.

This chapter describes the enormous changes that occurred in the 1980s and early 1990s. It highlights the economic and technological shifts that affected the daily lives of millions of Americans, bringing unprecedented prosperity to people at the top of the economic pyramid but leaving millions of less fortunate Americans behind. It explores the efforts of the Republican administrations of Ronald Reagan and George Bush to redefine the government's role in the economy, and assesses the impact it had on people like Andy Hjelmeland and Jerry Espinoza. And it examines how foreign policy initiatives brought a successful end to the Cold War.

# THE CONSERVATIVE TRANSFORMATION

In the 1980s and early 1990s, the Republican party reestablished itself as the dominant force in national politics. The Republican ascendancy that had begun in the Nixon era was now largely complete. The liberal agenda that had governed national affairs ever since the New Deal of Franklin Roosevelt gave way to a new Republican coalition determined to scale back the welfare state and prevent what it perceived as the erosion of the nation's moral values. Firmly in control of the presidency, sometimes in control of the Senate and later the whole Congress, the Republican party set the new national agenda.

## The New Politics

Conservatism gained respect in the 1980s. It attracted countless new adherents after the turbulence of the 1960s and the backlash of the Vietnam War. Innovative advertising and fund-raising techniques capitalized on national disaffection with liberal solutions to continuing social problems and made the conservative movement almost unstoppable.

Conservatives seized on Thomas Jefferson's maxim: "That government is best which governs least." They argued that the United States in the 1980s had entered an era of limits, with international competition making resources scarcer. The dramatic economic growth of the 1960s and 1970s, they believed, left a legacy of rising inflation, falling productivity, enormous waste, and out-of-control entitlements. The liberal solution of "throwing money at social problems" no longer worked, conservatives argued. They therefore sought to downsize government, reduce taxes, and roll back regulations they claimed hampered business competition in order to restore the focus on individual initiative and private enterprise.

The conservative philosophy had tremendous appeal. It promised profitability to those who worked hard and showed initiative. It attracted middle-class Americans, who were troubled that they were being forgotten in the commitment to assist minorities and the poor. It also offered hope for the revival of basic social and religious values that many citizens worried had been eaten away by rising divorce rates, legalized abortion, homosexuality, and media preoccupation with violence and sex.

The new conservative coalition covered a broad spectrum. Some followers embraced the economic doctrines of the University of Chicago's Milton Friedman, who promoted the free play of market forces and a sharp restriction of governmental activism in regulating the economy. Others applauded the social and political conservatism of North Carolina Senator Jesse Helms, a tireless foe of anything he deemed pornographic and a fervent campaigner for a limited federal role. Still others flocked to the Republican fold because of their conviction that civil rights activists and "bleeding heart liberals" practiced "reverse racism" with affirmative action, job quotas, and busing to promote equal opportunity.

The conservative coalition also drew deeply from religious fundamentalists who advocated a literal interpretation of Scriptures. Millions—devout Catholics, orthodox Jews, evangelical Protestants—demanded a return to stricter standards of morality. Muslims, relying on the Koran, took an equally fundamentalist approach. All groups worried about sexual permissiveness and gay rights. They were disturbed at the increase in the number of women working outside the home, a practice they believed eroded family life. They were bothered by a sizable increase in crime. They were likewise troubled by the increase in drug use. Marijuana was not simply a youthful fad but a recreational drug for a broad segment of society. Cocaine use was increasingly common. In short, fundamentalists objected to what they viewed as the liberalizing tendencies they saw all around them and sought to refashion society by reaffirming scriptural morality and the centrality of religion in American life.

Many of these activists belonged to the so-called Moral Majority. The Reverend Jerry Falwell of Virginia and other television evangelists who focused the concerns of religious fundamentalism attracted large followings in the 1980s. Emulating Father Charles E. Coughlin, the radio priest of the 1930s, they appealed to audiences who knew them only on the airwaves. Using electronic means to preach fiery sermons to enormous audiences, they focused their television congregations on specific political ends. They also used their fund-raising ability to support candidates sympathetic to their cause. Moral Majority money began to fund politicians who demanded reinstituting school prayer, ending legalized abortion, and defeating the Equal Rights Amendment. Later a group calling itself the Christian Coalition became even more powerful in supporting—and electing—candidates who met its litmus test on conservative values.

Conservatives from all camps capitalized on changing political techniques more successfully than their liberal opponents. They understood the importance of television in providing instant access to the American public. Politicians became increasingly adept at using "sound bytes," often lasting no more than 15 or 30 seconds, to state their views. By the 1990s, they were exploiting e-mail, fax, and the Internet to mobilize their followers.

Similarly, conservatives outdid liberals in using negative political advertising. Mudslinging has always been a part of the American political tradition, but now carefully crafted television ads concentrated not so much on conveying a positive image of a candidate's platform but on subtly attacking an opponent's character in order to create fundamental doubt in a voter's mind. That effort was visible in both presidential and congressional campaigns.

Conservatives likewise led the way in refining their appeal to voters. Polls, sometimes taken daily, showed which part of a candidate's image needed polishing or where an opponent was vulnerable. "Spin doctors" put the best possible gloss on what politicians said. Small wonder that Americans became increasingly cynical about politics and avoided voting booths in record numbers.

Conservatives also were most successful in raising unprecedented sums of money for their campaigns. Richard Viguerie, the New Right mastermind, understood how to tap the huge conservative constituency for political ends. A young Houston activist who later moved to Washington, he developed direct-mail appeals that assisted conservative candidates around the country.

At the same time, conservatives understood the need to provide an intellectual grounding for their positions. Conservative scholars worked in think tanks and other research organizations such as the Hoover Institution at Stanford University

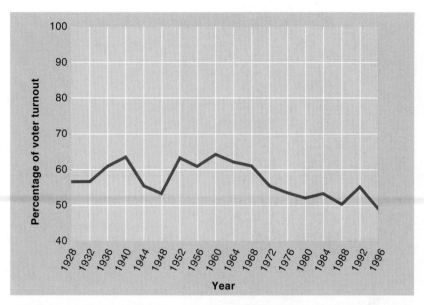

**VOTER TURNOUT, 1928–1996** Voter turnout was far lower in the twentieth century than it had been in the nineteenth century. The fact that barely 50 percent of the electorate voted in the last decade reflects a pervasive sense of disillusionment with the political process. (*Source:* Data from *Historical Statistics of the United States* and *Statistical Abstract of the United States.*)

or the American Enterprise Institute in Washington, D.C., that gave conservatism a solid institutional base. Their books, articles, and reports helped elect Ronald Reagan and other conservative politicians.

## Conservative Leadership

More than any other Republican, Ronald Reagan was responsible for the success of the conservative cause. An actor turned politician, he had been a radio broadcaster in his native Midwest, then gravitated to California, where he began a movie career. His success affected his political inclinations, and he changed his affiliation from Democrat to Republican. His visibility and ability to articulate corporate values as a public spokesman for General Electric attracted the attention of conservatives who recognized his political potential and helped him win election as governor of California in 1966. He failed in his first bid for the presidency in 1976 but consolidated his strength over the next four years. By 1980, he had the firm support of the growing right, which applauded his promise to reduce the size of the federal government but bolster military might.

Running against incumbent Jimmy Carter in 1980, Reagan scored a landslide victory, gaining a popular vote of 51 to 41 percent and a 489 to 49 Electoral College advantage. He also led the Republican party to control of the Senate for the first time since 1955. In 1984, he was reelected by an even larger margin. He received 59 percent of the popular vote and swamped Democratic candidate Walter Mondale in the Electoral College 525 to 13, losing only Minnesota, Mondale's home state,

Ronald Reagan drew on his experience in the movies to project an appealing, if old-fashioned, image. Though he was the nation's oldest president, he gave the appearance of vitality. Here he is pictured with his wife Nancy, who was one of his most influential advisers. (The White House, Courtesy White House Historical Association)

and the District of Columbia. The Democrats, however, netted two additional seats in the Senate and maintained superiority in the House of Representatives.

Reagan had a pleasing manner and a special skill as a media communicator. Relying on his acting experience, he used television as Franklin D. Roosevelt had used radio in the 1930s. He was a gifted storyteller who loved using anecdotes or one-liners to make his point. In 1980, for example, he quibbled playfully with Carter over definitions of economic doldrums. "I'm talking in human terms and he is hiding behind a dictionary," Reagan said. "If he wants a definition, I'll give him one. A recession is when your neighbor loses his job. A depression is when you lose yours. A recovery is when Jimmy Carter loses his."

Reagan enjoyed enormous popularity. People talked about a "Teflon" presidency, making a comparison with nonstick frying pans, for even serious criticisms failed to stick and disagreements over policy never diminished his personal approval ratings. When he left the White House, an overwhelming 68 percent of the American public approved of his performance over the past eight years.

But Reagan had a number of liabilities that surfaced over time. As the oldest president the nation had ever had, his attention often drifted, and he occasionally fell asleep during meetings. In press conferences, he was frequently unsure about what was being asked. Uninterested in governing, he delegated a great deal of authority, even if that left him unclear about policy decisions.

Worst of all, he suffered from charges of "sleaze" in his administration. In a period of several months during his last year in office, one former aide was convicted of lying under oath to conceal episodes of influence peddling. Another was convicted of illegally lobbying former government colleagues. His attorney general escaped indictment but nonetheless resigned after severe criticism for improprieties.

In 1988, Republican George Bush, who served eight years as Reagan's vice president, ran for the presidency. Though a New Englander, he had prospered in the Texas oil industry, then served in Congress, as top envoy to China, and as head of the CIA. Termed a preppy wimp by the press, he became a pit bull who ran a mudslinging campaign against his Democratic opponent, Governor Michael Dukakis of Massachusetts. On election day, Bush gained a 54–46 percent popular vote majority and carried 40 states, giving him a 426–112 electoral vote victory. But he did not have the kind of mandate Reagan had enjoyed eight years earlier, and Democrats controlled both houses of Congress.

Bush quickly put his own imprint on the presidency. Despite his upper-crust background, he was an unpretentious man who made a point of trying to appear down-to-earth. He also maintained his own network of friends and political contacts through handwritten notes, telephone calls, and personal visits. More than a year and a half into his term, he was still on his political honeymoon, with a personal approval rating of 67 percent. Support grew even stronger as he presided over the Persian Gulf War in 1991. Then, as the economy faltered and the results of the war seemed suspect, approval levels began to drop and he failed in his bid for reelection in 1992 (see Chapter 31).

## Republican Policies at Home

Republicans in the 1980s and early 1990s aimed to reverse the stagnation of the Carter years and to provide new opportunities for business to prosper. To that end Reagan proposed and implemented an economic recovery program that rested on the theory of supply-side economics. According to this much-criticized theory, reduction of taxes would encourage business expansion, which in turn would lead to a larger supply of goods to help stimulate the system as a whole. Even George Bush, during his brief run for the Republican nomination in 1980, was critical, charging that Reagan was promoting "voodoo economics." Despite such criticism, Republicans followed the president's lead and endorsed "Reaganomics" with its promise of a revitalized economy.

One early initiative involved tax reductions. A 5 percent cut in the tax rate was enacted to go into effect on October 1, 1981, followed by 10 percent cuts in 1982 and 1983. Although all taxpayers received some tax relief, the rich gained far more than middle- and lower-income Americans. Poverty-level Americans did not benefit at all. Tax cuts and enormous defense expenditures increased the budget deficit. From $74 billion in 1980, it jumped to $290 billion in 1992. Such massive deficits drove the gross federal debt—the total national indebtedness—upward from $909 billion in 1980 to $4.4 trillion in 1992. When Reagan assumed office, the per capita national debt was $4,035; 10 years later, in 1990, it was about $12,400.

Faced with the need to raise more money and rectify an increasingly skewed tax code, in 1986 Congress passed and Reagan signed the most sweeping tax reform since the federal income tax began in 1913. It lowered rates, consolidated brackets, and closed loopholes to expand the tax base. Though it ended up neither increasing nor decreasing the government's tax take, the measure was an important step toward treating low-income Americans more equitably. Still, most of the benefits went to the richest 5 percent of Americans.

At the same time, Reagan embarked on a major program of deregulation. In a campaign more comprehensive than Jimmy Carter's, he focused on agencies of

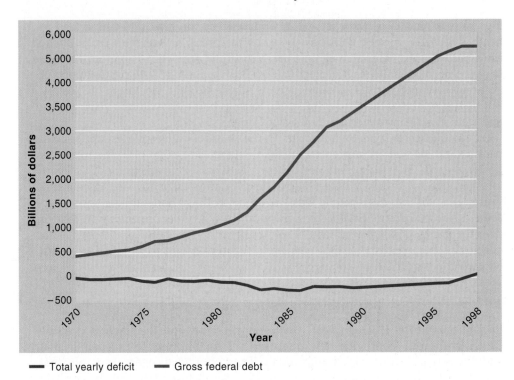

**FEDERAL BUDGET DEFICITS AND THE NATIONAL DEBT, 1970–1998**   In the 1970s, 1980s, and early 1990s, the yearly federal deficit grew steadily larger, and the gross federal debt skyrocketed. Although the deficit began to decline after 1992 and the government announced a budget surplus in 1998, the gross federal debt continued to climb, moving over $5 trillion. (*Source:* Data from *Statistical Abstract of the United States.*)

the 1970s such as the Environmental Protection Agency, the Consumer Product Safety Commission, and the Occupational Safety and Health Administration. The Republican administration argued that regulations pertaining to the consumer, the workplace, and the environment were inefficient, paternalistic, and excessively expensive. They impeded growth and needed to be eliminated.

Meanwhile, Reagan challenged the New Deal consensus that the federal government should monitor the economy and assist the least fortunate citizens. He had played by the rules of the system and had won fame and fortune. Others could do the same. He charged that government intruded too deeply into American life. It was time to eliminate "waste, fraud, and abuse" by cutting unnecessary programs.

Reagan needed to curtail social programs both because of sizable tax cuts and because of enormous military expenditures. Committed to a massive arms buildup, over a five-year period the administration sought an unprecedented military budget of $1.5 trillion. By 1985, with an allocation of $300 billion, the United States was spending half a million dollars a minute on defense and four times as much as at the height of the Vietnam War.

The huge cuts in social programs reversed the approach of liberals over the past 50 years. Republicans in the 1970s had begun to question the social policy goals of Lyndon Johnson's Great Society (see Chapter 28). In the 1980s, they attacked those liberal aims head-on. They eliminated public service jobs and reduced other aid to the cities, where the poor congregated. They cut back unemployment compensation and required Medicare patients to pay more for treatment. They lowered welfare benefits and food stamp allocations. They slashed the Legal Services Corporation, which provided legal services for the poor. They replaced grants for college students with loans. Spending on human resources fell by $101 billion between 1980 and 1982. The process continued even after Reagan left office. Between 1981 and 1992, federal spending (adjusted for inflation) fell 82 percent for subsidized housing, 63 percent for job training and employment services, and 40 percent for community services. Middle-class Americans, benefiting from the tax cuts, were not hurt by the slashes in social programs. But for millions of the nation's poorest citizens, the administration's approach caused real suffering.

As a political conservative distrustful of centralized government, Reagan wanted to place more power in the hands of state and local governments and to reduce the involvement of the federal government in people's lives. His "New Federalism" attempted to shift responsibilities from the federal to the state level. By eliminating federal funding and instead making grants to the states, which could spend the money as they saw fit, he hoped to fortify local initiative. Critics charged, with some justification, that the proposal was merely a back-handed way of moving programs from one place to another, while eliminating federal funding. When a prolonged recession began in 1990, the administration's policy contributed to the near-bankruptcy of a number of states and municipalities, which now bore responsibility for programs formerly funded in Washington.

Reagan took a conservative approach to social issues as well. Accepting the support of the New Right, he strongly endorsed conservative social goals. To avoid compromising his economic program, however, he provided only symbolic support at first. He spoke out for public prayer in the schools without expending political capital in Congress to support the issue. In the same way, he showed his opposition to abortion by making sure that the first nongovernmental group to receive an audience at the White House was an antiabortion March for Life contingent.

George Bush followed directly in his predecessor's footsteps. Having forsworn his objection to "voodoo economics" as soon as he received the vice-presidential nomination, Bush faithfully adhered to Reagan's general economic policy even after he became president. Running for president in 1988, he promised "no new taxes." Though he backed down from that pledge to join a bipartisan effort to bring the budget deficit under control, he later renounced his own agreement to modest tax increases when he went back on the campaign trail in 1992.

Like Reagan, Bush wanted deep cuts in social programs. Tireless in his criticism of the Democratic majorities in the Senate and House of Representatives, he vetoed measure after measure to assist those caught in the ravages of a troubling recession that sent unemployment rates up to 8 percent and left one of every four urban children living in poverty.

Bush was more outspoken than Reagan in his support of conservative social goals. At the start of the 1980s, conservatives had questioned Bush's commitment to their social agenda, and, indeed, Bush had been sympathetic to a woman's

In 1988 and again in 1992, George Bush and the Republicans emphasized traditional family values as a way of healing the social ills of the nation. In this campaign picture, Bush poses with his family at their home in Maine as a way of showing that he was a good family man. (Sipa Press)

right to choice in the abortion issue. As president, however, he firmly opposed abortion, and his Supreme Court appointments, like Reagan's, guaranteed that the effort to roll back or overturn *Roe* v. *Wade* would continue.

The Republican philosophy under Reagan and Bush dramatically reversed the nation's domestic agenda. Liberalism in the 1960s had reached a high-water mark in a time of steady growth, when hard choices about where to spend money had been less necessary. As limits began to loom, decisions about social programs became more difficult, and millions of Americans came to believe that most of the Great Society programs had failed to conquer poverty and in fact had created life-long welfare dependency. Conservatism offered a more attractive answer, particularly to those Americans in the middle and upper classes who were already comfortable.

But the transformation was accompanied by a number of serious problems that emerged in the early 1990s. Bush faced a crisis in the long-mismanaged savings and loan industry. The Republican deregulation policy had allowed owners of savings and loan institutions to operate without previous restrictions. Many, paying themselves lavish salaries, made unwise high-risk investments that proved profitable for a while but then produced tremendous losses. To protect depositors whose assets had been lost by these questionable lending practices, Congress approved a $166 billion rescue plan (that soon reached more than $250 billion) committing taxpayers to bail out the industry.

Republican policy also widened the gap between rich and poor. Tax breaks for the wealthy, deregulation initiatives, high interest rates for investors, permissiveness toward mergers, and an enormous growth in the salaries of top business executives all contributed to the disparity. So did more lenient antitrust enforcement and a general sympathy for speculative finance.

The results of the 1980s were clear. This was "a decade of money fever," according to author Tom Wolfe. It reflected "the triumph of upper America," analyst Kevin Phillips observed, "an ostentatious celebration of wealth, the political ascendancy of the rich and a glorification of capitalism, free markets and finance." The concentration of capital increased, and the sums involved took what Phillips termed a "megaleap" forward. Now there was an extraordinary amassing of wealth at the top levels, among the dekamillionaires, centmillionaires, half-billionaires, and billionaires. "Garden-variety millionaires," Phillips noted, "had become so common that there were about 1.5 million of them by 1989." According to one study, the share of national wealth of the richest 1 percent of the nation rose from about 18 percent in 1976 to 36 percent in 1989. The net worth of the *Forbes* magazine 400 richest Americans nearly tripled between 1981 and 1989.

Meanwhile, less fortunate Americans suffered more than they had since the Great Depression. Financial expert Felix Rohatyn decried the "huge transfer of wealth from lower-skilled, middle-class American workers to owners of capital assets and a new technological aristocracy." Millions of people, ranging from foreclosed farmers to laid-off industrial workers like Andy Hjelmeland and Jerry Espinoza, met at the start of the chapter, were struggling to make ends meet.

## AN END TO SOCIAL REFORM

The Republican attack on the welfare state included an effort to limit the commitment to social reform. Enough had been done already, conservatives argued, and gains for less fortunate Americans came at the expense of the middle class. It was time to end federal "intrusion" in this area.

### Slowdown in the Struggle for Civil Rights

Republican policies slowed the civil rights movement. Reagan opposed busing to achieve racial balance, and his attorney general worked to dismantle affirmative action programs. Initially reluctant to support extension of the enormously successful Voting Rights Act of 1965, Reagan relented only under severe bipartisan criticism. He directed the Internal Revenue Service to cease banning tax exemptions for private schools that discriminated against blacks, only to see that move overturned by the Supreme Court in 1983. He also launched an assault on the Civil Rights Commission and hampered its effectiveness by appointing members who did not support its main goals.

The courts similarly weakened commitments to equal rights. As a result of Reagan's and Bush's judicial appointments, federal courts stopped pushing for school integration. The Supreme Court's *Freeman* v. *Pitts* decision in 1992 granted a suburban Atlanta school board relief from a desegregation order on the grounds that it was not possible to counteract massive demographic shifts.

Yet African Americans kept the struggle alive. The Reverend Jesse Jackson, a longtime civil rights activist, established what he called the Rainbow Coalition in

Jesse Jackson demonstrated that an African American could attract a substantial level of support as he ran for president in 1984 and 1988. Here he is shown on the campaign trail in Chicago in 1988. (© Pokempner, 1999)

1984 and ran for the presidency. Though he lost in his bid for the Democratic nomination, he had the support of nearly 400 delegates and in a nationally televised speech at the convention he vowed not to forget his constituency of "the desperate, the damned, the disinherited, the disrespected, and the despised." All Americans, he went on, needed to work together for a common cause: "Our flag is red, white and blue, but our nation is a rainbow—red, yellow, brown, black and white—and we're all precious in God's sight." Four years later, in 1988, he sought the Democratic nomination again, this time with the support of 1200 delegates at the convention, before falling short of his goal once more.

Despite significant progress in other areas of the electoral arena—where African Americans won mayoral elections in major cities and captured the governor's office in Virginia—black-white relations remained tense. As Joseph Lattimore, an African American from Chicago, observed, "As far as integrating with you—we have sang 'We Shall Overcome,' we have prayed at the courthouse steps, we have made all these gestures, and the door is not open." Sylvia Matthews, from the same city, noted, "Today it seems more acceptable to be racist. Just in the kinds of things you hear people say."

A riot in Los Angeles in 1992 revealed the continuing racial polarization. The year before, Americans had watched a videotaped savage beating of black motorist Rodney King by white police officers, the most dramatic of a long string of incidents involving police brutality. When a California jury lacking any African Americans acquitted the policemen, many people throughout the country became convinced that people of color could not obtain equal justice under the law. In Los Angeles thousands reacted with uncontrolled fury. As widespread arson and looting swept through many neighborhoods, the police proved unable to control the mayhem. Much of it was led by gang members but it also involved hundreds of ordinary citizens who acted irresponsibly, yet with a sense that the social contract had been broken by politicians and the rich who were unresponsive to their plight. Several days later, after the riot had run its course, 51 people (most of them black and Hispanic) lay dead, 2,000 were injured, and $1 billion in damage had been done to the city. It was the worst riot in decades, more deadly even than the Watts riot 27 years before. Political candidates from both parties scurried around trying to define an urban policy, as the upheaval served notice that racial injustice, social inequality, and poverty could no longer be ignored.

## Obstacles to Women's Rights

Women had a similar experience in the 1980s and early 1990s. They, too, made significant electoral gains at the local, state, and national levels. In 1981, President Reagan named Sandra Day O'Connor as the first woman Supreme Court justice, and in 1984 Democrat Geraldine Ferraro became the first major-party female vice-presidential nominee.

Yet women still faced serious problems that were compounded by conservative social policies. Access to new positions did not change their concentration in lower-paying jobs. In 1985, most working women were still secretaries, cashiers, bookkeepers, registered nurses, and waitresses—the same jobs most frequently held 10 years before. Even when women moved into positions traditionally held by men, their progress often stopped at the lower and middle levels. Interruptions of work—to bear children or assume family responsibilities—impeded advancement. A "glass ceiling" seemed to prevent them from moving up.

Wage differentials between women and men continued to exist. In 1985, full-time working women still earned only 63.6 cents for every dollar earned by men. Their concentration in traditional women's jobs made further improvement difficult. Comparable-worth arguments that women should receive equal pay for different jobs of similar value met conservative resistance.

Conservatives also waged a dedicated campaign against the right to legal abortion. Despite the 1973 Supreme Court decision legalizing abortion, the issue remained very much alive. The number of abortions increased dramatically in the decade after the decision. In response, "pro-life" forces mobilized. Opponents lobbied to cut off federal funds that allowed the poor to obtain the abortions the better-off could pay for themselves; they insisted that abortions should be performed in hospitals and not in less expensive clinics; and they worked to reverse the original decision itself.

Though the Supreme Court underscored its judgment in 1983, the pro-life movement was not deterred. In 1989, a solidifying conservative majority on the Court ruled in *Webster* v. *Reproductive Health Services* that while women's right to abortion remained intact, state legislatures could impose limitations if they chose. With that judgment, a major legislative debate over the issue began, and numerous states began to mandate restrictions.

In 1992, in *Planned Parenthood* v. *Casey*, the Supreme Court reaffirmed what it termed the essence of the right to abortion, while permitting further state restrictions. It declared that a 24-hour waiting period for women seeking abortions was acceptable and required teenage girls to secure the permission of a parent (or a judge) before ending a pregnancy. The ruling clearly gave states greater latitude in the overall restrictive effort and made an abortion harder to obtain, particularly for poor women and young women.

In response to a conservative backlash, the women's movement became more inclusive and more sensitive to race. Black women now found more common ground with white feminists. While black women in the early 1990s still earned less, on a weekly basis, than white men and white women, that situation began to improve.

Women and men became more sensitive to the issue of sexual harassment. The dramatic confrontation between Supreme Court nominee Clarence Thomas and lawyer Anita Hill during confirmation hearings in 1991 dramatized both racial questions and the problem of sexual harassment. In the aftermath, Americans in Congress, in the business community, and in the larger workplace all became more aware of inappropriate behavior that could no longer be tolerated.

## The Limited Commitment to Latino Rights

Latinos likewise faced continuing problems in the 1980s and 1990s as the commitment to reform eroded. Spanish-speaking students often found it difficult to finish school. In 1987, fully 40 percent of all Latino high school students did not graduate, and only 31 percent of Latino seniors were enrolled in college-preparatory courses; those who were in such classes frequently received little help from guidance counselors. Anel Albarran, a Mexican immigrant who arrived in East Los Angeles when she was 11, applied to UCLA when a special high school teacher encouraged her and made sure that she received help in choosing the necessary courses. By contrast, her regular counselor took little interest in her, only asking her two months before graduation whether she had considered college. "All he had wanted to do during high school," Anel observed, "was give me my classes and get me out of the room."

College itself was another problem. Of those Latinos who went to college in the early 1990s, 56 percent attended community colleges. Graduation often proved difficult; fewer than 7 percent completed a course of study. When forced to take courses with little connection to their background and less relevance to their lives, many students became frustrated and dropped out.

Like other groups, Latinos slowly extended their political gains. In the 1980s, Henry Cisneros became mayor of San Antonio and Federico Peña was elected mayor of Denver. In New Mexico, Governor Toney Anaya called himself the nation's highest elected Hispanic. The number of Latinos holding elective offices nationwide increased 3.5 percent between 1986 and 1987, and the number of Latina women in such offices increased 20 percent in that time. The number of Latino public officials nationwide increased 73 percent between 1985 and 1994, and Lauro Cavazos became the first Latino Cabinet official when he was appointed secretary of education in 1988.

Latino workers, however, continued to have a hard time in the employment market. Even as the nation's overall unemployment rate dropped, the rate for the 12 million Latino workers barely budged—and worsened in relation to the rate for African Americans. Many found themselves suffering from outdated skills and weak educational backgrounds that limited economic opportunities.

## Continuing Problems for Native Americans

Native Americans likewise experienced the waning commitment to reform, and their gains came as a result of their own efforts. Some tribal communities developed business skills, although traditional Indian attitudes hardly fostered the capitalist perspective. As Dale Old Horn, an MIT graduate and department head at Little Big Horn College in Crow Agency, Montana, explained:

> The Crow Indian child is taught that he is part of a harmonious circle of kin relations, clans and nature. The white child is taught that he is the center of the circle. The Crow believe in sharing wealth, and whites believe in accumulating wealth.

Some Indian groups did adapt to the capitalist ethos. "Now we're beginning to realize that, if we want to be self-sufficient, we're going to have to become entrepreneurs ourselves," observed Iola Hayden, the Comanche executive director of Oklahomans for Indian Opportunity. The Choctaw in Mississippi were among the most successful. Before they began a drive toward self-sufficiency in 1979, their unemployment rate was 50 percent. By the middle of the 1980s, Choctaws owned all or part of three businesses on the reservation, employed 1,000 people, generated $30 million in work annually, and cut the unemployment rate in half. After Congress approved Native-American gambling in 1988, an increasing number of tribes became involved in this industry. The Pequots in Connecticut built a casino in the southeastern part of the state that became the most profitable one in the nation.

Despite entrepreneurial gains, Indians still remained, as the 1990 census showed, the nation's poorest group. As Ben Nighthorse Campbell, Republican senator from Colorado, noted in 1995, average Indian household income fell by 5 percent in the 1980s, while it rose for all other ethnic and racial groups. Median Indian household income, according to the 1990 census, was less than $20,000 a year.

## Pressures on the Environmental Movement

Environmentalists, too, were discouraged by the direction of public policy in the 1980s and early 1990s. Activists found that they faced fierce opposition in the Republican years. Reagan systematically restrained the EPA in his avowed effort to promote economic growth. The Department of the Interior opened forest lands, wilderness areas, and coastal waters to economic development, with no concern for preserving the natural environment. Bush initially proved more sympathetic to environmental causes and delighted environmentalists by signing new clean air legislation. Later, as the economy faltered, he was less willing to support environmental action that he claimed might slow economic growth. In 1992, he accommodated business by easing clean air restrictions. That same year, at a United

Nations-sponsored Earth Summit in Rio de Janeiro, Brazil, with 100 other heads of state, Bush stood alone in his refusal to sign a biological diversity treaty framed to conserve plant and animal species.

## ECONOMIC AND DEMOGRAPHIC CHANGE

Republicans sought to reorganize the government against the backdrop of an economy that was volatile in the 1980s and early 1990s. As patterns of employment changed in an increasingly mechanized workplace, millions of workers like Andy Hjelmeland and Jerry Espinoza, met at the start of the chapter, struggled to survive the shocks. Under Republican supply-side economics, the business cycle moved from recession to boom and back to recession again. When Reagan took office in 1980, the economy was reeling under the impact of declining productivity, galloping inflation, oil shortages, and high unemployment. It revived in the early 1980s but faltered in the last years of the decade and gave way to a deep recession that lasted from 1990 to 1992 and underscored the need for renewed productivity, full employment, and equitable distribution of wealth.

### The Changing Nature of Work

Automation and other technological advances had a powerful impact on the American workplace and brought about a shift in the occupational structure of the working class. Because of such advances, the *New York Times* reported in 1990 in an article on the industrial Midwest, "Some factories look as if they have been hit by a kind of economic neutron bomb, which left assembly lines running at full speed but eliminated most of the people who worked on them." Formerly profitable jobs disappeared. One pulp mill worker voiced gloom about the future: "I think the country has a problem. The managers want everything run by computers. But if no one has a job, no one will know how to do anything anymore. Who will pay the taxes? What kind of society will it be when people have lost their knowledge and depend on computers for everything?"

In human terms, the introduction of the computer had other consequences as well. Now workers sat for hours before their screens. Some described the feeling of "floating in space" as they worked, or of being "lost behind the screen." Others worried about radiation from the monitor or muscular fatigue from sitting at a keyboard all day. Still others complained that they could no longer touch their work.

Yet even as the nature of work changed, people seemed to be working more. In past decades leisure time had seemed to expand and there was talk of a four-day workweek in the 1950s. In subsequent years, however, the amount of time Americans worked steadily rose so that the mid-1990s American employees worked more hours each year than their counterparts in Germany or France.

In the process, they experienced more stress, as they attempted to juggle the pressures between employment and family life. Problems were particularly severe for women, still trying to cope with the pressures of a double load, as they maintained responsibility for the home even when working outside. Marriages came under significant strain. One 26-year-old legal secretary in California spoke for many as she summed up her frustration. Her husband, she noted, "does no cooking, no washing, no anything else. How do I feel? Furious. If our marriage ends, it will be on this issue."

## The Shift to a Service Economy

The scarcity of good jobs stemmed in part from the restructuring of the economy that occurred in the 1980s. In a trend underway for more than half a century, the United States continued its shift from an industrial base, where most workers actually produced things, to a service base, where most provided expertise or service to others in the workforce. By the mid-1980s, three-fourths of the 113 million employees in the country worked in the service sector as fast-food workers, clerks, computer programmers, doctors, lawyers, bankers, teachers, and bureaucrats.

That shift, in turn, had its roots in the decline of the country's industrial sector. The United States had been the world's industrial leader since the late nineteenth century. By the 1970s, however, the nation began to lose that predominant position. After 1973, productivity slowed in virtually all American industries, and remained lower than it had been in the past in the 1980s and early 1990s.

The causes of this decline in productivity were complex. The most important factor was a widespread and systematic failure on the part of the United States to invest sufficiently in its basic productive capacity. During the Reagan years, capital investment in real plants and equipment within the United States gave way to speculation, mergers, and spending abroad. Gross private domestic investment in national industries rose modestly during the boom years, though many companies became caught up in an acquisition mania that consumed even more resources. At the end of the 1980s, domestic investment was down—5.7 percent in 1990 and 9.5 percent in 1991. The energy crisis and rising oil prices (see Chapter 28) also contributed to the industrial decline. Finally, the war in Vietnam diverted federal funds from research and development with consequences that continued even after the conflict ended.

While American industry became less productive, other industrial nations moved forward. German and Japanese industries, rebuilt after World War II with U.S. aid and aggressively modernized thereafter, reached new heights of efficiency. As a result, the United States began to lose its share of the world market for industrial goods. In 1946, the country had provided 60 percent of the world's iron and steel. In 1978, it provided a mere 16 percent. So efficient and cost-effective were foreign steel producers that the United States found itself importing a fifth of its iron and steel. By 1980, Japanese car manufacturers had also captured nearly a quarter of the American automobile market, and they continued to hold a substantial share. The auto industry, which had been a mainstay of economic growth for much of the twentieth century, suffered plant shutdowns and massive layoffs. In 1991, its worst year ever, Ford lost a staggering $2.3 billion.

## Workers in Transition

In the 1980s and early 1990s, American labor struggled to hold on to the gains realized by the post–World War II generation of blue-collar workers. The largest problems involved adjusting to the nation's changing economic needs. The shift to a service economy, while providing new jobs, was difficult for many American workers. Millions of men and women who lost positions as a result of mergers, plant closings, and permanent economic contractions now found themselves in low-paying jobs with few opportunities for advancement. Entry-level posts were seldom located in the central cities, where most of the poor lived. Even when new jobs were created in the cities, minority residents often lacked the skills to acquire or hold them.

Meanwhile, the trade union movement faltered as the economy moved from an industrial to a service base. Unions had been most successful in organizing the nation's industrial workers in the years since the 1930s, and the United States emerged from World War II with unions strong. In the years that followed, the percentage of workers belonging to unions dropped, from just over 25 percent in 1980 to barely over 16 percent a decade later. As the total number of wage and salary workers rose substantially between 1983 and 1993, the overall number of union members dropped from 17.7 to 16.6 million.

The pattern was visible in the example of U.S. Steel. It had once relied on a unionized workforce of 200,000 employees. In the early 1980s, it reconstituted it-self as USX Corporation and shut many of its steel mills, while branching out into the more profitable oil business. The union—the United Steelworkers of America—lost half of its members in the process.

Union membership declined for a number of reasons. The shift from blue-col-lar to white-collar work contributed to the contraction. The increase in the work-force in the numbers of women and young people (groups that have historically been difficult to organize) was another factor, as was the more forceful opposition to unions by managers applying the provisions of the Taft-Hartley Act of 1947, which restricted the tactics labor leaders could use. At the same time, union or-ganizing efforts fell off significantly.

Union vulnerability was visible early in Reagan's first term, when the Profes-sional Air Traffic Controllers Organization (PATCO) went on strike. Charging that the strike violated the law, the president fired the strikers, decertified the union, and ordered the training of new controllers at a cost of $1.3 billion. The message was clear: government employees could not challenge the public interest.

Anti-union sentiments reverberated throughout the nongovernment sector as well, as a 1983 strike by Arizona miners demonstrated. Confronted by falling prices and company losses, the management of Phelps Dodge, one of the world's largest copper producers, decided to end the cost-of-living allowance that en-abled workers, many of them Mexican Americans, to earn $12 an hour. When ne-gotiations failed, workers struck, only to find that the company, working with anti-union experts at the University of Pennsylvania's Wharton School of Busi-ness, had hired permanent replacement workers. As the company president later acknowledged, "I had decided to break the union."

Strikers who kept their jobs found that their unions could not get favorable contracts. For example, in 1984 the United Auto Workers (UAW) ended a strike at General Motors by trading a pledge that GM would guarantee up to 70 percent of the production workers' lifetime jobs for a smaller wage increase than the union sought and a modification of the cost-of-living allowance that had been a part of UAW contracts since 1948.

Farmers also had to adjust as the larger workforce was reconstituted. Continuing a trend that began in the early twentieth century, the number of farms and farmers declined steadily. When Franklin Roosevelt took office in 1933, some 6.7 million farms covered the American landscape. Fifty years later, there were only 2.4 million. In 1980, farm residents made up 2.7 percent of the total population; by 1989, that figure had fallen to 1.9 percent. As family farms disappeared, farming income became more concentrated in the hands of the largest operators. In 1983, the top 1 percent of the nation's farmers produced 30 percent of all farm products, while the top 12 percent generated 90 percent of all farm income. The top 1 percent of the growers in the United States had average annual incomes of $572,000, but the small and medium-size farmers who were being forced off the land frequently had incomes below the official government poverty line.

The extraordinary productivity of the most successful American farmers derived in part from the use of chemical fertilizers, irrigation, pesticides, and scientific management. Government price support programs helped too. Yet that very productivity caused unexpected setbacks. In the 1970s, food shortages abroad made the United States the "breadbasket of the world." Farmers increased their output to meet multibillion-bushel grain export orders and profited handsomely from high prices. To increase production, farmers often borrowed heavily at high interest rates. When a worldwide economic slump began in 1980, overseas demand for American farm products declined sharply and farm prices dropped.

Thousands of farmers, caught in the cycle of overproduction, heavy indebtedness, and falling prices, watched helplessly as banks and federal agencies foreclosed on their mortgages and drove them out of business. Dale Christensen, an Iowa corn grower, faced foreclosure in 1983 when the Farmers Home Administration called in his overdue payments on debts totaling $300,000. "I am 58 years old," he said. "My whole life has gone into this farm." He was one of many struggling farmers, who, in spite of government crop support programs that cost more in 1982 than all welfare programs for the poor, could not make ends meet.

## The Roller Coaster Economy

The economy shifted back and forth during the 1980s and early 1990s. The Reagan years began with a recession that lasted for several years. An economic boom between 1983 and 1990 gave way to a punishing recession as the new decade began. It appeared that the United States had embarked on another boom-and-bust cycle as unsettling as that which had prevailed in the early years of the twentieth century.

The recession of 1980 to 1982 began during the Carter administration, when the Federal Reserve Board tried to deal with mounting deficits by increasing the money supply. Program cuts to counter inflation brought substantial unemployment in the workforce. During Reagan's first year, the job situation deteriorated further, and by the end of 1982, the unemployment rate had climbed to 10.8 percent (and over 20 percent among African Americans). Nearly a third of the nation's industrial capacity lay idle, and 12 million Americans were out of work.

# Technology Changes the American People

## The Internet and the World Wide Web

Today, the Internet is an integral part of our daily lives. More and more people use e-mail to communicate quickly with friends and colleagues around the world. Many Americans use the World Wide Web to make purchases ranging from books to automobiles. Others buy stocks online and rely on the Web to manage their portfolios. Historians and other scholars have come to depend on huge databases on the Web that are accessible from computers anywhere at the click of a mouse.

But the Internet is not new. Its roots extend back 30 years, to the mid-1960s, when Americans were worried about the nuclear arms race with the Soviet Union at the height of the Cold War. After the Russians launched their *Sputnik* satellite in 1957, American scientists dedicated themselves to catching up and surpassing the Soviets in space. To do so, they needed to develop their computer technology.

Scientists were also interested in figuring out how to maintain communication in the aftermath of a nuclear attack. The Department of Defense wanted to create a communications link that could withstand any such disaster.

A number of developments in the fledgling computer world were the first steps in creating an extended communications network. In the early 1960s, scientists at the Massachusetts Institute of Technology developed the concept of timesharing, whereby different users at widely separated sites could use the same central computer at the same time. Another step forward came in the mid-1960s, with the development of "packet-switching" technology, which broke down data into small, discrete packets which could be transmitted over telephone lines, using modems to connect the computers to the phone lines.

Building on those steps, the Department of Defense established the Advanced Research Projects Agency Network, known as the ARPANET, in 1969. It linked together the computers of four institutions—the University of California campuses at Los Angeles and Santa Barbara, the Stanford Research Institute, and the University of Utah. Two years later, the system had expanded to include 23 universities and research centers around the country.

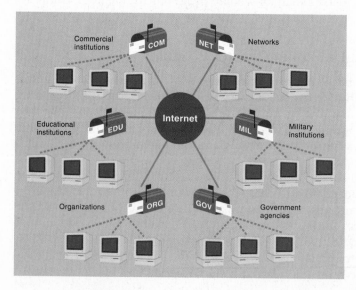

Internet and World Wide Web addresses are organized into domains, each indicated by a different three-letter suffix. Colleges and universities, for example, all use the "edu" designation.

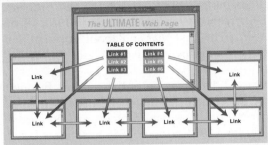

The World Wide Web links numerous Web pages together. By clicking the computer mouse on a highlighted item, a user can move easily from one linked page to another.

The system was hardly user-friendly in these early days. In an age before the advent of personal computers at home, or even office computers at work, only computer professionals or engineers or other scientists mastered the intricacies of what were very complex networks. Once they did, however, they were able to send research articles back and forth and to communicate with one another through what became known as electronic mail, or e-mail.

By 1981, the ARPANET connected 213 different institutions. The term "Internet" was first used to describe this decentralized network in 1982, and in 1986, the National Science Foundation created a network called the NSFNET that created a better-organized backbone for the entire system. In this new infrastructure, there were different domains, each marked by a different suffix at the end of an e-mail address, such as "edu" for educational establishments, "com" for commercial enterprises, and "gov" for government offices. With the development of the personal computer—IBM released its first PC in 1981—the system continued to grow.

But even with improvements, the Internet remained hard to use. Then, in 1991, the University of Minnesota developed a system for finding information by accessing a huge number of databases and named it after the university mascot—the golden gopher. Such gopher systems multiplied, until within a few years there were more than 10,000 around the world.

About the same time, another development made an even greater impact on Internet use. In 1989, Tim Berners-Lee and others at the European Laboratory for Particle Physics (known as CERN) in Geneva, Switzerland, developed a new system for information distribution. It was based on the concept of hypertext, which involved embedding links to other documents or pieces of information in the text of a document itself. While reading an article or essay on the computer, you could simply move to another document by selecting the appropriate link. This system became the basis for what came to be called the World Wide Web in 1991, and over the next few years it supplanted the gophers as the easiest way to maneuver the masses of information in cyberspace. In 1993, Mark Andreessen and others at the National Center for Superconducting Applications at the University of Illinois at Champaign-Urbana went a step further when they developed what they called Mosaic, which was a graphical Web browser that allowed you to click your mouse on graphics or icons as well as text in a document to move to another document or Web site.

**Reflecting on the Past**  Today, though the ARPANET and the NSFNET have been discontinued, the World Wide Web is more accessible than ever to computer users all over the world. But now, legal issues remain to be resolved. What kinds of censorship are acceptable on the Web? How can writers and artists and musicians maintain copyright protection for their work when the materials they produce are frequently instantly accessible on the Web? How can technology improve the access to the Web, as telephone lines become choked with Internet traffic? How can we protect systems from "hackers" who use their ingenuity to break into commercial or government computers?

How do you use the World Wide Web? What advantages does it provide you in your daily life? How has it helped you at school? What patterns in your own family's existence has it changed? What problems with the Web seem most important to you?

925

Inflation, accompanied by heavy unemployment, continued to be a problem. The inflation rate, which reached 12.4 percent a year under Carter in 1980, fell after Reagan assumed office, to 8.9 percent in his first year and about 5 percent during the remainder of his first term. But even the lower rate eroded the purchasing power of people already in difficulty.

The recession of 1980 to 1982 afflicted every region of the country. Business failures proliferated in every city and state, as large and small businesses closed their doors and fired employees. In 1982, business bankruptcies rose 50 percent from the previous year. In one week in June 1982, a total of 548 businesses failed, close to the 1932 weekly record of 612.

Detroit was one of the hardest-hit areas in the United States. An industrial city revolving around automobile manufacturing, it suffered both from Japanese competition and from the high interest rates that made car sales plummet. The Detroit unemployment rate rose to more than 19 percent and affected the entire city.

Even the Sun Belt—the vast southern region stretching from coast to coast— showed the effects of the recession. It had enjoyed economic growth fostered by the availability of cheap, nonunion labor, tax advantages that state governments offered corporations willing to locate plants there, and a favorable climate. Now it, too, began to suffer economic problems, and large areas began to stagnate. Overexpansion in the oil industry led to a collapse in prices that disrupted the economy in Texas, Oklahoma, Louisiana, and other oil-producing regions. Worldwide gluts of some minerals, copper for example, added to unemployment elsewhere in the Southwest.

Economic conditions improved in late 1983 and early 1984, particularly for Americans in the middle and upper income ranges. The federal tax cut Reagan pushed through encouraged consumer spending, and huge defense expenditures had a stimulating effect. The Republican effort to reduce restrictions and cut waste sparked business confidence. A voluntary Japanese quota on car exports assisted the ailing automobile industry. The stock market climbed as it reflected the optimistic buying spree. Inflation remained low, about 3 to 4 percent annually from 1982 to 1988. Interest rates likewise fell from 16.5 percent to 10.5 percent in the same period and remained thereafter under 11 percent. The unemployment rate at the end of the 1980s fell to below 6 percent nationally (though many of the new jobs created paid less than $13,000 per year). Between the start of the recovery and 1988, real GNP grew at an annual rate of 4.2 percent.

But the economic upswing masked a number of problems. Millions of Americans remained poor. Many families continued to earn a middle-class income, but only by having two full-time income earners. They also went deeply into debt. To buy homes, young people accepted vastly higher mortgage interest rates than their parents had. Stiff credit card debts, often at 20 percent interest, were common. Under such circumstances, some young families struggled to remain in the middle class. Blue-collar workers like Andy Hjelmeland and Jerry Espinoza, introduced at the start of this chapter, had to accept lower standards of living. Single mothers were hit hardest of all.

The huge and growing budget deficits reflected the fundamental economic instability. Those deficits provoked doubts that resulted in the stock market crash of 1987. Six weeks of falling prices culminated with a 22.6 percent drop on Monday, October 19, almost double the plunge of "Black Tuesday," October 29, 1929. The deficits, negative trade balances, and exposures of Wall Street fraud all combined to puncture the bubble. The stock market revived, but the crash foreshadowed further problems.

Those problems surfaced in the early 1990s, as the country experienced another recession. The combination of extravagant military spending, the uncontrolled growth of entitlements—programs such as Medicare and Medicaid which provided benefits for millions of Americans on the basis of need—and the tax cuts sent budget deficits skyward. As bond traders in the 1980s speculated recklessly and pocketed huge profits, the basic productive structure of the country continued to decline. The huge increase in the national debt eroded business confidence, and this time the effects were felt not simply in the stock market but in the economy as a whole.

American firms suffered a serious decline as corporate profits fell from $327 billion in 1989 to $315.5 billion in 1991. To cope with declining profits and decreased consumer demand, companies scaled back dramatically. In late 1991, General Motors announced that it would close 21 plants, lay off 9,000 white-collar employees the next year, and eliminate more than 70,000 jobs in the next several years. Hundreds of other companies did the same thing, trimming corporate fat but also cutting thousands of jobs.

The unemployment rate rose once again. In mid-1991, it reached 7 percent, the highest level in nearly five years. About 8.7 million Americans were without jobs, up 2 million in the year since the recession began.

Around the nation, state governments found it impossible to balance their budgets without resorting to massive spending cuts. Reagan's efforts to move programs from the federal to the state level worked as long as funding lasted, but as national support dropped and state tax revenues declined, states found themselves in a budgetary gridlock. Most had constitutional prohibitions against running deficits, and so they had to slash spending for social services and education, even after yearly budgets had been approved.

After a number of false starts, the economy began to recover in mid-1992. The unemployment rate dropped, the productivity index rose, and a concerted effort began to bring the federal deficit down.

## Population Shifts

As the American people dealt with the swings of the economy, demographic patterns changed significantly. The nation's population increased from 228 million to approximately 250 million between 1980 and 1990—a rise of 9.6 percent (as opposed to 11.5 percent in the 1970s) that was one of the lowest rates of growth in American history. At the same time, the complexion of the country changed. In 1992 the country's non-white population—blacks, Latinos, Asians, and Native Americans—stood at an all-time high of 25 percent, the result of increased immigration and of minority birthrates significantly above the white rate.

The population shifted as well. American cities increasingly filled with members of the nation's minorities. White families continued to leave for the steadily growing suburbs, which by 1990 contained almost half the population, more than ever before. In 15 of the nation's 28 largest cities—New York, Chicago, and Houston among them—minorities made up at least half the population. Minority representation varied by urban region. In Detroit, Washington, New Orleans, and Chicago,

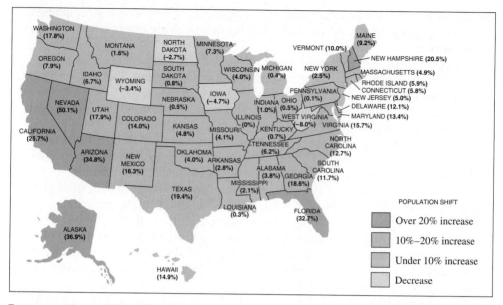

**POPULATION SHIFTS, 1980–1990**   This map shows the population shifts between 1980 and 1990. Note the substantial increases in western regions of the country and the much smaller increases along the Atlantic seaboard.

blacks were the largest minority; in Phoenix, El Paso, San Antonio, and Los Angeles, Latinos held that position; in San Francisco, Asians outnumbered other groups.

The cities also grew steadily poorer. In Houston, for example, although increasing numbers of blacks, Latinos, and Asians lived in the suburbs, most of the poorest minority families concentrated in the city itself. As had been the case since World War II, commuters from the suburbs took the better-paying jobs, while people living in the cities held lower-paying positions. Mario Perez, a 27-year-old Latino immigrant, noted in 1991 that the increase in the number of Spanish-speaking immigrants in the nine years since he arrived in Houston made it easier to find a job but harder to secure well-paying work. Perez himself worked seven days a week sweeping streets downtown and tending plants for $5.50 an hour.

At the same time, the population was moving west. In 1900, the Mountain and Pacific states contained about 5 percent of the nation's population. By 1990 that figure stood at 21 percent. The population of the nation as a whole rose by less than 10 percent in the 1980s, but the population of the West increased by 22 percent.

That population was becoming much more urbanized. In the 50 years following 1940, the six largest metropolitan areas in the West grew by 380 percent; the six largest in the East expanded by only 64 percent. By 1990, 80 percent of all westerners lived in metropolitan areas, compared to 76 percent of the people in the rest of the United States. Writer Wallace Stegner observed, the West "*is* urban; it's an oasis civilization."

With its urban development, the West became a pacesetter for the rest of the country. If the New England village had been a representative symbol of the eighteenth century and the midwestern town a similar symbol of the nineteenth century, now in the late twentieth century the western metropolis had special symbolic importance. Western cities were unbounded, open-ended, sprawling in all directions. They seemed capable of expanding indefinitely. Horizontal, low-slung homes made western neighborhoods look very different from those in the Northeast. Tourism became a dynamic industry, with the West in the forefront. The motel, a western invention, made automobile travel easier. Western cities were among the most popular tourist destinations, drawing visitors from all over the world.

California was the nation's fastest-growing state, its population increasing in the 1980s by nearly 26 percent. Responding to a question about California's impact on the rest of the country, Wallace Stegner replied, "We *are* the national culture, at its most energetic end." Los Angeles became the most dynamic example of American vitality and creativity. The motion picture industry exerted a worldwide impact. The city became a capital of consumption.

## FOREIGN POLICY AND THE END OF THE COLD WAR

In the early 1990s, the United States emerged triumphant in the Cold War that had dominated international politics since the end of World War II. In one of the most momentous turns in modern world history, Communism collapsed in Eastern Europe and in the Soviet Union, and the various republics in the Soviet orbit moved toward capitalism and democracy. Other regions—the Middle East and Africa—experienced equally breathtaking change.

### Reagan, Bush, and the Soviet Union

The Cold War was very much alive when Ronald Reagan assumed power in 1981. The new president asserted U.S. interests far more aggressively than had Jimmy Carter. Like most of his compatriots, Reagan believed in large defense budgets and a militant approach toward the Soviet Union. He wanted to cripple the USSR economically by forcing it to spend more than it could afford on defense.

Viewing the Soviet Union as an "evil empire" in his first term, Reagan promoted a larger atomic arsenal by arguing that a nuclear war could be fought and won. The administration dropped efforts to obtain Senate ratification of SALT II, the arms reduction plan negotiated under Carter, although it observed the pact's restrictions. Then Reagan proposed the enormously expensive and bitterly criticized Strategic Defense Initiative, popularly known as "Star Wars" after a 1977 movie, to intercept Soviet missiles in outer space.

In his second term, Reagan softened his belligerence. Mikhail Gorbachev, the new Soviet leader, watching his own economy collapse under the pressure of the superheated arms race, realized the need for greater accommodation with the West. He understood that the only way the Soviet Union could survive was through arms negotiations with the United States that would help reduce his overextended budget. He therefore proposed a policy of *perestroika* (restructuring the economy) and *glasnost* (political openness to encourage personal initiative). His overtures opened the way to better relations with the United States.

Concerned with his own place in history, Reagan met with Gorbachev, and the two developed a close working relationship. Summit meetings led to an Intermediate-Range Nuclear Forces Treaty in 1987 that provided for the withdrawal and destruction of 2,500 Soviet and American nuclear missiles in Europe.

George Bush maintained Reagan's comfortable relationship with Gorbachev. At several summit meetings in 1989 and 1990, the two leaders signed agreements reducing the number of long-range nuclear weapons, ending manufacture of chemical weapons, and easing trade restrictions. The Strategic Arms Reduction Treaty (START) signed in 1991 dramatically cut stockpiles of long-range weapons.

## The End of the Cold War

The Cold War ended with astonishing speed. Gorbachev's efforts to restructure Soviet society and to work with the United States brought him acclaim around the world but led to trouble at home. In mid-1991, he faced an old-guard Communist coup, led by those who opposed *glasnost* and *perestroika* and wanted to slow the process of change. He survived this right-wing challenge, but he could not resist those who wanted to go even further to establish democracy and capitalism. The forces he had unleashed finally destroyed the Soviet system and tore the USSR apart.

Boris Yeltsin, president of Russia, the strongest and largest of the Soviet republics, emerged as the dominant leader, but even he could not contain the forces of disintegration. Independence movements in the tiny Baltic republics of Latvia, Lithuania, and Estonia began the dismantling of the Soviet Union, and other republics likewise went their own way. The once-powerful superpower was now a collection of separate states. Although the republics coalesced loosely in a Commonwealth of Independent States, led by Russia, they retained their autonomy—and independent leadership—in domestic and foreign affairs.

Early in 1992, Bush and Yeltsin proclaimed a new era of "friendship and partnership" and formally declared an end to the Cold War. After half a century of confrontation, the United States had won. Yeltsin abandoned the quest for nuclear parity—maintaining an arsenal equal to that of the United States—and agreed to cut back Russian conventional forces. The United States then extended aid to the former Soviet republics, which needed help in reorganizing their economies as free enterprise systems.

Meanwhile, Communist regimes throughout Europe collapsed. In a series of remarkable developments that occurred at the same time and intertwined with the turbulence in the Soviet Union, many of the Communist satellites broke loose, rejected Communism, and proclaimed a new commitment to democracy.

The most dramatic chapter in this story unfolded in Germany in November 1989. Responding to Gorbachev's softening stance toward the West, East Germany's Communist party boss announced unexpectedly that citizens of his country would be free to leave East Germany. Within hours, thousands of people gathered on both sides of the 28-mile Berlin Wall—the symbol of the Cold War that divided Berlin into east and west sectors. As the border guards stepped aside, East Germans flooded into West Berlin amidst dancing, shouting, and fireworks. All through the night noisy celebrators reveled in what one observer called the "greatest street party in the history of the world."

Within days, sledgehammer-wielding Germans pulverized the Berlin Wall, and soon the Communist government itself came tumbling down. By October 1990, less than a year after the free movement of East Germans across their borders began, the two Germanys were reunited.

The destruction of the Berlin Wall in November 1989 was a symbolic blow to the entire Cold War structure that had solidified in Europe in the postwar years. People grabbed hammers and joined together in tearing down the hated wall. Joyous celebrations marked the reunification of a city that had been divided for decades. (Alexandria Avakian/Woodfin Camp & Associates)

The fall of the Berlin Wall reverberated all over Eastern Europe. Everywhere it brought in its wake the pell-mell overthrow of Communist regimes. In Poland, the 10-year-old Solidarity movement led by Lech Walesa triumphed in its long struggle against Soviet domination and found itself in power, with Walesa as president. Governing, however, sometimes proved more difficult than leading the revolt. The nation faced enormous economic problems, and Americans had to decide just how much help they could afford to give.

In Czechoslovakia, two decades after Soviet tanks had rolled into the streets of Prague to suppress a policy of liberalization, the forces of freedom were victorious. A month after the Berlin Wall dismantlement, playwright Vaclav Havel was elected president of Czechoslovakia. Like Walesa, he sought and received aid from the United States. But not even economic assistance could keep the nation intact, as turbulence led to the creation of separate and independent Czech and Slovak republics. The same forces that culminated in the independence of Czechoslovakia brought new regimes in Bulgaria, Hungary, Romania, and Albania.

Yugoslavia, held together by a Communist dictatorship since 1945, proved to be the extreme case of ethnic hostility resurging amid collapsing central authority. In 1991, Yugoslavia splintered into its ethnic components. In Bosnia, the decision of the Muslim and Croatian majority to secede from Serbian-dominated Yugoslavia led

**THE FALL OF COMMUNISM**   In the late 1980s and early 1990s, the Soviet Union fragmented and lost control of its satellites in eastern Europe. As many countries shown above declared their independence, Czechoslovakia broke into two nations, while Yugoslavia ruptured into a group of feuding states.

Bosnian Serbs, backed by the Serbian republic, to embark upon a brutal siege of the city of Sarajevo and an even more ruthless "ethnic cleansing" campaign to liquidate opponents. The United States remained out of the conflict, unsure what to do.

## American Involvement Overseas

As the United States struggled to keep abreast of the monumental changes in Eastern Europe, it was equally involved with events in the rest of the world. Here again the nation sought to preserve stability as the Cold War drew to an end.

A dramatic crisis occurred in the Middle East in 1990 when Saddam Hussein, the dictator of Iraq, invaded and annexed his oil-rich neighbor Kuwait. Saddam seemed intent on unifying Arab nations, threatening Israel, and dominating the Middle Eastern oil on which the West, including the United States, relied.

President Bush reacted vigorously. Working through the United Nations, as Harry Truman had done in Korea, the United States persuaded the Security Council to vote unanimously to condemn the attack and impose an embargo on Iraq. After Saddam refused to relinquish Kuwait, in mid-January 1991 a 28-nation coalition struck at Iraq with an American-led multinational army of nearly half a million troops. In Operation Desert Storm, the coalition forces' sophisticated missiles, aircraft, and tanks swiftly overwhelmed the Iraqis. Americans were initially jubilant. Then the euphoria soured as Saddam used his remaining military power against minorities in Iraq. Bush's unwillingness to become bogged down in an Iraqi civil war and his eagerness to return U.S. troops home left the conflict unfinished. A year after his defeat, Saddam was as strongly entrenched as ever.

Meanwhile, the United States was involved in a larger, and ultimately more important, effort to bring peace to the Middle East. In the early 1990s, Secretary of State James Baker finally secured agreement from the major parties in the region to speak to one another face-to-face. A victory in the Israeli parliamentary elections in mid-1992 for Yitzhak Rabin, a soldier who recognized the need for peace and was ready to compromise, offered further hope for the talks.

In Latin America, the United States intervened frequently as it had in the past, hoping to impose stability on the volatile region. Viewing Central America as a Cold War battlefield early in his presidency, Reagan openly opposed left-wing guerrillas in El Salvador who fought to overthrow a repressive right-wing regime. He was fearful that still another nation might follow the Marxist examples of Cuba and Nicaragua. The United States increased its assistance to the antirevolutionary Salvadoran government, heedless of a similar course followed years before in Vietnam. Efforts to destroy the radical forces failed, despite the expenditure of about $1 million a day. Then in 1989, a far-right faction won Salvadoran elections and polarized the country. As fighting continued, U.S. officials despaired of finding a solution.

Nicaragua became an even bloodier battleground in the effort to promote stability. In 1979, revolutionaries calling themselves Sandinistas (after César Sandino, who fought in the 1920s against U.S. occupation troops) overthrew the repressive Somoza family, which had ruled for three decades. President Carter initially extended aid to the Sandinistas and recognized the new regime, then cut off support to show his disapproval of their curbs on civil liberties and their alleged efforts to assist rebels in El Salvador. The Republicans adopted a far stronger position. Their 1980 platform pledged to replace the Sandinistas with a "free and independent" government. Once in office, Reagan circumvented congressional opposition to his efforts to defeat the revolutionary reformers and signed a National Security directive in November 1981 authorizing the CIA to arm and train counterrevolutionaries known as *contras*.

The *contras* began to attack from bases outside the country and Nicaragua became enmeshed in a bitter civil war. When the war went badly for the *contras*, the CIA assumed the military initiative and mined Nicaraguan harbors, violating international law. Upon discovering these secret missions, Congress cut off military aid to the *contras*. Peaceful elections in early 1990 finally drove the Sandinistas out and brought the fighting to an end. Though the economy remained in desperate straits, the new regime seemed to offer the best hope of healing the wounds of the bloody conflict.

Middle Eastern and Central American concerns became entangled in the Iran-*contra* affair. In 1987, Congress learned that the National Security Council had launched an effort to free American hostages in the Middle East by selling arms to Iran and then using the funds to aid the *contras*, in direct violation of both the law and congressional will. The trial of Oliver North, the National Security Council official responsible for the policy, focused on his distortions and falsifications before congressional committees and on his destruction of official documents that could have substantiated charges of wrongdoing by top officials. Convicted in 1989, North received a light sentence requiring no time in prison from a judge who recognized that North was not acting entirely on his own.

Reagan found it easier to maintain stability on the tiny Caribbean island of Grenada. The president ordered marines there in October 1983, after a coup installed a government sympathetic to Fidel Castro's Cuba. Concerned about the construction of a large airfield there, 2,000 marines invaded the island, rescued a number of American medical students, and claimed triumph. Though the United Nations condemned it, Americans cheered what the administration called its "rescue mission."

Bush took credit for a similar incursion in Panama. Despite memories of past imperialism, the United States invaded Panama, it said, to protect the Canal, defend American citizens, and stop drug traffic. The campaign resulted in the capture of military leader Manuel Noriega, notorious for his involvement in the drug trade. Noriega was brought to the United States, tried, and after a lengthy trial, convicted of drug-trafficking charges.

The United States likewise found itself drawn into turbulent African affairs. In South Africa, the United States supported the long and ultimately successful struggle against apartheid. This policy, whereby the white minority (only 15 percent of the population) segregated, suppressed, and denied basic human rights to the black majority, was part of South African law. While the United States had long expressed its dislike of this ruthless system of segregation, in past years it had refused to go further. Large investments, naval ports, and a reluctance to oppose allies who still controlled African territory tempered U.S. resistance. Then the ferment within the United States, sparked by the civil rights movement and opposition to dictatorships in Central America, generated domestic pressure for a stronger stand. In 1986, over Reagan's objections, Congress imposed sanctions, including a rule prohibiting new American investments. The economic pressure damaged the South African economy and persuaded more than half of the 300 American firms doing business there to leave.

The final blow to apartheid came from the efforts of Nelson Mandela. The black activist, who had become a symbol of the militant resistant movement during his 27 years in prison, steered his nation through a stunning transformation. In 1990, Prime Minister Frederik W. De Klerk succumbed to pressure from the United States and the rest of the world. He freed Mandela and announced plans gradually to overturn apartheid. Talks in South Africa between the white government and the African National Congress that Mandela led laid the groundwork for a smooth transition to a biracial democracy and Mandela and De Klerk worked together to ensure peaceful elections in 1994, in which blacks voted for the first time. After years of struggle, the African National Congress assumed power and dismantled the apartheid system. Mandela himself became president of this nation that was building itself anew. American aid provided support in transitional times.

Elsewhere in Africa, U.S. policy makers had greater difficulty in maintaining post–Cold War stability. Somalia, an impoverished East African nation, suffered from a devastating famine, compounded by struggles between warlords that led to an almost total disintegration of order. In 1992, Bush sent U.S. troops to assist a

# Timeline

| | | | |
|---|---|---|---|
| **1980** | Ronald Reagan elected president | **1989** | Federal bailout of savings and loan industry |
| **1980–1982** | Recession | | Fall of the Berlin Wall |
| **1981** | Reagan breaks air controllers' strike | **1990** | National debt reaches $3.1 trillion |
| | AIDS (acquired immune deficiency syndrome) discovered | | Immigration Act of 1990 |
| **1981–1983** | Tax cuts; deficit spending increases | | Sandinistas driven from power in Nicaragua |
| **1982** | U.S. invasion of Lebanon | | Nelson Mandela freed in South Africa |
| **1983** | Reagan proposes Strategic Defense Initiative ("Star Wars") | | U.S. population reaches 250 million |
| **1984** | Reagan reelected | **1990–1992** | Recession |
| **1986** | Tax reform measure passed | **1991** | Persian Gulf War |
| | Immigration Reform and Control Act | | Failed coup in Soviet Union |
| **1987** | Iran-*contra* affair becomes public | | Disintegration of the Soviet Union |
| | Stock market crashes | | Strategic Arms Reduction Treaty (START) signed |
| | Intermediate Range Nuclear Forces Treaty signed | | Ethnic turbulence in fragmented former Yugoslavia |
| **1988** | George Bush elected president | | |

United Nations effort to stop the starvation and stabilize the country, but those efforts proved unsuccessful.

❧ ❧ ❧ ❧

# CONCLUSION

## *The Conservative Transformation*

In the 1980s and early 1990s, the United States witnessed the resurgence of conservatism. The assault on the welfare state, dubbed the "Reagan Revolution," created a less regulated economy, whatever the implications for less fortunate Americans. The policies of Ronald Reagan and George Bush continued the trend begun by Richard Nixon in the 1970s. They reshaped the political agenda and reversed the liberal approach that had held sway since the New Deal of Franklin Roosevelt in the 1930s. In foreign affairs, Republican administrations likewise shifted course. Reagan first assumed a steel-ribbed posture toward the Soviet Union, then moved toward détente, and watched as his successor declared victory in the Cold War.

To be sure, there were limits to the transformation. Such fundamental programs as Social Security and Medicare remained securely in place, accepted by all but the most implacable splinter groups. Even the most conservative presidents of the past half century could not return to an imagined era of unbridled individualism and puny federal government. On the international front, despite the end of the Cold

War, the nation's defense budget remained far higher than many Americans wished, and the nuclear arsenal continued to pose a threat to the human race.

Nor was the transformation beneficial to everyone. Periods of deep recession wrought havoc on the lives of blue-collar and white-collar workers alike. Working-class Americans like Andy Hjelmeland and Jerry Espinoza, introduced at the start of the chapter, were caught in the spiral of downward mobility that made them question the ability of the nation's economy to reward hard work. Liberals and conservatives both worried about the mounting national debt and the capacity of the economy to compete with Japan, South Korea, Germany, and other countries. Countless Americans fretted about the growing gaps between rich and poor. They fought with one another over what rules should govern a woman's right to an abortion. For the first time in American history, many children could not hope to do better than their parents had done. Reluctantly they tried to prepare themselves to accept a scaled-down version of the American dream

## Discovering U.S. History Online

*Ronald Wilson Reagan*    http://www.ipl.org/ref/POTUS/rwreagan.html
This site contains basic factual data about Reagan's election and presidency, speeches, and online biographies.

*The Reagan Years*    http://www.reagan.utexas.edu/resource.htm
This site from the Ronald Reagan Presidential Library provides both pictures and written documents from the Reagan years.

*George Herbert Walker Bush*    http://www.ipl.org/ref/POTUS/ghwbush.html
This site contains basic factual data about Bush's election and presidency, speeches, and online biographies.

*Cold War*    http://cnn.com/SPECIALS/cold.war/
This is the companion site to the CNN series on the Cold War. It contains some material on the end of the struggle.

*The Gulf War*    http://www.pbs.org/pages/frontline/gulf/index.html
This PBS site combines personal accounts with a chronology and general information about the war.

## Fiction and Film

Sherman Alexie, *The Lone Ranger and Tonto Fistfight in Heaven* (1993) is a collection of stories about contemporary Indian life; Julia Alvarez, *How the Garcia Girls Lost Their Accents* (1992) is the fictional account of four young women from the Dominican Republic and their transition to American life; Tom Wolfe, *The Bonfire of the Vanities* (1987) is a novel about the arrogance of the upper class in New York—the masters of the universe—and the consequences when an accident occurs.

*Bedtime for Bonzo* (1951) shows Ronald Reagan the actor playing the part of a professor trying to teach morals to a chimpanzee. *Wall Street* (1987) captures the sense of greed and corporate arrogance that created the tone for the 1980s.

## Recommended Reading

### The Conservative Transformation

Samuel G. Freedman, *The Inheritance: How Three Families and America Moved From Roosevelt to Reagan and Beyond* (1996); U.S. Bureau of the Census, *U.S. Census of Population, 1990;* Vincent Virga, *The Eighties: Images of America* (1992).

David Chidester, *Patterns of Power: Religion and Politics in American Culture* (1988); Erling Jorstad, *Holding Fast/Pressing On: Religion in America in the 1980s* (1990); R. Laurence Moore, *Selling God: American Religion in the Marketplace of Culture* (1994); Garry Wills, *Under God: Religion and American Politics* (1990).

Paul Boyer, ed., *Reagan as President: Contemporary Views of the Man, His Politics, and His Policies* (1990); Lou Cannon, *President Reagan: The Role of a Lifetime* (1991); Ronnie Dugger, *On Reagan: The Man and His Presidency* (1983); Fred I. Greenstein, ed., *The Reagan Presidency: An Early Assessment* (1983); Godfrey Hodgson, *The World Turned Right Side Up: A History of the Conservative Ascendency in America* (1997); Haynes Johnson, *Sleepwalking Through History: America Through the Reagan Years* (1991); Edmund Morris, *Dutch: A Memoir of Ronald Reagan* (1999); William E. Pemberton, *Exit with Honor: The Life and Presidency of Ronald Reagan* (1998); Garry Wills, *Reagan's America: Innocents at Home* (1985).

Colin Campbell, S.J. and Bert A. Rockman, eds., *The Bush Presidency: First Appraisals* (1991); Herbert S. Parmet, *George Bush: The Life of a Lone Star Yankee* (1997).

## An End to Social Reform

Rodolfo Acuña, *Occupied America: A History of Chicanos*, 4th ed. (2000); Stephen Cornell, *The Return of the Native: American Indian Political Resurgence* (1988); Susan Faludi, *Backlash: The Undeclared War Against American Women* (1991); John Hope Franklin and Alfred A. Moss, Jr., *From Slavery to Freedom: A History of African Americans*, 8th ed. (2000); David G. Gutiérrez, *Walls and Mirrors: Mexican Americans, Mexican Immigrants, and the Politics of Identity* (1995); Jacqueline Jones, *Labor of Love, Labor of Sorrow: Black Women, Work, and the Family from Slavery to the Present* (1985); Peter Skerry, *Mexican Americans: The Ambivalent Minority* (1993); David Hurst Thomas, Jay Miller, Richard White, Peter Nabokov, and Philip J. Deloria, *The Native Americans: An Illustrated History* (1993).

## Economic and Demographic Change

Kathryn Marie Dudley, *The End of the Line: Lost Jobs, New Lives in Postindustrial America* (1994); Arlie Russell Hochschild, *The Time Bind: When Work Becomes Home and Home Becomes Work* (1997); Jacqueline Jones, *American Work: Four Centuries of Black and White Labor* (1998) and *The Dispossessed: America's Underclasses from the Civil War to the Present* (1992); Michael B. Katz, *The Undeserving Poor: From the War on Poverty to the War on Welfare* (1990); Katherine S. Newman, *Falling from Grace: The Experience of Downward Mobility in the American Middle Class* (1988); James T. Patterson, *America's Struggle Against Poverty in the Twentieth Century* (2000); Kevin P. Phillips, *The Politics of Rich and Poor: Wealth and the American Electorate in the Reagan Aftermath* (1990); Juliet B. Schor, *The Overworked American: The Unexpected Decline of Leisure* (1991); John C. Teaford, *Cities of the Heartland: The Rise and Fall of the Industrial Midwest* (1993).

Richard B. Freeman and James L. Medoff, *What Do Unions Do?* (1984); Arthur B. Shostak, *Robust Unionism: Innovations in the Labor Movement* (1991).

Carl Abbott, *The Metropolitan Frontier: Cities in the Modern American West* (1993); Timothy Egan, *Lasso the Wind: Away to the New West* (1998); John M. Findlay, *Magic Lands: Western Cityscapes and American Culture After 1940* (1992); William G. Robbins, *Colony and Empire: The Capitalist Transformation of the American West* (1994); Richard White, *"It's Your Misfortune and None of My Own": A New History of the American West* (1991).

## Foreign Policy and the End of the Cold War

George Bush and Brent Scowcroft, *A World Transformed* (1998); Paul Kennedy, *The Rise and Fall of the Great Powers: Economic Change and Military Conflict from 1500 to 2000* (1987); Walter LaFeber, *America, Russia, and the Cold War, 1945–1996*, 8th ed. (1993) and *Inevitable Revolutions: The United States in Central America* (1983); Robert Scheer, *With Enough Shovels: Reagan, Bush & Nuclear War* (1982); Laura Silber and Alan Little, *Yugoslavia: Death of a Nation* (1996); Strobe Talbott, *The Russians and Reagan* (1984); Allan M. Winkler, *The Cold War: A History in Documents* (2000).

# CHAPTER 31
# The Post–Cold War World

## CHAPTER OUTLINE

- The Changing Face of the American People
- Economic and Social Change
- Democratic Revival

- The Election of 2000
- Foreign Policy in the Post–Cold War Era
- Conclusion: The Recent Past in Perspective

## AMERICAN STORIES
### An Immigrant Family Struggles as the Economy Improves

In 1997, Marlene Garrett bundled up her three sleepy children—aged four, three, and one—and took them to the babysitter's home every morning at 5 A.M.. "Mama has to go to work so she can buy you shoes," she told them as she left for a job behind the counter at a bagel café in Fort Lauderdale, Florida, that began at 6 A.M.. This was a new position and she did not want to be late.

Marlene had come to the United States from Jamaica eight years before. She and her husband Rod had high hopes for a better life in the United States, and were fortunate enough to be employed. But both of them held entry-level jobs and had to struggle to make ends meet. Rod worked in a factory making hospital curtains and brought home about $250 a week. Marlene had just left a $5.25 job selling sneakers for her $6 an hour job at the bagel café. It was a small improvement, but the $200 she earned made it possible to pay the monthly rent of $400 and buy groceries. With luck, they could repair or replace the car which had recently died and perhaps begin to pay off their $5,000 debt from medical bills. They had no health insurance and could only hope that no one got sick.

Marlene was not happy about her babysitting arrangements. Her real preference was to stay at home. "Who's a better caretaker than mom?" she asked. But remaining at home was out of the question. Welfare might have been a possibility in the past, but the United States was in the process of cutting back drastically on its welfare rolls, and, in any event, Marlene was not comfortable with that alternative. "I don't want to plant that seed in my children," she said. "I want to work."

Marlene had few day care options. She would have liked to have taken Scherrod, Angelique, and Hasia to the Holy Temple Christian Academy—her church day care center

938

and preschool—but it cost $180 a week for three children and was beyond reach. Several months before, when she had been earning $8 an hour as a home health aide for the elderly, she had thought she could afford the church center and she even put money down for school uniforms for the kids. Then her car gave out, and made it impossible to continue that job.

Instead of the Holy Temple Christian Academy, Marlene took the children to the home of Vivienne, a woman from the Bahamas who worked nights at the self-service laundry where Marlene did her wash. Vivienne's apartment was simple and clean, but had no toys or books anywhere in sight. Most days the children spent the 10 hours Marlene was away watching television.

The Garretts knew how important it was to stimulate the kids. Reflecting longingly on the church center and what it offered, Marlene said, "The children play games. They go on field trips. They teach them, they train them. My children are bright. You would be amazed at what they would acquire in a year." But instead of a stimulating center, the Garretts had to settle for a place that was simply safe.

At a time when the administration of Bill Clinton was trying to reconfigure the welfare system, people like the Garretts found themselves left out. Florida, like many states, budgeted most of its child care money for families moving off of welfare to jobs. People who had never been on welfare received nothing. As the executive director of a Florida child care referral agency observed, "Many of these parents have no choice but to leave their children in substandard arrangements that are rotting their brains, and jeopardizing their futures."

Marlene refused to give up hope. Her children were on a waiting list for help from the state that might make the Holy Temple Christian Academy accessible. Meanwhile, she took a second job working nights at the local Marriott Hotel. She had to pay Vivienne more money for the extra hours, and worried even more about the additional time away from the children, but felt she had no choice. "It is temporary," she said. "I am doing what I have to do."

Marlene and Rod Garrett were like millions of poor Americans who found themselves left out of the prosperity that returned to the United States in the mid-1990s. Despite rosy economic indicators, more than 35 million Americans still lived below the federally defined poverty line. Life was hardly easy for the Garretts or for other families who found themselves on the bottom side of the line.

❦ ❦ ❦ ❦

The Garretts' struggle to care for their children—and for themselves—unfolded against the backdrop of the longest period of economic growth in American history. As a deep recession in the early 1990s lifted, the economy went on a tear. With inflation low, the Federal Reserve Board kept interest rates down, and the easy availability of money encouraged middle- and upper-class Americans to invest in the stock market and mutual funds and to realize large gains. The troubling budget deficit that had soared in the Reagan administration disappeared as the government, guided by Democratic president Bill Clinton, ran a surplus for the first time in years. The unemployment level dropped, yet for Americans at the bottom of the economic ladder, many of the jobs now available as a result of the relentless shift toward a service economy paid little more than the minimum wage, and people like the Garretts still found themselves struggling to survive. Conditions became even more difficult when the Democratic party cut back and reconfigured the welfare system to preempt the issue for their own political ends.

At the same time, the cataclysmic events in Europe that ended nearly a half century of Cold War required the United States to redefine its international role. This led to substantial debate, as both Republicans, who controlled Congress for most of the 1990s, and Democrats, who controlled the White House for the same period, voiced reservations about playing an activist, and potentially expensive, role abroad. Then, as the new decade began, the United States confronted the menace of terrorism on a scale never known before.

This chapter describes demographic shifts, reflected in the census of 2000, that changed the face of the American people. It highlights the revival of the economy that brought unprecedented prosperity for many but still failed to accommodate the needs of less fortunate Americans like the Garretts. It examines the political struggle between Democrats and Republicans that brought the second presidential impeachment in American history. It notes the bitterly contested national election of 2000. Finally, it explores the continuing effort to define the American role in the turbulent post–Cold War world.

## THE CHANGING FACE OF THE AMERICAN PEOPLE

The United States changed in significant ways in the 1990s, as the influx of new immigrants altered demographic patterns. The overall population, as reported in the census of 2000, grew more rapidly than it had in the past several decades, and reflected the continuing increase in the number of non-white Americans.

## The New Pilgrims

The second great wave of immigrants in the twentieth century played a major role in the demographic shift. The number of immigrants to the United States has risen dramatically in the past 30 years. In the 1970s the number averaged 450,000 a year, far higher than in the decade before. In the 1980s, it averaged 730,000, while in the 1990s, it averaged 950,000. Altogether, nearly a third of the population growth in the 1990s stemmed from immigration.

The influx was spurred by the Immigration Act of 1965 (see Chapter 28). Part of Lyndon Johnson's Great Society program, this act authorized the acceptance of immigrants impartially from all parts of the world. The result in the 1980s and 1990s, as in the 1970s, was far greater numbers of Asians and Latin Americans. In the 1990s, 32 percent of the new arrivals came from Asia, and 48 percent came from Mexico, the Caribbean, and Central and South America. Always a nation of immigrants, the United States was once again receiving new, and very different, ethnic infusions.

As has long been true, the desire for jobs fostered immigration. But foreign crises also fueled the influx. After 1975, the United States accepted more than a half million Vietnamese refugees. In 1980, the nation admitted 125,000 Cuban and Haitian refugees.

Asian immigrants often brought skills and professional expertise, although Southeast Asian refugees were frequently less well off when they arrived. The Asian arrivals, following a pattern established decades before, sought better oppor-

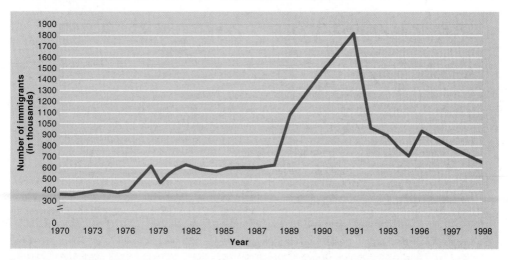

**IMMIGRATION, 1970–1998** This chart shows the significant rise in immigration after 1970, as the tightly restricted quotas in force from the 1920s to 1965 were liberalized. The steady rise in the 1970s and 1980s reflected the arrival of Asian and Latin Americans, while the spike in the early 1990s occurred because of the amnesty that legalized the status of many illegal immigrants who were now officially counted. (*Source:* Data from *Statistical Abstract of the United States*)

tunities for their children, and in California they became the largest group of entering students at a number of college campuses.

Sometimes the media highlighted the successes of Asian immigrants, particularly in contrast to the problems encountered by other groups. Asian Americans were proud of the exposure that highlighted their accomplishments, but pointed out that many members of the working class still struggled for a foothold, especially in the Chinatowns of San Francisco, Los Angeles, and New York. Chinese immigrant women, in particular, often had little choice but to work as seamstresses, just as women from other nationalities had earlier in the century.

Many professionals had a hard time. Frequently, training in their country of birth had little bearing in the United States. One Vietnamese physician who resettled in Oklahoma noted, "When I come here, I am told that I must be a beginner again and serve like an apprentice for two years. I have no choice, so I will do it, but I have been wronged to be asked to do this."

Other immigrants arrived from Latin America. As populations of nations to the south soared and as economic conditions deteriorated, more and more people looked to the United States for relief. The influx had a powerful impact on southern California as well as other parts of the country. In 1966, when Adolph Macias, an immigrant from Mexico, opened a barbershop in Anaheim, he was just another new arrival who looked white. He spoke English with his customers and reserved Spanish for his family. In the mid-1990s, he finally hung a sign in Spanish that read: "*Se habla español*" —"We speak Spanish."

Many Latin Americans came as legal immigrants. Many more arrived illegally. In the mid-1970s, it was estimated that there might be 12 million foreigners in the nation illegally, and that number increased in subsequent years.

Several legislative measures sought to rationalize the immigration process. In 1986, Congress passed the Immigration Reform and Control Act, aimed at curbing

# Recovering the Past

## Autobiography

As we reach our own time, the historical past most worth recovering, perhaps, is our own. Our own story is as valid a part of the story of American history as the tale of Revolutionary War soldiers, frontier women, reform politicians, and immigrant grandparents. In this computerized age, the person we need to recover is ourself, a self that has been formed, at least in part, by the entire American experience we have been studying.

Autobiography is the form of writing in which people tell their own life's history. Although written autobiographies are at least as old as the literature of the early Christians, for example, *The Confessions of St. Augustine,* the word *autobiography* dates from the late eighteenth century, around the time of the French and American revolutions. That is no accident. These momentous events represented the triumph of individual liberty and the sovereignty of the self. *The Autobiography of Benjamin Franklin,* written between 1771 and his death in 1790, and excerpted here, is a classic celebration of the American success story. Franklin's work set the standard for one autobiographical form, the memoir of one's public achievements and success. The other brief autobiographical memoir, from the reminiscences of Elizabeth Cady Stanton, also reflects the tone and range of this tradition.

Not all autobiographies are written late in life to celebrate one's accomplishments. The confessional autobiography, unlike most memoirs, explores the author's interior life, acknowledging flaws and failures as well as successes; it may be written at any age. The purpose of this type of autobiography is not just to reconstruct one's past to preserve it for posterity, but to find from one's past an identity in order to know better how to live one's future. The story of religious confessions and conversions is an obvious example. This form also includes secular self-examinations such as those by Maxine Hong Kingston in *The Woman Warrior* (1976), Piri Thomas in *Down These Mean Streets* (1967), or Maya Angelou in a series of five autobiographical sketches beginning with *I Know Why the Caged Bird Sings* (1969). The other two excerpts presented here are among the finest examples of confessional autobiography and suggest its variety.

These examples hardly convey the full range of the autobiographical form or how available to all people is the opportunity to tell the story of one's life. In 1909, William Dean Howells called autobiography the "most democratic province in the republic of letters." A recent critic agrees, pointing out:

> To this genre have been drawn public and private figures: poets, philosophers, prizefighters; actresses, artists, political activists; statesmen and penitentiary prisoners; financiers and football players; Quakers and Black Muslims; immigrants and Indians. The range of personality, experience, and profession reflected in the forms of American autobiography is as varied as American life itself.

Your story, too, is a legitimate part of American history. But writing an autobiography, while open to all, is deceptively difficult. Like historians, autobiographers face problems of sources, selection, interpretation, and style. As in the writing of any history, the account of one's past must be objective, not only in the verifiable accuracy of details but also in the honest selection of representative events to be described. Moreover, in fiction as well as history, the autobiographer must provide a structured form, an organizing principle, literary merit, and thematic coherence to the story. Many other challenges face the would-be autobiographer, such as finding a balance between one's public life and the private self and handling problems of memory, ego (should one, for example, use the first or third person?), and death.

**Reflecting on the Past**  To get an idea of the difficulties of writing an autobiography, try writing your own. Limit yourself to 1,000 words. Good luck.

## Autobiographical Memoirs

### Benjamin Franklin

DEAR SON,

I have ever had a pleasure in obtaining any little anecdotes of my ancestors. . . . Imagining it may be equally agreeable to you to know the circumstances of my life—many of which you are yet unacquainted with—and expecting a week's uninterrupted leisure in my present country retirement, I sit down to write them for you. Besides, there are some other inducements that excite me to this undertaking. From the poverty and obscurity in which I was born and in which I passed my earliest years, I have raised myself to a state of affluence and some degree of celebrity in the world. As constant good fortune has accompanied me even to an advanced period of life, my posterity will perhaps be desirous of learning the means, which I employed, and which, thanks to Providence, so well succeeded with me. They may also deem them fit to be imitated, should any of them find themselves in similar circumstances.

Source: The Autobiography of Benjamin Franklin (1771).

### Elizabeth Cady Stanton

It was 'mid such exhilarating scenes that Miss Anthony and I wrote addresses for temperance, anti-slavery, educational and woman's rights conventions. Here we forged resolutions, protests, appeals, petitions, agricultural reports, and constitutional arguments; for we made it a matter of conscience to accept every invitation to speak on every question, in order to maintain woman's right to do so. . . .

It is often said, by those who know Miss Anthony best, that she has been my good angel, always pushing and goading me to work, and that but for her pertinacity I should never have accomplished the little I have. On the other hand it has been said that I forged the thunderbolts and she fired them. Perhaps all this is, in a measure, true. With the cares of a large family I might, in time, like too many women, have become wholly absorbed in a narrow family selfishness, had not my friend been continually exploring new fields for missionary labors.

Source: Elizabeth Cady Stanton, Eighty Years and More: Reminiscences, 1815–1897 (1898).

## Confessional Autobiographies

### Black Elk

And so it was all over.

I did not know then how much was ended. When I look back now from this high hill of my old age, I can still see the butchered women and children lying heaped and scattered all along the crooked gulch as plain as when I saw them with eyes still young. And I can see that something else died there in the bloody mud, and was buried in the blizzard. A people's dream died there. It was a beautiful dream.

And I, to whom so great a vision was given in my youth,—you see me now a pitiful old man who has done nothing, for the nation's hoop is broken and scattered. There is no center any longer, and the sacred tree is dead.

Source: Black Elk Speaks, as told through John G. Neihardt (1932).

### Malcolm X

I want to say before I go on that I have never previously told anyone my sordid past in detail. I haven't done it now to sound as though I might be proud of how bad, how evil, I was.

But people are always speculating—why am I as I am? To understand that of any person, his whole life, from birth, must be reviewed. All of our experiences fuse into our personality. Everything that ever happened to us is an ingredient.

Today, when everything that I do has an urgency, I would not spend one hour in the preparation of a book which has the ambition to perhaps titillate some readers. But I am spending many hours because the full story is the best way that I know to have it seen, and understood, that I had sunk to the very bottom of the American white man's society when—soon now, in prison—I found Allah and the religion of Islam and it completely transformed my life.

Source: The Autobiography of Malcolm X, with the assistance of Alex Haley (1964).

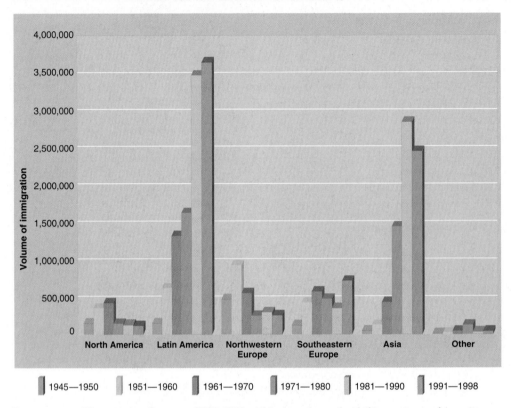

**IMMIGRATION: VOLUME AND SOURCES, 1945–1998**   This chart shows the shifting patterns of American immigration in the postwar years. In particular, note the large increase in Asian and Latin American immigration in the past several decades.

illegal immigration while offering amnesty to aliens who had lived in the United States since 1982. As the mid-1988 deadline approached, 50,000 per week applied to stay. The Immigration Act of 1990 revised the level and preference system for admitting immigrants and refined naturalization procedures. Raising immigration quotas by 40 percent per year, the act cut back on restrictions based on ideology or sexual orientation that had denied entry in the past. It also set aside a substantial number of visas for large investors and provided for swift deportation of aliens who committed crimes. In 2001, the United States and Mexico began to talk about how to ease the plight of Mexican immigrants and permit illegal arrivals to stay.

In the 1970s and 1980s, America's efforts to help immigrants coincided with still-intact social assistance programs of the liberal welfare state. Affirmative action programs aided both legal and illegal arrivals. Bilingual classrooms became more common, and multiculturalism, stressing the different values that made up a larger American identity, became a dominant theme in many schools.

Yet those efforts brought increasing resistance from Americans already here, particularly as the structure of the economy changed and good jobs became more scarce. That opposition, which echoed the anti-immigrant feeling of the past, included strenuous efforts to restrict illegal immigration and a move to lower annual quotas for new arrivals. Resistance came to a head in California in 1994, where a referendum issue, Proposition 187, was passed, requiring teachers and clinic doctors to deny assistance to illegal aliens and to report them to police. It provided a model for other states to follow, and caught the attention of national legislators as the Republicans took control of Congress. Meanwhile, toward the end of the decade, California ended its support for bilingual education, mandating English immersion instead, and sparked a similar national drive.

## The Census of 2000

The 2000 census reported a 13 percent increase in the national population, as the United States gained 32.7 million people in the 1990s to give a total of 281.4 million inhabitants. This expansion surpassed the previous 10-year record of 28 million people in the 1950s, in the midst of the baby boom after World War II. The rate of growth, which had slowed down over the past three decades, now accelerated in the 1990s. While every state had a net increase in population, growth was greatest in the West, which gained 10.4 million people and expanded by 19 percent. Some areas showed extraordinary expansion. The Phoenix, Arizona, metropolitan area grew by 45 percent, while the Las Vegas, Nevada, metropolitan region expanded by 83 percent.

Nationally, the United States remained about 69 percent white, with a 12 percent African American and 11 percent Latino population. But Latinos and blacks both predominated in major urban centers and immigration entry areas. Latinos continued to flock to southern California, the Texas border region, and the south of Florida, and also began to congregate in increasing numbers in places like Chicago and Denver. African Americans maintained their dominance in older northern cities such as Detroit, while continuing to move into metropolitan suburbs where they found changing employment and housing opportunities.

In California, Asians showed the largest increase of any group. They now comprised nearly 13 percent of the total state population, and maintained their position as the third largest population group, after whites and Latinos. Much of the Asian population growth occurred in the suburbs, where the more affluent moved, though large pockets of poverty remained in places like Chinatown in Los Angeles and Little Phom Penh in Long Beach.

One new feature of the 2000 census was the ability of people to identify themselves as part of more than one racial or ethnic group. Nationwide, 2.4 percent of the American people identified themselves as multiracial. In Hawaii, 21 percent of all residents traced their heritage to two or more racial or ethnic groups.

## ECONOMIC AND SOCIAL CHANGE

In the 1990s, the economy improved dramatically. Yet despite the revival, millions of Americans remained poor, and homelessness became an increasingly visible problem. Meanwhile outsiders continued to face resistance in their long and continuing struggle for equality in the United States.

## The Boom Economy

Economic recovery began in mid-1992. The lowering of interest rates by the Federal Reserve Board revived confidence and promoted significant consumer spending. Productivity rose steadily throughout the decade, though not quite as quickly as it had in the 1950s and 1960s. Similarly, the national economic growth rate began to rise again, reaching 3.9 percent in 1997, while averaging 3 percent in the years since the recovery began. Growth, like productivity, was not as dramatic as it had sometimes been in the golden years of industrial development, but it was steady and sustained and gave no signs of flagging in the longest expansion in American history. Inflation fell, and in 1998 stood at the lowest rate since 1965. The unemployment rate also declined, dropping from 7.8 percent in 1992 to 4.6 percent in 1997, with monthly rates occasionally even lower in the next several years. Taking credit for the recovery, President Clinton declared that the drop in unemployment was "the latest evidence that our economy is growing, steady and strong, that the American dream is in fact alive and well."

One reflection of the return of prosperity was the soaring stock market. A willingness to invest in the market is often a good indicator of confidence in the nation's economic health. In the 1990s, Americans became emboldened by the positive economic indicators and invested billions of dollars in mutual funds and stocks. The market, which had inched upward in past years, now began a dramatic rise. The Dow Jones average topped the once-unimaginable 10,000 barrier in 1999 and quickly moved on past the 11,000 mark. Investors, most from the middle and upper classes, made considerable amounts of money in the market.

The homeless became far more visible in the 1990s. Here a man lies sleeping under a thin sheet of plastic serving as a blanket right in front of the White House in Washington, D.C. (Bettmann/CORBIS)

An even more important sign of economic health was the steady reduction in the budget deficit. A Democratic effort to preempt a Republican issue and hold down spending paid off, particularly as low interest rates encouraged economic expansion. In 1998, the United States finished with a budget surplus for the first time in 29 years. With $70 billion—the largest surplus ever—left over at the end of the fiscal year, Democrats and Republicans began arguing with one another about how the money should be used. The president and most Democrats favored using funds to bolster the social security system, which seemed likely to run out of money, while Republicans, who controlled Congress, preferred a politically attractive tax cut. Forgotten in the euphoria was the fact that the national debt—the total of all past deficits—remained over $5.4 trillion.

In these prosperous times, American companies embarked upon a wave of mergers like those around the turn of the century that created the great oil and steel corporations. In the defense industry, for example, Lockheed and Martin Marietta merged in 1994, while Boeing merged with McDonnell Douglas in 1996. In 1997, a record $1 trillion in mergers involving American companies took place as huge conglomerates swallowed up smaller competitors in the interests of efficiency and ever-larger profits. One consequence of the mergers, however, was layoffs of workers who duplicated tasks and seemed superfluous. The jobs available as they looked for other work were often positions like those held by Marlene Garrett and her husband, met earlier in the chapter, which paid far less.

## Poverty and Homelessness

Meanwhile, despite the increase in wealth enjoyed by the already-rich, many Americans were growing poorer. The Census Bureau reported in 1997 that 35.6 million people in the United States still lived below what was defined as the poverty line of about $16,000 a year for a family of four. The percentage—13.3 percent—had fallen slightly in each of the past few years, but was still sizable, especially considering that it included one out of every three *working* Americans. As always, minorities fared worse than whites. The net worth of a typical white household at the beginning of the decade was 12 times greater than the net worth of a typical black household and eight times greater than the net worth of a typical Latino household. Minorities and women continued to lose ground faster than the rest of the population.

Just as the United States rediscovered its poor in the 1960s, so it rediscovered its homeless in the 1980s and 1990s. Even as unemployment dropped in the 1980s, the number of homeless quadrupled during that time. Numbers were hard to ascertain, for the homeless had no fixed addresses, but one estimate in 1990 calculated that 6 or 7 million people had been homeless at some point in the past five years. A more careful study in 1994 scaled that figure down to 500,000, still a huge number in the richest nation on earth. Still another study noted that family homelessness in New York had risen between 1990 and 1995, with the largest increase coming among children nine years old and younger.

People became homeless for a variety of reasons. Some started life in seriously disturbed families. Others fell prey to alcohol and drugs. Still others had health or learning problems that eroded the possibility of a stable life. For millions of working Americans, homelessness was just a serious and unaffordable illness away. Though many Americans initially regarded the homeless as "bag ladies, winos, and junkies," they gradually came to realize that the underclass category included others as well.

One homeless single mother described the plight so many people faced. Deborah M., interviewed on television in 1991, observed, "This could happen to anyone. As for me, I finished high school. I've done a year and a half of college. I'm a certified nurse's aid and a bank teller, and I'm homeless." Her four children suffered most of all. "From the little timid children that they were," Deborah noted, "they're not that anymore." She was lucky; a city agency found an affordable apartment for her family. Others in the 1990s were less fortunate.

## Illness and Aging

Illness was a growing problem as the century came to an end. The discovery of AIDS (acquired immune deficiency syndrome) in 1981 marked the start of one of the most serious diseases in the history of the United States—and the world. The sexual revolution of the 1960s had brought a major change in sexual patterns, particularly among the young, but now sexual experimentation was threatened by this deadly new disease. Although it seemed to strike intravenous drug users and homosexuals with numerous partners more than other groups at first, it soon spread to the heterosexual population as well. Babies with AIDS were born to mothers with the illness. AIDS became the leading cause of death in Americans between the ages of 25 and 44. The growing number of deaths—more than 250,000 by 1995—suggested that the disease would reach epic proportions. Advertisements in the national media advised the use of condoms, and the U.S. surgeon general mailed a brochure, *Understanding AIDS*, to every household in the United States. New drugs, taken in combination, extended the life-span of those with the HIV virus and reduced the death rate in the 1990s, but AIDS remained a lethal, and ultimately fatal, disease. Despite medical advances, a cure remained elusive.

Meanwhile, there was a growing awareness of the plight of the elderly. Between 1900 and 1980, when the population of the country tripled, the number of people over 65 rose eightfold and continued to rise in the next two decades. In the 1980s, the number of Americans over 75 grew by more than 27 percent. Underlying the rapid increase was the steady advance in medical care, which in the twentieth century had increased life expectancy from 47 to 74 years. Americans became aware of the "aging revolution," which promised to become the most lasting of all twentieth-century social changes.

One component of that revolution was Viagra, a new drug designed to help men suffering from impotence, that came on the market in the 1990s. Whether sexual dysfunction was a result of prostate illness, common among older males, or emotional distress, Viagra helped ailing men enjoy normal sex lives. Bob Dole, the defeated presidential candidate in 1996 when he was in his 70s, participated in a national advertising campaign extolling the benefits of Viagra in his own life. Americans, including the elderly, now talked frankly about erectile dysfunction, just as they had talked openly about birth control when the birth control pill was introduced three and a half decades before. *Newsweek* magazine noted in 1998 that Viagra was the fastest-selling drug in history.

As the AIDS epidemic caused more and more deaths, family members and friends began a huge quilt to celebrate the lives of those who had died. Each panel represented a different person. The quilt, shown here in Washington, D.C., was on display around the country and drew millions of viewers who came to remember those lost to the disease. (Lisa Quinones/Black Star)

The elderly raised new issues in a nation suffering periodic recession. Many wanted to continue working and opposed mandatory retirement rules that drove them from their jobs. Legislation in 1978 that raised the mandatory retirement age from 65 to 70 helped older workers but decreased employment opportunities for younger workers seeking jobs, a pattern that became even more problematical in the 1990s.

Generational resentment over jobs was compounded by the knotty problems faced by the social security system established a half century before. As more and more Americans retired, the system could not generate sufficient revenue to make the payments due without assistance from the general governmental fund. In the early 1980s, it appeared that the entire system might collapse. A government solution involving higher taxes for those still employed and a later age for qualifying for benefits rescued the fund for a time, but many Americans in the 1990s wondered whether Social Security would survive. In 2001, the nation began to consider establishing private retirement accounts as one part of the solution to the problem, but political agreement proved hard to attain. Meanwhile, millions of elderly people wondered how they could afford the rapidly increasing cost of prescription drugs.

As Americans lived longer, they suffered increasingly from Alzheimer's disease, an affliction that gradually destroyed a patient's memory and brought on infantile behavior. Diagnosis was difficult and there was no treatment to reverse the ailment's course. The illness gained exposure in 1995 when the family of

Ronald Reagan disclosed that the former president was suffering from the incurable disease.

## Continuing Problems for Minorities and Women

Outsiders continued to face problems in the 1990s. African Americans made some gains, but faced constant reminders that there was still work to be done. Incidents like the beating of black motorist Rodney King in Los Angeles and the rioting that subsequently occurred (see Chapter 30) made many people wonder just how much progress the civil rights movement had made. African-American historian John Hope Franklin, looking back in 1995 at the eight decades of his life, said, "Just about the time you sit down or sit back and say, 'Oh, yes, we're really moving,' you get slapped back down."

Affirmative action was one area where blacks faced a backlash. Resistance began at the state level and spread around the nation. Energized by their political victories in 1994, conservatives launched a powerful attack on the policy of giving preferential treatment to groups that had suffered discrimination in the past. Arguing that government leaders had never intended affirmative action to be a permanent policy, they pushed ballot initiatives and pressured public agencies to bring the practice to an end. The most visible of those was Proposition 209 in California, approved by voters in the election of 1996, which prohibited using gender or race in awarding state government contracts or admitting students to state colleges and universities. After victory in California, businessman Ward Connerly, who had spearheaded the effort, established an organization called, ironically, the American Civil Rights Institute to help other states enact similar bans on preferences. When he declared that he wanted to create the kind of colorblind society Martin Luther King, Jr., had sought, black lawmakers and civil rights leaders blasted him for "spitting on the grave" of King's legacy.

Meanwhile, the Supreme Court waded into the controversy. In 1995, the Court let stand a lower court ruling prohibiting colleges and universities from awarding special scholarships to African Americans or other minorities. In 1996, it declined to hear an appeal of a U.S. District Court decision two years before in *Hopwood* v. *Texas*, which prohibited the use of affirmative action in higher education. As other cases moved through the legal system in the first years of the twenty-first century, both proponents and opponents awaited a more definitive ruling from the Court.

The court rulings and ballot initiatives had a chilling effect on the number of minority candidates seeking admission to colleges and universities. At the University of California at Berkeley, the number of first-year African-American students arriving in 1998 dropped by about 60 percent, and universities around the country reported a similar pattern.

In an effort to promote racial harmony, President Bill Clinton launched a nationwide dialogue on race in 1997. He appointed a multiracial advisory panel, headed by John Hope Franklin, to convene discussions around the country to try to get all Americans to talk frankly about race.

Conversation was a first step in fostering better relations. Even more helpful was a booming job market in the late 1990s that provided new opportunities for people who had been unemployed. A survey in 1999 reported that young black men in particular were moving back into the economic mainstream at a faster rate than their white counterparts, and crime levels were falling in areas where joblessness was declining. The jobless rate for young black men was still twice that for young white men, but the improvement was encouraging. Even so, tensions persisted. In the spring of 2001, a series of hostile confrontations in Cincinnati, Ohio engulfed the city when a white policeman killed an unarmed black youth in a bitter reminder of riots in the past.

Women, too, faced continuing problems. Abortion remained a polarizing issue, particularly as anti-abortion activists sought to disrupt abortion clinics. They launched around-the-clock pickets, aimed at frightening away women seeking abortions. Physicians performing abortions found their lives at risk, and Barnet Slepian, a Buffalo doctor, became the latest casualty when he was killed in 1998 in his own home by a sniper shooting through a window.

The backlash had an impact on the larger women's liberation movement. After two decades in which the gap in wages between men and women gradually narrowed, reaching 77 percent in 1993, it fell back to 75 percent in 1997. In 1998, only 26 percent of working women said "To me, a career is as important as being a wife and mother," down from 36 percent in 1979. While young women took for granted the gains fought for and won by their mothers and grandmothers, fewer wanted to call themselves feminists.

Yet the movement persisted and brought continued improvements in the lives of women. The glass ceiling, preventing women from rising to the top of the corporate ladder, began to crumble in the 1990s, as women gained top managerial positions in some industries.

Latinos faced many of the same difficulties as blacks. Proposition 209 in California, ending affirmative action at the state level, led to a drop in the percentage of Latino students in the first-year class at the University of California at Berkeley from 13 percent in 1997 to 7 percent in 1998.

Yet Latinos still managed to extend their political gains. In 1993, Henry Cisneros became secretary of housing and urban development and Federico Peña became secretary of transportation in Bill Clinton's administration. At the end of the decade, with Latinos projected to become the nation's largest minority by 2005, Latino political figures became even more numerous and visible. In California, for example, both the lieutenant governor and the speaker of the Assembly were Chicano, as was the mayor of San Jose. Democrat Loretta Sanchez, who defeated eight-term congressman Robert Dornan in Orange County, served in the U.S. House of Representatives.

As the nation's overall unemployment rate dropped in the mid-1990s, the rate for the 12 million Latino workers likewise fell—from 9.8 percent in 1992 to 7.3 percent in 1997. Despite that drop, the rate remained higher than the rate for white workers. Meanwhile, median household income fell, even as it rose for every other ethnic and racial group. Many Latinos, like Marlene Garrett, met at the start of the chapter, found it difficult to make ends meet.

Native Americans continued their legal efforts to regain lost land. In 1999, the federal government joined the Oneida Indians in a lawsuit arguing that state and local governments in central New York had illegally acquired 270,000 acres of land from the Indians in the late eighteenth and early nineteenth centuries. Now it was the turn of 20,000 landowners to be worried about the fate of their property.

Indians also pressed successfully for the return of Indian remains, removed by white scientists and museum officials over the course of the last century. Ever since passage of the Native American Graves Protection and Repatriation Act of 1990, skeletons and sacred objects flowed back to the tribes where they belonged. In 1997, Harvard's Peabody Museum sent back the bones of nearly 2,000 Pueblo Indians in the largest single return of these remains.

Many Indians still felt a sense of dislocation, captured by novelist Sherman Alexie in 1993. Asked what it was like to return from the city to the reservation, he responded through the narrator in one of the stories in *The Lone Ranger and Tonto Fistfight in Heaven:*

> "It's like a bad dream you never wake up from," I said, and it's true. Some-times I still feel like half of me is lost in the city, with its foot wedged into a steam grate or something. Stuck in one of those revolving doors, going round and round while all the white people are laughing. Standing completely still on an escalator that will not move, but I didn't have the courage to climb the stairs by myself.

The struggle for gay rights continued, but also encountered a backlash. In 1998, 21-year-old University of Wyoming student Matthew Shepherd died after being brutally beaten and tortured by two men troubled by his lifestyle. When actress Ellen DeGeneres came out as lesbian on television, both as a character in her sitcom and in real life, some viewers wondered if her public decision accounted for the eventual canceling of her show. Most American cities had thriving gay communities and many institutions began to grant domestic partner benefits to gays and lesbians, but there was still deep-seated resistance in some quarters.

## DEMOCRATIC REVIVAL

The 1990s saw a Democratic revival. After the conservative onslaught of the 1980s, Democrats regrouped, reformulated their message, and followed the lead of the Republicans in relying on new forms of media to broadcast political appeals. But for much of the decade, even as the Democrats regained the White House, the Republicans maintained control of Congress and bitter partisan fighting was the result.

### Democratic Victory

In 1992, the Democratic Party mounted an aggressive challenge to Republican rule. After a fierce primary campaign, Governor Bill Clinton of Arkansas triumphed over a crowded field of candidates. Overcoming allegations of marital instability, marijuana use, and draft evasion, he argued that it was time for a new generation to take command. Forty-six years old, he had reached maturity in the 1960s and stood in stark contrast to President George Bush, now running for re-election, who had come of age during World War II. The third candidate in what became a three-way race was H. Ross Perot, a billionaire businessman from Texas who had made a fortune in the computer data-processing field and declared that he alone could provide the leadership the nation needed.

This campaign, more than any in the past, was fought on television. In addition to three televised presidential debates, the candidates appeared on talk shows

Bill Clinton was an exuberant campaigner who used his musical talent to attract support as he ran for president in 1992. Here he plays his saxophone on nationwide television on "The Arsenio Hall Show" in Los Angeles. (AP/Wide World Photos)

and interview programs. Perot energized his campaign with appearances on "Larry King Live." Bill Clinton used a post–Super Bowl appearance on "60 Minutes" to answer charges questioning his character and later played his saxophone on the "Arsenio Hall Show" and appeared on MTV. This reliance on the electronic marketplace reoriented American campaign politics. Although Bush's popularity rating was high after the success of the Persian Gulf War, many Americans were turned off when he reneged on his campaign promise of "no new taxes."

On election day, Clinton won 43 percent of the popular vote to 38 percent for Bush and 19 percent for Perot. The electoral vote margin was even larger: 357 for Clinton, 168 for Bush, 0 for Perot. The Democrats retained control of both houses of Congress, with more women and minority members than ever before.

The president-elect wanted to check the cynicism that was poisoning political life. In 1964, three-quarters of the American public trusted the government to do the right thing most of the time. Three decades later, the number was closer to one-quarter. Clinton sought to shift the nation's course after 12 years of Republican rule with Cabinet nominations that included four women, four African Americans, and two Latinos. He held a televised "economic summit" to explore national options and demonstrated a keen grasp of the details of policy. In his inaugural address, Clinton declared that "a new season of American renewal has begun." He also spoke out on behalf of a "communitarian" initiative, in which Americans would be more concerned with their responsibilities to the larger national community than with their individual and collective rights

Clinton soon found his hands full at home. Although the economy finally began to improve, the public gave the president little credit for the upturn. He gained

Senate ratification of the North American Free Trade Agreement (NAFTA)—aimed at promoting free trade between Canada, Mexico, and the United States—in November 1993 after a bitter battle. He secured passage of a crime bill banning manufacture, sale, or possession of 19 different assault weapons (though not of a much larger number of semiautomatic guns). But he failed to win approval of his major legislative initiative: health care reform. "This health-care system of ours is badly broken," he said in September 1993, "and it's time to fix it." Particularly troublesome were escalating costs and the lack of universal medical care, which left 35 million Americans with no medical insurance. Clinton's complicated proposal for a system of health alliances in each state provoked intense opposition from the health care and insurance industries and from politicians with plans of their own. In the end he was unable to persuade Congress either to accept his approach or adopt a workable alternative.

## Republican Resurgence

Voters demonstrated their dissatisfaction in the midterm elections of 1994. Republicans swept control of both the Senate and the House for the first time in over 40 years. In the House, they made the largest gains since 1946, winning over 50 races against Democratic incumbents. Some of the strongest and most senior Representatives, including Speaker Thomas Foley, lost their seats. At the state level, Republicans picked up 12 governorships and took control in seven of the eight largest states.

The election marked the end of the commitment to the welfare state. The 104th Congress moved aggressively to make good on its promises—outlined during the campaign in the Republicans' "Contract with America"—to scale back the role of the federal government, eliminate environmental regulations, cut funding for educational programs like Head Start, reduce taxes, and balance the budget. Newt Gingrich, as the new Speaker of the House of Representatives, pushed through changes in the House rules that provided him with far greater power in appointing committee members and moving legislation along. Under his leadership, Congress launched a frontal attack on the budget, proposing massive cuts in virtually all social services. It demanded the elimination of three Cabinet departments and insisted on gutting the National Endowment for the Humanities, the National Endowment for the Arts, and the Public Broadcasting System. When, at the end of 1995 the president and the speaker tangled with one another on the size of the cuts and refused to compromise on a budget, the government shut down and 800,000 federal employees found themselves temporarily "furloughed."

While the House of Representatives passed many of the measures proposed in the "Contract with America," only a few of them became law. The Senate balked at some; the president vetoed others. As the election of 1996 approached, Newt Gingrich found himself out of favor as millions of Americans began to realize that they would suffer from the cuts more aggressive Republicans sought.

## A Second Term for Clinton

As Bill Clinton sought a second term in 1996, the Republicans nominated Senate Minority Leader Robert Dole as their presidential candidate. The 73-year-old Dole ran a lackluster campaign. His pledge to push through a sweeping 15 percent tax reduction failed to excite voter interest. Even supporters wondered how he would balance the budget at the same time. Stung by Democratic congressional defeats two years before, Clinton reshaped his own image and announced that the "era of big government is over." He co-opted Republican issues, pledging to balance the budget himself and enraging liberal supporters by signing a welfare reform bill that slashed benefits and removed millions of people from the rolls. At the same time, he posed as the protector of Medicare and other programs that were threatened by proposed Republican cuts.

Clinton's strategy worked. On election day, he won a resounding victory over Dole. He received 49 percent of the popular vote to 41 percent for Dole and 8 percent for Ross Perot, who ran again, though this time less successfully than four years before. In the electoral tally, Clinton received 379 votes to 159 for Dole. Yet the Republicans kept control of Congress. In the House of Representatives, they lost a number of seats but retained a majority. In the Senate, they added two seats to what they had won in 1994. Around the country, voters seemed willing to support Clinton, but not to give him the blanket mandate he sought.

## Partisan Politics and Impeachment

Democrats made small gains in the mid-term elections of 1998. They worried about their prospects as election day approached, for Clinton had been accused by an independent prosecutor, appointed by the Justice Department, of having engaged in an improper sexual relationship with Monica Lewinsky, a White House intern. While Clinton denied the relationship at first, the lengthy report presented to Congress left little doubt that such a connection existed, and Clinton finally admitted to the relationship in a nationally televised address.

As Congress began to consider impeachment, Americans outside of Washington felt differently. Disturbed at what Clinton had done in his personal life, they nonetheless approved overwhelmingly of the job he was doing as president, and his approval ratings were higher than any of his presidential predecessors in the recent past.

Those sentiments were reflected in the 1998 vote. Republicans, who had hoped to score sizable gains in both house of Congress, maintained their 55–45 margin in the Senate, but lost five seats in the House of Representatives, ending up with a 223-211 margin that made it even more difficult to pursue their own agenda.

Despite that clear signal from the voters, House Republicans continued their efforts to remove the president. Just weeks after the election, a majority impeached him on counts of perjury and obstruction of justice. At the start of 1999, the case moved to the Senate for a trial, where Clinton fought to retain his office, just as Andrew Johnson had done 131 years before. In the Senate, presided over by the Chief Justice of the Supreme Court, a two-thirds vote was necessary to find the president guilty and remove him from office. After weeks of testimony, despite universal condemnation of Clinton's personal behavior, the Senate voted for acquittal. Democrats, joined by a number of Republicans, stood by the president, and with that coalition, neither charge managed to muster even a majority. The count of perjury was decided by a 45–55 vote, while the count of obstruction of justice failed on a 50–50 vote. At long last, the nightmare was over, and the country could deal with more pressing issues again.

Clinton was an enormously successful politician. Not only had he escaped conviction in the highly visible—and embarrassing—impeachment case, but he also managed to co-opt Republican issues and seize the political center. When he moved to reconfigure the national welfare system, to limit the number of years a person could receive benefits and to pare down the number of people on welfare rolls, conservatives were pleased while liberals were furious. Yet in other ways he quietly advanced liberal goals, with incremental appropriations, even when he was unable to push major programs, such as his medical insurance scheme, through the Congress. His administration's antitrust suit against the Microsoft Corporation aroused controversy. It was initially successful in court, only to be partially overturned on appeal, and eventually circumscribed after he left the White House. Polls showed that Clinton remained popular, even when people disapproved of his personal conduct, to the end of his term in office.

## THE ELECTION OF 2000

The election of 2000 promised to be close. The strong economy gave Vice President Al Gore, the Democratic nominee, an initial advantage. Yet the Republicans, led by Texas Governor George W. Bush (son of former President George H. W. Bush), promised to return morality and respect to the White House, and appealed to those who had been disturbed by Clinton's behavior.

The campaign revolved around what the government should do with the federal budget surplus. Republicans argued that much of the money should be returned to the public in the form of a tax cut. Democrats countered that such a tax cut would benefit only the wealthiest Americans, not ordinary workers, and said

In Florida—and other states—punch card ballots were sometimes defective, and if the little stubs of cardboard—called chads—were not pushed out entirely, the vote might be counted inaccurately. Here the chairman of the Palm Beach County canvassing board holds up a ballot during the manual recount in Florida, as Democratic and Republican lawyers look on. (Charles Rex Arbogast/AP/Wide World Photos)

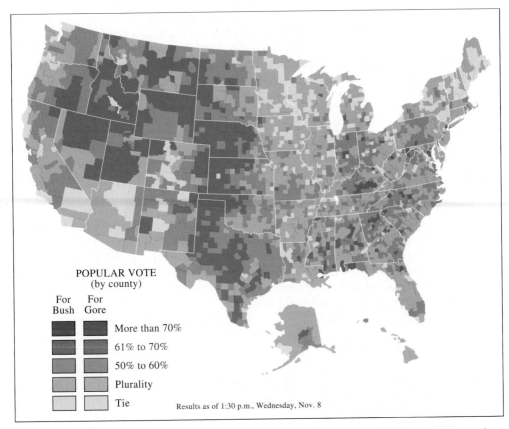

POPULAR VOTE
(by county)

For Bush · For Gore

More than 70%

61% to 70%

50% to 60%

Plurality

Tie      Results as of 1:30 p.m., Wednesday, Nov. 8

**THE ELECTION OF 2000**   The popular vote in the election of 2000 was evenly split between Al Gore and George W. Bush. The split in the vote for president reflected a larger split on many national issues. (*Newsweek*, 11/20/00 "Divided We Stand," p. 19 © Newsweek, Inc. All rights reserved. Reprinted with permission.)

that the surplus should be used to bolster the ailing Social Security program and to pay down the national debt.

In the weeks before the election, polls showed that the two candidates were virtually tied with one another. They also showed that many Americans were not very enthusiastic about either nominee.

On election night, returns in several states were so close that it was impossible to say who won. As a result, neither Bush nor Gore captured the 270 electoral votes necessary to win the presidency. The electoral vote in Florida, one of the undecided states, was large enough to give the winner a victory in the entire election. A recount, required by law, began, and Florida became a battleground as lawyers for both sides swarmed to the state to monitor the counting. Democrats and Republicans argued bitterly, in court and in the media, about how the recount should proceed.

Eventually the case reached the Supreme Court. In *Bush* v. *Gore*, the justices overturned a Florida Supreme Court decision allowing the recount to proceed, and ruled, by a 5–4 vote, that the recount should be curtailed, leaving Bush the winner. Although Gore won the popular vote, Bush triumphed in the Electoral College by a 271–266 majority.

The voting in congressional races was equally close. The new Senate was evenly split, with each party holding 50 seats. Republicans organized the states, and gained all committee chairs, since Vice President Dick Cheney broke the tie, though five months after the new session began, Senator James Jeffords of Vermont left the Republican party, giving control to the Democrats. Republicans also lost seats in the House of Representatives, leaving them with but a nine-vote majority.

## FOREIGN POLICY IN THE POST–COLD WAR WORLD

As the Cold War ended, the United States had to examine its own assumptions about its role in the world. What kind of leadership would the United States exert as the one remaining superpower on the globe? How involved would it become in peacekeeping missions in troubled lands? What kind of assistance would it extend to developing nations once the competition with the Soviet Union that had fueled foreign aid was over? How would it deal with the threat of terrorism? These questions, asked in different forms over the course of past centuries, helped shape foreign policy in transitional times.

In the area that had formerly been the Soviet Union, the United States continued to try to promote both democracy and free market capitalism. It worked closely with Boris Yeltsin in Russia, and then with his successor, Vladimir Putin, who assumed power on the last day of the twentieth century, and was then elected president in his own right in 2001. But Russia remained unstable, still caught up in the complications of a huge political, social, and economic transformation that was far from over.

In the Balkans, in Eastern Europe, ethnic and religious violence worsened in the mid-1990s. Brutal killing escalated out of control, rape became commonplace, and civilians suffered most from the uncurbed violence. As the region became increasingly volatile, the United States remained out of the conflict, while the United Nations proved unable to bring about peace. In mid-1995, the North Atlantic Treaty Organization (NATO) bombing campaign forced the Bosnian Serbs into negotiations, and a peace conference held in Dayton, Ohio, led to the commitment of American troops, along with soldiers from other countries, to stabilize the region.

In 1999, a smoldering conflict in Kosovo, one of the provinces of Yugoslavia, led to war. In an effort to stop Slobodan Milosevic, the Serbian leader responsible for the devastation of Bosnia, from squelching a movement for autonomy in Kosovo, NATO, now 50 years old, launched an American-led bombing campaign. Milosevic responded with an even more violent "ethnic cleansing" campaign that drove hundreds of thousands of Kosovars from their homes. Even without the introduction of ground troops, this ultimately successful air assault was the largest allied operation in Europe since World War II.

Milosevic finally succumbed. When he refused to recognize the election victory of the opposition leader in 2000, hundreds of thousands of people demonstrated in the streets and declared a national strike. A week and a half after the election, protesters set fire to both the parliament and the state TV station. Policemen joined the protesters and overthrew the leader who had wrought such havoc.

President Bill Clinton helped orchestrate this famous handshake between Israeli Prime Minister Yitzhak Rabin and Palestine Liberation Organization Chairman Yasir Arafat in 1993. Though the two men had long been adversaries, they now began to work together to settle the bitter conflicts in the Middle East. (AP/Wide World Photos)

Milosevic was arrested in 2001, and brought to the Netherlands to stand trial for crimes against humanity at the International Court of Justice in The Hague.

In the Middle East, Clinton tried to play the part of peacemaker, just as Jimmy Carter had done 15 years before. On September 13, 1993, in a dramatic ceremony on the White House lawn, Palestine Liberation Organization leader Yasir Arafat and Israeli prime minister Yitzhak Rabin took the first public step toward ending years of conflict as they shook hands and signed a peace agreement that led to Palestinian self-rule in the Gaza strip. In 1995, Israel and the PLO signed a further agreement and the Israelis handed over control of the West Bank of the Jordan River to the Palestinians. A treaty between Jordan and Israel brought peace on still another border. While extremists tried to destroy the peace process by continued violence, and assassinated Rabin in a move deplored worldwide, the effort to heal old animosities continued. In 1998, Clinton once again played the role of mediator, this time facilitating an agreement between Arafat and Israeli leader Benjamin Netanyahu that moved the peace process along. As he prepared to leave office, he sought to seal a final agreement between the Israelis and the Palestinians, but this time he was not successful, and the smoldering Middle Eastern tensions burst once more in flames that threatened to engulf the entire region.

Africa also remained troubled. The AIDS epidemic devastated the continent, infecting and killing far more people than in other parts of the world. Bill Clinton became the first president to travel to Africa, as he sought to dramatize international responsibility for assisting the continent, and watched with satisfaction as Nelson Mandela handed over power in South Africa to his successor in a peaceful transition. But other areas proved more problematical. Six months after Clinton became president, a firefight with one faction in war-ravaged Somalia, in East Africa, resulted in several dozen American casualties. The shooting prompted some Americans, still haunted by the memory of Vietnam, to demand withdrawal. Reluctant to back down as he groped to define his policy, Clinton first increased the number of U.S. troops, then in 1993 recalled the soldiers without having restored order.

The United States was similarly baffled by a crisis in Rwanda, in central Africa. There a fragile balance of power between two ethnic groups—the Tutsis and the Hutus—broke down. When the Hutu president died in a suspicious plane crash in 1994, hard-line Hutus blamed Tutsi rebels and embarked on a massive genocidal campaign that resulted in the slaughter of hundreds of thousands of innocent Tutsis and moderate Hutus. As the world followed the carnage on television, the United States, like many European nations, debated the possibility of intervention on humanitarian grounds but decided to do nothing. Eventually the killing stopped, although the friction between the rival groups remained.

The post–Cold War world remained an unsettled and uncertain place. While the United States was committed to nourishing democracy and protecting its economic interests, Americans remained wary of foreign intervention, even to prevent genocide or massive violations of human rights. They continued to be haunted by the specter of Vietnam, 20 years after the war's end. Yet powerful political, military, and economic interests still required attention, just as they had for the past 50 years, and the United States remained deeply involved in the effort to promote international stability.

## *Timeline*

| | | | |
|---|---|---|---|
| **1991–1999** | Ethnic turbulence in fragmented former Yugoslavia | **1998** | Budget surplus announced |
| **1992** | Bill Clinton elected president | | Bill Clinton impeached by the House of Representatives |
| | Czechoslovakia splits into separate Czech and Slovak Republics | **1999** | Bill Clinton acquitted by the Senate |
| | Riots erupt in Los Angeles | | Stock market soars as Dow Jones average passes 10,000 |
| **1993** | North American Free Trade Agreement (NAFTA) ratified | **2000** | George W. Bush elected president |
| | Palestine Liberation Organization and Israel sign peace treaty | **2001** | Economy falters |
| | | | Stock market dips below 10,000 |
| **1994** | Nelson Mandela elected president of South Africa | | Terrorists strike New York City and Washington, D.C. |
| **1996** | Bill Clinton reelected | | |

That commitment was underscored in September 2001, after a brutal terrorist attack that destroyed the two World Trade Center towers in New York City and damaged the Pentagon in Washington, D.C., killing approximately 3,000 people. As the nation—and the world—watched with horror, hijacked commercial airplanes slammed into all three buildings, setting off explosions that reduced the structures to rubble. A fourth plane was downed in Pennsylvania. In the space of an hour, America's sense of security, at least within its own borders, disappeared. Furious at the unprovoked attacks, President George W. Bush vowed to find and punish the terrorists, and put together a worldwide coalition to assist in the process. Though the Cold War was over, global responsibilities remained, and now the stakes were even greater than before.

ᠷᡝ ᠷᡝ ᠷᡝ ᠷᡝ

# CONCLUSION

## *The Recent Past in Perspective*

In the 1990s, the United States prospered in a period of economic growth longer than any in its history. After weathering a recession at the start of the decade, the economy began to boom and the boom continued for the next 10 years. Most middle- and upper-class Americans prospered. The budget deficit disappeared, and the government ran a sizable surplus. Yet not all Americans shared in the prosperity. Despite the drop in the unemployment level, many of the available jobs paid little more than the minimum wage, and people like the Garretts, met at the start of the chapter, had trouble making ends meet. Members of minority groups, whose numbers grew throughout the decade, had the toughest time of all.

Meanwhile, Americans worried about their role in the outside world. As they enjoyed their new-found prosperity, some were reluctant to spend money in an activist role abroad. They debated what to do about the defense establishment, which had begun to deteriorate, and were hesitant to become deeply involved in foreign conflicts where they had trouble ascertaining American interests. Then, in 2001, the brutal terrorist attack on New York City and Washington, D.C., mobilized the nation. Recognizing at long last that terrorism threatened the entire globe, including the United States, they prepared themselves for an extended effort to try to bring it under control and to make the world a safer place. As they had in years past, in both World War I and World War II, the United States again sought to protect the democratic way of life for both the American people, and for people elsewhere as well.

## *Discovering U.S. History Online*

*William Jefferson Clinton*   http://www.ipl.org/ref/POTUS/wjclinton.html
This site contains basic factual data about Clinton's election and presidency, speeches, and online biographies.

*Investigating the President: The Trial*   http://www.cnn.com/ALLPOLITICS/resources/1998/lewinsky/
This site from CNN provides information and documents about the scandals surrounding President Clinton and his impeachment.

*Election Collection 2000*    http://archive0.alexa.com/collections/e2k.html
This site contains links to all of the candidate websites and coverage of the Election Day itself and its aftermath.

*George Walker Bush*    http://www.ipl.org/ref/POTUS/gwbush.html
This site contains basic factual data about Bush's election and presidency, speeches, and online biographies.

*A Special Report: The Attack on America*
http://www.nytimes.com/pages/national/dayofterror/
This site from the *New York Times* contains stories and accounts, including video images and pictures, of the September 11, 2001, terrorist attack on the World Trade Center towers in New York City and the Pentagon in Washington, D.C. Look particularly at the right hand column called "Since September 11," where you will find video, stories and images from that day.

## Fiction and Film

Alice Mattison, *Men Giving Money, Women Yelling* (1997) is a series of intersecting stories about the complexities of people's lives and relationships; Lorrie Moore, *Birds of America: Stories* (1998) is another collection of stories about modern culture and life, including one about a nuclear family involved in a meltdown.

Philadelphia (1993) is a movie about a lawyer who contracts the AIDS virus; *When Harry Met Sally* (1989) is a film about the difficulties of relationships between men and women.

## Recommended Reading

Historians have not yet had a chance to deal in detail with the developments of the immediate past, so full descriptions must be found in other sources, such as newspaper and magazine accounts. But a number of useful treatments about selected topics provide good starting points in various areas.

### The Changing Face of the American People
Stephanie Coontz, *The Way We Really Are: Coming to Terms with America's Changing Families* (1997); Roger Daniels, *Coming to America: A History of Immigration and Ethnicity in American Life* (1990); David M. Reimers, *Still the Golden Door: The Third World Comes to America* (1985); Paul James Rutledge, *The Vietnamese Experience in America* (1992); Al Santoli, *New Americans: An Oral History: Immigrants and Refugees in the U.S. Today* (1988); Ronald Takaki, *A Different Mirror: A History of Multicultural America* (1993) and *A Larger Memory: A History of Our Diversity, With Voices* (1998); Susan J. Tolchin, *The Angry American: How Voter Rage is Changing the Nation*, 2nd ed. (1999); U.S. Bureau of the Census, *Statistical Abstract of the United States: 1994 & 1998*; U.S. Bureau of the Census, *U.S. Census of Population, 1990*; U.S. Bureau of the Census, *U.S. Census of Population, 2000* (as excerpted in the popular press); Alan Wolfe, *One Nation, After All: What Middle-Class Americans Really Think About: God, Country, Family, Racism, Welfare, Immigration, Homosexuality, Work, the Right, the Left, and Each Other* (1998); Reed Ueda, *Postwar Immigrant America: A Social History* (1994).

### Economic and Social Change
William Bamberger and Cathy N. Davidson, *Closing: The Life and Death of an American Factory* (1998); Kathryn Marie Dudley, *The End of the Line: Lost Jobs, New Lives in Postindustrial America* (1994); Arlie Russell Hochschild, *The Time Bind: When Work Becomes Home and Home Becomes Work* (1997); Christopher Jencks, *The Homeless* (1994); Jacqueline Jones, *American Work: Four Centuries of Black and White Labor* (1998) and *The Dispossessed: America's Underclasses from the Civil War to the Present* (1992); Michael B. Katz, *The Undeserving Poor: From the War on Poverty to the War on Welfare* (1990); James T. Patterson,

*America's Struggle Against Poverty in the Twentieth Century* (2000); John C. Teaford, *Cities of the Heartland: The Rise and Fall of the Industrial Midwest* (1993); William Julius Wilson, *When Work Disappears: The World of the New Urban Poor* (1996).

### Democratic Revival
Christopher Hitchens, *No One Left to Lie To: The Triangulations of William Jefferson Clinton* (1999); David Maraniss, *First in His Class: A Biography of Bill Clinton* (1995); George Stephanopoulos, *All Too Human: A Political Education* (1999).

### The Election of 2000
E. J. Dionne, Jr., ed., *The Election 2000: Reports and Interpretations* (2001); David A. Kaplan, *The Accidental President* (2001); The New York Times, *36 Days: The Complete Chronicle of the 2000 Presidential Election* (2001); Larry Sabato, *Overtime! The Election 2000 Thriller* (2001); Jeffrey Toobin, *Too Close to Call: The 36-Day Battle to Decide the 2000 Election* (2001).

### Foreign Policy in the Post-Cold War Era
George Bush and Brent Scowcroft, *A World Transformed* (1998); Paul Kennedy, *The Rise and Fall of the Great Powers: Economic Change and Military Conflict from 1500 to 2000* (1987); Walter LaFeber, *America, Russia, and the Cold War, 1945–1996*, 8th ed. (1993) and *Inevitable Revolutions: The United States in Central America* (1983); Laura Silber and Alan Little, *Yugoslavia: Death of a Nation* (1996); Ronald Steel, *Temptations of a Superpower* (1995).

# APPENDIX

❧❧ ❧❧ ❧❧ ❧❧

## The Declaration of Independence In Congress, July 4, 1776

### THE UNANIMOUS DECLARATION OF THE THIRTEEN UNITED STATES OF AMERICA

When, in the course of human events, it becomes necessary for one people to dissolve the political bonds which have connected them with another, and to assume, among the powers of the earth, the separate and equal station to which the laws of nature and of nature's God entitle them, a decent respect to the opinions of mankind requires that they should declare the causes which impel them to the separation.

We hold these truths to be self-evident: That all men are created equal; that they are endowed by their Creator with certain unalienable rights; that among these are life, liberty, and the pursuit of happiness; that, to secure these rights, governments are instituted among men, deriving their just powers from the consent of the governed; that whenever any form of government becomes destructive of these ends, it is the right of the people to alter or to abolish it, and to institute new government, laying its foundation on such principles, and organizing its powers in such form, as to them shall seem most likely to effect their safety and happiness. Prudence, indeed, will dictate that governments long established should not be changed for light and transient causes; and accordingly all experience hath shown that mankind are more disposed to suffer, while evils are sufferable, than to right themselves by abolishing the forms to which they are accustomed. But when a long train of abuses and usurpations, pursuing invariably the same object, evinces a design to reduce them under absolute depotism, it is their right, it is their duty, to throw off such government, and to provide new guards for their future security. Such has been the patient sufferance of these colonies; and such is now the necessity which constrains them to alter their former systems of government. The history of the present King of Great Britain is a history of repeated injuries and usurpations, all having in direct object the establishment of an absolute tyranny over these states. To prove this, let facts be submitted to a candid world.

He has refused his assent to laws, the most wholesome and necessary for the public good.

He has forbidden his governors to pass laws of immediate and pressing importance, unless suspended in their operation till his assent should be obtained; and, when so suspended, he has utterly neglected to attend to them.

He has refused to pass other laws for the accommodation of large districts of people, unless those people would relinquish the right of representation in the legislature, a right inestimable to them, and formidable to tyrants only.

He has called together legislative bodies at places unusual, uncomfortable, and distant from the depository of their public records, for the sole purpose of fatiguing them into compliance with his measures.

He has dissolved representative houses repeatedly, for opposing, with manly firmness, his invasions on the rights of the people.

He has refused for a long time, after such dissolutions, to cause others to be elected; whereby the legislative powers, incapable of annihilation, have returned to the people at large for their exercise; the state remaining, in the mean time, exposed to all the dangers of invasions from without and convulsions within.

He has endeavored to prevent the population of these states; for that purpose obstructing the laws for naturalization of foreigners; refusing to pass others to encourage their migration hither, and raising the conditions of new appropriations of lands.

He has obstructed the administration of justice, by refusing his assent to laws for establishing judiciary powers.

He has made judges dependent on his will alone, for the tenure of their offices, and the amount and payment of their salaries.

He has erected a multitude of new offices, and sent hither swarms of officers to harass our people and eat out their substance.

He has kept among us, in times of peace, standing armies, without the consent of our legislatures.

He has affected to render the military independent of, and superior to, the civil power.

He has combined with others to subject us to a jurisdiction foreign to our constitution, and unacknowledged by our laws, giving his assent to their acts of pretended legislation:

For quartering large bodies of armed troops among us;

For protecting them, by a mock trial, from punishment for any murder which they should commit on the inhabitants of these states;

For cutting off our trade with all parts of the world;

For imposing taxes on us without our consent;

For depriving us, in many cases, of the benefits of trial by jury;

For transporting us beyond seas, to be tried for pretended offenses;

For abolishing the free system of English laws in a neighboring province, establishing therein an arbitrary government, and enlarging its boundaries, so as to render it at once an example and fit instrument for introducing the same absolute rule into these colonies;

For taking away our charters abolishing our most valuable laws, and altering fundamentally the forms of our governments;

For suspending our own legislatures, and declaring themselves invested with power to legislate for us in all cases whatsoever.

He has abdicated government here, by declaring us out of his protection and waging war against us.

He has plundered our seas, ravaged our coasts, burned our towns, and destroyed the lives of our people.

He is at this time transporting large armies of foreign mercenaries to complete the works of death, desolation, and tyranny already begun with circumstances of cruelty and perfidy scarcely paralleled in the most barbarous ages, and totally unworthy the head of a civilized nation.

He has constrained our fellow-citizens, taken captive on the high seas, to bear arms against their country, to become the executioners of their friends and brethren, or to fall themselves by their hands.

He has excited domestic insurrection among us, and has endeavored to bring on the inhabitants of our frontiers the merciless Indian savages, whose known rule of warfare is an undistinguished destruction of all ages, sexes, and conditions.

In every stage of these oppressions we have petitioned for redress in the most humble terms; our repeated petitions have been answered only by repeated injury. A prince, whose character is thus marked by every act which may define a tyrant, is unfit to be the ruler of a free people.

Nor have we been wanting in our attentions to our British brethren. We have warned them, from time to time, of attempts by their legislature to extend an unwarrantable jurisdiction over us. We have reminded them of the circumstances of our emigration and settlement here. We have appealed to their native justice and magnanimity; and we have conjured them, by the ties of our common kindred, to disavow these usurpations, which would inevitably interrupt our connections and correspondence. They, too, have been deaf to the voice of justice and of consanguinity. We must, therefore, acquiesce in the necessity which denounces our separation, and hold them, as we hold the rest of mankind, enemies in war, in peace friends.

We, therefore, the representatives of the United States of America, in General Congress assembled, appealing to the Supreme Judge of the world for the rectitude of our intentions, do, in the name and by the authority of the good people of these colonies, solemnly publish and declare, that these United Colonies are, and of right, ought to be, FREE AND INDE-PENDENT STATES; that they are absolved from all allegiance to the British crown, and that all political connection between them and the state of Great Britain is, and ought to be, totally dissolved; and that, as free and independent states, they have full power to levy war, conclude peace, contract alliances, establish commerce, and do all other acts and things which independent states may of right do. And for the support of this declaration, with a firm reliance on the protection of Devine Providence, we mutually pledge to each other our lives, our fortunes, and our sacred honor.

JOHN HANCOCK

| | | |
|---|---|---|
| BUTTON GWENNETT | THS. NELSON, JR. | RICHD. STOCKTON |
| LYMAN HALL | FRANCIS LIGHTFOOT LEE | JNO. WITHERSPOON |
| GEO. WALTON | CARTER BRAXTON | FRAS. HOPKINSON |
| WM. HOOPER | ROBT. MORRIS | JOHN HART |
| JOSEPH HEWES | BENJAMIN RUSH | ABRA. CLARK |
| JOHN PENN | BENJA. FRANKLIN | JOSIAH BARTLETT |
| EDWARD RUTLEDGE | JOHN MORTON | WM. WHIPPLE |
| THOS. HEYWARD, JUNR. | GEO. CLYMER | SAML. ADAMS |
| THOMAS LYNCH, JUNR. | JAS. SMITH | JOHN ADAMS |
| ARTHUR MIDDLETON | GEO. TAYLOR | ROBT. TREAT PAINE |
| SAMUEL CHASE | JAMES WILSON | ELBRIDGE GERRY |
| WM. PACA | GEO. ROSS | STEP. HOPKINS |
| THOS. STONE | CAESAR RODNEY | WILLIAM ELLERY |
| CHARLES CARROLL | GEO. READ | ROGER SHERMAN |
| OF CARROLLTON | THO. MÍKEAN | SAMÍEL. HUNTINGTON |
| GEORGE WYTHE | WM. FLOYD | WM. WILLIAMS |
| RICHARD HENRY LEE | PHIL. LIVINGSTON | OLIVER WOLCOTT |
| TH. JEFFERSON | FRANS. LEWIS | MATHEW THORNTON |
| BENJA. HARRISON | LEWIS MORRIS | |

# The Constitution of the United States of America

## PREAMBLE

We the People of the United States, in Order to form a more perfect Union, establish Justice, insure domestic Tranquility, provide for the common defence, promote the general Welfare, and secure the Blessings of Liberty to ourselves and our Posterity, do ordain and establish this Constitution for the United States of America.

## ARTICLE I.

**Section 1**  All legislative Powers herein granted shall be vested in a Congress of the United States, which shall consist of a Senate and House of Representatives.

**Section 2**    The House of Representatives shall be composed of Members chosen every second Year by the People of the several States, and the Electors in each State shall have the Qualifications requisite for Electors of the most numerous Branch of the State Legislature.

No Person shall be a Representative who shall not have attained to the Age of twenty five Years, and been seven Years a Citizen of the United States, and who shall not, when elected, be an Inhabitant of that State in which he shall be chosen.

Representatives and direct Taxes shall be apportioned among the several States which may be included within this Union, according to their respective Numbers, *which shall be determined by adding to the whole Number of free Persons, including those bound to Service for a Term of Years, and excluding Indians not taxed, three fifths of all other Persons.* The actual Enumeration shall be made within three Years after the first Meeting of the Congress of the United States, and within every subsequent Term of ten Years, in such Manner as they shall by Law direct. The Number of Representatives shall not exceed one for every thirty Thousand, but each State shall have at Least one Representative; *and until such enumeration shall be made, the State of New Hampshire shall be entitled to chuse three, Massachusetts eight, Rhode-Island and Providence Plantations one, Connecticut five, New-York six, New Jersey four, Pennsylvania eight, Delaware one, Maryland six, Virginia ten, North Carolina five, South Carolina five, and Georgia three.*

When vacancies happen in the Representation from any State, the Executive Authority thereof shall issue Writs of Election to fill such Vacancies.

The House of Representatives shall chuse their Speaker and other Officers; and shall have the sole Power of Impeachment.

**Section 3**    The Senate of the United States shall be composed of two Senators from each State, chosen by the Legislature thereof, for six Years; and each Senator shall have one Vote.

*Immediately after they shall be assembled in Consequence of the first Election, they shall be divided as equally as may be into three Classes. The Seats of the Senators of the first Class shall be vacated at the Expiration of the second Year, of the second Class at the Expiration of the fourth Year, and of the third Class at the Expiration of the sixth Year, so that one third may be chosen every second Year; and if Vacancies happen by Resignation, or otherwise, during the Recess of the Legislature of any State, the Executive thereof may make temporary Appointments until the next Meeting of the Legislature, which shall then fill such Vacancies.*

No Person shall be a Senator who shall not have attained to the Age of thirty Years, and been nine Years a Citizen of the United States, and who shall not, when elected, be an Inhabitant of that State for which he shall be chosen.

The Vice President of the United States shall be President of the Senate, but shall have no Vote, unless they be equally divided.

The Senate shall choose their other Officers, and also a President *pro tempore*, in the Absence of the Vice President, or when he shall exercise the Office of President of the United States.

The Senate shall have the sole Power to try all Impeachments. When sitting for that Purpose, they shall be on Oath or Affirmation. When the President of the United States is tried the Chief Justice shall preside: And no Person shall be convicted without the Concurrence of two thirds of the Members present.

Judgment in Cases of Impeachment shall not extend further than to removal from Office, and disqualification to hold and enjoy any Office of honor, Trust or Profit under the United States: but the Party convicted shall nevertheless be liable and subject to Indictment, Trial, Judgment and Punishment, according to Law.

**Section 4**    The Times, Places and Manner of holding Elections for Senators and Representatives, shall be prescribed in each State by the Legislature thereof; but the Congress may at any time by Law make or alter such Regulations, except as to the Places of chusing Senators.

The Congress shall assemble at least once in every Year, and such Meeting *shall be on the first Monday in December, unless they shall by Law appoint a different Day.*

**Section 5**    Each House shall be the Judge of the Elections, Returns and Qualifications of its own Members, and a Majority of each shall constitute a Quorum to do Business; but a smaller Number may adjourn from day to day, and may be authorized to compel the Attendance of absent Members, in such Manner, and under such Penalties as each House may provide.

Each House may determine the Rules of its Proceedings, punish its Members for disorderly Behaviour, and, with the Concurrence of two thirds, expel a Member.

Each House shall keep a Journal of its Proceedings, and from time to time publish the same, excepting such Parts as may in their Judgment require Secrecy; and the Yeas and Nays of the Members of either House on any question shall, at the Desire of one fifth of those Present, be entered on the Journal.

Neither House, during the Session of Congress, shall, without the Consent of the other, adjourn for more than three days, nor to any other Place than that in which the two Houses shall be sitting.

**Section 6**    The Senators and Representatives shall receive a Compensation for their Services, to be ascertained by Law, and paid out of the Treasury of the United States. They shall in all Cases, except Treason, Felony and Breach of the Peace, be privileged from Arrest during their Attendance at the Session of their respective Houses, and in going to and returning from the same; and for any Speech or Debate in either House, they shall not be questioned in any other Place.

No Senator or Representative shall, during the Time for which he was elected, be appointed to any civil Office under the Authority of the United States, which shall have been created, or the Emoluments whereof shall have been encreased during such time; and no Person holding any Office under the United States, shall be a Member of either House during his Continuance in Office.

**Section 7**    All Bills for raising Revenue shall originate in the House of Representatives; but the Senate may propose or concur with Amendments as on other Bills.

Every Bill which shall have passed the House of Representatives and the Senate, shall, before it become a Law, be presented to the President of the United States; If he approve he shall sign it, but if not he shall return it, with his Objections to that House in which it shall have originated, who shall enter the Objections at large on their Journal, and proceed to reconsider it. If after such Reconsideration two thirds of that House shall agree to pass the Bill, it shall be sent, together with the Objections, to the other House, by which it shall likewise be reconsidered, and if approved by two thirds of that House, it shall become a Law. But in all such Cases the Votes of both Houses shall be determined by yeas and Nays, and the Names of the Persons voting for and against the Bill shall be entered on the Journal of each House respectively. If any Bill shall not be returned by the President within ten Days (Sundays excepted) after it shall have been presented to him, the Same shall be a Law, in like Manner as if he had signed it, unless the Congress by their Adjournment prevent its Return, in which Case it shall not be a Law.

Every Order, Resolution, or Vote to which the Concurrence of the Senate and House of Representatives may be necessary (except on a question of Adjournment) shall be presented to the President of the United States; and before the Same shall take Effect, shall be approved by him, or being disapproved by him, shall be repassed by two thirds of the Senate and House of Representatives, according to the Rules and Limitations prescribed in the Case of a Bill.

**Section 8**    The Congress shall have Power:

To lay and collect Taxes, Duties, Imposts and Excises, to pay the Debts and provide for the common Defence and general Welfare of the United States; but all Duties, Imposts and Excises shall be uniform throughout the United States;

To borrow Money on the credit of the United States;

To regulate Commerce with foreign Nations, and among the several States, and with the Indian Tribes;

To establish an uniform Rule of Naturalization, and uniform Laws on the subject of Bankruptcies throughout the United States;

To coin Money, regulate the Value thereof, and of foreign Coin, and fix the Standard of Weights and Measures;

To provide for the Punishment of counterfeiting the Securities and current Coin of the United States;

To establish Post Offices and post Roads;

To promote the Progress of Science and useful Arts, by securing for limited Times to Authors and Inventors the exclusive Right to their respective Writings and Discoveries;

To constitute Tribunals inferior to the supreme Court;

To define and punish Piracies and Felonies committed on the high Seas, and Offences against the Law of Nations;

To declare War, grant Letters of Marque and Reprisal, and make Rules concerning Captures on Land and Water;

To raise and support Armies, but no Appropriation of Money to that Use shall be for a longer Term than two Years;

To provide and maintain a Navy;

To make Rules for the Government and Regulation of the land and naval Forces;

To provide for calling forth the Militia to execute the Laws of the Union, suppress Insurrections and repel Invasions;

To provide for organizing, arming, and disciplining, the Militia, and for governing such Part of them as may be employed in the Service of the United States, reserving to the States respectively, the Appointment of the Officers, and the Authority of training the Militia according to the discipline prescribed by Congress;

To exercise exclusive Legislation in all Cases whatsoever, over such District (not exceeding ten Miles square) as may, by Cession of particular States, and the Acceptance of Congress, become the Seat of the Government of the United States, and to exercise like Authority over all Places purchased by the Consent of the Legislature of the State in which the Same shall be, for the Erection of Forts, Magazines, Arsenals, dock-Yards, and other needful Buildings;—And

To make all Laws which shall be necessary and proper for carrying into Execution the foregoing Powers, and all other Powers vested by this Constitution in the Government of the United States, or in any Department or Officer thereof.

**Section 9**  *The Migration or Importation of such Persons as any of the States now existing shall think proper to admit, shall not be prohibited by the Congress prior to the Year one thousand eight hundred and eight, but a Tax or duty may be imposed on such Importation, not exceeding ten dollars for each Person.*

The Privilege of the Writ of Habeas Corpus shall not be suspended, unless when in Cases of Rebellion or Invasion the public Safety may require it.

No Bill of Attainder or ex post facto Law shall be passed.

No Capitation, or other direct, Tax shall be laid, unless in Proportion to the Census or Enumeration herein before directed to be taken.

No Tax or Duty shall be laid on Articles exported from any State.

No Preference shall be given by any Regulation of Commerce or Revenue to the Ports of one State over those of another: nor shall Vessels bound to, or from, one State, be obliged to enter, clear, or pay Duties in another.

No Money shall be drawn from the Treasury, but in Consequence of Appropriations made by Law; and a regular Statement and Account of the Receipts and Expenditures of all public Money shall be published from time to time.

No Title of Nobility shall be granted by the United States: And no Person holding any Office of Profit or Trust under them, shall, without the Consent of the Congress, accept of any present, Emolument, Office, or Title, of any kind whatever, from any King, Prince, or foreign State.

**Section 10**   No State shall enter into any Treaty, Alliance, or Confederation; grant Letters of Marque and Reprisal; coin Money; emit Bills of Credit; make any Thing but gold and silver Coin a Tender in Payment of Debts; pass any Bill of Attainder, ex post facto Law, or Law impairing the Obligation of Contracts, or grant any Title of Nobility.

No State shall, without the Consent of the Congress, lay any Imposts or Duties on Imports or Exports, except what may be absolutely necessary for executing it's inspection Laws: and the net Produce of all Duties and Imposts, laid by any State on Imports or Exports, shall be for the Use of the Treasury of the United States; and all such Laws shall be subject to the Revision and Controul of the Congress.

No State shall, without the Consent of Congress, lay any Duty of Tonnage, keep Troops, or Ships of War in time of Peace, enter into any Agreement or Compact with another State, or with a foreign Power, or engage in War, unless actually invaded, or in such imminent Danger as will not admit of delay.

# ARTICLE II.

**Section 1**   The executive Power shall be vested in a President of the United States of America. He shall hold his Office during the Term of four Years, and, together with the Vice President, chosen for the same Term, be elected, as follows

Each State shall appoint, in such Manner as the Legislature thereof may direct, a Number of Electors, equal to the whole Number of Senators and Representatives to which the State may be entitled in the Congress: but no Senator or Representative, or Person holding an Office of Trust or Profit under the United States, shall be appointed an Elector.

*The Electors shall meet in their respective States, and vote by Ballot for two Persons, of whom one at least shall not be an Inhabitant of the same State with themselves. And they shall make a List of all the Persons voted for, and of the Number of Votes for each; which List they shall sign and certify, and transmit sealed to the Seat of Government of the United States, directed to the President of the Senate. The President of the Senate shall, in the Presence of the Senate and House of Representatives, open all the Certificates, and the Votes shall then be counted. The Person having the greatest Number of Votes shall be the President, if such Number be a Majority of the whole Number of Electors appointed; and if there be more than one who have such Majority, and have an equal Number of Votes, then the House of Representatives shall immediately chuse by Ballot one of them for President; and if no Person have a Majority, then from the five highest on the List the said House shall in like Manner chuse the President. But in chusing the President, the Votes shall be taken by States, the Representation from each State having one Vote; A quorum for this Purpose shall consist of a Member or Members from two thirds of the States, and a Majority of all the States shall be necessary to a Choice. In every Case, after the Choice of the President, the Person having the greatest Number of Votes of the Electors shall be the Vice President. But if there should remain two or more who have equal Votes, the Senate shall chuse from them by Ballot the Vice President.*

The Congress may determine the Time of chusing the Electors, and the Day on which they shall give their Votes; which Day shall be the same throughout the United States.

No Person except a natural born Citizen, *or a Citizen of the United States, at the time of the Adoption of this Constitution,* shall be eligible to the Office of President; neither shall any Person be eligible to that Office who shall not have attained to the Age of thirty five Years, and been fourteen Years a Resident within the United States.

In Case of the Removal of the President from Office, or of his Death, Resignation, or Inability to discharge the Powers and Duties of the said Office, the Same shall devolve on the Vice President, and the Congress may by Law provide for the Case of Removal, Death,

Resignation or Inability, both of the President and Vice President declaring what Officer shall then act as President, and such Officer shall act accordingly, until the Disability be removed, or a President shall be elected.

The President shall, at stated Times, receive for his Services, a Compensation, which shall neither be encreased nor diminished during the Period for which he shall have been elected, and he shall not receive within that Period any other Emolument from the United States, or any of them.

Before he enter on the Execution of his Office, he shall take the following Oath or Affirmation: "I do solemnly swear (or affirm) that I will faithfully execute the Office of President of the United States, and will to the best of my Ability, preserve, protect and defend the Constitution of the United States."

**Section 2**  The President shall be Commander in Chief of the Army and Navy of the United States, and of the Militia of the several States, when called into the actual Service of the United States; he may require the Opinion, in writing, of the principal Officer in each of the executive Departments, upon any Subject relating to the Duties of their respective Offices, and he shall have Power to grant Reprieves and Pardons for Offences against the United States, except in Cases of Impeachment.

He shall have Power, by and with the Advice and Consent of the Senate, to make Treaties, provided two thirds of the Senators present concur; and he shall nominate, and by and with the Advice and Consent of the Senate, shall appoint Ambassadors, other public Ministers and Consuls, Judges of the supreme Court, and all other Officers of the United States, whose Appointments are not herein otherwise provided for, and which shall be established by Law: but the Congress may by Law vest the Appointment of such inferior Officers, as they think proper, in the President alone, in the Courts of Law, or in the Heads of Departments.

The President shall have Power to fill up all Vacancies that may happen during the Recess of the Senate, by granting Commissions which shall expire at the End of their next Session.

**Section 3**  He shall from time to time give to the Congress Information of the State of the Union, and recommend to their Consideration such Measures as he shall judge necessary and expedient; he may, on extraordinary Occasions, convene both Houses, or either of them, and in Case of Disagreement between them, with Respect to the Time of Adjournment, he may adjourn them to such Time as he shall think proper; he shall receive Ambassadors and other public Ministers; he shall take Care that the Laws be faithfully executed, and shall Commission all the Officers of the United States.

**Section 4**  The President, Vice President and all civil Officers of the United States, shall be removed from Office on Impeachment for, and Conviction of, Treason, Bribery, or other high Crimes and Misdemeanors.

# ARTICLE III.

**Section 1**  The judicial Power of the United States, shall be vested in one supreme Court, and in such inferior Courts as the Congress may from time to time ordain and establish. The Judges, both of the supreme and inferior Courts, shall hold their Offices during good Behaviour, and shall, at stated Times, receive for their Services, a Compensation which shall not be diminished during their Continuance in Office.

**Section 2**  The judicial Power shall extend to all Cases, in Law and Equity, arising under this Constitution, the Laws of the United States, and Treaties made, or which shall be made, under their Authority;—to all Cases affecting Ambassadors, other public Ministers and Consuls;— to all Cases of admiralty and maritime Jurisdiction;—to Controversies to which the United States shall be a Party;—to Controversies between two or more States;—*between a State and Citizens of another State;*—between Citizens of different States;—between Citizens of the same State claiming Lands under Grants of different States, and between a State, or the Citizens thereof, and foreign States, Citizens or Subjects.

In all Cases affecting Ambassadors, other public Ministers and Consuls, and those in which a State shall be Party, the supreme Court shall have original Jurisdiction. In all the other Cases before mentioned, the supreme Court shall have appellate Jurisdiction, both as to Law and Fact, with such Exceptions, and under such Regulations as the Congress shall make.

The Trial of all Crimes, except in Cases of Impeachment, shall be by Jury; and such Trial shall be held in the State where the said Crimes shall have been committed; but when not committed within any State, the Trial shall be at such Place or Places as the Congress may by Law have directed.

**Section 3**   Treason against the United States, shall consist only in levying War against them, or in adhering to their Enemies, giving them Aid and Comfort. No Person shall be convicted of Treason unless on the Testimony of two Witnesses to the same overt Act, or on Confession in open Court.

The Congress shall have Power to declare the Punishment of Treason, but no Attainder of Treason shall work Corruption of Blood, or Forfeiture except during the Life of the Person attainted.

# ARTICLE IV

**Section 1**   Full Faith and Credit shall be given in each State to the public Acts, Records, and judicial Proceedings of every other State. And the Congress may by general Laws prescribe the Manner in which such Acts, Records and Proceedings shall be proved, and the Effect thereof.

**Section 2**   The Citizens of each State shall be entitled to all Privileges and Immunities of Citizens in the several States.

A Person charged in any State with Treason, Felony, or other Crime, who shall flee from Justice, and be found in another State, shall on Demand of the executive Authority of the State from which he fled, be delivered up, to be removed to the State having Jurisdiction of the Crime.

*No Person held to Service or Labour in one State, under the Laws thereof, escaping into another, shall, in Consequence of any Law or Regulation therein, be discharged from such Service or Labour, but shall be delivered up on Claim of the Party to whom such Service or Labour may be due.*

**Section 3**   New States may be admitted by the Congress into this Union; but no new State shall be formed or erected within the Jurisdiction of any other State; nor any State be formed by the Junction of two or more States, or Parts of States, without the Consent of the Legislatures of the States concerned as well as of the Congress.

The Congress shall have Power to dispose of and make all needful Rules and Regulations respecting the Territory or other Property belonging to the United States; and nothing in this Constitution shall be so construed as to Prejudice any Claims of the United States, or of any particular State.

**Section 4**   The United States shall guarantee to every State in this Union a Republican Form of Government, and shall protect each of them against Invasion; and on Application of the Legislature, or of the Executive (when the Legislature cannot be convened) against domestic Violence.

# ARTICLE V

The Congress, whenever two thirds of both Houses shall deem it necessary, shall propose Amendments to this Constitution, or, on the Application of the Legislatures of two thirds of the several States, shall call a Convention for proposing Amendments, which, in either Case, shall be valid to all Intents and Purposes, as Part of this Constitution, when ratified by the Legislatures of three fourths of the several States, or by Conventions in three fourths thereof, as the one or the other Mode of Ratification may be proposed by the Congress; Provided *that no Amendment which may be made prior to the Year One thousand eight hundred and eight shall in any Manner affect the first and fourth Clauses in the Ninth Section of the first Article; and* that no State, without its Consent, shall be deprived of its equal Suffrage in the Senate.

# ARTICLE VI

All Debts contracted and Engagements entered into, before the Adoption of this Constitution, shall be as valid against the United States under this Constitution, as under the Confederation.

This Constitution, and the Laws of the United States which shall be made in Pursuance thereof; and all Treaties made or which shall be made, under the Authority of the United States, shall be the supreme Law of the Land; and the Judges in every State shall be bound thereby, any Thing in the Constitution or Laws of any State to the Contrary notwithstanding.

The Senators and Representatives before mentioned, and the Members of the several State Legislatures, and all executive and judicial Officers, both of the United States and of the several States, shall be bound by Oath or Affirmation, to support this Constitution; but no religious Test shall ever be required as a Qualification to any Office or public Trust under the United States.

# ARTICLE VII

The Ratification of the Conventions of nine States, shall be sufficient for the Establishment of this Constitution between the States so ratifying the Same.

Done in Convention by the Unanimous Consent of the States present the Seventeenth Day of September in the Year of our Lord one thousand seven hundred and Eighty seven and of the Independence of the United States of America the Twelfth. IN WITNESS whereof We have hereunto subscribed our Names,

GEORGE WASHINGTON,
President and Deputy from Virginia

*North Carolina*
WILLIAM BLOUNT
RICHARD DOBBS
SPRAIGHT
HU WILLIAMSON

*Pennsylvania*
BENJAMIN FRANKLIN
THOMAS MIFFLIN
ROVERT MORRIS
GEORGE CLYMER
THOMAS FITZSIMONS
JARED INGERSOLL
JAMES WILSON
GOUVERNEUR MORRIS

*Delaware*
GEORGE READ
GUNNING BEDFORD, JR.
JOHN DICKINSON
RICHARD BASSETT
JACOB BROOM

*South Carolina*
J. RUTLEDGE
CHARLES C. PINCKNEY
PIERCE BUTLER

*Virginia*
JOHN BLAIR
JAMES MADISON, JR.

*New Jersey*
WILLIAM LIVINGSTON
DAVID BREARLEY
WILLIAM PATERSON
JONATHAN DAYTON

*Maryland*
JAMES MCHENRY
DANIEL OF ST. THOMAS
JENIFER
DANIEL CARROLL

*Massachusetts*
NATHANIEL GORHAM
RUFUS KING

*Connecticut*
WILLIAM S. JOHNSON
ROGER SHERMAN

*New York*
ALEXANDER HAMILTON

*New Hampshire*
JOHN LANGDON
NICHOLAS GILMAN

*Georgia*
WILLIAM FEW
ABRAHAM BALDWIN

# AMENDMENTS TO THE CONSTITUTION*

*The first ten amendments (the Bill of Rights) were adopted in 1791.

### Amendment I
Congress shall make no law respecting an establishment of religion, or prohibiting the free exercise thereof; or abridging the freedom of speech, or of the press; or the right of the people peaceably to assemble, and to petition the Government for a redress of grievances.

### Amendment II
A well regulated Militia, being necessary to the security of a free State, the right of the people to keep and bear Arms, shall not be infringed.

### Amendment III
No Soldier shall, in time of peace be quartered in any house, without the consent of the Owner, nor in time of war, but in a manner to be prescribed by law.

### Amendment IV
The right of the people to be secure in their persons, houses, papers, and effects, against unreasonable searches and seizures, shall not be violated, and no Warrants shall issue, but upon probable cause, supported by Oath or affirmation, and particularly describing the place to be searched, and the persons or things to be seized.

### Amendment V
No person shall be held to answer for a capital, or otherwise infamous crime, unless on a presentment or indictment of a Grand Jury, except in cases arising in the land or naval forces, or in the Militia, when in actual service in time of War or public danger; nor shall any person be subject for the same offence to be twice put in jeopardy of life or limb; nor shall be compelled in any criminal case to be a witness against himself, nor be deprived of life, liberty, or property, without due process of law; nor shall private property be taken for public use, without just compensation.

### Amendment VI
In all criminal prosecutions, the accused shall enjoy the right to a speedy and public trial, by an impartial jury of the State and district wherein the crime shall have been committed, which district shall have been previously ascertained by law, and to be informed of the nature and cause of the accusation; to be confronted with the witnesses against him; to have compulsory process for obtaining witnesses in his favor, and to have the Assistance of Counsel for his defence.

### Amendment VII
In Suits at common law, where the value in controversy shall exceed twenty dollars, the right of trial by jury shall be preserved, and no fact tried by a jury, shall be otherwise re-examined in any Court of the United States, than according to the rules of the common law.

### Amendment VIII
Excessive bail shall not be required, nor excessive fines imposed, nor cruel and unusual punishments inflicted.

### Amendment IX
The enumeration in the Constitution, of certain rights, shall not be construed to deny or disparage others retained by the people.

### Amendment X
The powers not delegated to the United States by the Constitution, nor prohibited by it to the States, are reserved to the States respectively, or to the people.

**Amendment XI [Adopted 1798]**

The Judicial power of the United States shall not be construed to extend to any suit in law or equity, commenced or prosecuted against one of the United States by Citizens of another State, or by Citizens or Subjects of any Foreign State.

**Amendment XII [Adopted 1804]**

The Electors shall meet in their respective states, and vote by ballot for President and Vice-President, one of whom, at least, shall not be an inhabitant of the same state with themselves; they shall name in their ballots the person voted for as President, and in distinct ballots the person voted for as Vice-President, and they shall make distinct lists of all persons voted for as President, and of all persons voted for as Vice-President, and of the number of votes for each, which list they shall sign and certify, and transmit sealed to the seat of the government of the United States, directed to the President of the Senate;—The President of the Senate shall, in the presence of the Senate and House of Representatives, open all the certificates and the votes shall then be counted;—The person having the greatest number of votes for President, shall be the President, if such number be a majority of the whole number of Electors appointed; and if no person have such majority, then from the persons having the highest numbers not exceeding three on the list of those voted for as President, the House of Representatives shall choose immediately, by ballot, the President. But in choosing the President, the votes shall be taken by states, the representation from each state having one vote; a quorum for this purpose shall consist of a member or members from two thirds of the states, and a majority of all the states shall be necessary to a choice. And if the House of Representatives shall not choose a President whenever the right of choice shall devolve upon them, before *the fourth day of March* next following, then the Vice-President shall act as President, as in the case of the death or other constitutional disability of the President.

The person having the greatest number of votes as Vice-President, shall be the Vice-President, if such number be a majority of the whole number of Electors appointed, and if no person have a majority, then from the two highest numbers on the list, the Senate shall choose the Vice-President; a quorum for the purpose shall consist of two thirds of the whole number of Senators, and a majority of the whole number shall be necessary to a choice. But no person constitutionally ineligible to the office of President shall be eligible to that of Vice-President of the United States.

**Amendment XIII [Adopted 1865]**

**Section 1** Neither slavery nor involuntary servitude, except as a punishment for crime whereof the party shall have been duly convicted, shall exist within the United States, or any place subject to their jurisdiction.

**Section 2** Congress shall have power to enforce this article by appropriate legislation.

**Amendment XIV [Adopted 1868]**

**Section 1** All persons born or naturalized in the United States, and subject to the jurisdiction thereof, are citizens of the United States and of the State wherein they reside. No State shall make or enforce any law which shall abridge the privileges or immunities of citizens of the United States; nor shall any State deprive any person of life, liberty, or property, without due process of law; nor deny to any person within its jurisdiction the equal protection of the laws.

**Section 2** Representatives shall be apportioned among the several States according to their respective numbers, counting the whole number of persons in each State, excluding Indians not taxed. But when the right to vote at any election for the choice of electors for President and Vice-President of the United States, Representatives in Congress, the Executive and Judicial officers of a State, or the members of the Legislature thereof, is denied to any of the male inhabitants of such State, being twenty-one years of age, and citizens of the United States, or in any way abridged, except for participation in rebellion, or other crime, the basis of representation therein shall be reduced in the proportion which the number of such male citizens shall bear to the whole number of male citizens twenty-one years of age in such State.

**Section 3**   No person shall be a Senator or Representative in Congress, or elector of President and Vice-President, or hold any office, civil or military, under the United States, or under any State, who, having previously taken an oath, as a member of Congress, or as an officer of the United States, or as a member of any State legislature, or as an executive or judicial officer of any State, to support the Constitution of the United States, shall have engaged in insurrection or rebellion against the same, or given aid or comfort to the enemies thereof. But Congress may by a vote of two thirds of each House, remove such disability.

**Section 4**   The validity of the public debt of the United States, authorized by law, including debts incurred for payment of pensions and bounties for services in suppressing insurrection or rebellion, shall not be questioned. But neither the United States nor any State shall assume or pay any debt or obligation incurred in aid of insurrection or rebellion against the United States, or any claim for the loss or emancipation of any slave; but all such debts, obligations and claims shall be held illegal and void.

**Section 5**   The Congress shall have power to enforce, by appropriate legislation, the provisions of this article.

## Amendment XV [Adopted 1870]
**Section 1**   The right of citizens of the United States to vote shall not be denied or abridged by the United States or by any State on account of race, color, or previous condition of servitude.

**Section 2**   The Congress shall have power to enforce this article by appropriate legislation.

## Amendment XVI [Adopted 1913]
The Congress shall have power to lay and collect taxes on incomes, from whatever source derived, without apportionment among the several States, and without regard to any census or enumeration.

## Amendment XVII [Adopted 1913]
The Senate of the United States shall be composed of two Senators from each State, elected by the people thereof, for six years; and each Senator shall have one vote. The electors in each State shall have the qualifications requisite for electors of the most numerous branch of the State legislatures.

When vacancies happen in the representation of any State in the Senate, the executive authority of such State shall issue writs of election to fill such vacancies: *Provided,* That the legislature of any State may empower the executive thereof to make temporary appointments until the people fill the vacancies by election as the legislature may direct.

This amendment shall not be so construed as to affect the election or term of any Senator chosen before it becomes valid as part of the Constitution.

## Amendment XVIII [Adopted 1919; Repealed 1933]
**Section 1**   After one year from the ratification of this article the manufacture, sale, or transportation of intoxicating liquors within, the importation thereof into, or the exportation thereof from the United States and all territory subject to the jurisdiction thereof for beverage purposes is hereby prohibited.

**Section 2**   The Congress and the several States shall have concurrent power to enforce this article by appropriate legislation.

**Section 3**   This article shall be inoperative unless it shall have been ratified as an amendment to the Constitution by the legislatures of the several States, as provided in the Constitution, within seven years from the date of the submission hereof to the States by the Congress.

## Amendment XIX [Adopted 1920]
**Section 1**   The right of citizens of the United States to vote shall not be denied or abridged by the United States or by any State on account of sex.

**Section 2**   Congress shall have power to enforce this article by appropriate legislation.

## Amendment XX [Adopted 1933]
**Section 1**   The terms of the President and Vice-President shall end at noon on the 20th day of January, and the terms of Senators and Representatives at noon on the third day of January, of the years in which such terms would have ended if this article had not been ratified; and the terms of their successors shall then begin.

**Section 2**   The Congress shall assemble at least once in every year, and such meeting shall begin at noon on the third day of January, unless they shall by law appoint a different day.

**Section 3**   If, at the time fixed for the beginning of the term of the President, the President elect shall have died, the Vice-President elect shall become President. If a President shall not have been chosen before the time fixed for the beginning of his term, or if the President elect shall have failed to qualify, then the Vice-President elect shall act as President until a President shall have qualified; and the Congress may by law provide for the case wherein neither a President elect nor a Vice-President elect shall have qualified, declaring who shall then act as President, or the manner in which one who is to act shall be selected, and such person shall act accordingly until a President or Vice-President shall have qualified.

**Section 4**   The Congress may by law provide for the case of the death of any of the persons from whom the House of Representatives may choose a President whenever the right of choice shall have devolved upon them, and for the case of the death of any of the persons from whom the Senate may choose a Vice-President whenever the right of choice shall have devolved upon them.

**Section 5**   Sections 1 and 2 shall take effect on the 15th day of October following the ratification of this article.

**Section 6**   This article shall be inoperative unless it shall have been ratified as an amendment to the Constitution by the legislatures of three fourths of the several States within seven years from the date of its submission.

## Amendment XXI [Adopted 1933]
**Section 1**   The eighteenth article of amendment to the Constitution of the United States is hereby repealed.

**Section 2**   The transportation or importation into any State, Territory, or possession of the United States for delivery or use therein of intoxicating liquors, in violation of the laws thereof, is hereby prohibited.

**Section 3**   This article shall be inoperative unless it shall have been ratified as an amendment to the Constitution by conventions in the several States, as provided in the Constitution, within seven years from the date of the submission hereof to the States by the Congress.

## Amendment XXII [Adopted 1951]
**Section 1**   No person shall be elected to the office of the President more than twice, and no person who has held the office of President, or acted as President, for more than two years of a term to which some other person was elected President shall be elected to the office of

the President more than once. But this Article shall not apply to any person holding the office of President when this Article was proposed by the Congress, and shall not prevent any person who may be holding the office of President, or acting as President, during the term within which this Article becomes operative from holding the office of President or acting as President during the remainder of such term.

**Section 2**   This article shall be inoperative unless it shall have been ratified as an amendment to the Constitution by the legislatures of three fourths of the several States within seven years from the date of its submission to the States by the Congress.

### Amendment XXIII [Adopted 1961]

**Section 1**   The District constituting the seat of Government of the United States shall appoint in such manner as the Congress may direct:

A number of electors of President and Vice-President equal to the whole number of Senators and Representatives in Congress to which the District would be entitled if it were a State, but in no event more than the least populous State; they shall be in addition to those appointed by the States, but they shall be considered, for the purposes of the election of President and Vice-President, to be electors appointed by a State; and they shall meet in the District and perform such duties as provided by the twelfth article of amendment.

**Section 2**   The Congress shall have power to enforce this article by appropriate legislation.

### Amendment XXIV [Adopted 1964]

**Section 1**   The right of citizens of the United States to vote in any primary or other election for President or Vice-President, for electors for President or Vice-President, or for Senator or Representative in Congress, shall not be denied or abridged by the United States or any State by reason of failure to pay any poll tax or other tax.

**Section 2**   The Congress shall have power to enforce this article by appropriate legislation.

### Amendment XXV [Adopted 1967]

**Section 1**   In case of the removal of the President from office or his death or resignation, the Vice-President shall become President.

**Section 2**   Whenever there is a vacancy in the office of the Vice-President, the President shall nominate a Vice-President who shall take the office upon confirmation by a majority vote of both houses of Congress.

**Section 3**   Whenever the President transmits to the President pro tempore of the Senate and the Speaker of the House of Representatives his written declaration that he is unable to discharge the powers and duties of his office, and until he transmits to them a written declaration to the contrary, such powers and duties shall be discharged by the Vice-President as Acting President.

**Section 4**   Whenever the Vice-President and a majority of either the principal officers of the executive departments, or of such other body as Congress may by law provide, transmit to the President pro tempore of the Senate and the Speaker of the House of Representatives their written declaration that the President is unable to discharge the powers and duties of his office, the Vice-President shall immediately assume the powers and duties of the office as Acting President.

Thereafter, when the President transmits to the President pro tempore of the Senate and the Speaker of the House of Representatives his written declaration that no inability exists, he shall resume the powers and duties of his office unless the Vice-President and a majority of either the principal officers of the executive department, or of such other body as Congress may by law provide, transmit within four days to the President pro tempore of the Senate and the Speaker of the House of Representatives their written declaration that the President is unable to discharge the powers and duties of his office. Thereupon Congress shall decide the issue, assembling within 48 hours for that purpose if not in session. If the Congress, within 21 days after receipt of the latter written declaration, or, if Congress is not in session, within 21 days after Congress is required to assemble, determines by two-thirds vote of both houses that the President is unable to discharge the powers and duties of his office, the Vice-President shall continue to discharge the same as Acting President; otherwise, the President shall resume the powers and duties of his office.

**Amendment XXVI [Adopted 1971]**
**Section 1**   The right of citizens of the United States, who are eighteen years of age or older, to vote shall not be denied or abridged by the United States or any state on account of age.

**Section 2**   The Congress shall have power to enforce this article by appropriate legislation.

**Amendment XXVII [Adopted 1992]**
No law, varying the compensation for the services of Senators and Representatives, shall take effect until an election of Representatives have intervened.

# Presidential Elections

| Year | Candidates | Parties | Popular Vote | Electoral Vote | Voter Participation |
|------|-----------|---------|--------------|----------------|---------------------|
| 1789 | GEORGE WASHINGTON | | * | 69 | |
| | John Adams | | | 34 | |
| | Others | | | 35 | |
| 1792 | GEORGE WASHINGTON | | * | 132 | |
| | John Adams | | | 77 | |
| | George Clinton | | | 50 | |
| | Others | | | 5 | |
| 1796 | JOHN ADAMS | Federalist | * | 71 | |
| | Thomas Jefferson | Democratic-Republican | | 68 | |
| | Thomas Pinckney | Federalist | | 59 | |
| | Aaron Burr | Dem.-Rep. | | 30 | |
| | Others | | | 48 | |
| 1800 | THOMAS JEFFERSON | Dem.-Rep. | * | 73 | |
| | Aaron Burr | Dem.-Rep. | | 73 | |
| | C. C. Pinckney | Federalist | | 64 | |
| | John Jay | Federalist | | 1 | |
| 1804 | THOMAS JEFFERSON | Dem.-Rep. | * | 162 | |
| | C. C. Pinckney | Federalist | | 14 | |
| 1808 | JAMES MADISON | Dem.-Rep. | * | 122 | |
| | C. C. Pinckney | Federalist | | 47 | |
| | George Clinton | Dem.-Rep. | | 6 | |
| 1812 | JAMES MADISON | Dem.-Rep. | * | 128 | |
| | De Witt Clinton | Federalist | | 89 | |
| 1816 | JAMES MONROE | Dem.-Rep. | * | 183 | |
| | Rufus King | Federalist | | 34 | |
| 1820 | JAMES MONROE | Dem.-Rep. | * | 231 | |
| | John Quincy Adams | Dem.-Rep. | | 1 | |
| 1824 | JOHN Q. ADAMS | Dem.-Rep. | 108,740 (10.5%) | 84 | 26.9% |
| | Andrew Jackson | Dem.-Rep. | 153,544 (43.1%) | 99 | |
| | William H. Crawford | Dem.-Rep. | 46,618 (13.1%) | 41 | |
| | Henry Clay | Dem.-Rep. | 47,136 (13.2%) | 37 | |

| Year | Candidates | Parties | Popular Vote | Electoral Vote | Voter Participation |
|------|-----------|---------|--------------|----------------|---------------------|
| 1828 | ANDREW JACKSON | Democratic | 647,286 (56.0%) | 178 | 57.6% |
|      | John Quincy Adams | National Republican | 508,064 (44.0%) | 83 | |
| 1832 | ANDREW JACKSON | Democratic | 687,502 (55.0%) | 219 | 55.4% |
|      | Henry Clay | National Republican | 530,189 (42.4%) | 49 | |
|      | John Floyd | Independent | | 11 | |
|      | William Wirt | Anti-Mason | 33,108 (2.6%) | 7 | |
| 1836 | MARTIN VAN BUREN | Democratic | 765,483 (50.9%) | 170 | 57.8% |
|      | W. H. Harrison | Whig | | 73 | |
|      | Hugh L. White | Whig | 739,795 (49.1%) | 26 | |
|      | Daniel Webster | Whig | | 14 | |
|      | W. P. Magnum | Independent | | 11 | |
| 1840 | WILLIAM H. HARRISON | Whig | 1,274,624 (53.1%) | 234 | 80.2% |
|      | Martin Van Buren | Democratic | 1,127,781 (46.9%) | 60 | |
|      | J. G. Birney | Liberty | 7069 | — | |
| 1844 | JAMES K. POLK | Democratic | 1,338,464 (49.6%) | 170 | 78.9% |
|      | Henry Clay | Whig | 1,300,097 (48.1%) | 105 | |
|      | J. G. Birney | Liberty | 62,300 (2.3%) | — | |
| 1848 | ZACHARY TAYLOR | Whig | 1,360,967 (47.4%) | 163 | 72.7% |
|      | Lewis Cass | Democratic | 1,222,342 (42.5%) | 127 | |
|      | Martin Van Buren | Free-Soil | 291,263 (10.1%) | — | |
| 1852 | FRANKLIN PIERCE | Democratic | 1,601,117 (50.9%) | 254 | 69.6% |
|      | Winfield Scott | Whig | 1,385,453 (44.1%) | 42 | |
|      | John P. Hale | Free-Soil | 155,825 (5.0%) | — | |
| 1856 | JAMES BUCHANAN | Democratic | 1,832,955 (45.3%) | 174 | 78.9% |
|      | John C. Fremont | Republican | 1,339,932 (33.1%) | 114 | |
|      | Millard Fillmore | American | 871,731 (21.6%) | 8 | |
| 1860 | ABRAHAM LINCOLN | Republican | 1,865,593 (39.8%) | 180 | 81.2% |
|      | Stephen A. Douglas | Democratic | 1,382,713 (29.5%) | 12 | |
|      | John C. Breckinridge | Democratic | 848,356 (18.1%) | 72 | |
|      | John Bell | Union | 592,906 (12.6%) | 39 | |
| 1864 | ABRAHAM LINCOLN | Republican | 2,213,655 (55.0%) | 212 | 73.8% |
|      | George B. McClellan | Democratic | 1,805,237 (45.0%) | 21 | |
| 1868 | ULYSSES S. GRANT | Republican | 3,012,833 (52.7%) | 214 | 78.1% |
|      | Horatio Seymour | Democratic | 2,703,249 (47.3%) | 80 | |
| 1872 | ULYSSES S. GRANT | Republican | 3,597,132 (55.6%) | 286 | 71.3% |
|      | Horace Greeley | Democratic; Liberal Republican | 2,834,125 (43.9%) | 66 | |
| 1876 | RUTHERFORD B. HAYES | Republican | 4,036,298 (48.0%) | 185 | 81.8% |
|      | Samuel J. Tilden | Democratic | 4,300,590 (51.0%) | 184 | |
| 1880 | JAMES A. GARFIELD | Republican | 4,454,416 (48.5%) | 214 | 79.4% |
|      | Winfield S. Hancock | Democratic | 4,444,952 (48.1%) | 155 | |
| 1884 | GROVER CLEVELAND | Democratic | 4,874,986 (48.5%) | 219 | 77.5% |
|      | James G. Blaine | Republican | 4,851,981 (48.2%) | 182 | |
| 1888 | BENJAMIN HARRISON | Republican | 5,439,853 (47.9%) | 233 | 79.3% |
|      | Grover Cleveland | Democratic | 5,540,309 (48.6%) | 168 | |
| 1892 | GROVER CLEVELAND | Democratic | 5,556,918 (46.1%) | 277 | 74.7% |
|      | Benjamin Harrison | Republican | 5,176,108 (43.0%) | 145 | |
|      | James B. Weaver | People's | 1,041,028 (8.5%) | 22 | |

| Year | Candidates | Parties | Popular Vote | Electoral Vote | Voter Participation |
|------|-----------|---------|--------------|----------------|---------------------|
| 1896 | WILLIAM McKINLEY | Republican | 7,104,779 (51.1%) | 271 | 79.3% |
|      | William J. Bryan | Democratic | 6,502,925 (47.7%) | 176 | |
|      |  | People's | | | |
| 1900 | WILLIAM McKINLEY | Republican | 7,207,923 (51.7%) | 292 | 73.2% |
|      | William J. Bryan | Dem.-Populist | 6,358,133 (45.5%) | 155 | |
| 1904 | THEODORE ROOSEVELT | Republican | 7,623,486 (57.9%) | 336 | 65.2% |
|      | Alton B. Parker | Democratic | 5,077,911 (37.6%) | 140 | |
|      | Eugene V. Debs | Socialist | 402,283 (3.0%) | — | |
| 1908 | WILLIAM H. TAFT | Republican | 7,678,908 (51.6%) | 321 | 65.4% |
|      | William J. Bryan | Democratic | 6,409,104 (43.1%) | 162 | |
|      | Eugene V. Debs | Socialist | 420,793 (2.8%) | — | |
| 1912 | WOODROW WILSON | Democratic | 6,293,454 (41.9%) | 435 | 58.8% |
|      | Theodore Roosevelt | Progressive | 4,119,538 (27.4%) | 88 | |
|      | William H. Taft | Republican | 3,484,980 (23.2%) | 8 | |
|      | Eugene V. Debs | Socialist | 900,672 (6.0%) | — | |
| 1916 | WOODROW WILSON | Democratic | 9,129,606 (49.4%) | 277 | 61.6% |
|      | Charles E. Hughes | Republican | 8,538,221 (46.2%) | 254 | |
|      | A. L. Benson | Socialist | 585,113 (3.2%) | — | |
| 1920 | WARREN G. HARDING | Republican | 16,152,200 (60.4%) | 404 | 49.2% |
|      | James M. Cox | Democratic | 9,147,353 (34.2%) | 127 | |
|      | Eugene V. Debs | Socialist | 919,799 (3.4%) | — | |
| 1924 | CALVIN COOLIDGE | Republican | 15,725,016 (54.0%) | 382 | 48.9% |
|      | John W. Davis | Democratic | 8,386,503 (28.8%) | 136 | |
|      | Robert M. La Follette | Progressive | 4,822,856 (16.6%) | 13 | |
| 1928 | HERBERT HOOVER | Republican | 21,391,381 (58.2%) | 444 | 56.9% |
|      | Alfred E. Smith | Democratic | 15,016,443 (40.9%) | 87 | |
|      | Normal Thomas | Socialist | 267,835 (0.7%) | — | |
| 1932 | FRANKLIN D. ROOSEVELT | Democratic | 22,821,857 (57.4%) | 472 | 56.9% |
|      | Herbert Hoover | Republican | 15,761,841 (39.7%) | 59 | |
|      | Norman Thomas | Socialist | 881,951 (2.2%) | — | |
| 1936 | FRANKLIN D. ROOSEVELT | Democratic | 27,751,597 (60.8%) | 523 | 61.0% |
|      | Alfred M. Landon | Republican | 16,679,583 (36.5%) | 8 | |
|      | William Lemke | Union | 882,479 (1.9%) | — | |
| 1940 | FRANKLIN D. ROOSEVELT | Democratic | 27,244,160 (54.8%) | 449 | 62.5% |
|      | Wendell L. Willkie | Republican | 22,305,198 (44.8%) | 82 | |
| 1944 | FRANKLIN D. ROOSEVELT | Democrat | 25,602,504 (53.5%) | 432 | 55.9% |
|      | Thomas E. Dewey | Republican | 22,006,285 (46.0%) | 99 | |
| 1948 | HARRY S TRUMAN | Democratic | 24,105,695 (49.5%) | 303 | 53.0% |
|      | Thomas E. Dewey | Republican | 21,969,170 (45.1%) | 189 | |
|      | J. Strom Thurmond | State-Rights Democratic | 1,169,021 (2.4%) | 39 | |
|      | Henry A. Wallace | Progressive | 1,156,103 (2.4%) | — | |
| 1952 | DWIGHT D. EISENHOWER | Republican | 33,936,252 (55.1%) | 442 | 63.3% |
|      | Adlai E. Stevenson | Democratic | 27,314,992 (44.4%) | 89 | |
| 1956 | DWIGHT D. EISENHOWER | Republican | 35,575,420 (57.6%) | 457 | 60.5% |
|      | Adlai E. Stevenson | Democratic | 26,033,066 (42.1%) | 73 | |
|      | Other | — | — | 1 | |

| Year | Candidates | Parties | Popular Vote | Electoral Vote | Voter Participation |
|------|-----------|---------|-------------|----------------|---------------------|
| 1960 | JOHN F. KENNEDY | Democratic | 34,227,096 (49.9%) | 303 | 62.8% |
|      | Richard M. Nixon | Republican | 34,108,546 (49.6%) | 219 | |
|      | Other | — | — | 15 | |
| 1964 | LYNDON B. JOHNSON | Democratic | 43,126,506 (61.1%) | 486 | 61.7% |
|      | Barry M. Goldwater | Republican | 27,176,799 (38.5%) | 52 | |
| 1968 | RICHARD M. NIXON | Republican | 31,770,237 (43.4.%) | 301 | 60.6% |
|      | Hurbert H. Humphrey | Democratic | 31,270,633 (42.7%) | 191 | |
|      | George Wallace | American Indep. | 9,906,141 (13.5%) | 46 | |
| 1972 | RICHARD M. NIXON | Republican | 47,169,911 (60.7%) | 520 | 55.2% |
|      | George S. McGovern | Democratic | 29,170,383 (37.5%) | 17 | |
|      | Other | — | — | 1 | |
| 1976 | JIMMY CARTER | Democratic | 40,828,587 (50.0%) | 297 | 53.5% |
|      | Gerald R. Ford | Republican | 39,147,613 (47.9%) | 240 | |
|      | Other | — | 1,575,459 92.1%) | — | |
| 1980 | RONALD REAGAN | Republican | 43,901,812 (50.7%) | 489 | 52.6% |
|      | Jimmy Carter | Democratic | 35,483,820 (41.0%) | 49 | |
|      | John B. Anderson | Independent | 5,719,722 (6.6%) | — | |
|      | Ed Clark | Libertarian | 921,188 (1.1%) | — | |
| 1984 | RONALD REAGAN | Republican | 54,455,075 (59.0%) | 525 | 53.3% |
|      | Walter Mondale | Democratic | 37,577,185 (41.0%) | 13 | |
| 1988 | GEORGE H. W. BUSH | Republican | 48,886,000 (45.6%) | 426 | 57.4% |
|      | Michael S. Dukakis | Democratic | 41,809,000 (45.6%) | 112 | |
| 1992 | WILLIAM J. CLINTON | Democratic | 43,728,375 (43%) | 370 | 55.0% |
|      | George H. W. Bush | Republican | 38,167,416 (38%) | 168 | |
|      | Ross Perot | — | 19,237,247 (19%) | — | |
| 1996 | WILLIAM J. CLINTON | Democratic | 45,590,703 (50%) | 379 | 48.8% |
|      | Robert Dole | Republican | 37,816,307 (41%) | 159 | |
|      | Ross Perot | Independent | 7,866,284 (9%) | — | |
| 2000 | GEORGE W. BUSH | Republican | 50,456,062 (47%) | 271 | 51.0% |
|      | Albert Gore | Democratic | 50,996,582 (49%) | 267 | |
|      | Ralph Nader | Independent | 2,858,843 (3%) | — | |

# INDEX

983

996

# The World

## Central America and the Caribbean

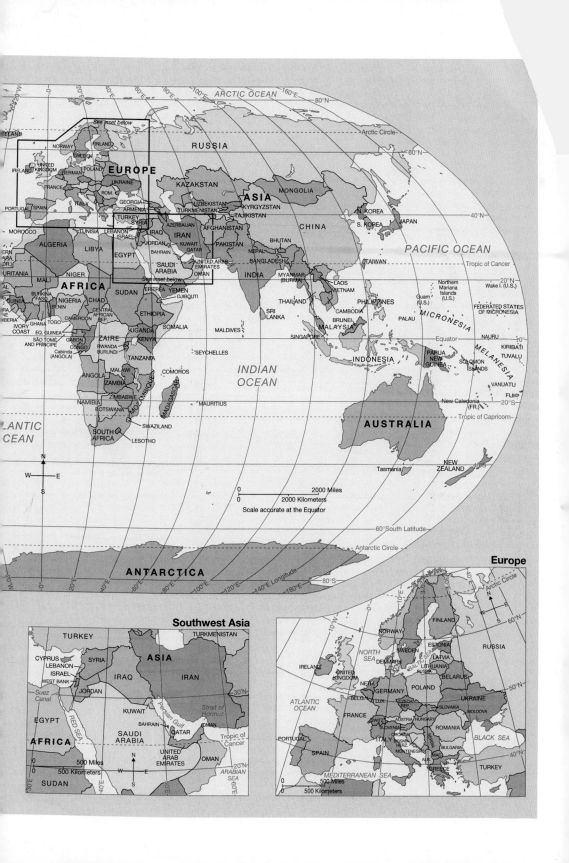

ARCTIC OCEAN

80°N

Arctic Circle

60°N

See inset below

NORWAY    FINLAND

SWEDEN

RUSSIA

IRELAND

UNITED
KINGDOM    GERMANY    POLAND

EUROPE

FRANCE

ITALY    ROM.

UKRAINE

KAZAKSTAN

ASIA    MONGOLIA

40°N

PORTUGAL    SPAIN

GEORGIA

ARMENIA

TURKEY    SYRIA

AZERBAIJAN

UZBEKISTAN

TURKMENISTAN

KYRGYZSTAN

TAJIKISTAN

N. KOREA    JAPAN

CHINA    S. KOREA

MOROCCO    TUNISIA

LEBANON    IRAQ    IRAN

ISRAEL

JORDAN    KUWAIT

AFGHANISTAN

PAKISTAN

BHUTAN

PACIFIC OCEAN

ALGERIA    LIBYA

EGYPT    BAHRAIN    QATAR

NEPAL

Tropic of Cancer

TAIWAN

MAURITANIA

NIGER

SAUDI
ARABIA

UNITED ARAB
EMIRATES

OMAN

BANGLADESH

INDIA    MYANMAR
(BURMA)

LAOS

Northern
Mariana
Islands

Wake I. (U.S.)

20°N

MALI

AFRICA    SUDAN

ERITREA    YEMEN

See inset below

VIETNAM

Guam
(U.S.)    (U.S.)

FEDERATED STATES
OF MICRONESIA

BURKINA
FASO    NIGERIA    CHAD

DJIBOUTI

THAILAND

CAMBODIA

PHILIPPINES

BENIN

CENTRAL
AFRICAN
REP.

ETHIOPIA

SRI
LANKA

PALAU

MICRONESIA

IVORY
COAST    GHANA    TOGO    CAMEROON

EQ. GUINEA

SÃO TOMÉ
AND PRINCIPE    GABON    CONGO

ZAIRE

UGANDA    KENYA

SOMALIA

MALDIVES

SINGAPORE

MALAYSIA

BRUNEI

Equator

NAURU    KIRIBATI

TUVALU

Cabinda
(ANGOLA)

RWANDA

BURUNDI

TANZANIA

SEYCHELLES

INDONESIA

PAPUA
NEW
GUINEA

SOLOMON
ISLANDS

MELANESIA

ANGOLA    MALAWI

ZAMBIA

COMOROS

INDIAN
OCEAN

VANUATU

NAMIBIA

ZIMBABWE

BOTSWANA

MADAGASCAR

MOZAMBIQUE

MAURITIUS

AUSTRALIA

Tropic of Capricorn

20°S

New Caledonia
(FR.)

FIJI

SOUTH
AFRICA    SWAZILAND

LESOTHO

ATLANTIC
OCEAN

N

W    E

S

0    2000 Miles

0    2000 Kilometers

Scale accurate at the Equator

Tasmania

NEW
ZEALAND

60° South Latitude

Antarctic Circle

ANTARCTICA

40°E    60°E    80°E    100°E    120°E    140°E Longitude    160°E

80°S

## Southwest Asia

TURKEY

TURKMENISTAN

CYPRUS

LEBANON

ISRAEL

WEST BANK

SYRIA

JORDAN

IRAQ

ASIA

IRAN

Suez
Canal

30°N

KUWAIT

Strait of
Hormuz

Persian Gulf

EGYPT

RED SEA

AFRICA

SAUDI
ARABIA

BAHRAIN    OMAN

QATAR

UNITED
ARAB
EMIRATES

Tropic of
Cancer

0    500 Miles

0    500 Kilometers

N

W    E

S

OMAN

20°N

SUDAN

ARABIAN
SEA

## Europe

Arctic Circle

N

W    E

S

60°N

FINLAND

NORWAY

ESTONIA

RUSSIA

NORTH
SEA

SWEDEN

DENMARK

LATVIA

IRELAND    UNITED
KINGDOM

NETH.

RUSSIA

LITHUANIA

BELARUS

50°N

GERMANY

POLAND

ATLANTIC
OCEAN

BELG.    LUX.

CZECH
REP.

UKRAINE

FRANCE

SWITZ.

SLOVENIA

AUSTRIA

SLOVAKIA

HUNGARY

MOLDOVA

ROMANIA

CROATIA

BOSNIA-
HERZ.

SERBIA

BLACK SEA

PORTUGAL

ITALY

MONTENEGRO

MAC.

BULGARIA

SPAIN

ALB.

40°N

MEDITERRANEAN SEA

GREECE

TURKEY

0    500 Miles

0    500 Kilometers